Beginning PHP and PostgreSQL E-Commerce

From Novice to Professional

Cristian Darie, Emilian Balanescu,
Mihai Bucica

Apress®

Beginning PHP and PostgreSQL E-Commerce: From Novice to Professional

Copyright © 2006 by Cristian Darie, Emilian Balanescu, Mihai Bucica

ISBN-13 (pbk): 978-1-59059-648-7

ISBN-10 (pbk): 1-59059-648-X

Printed and bound in the United States of America 9 8 7 6 5 4 3 2 1

Lead Editor: Jason Gilmore
Technical Reviewer: Greg Sabino Mullane
Editorial Board: Steve Anglin, Ewan Buckingham, Gary Cornell, Jason Gilmore, Jonathan Gennick, Jonathan Hassell, James Huddleston, Chris Mills, Matthew Moodie, Dominic Shakeshaft, Jim Sumser, Keir Thomas, Matt Wade
Project Manager: Kylie Johnston
Copy Edit Manager: Nicole Flores
Copy Editor: Julie McNamee
Assistant Production Director: Kari Brooks-Copony
Production Editor: Lori Bring
Compositor: Gina Rexrode
Proofreader: April Eddy
Indexer: John Collin
Artist: April Milne
Cover Designer: Kurt Krames
Manufacturing Director: Tom Debolski

Distributed to the book trade worldwide by Springer-Verlag New York, Inc., 233 Spring Street, 6th Floor, New York, NY 10013. Phone 1-800-SPRINGER, fax 201-348-4505, e-mail orders-ny@springer-sbm.com, or visit http://www.springeronline.com.

For information on translations, please contact Apress directly at 2560 Ninth Street, Suite 219, Berkeley, CA 94710. Phone 510-549-5930, fax 510-549-5939, e-mail info@apress.com, or visit http://www.apress.com.

The source code for this book is available to readers at http://www.apress.com in the Source Code/ Download section.

Contents at a Glance

Contents

PART 1 ■ ■ ■ Phase 1 of Development

PART 2 ■■■ Phase II of Development

PART 3 ■ ■ ■ Phase III of Development

About the Authors

CRISTIAN DARIE is a software engineer with experience in a wide range of modern technologies, and he is the author of numerous technical books. Cristian is studying distributed application architectures for his PhD and is getting involved with various commercial and research projects. When not planning to buy Google, he enjoys his bit of social life. If you want to say "hi," you can reach Cristian through his personal web site at http://www.cristiandarie.ro.

EMILIAN BALANESCU is a programmer experienced in many technologies, such as PHP, Java, .NET, AJAX, PostgreSQL, MySQL, and MS SQL Server. He currently works as a Fault Handling Engineer at AccessNET International. You can reach Emilian at http://www.emilianbalanescu.ro.

MIHAI BUCICA started programming and competing in programming contests (winning many of them) at age 12. With a bachelor's degree in computer science from the Automatic Control and Computers Faculty of the Politehnica University of Bucharest, Romania, Mihai works on building communication software with various electronic markets.

Even after working with a multitude of languages and technologies, Mihai's programming language of choice remains C++, and he loves the LGPL world. Mihai also co-authored *Beginning PHP 5 and MySQL E-Commerce.* He can be contacted through his personal web site, http://www.valentinbucica.ro.

About the Technical Reviewer

GREG SABINO MULLANE has used many databases but believes that none compare to PostgreSQL (and advocates calling it "Postgres"). He helps maintain the Postgres mailing lists and web sites, has spoken at OSCon and other events on Postgres topics, and has contributed code to the Postgres core. He is the primary developer of the DBD::Pg module, has ported MediaWiki to Postgres, and has been recognized as a Postgres Major Developer for all of his Postgres work. He has a strong interest in PGP and cryptography, and he attends keysignings as often as possible.

His PGP fingerprint is 2529 DF6A B8F7 9407 E944 45B4 BC9B 9067 1496 4AC8, and he has been known to sneak it into code he has written. He currently works as a software developer for End Point, primarily doing Postgres, Perl, and PHP work. He and his wife Joy enjoy traveling and try to make at least one overseas trip a year.

Acknowledgments

We would like to thank Kylie, our project manager, for guiding everyone through the process of building this book; Julie, for her constantly wonderful edits; Lori and April, for the final magic touch; and Greg and Jason, for giving us excellent technical feedback that contributed decisively to the quality of this book.

Introduction

Welcome to *Beginning PHP and PostgreSQL E-Commerce: From Novice to Professional*! The explosive growth of retail over the Internet is encouraging more small- to medium-sized businesses to consider the benefits of setting up e-commerce web sites. Although there are great and obvious advantages to online retail, there are also many hidden pitfalls that you might encounter when developing a retail web site. This book provides you with a practical, step-by-step guide to setting up an e-commerce web site. Guiding you through every step of the design and build process, this book will have you building high quality, extendable e-commerce web sites quickly and easily.

Over the course of the book, you will develop all the skills necessary to get your business up on the web and available to a worldwide audience. We present this information in a book-long case study, the complexity of which develops as your knowledge increases through the book.

The case study is presented in three phases. The first phase focuses on getting the site up and running as quickly as possible and at a low cost. Although not yet full-featured, at the conclusion of this phase, your site will be capable of accepting PayPal payments, enabling you to begin generating revenue immediately.

The second phase concentrates on increasing revenue by improving the shopping experience. In this phase, you'll learn how to proactively encourage customers to buy more by implementing product recommendations. We'll also begin laying the groundwork for handling credit card transactions by developing and integrating custom shopping cart functionality.

In the third phase, we'll show you how to increase your profit margins by reducing costs through automating and streamlining order processing and administration and by handling credit card transactions yourself. You also learn how to integrate external functionality through Web Services and how to improve your customer's shopping experience by adding product reviews functionality.

Who This Book Is For

Beginning PHP and PostgreSQL E-Commerce: From Novice to Professional is aimed at developers looking for a tutorial approach to building a full e-commerce web site from design to deployment. However, it's assumed that you have some knowledge of building web sites with PHP and PostgreSQL. *Beginning PHP and PostgreSQL 8: From Novice to Professional* (Apress, 2006), authored by W. Jason Gilmore and Robert Treat, can provide this foundation knowledge for you.

This book will also prove valuable for PHP 4 developers who learn best by example and want to experience PHP 5 development techniques first hand.

How This Book Is Structured

This book is divided into three parts consisting of 17 chapters and 2 appendixes. We cover a wide variety of topics, showing you how to

- Build an online product catalog that can be browsed and searched

- Implement the catalog administration pages that allow adding, modifying, and removing products, categories, and departments

- Create your own shopping basket and checkout in PHP

- Increase sales by implementing product recommendations and product reviews

- Handle payments using PayPal, DataCash, and Authorize.net

- Implement a customer accounts system

- Integrate external functionality through Web Services

The following brief roadmap highlights how we'll take you from novice to professional regarding each of the topics in the previous list.

Part 1: Phase I of Development

Chapter 1: Starting an E-Commerce Site

In this chapter, we'll introduce some of the principles of e-commerce in the real world. You see the importance of focusing on short-term revenue and keeping risks down. We look at the three basic ways in which an e-commerce site can make money. We then apply those principles to a three-phase plan that provides a deliverable, usable site at each phase of this book.

Chapter 2: Laying Out the Foundations

The first chapter offered an overview of e-commerce in the real world. Now that you've decided to develop a web site, we start to look in more detail at laying down the foundations for its future. We'll talk about what technologies and tools you'll use, and even more importantly, how you'll use them.

Chapter 3: Creating the Product Catalog: Part I

After learning about the three-tier architecture and implementing a bit of your web site's main page, it's time to continue your work by starting to create the HatShop product catalog. Because the product catalog is composed of many components, you'll create it over two chapters. In Chapter 3, you'll create the first database table and implement the data access code. By the end of this chapter, you'll have something dynamically generated on your web page.

Chapter 4: Creating the Product Catalog: Part II

The fun isn't over yet! In the previous chapter, you created a selectable list of departments for HatShop. However, a product catalog is much more than a list of departments. In Chapter 4, you'll add the rest of the product catalog features.

Chapter 5: Searching the Catalog

In the preceding two chapters, you will have implemented a functional product catalog for HatShop. However, the site still lacks the all-important search feature. The goal in this chapter is to allow the visitor to search the site for products by entering one or more keywords. You'll learn how to implement search results rankings and how to browse through the search results page by page. You'll see how easy it is to add new functionality to a working site by integrating the new components into the existing architecture.

Chapter 6: Receiving Payments Using PayPal

Let's make some money! Your e-commerce web site needs a way to receive payments from customers. The preferred solution for established companies is to open a merchant account, but many small businesses choose to start with a solution that's simpler to implement, where they don't have to process credit card or payment information themselves.

A number of companies and web sites exist to help individuals or small businesses that don't have the resources to process credit card and wire transactions. These companies can be used to process the payment between companies and their customers. In this chapter, we'll demonstrate some of the functionality provided by one such company, PayPal, as we use it on the HatShop web site in the first two stages of development.

Chapter 7: Catalog Administration

The final detail to take care of before launching a web site is to create its administrative interface. Although this is a part visitors will never see, it's still key to delivering a quality web site to your client.

Part 2: Phase II of Development

Chapter 8: The Shopping Cart

With this chapter, you enter the second phase of development, where you start improving and adding new features to the already existing, fully functional e-commerce site. In Chapter 8, you'll implement the custom shopping cart, which stores its data in the local database. This provides you with more flexibility than the PayPal shopping basket, over which you have no control and which you can't save into your database for further processing and analysis.

Chapter 9: Dealing with Customer Orders

The good news is that the brand new shopping cart implemented in Chapter 8 looks good and is fully functional. The bad news is that it doesn't allow the visitor to actually place an order, making it totally useless in the context of a production system. As you have probably already guessed, you'll deal with that problem in this chapter, in two separate stages. In the first part of the chapter, you'll implement the client-side part of the order-placing mechanism. In the second part of the chapter, you'll implement a simple orders administration page where the site administrator can view and handle pending orders.

Chapter 10: Product Recommendations

One of the best advantages of an Internet store compared to a brick-and-mortar store is the capability to customize the web site for each visitor based on his or her preferences, or based on data gathered from other visitors with similar preferences. If your web site knows how to suggest additional products to your visitor in a clever way, he or she might end up buying more than initially planned. In Chapter 10, you'll learn how to implement a dynamic product recommendation system.

Part 3: Phase III of Development

Chapter 11: Managing Customer Details

In the first two stages of development, you've built a basic (but functional) site and have hooked it into PayPal for taking payments and confirming orders. In the third section of the book, you'll take things a little further. By cutting out PayPal from the ordering process, you can gain better control as well as reduce overhead. This isn't as complicated as you might think, but you must be careful to do things right. Chapter 11 lays the groundwork by implementing a customer account system, as well as looking into the security aspects of exchanging and storing customer and credit card details.

Chapter 12: Storing Customer Orders

In this chapter, you'll make the modifications required for customers to place orders that are associated with their user profiles. The main modification here is that the customer associated with an order will be identified by a new piece of information in the orders table, and much of the rest of the modifications will be made to use this information.

Also in this chapter, you'll take a look at dealing with another common feature of e-commerce sites: tax and shipping charges. Many options are available for implementing this functionality, but we'll just examine a simple way of doing things and lay the groundwork for your own further development.

Chapter 13: Implementing the Order Pipeline: Part I

The HatShop e-commerce application is shaping up nicely. You've added customer account functionality, and you're keeping track of customer addresses and credit card information, which is stored in a secure way. However, you're not currently using this information—you're delegating responsibility for this to PayPal. In this and the next chapter, you'll build your own order-processing pipeline that deals with authorizing credit cards, stock checking, shipping, providing email notifications, and so on. We'll leave the credit card processing specifics until Chapter 15, but we'll show you where this process fits in before then.

Chapter 14: Implementing the Order Pipeline: Part II

In this chapter, you'll add the required pipeline sections so that you can process orders from start to finish, although you won't be adding full credit card transaction functionality until the next chapter. We'll also look at the web administration of orders by modifying the order admin pages added earlier in the book to take into account the new order-processing system.

Chapter 15: Credit Card Transactions

The last thing you need to do before launching the e-commerce site is enable credit card processing. In this chapter, we'll look at how you can build this into the pipeline you created in Chapters 13 and 14. You'll see how to use two popular credit card gateways to do this: Data-Cash and Authorize.net. By the end of this chapter, HatShop will be a fully functioning, secure, and usable e-commerce application.

Chapter 16: Product Reviews

At this point, you have a complete and functional e-commerce web site. However, this doesn't stop you from adding even more features to it, making it more useful and pleasant for visitors. By adding a product reviews system to your web site, you increase the chances that visitors will get back to your site, either to write a review for a product they bought or to see what other people think about that product.

Chapter 17: Connecting to Web Services

In the dynamic world of the Internet, sometimes it isn't enough to just have an important web presence; you also need to interact with functionality provided by third parties to achieve your goals. So far in this book, you already saw how to integrate external functionality to process payments from your customers. In Chapter 17, you'll learn how to use Amazon.com functionality from and through Web Services. A *Web Service* is exposed through a web interface using standard Internet protocols such as HTTP. The messages exchanged by the client and the server are encoded using an XML-based protocol named SOAP (Simple Object Access Protocol), or by using REST (Representational State Transfer). These messages are sent over HTTP. You'll learn more about these technologies in this chapter.

Prerequisites

The code in this book has been built and tested with PHP 5 and PostgreSQL 8. It will not work with PHP 4 or older versions. You'll find detailed information about the required software in Appendix A.

Downloading the Code

The code for this book can be downloaded in zip file format from the Source Code/Downloads section of the Apress web site (http://www.apress.com). You also can find the code, errata, and other resources related to the book on Cristian's web site at http://www.cristiandarie.ro/php-postgresql-ecommerce/, or on Emilian's web site at http://www.emilianbalanescu.ro/beginning-php-postgresql-ecommerce/.

Contacting the Authors

You can contact the authors through their web sites, as follows:

- Cristian Darie, http://www.cristiandarie.ro

- Emilian Balanescu, http://www.emilianbalanescu.ro

- Mihai Valentin Bucica, http://www.valentinbucica.ro

PART 1

Phase 1 of Development

■ ■ ■

CHAPTER 1

Starting an E-Commerce Site

The word "e-commerce" has had a remarkable fall from grace in the past few years. Just the idea of having an e-commerce web site was enough to get many businessmen salivating with anticipation. But now, it's no longer enough to say, "e-commerce is the future—get online or get out of business." You now need compelling, realistic, and specific reasons to take your business online.

This book focuses on programming and associated disciplines, such as creating, accessing, and manipulating databases. But before we jump into that, we need to understand the business decisions that lead to the creation of an e-commerce site in the first place.

If you want to build an e-commerce site today, you must answer some tough questions. The good news is that these questions do have answers, and we're going to have a go at answering them in this chapter:

- So many big e-commerce sites have failed. What can e-commerce possibly offer me in today's tougher environment?

- Most e-commerce companies seemed to need massive investment. How can I produce a site on my limited budget?

- Even successful e-commerce sites expect to take years before they turn a profit. My business can't wait that long. How can I make money now?

Deciding Whether to Go Online

Although there are hundreds of possible reasons to go online, they tend to fall into the following groups:

- Get more customers

- Make existing customers spend more

- Reduce the costs of fulfilling orders

We'll look at each of these in the following sections.

Get More Customers

Getting more customers is immediately the most attractive reason. With an e-commerce site, even small businesses can reach customers all over the world. This reason can also be the most dangerous, however, because many people set up e-commerce sites assuming that the site will reach customers immediately. It won't. In the offline world, you need to know a shop exists before you can go into it. This is still true in the world of e-commerce—people must know your site exists before you can hope to get a single order.

Addressing this issue is largely a question of advertising, rather than the site itself. Popular methods of getting more customers include registering the web site with the popular search engines and directory listings, optimizing the site for search-engine ranking, creating forums, sending newsletters, and so on.

We don't cover many of these aspects of e-commerce in this book, as we try to stay focused on e-commerce development. A simple web search for "web site advertising tutorial" will point you to many useful resources.

Make Customers Spend More

Assuming your company already has customers, you probably wish that they bought more. What stops them? If the customers don't want any more of a certain product, there's not a lot that e-commerce can do, but chances are there are other reasons, too:

- Getting to the shop/placing an order by mail is a hassle.

- Some of the things you sell can be bought from more convenient places.

- You're mostly open while your customers are at work.

- It's harder to implement an efficient product recommendations system in a physical store.

A quality e-commerce site (because there are so many buggy, insecure, or hard-to-use web sites out there) can fix those problems. People with Internet access will find placing an order online far easier than any other method—meaning that when the temptation to buy strikes, it's much easier for them to give in. Of course, the convenience of being online also means that people are more likely to choose you over other local suppliers.

Because your site is online 24 hours a day, rather than the usual 9 to 5, your customers can shop with you outside of their working hours. Having an online store brings a double blessing to you if your customers work in offices because they can indulge in retail therapy directly from their desks.

Skillful e-commerce design can encourage your customers to buy things they wouldn't usually think of. You can easily update your site to suggest items of particular seasonal interest, to announce interesting new products, or to recommend products similar to what that specific customer has already bought.

Many of the large e-commerce sites encourage customers to buy useful accessories along with the main product or to buy a more expensive alternative to the one they're considering. Others give special offers to regular shoppers or suggest impulse purchases during checkout. You'll learn how to use some of these methods in later chapters; by the end of the book, you'll have a good idea of how to add more features for yourself.

Finally, it's much easier to learn about your customers via e-commerce than in face-to-face shops, or even mail order. Even if you just gather email addresses, you can use these to send out updates and news. More sophisticated sites can automatically analyze a customer's buying habits to make suggestions on other products the customer might like to buy.

Another related benefit of e-commerce is that there's no real cost in having people browse without buying. In fact, getting people to visit the site as often as possible can be valuable. You should consider building features into the site that are designed purely to make people visit regularly; for example, you might include community features such as forums or free content related to the products you're selling.

Reduce the Costs of Fulfilling Orders

A well-built e-commerce site will be much cheaper to run than a comparable offline business. Under conventional business models, a staff member must feed an order into the company's order-processing system. With e-commerce, the customer can do this for you—the gateway between the site and the order processing can be seamless.

Of course, after your e-commerce site is up and running, the cost of actually taking orders gets close to zero—you don't need to pay for checkout staff, assistants, security guards, or rent in a busy shopping mall.

If you have a sound business idea, and you execute the site well, you can receive these benefits without a massive investment. What's important is to always focus on the almighty dollar: Will your site, or any particular feature of it, really help you get more customers, get customers to spend more, or reduce the costs and therefore increase your margins?

Now it's time to introduce the site we'll be using as the example in this book, and see just how all of these principles relate to our own shop.

Let's Make Money

We're going to build an e-commerce store that sells hats. On all the e-commerce sites we've worked on, there's always been a trade-off to make between building an amazing site that everybody will love and creating a site on a limited budget that will make money. Usually, I'm on the trigger-happy, really amazing site side, but I'm always grateful that my ambitions are reined in by the actual business demands. If you're designing and building the site for yourself and you are the client, then you have a challenge—keeping your view realistic while maintaining your enthusiasm for the project.

This book shows you a logical way to build an e-commerce site that will deliver what it needs to be profitable. However, when designing your own site, you need to think carefully about exactly who your customers are, what they need, how they want to place orders, and what they are most likely to buy. Most important, you need to think about how they will come to your site in the first place. You should consider the following points before you start to visualize or design the site and certainly before you start programming:

Getting customers: How will you get visitors to the site in the first place?

Offering products: What will you offer, and how will you expect customers to buy? Will they buy in bulk? Will they make a lot of repeat orders? Will they know what they want before they visit, or will they want to be inspired? These factors will influence how you arrange your catalog and searching as well as what order process you use. A shopping basket is great if people want to browse. If people know exactly what they want, then they might prefer something more like an order form.

Processing orders: How will you turn a customer order into a parcel ready for mailing? Your main consideration here is finding an efficient way to process payments and deliver orders to whoever manages your stock or warehouse. How will you give your customers confidence in your ability to protect their data and deliver their purchases on time?

Serving customers: Will customers require additional help with products that they buy from you? Do you need to offer warranties, service contracts, or other support services?

Bringing customers back: How will you entice customers back to the site? Are they likely to only visit the site to make a purchase, or will there be e-window shoppers? Are your products consumables, and can you predict when your customers will need something new?

After you've answered these questions, you can start designing your site, knowing that you're designing for your customers—not just doing what seems like a good idea at the time. Determining the answers to these questions will also help ensure that your design covers all the important areas, without massive omissions that will be a nightmare to fix later.

The example site presented in this book has taken a deliberate generic approach to show you the most common e-commerce techniques. To really lift yourself above the competition, however, you don't need fancy features or Flash movies—you just need to understand, attract, and serve your customers better than anybody else. Think about this before you launch into designing and building the site itself.

Risks and Threats

All this might make it sound as if your e-commerce business can't possibly fail. Well, it's time to take a cold shower and realize that even the best-laid plans often go wrong. Some risks are particularly relevant to e-commerce companies, such as

- Hacking

- Credit card scams

- Hardware failures

- Unreliable shipping services

- Software errors

- Changing laws

You can't get rid of these risks, but you can try to understand them and defend yourself from them. The software developed in this book goes some way to meeting these issues, but many of the risks have little to do with the site itself.

An important way to defend your site from many risks is to maintain backups. You already know backups are important. But if you're anything like me, when it gets to the end of the day, saving five minutes and going home earlier seems even more important. When you have a live web site, this simply isn't an option.

We haven't talked much about the legal side of e-commerce in this book because we are programmers, not lawyers. However if you are setting up an e-commerce site that goes much beyond an online garage sale, you'll need to look into these issues before putting your business online.

While we're on the subject of risks and threats, one issue that can really damage your e-commerce site is unreliable order fulfillment. This is a programming book, which focuses on offering products to customers and communicating their orders to the site's owner. An essential part of the processes is delivering the products, and to do this, you need a good logistics network set up before launching your shop. If your store doesn't deliver the goods, customers won't come back or refer their friends.

Tip Webmonkey provides an excellent general e-commerce tutorial, which covers taxation, shipping, and many of the issues you'll face when designing your site, at `http://www.webmonkey.com/webmonkey/e-business/building/tutorials/tutorial3.html`. Check this out before you start designing your site.

Designing for Business

Building an e-commerce site requires a significant investment. If you design the site in phases, you can reduce the initial investment and therefore cut your losses if the idea proves unsuccessful. You can use the results from an early phase to assess whether it's worthwhile to add extra features, and even use revenue from the site to fund future development. If nothing else, planning to build the site in phases means that you can get your site online and receiving orders much earlier than if you build every possible feature into the first release.

Even after you've completed your initial planned phases, things might not end there. Whenever planning a large software project, it's important to design in a way that makes unplanned future growth easy. In Chapter 2, where we'll start dealing with the technical details of building e-commerce sites, you'll learn how to design the web site architecture to allow for long-term development flexibility.

If you're building sites for clients, they will like to think their options are open. Planning the site, or any other software, in phases will help your clients feel comfortable doing business with you. They will be able to see that you are getting the job done and can decide to end the project at the end of any phase if they feel—for whatever reason—that they don't want to continue to invest in development.

Phase I: Getting a Site Up

Chapters 2 through 7 concentrate on establishing the basic framework for the site and putting a product catalog online. We'll start by putting together the basic site architecture and deciding how the different parts of the application will work together. We'll then build the product catalog into this architecture. You'll learn how to

- Design a database for storing the product catalog, containing departments, categories, and products

- Write the SQL (Structured Query Language) and PHP (Hypertext Preprocessor) code for accessing that data and making the product catalog functional

- Provide a product search engine

- Receive payments through PayPal Website Payments Standard

- Give the site's administrators a private section of the site where they can administer the catalog online

After you've built this catalog, you'll see how to offer the products for sale by integrating it with PayPal's shopping cart and order-processing system, which will handle credit card transactions for you and email you with details of orders. These orders will be processed manually, but in the early stages of an e-commerce site, the time you lose processing orders will be less than the time it would have taken to develop an automated system.

Phase II: Creating Your Own Shopping Cart

Using PayPal's shopping cart is okay and really easy, but it does mean you miss out on a lot of advantages. For example, you can't control the look and feel of PayPal's shopping cart, whereas if you use your own, you can make it an integral part of the site.

This is a significant advantage, but it's superficial compared to some of the others. For example, with your own shopping cart, you can store complete orders in the database as part of the order process and then use that data to learn about the customers. With additional work, you also can use the shopping basket and checkout as a platform for selling more products. How often have you been tempted by impulse purchases near the checkout of your local store? Well, impulse shopping also works with e-commerce. Having your own shopping cart and checkout gives you the option of offering low-cost special offers from the shopping cart at checkout. You can even analyze the contents of the cart and make suggestions based on this.

Chapters 8 through 10 show you how to

- Build your own shopping cart

- Pass a complete order through to PayPal for credit card processing

- Create an orders administration page

- Implement a product recommendations system

Once again, at the end of Phase II, our site will be fully operational. If you want, you can leave it as it is or add features within the existing PayPal-based payment system. But when the site gets serious, you'll want to start processing orders and credit cards yourself. This is the part where things get complicated, and you need to be serious and careful about your site's security.

Phase III: Processing Orders and Adding Features

The core of e-commerce—and the bit that really separates it from other web-development projects—is handling orders and credit cards. PayPal has helped us put this off, but there are many good reasons why—eventually—you'll want to part company with PayPal:

Cost: PayPal is not expensive, but the extra services it offers must be paid for somehow. Moving to a simpler credit card processing service can mean lower transaction costs (this is not a rule though), although developing your own system will obviously incur upfront costs.

Freedom: PayPal has a fairly strict set of terms and conditions and is designed for residents of a limited number of countries. By taking on more of the credit card processing responsibility yourself, you can better control the way your site works. As an obvious example, you can accept payment using regional methods such as the Switch debit cards common in the United Kingdom.

Integration: If you deal with transactions and orders using your own system, you can integrate your store and your warehouse to whatever extent you require. You could even automatically contact a third-party supplier and have the supplier ship the goods straight to the customer.

Information: When you handle the whole order yourself, you can record and collate all the information involved in the transaction—and then use it for marketing and research purposes.

By integrating the order processing with the warehouse, fulfillment center, or suppliers, you can reduce costs significantly. This might reduce the need for staff in the fulfillment center or allow the business to grow without requiring additional staff.

Acquiring information about customers can feed back into the whole process, giving you valuable information about how to sell more. At its simplest, you could email customers with special offers or just keep in touch with a newsletter. You also could analyze buying patterns and use that data to formulate targeted marketing campaigns.

During Phase III, you will learn how to

- Build a customer accounts module so that customers can log in and retrieve their details every time they make an order

- Allow customers to add product reviews

- Integrate Amazon.com products into your web site using XML Web Services

- Establish secure connections using SSL (Secure Socket Layer) so that data sent by users is encrypted on its travels across the Internet

- Charge credit cards using DataCash and Authorize.net

- Store credit card numbers securely in a database

This third phase is the most involved of all of them and requires some hard and careful work. By the end of Phase III, however, you will have an e-commerce site with a searchable product catalog, shopping cart, secure check out, and complete order-processing system.

HatShop

As we said earlier, we're going to build an online shop called HatShop (which will sell, surprisingly enough, hats). Figure 1-1 shows how HatShop will look at some point during the second stage of development.

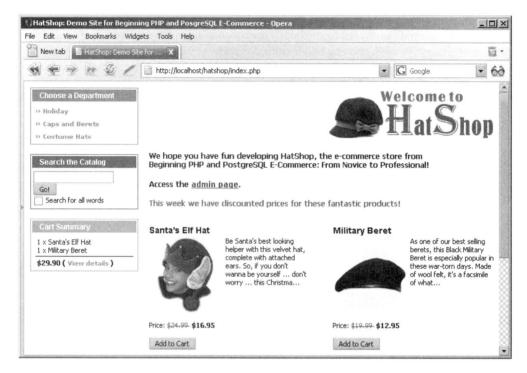

Figure 1-1. *HatShop during Phase II of development*

■**Tip** You can find a link to an online version of HatShop at `http://www.cristiandarie.ro/php-postgresql-ecommerce/`. Many thanks go to the folks at Hats in the Belfry (`http://www.hatsinthebelfry.com`) who allowed us to use some of their products to populate our virtual HatShop store.

For the purposes of this book, we'll assume that the client already exists as a mail-order company and has a good network of customers. The company is not completely new to the business, and wants the site to make it easier and more enjoyable for its existing customers to buy—with the goal that they'll end up buying more.

Knowing this, I suggest the phased development because

- The company is unlikely to get massive orders initially—we should keep the initial cost of building the web site down as much as possible.

- The company is accustomed to manually processing mail orders, so manually processing orders emailed by PayPal will not introduce many new problems.

- The company doesn't want to invest all of its money in a massive e-commerce site, only to find that people actually prefer mail order after all! Or it might find that, after Phase I, the site does exactly what it wants, and there's no point in expanding it further. Either way, I hope that offering a lower initial cost gives my bid the edge. (It might also mean I can get away with a higher total price.)

Because this company is already a mail-order business, it probably already has a merchant account and can process credit cards. Therefore, moving on to Phase III as soon as possible would be best for this company so it can benefit from the preferential card-processing rates.

Summary

In this chapter, we've seen some of the principles of e-commerce in the real, hostile world where it's important to focus on short-term revenue and keeping risks down. We've looked at the three basic reasons an e-commerce site can make money:

- Acquiring more customers

- Making customers spend more

- Reducing the costs of fulfilling orders

We've applied those principles to a three-phase plan that provides a deliverable, usable site at each stage and continues to expand throughout the book.

At this point, you've presented your plan to the owners of the hat shop. In the next chapter, you'll put on your programming hat and start to design and build the web site (assuming you get the contract, of course).

CHAPTER 2

■■■

Laying Out the Foundations

Now that you've convinced the client that you can create a cool web site to complement his or her activity, it's time to stop celebrating and start thinking about how to put into practice all the promises you've made. As usual, when you lay down on paper the technical requirements you must meet, everything starts to seem a bit more complicated than initially anticipated.

Note Be warned that this and the next are dense chapters, and you may found them pretty challenging if you don't have much experience with PHP or PostgreSQL. Books such as *Beginning PHP and PostgreSQL 8: From Novice to Professional* (Apress, 2006) do a good job at preparing you to build your first e-commerce web site. We strongly recommend that you consistently follow an efficient project-management methodology to maximize the chances of the project's success, on budget and on time. Most project-management theories imply that you and your client have signed an initial requirements/specifications document containing the details of the project you're about to create. You can use this document as a guide while creating the solution; it also allows you to charge extra in case the client brings new requirements or requests changes after development has started. See Appendix B for more details.

To ensure this project's success, you need to come up with a smart way to implement what you have signed the contract for. You want to develop the project smoothly and quickly, but the ultimate goal is to make sure the client is satisfied with your work. Consequently, you should aim to provide your site's increasing number of visitors with a positive web experience by creating a pleasant, functional, and responsive web site.

The requirements are high, but this is normal for an e-commerce site today. To maximize the chances of success, we'll analyze and anticipate as many of the technical requirements as possible, and implement solutions in a way that supports changes and additions with minimal effort.

This chapter lays down the foundations for the future HatShop web site. We will talk about the technologies and tools you'll use, and even more importantly, how you'll use them. Your goals for this chapter are to

- Analyze the project from a technical point of view

- Analyze and choose an architecture for your application

- Decide which technologies, programming languages, and tools to use

- Consider naming and coding conventions

- Create the basic structure of the web site and set up the database

- Implement an error-handling routine and a reporting routine in the site skeleton

Designing for Growth

The word *design* in the context of a web application can mean many things. Its most popular usage probably refers to the visual and user interface design of a web site.

This aspect is crucial because, let's face it, the visitor is often more impressed with how a site looks and how easy it is to use than about which technologies and techniques are used behind the scenes or what operating system the web server is running. If the site is slow, hard to use, or easy to forget, it just doesn't matter what rocket science was used to create it.

Unfortunately, this truth makes many inexperienced programmers underestimate the importance of the way the invisible part of the site is implemented—the code, the database, and so on. The visual part of a site gets visitors interested to begin with, but its functionality makes them come back. A web site can sometimes be implemented very quickly based on certain initial requirements, but if not properly architected, it can become difficult, if not impossible, to change.

For any project of any size, some preparation must be done before starting to code. Still, no matter how much preparation and design work is done, the unexpected does happen, and hidden catches, new requirements, and changing rules always seem to work against deadlines. Even without these unexpected factors, site designers are often asked to change or add new functionality many times after the project is finished and deployed. This will also be the case for HatShop, which will be implemented in three separate stages, as discussed in Chapter 1.

You will learn how to create the web site so that the site (or you) will not fall apart when functionality is extended or updates are made. Because this is a programming book, instead of focusing on how to design the user interface or on marketing techniques, we'll pay close attention to designing the code that makes them work.

The phrase, **designing the code**, can have different meanings; for example, we'll need to have a short talk about naming conventions. Still, the most important aspect that we need to take a look at is the application architecture. The architecture refers to the way you split the code for a simple piece of functionality (for example, the product search feature) into smaller components. Although it might be easier to implement that functionality as quickly and as simply as possible in a single component, you gain great long-term advantages by creating more components that work together to achieve the desired result.

Before talking about the architecture itself, you must determine what you want from this architecture.

Meeting Long-Term Requirements with Minimal Effort

Apart from the fact that you want a fast web site, each of the phases of development we talked about in Chapter 1 brings new requirements that must be met.

Every time you proceed to a new stage, you want to be able to **reuse** most of the already existing solution. It would be very inefficient to redesign the whole site (not just the visual part but the code as well!) just because you need to add a new feature. You can make it easier to reuse the solution by planning ahead, so any new functionality that needs to be added can slot in with ease, rather than each change causing a new headache.

When building the web site, implementing a **flexible architecture** composed of pluggable components allows you to add new features—such as the shopping cart, the departments list, or the product search feature—by coding them as separate components and plugging them into the existing application. Achieving a good level of flexibility is one of the goals regarding the application's architecture, and this chapter shows how you can put this into practice. You'll see that the flexibility level is proportional to the amount of time required to design and implement it, so we'll try to find a compromise that will provide the best gains without complicating the code too much.

Another major requirement that is common to all online applications is having a **scalable architecture**. Scalability is defined as the capability to increase resources to yield a linear increase in service capacity. In other words, ideally, in a scalable system, the ratio (proportion) between the number of client requests and the hardware resources required to handle those requests is constant, even when the number of clients increases. An unscalable system can't deal with an increasing number of clients, no matter how many hardware resources are provided. Because we're optimistic about the number of customers, we must be sure that the site will be capable of delivering its functionality to a large number of clients without throwing out errors or performing sluggishly.

Reliability is also a critical aspect for an e-commerce application. With the help of a coherent error-handling strategy and a powerful relational database, you can ensure data integrity and ensure that noncritical errors are properly handled without bringing the site to its knees.

The Magic of the Three-Tier Architecture

Generally, the architecture refers to splitting each piece of the application's functionality into separate components based on what they do and grouping each kind of component into a single logical tier.

Almost every module that you'll create for your site will have components in these three tiers from the application server:

- The presentation tier

- The business tier

- The data tier

The **presentation tier** contains the user interface elements of the site and includes all the logic that manages the interaction between the visitor and the client's business. This tier makes the whole site feel alive, and the way you design it has a crucial importance for the site's success. Because your application is a web site, its presentation tier is composed of dynamic web pages.

The **business tier** (also called the *middle tier*) receives requests from the presentation tier and returns a result to the presentation tier depending on the business logic it contains. Almost any event that happens in the presentation tier usually results in the business tier being called (except events that can be handled locally by the presentation tier, such as simple input data validation, and so on). For example, if the visitor is doing a product search, the presentation tier calls the business tier and says, "Please send me back the products that match this search criterion." Almost always, the business tier needs to call the data tier for information to be able to respond to the presentation tier's request.

The **data tier** (sometimes referred to as the *database tier*) is responsible for managing the application's data and sending it to the business tier when requested. For the HatShop e-commerce site, you'll need to store data about products (including their categories and their departments), users, shopping carts, and so on. Almost every client request finally results in the data tier being interrogated for information (except when previously retrieved data has been cached at the business tier or presentation tier levels), so it's important to have a fast database system. In Chapters 3 and 4, you'll learn how to design the database for optimum performance.

These tiers are purely logical—there is no constraint on the physical location of each tier. In theory, you are free to place all of the application, and implicitly all of its tiers, on a single server machine, or you can place each tier on a separate machine if the application permits this. Chapter 17 explains how to integrate functionality from other web sites using XML Web Services. XML Web Services permit easy integration of functionality across multiple servers.

An important constraint in the three-layered architecture model is that information must flow in sequential order between tiers. The presentation tier is only allowed to access the business tier, and it can never directly access the data tier. The business tier is the "brain" in the middle that communicates with the other tiers and processes and coordinates all the information flow. If the presentation tier directly accessed the data tier, the rules of three-tier architecture programming would be broken. When you implement a three-tier architecture, you must be consistent and obey its rules to reap the benefits.

Figure 2-1 is a simple representation of the way data is passed in an application that implements the three-tier architecture.

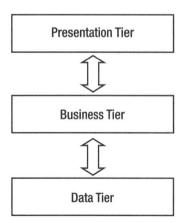

Figure 2-1. *Simple representation of the three-tier architecture*

A Simple Example

It's easier to understand how data is passed and transformed between tiers if you take a closer look at a simple example. To make the example even more relevant to our project, let's analyze a situation that will actually happen in HatShop. This scenario is typical for three-tier applications.

Like most e-commerce sites, HatShop will have a shopping cart, which we will discuss later in the book. For now, it's enough to know that the visitor will add products to the shopping cart by clicking an Add to Cart button. Figure 2-2 shows how the information flows through the application when that button is clicked.

When the user clicks on the Add to Cart button for a specific product (step 1), the presentation tier (which contains the button) forwards the request to the business tier—"Hey, I want this product added to my shopping cart!" (step 2). The business tier receives the request, understands that the user wants a specific product added to the shopping cart, and handles the request by telling the data tier to update the visitor's shopping cart by adding the selected product (step 3). The data tier needs to be called because it stores and manages the entire web site's data, including users' shopping cart information.

The data tier updates the database (step 4) and eventually returns a success code to the business tier. The business tier (step 5) handles the return code and any errors that might have occurred in the data tier while updating the database and then returns the output to the presentation tier.

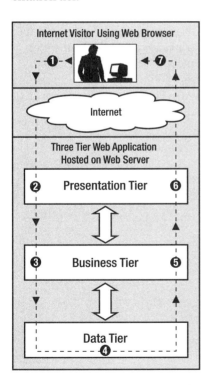

Figure 2-2. *Internet visitor interacting with a three-tier application*

Finally, the presentation tier generates an updated view of the shopping cart (step 6). The results of the execution are wrapped up by generating an HTML (Hypertext Markup Language) web page that is returned to the visitor (step 7), where the updated shopping cart can be seen in the visitor's web browser.

Note that in this simple example, the business tier doesn't do a lot of processing, and its business logic isn't very complex. However, if new business rules appear for your application, you would change the business tier. If, for example, the business logic specified that a product could only be added to the shopping cart if its quantity in stock was greater than zero, an additional data tier call would have been made to determine the quantity. The data tier would only be requested to update the shopping cart if products are in stock. In any case, the presentation tier is informed about the status and provides human-readable feedback to the visitor.

What's in a Number?

It's interesting to note how each tier interprets the same piece of information differently. For the data tier, the numbers and information it stores have no significance because this tier is an engine that saves, manages, and retrieves numbers, strings, or other data types—not product quantities or product names. In the context of the previous example, a product quantity of 0 represents a simple, plain number without any meaning to the data tier (it is simply 0, a 32-bit integer).

The data gains significance when the business tier reads it. When the business tier asks the data tier for a product quantity and gets a "0" result, this is interpreted by the business tier as "Hey, no products in stock!" This data is finally wrapped in a nice, visual form by the presentation tier, such as a label reading, "Sorry, at the moment the product cannot be ordered."

Even if it's unlikely that you want to forbid a customer from adding a product to the shopping cart if the product is not in stock, the example (described in Figure 2-3) is good enough to present in yet another way how each of the three tiers has a different purpose.

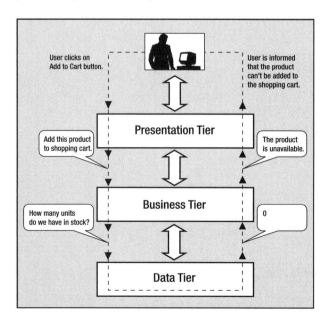

Figure 2-3. *Internet visitor interacting with a three-tier application*

The Right Logic for the Right Tier

Because each layer contains its own logic, sometimes it can be tricky to decide where exactly to draw the line between the tiers. In the previous scenario, instead of reading the product's quantity in the business tier and deciding whether the product is available based on that number (resulting in two data tier, and implicitly, database, calls), you could have a single data tier method named `add_product_if_available` that adds the product to the shopping cart only if it's available in stock.

In this scenario, some logic is transferred from the business tier to the data tier. In many other circumstances, you might have the option to place some logic in one tier or another or maybe in both. In most cases, there is no single best way to implement the three-tier architecture, and you'll need to make a compromise or a choice based on personal preference or external constraints.

Furthermore, there are occasions in which even though you know the *right* way (in respect to the architecture) to implement something, you might choose to break the rules to get a performance gain. As a general rule, if performance can be improved this way, it is okay to break the strict limits between tiers *just a little bit* (for example, add some of the business rules to the data tier or vice versa), *if* these rules are not likely to change in time. Otherwise, keeping all the business rules in the middle tier is preferable because it generates a "cleaner" application that is easier to maintain.

Finally, don't be tempted to access the data tier directly from the presentation tier. This is a common mistake that is the shortest path to a complicated, hard-to-maintain, and inflexible system. In many data access tutorials or introductory materials, you'll be shown how to perform simple database operations using a simple user interface application. In these kinds of programs, all the logic is probably written in a short, single file, instead of separate tiers. Although the materials might be very good, keep in mind that most of these texts are meant to teach you how to do different individual tasks (for example, access a database), and not how to correctly create a flexible and scalable application.

A Three-Tier Architecture for HatShop

Implementing a three-tiered architecture for the HatShop web site will help achieve the goals listed at the beginning of the chapter. The coding discipline imposed by a system that might seem rigid at first sight allows for excellent levels of flexibility and extensibility in the long run.

Splitting major parts of the application into separate smaller components encourages reusability. More than once when adding new features to the site, you'll see that you can reuse some of the already existing bits. Adding a new feature without needing to change much of what already exists is, in itself, a good example of reusability.

Another advantage of the three-tiered architecture is that, if properly implemented, the overall system is resistant to changes. When bits in one of the tiers change, the other tiers usually remain unaffected, sometimes even in extreme cases. For example, if for some reason the backend database system is changed (say, the manager decides to use Oracle instead of PostgreSQL), you only need to update the data tier and maybe just a little bit of the business tier.

Why Not Use More Tiers?

The three-tier architecture we've been talking about so far is a particular (and the most popular) version of the *n*-Tier Architecture. ***n*-Tier Architecture** refers to splitting the solution into a number (*n*) of logical tiers. In complex projects, sometimes it makes sense to split the business layer into more than one layer, thus resulting in architecture with more than three layers. However, for our web site, it makes the most sense to stick with the three-layered design, which offers most of the benefits while not requiring too many hours of design or a complex hierarchy of framework code to support the architecture.

Maybe with a more involved and complex architecture, you could achieve even higher levels of flexibility and scalability for the application, but you would need much more time for design before starting to implement anything. As with any programming project, you must find a fair balance between the time required to design the architecture and the time spent to implement it. The three-tier architecture is best suited to projects with average complexity, such as the HatShop web site.

You also might be asking the opposite question, "Why not use fewer tiers?" A two-tier architecture, also called *client-server* architecture, can be appropriate for less complex projects. In short, a two-tier architecture requires less time for planning and allows quicker development in the beginning, although it generates an application that's harder to maintain and extend in the long run. Because we're expecting to have to extend the application in the future, the client-server architecture is not appropriate for our application, so it won't be discussed further in this book.

Now that the general architecture is known, let's see what technologies and tools you will use to implement it. After a brief discussion of the technologies, you'll create the foundation of the presentation and data tiers by creating the first page of the site and the backend database. You'll start implementing some real functionality in each of the three tiers in Chapter 3 when you start creating the web site's product catalog.

Choosing Technologies and Tools

No matter which architecture is chosen, a major question that arises in every development project is which technologies, programming languages, and tools are going to be used, bearing in mind that external requirements can seriously limit your options.

■**Note** In this book, we're creating a web site using PHP, PostgreSQL, and related technologies. We really like these technologies, but it doesn't necessarily mean they're the best choice for any kind of project, in any circumstances. Additionally, there are many situations in which you must use specific technologies because of client requirements. The System Requirements and Software Requirements stages in the software development process will determine which technologies you must use for creating the application. See Appendix B for more details.

Although the book assumes some previous experience with PHP and PostgreSQL, we'll take a quick look at them and see how they fit into our project and into the three-tier architecture.

■**Note** We included complete environment installation instructions (including Apache, PHP, and PostgreSQL) in Appendix A.

Using PHP to Generate Dynamic Web Content

PHP is an open source technology for building dynamic, interactive web content. Its short description (on the official PHP web site, `http://www.php.net`) is "PHP is a widely-used general-purpose scripting language that is especially suited for Web development and can be embedded into HTML."

PHP stands for *PHP: Hypertext Preprocessor* (yes, it's a recursive acronym), and is available for free download at its official web site. We included complete installation instructions for PHP in Appendix A. Because we're using PHP to build a dynamic web site, you'll also learn how to install Apache and how to integrate PHP with it in Appendix A.

The story of PHP, having its roots somewhere in 1994, is a successful one. Among the factors that led to its success are the following:

- PHP is free; especially when combined with Linux server software, PHP can prove to be a very cost-efficient technology to build dynamic web content.

- PHP has a shorter learning curve than other scripting languages.

- The PHP community is agile, many useful helper libraries or new versions of the existing libraries are being developed (such as those you can find in the PEAR repository or at `http://www.phpclasses.org`), and new features are added frequently.

- PHP works very well on a variety of web servers and operating systems (Unix-like platforms, Windows, Mac OS X).

However, PHP is not the only server-side scripting language around for creating dynamic web pages. Among its most popular competitors are JSP (Java Server Pages), Perl, ColdFusion, and ASP.NET. Among these technologies are many differences but also some fundamental similarities. For example, pages written with any of these technologies are composed of basic HTML, which draws the static part of the page (the template), and code that generates the dynamic part.

▓**Note**   You might want to check out *Beginning ASP.NET 2.0 E-Commerce in C# 2005* (Apress, 2005), which explains how to build e-commerce web sites with ASP.NET 2.0, C#, and SQL Server 2005.

Using Smarty to Separate Layout from Code

Because PHP is simple and easy to start with, it has always been tempting to start coding without properly designing an architecture and framework that would be beneficial in the long run.

What makes things even worse is that the straightforward method of building PHP pages is to mix PHP instructions with HTML because PHP doesn't have by default an obvious technique of separating the PHP code from the HTML layout information.

Mixing the PHP logic with HTML has two important disadvantages:

- This technique often leads to long, complicated, and hard-to-manage code. Maybe you have seen those kilometric source files with an unpleasant mixture of PHP and HTML, which are hard to read and impossible to understand after a week.

- These mixed files are the subject of both designers' and programmers' work, which complicates the collaboration more than necessary. This also increases the chances of the designer creating bugs in the code logic while working on cosmetic changes.

These kinds of problems led to the development of template engines, which offer frameworks separating the presentation logic from the static HTML layout. Smarty (http://smarty.php.net) is the most popular and powerful template engine for PHP. Its main purpose is to offer you a simple way to separate application logic (PHP code) from its presentation code (HTML).

This separation permits the programmer and the template designer to work independently on the same application. The programmer can change the PHP logic without needing to change the template files, and the designer can change the templates without caring how the code that makes them alive works.

Figure 2-4 shows the relationship between the Smarty Design Template file and its Smarty plugin file.

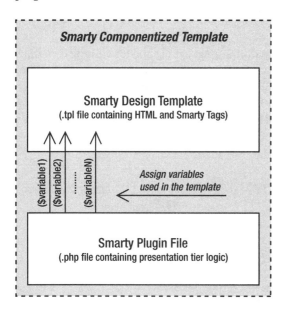

Figure 2-4. *Smarty Componentized Template*

The Smarty Design Template (a .tpl file containing the HTML layout and Smarty-specific tags and code) and its Smarty plugin file (a .php file containing the associated code for the template) form a **Smarty Componentized Template**. You'll learn more about how Smarty works while you're building the e-commerce web site. For a comprehensive Smarty tutorial, read *Smarty PHP Template Programming and Applications* (Packt, 2006).

■**Note** Adding Smarty or another template engine to a web application's architecture adds some initial coding effort and also implies a learning curve. However, you should try it anyway because the advantages of using such a modern development technique will prove to be significant later in the process.

What About the Alternatives?

Smarty is not the only template engine available for PHP. Other popular template engines are

- Yapter (`http://yapter.sourceforge.net/`)

- EasyTemplate (`http://www.onlinetools.org/tools/easytemplate/index.php`)

- phpLib (`http://phplib.sourceforge.net/`)

- TemplatePower (`http://templatepower.codocad.com/`)

Although all template engines follow the same basic principles, we chose to use Smarty in the PHP e-commerce project for this book because of its very good performance results, powerful features (such as template compilation and caching), and wide acceptance in the industry.

Using PostgreSQL to Store Web Site Data

Most of the data your visitors will see while browsing the web site will be retrieved from a relational database. A Relational Database Management System (RDBMS) is a complex software program, the purpose of which is to store, manage, and retrieve data as quickly and reliably as possible. For the HatShop web site, it will store all data regarding the products, departments, users, shopping carts, and so on.

Many RDBMSs are available for you to use with PHP, including PostgreSQL, MySQL, Oracle, and so on. PostgreSQL is arguably the world's most advanced open source database, and it's a free, fast, and reliable database. Another important advantage is that many web hosting providers offer access to a PostgreSQL database, which makes your life easier when going live with your newly created e-commerce web site. We'll use PostgreSQL as the backend database when developing the HatShop e-commerce web site.

The language used to communicate with a relational database is SQL (Structured Query Language). However, each database engine recognizes a particular dialect of this language. If you decide to use a different RDBMS than PostgreSQL, you'll probably need to update some of the SQL queries.

Getting in Touch with PostgreSQL

You talk with the database server by formulating an SQL query, sending it to the database engine, and retrieving the results. The SQL query can say anything related to the web site data, or its data structures, such as "give me the list of departments," "remove product no. 223," "create a data table," or "search the catalog for yellow hats."

No matter what the SQL query says, we need a way to send it to PostgreSQL. PostgreSQL ships with a simple, text-based interface (named "psql") that permits executing SQL queries and getting back the results. The command-line interface isn't particularly easy to use, but it is functional. However, there are alternatives.

Several free, third-party database administration tools allow you to manipulate data structures and execute SQL queries via an easy-to-use graphical interface. In this book, we'll show you how to use pgAdmin III, which is an admin tool that ships together with PostgreSQL.

Apart from needing to interact with PostgreSQL with a direct interface to its engine, you also need to learn how to access PostgreSQL programmatically, from PHP code. This require-ment is obvious, because the e-commerce web site will need to query the database to retrieve catalog information (departments, categories, products, and so on) when building pages for the visitors.

As for querying PostgreSQL databases through PHP code, the tool you'll rely on here is PDO (PHP Data Objects).

Implementing Database Integration Using PDO

PDO (PHP Data Objects) is a native data-access abstraction library that ships with PHP 5.1 and is offered as a PECL extension for PHP 5.0. (PECL is a repository of PHP extensions, located at http://pecl.php.net/.) The official PDO manual, together with installation instructions (which can also be found in Appendix A), is available at http://php.net/pdo.

PDO offers a uniform way to access a variety of data sources. Using PDO increases your application's portability and flexibility because if the backend database changes, the effects on your data access code are kept to a minimum (in many cases, all that needs to change is the connection string for the new database).

After you become familiar with the PDO data-access abstraction layer, you can use the same programming techniques on other projects that might require a different database solution.

To demonstrate the difference between accessing the database using the old PHP func-tions and PDO, let's take a quick look at two short PHP code snippets.

■**Note** If you aren't familiar with how the code works, don't worry—we'll analyze everything in greater detail in the following chapters.

The following shows database access using PHP native (PostgreSQL-specific) functions:

```
// Connecting to PostgreSQL
$link = pg_connect('host=localhost dbname=hatshop' .
                   'user=' . $username . ' password=' . $password)
       or die('Could not connect: ' . pg_last_error($link));

// Execute SQL query
$queryString = 'SELECT * FROM product';
```

```
$result = pg_query($link, $queryString)
          or die('Query failed : ' . pg_last_error($link));

// Close connection
pg_close($link);
```

Next, the same action is shown, this time using PDO:

```
try
{
  // Create a new PDO instance
  $database_handler =
    new PDO('pgsql:host=localhost;dbname=hatshop',
            $username, $password);

  // Prepare the SQL query
  $statement_handler =
    $database_handler->prepare('SELECT * FROM product');

  // Execute SQL query
  $statement_handler->execute();

  // Retrieve result
  $result = $statement_handler->fetchAll();

  // Clear the PDO object instance
  $database_handler = null;
}
catch (PDOException $e)
{
  /* If something goes wrong we catch the exception thrown by
     the object, print the message and stop the execution of
     script */
  print 'Error! <br />' . $e->getMessage() . '<br />';

  exit;
}
```

The version of the code that uses PDO is longer, but it includes a powerful error-handling mechanism and *prepared statements* (which protect you from injection-based attacks). If these concepts sound foreign, once again, wait until the later chapters where we'll put PDO to work, and you'll learn more about it there.

Also, when using PDO, you won't need to change the data access code if, for example, you decide to use MySQL instead of PostgreSQL. On the other hand, the first code snippet, which uses PostgreSQL-specific functions, would need to change completely (use mysql_connect and mysql_query instead of pg_connect and pg_query, and so on). In addition, some MySQL-specific functions have different parameters than the similar PostgreSQL functions.

When using a database abstraction layer (such as PDO), you'll probably only need to change the connection string when changing the database backend. Note that here we're only talking about the PHP code that interacts with the database. In practice, you might also need to update some SQL queries if the database engines support different dialects of SQL.

■**Note** To keep your SQL queries as portable as possible, keep their syntax as close as possible to the SQL-92 standard. You'll learn more about SQL details in Chapter 3.

PostgreSQL and the Three-Tier Architecture

It is clear by now that PostgreSQL is somehow related to the data tier. However, if you haven't worked with databases until now, it might be less than obvious that PostgreSQL is more than a simple store of data. Apart from the actual data stored inside, PostgreSQL is also capable of storing logic in the form of stored procedures, maintaining table relationships, ensuring various data integrity rules are obeyed, and so on.

You can communicate with PostgreSQL through SQL (Structured Query Language), which is a language used to interact with the database. SQL is used to transmit to the database instructions such as "Send me the last 10 orders" or "Delete product #123."

Although it's possible to compose SQL statements in your PHP code and then submit them for execution, this is generally a *bad practice*, because it incurs security, consistency, and performance penalties. In our solution, we'll store all data tier logic using **database functions**.

The code presented in this book was designed to work with PostgreSQL 8.1 (the most recent stable version at the time of writing). PostgreSQL consists of the data store in the e-commerce software project, as shown in Figure 2-5.

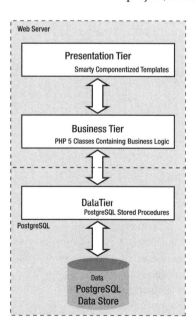

Figure 2-5. *The technologies you'll use to develop HatShop*

Choosing Naming and Coding Standards

Although coding and naming standards might not seem that important at first, they definitely shouldn't be overlooked. Not following a set of rules for your code will almost always result in code that's hard to read, understand, and maintain. On the other hand, when you follow a consistent way of coding, you can almost say your code is already half documented, which is an important contribution toward the project's maintainability, especially when more people are working on the same project at the same time.

■Tip Some companies have their own policies regarding coding and naming standards, whereas in other cases, you'll have the flexibility to use your own preferences. In either case, the golden rule to follow is *be consistent in the way you code*. Commenting your code is another good practice that improves the long-term maintainability of your code.

Naming conventions refer to many elements within a project, simply because almost all of a project's elements have names: the project itself, files, classes, variables, methods, method parameters, database tables, database columns, and so on. Without some discipline when naming all those elements, after a week of coding you won't understand a single line of what you've written.

When developing HatShop, we followed a set of naming conventions that are popular among PHP developers. Some of the most important rules are summarized here and in the following piece of code:

```php
class WarZone
{
  public  $mSomeSoldier;
  private $_mSomeOtherSoldier;

  function SearchAndDestroy($someEnemy, $someOtherEnemy)
  {
    $master_of_war = 'Soldier';
    $this->mSomeSoldier = $someEnemy;
    $this->_mSomeOtherSoldier = $someOtherEnemy;
  }
}
```

- Class names and method names should be written using Pascal casing (uppercase letters for the first letter in every word), such as in `WarZone` or `IsDataValid`.

- Public class attribute names follow the same rules as class names but should be prepended with the character "m". So, valid public attribute names look like this: `$mSomeSoldier`.

- Private class attribute names follow the same rules as public class attribute names, except they're also prepended with an underscore, such as in `$_mSomeOtherSoldier`.

- Method argument names should use camel casing (uppercase letters for the first letter in every word except the first one), such as $someEnemy, $someOtherEnemy.

- Variable names should be written in lowercase, with an underscore as the word separator, such as $master_of_war.

- Database objects use the same conventions as variable names (the department_id column).

- Try to indent your code using a fixed number of spaces (say, four) for each level. (The code in this book uses two spaces because of physical space limitations.)

Among the decisions that need to be made is whether to use quotes for strings. JavaScript, HTML, and PHP allow using both single quotes and double quotes. For the code in this book, we'll use double quotes in HTML and JavaScript code, and we'll use single quotes in PHP. Although for JavaScript it's a matter of taste (you can use single quotes, as long as you use them consistently), in PHP, the single quotes are processed faster, they are more secure, and they are less likely to cause programming errors. Learn more about PHP strings at http://php.net/types.string. You can find two useful articles on PHP strings at http://www.sitepoint.com/print/quick-php-tips and http://www.jeroenmulder.com/weblog/2005/04/php_single_and_double_quotes.php.

Starting the HatShop Project

So far, we have dealt with theory regarding the application you're going to create. It was fun, but it's going to be even more interesting to put into practice what you've learned up until now.

Start your engines!

Installing the Required Software

The code in this book has been tested with

- PHP 5.1

- Apache 2.2

- PostgreSQL 8.1

Caution The code is most likely to be compatible with newer versions of the mentioned software, but it won't work with versions of PHP older than PHP 5.

The project should work with other web servers as well, as long as they're compatible with PHP 5.1 (see http://www.php.net/manual/en/installation.php). However, Apache is the web server of choice for the vast majority of PHP projects.

See Appendix A for detailed installation instructions for PHP, Apache, and PostgreSQL.

Getting a Code Editor

Before writing the first line of code, you'll need to install a code editor, if you don't already have a favorite. Many free editors are available, and there is an ever longer list of commercial editors. It's a matter of taste and money. You can find a list of PHP editors at `http://www.php-editors.com`. Here are a few of the more popular:

- Zend Studio (`http://www.zend.com/products/zend_studio`) is perhaps the most powerful IDE (Integrated Development Environment) available for developing PHP web applications.

- phpEclipse (`http://www.phpeclipse.net`) is an increasingly popular environment for developing PHP web applications. Zend is a member of the Eclipse foundation.

- Emacs (`http://www.gnu.org/software/emacs/`) is, as defined on its web site, an "extensible, customizable, self-documenting real-time display editor." Emacs is a very powerful, free, and cross-platform editor.

- SciTe (`http://scintilla.sourceforge.net/SciTEDownload.html`) is a free and cross-platform editor.

- PSPad (`http://www.pspad.com/`) is a freeware editor popular among Windows developers. The editor knows how to highlight the syntax for many existing file formats. Additional plugins can add integrated CSS editing functionality and spell checking.

- PHP Designer 2006 (`http://www.mpsoftware.dk`) is a Windows editor that contains an integrated debugger.

Preparing the hatshop Virtual Folder

One of the advantages of working with open source, platform-independent technologies is that you can choose the operating system to use for development. You should be able to develop and run HatShop on Windows, Unix, Linux, Mac, and others. However, this also means that you may struggle a little bit to set up your initial environment, especially if you're a beginner.

When setting up the project's virtual folder, a few details differ depending on the operating system (mostly because of the different file paths), so we'll cover them separately for Windows and for Unix systems in the following pages. However, the main steps are the same:

1. Create a folder in the file system named `hatshop` (we use lowercase for folder names), which will contain the HatShop project's files (such as PHP code, image files, and so on).

2. Edit Apache's configuration file (`httpd.conf`) to create a virtual folder named `hatshop` that points to the `hatshop` physical folder created earlier. This way, when pointing a web browser to `http://localhost/hatshop`, the project in the `hatshop` physical folder will be loaded. This functionality is implemented in Apache using aliases, which are configured through the `httpd.conf` configuration file. The syntax of an alias entry is as follows:

```
Alias virtual_folder_name real_folder_name
```

■**Tip** The `httpd.conf` configuration file is well documented, but you can also check the Apache 2 documentation available at `http://httpd.apache.org/docs-2.0/`.

If you're working on Windows, follow the steps in the following exercise. The steps for Unix systems will follow after this exercise.

Exercise: Preparing the hatshop Virtual Folder on Windows

1. Create a new folder named `hatshop`, which will be used for all the work you'll do in this book. You might find it easiest to create it in the root folder (`C:\`), but because we'll use relative paths in the project, feel free to create it in any location.

2. The default place used by Apache to serve client requests from is usually something like `C:\Program Files\Apache Software Foundation\ApacheX.Y\htdocs`. This location is defined by the `DocumentRoot` directive in the Apache configuration file, which is located in the `APACHE_BASE/conf/httpd.conf` file (where `APACHE_BASE` is the Apache installation folder).

   Because we want to use our folder instead of the default folder mentioned by `DocumentRoot`, we need to create a virtual folder named `hatshop` that points to the `hatshop` physical folder you created in step 1. Open the Apache configuration file (`httpd.conf`), and add the following lines:

   ```
   <IfModule alias_module>
     # ...
     Alias /hatshop/ "C:/hatshop/"
     Alias /hatshop "C:/hatshop"
   </IfModule>
   <Directory "C:/hatshop">
     Allow from all
   </Directory>
   ```

   After adding these lines and restarting the Apache web server, a request for `http://localhost/hatshop` or `http://localhost/hatshop/` will result in the application in the `hatshop` folder (if it existed) being executed.

3. Create a file named `test.php` in the `hatshop` folder, with the following line inside:

   ```
   <?php phpinfo(); ?>
   ```

4. Restart the Apache web server, and load `http://localhost/hatshop/test.php` (or `http://localhost:8080/hatshop/test.php` if Apache works on port 8080) in a web browser.

Exercise: Preparing the hatshop Virtual Folder on Unix Systems

1. Create a new folder named `hatshop`, which will be used for all the work you'll do in this book. You might find it easiest to create it in your home directory (in which case the complete path to your `hatshop` folder will be something like `/home/username/hatshop`), but because we'll use relative paths in the project, feel free to create it in any location.

2. The default place used by Apache to serve client requests from is usually something like `/usr/local/apache2/htdocs/`. This location is defined by the `DocumentRoot` directive in the Apache configuration file, whose complete path is usually `/usr/local/apache/conf/httpd.conf`.

   Because we want to use our folder instead of the default folder mentioned by `DocumentRoot`, we need to create a virtual folder named `hatshop` that points to the `hatshop` physical folder you created in step 1. Open the Apache configuration file (`httpd.conf`), find the Aliases section, and add the following lines:

   ```
   <IfModule alias_module>
     # ...
     Alias /hatshop/ "/home/username/hatshop/"
     Alias /hatshop "/home/username/hatshop"
   </IfModule>
   <Directory "/home/username/hatshop">
     Allow from all
   </Directory>
   ```

   After adding these lines, a request for `http://localhost/hatshop` or `http://localhost/hatshop/` will result in the application in the `hatshop` folder (if it existed) being executed.

3. Create a file named `test.php` in the `hatshop` folder, with the following line inside:

   ```
   <?php phpinfo(); ?>
   ```

4. Restart the Apache web server, and load `http://localhost/hatshop/test.php` (or `http://localhost:8080/hatshop/test.php` if Apache works on port 8080) in a web browser.

How It Works: The Virtual Folder

This first step toward building the HatShop e-commerce site is a small, but important, one because it allows you to test that Apache, PHP, and the `hatshop` alias work okay. If you have problems running the test page, make sure you followed the installation steps in Appendix A correctly.

No matter whether you're working on Windows or a Unix flavor, loading `test.php` in a web browser should give you the PHP information returned by the `phpinfo` function as shown in Figure 2-6.

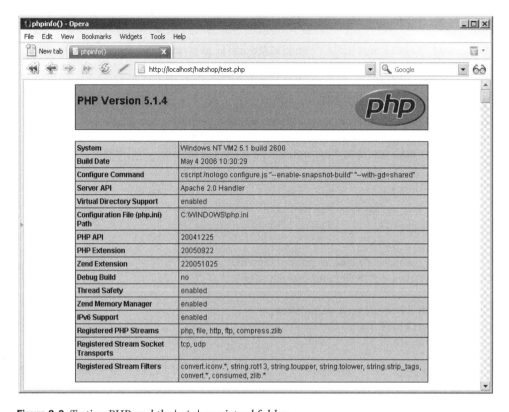

Figure 2-6. *Testing PHP and the* hatshop *virtual folder*

You also ensured that the hatshop directory and all its contents can be accessed properly by the web server.

Installing Smarty

Installing Smarty implies simply copying the Smarty PHP classes to your project's folder. Many web-hosting companies provide these classes for you, but it's better to have your own installation for two reasons:

- It's always preferable to make your project independent of the server's settings, when possible.

- Even if the hosting system has Smarty installed, that company's version might be changed in time, perhaps without notice, possibly affecting your web site's functionality.

You'll install Smarty into a subfolder of the `hatshop` folder named `libs` in the following exercise. The steps should work the same no matter what operating system you're running on.

Exercise: Installing Smarty

1. Create a folder named `libs` inside the `hatshop` folder, and then create a folder named `smarty` inside the `libs` folder.

2. Download the latest version of Smarty from `http://smarty.php.net/download.php`, and download the latest stable release. The archive is a .tar.gz file. To open it under Windows, you'll need a program such as WinZip (`http://www.winzip.com`) or WinRar (`http://www.rarlabs.com`). Open the archive, and copy the contents of the `Smarty-2.X.Y/libs` directory from the archive to the folder you created earlier (`hatshop/libs/smarty`). You only need to copy the contents of the mentioned `libs` folder, nothing more.

3. To operate correctly, Smarty needs three folders, which you need to create: `templates`, `templates_c`, and `configs`. Create a folder named `presentation` inside the `hatshop` directory, and in this folder create two folders named `templates` and `templates_c`. The `presentation` folder will contain all the presentation files.

4. Create a folder named `include` in the `hatshop` folder. This will have all the config files of the application. Inside this folder create a folder named `configs`.

5. If you're using a Unix operating system, you'll also need to set some security options. You need to ensure that Apache has write access to the `templates_c` directory, where the Smarty engine needs to save its compiled template files (you'll learn more about this a bit later).

   If you're building your project under a Unix system, you should execute the following command to ensure that your Apache server can access your project's files and has write permissions to the `templates_c` directory:

   ```
   chmod a+w /home/username/hatshop/presentation/templates_c
   ```

■**Note** Setting permissions on Unix systems as shown here allows any user with a shell account on your Unix box to view the source code of any files in your folder, including PHP code and other data (which might include sensitive information such as database passwords, keys used to encrypt/decrypt credit card information, and so on). To fine-tune the security settings, consult your system administrator.

How It Works: The Smarty Installation

In this exercise, you created these three folders used by Smarty:

- The `templates` folder will contain the Smarty templates for your web site (`.tpl` files).

- The `templates_c` folder will contain the compiled Smarty templates; these are files generated automatically by the Smarty engine.

- The `configs` folder will contain configuration files you might need for templates.

After adding these folders, your folder structure should look like this:

```
hatshop/
   include/
      configs/
   libs/
      smarty/
         internals/
         plugins/
   presentation/
      templates/
      templates_c/
```

Implementing the Site Skeleton

The visual design of the site is usually agreed upon after a discussion with the client, and in collaboration with a professional web designer. Alternatively, you can buy a web site template from one of the many companies that offer this kind of service for a reasonable price.

This is a programming book, so we won't focus on web design issues. We will implement a simple, yet friendly and usable design, which will allow for easy customization (if you'll need to apply your layout on top of the one we're creating here) and will allow you to focus on the technical details of the site.

All pages in HatShop, including the first page, will have the structure shown in Figure 2-7.

Although the detailed structure of the product catalog is covered in the next chapter, right now we know that a main list of departments needs to be displayed on every page of the site. When the visitor clicks on a department, the list of categories for that department will appear below the departments list. The site also has the search box that will allow visitors to perform product searches. At the top of the page, the site header will be visible in any page the visitor browses.

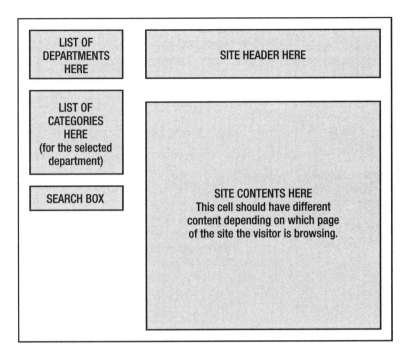

Figure 2-7. *Structure of web pages in HatShop*

To implement this structure as simply as possible, we'll use Smarty Componentized Templates (or simple Smarty Design Templates) to create the separate parts of the page as shown in Figure 2-8.

As Figure 2-8 suggests, you will create a Smarty componentized template named departments_list and a simple Smarty design template file named header.tpl, which will help you populate the first page.

Using Smarty templates to implement different pieces of functionality provides benefits discussed earlier in the chapter. Having different, unrelated pieces of functionality logically separated from one another gives you the flexibility to modify them independently and even reuse them in other pages without having to write their code again. It's also extremely easy to change the place in the parent web page of a feature implemented as a Smarty template.

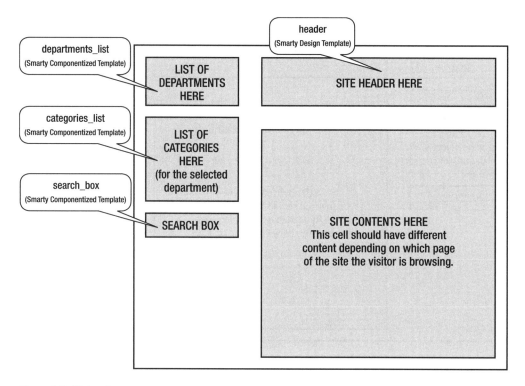

Figure 2-8. *Using Smarty to generate content*

▌**Note** We call **Smarty Componentized Template** the combination of a **Smarty Design Template** (the .tpl file) and its associated **Smarty Plugin file**, which contains the presentation tier logic (a .php file). In cases of simple pages that don't need an associated .php code file, such as the header, we'll use just a Smarty Design Template file. You'll meet Smarty plugins in Chapter 3, and you can learn more about them at http://smarty.php.net/manual/en/plugins.php.

The list of departments, the search box, and the site header are elements that will be present in every page of the site. The list of categories appears only when the visitor selects a department from the list. The most dynamic part of the web site that changes while browsing through the site will be the contents cell, which will update itself depending on the site location requested by the visitor. There are two main options for implementing that cell: add a componentized template that changes itself depending on the location or use different componentized templates to populate the cell depending on the location being browsed. There is no rule of thumb about which method to use because it mainly depends on the specifics of the project. For HatShop, you will create a number of componentized templates that will fill that location.

In the remainder of this chapter, you will

- Create the main web page and the header template.

- Implement the foundations of the error-handling system in HatShop.

- Create the HatShop database.

Building the First Page

The main page in HatShop will be generated by the files `index.php` and `index.tpl`.

You'll write the `index.tpl` Smarty template with placeholders for the three major parts of the site—the header, the table of departments, and the page contents cell. Implement the main page in the following exercise, and we'll discuss the details in the "How It Works" section thereafter.

Exercise: Implementing the First Page and Its Header

1. Create a new folder named `images` inside the `hatshop` folder.

2. Copy the files in `images_folder/images` from the Source Code/Download of the book (which you can find at the book details page on `http://www.apress.com` or `http://www.cristiandarie.ro`) to `hatshop/images` (the folder you just created).

3. Create a file named `site.conf` in the `hatshop/include/configs` folder (used by the Smarty templates engine), and add the following line to it:

```
site_title = "HatShop : Demo Site for Beginning PHP and PostgreSQL E-Commerce"
```

4. Create a file named `index.tpl` in `hatshop/presentation/templates`, and add the following code to it:

```
{* smarty *}
{config_load file="site.conf"}
<!DOCTYPE html PUBLIC "-//W3C//DTD XHTML 1.1//EN"
 "http://www.w3.org/TR/xhtml11/DTD/xhtml11.dtd">
<html>
  <head>
    <title>{#site_title#}</title>
    <link href="hatshop.css" type="text/css" rel="stylesheet" />
  </head>
  <body>
    <div>
      <div class="left_box">
        Place list of departments here
      </div>
      {include file="header.tpl"}
      <div id="content">
        Place contents here
```

```
        </div>
      </div>
    </body>
  </html>
```

5. Create a template file named `header.tpl` in `hatshop/presentation/templates`, and add the following contents to it:

```
<div id="header">
  <a href="index.php">
    <img src="images/title.png" alt="Site title" />
  </a>
</div>
```

6. Create a file named `hatshop.css` in the root folder of your project (`hatshop`), and write this code:

```
body
{
  font-family: tahoma, verdana, arial;
  font-size: 11px;
  margin: 0px;
  padding: 5px;
  text-align: center;
}
body div
{
  margin: 0px;
  padding: 5px;
  text-align: left;
}
.left_box
{
  margin: 0px 15px 15px 0px;
  padding: 2px;
  width: 170px;
}
img
{
  border: 0;
}
#header
{
  left: 194px;
  margin: 0px;
  padding: 0px;
  position: absolute;
  text-align: right;
  top: 10px;
  width: 570px;
}
```

```
}
#content
{
  left: 194px;
  margin: 0px;
  padding: 0px 0px 10px 10px;
  position: absolute;
  top: 110px;
  width: 558px;
}
```

7. Add a file named config.php to the hatshop/include folder, with the following contents:

```php
<?php
// SITE_ROOT contains the full path to the hatshop folder
define('SITE_ROOT', dirname(dirname(__FILE__)));

// Application directories
define('PRESENTATION_DIR', SITE_ROOT . '/presentation/');
define('BUSINESS_DIR', SITE_ROOT . '/business/');

// Settings needed to configure the Smarty template engine
define('SMARTY_DIR', SITE_ROOT . '/libs/smarty/');
define('TEMPLATE_DIR', PRESENTATION_DIR . '/templates');
define('COMPILE_DIR', PRESENTATION_DIR . '/templates_c');
define('CONFIG_DIR', SITE_ROOT . '/include/configs');
?>
```

Before moving on, let's see what happens here. dirname(__FILE__) returns the parent directory of the current file; naturally, dirname(dirname(__FILE__)) returns the parent of the current file's directory. This way our SITE_ROOT constant will be set to the full path of hatshop. With the help of the SITE_ROOT constant, we set up absolute paths of Smarty folders.

8. Create a file named app_top.php in the hatshop/include folder, and add the following contents to it:

```php
<?php
// Include utility files
require_once 'include/config.php';

// Load the page template
require_once PRESENTATION_DIR . 'page.php';
?>
```

This file (app_top.php) will be included at the top of the main web pages to perform the necessary initializations.

9. Create a file named page.php in the hatshop/presentation folder, and add the following contents to it:

```php
<?php
// Reference Smarty library
require_once SMARTY_DIR . 'Smarty.class.php';
```

```
/* Class that extends Smarty, used to process and display Smarty
   files */
class Page extends Smarty
{
  // Class constructor
  public function __construct()
  {
    // Call Smarty's constructor
    parent::Smarty();

    // Change the default template directories
    $this->template_dir = TEMPLATE_DIR;
    $this->compile_dir = COMPILE_DIR;
    $this->config_dir = CONFIG_DIR;
  }
}
?>
```

In page.php, you extend the Smarty class with a wrapper class named Page, which changes Smarty's default behavior. The Page class configures in its constructor the Smarty folders you created earlier.

Tip As mentioned earlier, Smarty requires three folders to operate: templates, templates_c, and configs. In the constructor of the Page class, we set a separate set of these directories for our application. If you want to turn on caching, then Smarty also needs a directory named cache. We will not be using Smarty caching for HatShop, but you can read more details about this in the Smarty manual at http://smarty.php.net/manual/en/caching.php.

---

10. Add the index.php file to the hatshop folder. The role of this file is to load the index.tpl template by using the Page class you created earlier. Here's the code for index.php:

```
<?php
// Load Smarty library and config files
require_once 'include/app_top.php';

// Load Smarty template file
$page = new Page();

// Display the page
$page->display('index.tpl');
?>
```

11. Now it's time to see some output from this thing. Load http://localhost/hatshop/ in your favorite web browser, and admire the results as shown in Figure 2-9.

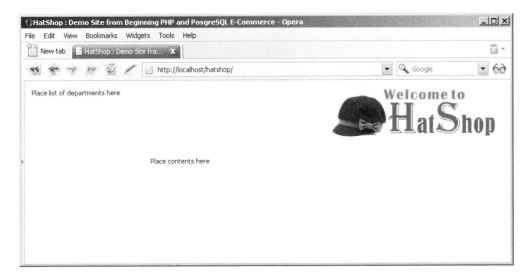

Figure 2-9. *Running HatShop*

How It Works: The First Page of HatShop

The main web page contains three major sections. There are two table cells that you'll fill with componentized templates—one for the list of departments and one for the page contents—in the following chapters.

Notice the departments list placed on the left side, the header at the top, and the contents cell filled with information regarding the first page. As previously mentioned, this contents cell is the only one that changes while browsing the site; the other two cells will look exactly the same no matter what page is visited. This implementation eases your life as a programmer and keeps a consistent look and feel for the web site.

Before you move on, it's important to understand how the Smarty template works. Everything starts from index.php, so you need to take a close look at it. Here's the code again:

```php
<?php
// Load Smarty library and config files
require_once 'include/app_top.php';

// Load Smarty template file
$page = new Page();

// Display the page
$page->display('index.tpl');
?>
```

At this moment, this file has very simple functionality. First, it loads app_top.php, which sets some global variables, and then it loads the Smarty template file, which will generate the actual HTML content when a client requests index.php.

The standard way to create and configure a Smarty page is shown in the following code snippet:

```php
<?php
// Load the Smarty library
require_once SMARTY_DIR . 'Smarty.class.php';

// Create a new instance of the Smarty class
$smarty = new Smarty();
$smarty->template_dir = TEMPLATE_DIR;
$smarty->compile_dir = COMPILE_DIR;
$smarty->config_dir = CONFIG_DIR;
?>
```

In HatShop, we created a class named Page that inherits from Smarty, which contains the initialization procedure in its constructor. This makes working with Smarty templates easier. Here's again the code of the Page class:

```php
class Page extends Smarty
{
  // Class constructor
  public function __construct()
  {
    // Call Smarty's constructor
    parent::Smarty();

    // Change the default template directories
    $this->template_dir = TEMPLATE_DIR;
    $this->compile_dir = COMPILE_DIR;
    $this->config_dir = CONFIG_DIR;
  }
}
```

■**Note** The notion of constructor is specific to object-oriented programming terminology. The constructor of a class is a special method that executes automatically when an instance of that class is created. In PHP, the constructor of a class is called __construct(). Writing that code in the constructor of the Page class guarantees that it gets executed automatically when a new instance of Page is created.

The Smarty template file (index.tpl), except for a few details, contains simple HTML code. Those details are worth analyzing. In index.tpl, before the HTML code begins, the configuration file site.conf is loaded.

```
{* smarty *}
{config_load file="site.conf"}
```

Tip Smarty comments are enclosed between {* and *} marks.

At this moment, the only variable set inside the `site.conf` file is `site_title`, which contains the name of the web site. The value of this variable is used to generate the title of the page in the HTML code:

```
<!DOCTYPE html PUBLIC "-//W3C//DTD XHTML 1.1//EN"
  "http://www.w3.org/TR/xhtml11/DTD/xhtml11.dtd">
<html>
  <head>
    <title>{#site_title#}</title>
    <link href="hatshop.css" type="text/css" rel="stylesheet" />
  </head>
```

Variables that are loaded from the config files are referenced by enclosing them within hash marks (#), or with the smarty variable `$smarty.config`, as in:

```
<head>
  <title>{$smarty.config.site_title}</title>
</head>
```

We loaded the `site.conf` config file using `{config_load file="site.conf"}` and accessed the `site_title` variable with `{#site_title#}`, which you'll use whenever you need to obtain the site title. If you want to change the site title, all you have to do is edit `site.conf`.

Finally, it's important to notice how to include a Smarty template in another Smarty template. `index.tpl` references `header.tpl`, which will also be reused in a number of other pages:

```
<body>
  <div>
    <div class="left_box">
      Place list of departments here
    </div>
    {include file="header.tpl"}
    <div id="content">
      Place contents here
    </div>
  </div>
</body>
</html>
```

Last, it's worth noting that we're using CSS (Cascading Style Sheets). CSS allows setting formatting options in a centralized document that is referenced from HTML files. If the job is done right, and CSS is used consistently in a web site, CSS will allow you to make visual changes to the entire site (or parts of the site) with very little effort, just by editing the CSS file. There are many books and tutorials on CSS, including the free ones you can find at `http://www.w3.org/Style/CSS/` and `http://www.w3schools.com/css/default.asp`. Many useful CSS-related resources can be found at `http://www.csszengarden.com/`. Using CSS is highly recommended because of the significant benefits it brings. You'll see much more action with CSS in Chapter 3.

Handling and Reporting Errors

Although the code will be written to run without any unpleasant surprises, there's always a possibility that something might go wrong when processing client requests. The best strategy to deal with these unexpected problems is to find a centralized way to handle these errors and perform certain actions when they do happen.

PHP is known for its confusing error messages. If you've worked with other programming languages, you probably appreciate the information you can get from displaying the stack trace when you have an error. Tracing information is not displayed by default when you have a PHP error, so you'll want to change this behavior. In the development stage, tracing information will help you debug the application, and in a release version, the error message must be reported to the site administrator. Another problem is the tricky E_WARNING error message type because it's hard to tell whether it's fatal or not for the application.

Tip If you don't remember or don't know what a PHP error message looks like, try adding the following line in your include/app_top.php file:

require_once 'inexistent_file.php';

Load the web site in your favorite browser, and notice the error message you get. If you do this test, make sure to remove the problematic line afterwards!

In the context of a live web application, errors can happen unexpectedly for various reasons, such as software failures (operating system or database server crashes, viruses, and so on) and hardware failures. It's important to be able to log these errors and eventually inform the web site administrator (perhaps by sending an email message), so the error can be taken care of as fast as possible.

For these reasons, we'll start establishing an efficient error-handling and reporting strategy. You'll create a class named ErrorHandler that will manage the error handling. In this class, you'll create a static user-defined error handler method named Handler, which will get executed anytime a PHP error happens during runtime. In PHP, you define a custom error handler using the set_error_handler() function.

Caution As you'll see, the second parameter of set_error_handler() is used to specify the error types that the specified handler function should handle. However, this second parameter is supported only since PHP 5. Read more details at http://www.php.net/set_error_handler. You can also find more info about PHP errors and logging in the PHP manual at http://www.php.net/manual/en/ ref.errorfunc.php.

Serious error types (E_ERROR, E_PARSE, E_CORE_ERROR, E_CORE_WARNING, E_COMPILE_ERROR, and E_COMPILE_WARNING) cannot be intercepted and handled by ErrorHandler::Handler, but the other types of PHP errors (E_WARNING for example) can be.

The error-handling method, `Handler`, will behave like this:

- It creates a detailed error message.

- If configured to do so, the error is emailed to the site administrator.

- If configured to do so, the error is logged to an errors log file.

- If configured to do so, the error is shown in the response web page.

- Serious errors will halt the execution of the page. The other ones will allow the page to continue processing normally.

Let's implement the `ErrorHandler` class in the next exercise.

Exercise: Implementing the ErrorHandler Class

1. Add the following error-handling related configuration variables to `include/config.php`:

```php
<?php
// SITE_ROOT contains the full path to the hatshop folder
define('SITE_ROOT', dirname(dirname(__FILE__)));

// Application directories
define('PRESENTATION_DIR', SITE_ROOT . '/presentation/');
define('BUSINESS_DIR', SITE_ROOT . '/business/');

// Settings needed to configure the Smarty template engine
define('SMARTY_DIR', SITE_ROOT . '/libs/smarty/');
define('TEMPLATE_DIR', PRESENTATION_DIR . '/templates');
define('COMPILE_DIR', PRESENTATION_DIR . '/templates_c');
define('CONFIG_DIR', SITE_ROOT . '/include/configs');

// These should be true while developing the web site
define('IS_WARNING_FATAL', true);
define('DEBUGGING', true);

// The error types to be reported
define('ERROR_TYPES', E_ALL);

// Settings about mailing the error messages to admin
define('SEND_ERROR_MAIL', false);
define('ADMIN_ERROR_MAIL', 'admin@example.com');
define('SENDMAIL_FROM', 'errors@example.com');
ini_set('sendmail_from', SENDMAIL_FROM);

// By default we don't log errors to a file
define('LOG_ERRORS', false);
define('LOG_ERRORS_FILE', 'c:\\hatshop\\errors_log.txt'); // Windows
// define('LOG_ERRORS_FILE', '/var/tmp/hatshop_errors.log'); // Unix
```

```
   /* Generic error message to be displayed instead of debug info
      (when DEBUGGING is false) */
   define('SITE_GENERIC_ERROR_MESSAGE', '<h2>HatShop Error!</h2>');
   ?>
```

2. In the hatshop folder, create a subfolder named business.

3. In the business folder, create a file named error_handler.php file, and write the following code:

```php
<?php
class ErrorHandler
{
  // Private constructor to prevent direct creation of object
  private function __construct()
  {
  }

  /* Set user error handler method to ErrorHandler::Handler method */
  public static function SetHandler($errTypes = ERROR_TYPES)
  {
    return set_error_handler(array ('ErrorHandler', 'Handler'), $errTypes);
  }

  // Error handler method
  public static function Handler($errNo, $errStr, $errFile, $errLine)
  {
    /* The first two elements of the backtrace array are irrelevant:
         - ErrorHandler.GetBacktrace
         - ErrorHandler.Handler */
    $backtrace = ErrorHandler::GetBacktrace(2);

    // Error message to be displayed, logged, or mailed
    $error_message = "\nERRNO: $errNo\nTEXT: $errStr" .
                     "\nLOCATION: $errFile, line " .
                     "$errLine, at " . date('F j, Y, g:i a') .
                     "\nShowing backtrace:\n$backtrace\n\n";

    // Email the error details, in case SEND_ERROR_MAIL is true
    if (SEND_ERROR_MAIL == true)
      error_log($error_message, 1, ADMIN_ERROR_MAIL, "From: " .
              SENDMAIL_FROM . "\r\nTo: " . ADMIN_ERROR_MAIL);

    // Log the error, in case LOG_ERRORS is true
    if (LOG_ERRORS == true)
      error_log($error_message, 3, LOG_ERRORS_FILE);
```

```php
    /* Warnings don't abort execution if IS_WARNING_FATAL is false
       E_NOTICE and E_USER_NOTICE errors don't abort execution */
    if (($errNo == E_WARNING && IS_WARNING_FATAL == false) ||
        ($errNo == E_NOTICE || $errNo == E_USER_NOTICE))
    // If the error is nonfatal ...
    {
      // Show message only if DEBUGGING is true
      if (DEBUGGING == true)
        echo '<pre>' . $error_message . '</pre>';
    }
    else
    // If error is fatal ...
    {
      // Show error message
      if (DEBUGGING == true)
        echo '<pre>' . $error_message . '</pre>';
      else
        echo SITE_GENERIC_ERROR_MESSAGE;

      // Stop processing the request
      exit;
    }
  }

  // Builds backtrace message
  public static function GetBacktrace($irrelevantFirstEntries)
  {
    $s = '';
    $MAXSTRLEN = 64;
    $trace_array = debug_backtrace();

    for ($i = 0; $i < $irrelevantFirstEntries; $i++)
      array_shift($trace_array);
    $tabs = sizeof($trace_array) - 1;

    foreach ($trace_array as $arr)
    {
      $tabs -= 1;
      if (isset ($arr['class']))
        $s .= $arr['class'] . '.';
      $args = array ();

      if (!empty ($arr['args']))
```

```
          foreach ($arr['args']as $v)
          {
            if (is_null($v))
              $args[] = 'null';
            elseif (is_array($v))
              $args[] = 'Array[' . sizeof($v) . ']';
            elseif (is_object($v))
              $args[] = 'Object: ' . get_class($v);
            elseif (is_bool($v))
              $args[] = $v ? 'true' : 'false';
            else
            {
              $v = (string)@$v;
              $str = htmlspecialchars(substr($v, 0, $MAXSTRLEN));
              if (strlen($v) > $MAXSTRLEN)
                $str .= '...';
              $args[] = '"' . $str . '"';
            }
          }

      $s .= $arr['function'] . '(' . implode(', ', $args) . ')';
      $line = (isset ($arr['line']) ? $arr['line']: 'unknown');
      $file = (isset ($arr['file']) ? $arr['file']: 'unknown');
      $s .= sprintf(' # line %4d, file: %s', $line, $file);
      $s .= "\n";
    }

    return $s;
  }
}
?>
```

4. Modify the include/app_top.php file to include the newly created error_handler.php file, and set the error handler:

```
<?php
// Include utility files
require_once 'include/config.php';
require_once BUSINESS_DIR . 'error_handler.php';

// Sets the error handler
ErrorHandler::SetHandler();

// Load the page template
require_once PRESENTATION_DIR . 'page.php';
?>
```

5. Great! You just finished writing the new error-handling code. Let's test it. First, load the web site in your browser to see that you typed in everything correctly. If you get no errors, test the new error-handling system by adding the following line to include/app_top.php:

```php
<?php
// Include utility files
require_once 'include/config.php';
require_once BUSINESS_DIR . 'error_handler.php';

// Sets the error handler
ErrorHandler::SetHandler();

// Load the page template
require_once PRESENTATION_DIR . 'page.php';

// Try to load inexistent file
require_once 'inexistent_file.php';
?>
```

Now load again index.php in your browser, and admire your brand new error message as shown in Figure 2-10.

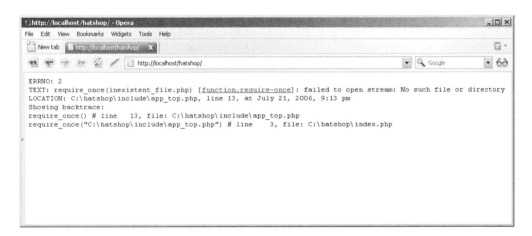

Figure 2-10. *Error message showing backtrace information*

Don't forget to remove the buggy line from app_top.php before moving on.

How It Works: Error Handling

The method that intercepts web site errors and deals with them is ErrorHandler::Handler (located in error_handler.php). The code that registers the ErrorHandler::Handler function to be the one that handles errors in your site is in the ErrorHandler::SetHandler method that is invoked in app_top.php:

```
/* Set user error handler method to ErrorHandler::Handler method */
public static function SetHandler($errTypes = ERROR_TYPES)
{
  return set_error_handler(array ('ErrorHandler', 'Handler'), $errTypes);
}
```

■**Note** The second parameter of set_error_handler specifies the range of errors that should be inter-cepted. E_ALL specifies all types of errors, including E_NOTICE errors, which should be reported during web site development.

When called, ErrorHandler::Handler constructs the error message with the help of a method named ErrorHandler::GetBacktrace, and forwards the error message to the client's browser, a log file, the administrator (by email), or a combination of these, which can be configured by editing config.php.

GetBacktrace gets the backtrace information from the debug_backtrace function (which was introduced in PHP 4.3.0) and changes its output format to generate an HTML error message similar to a Java error. It isn't important to understand every line in GetBacktrace unless you want to personalize the backtrace displayed in case of an error. The 2 parameter sent to GetBacktrace specifies that the backtrace results should omit the first two entries (the calls to ErrorHandler::Handler and ErrorHandler::GetBacktrace).

You build the detailed error string in ErrorHandler::Handler, including the backtrace information:

```
$backtrace = ErrorHandler::GetBacktrace(2);

// Error message to be displayed, logged or mailed
$error_message = "\nERRNO: $errNo\nTEXT: $errStr" .
                 "\nLOCATION: $errFile, line " .
                 "$errLine, at " . date('F j, Y, g:i a') .
                 "\nShowing backtrace:\n$backtrace\n\n";
```

Depending on the configuration options from the config.php file, you decide whether to display, log, and/or email the error. Here we use PHP's error_log method, which knows how to email or write the error's details to a log file:

```
    // Email the error details, in case SEND_ERROR_MAIL is true
    if (SEND_ERROR_MAIL == true)
      error_log($error_message, 1, ADMIN_ERROR_MAIL, "From: " .
                SENDMAIL_FROM . "\r\nTo: " . ADMIN_ERROR_MAIL);

    // Log the error, in case LOG_ERRORS is true
    if (LOG_ERRORS == true)
      error_log($error_message, 3, LOG_ERRORS_FILE);
```

■**Note** If you want to be able to send an error email to a localhost mail account (your_name@
localhost), then you should have an SMTP (Simple Mail Transfer Protocol) server started on your machine.
On a Red Hat (or Fedora) Linux distribution, you can start an SMTP server with the following command:

```
service sendmail start
```

■**Note** On Windows systems, you should check in IIS (Internet Information Services) Manager for Default
SMTP Virtual Server and make sure it's started.

While you are developing the site, the DEBUGGING constant should be set to true, but after launching the site in
the "wild," you should make it false, causing a user-friendly error message to be displayed instead of the
debugging information in case of serious errors, and no message shown at all in case of
nonfatal errors.

The errors of type E_WARNING are pretty tricky because you don't know which of them should stop the execution
of the request. The IS_WARNING_FATAL constant set in config.php decides whether this type of error should
be considered fatal for the project. Also, errors of type E_NOTICE and E_USER_NOTICE are not considered fatal:

```
/* Warnings don't abort execution if IS_WARNING_FATAL is false
   E_NOTICE and E_USER_NOTICE errors don't abort execution */
if (($errNo == E_WARNING && IS_WARNING_FATAL == false) ||
    ($errNo == E_NOTICE || $errNo == E_USER_NOTICE))
// If the error is nonfatal ...
{
  // Show message only if DEBUGGING is true
  if (DEBUGGING == true)
    echo '<pre>' . $error_message . '</pre>';
}
else
// If error is fatal ...
{
  // Show error message
  if (DEBUGGING == true)
    echo '<pre>' . $error_message . '</pre>';
  else
    echo SITE_GENERIC_ERROR_MESSAGE;

  // Stop processing the request
  exit;
}
```

In the following chapters, you'll need to manually trigger errors using the trigger_error PHP function, which
lets you specify the kind of error to generate. By default, it generates E_USER_NOTICE errors, which are not
considered fatal but are logged and reported by ErrorHandler::Handler code.

Preparing the Database

The final step in this chapter is to create the PostgreSQL database, although you won't use it until the next chapter. We will show you the steps to create your database and create a user with full privileges to it using the pgAdmin III utility that ships with PostgreSQL. If you're working with a database hosted by a hosting service, the service may give you access to your database through a web-based utility such as phpPgAdmin. See `http://phppgadmin.sourceforge.net/` for more details about using phpPgAdmin.

Before moving on, make sure you have PostgreSQL 8 installed. Consult Appendix A for installation instructions. Follow the steps in the exercise to create the database and a new user account.

Exercise: Creating the hatshop Database and a New User Account

1. Start the pgAdmin III utility, and select your database server from the left pane (in Windows, you start pgAdmin III by choosing Start ➤ Programs ➤ PostgreSQL ➤ pgAdmin III). The window should then look like the one in Figure 2-11.

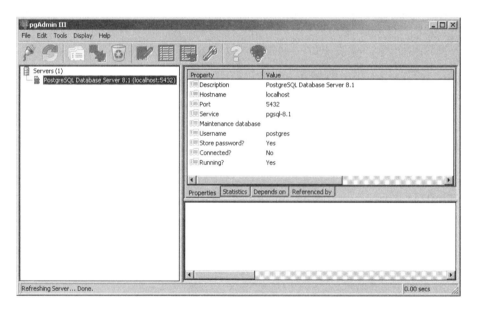

Figure 2-11. *The main pgAdmin III page*

2. While the database server is selected, choose Tools ➤ Connect. Alternatively, you can right-click the database server entry, and select Connect from the context menu. If asked, enter the root password and click OK.

3. You connected to the database server using the superuser account. For our project, we want to create a regular user account that will have access just to the `hatshop` database. Extend the database server node, right-click the Login Roles node, and select New Login Role from the context menu. Type **hatshopadmin** for the role name and for its password, and check the Superuser check box, as shown in Figure 2-12. Then click OK.

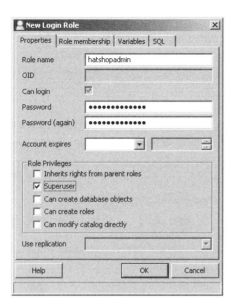

Figure 2-12. *Creating a new database role*

4. Now create the `hatshop` database. Right-click the Databases node, and choose New Database from the context menu. Type **hatshop** for its name, and select hatshopadmin from the Owner drop-down list. If you intend to store non-ASCII data, you should also choose the UTF-8 encoding, as shown in Figure 2-13. Click OK, and wait until the process completes and the New Database dialog box closes.

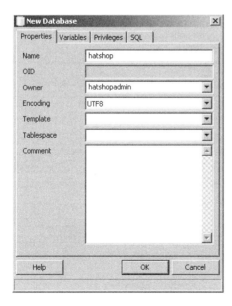

Figure 2-13. *Creating a new database*

■**Note** All operations performed with the pgAmin III utility can be also done by executing SQL code. SQL is the language used to interact with the database, and pgAdmin III can be used as an interface for executing SQL commands into your database. You'll learn more about SQL while following the exercises in this book.

5. In the end, select the hatshop node. You can browse the tree to see how an empty database looks, but don't worry, you'll start filling it with data in the next chapter. pgAdmin III is nice enough to even show you the SQL query it used to create your database (see Figure 2-14).

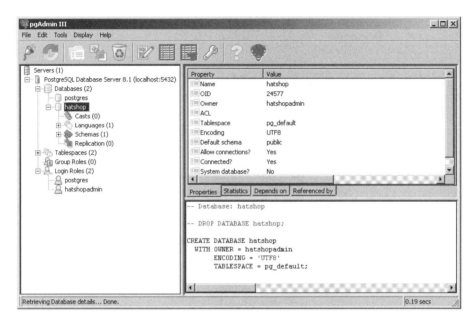

Figure 2-14. *Your brand new database*

6. From now on, when connecting to the hatshop database, you won't use the PostgreSQL superuser any more, but you'll use the hatshopadmin account instead. For a quick test, select the database server, and then choose Tools ➤ Disconnect. Right-click the database server, choose Properties, and type **hatshopadmin** in the Username text box, as shown in Figure 2-15. Click OK. On the next attempt to connect to the server, you'll be asked for the password of the hatshopadmin user. After logging in, you'll have access only to the hatshop database and to the public objects of any other databases.

Figure 2-15. *Logging in as hatshopadmin*

Downloading the Code

You can find the latest code downloads and a link to an online version of HatShop at the authors' web sites, at http://www.emilianbalanescu.ro or http://www.cristiandarie.ro, or in the Source Code/Download section of the Apress web site at http://www.apress.com. It should be easy to read through this book and build your solution as you go; however, if you want to check something from our working version, you can. Instructions on loading the chapters are available in the welcome.html document in the download.

Summary

Hey, we covered a lot of ground in this chapter, didn't we? We talked about the three-tier architecture and how it helps you create great flexible and scalable applications. We also saw how each of the technologies used in this book fits into the three-tier architecture.

So far, we have a very flexible and scalable application because it doesn't have much functionality, but you'll feel the real advantages of using a disciplined way of coding in the next chapters. In this chapter, you have only coded the basic, static part of the presentation tier, implemented a bit of error-handling code, and created the hatshop database, which is the support for the data tier. In the next chapter, you'll start implementing the product catalog and learn a lot about how to dynamically generate visual content using data stored in the database with the help of the middle tier and with smart and fast controls and components in the presentation tier.

CHAPTER 3

Creating the Product Catalog: Part I

After learning about the three-tier architecture and implementing a bit of your web site's main page, it's time to continue your work by starting to create the HatShop product catalog.

Because the product catalog is composed of many components, you'll create it over two chapters. In this chapter, you'll create the first data table, implement access methods in the middle tier, and learn how to deal with the data tier. By the end of this chapter, you'll finally have something dynamically generated on your web page. In Chapter 4, you'll finish building the product catalog by adding support for categories, product lists, a product details page, and more!

The main topics we'll touch on in this chapter are

- Analyzing the structure of the product catalog and the functionality it should support

- Creating the database structures for the catalog and the data tier of the catalog

- Implementing the business tier objects required to make the catalog run

- Implementing a functional user interface for the product catalog

Showing Your Visitors What You've Got

One of the essential features required in any e-store is to allow the visitor to easily browse through the products. Just imagine what Amazon.com would be like without its excellent product catalog!

Whether your visitors are looking for something specific or just browsing, it's important to make sure their experience with your site is a pleasant one. After all, you want your visitors to find what they are looking for as easily and painlessly as possible. This is why you'll want to add search functionality to the site and also find a clever way of structuring products into categories so they can be quickly and intuitively accessed.

Depending on the size of the store, it might be enough to group products under a number of categories, but if there are a lot of products, you'll need to find even more ways to categorize and structure the product catalog.

Determining the structure of the catalog is one of the first tasks to accomplish in this chapter. Keep in mind that in a professional approach, these details would have been established before starting to code when building the requirements document for the project, as explained in Appendix B. However, for the purposes of this book, we prefer to deal with things one at a time.

After the structure of the catalog is established, you'll start writing the code that makes the catalog work as planned.

What Does a Product Catalog Look Like?

Today's web surfers are more demanding than they used to be. They expect to find information quickly on whatever product or service they have in mind, and if they don't find it, they are likely to go to the competition before giving the site a second chance. Of course, you don't want this to happen to *your* visitors, so you need to structure the catalog to make it as intuitive and helpful as possible.

Because the e-store will start with around 100 products and will probably have many more in the future, it's not enough to just group them in categories. The store also has a number of departments and each department will contain a number of categories. Each category can then have any number of products attached to it.

■**Note** Later in the book, you'll also create the administrative part of the web site, often referred to as the *Control Panel*, which allows the client to update department, category, and product data. Until then, you'll manually fill in the database with data (or you can "cheat" by using the SQL scripts provided as part of the Source Code/Download section of the Apress web site at `http://www.apress.com`, as you'll see).

Another particularly important detail that you need to think about is whether a category can exist in more than one department and whether a product can exist in more than one category. As you might suspect, this is the kind of decision that has implications on the way you code the product catalog, so you need to consult your client on this matter.

For the HatShop product catalog, each category can exist in only one department, but a product can exist in more than one category. For example, the product "Military Beret" will appear in both "Berets" and "Military Hats" categories. This decision will have implications in the way you'll design the database, and we'll highlight those implications when we get there.

Finally, apart from having the products grouped in categories, you also want to have featured products. For this web site, a product can be featured either on the front page or in the department pages. The next section shows a few screenshots that explain this.

Previewing the Product Catalog

Although you'll have the fully functional product catalog finished by the end of Chapter 4, taking a look at it right now will give you a better idea about where you're heading. In Figure 3-1, you can see the HatShop front page and two of its featured products.

Note the departments list in the upper-left corner of the page. The list of departments is dynamically generated with data gathered from the database; you'll implement the list of departments in this chapter.

When site visitors click a department in the departments list, they go to the main page of the specified department. This replaces the store's list of catalog-featured products with a page containing information specific to the selected department—including the list of featured products for that department. In Figure 3-2, you see the page that will appear when the Holiday department is clicked.

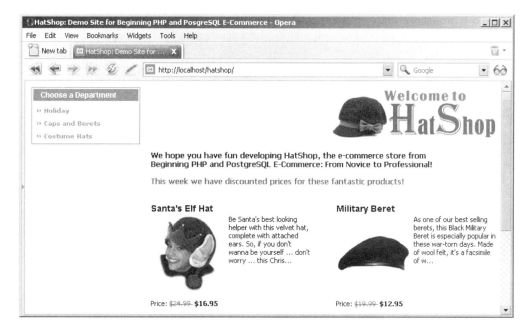

Figure 3-1. *HatShop front page and two of its featured products*

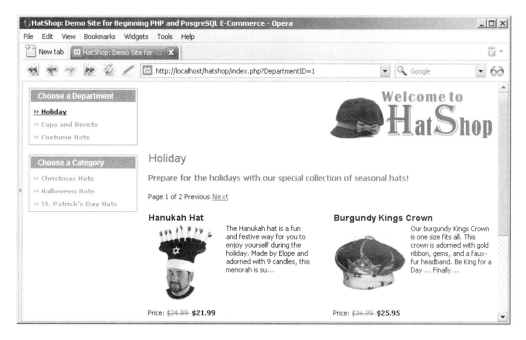

Figure 3-2. *Visiting the Holiday department*

Under the list of departments, you can now see the list of categories that belong to the selected department. In the right side of the screen, you can see the name of the selected department, its description, and its featured products. We decided to list only the featured products in the department page, in part because the complete list would be too long. The text above the list of featured products is the description for the selected department, which means you'll need to store both a name and a description for each department in the database.

In this page, when a particular category from the categories list is selected, all of its products are listed, along with updated title and description text.

Clicking a product's image in any of the products lists takes you to a product details page, which you can see in Figure 3-3.

Figure 3-3. *Visiting the Halloween Hats category*

When a category is selected, all its products are listed—you no longer see featured products. Note that the description text also changes. This time, this is the description of the selected category.

Roadmap for This Chapter

As you can see, the product catalog, although not very complicated, has more parts that need to be covered. In this chapter, you'll only create the departments list (see Figure 3-4).

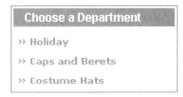

Figure 3-4. *The departments list*

The departments list will be the first dynamically generated data in your site (the names of the departments will be extracted from the database).

In this chapter, you'll implement just the departments list part of the web site. After you understand what happens behind the list of departments, you'll quickly implement the other components of the product catalog in Chapter 4.

In Chapter 2, we discussed the three-tiered architecture that you'll use to implement the web application. The product catalog part of the site makes no exception to the rule, and its components (including the departments list) will be spread over the three logical layers. Figure 3-5 previews what you'll create at each tier in this chapter to achieve a functional departments list.

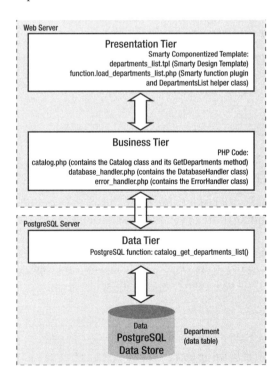

Figure 3-5. *The components of the departments list*

So far, you've only played a bit with the presentation and business tiers in Chapter 2. Now, when building the catalog, you'll finally meet the final tier and work further with the hatshop database. (Depending on whom you ask, the data store may or may not be considered an integral part of the three-tiered architecture.)

These are the main steps you'll take toward having your own dynamically generated departments list. Note that you start with the database and make your way to the presentation tier:

1. Create the `department` table in the database. This table will store data regarding the store's departments. Before adding this table, you'll learn the basic concepts of working with relational databases.

2. Write a PostgreSQL function named `catalog_get_departments_list`, which returns the IDs and names of the departments from the `department` table. PHP scripts will call this function to generate the departments list for your visitor. PostgreSQL functions are logically located in the data tier of your application. At this step, you'll learn how to speak to your relational database using SQL.

3. Create the `DatabaseHandler` class, which will be your helper class that performs common database interaction operations. `DatabaseHandler` is a wrapper class for some PDO functions and includes consistent error-handling techniques that deal with database-related errors.

4. Create the business tier components of the departments list (the `Catalog` class and its `GetDepartments` method). You'll see how to communicate with the database, through the `DatabaseHandler` helper class, to retrieve the necessary data.

5. Implement the `departments_list` Smarty template and its Smarty plugin function, which build on the lower layers to generate a good-looking list of departments for your visitor. The Smarty plugin function file will also contain a helper class named `DepartmentsList`.

So, let's start by creating the `department` table.

Storing Catalog Information

The vast majority of web applications, e-commerce web sites being no exception, live around the data they manage. Analyzing and understanding the data you need to store and process is an essential step in successfully completing your project.

The typical data storage solution for this kind of application is a relational database. However, this is not a requirement—you have the freedom to create your own data access layer and have whatever kind of data structures you want to support your application.

■**Note** In some particular cases, it may be preferable to store your data in plain text files or XML files instead of databases, but these solutions are generally not suited for applications such as HatShop, so we won't cover them in this book. However, it's good to know your options.

Although this is not a book about databases or relational database design, you'll learn all you need to know to understand the product catalog and make it work.

Essentially, a relational database is made up of **data tables** and the **relationships** that exist between them. Because you'll work with a single data table in this chapter, we'll cover only the database theory that applies to the table as a separate, individual database item. In the next chapter, when you'll add the other tables to the picture, we'll take a closer look at the theory behind relational databases by analyzing how the tables relate to each other and how PostgreSQL helps you deal with these relationships.

■**Note** In a real-world situation, you would probably design the whole database (or at least all the tables relevant to the feature you build) from the start. In this book, we chose to split the development over two chapters to maintain a better balance of theory and practice.

So, let's start with a little bit of theory, after which you'll create the department data table and the rest of the required components:

Understanding Data Tables

This section provides a quick database lesson covering the essential information you need to know to design simple data tables. We'll briefly discuss the main parts that make up a database table:

- Primary keys

- PostgreSQL data types

- UNIQUE columns

- NOT NULL columns and default values

- Serial columns and sequences

- Indexes

■**Note** If you have enough experience with PostgreSQL, you might want to skip this section and go directly to the "Creating the department Table" section.

A data table is made up of columns and rows. Columns are also referred to as **fields**, and rows are sometimes also called **records**.

Because this chapter only covers the departments list, you'll only need to create one data table: the department table. This table will store your departments' data and is one of the simplest tables you'll work with.

With the help of tools such as pgAdmin III, it's easy to create a data table in the database *if* you know for sure what kind of data it will store. When designing a table, you must consider which fields it should contain and which data types should be used for those fields. Besides a field's data type, there are a few more properties to consider, which you'll learn about in the following pages.

To determine which fields you need for the department table, write down a few examples of records that would be stored in that table. Remember from the previous figures that there isn't much information to store about a department—just the name and description for each department. The table containing the departments' data might look like Figure 3-6 (you'll implement the table in the database later, after we discuss the theory).

Holiday	Prepare for the holidays with our special collection of seasonal hats!
Caps and Berets	The perfect hats to wear at work and costume parties!
Costume Hats	Find the matching hat for your new costume!

Figure 3-6. *Data from the* department *table*

From a table like this, the names would be extracted to populate the list in the upper-left part of the web page, and the descriptions would be used as headers for the featured products list.

Primary Keys

The way you work with data tables in a relational database is a bit different from the way you usually work on paper. A fundamental requirement in relational databases is that each data row in a table must be *uniquely identifiable*. This makes sense because you usually save records into a database so that you can retrieve them later; however, you can't always do that if each table row doesn't have something that makes it unique. For example, suppose you add another record to the department table shown previously in Figure 3-6, making it look like the table shown in Figure 3-7.

Holiday	Prepare for the holidays with our special collection of seasonal hats!
Caps and Berets	The perfect hats to wear at work and costume parties!
Costume Hats	Find the matching hat for your new costume!
Costume Hats	Don't try this at home!

Figure 3-7. *Two departments with the same name*

Look at this table, and then find the description of the "Costume Hats" department. Yep, we have a problem—two departments with the same name "Costume Hats" (the name isn't unique). If you queried the table using the name column, you would get two results.

To solve this problem, you use a **primary key**, which allows you to uniquely identify a specific row out of many rows. Technically, the primary key is not a column itself. Instead, the PRIMARY KEY is a **constraint** that when applied on a column guarantees that the column will have unique values across the table.

■Note Applying a PRIMARY KEY constraint on a field also generates a unique index created on it by default. Indexes are objects that improve performance of many database operations, dramatically speeding up your web application (you'll learn more about this later in the "Indexes" section of this chapter).

Constraints are rules that apply to data tables and make up part of the **data integrity** rules of the database. The database takes care of its own integrity and makes sure these rules aren't broken. If, for example, you try to add two identical values for a column that has a PRIMARY KEY constraint, the database refuses the operation and generates an error. We'll do some experiments later in this chapter to show this.

■Note A primary key is not a column but a constraint that applies to that column; however, from now on and for convenience, when referring to the primary key, we'll be talking about the column that has the PRIMARY KEY constraint applied to it.

Back to the example, setting the name column as the primary key of the department table would solve the problem because two departments would not be allowed to have the same name. If name is the primary key of the department table, searching for a product with a specific name will always produce exactly one result if the name exists, or no results if no records have the specified name.

■Tip This is common sense, but it has to be said: a primary key column will never allow NULL values.

An alternative solution, and usually the preferred one, is to have an additional column in the table, called an ID column, to act as its primary key. With an ID column, the department table would look like Figure 3-8.

1	Holiday	Prepare for the holidays with our special collection of seasonal hats!
2	Caps and Berets	The perfect hats to wear at work and costume parties!
3	Costume Hats	Find the matching hat for your new costume!

Figure 3-8. *Adding an* ID *column as the primary key of* department

The primary key column is named department_id. We'll use this naming convention for primary key columns in all data tables we'll create.

There are two main reasons it's better to create a separate numerical primary key column than to use the name (or another existing column) as the primary key:

Performance: The database engine handles sorting and searching operations much faster with numerical values than with strings. This becomes even more relevant in the context of working with multiple related tables that need to be frequently joined (you'll learn more about this in Chapter 4).

Department name changes: If you need to rely on the ID value being stable in time, creating an artificial key solves the problem because it's unlikely you'll ever want to change the ID.

In Figure 3-8, the primary key is composed of a single column, but this is not a requirement. If the primary key is set on more than one column, the group of primary key columns (taken as a unit) is guaranteed to be unique, but the individual columns that form the primary key can have repeating values in the table. In Chapter 4, you'll see an example of a multivalued primary key. For now, it's enough to know that they exist.

Unique Columns

UNIQUE is yet another kind of constraint that can be applied to table columns. This constraint is similar to the PRIMARY KEY constraint in that it doesn't allow duplicate data in a column. Still, there are differences. Although there is only one PRIMARY KEY constraint per table, you are allowed to have as many UNIQUE constraints as you like.

Columns that have the UNIQUE constraint are useful when you already have a primary key but still have columns (or groups of columns) for which you want to have unique values. You can set name to be unique in the department table if you want to forbid repeating values.

We won't use the UNIQUE constraint in this book, but we mention it here for completeness. We decided to allow identical department names because only site administrators will have the privilege to modify or change department data.

The facts that you need to remember about UNIQUE constraints are

- The UNIQUE constraint forbids having identical values on the field.

- You can have more that one UNIQUE field in a data table.

- A UNIQUE field is allowed to accept NULL values, in which case, it will accept any number of them.

- Indexes are automatically created on UNIQUE and PRIMARY KEY columns.

Columns and Data Types

Each column in a table has a particular data type. By looking at the previously shown Figure 3-8 with the department table, department_id has a numeric data type, whereas name and description contain text.

It's important to consider the many data types that PostgreSQL Server supports so that you'll be able to make correct decisions about how to create your tables. Table 3-1 isn't an exhaustive list of PostgreSQL data types, but it focuses on the main types you might come across in your project. Refer to the PostgreSQL documentation for a more detailed list at http://www.postgresql.org/docs/current/interactive/datatype.html.

Tip For more information about any specific detail regarding PostgreSQL or PHP, including PostgreSQL data types, you can always refer to W. Jason Gilmore's *Beginning PHP and PostgreSQL 8: From Novice to Professional* (Apress, 2006), which is an excellent reference.

To keep the table short, under the "Data Type" heading, we have listed the used types in this project, while similar data types are explained under the "Description and Notes" heading. You don't need to memorize the list, but you should get an idea of which data types are available.

Table 3-1. *PostgreSQL Server Data Types for Use in HatShop*

Data Type	Size in Bytes	Description and Notes
integer	4 bytes	Signed 4-byte integer that stores numbers from -2,147,483,648 to 2,147,483,647. You can also refer to it using the int and int4 aliases. Related types are bigint(8 bytes) and smallint (2 bytes).
numeric (precision, scale)	variable	Stores numbers with exact precision. The precision specifies the total number of digits the number can have (including the digits to the right of the decimal point). The scale specifies the number of digits for the fractional part of the number. An integer number has a scale of 0. The PostgreSQL documentation gives as an example the number 23.5141, which has a precision of 6 and a scale of 4. You'll use the numeric type to store monetary information because it has exact precision.
timestamp	8 bytes	Stores date and time data from 4713 BC to 5874897 AD.
character	variable	Stores fixed-length character data. Strings shorter than the maximum value are completed with spaces, and longer strings are truncated. The trailing spaces aren't taken into account when comparing values of this type. A commonly used alias of this data type is char.
character varying	variable	Stores variable-length character data. A commonly used alias of this data type is varchar. The dimension you set represents the maximum length of strings it can accept (longer strings are truncated).
text	unlimited	Stores strings of unlimited value. The PostgreSQL documentation states that there are no performance differences between the text and character varying string data types.
serial	4 bytes	This is not a "true" data type, but a convention used to define an autonumbered integer column, similar to the AUTO_INCREMENT in MySQL or IDENTITY in SQL Server. In PostgreSQL 7.3 or newer, serial doesn't imply UNIQUE, and you must (and should) specify this explicitly if you want the column to store unique values. A variation of serial is the bigserial type, which implements the autonumbering feature over bigint.

Keep in mind that data type names are case insensitive, so you might see them capitalized differently depending on the database console program you're using.

Now let's get back to the department table and determine which data types to use. Don't worry that you don't have the table yet in your database; you'll create it a bit later. Figure 3-9 shows the design of department in pgAdmin III. department_id is a serial data type, and name and description are varchar data types.

Column name	Definition
department_id	serial NOT NULL
name	varchar(50) NOT NULL
description	varchar(1000)

Figure 3-9. *Designing the* department *table*

For character varying, the associated dimension—such as in character varying(50)—represents the maximum length of the stored strings. We'll choose to have 50 characters available for the department's name and 1,000 for the description. An integer record, as shown in the table, always occupies 4 bytes.

NOT NULL Columns and Default Values

For each column of the table, you can specify whether it is allowed to be NULL. The best and shortest definition for NULL is "undefined." For example, in your department table, only department_id and name are really required, whereas description is optional—meaning that you are allowed to add a new department without supplying a description for it. If you add a new row of data without supplying a value for columns that allow nulls, NULL is automatically supplied for them.

Especially for character data, there is a subtle difference between the NULL value and an "empty" value. If you add a product with an empty string for its description, this means that you actually set a value for its description; it's an empty string, not an undefined (NULL) value.

The primary key field never allows NULL values. For the other columns, it's up to you to decide which fields are required and which are not.

In some cases, instead of allowing NULLs, you'll prefer to specify default values. This way, if the value is unspecified when creating a new row, it will be supplied with the default value. The default value can be a literal value (such as 0 for a salary column or "unknown" for a description column), a system value, or a function.

Serial Columns and Sequences

Serial columns are "autonumbered" columns. When a column is declared a serial column, PostgreSQL automatically provides values for it when inserting new records into the table. Usually if max is the largest value currently in the table for that column, then the next generated value will be max+1.

This way, the generated values are always unique, which makes them especially useful when used in conjunction with the PRIMARY KEY constraint. You already know that primary keys are used on columns that uniquely identify each row of a table. If you set a primary key column to also be a serial column, PostgreSQL Server automatically fills that column with values when adding new rows (in other words, it generates new IDs), ensuring that the values are unique.

Serial columns are defined using the serial data type. This data type is not a "real" data type but a notation that automatically defines a SEQUENCE structure over the integer data type. The following SQL code creates a table named department with a serial column that is also the primary key:

```
CREATE TABLE department
(
  department_id SERIAL NOT NULL,
  name          VARCHAR(50) NOT NULL,
  description   VARCHAR(1000),
  CONSTRAINT pk_department_id PRIMARY KEY (department_id)
);
```

This is in fact a shorter form of

```
CREATE SEQUENCE department_department_id_seq;

CREATE TABLE department
(
  department_id INTEGER NOT NULL DEFAULT nextval('department_department_id_seq'),
  name          VARCHAR(50) NOT NULL,
  description   VARCHAR(1000),
  CONSTRAINT pk_department PRIMARY KEY (department_id)
);
```

When setting a serial column, the first value that PostgreSQL Server provides for that column is 1, but you can change this before adding data to your table with an SQL statement like the following:

```
ALTER SEQUENCE department_department_id_seq RESTART WITH 123;
```

This way, your PostgreSQL server will start generating values with 123. Now you understand that the default value shown in Figure 3-9 for department_id uses the sequence to generate new values for the column.

For more details about the serial data type, see its official documentation at http://www.postgresql.org/docs/current/interactive/datatype.html#DATATYPE-SERIAL. The documentation for updating the sequence can be found at http://www.postgresql.org/docs/current/interactive/sql-altersequence.html.

▪Note Unlike other database servers, PostgreSQL still allows you to manually specify for an autonumbered field when adding new rows, if you want.

Indexes

Indexes are related to PostgreSQL performance tuning, so we'll mention them only briefly here.

Indexes are database objects meant to increase the overall speed of database operations. Indexes work on the presumption that the vast majority of database operations are read operations. Indexes increase the speed of search operations but slow down insert, delete, and update operations. Usually, the gains of using indexes considerably outweigh the drawbacks.

On a table, you can create one or more indexes, with each index working on one column or on a set of columns. When a table is indexed on a specific column, its rows are either indexed or physically arranged based on the values of that column and the type of index. This makes search operations on that column very fast. If, for example, an index exists on depart-ment_id and then you do a search for the department with the ID value 934, the search would be performed very quickly.

The drawback of indexes is that they can slow down database operations that add new rows or update existing ones because the index must be actualized (or the table rows rearranged) each time these operations occur.

You should keep the following in mind about indexes:

- Indexes greatly increase search operations on the database, but they slow down operations that change the database (delete, update, and insert operations).

- Having too many indexes can slow down the general performance of the database. The general rule is to set indexes on columns frequently used in WHERE, ORDER BY, and GROUP BY clauses or used in table joins.

- By default, unique indexes are automatically created on primary key table columns.

You can use dedicated tools to test the performance of a database under stress conditions with and without particular indexes; in fact, a serious database administrator will want to run some of these tests before deciding on a winning combination for indexes.

Creating the department Table

You created the hatshop database in Chapter 2. In the following exercise, you'll add the department table to it using pgAdmin III. Alternatively, you can use the SQL scripts from the Source Code/Download to create and populate the department table (you can also execute them through pgAdmin III).

■**Note** You can find the database creation scripts in the Source Code/Download section for this book, which you can find on the Apress web site (http://www.apress.com). You can find the files on the authors' web sites as well, at http://www.cristiandarie.ro and http://www.emilianbalanescu.ro.

Exercise: Creating the department Table

1. Start pgAdmin III, and log into your database server using the hatshopadmin username, as you did in the last exercise of Chapter 2.

2. Expand the hatshop database node, expand Schemas, expand public, and then select the Tables node. Right-click this node, and choose New Table from the context menu.

3. Type **department** in the Name text box, and then click the Columns tab.

4. In the Columns window, click Add. Complete the details as shown in Figure 3-10, and then click OK.

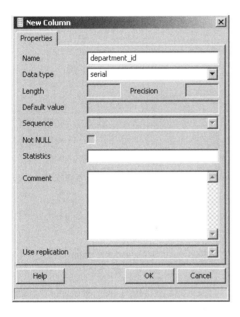

Figure 3-10. *Adding the* department_id *field*

5. Click Add again to add the name field, as shown in Figure 3-11.

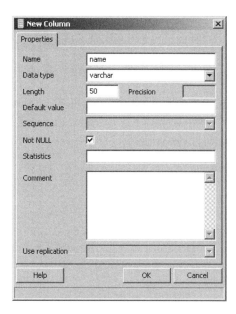

Figure 3-11. *Adding the name field*

6. Click Add again to add the description field. This should also be a `varchar` field, with a maximum length of 1000. Let the Not NULL check box stay unchecked, and click OK.

7. The final step for creating the table is to specify a primary key. Click the Constraints tab, make sure Primary Key is selected in the combo box, and click Add.

8. Type **pk_department** for the key's name, then switch to the Columns tab, and add **department_id** to the list. Click OK to close the dialog box.

9. Click OK again to create the table. Your new table should now appear in the Tables list of your database (see Figure 3-12). As you can see, apart from your new table, there are a few tables created by default by PostgreSQL—it's safe to ignore them. If you select the `department` table from the list, pgAdmin III shows you the SQL code that creates the structure you've just built using the visual interface. You can check that you see the same code on your computer to ensure you've followed the steps of the exercise correctly.

▥**Note** You'll learn more about SQL in the following chapters, but for now it's enough to know that SQL is a language that can be used to interact with the database, to create data tables, to read data from these tables, and so on.

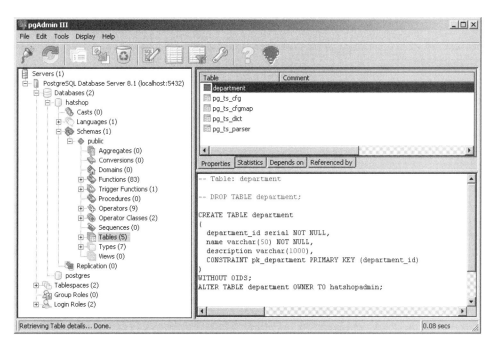

Figure 3-12. *The* department *table in pgAdmin III*

10. Let's populate the table with some sample data. Right-click on the department table, and select View Data.

11. Using the form that shows up, add the records mentioned in Table 3-2.

Table 3-2. *Three Records for the* department *Table*

department_id	name	description
1	Holiday	Prepare for the holidays with our special collection of seasonal hats!
2	Caps and Berets	The perfect hats to wear at work and costume parties!
3	Costume Hats	Find the matching hat for your new costume!

■**Caution** Because you have a sequence in place, it's better to let it generate the department IDs, rather than typing the values yourself. You just need to type in the names and descriptions. If you write the department_id value manually instead of letting the sequence generate it, you'll also need to update the sequence because this doesn't happen automatically. If you don't update the sequence, it will generate values that already exist in the database.

How It Works: Creating PostgreSQL Data Tables

You have just created your first database table! You also set a primary key, set a `serial` column, and filled the table with some data.

As you can see, as soon as you have a clear idea about the structure of a table, it's relatively easy to use pgAdmin III to create it into your database. Let's move on!

Communicating with the Database

Now that you have a table filled with data, let's do something useful with it! The ultimate goal with this table is to get the list of department names from a PHP page and populate the Smarty template with that list.

To get data from a database, you first need to know how to communicate with the database. Relational databases understand dialects and variants of **SQL**. The usual way of communicating with PostgreSQL is to write an SQL command, send it to the PostgreSQL server, and get the results back.

In practice, as you'll see later, we prefer to centralize the data access code using PostgreSQL **functions**, but before you can learn about them, you need to know the basics of SQL.

The Structured Query Language (SQL)

SQL is the language used to communicate with modern Relational Database Management Systems (RDBMS). However, we haven't seen a database system yet that supports exactly the SQL 99 and SQL 2003 standards. This means that in many cases, the SQL code that works with one database will not work with the other. Currently, PostgreSQL supports most of SQL 92 and SQL 99.

The most commonly used SQL commands are `SELECT`, `INSERT`, `UPDATE`, and `DELETE`. These commands allow you to perform the most basic operations on the database.

The basic syntax of these commands is very simple, as you'll see in the following pages. However, keep in mind that SQL is a very flexible and powerful language that can be used to create much more complicated and powerful queries than what you see here. You'll learn more while building the web site, but for now let's take a quick look at the basic syntax. For more details about any of these commands, you can always refer to the official documentation at

- `http://www.postgresql.org/docs/current/interactive/sql-select.html`

- `http://www.postgresql.org/docs/current/interactive/sql-insert.html`

- `http://www.postgresql.org/docs/current/interactive/sql-update.html`

- `http://www.postgresql.org/docs/current/interactive/sql-delete.html`

SELECT

The `SELECT` statement is used to query the database and retrieve selected data that match the criteria you specify. Its basic structure is

```
SELECT <column list>
[FROM <table name(s)>]
[WHERE <restrictive condition(s)>]
```

■**Note**   In this book, the SQL commands and queries appear in uppercase for consistency and clarity although SQL is not case sensitive. The WHERE and FROM clauses appear in brackets because they are optional.

The following command returns the name of the department that has the `department_id` of 1. In your case, the returned value is `Holiday`, but you would receive no results if there was no department with an `ID` of 1.

```
SELECT name FROM department WHERE department_id = 1;
```

■**Tip**   You can easily test these queries to make sure they actually work by using the Query tool, accessible from the Tools menu of pgAdmin III.

If you want more columns to be returned, you simply list them, separated by commas. Alternatively, you can use *, which means "all columns." However, for performance reasons, if you need only certain columns, you should list them separately instead of asking for them all. Using * is not advisable even if at a particular moment you do want all the columns for a query because in future you may add even more columns to the table, and your query would end up asking for more data than is needed. Finally, using * doesn't guarantee the order in which the columns are returned, as one may change the order of the columns in a table (although this is not likely to happen). For these reasons, we don't use * in this book.

With your current `department` table, the following two statements return the same results:

```
SELECT department_id, name, description
FROM   department
WHERE  department_id = 1;

SELECT * FROM department WHERE department_id = 1;
```

■**Tip**   You can split an SQL query on more lines, if you prefer—PostgreSQL won't mind.

If you don't want to place any condition on the query, simply remove the WHERE clause, and you'll get all the rows. The following SELECT statement returns all rows and all columns from the product table:

```
SELECT * FROM product;
```

■**Tip** If you are impatient and can't wait until later in the chapter, you can test the SQL queries right now by using the pgAdmin III tool! After connecting to the hatshop database, choose Tools ➤ Query tool. This will open a window where you can type and execute SQL queries on your database. Be careful, though, because in the rest of the book we'll assume the data in your department table is the same as shown previously in the chapter.

Unless a sorting order is specified, the order in which the rows are returned by a SELECT clause can't be determined. Moreover, executing the same query twice could generate different results! To sort the results, you use ORDER BY. The following query will return the list of departments sorted alphabetically by the department name:

```
SELECT    department_id, name, description
FROM      department
ORDER BY department_id;
```

INSERT

The INSERT statement is used to insert a row of data into the table. Its syntax is as follows:

```
INSERT INTO <table name> [(column list)] VALUES (column values)
```

■**Tip** Although the column list is optional (in case you don't include it, column values are assigned to columns in the order in which they appear in the table's definition), you should always include it. This ensures that changing the table definition doesn't break the existing INSERT statements.

The following INSERT statement adds a department named Seasonal Hats Department to the department table:

```
INSERT INTO department (name) VALUES ('Seasonal Hats Department');
```

No value was specified for the description field because it was marked to allow NULLs in the department table. This is why you can omit specifying a value, if you want to. Also, you're allowed to omit specifying a department ID because the department_id column was created with the serial option, which means the database takes care of automatically generating a value for it when adding new records. However, you're allowed to manually specify a value, if you prefer.

■Tip Because department_id is the primary key column, trying to add more records with the same ID would cause the database to generate an error. The database doesn't permit having duplicate values in the primary key field.

When letting PostgreSQL generate values for serial columns, you can obtain the last generated value using the currval function. Here's an example of how this works:

```
INSERT INTO department (name) VALUES ('Some New Department');
SELECT currval('department_department_id_seq');
```

■Tip In PostgreSQL, ";" is the delimiter between SQL commands.

UPDATE

The UPDATE statement is used to modify existing data and has the following syntax:

```
UPDATE   <table name>
SET <column name> = <new value> [, <column name> = <new value> ... ]
[WHERE <restrictive condition>]
```

The following query changes the name of the department with the ID of 43 to "Cool Department." If there were more departments with that ID, all of them would have been modified, but because department_id is the primary key, you can't have more departments with the same ID.

```
UPDATE department SET name='Cool Department' WHERE department_id = 43;
```

Be careful with the UPDATE statement because it makes it easy to mess up an entire table. If the WHERE clause is omitted, the change is applied to every record of the table, which you usually don't want to happen. PostgreSQL will be happy to change all of your records; even if all departments in the table would have the same name and description, they would still be perceived as different entities because they have different department_id values.

DELETE

The syntax of the DELETE command is actually very simple:

```
DELETE FROM <table name>
[WHERE <restrictive condition>]
```

Most of the time, you'll want to use the WHERE clause to delete a single row:

```
DELETE FROM department WHERE department_id = 43;
```

As with `UPDATE`, be careful with this command because if you forget to specify a `WHERE` clause, you'll end up deleting all of the rows in the table. The following query deletes all the records in `department`. The table itself isn't deleted by the `DELETE` command.

```
DELETE FROM department;
```

PostgreSQL Functions and Types

Database functions are objects that store programs written in a language that PostgreSQL understands. PostgreSQL knows how to deal with functions written in more languages, such as Perl or Python, but we'll stick to the standard, which is an SQL-based language called **PL/pgSQL**. You can find an introduction to the language at `http://www.postgresql.org/docs/ current/interactive/plpgsql.html#PLPGSQL-OVERVIEW`.

You don't need to use database functions if you want to perform database operations. You can directly send SQL commands from an external application (such as a PHP script of your HatShop application) to your PostgreSQL database. When using functions, instead of passing the SQL code you want executed, you just call the function and the values for any parameters it might have. Using functions for data operations has the following advantages:

- The performance can be better because PostgreSQL generates and caches the function's execution plan when it's first executed.

- Using functions allows for better maintainability of the data access and manipulation code, which is stored in a central place, and permits easier implementation of the three-tier architecture (the database functions forming the data tier).

- Security can be better controlled because PostgreSQL permits setting different security permissions for each individual function.

- SQL queries created ad hoc in PHP code are more vulnerable to SQL injection attacks, which is a major security threat. (Many Internet resources cover this security subject, such as the article at `http://www.sitepoint.com/article/ sql-injection-attacks-safe`.)

- This might be a matter of taste, but separating the SQL logic from the PHP code keeps the PHP code cleaner and easier to manage; it looks better to just query a function, than to join strings to build SQL queries to pass to the database.

When developing HatShop, we'll save all the data access code as PostgreSQL **functions** inside the `hatshop` database. These functions, as functions in any respectable language, have input parameters and return types. In some of our examples, we'll define custom types for returning the results.

The syntax for creating functions is

```
CREATE FUNCTION <name>(<param1 type>, <param2 type> ... )
RETURNS [SETOF] <return type> LANGUAGE plpgsql AS $$
  <code>
$$
```

Alternatively, you can specify the language (`LANGUAGE plpgsql`) at the end of the function code, after the closing $$.

Note that you can't create a function if your database already has a function with the same name and parameter number and types. You can, however, have multiple functions with the same name but different parameters (this method is called *overloading* in OOP [Object Oriented Programming] terminology). The key is that when calling the function, PostgreSQL must know which version of the function to call, and it can do that if the parameters are different.

To change an existing function, you should use CREATE OR REPLACE FUNCTION instead of CREATE FUNCTION, which creates the function if it doesn't already exist or updates the function if it does exist.

We'll use types to specify what kind of data the function returns. A type is defined like this:

```
CREATE TYPE name AS
   ( attribute_name data_type [, ... ] )
```

For the data tier of the departments list, you need to create a type called department_list and a function called catalog_get_departments_list. Let's do this in the following exercise.

Exercise: Creating PostgreSQL Types and Functions

1. Start pgAdmin III, and connect to the hatshop database using the hatshopadmin username.

2. pgAdmin III has the interface elements that you can use to create types without writing code (you can check by right-clicking on Types, and selecting New Type). However, because the interface is not particularly friendly, we prefer to write and execute the code that performs the same actions. Choose Tools ➤ Query Tool, and write this code:

```
CREATE TYPE department_list AS
(
   department_id INTEGER,
   name          VARCHAR(50)
);
```

3. Press F5 to execute the command. The output should be similar to "Query returned successfully with no result in 30 ms."

4. Choose Edit ➤ Clear Window to clear the current contents, and write the following code that creates the catalog_get_departments_list function:

```
CREATE FUNCTION catalog_get_departments_list()
RETURNS SETOF department_list LANGUAGE plpgsql AS $$
   DECLARE
     outDepartmentListRow department_list;
   BEGIN
     FOR outDepartmentListRow IN
       SELECT department_id, name
       FROM department
       ORDER BY department_id
     LOOP
       RETURN NEXT outDepartmentListRow;
     END LOOP;
   END;
$$;
```

5. Press F5 to execute the command. The output should once again say that the command executed successfully with no result.

6. To test that the new function returns what it's supposed to, clear again the contents of the window, and type the following query. The list of departments should be retrieved (see Figure 3-13).

```
SELECT * FROM catalog_get_departments_list();
```

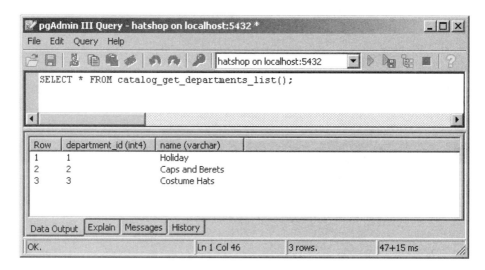

Figure 3-13. *Executing a function using pgAdmin III*

7. Close the Query tool window. If asked to save the changes, click No.

How It Works: PostgreSQL Types and Functions

Let's break down in parts the `catalog_get_departments_list` function. The first line is the one that defines the function name. Remember that you could use `CREATE OR REPLACE FUNCTION` if you have already created the function and want to change it.

```
CREATE FUNCTION catalog_get_departments_list()
```

The next line defines the return type and the language used in the function. The language we're using for this function, and for all the others in this book, is PL/pgSQL (LANGUAGE `plpgsql`).

```
RETURNS SETOF department_list LANGUAGE plpgsql AS $$
```

The return type is `SETOF department_list`, which means the function is supposed to return one or more records that have the structure defined by the `department_list` type. The `department_list` type is a simple type composed of `DepartmentID` and `Description`, defined like this:

```
CREATE TYPE department_list AS
(
  department_id INTEGER,
```

```
  name            VARCHAR(50)
);
```

The body of the function is between the beginning and ending $$. The following code snippet represents the typical way we'll code our functions that return data. The bold line executes the query we're interested in, and the rest is auxiliary code required to return the results of that query.

```
DECLARE
  outDepartmentListRow department_list;
BEGIN
  FOR outDepartmentListRow IN
    SELECT department_id, name FROM department
  LOOP
    RETURN NEXT outDepartmentListRow;
  END LOOP;
END;
```

So what happens here? The body of the function starts with the DECLARE section, which declares the variables that will be used by the function. Unlike with functions in other languages, a PL/pgSQL function has a special place where you can declare variables. In this case, the name of the variable is outDepartmentListRow, and its type is department_list.

The code that performs the actual functionality is written between BEGIN and END. The syntax may look weird at first, but what it does is pretty straightforward. If you remember, the function is declared to return a set of values of the department_list type, and this is what it does.

The function executes the SELECT statement, fetches each row of the results into the outDepartmentListRow variable (which is of the department_list type), and returns this variable. When this function finishes executing, it will have returned a set of department_list values.

Adding Logic to the Site

The business tier (or middle tier) is said to be the brains of the application because it manages the application's business logic. However, for simple tasks such as getting a list of departments from the data tier, the business tier doesn't have much logic to implement. It just requests the data from the database and passes it to the presentation tier.

In this chapter, we're building the foundation of the business layer, which includes the functionality to open and close database connections, store SQL logic as PostgreSQL functions, and access these functions from PHP.

For the business tier of the departments list, you'll implement two classes:

- DatabaseHandler will store the common functionality that you'll reuse whenever you need to access the database. Having this kind of generic functionality packed in a separate class saves keystrokes and avoids bugs in the long run.

- Catalog contains product catalog-specific functionality, such as the GetDepartments method that will retrieve the list of departments from the database.

Connecting to PostgreSQL

The SQL queries you write must be sent somehow to the database engine for execution. As you learned in Chapter 2, you'll use PHP PDO to access the PostgreSQL server.

Before writing the business tier code, you need to analyze and understand the possibilities for implementation. The important questions to answer before writing any code include the following:

- What strategy should you adopt for opening and closing database connections, when you need to execute an SQL query?

- Which methods of PHP PDO should you use for executing database functions and returning the results?

- How should you handle possible errors and integrate the error-handling solution with the error-handling code you wrote in Chapter 2?

Let's have a look at each of these questions one by one, and then we'll start writing some code.

Opening and Closing Connections to the PostgreSQL Server

There are two main possible approaches you can take for this. The first is illustrated by the following sequence of actions, which needs to be executed each time the database needs to be accessed.

1. *Open* a connection to the database exactly before you need to execute a command on the database.

2. *Execute* the SQL query (or the database function) using the open connection, and get back the results. At this stage, you also need to handle any possible errors.

3. *Close* the database connection immediately after executing the command.

This method has the advantage that you don't keep database connections for a long time (which is good because database connections consume server resources) and is also encouraged for servers that don't allow many simultaneous database connections. The disadvantage is the overhead implied by opening and closing the database connection all the time, which can be partially reduced by using persistent connections.

■**Note** Persistent connections refers to a technology that attempts to improve the efficiency of opening and closing database connections with no impact on functionality. You can learn more about this technology at http://www.php.net/manual/en/features.persistent-connections.php.

The alternative solution, and the one you'll use when implementing HatShop, can be described like this:

1. *Open* a connection to the database the first time you need to access the database during a request.

2. *Execute* all database functions (or SQL queries) through that connection without closing it. Here you also need to handle any possible errors.

3. *Close* the database connection when the client request finishes processing.

Using this method, all database operations that happen for a single client request (which happens each time a user visits a new page of our site) will go through a single database connection, avoiding opening and closing the connection each time you need something from the database. You'll still use persistent connections to improve the efficiency of opening a new database connection for each client request.

This solution is the one you will use for data access in the HatShop project.

Using PHP PDO for Database Operations

Now you should learn the theory about how to put this in practice using PHP PDO. You'll effectively write the code a bit later, when building the added functionality into the web site.

As explained in Chapter 2, you won't access PostgreSQL through PHP's PostgreSQL-specific database functions but through a database abstraction layer (PHP PDO). The PDO classes permit accessing various data sources using the same API (Application Programming Interface), so you won't need to change the PHP data access code or learn different data-access techniques when working with database systems other than PostgreSQL (but you might need to change the SQL code itself if the database you migrate to uses a different dialect). Using PHP PDO makes your life as a programmer easier in the long run.

The important PHP PDO class you'll work with is PDO, which provides methods for performing various database operations.

■**Note** In this book, you'll learn about the PHP PDO functionality as used in HatShop. For more details about PHP PDO, see the PHP Manual documentation at http://www.php.net/manual/en/ref.pdo.php.

The PDO class provides the functionality to connect to the PostgreSQL server and execute SQL queries. The function that opens a database connection is PDO's constructor, which receives as parameters the connection string to the database server and an optional parameter that specifies whether the connection is a persistent connection. The connection string contains the data required to connect to the database server. You create a new PDO object like this:

```
$dbh = new PDO('pgsql:dbname=' . $db_name . ';host=' . $db_host,
               $db_user,
               $db_pass,
               array(PDO::ATTR_PERSISTENT => $persistent));
```

■**Note** The constructor of the PDO class returns an initialized database connection object (which is specific to the type of database you're connecting to, such as pgsql) if the connection is successful; otherwise, an exception is thrown.

The previous code snippet shows the standard data you need to supply when connecting to a PostgreSQL server and uses five variables:

- $db_user represents the username.

- $db_pass represents the user's password.

- $db_host is the hostname of your PostgreSQL server.

- $db_name is the name of the database you're connecting to.

- $persistent is true if we want to create a persistent database connection or false otherwise.

To disconnect from the database, you need to make $dbh = null.

The following code snippet demonstrates how to create, open, and then close a PostgreSQL database connection and also catch any exceptions that are thrown:

```
try
{
  // Open connection
  $dbh = new PDO('pgsql:dbname=' . $db_name . ';host=' . $db_host,
                 $db_user, $db_pass);

  // Close connection
  $dbh = null;
}
catch (PDOException $e)
{
  echo 'Connection failed: ' . $e->getMessage();
}
```

The try and catch keywords are used to handle **exceptions**.

PHP 5 EXCEPTION HANDLING

In Chapter 2, you implemented the code that intercepts and handles (and eventually reports) errors that happen in the HatShop site. **PHP errors** are the standard mechanism that you can use to react with an error happening in your PHP code. When a PHP error occurs, the execution stops; you can, however, define an error-handling function that is called just before the execution is terminated. You added such a function in Chapter 2, where you obtain as many details as possible about the error and log them for future reference. Having those details, a programmer can fix the code to avoid the same error happening in the future.

PHP 5 introduced, along with other OOP features, a new way to handle runtime errors: enter exceptions. Exceptions represent the modern way of managing runtime errors in your code and are much more powerful and flexible than PHP errors. Exceptions are a very important part of the OO (Object Oriented) model, and PHP 5 introduces an exception model resembling that of other OOP languages such as Java and C#. However, exceptions in PHP coexist with the standard PHP errors in a strange combination, and you can't solely rely on exceptions for dealing with runtime problems. Some PHP extensions, such as PDO, can be configured to generate exceptions to signal problems that happen at runtime, whereas in other cases, your only option is to deal with standard PHP errors.

The advantages of exceptions over errors lies in the flexibility you're offered in handling them. When an exception is generated, you can handle it locally and let your script continue executing normally, or you can pass the exception to another class for further processing. With exceptions, your script isn't terminated like what happens when a PHP error appears. When using exceptions, you place the code that you suspect could throw an exception inside a `try` block and handle potential exceptions in an associated `catch` block:

```
try
{
  // Code that could generate an exception that you want to handle
}
catch (Exception $e)
{
  // Code that is executed when an exception is generated
  // (exception details are accessible through the $e object)
}
```

When an exception is generated by any of the code in the `try` block, the execution is passed directly to the `catch` block. Unless the code in the `catch` block rethrows the exception, it is assumed that it handled the exception, and the execution of your script continues normally. This kind of flexibility allows you to prevent many causes that could make your pages stop working, and you'll appreciate the power exceptions give you when writing PHP code!

A PHP 5 exception is represented by the `Exception` class, which contains the exception's details. You can generate (throw) an exception yourself using the `throw` keyword. The `Exception` object that you throw is propagated through the call stack until it is intercepted using the `catch` keyword. The call stack is the list of methods being executed. So if a function `A()` calls a function `B()`, which in turn calls a function `C()`, then the call stack will be formed of these three methods. In this scenario, an exception that is raised in function `C()` can be handled in the same function, provided the offending code is inside a `try-catch` block. If this is not the case, the exception propagates to method `B()`, which has a chance to handle the exception, and so on. If no method handles the exception, the exception is finally intercepted by the PHP interpreter, which transforms the exception into a PHP fatal error.

In our database handling code, we'll catch the potential exceptions that could be generated by PDO. Although it doesn't do it by default, PDO can be instructed to generate exceptions in case something goes wrong when executing an SQL command or opening a database connection, like this:

```
// Create a new PDO class instance
$handler = new PDO( ... );

// Configure PDO to throw exceptions
self::$_mHandler->setAttribute(PDO::ATTR_ERRMODE,
                               PDO::ERRMODE_EXCEPTION);
```

We catch these exceptions, and we pass the error details to the error-handling code you wrote in Chapter 2. The following code snippet shows a short function with this functionality implemented:

```
// Wrapper method for PDOStatement::fetch
public static function GetRow($statementHandler, $params = null,
                              $fetchStyle = PDO::FETCH_ASSOC)
{
  // Initialize the return value to null
  $result = null;

  // Try executing the prepared statement received as parameter
  try
  {
    self::Execute($statementHandler, $params);

    $result = $statementHandler->fetch($fetchStyle);
  }
  catch(PDOException $e)
  {
    // Close the database handler and trigger an error
    self::Close();
    trigger_error($e->getMessage(), E_USER_ERROR);
  }

  // Return the query results
  return $result;
}
```

Issuing Commands Using the Connection

After opening the connection, you're now at the stage we've been aiming for from the start: executing SQL commands through the connection.

You can execute the command in many ways, depending on the specifics. Does the SQL query you want to execute return any data? If so, what kind of data, and in which format? The PDO methods that we'll use to execute SQL queries are

- PDOStatement::execute is used to execute an INSERT, an UPDATE, or DELETE query.

- PDOStatement::fetch is used to retrieve one row of data from the database.

- PDOStatement::fetchAll is used to retrieve multiple rows of data from the database.

- PDO::prepare prepares an SQL query to be executed, creating a so-called *prepared statement*.

A **prepared statement** is a parameterized SQL query whose parameter values are replaced by either parameter markers (?) or named variables (:variable_name), like in these examples:

```
$query1 = "SELECT name FROM department WHERE department_id = ?"
$query1 = "SELECT name FROM department WHERE department_id = :dept_id"
```

To execute a prepared statement, you supply the parameter values to the functions that execute your query, which take care to build the complete SQL query for you. To implement the list of departments, you won't need to work with parameters, but you'll learn how to handle them in Chapter 4.

Nonprepared statements can be executed with PDO using the PDO::exec, in which case, you need to create the string of the SQL query, including its parameters. In this book, we'll always use prepared statements because they bring two important benefits:

- Parameter values are checked to prevent injection attacks.

- The query will likely execute faster with prepared statements because the database server can reuse the access plan it builds for a prepared statement.

To be able to reuse more of the database handling code and to have a centralized error-handling mechanism for the database code, we won't be using the PDO methods directly from the business tier of our application. Instead, we'll wrap the PDO functionality into a class named DatabaseHandler, and we'll use this class from the other classes of the business tier.

Writing the Business Tier Code

Okay, let's write some code! You'll start by writing the DatabaseHandler class, which will be a support class that contains generic functionality needed in the other business tier methods. Then you'll create a business tier class named Catalog, which uses the DatabaseHandler class to provide the functionality required by the presentation tier. The Catalog class will contain methods such as GetDepartments (which will be used to generate the list of departments), GetCategories, and so on. The only method we'll need to add to the Catalog class in this chapter is GetDepartments.

Although in this chapter we won't need all this functionality, we'll write the complete code of the DatabaseHandler class. DatabaseHandler will have the following methods:

- Prepare is a wrapper for the PDO::prepare method, which is used to create a prepared statement.

- Execute executes an SQL command that doesn't return records from the database, such as INSERT, DELETE, or UPDATE statements.

- GetOne returns a single value from the database. We can use this method to call database functions that return a single value, such as one that returns the subtotal of a shopping cart.

* GetRow is used to execute queries that return a single row of data.

- GetAll is used to execute queries that return more rows of data, such as when requesting the list of departments.

Exercise: Creating and Using the DatabaseHandler Class

1. Add the database login information at the end of hatshop/include/config.php, modifying the constants' values to fit your server's configuration. The following code assumes you created the admin user account as instructed in Chapter 2:

```
// Database login info
define('DB_PERSISTENCY', 'true');
define('DB_SERVER', 'localhost');
define('DB_USERNAME', 'hatshopadmin');
define('DB_PASSWORD', 'hatshopadmin');
define('DB_DATABASE', 'hatshop');
define('PDO_DSN', 'pgsql:host=' . DB_SERVER . ';dbname=' . DB_DATABASE);
```

2. Create a new file named database_handler.php in the hatshop/business folder, and create the DatabaseHandler class as shown in the following code listing. At this moment, we only included its constructor (which is private, so the class can't be instantiated), and the static GetHandler method, which creates a new database connection, saves it into the $_mHandler member, and then returns this object. (Find more explanations about the process in the upcoming "How It Works" section.)

```php
<?php
// Class providing generic data access functionality
class DatabaseHandler
{
  // Hold an instance of the PDO class
  private static $_mHandler;

  // Private constructor to prevent direct creation of object
  private function __construct()
  {
  }

  // Return an initialized database handler
  private static function GetHandler()
  {
    // Create a database connection only if one doesn't already exist
    if (!isset(self::$_mHandler))
    {
      // Execute code catching potential exceptions
      try
      {
        // Create a new PDO class instance
        self::$_mHandler =
          new PDO(PDO_DSN, DB_USERNAME, DB_PASSWORD,
                  array(PDO::ATTR_PERSISTENT => DB_PERSISTENCY));

        // Configure PDO to throw exceptions
        self::$_mHandler->setAttribute(PDO::ATTR_ERRMODE,
```

```
                              PDO::ERRMODE_EXCEPTION);
    }
    catch (PDOException $e)
    {
      // Close the database handler and trigger an error
      self::Close();
      trigger_error($e->getMessage(), E_USER_ERROR);
    }
  }

  // Return the database handler
  return self::$_mHandler;
  }
}
?>
```

3. Add the `Close` method to the `DatabaseHandler` class. This method will be called to close the database connection:

```
// Clear the PDO class instance
public static function Close()
{
  self::$_mHandler = null;
}
```

4. Add the `Prepare` method to `DatabaseHandler`. This method uses PDO's `prepare` method, and you'll use it for preparing SQL statements for execution.

```
// Wrapper method for PDO::prepare
public static function Prepare($queryString)
{
  // Execute code catching potential exceptions
  try
  {
    // Get the database handler and prepare the query
    $database_handler = self::GetHandler();
    $statement_handler = $database_handler->prepare($queryString);

    // Return the prepared statement
    return $statement_handler;
  }
  catch (PDOException $e)
  {
    // Close the database handler and trigger an error
    self::Close();
    trigger_error($e->getMessage(), E_USER_ERROR);
  }
}
```

5. Add the Execute method to DatabaseHandler. This method uses the PDOStatement::execute method to run queries that don't return records (INSERT, DELETE, or UPDATE queries):

```
// Wrapper method for PDOStatement::execute
public static function Execute($statementHandler, $params = null)
{
  try
  {
    // Try to execute the query
    $statementHandler->execute($params);
  }
  catch(PDOException $e)
  {
    // Close the database handler and trigger an error
    self::Close();
    trigger_error($e->getMessage(), E_USER_ERROR);
  }
}
```

6. Add the GetAll function, which is the wrapper method for fetchAll. You'll call this function for retrieving a complete result set from a SELECT query.

```
// Wrapper method for PDOStatement::fetchAll
public static function GetAll($statementHandler, $params = null,
                             $fetchStyle = PDO::FETCH_ASSOC)
{
  // Initialize the return value to null
  $result = null;

  // Try executing the prepared statement received as parameter
  try
  {
    self::Execute($statementHandler, $params);

    $result = $statementHandler->fetchAll($fetchStyle);
  }
  catch(PDOException $e)
  {
    // Close the database handler and trigger an error
    self::Close();
    trigger_error($e->getMessage(), E_USER_ERROR);
  }

  // Return the query results
  return $result;
}
```

7. Add the GetRow function, which is the wrapper class for fetchRow, as shown. This will be used to get a row of data resulted from a SELECT query.

```
// Wrapper method for PDOStatement::fetch
public static function GetRow($statementHandler, $params = null,
                                $fetchStyle = PDO::FETCH_ASSOC)
{
  // Initialize the return value to null
  $result = null;

  // Try executing the prepared statement received as parameter
  try
  {
    self::Execute($statementHandler, $params);

    $result = $statementHandler->fetch($fetchStyle);
  }
  catch(PDOException $e)
  {
    // Close the database handler and trigger an error
    self::Close();
    trigger_error($e->getMessage(), E_USER_ERROR);
  }

  // Return the query results
  return $result;
}
```

8. Add the GetOne function, which is the wrapper class for fetch, as shown. This will be used to get a single value resulted from a SELECT query.

```
// Return the first column value from a row
public static function GetOne($statementHandler, $params = null)
{
  // Initialize the return value to null
  $result = null;

  // Try executing the prepared statement received as parameter
  try
  {
    /* Execute the query, and save the first value of the result set
       (first column of the first row) to $result */
    self::Execute($statementHandler, $params);

    $result = $statementHandler->fetch(PDO::FETCH_NUM);
    $result = $result[0];
  }
  catch(PDOException $e)
  {
```

```
      // Close the database handler and trigger an error
      self::Close();
      trigger_error($e->getMessage(), E_USER_ERROR);
    }

    // Return the query results
    return $result;
  }
}
```

9. Create a file named `catalog.php` inside the `business` folder. Add the following code into this file:

```php
<?php
// Business tier class for reading product catalog information
class Catalog
{
  // Retrieves all departments
  public static function GetDepartments()
  {
    // Build SQL query
    $sql = 'SELECT * FROM catalog_get_departments_list();';

    // Prepare the statement with PDO-specific functionality
    $result = DatabaseHandler::Prepare($sql);

    // Execute the query and return the results
    return DatabaseHandler::GetAll($result);
  }
}
?>
```

10. You need to include the newly created `database_handler.php` in `app_top.php` so you can make the class available for the application. To do this, add the highlighted code to the `include/app_top.php` file:

```php
<?php
// Include utility files
require_once 'include/config.php';
require_once BUSINESS_DIR . 'error_handler.php';

// Sets the error handler
ErrorHandler::SetHandler();

// Load the page template
require_once PRESENTATION_DIR . 'page.php';

// Load the database handler
require_once BUSINESS_DIR . 'database_handler.php';
?>
```

11. Create a new file named `hatshop/include/app_bottom.php`, and add the following in it:

```php
<?php
DatabaseHandler::Close();
?>
```

12. This file must be included at the end of the main page `index.php` to close the connection. Modify your `index.php` file as follows:

```php
<?php
// Load Smarty library and config files
require_once 'include/app_top.php';

// Load Smarty template file
$page = new Page();

// Display the page
$page->display('index.tpl');

// Load app_bottom which closes the database connection
require_once 'include/app_bottom.php';
?>
```

How It Works: The Business Tier Code

After adding the database connection data to `config.php`, you created the `DatabaseHandler` class. This class contains a number of wrapper methods that access PDO functions and provide the functionality needed for the rest of the business tier methods.

The `DatabaseHandler` class has a **private constructor**, meaning that it can't be instantiated; you can't create `DatabaseHandler` objects, but you can execute the **static methods** for the class. Static class members and methods, as opposed to instance members and methods, are called directly using the class name, instead of an object of the class. For example, this is how you would call the instance method `myMethod` of a hypothetical class named `MyClass`:

```php
$myObject = new MyClass;
$myObject->myMethod();
```

If `myMethod` was a static method, you would call it like this:

```php
MyClass::MyMethod();
```

■**Note**   Static members are OOP-specific features that aren't supported by PHP 4 and older versions. You can find a very good introduction to the OOP features in PHP 5 at `http://php.net/manual/en/language.oop5.php`.

The database functions themselves have a standard structure, taking advantage of the fact that PDO has been configured to throw exceptions. Let's take a closer look at the GetRow method.

```
// Wrapper method for PDOStatement::fetch
public static function GetRow($statementHandler, $params = null,
                              $fetchStyle = PDO::FETCH_ASSOC)
{
  // Initialize the return value to null
  $result = null;

  // Try executing the prepared statement received as parameter
  try
  {
    self::Execute($statementHandler, $params);

    $result = $statementHandler->fetch($fetchStyle);
  }
  catch(PDOException $e)
  {
    // Close the database handler and trigger an error
    self::Close();
    trigger_error($e->getMessage(), E_USER_ERROR);
  }

  // Return the query results
  return $result;
}
```

This method generates an error (using the `trigger_error` function) if the database command didn't execute successfully. The error is captured by the error-handling mechanism you implemented in Chapter 2.

Because of the way you implemented the error-handling code in Chapter 2, generating an E_USER_ERROR error freezes the execution of the request, eventually logging and/or emailing the error data, and showing the visitor a nice "Please come back later" message (if there is such thing as a nice "Please come back later" message, anyway).

Note that before the error is generated, we also close the database connection to ensure that we're not leaving any database resources occupied by the script.

By default, if you don't specify to `trigger_error` the kind of error to generate, an E_USER_NOTICE message is generated, which doesn't interfere with the normal execution of the request (the error is eventually logged, but execution continues normally afterwards).

The functionality in the DatabaseHandler class is meant to be used in the other business tier classes, such as Catalog. At this moment, Catalog contains a single method: GetDepartments.

```
// Business tier class for reading product catalog information
class Catalog
{
  // Retrieves all departments
  public static function GetDepartments()
```

```
{
  // Build SQL query
  $sql = 'SELECT * FROM catalog_get_departments_list();';

  // Prepare the statement with PDO-specific functionality
  $result = DatabaseHandler::Prepare($sql);

  // Execute the query and return the results
  return DatabaseHandler::GetAll($result);
  }
}
```

Because it relies on the functionality you've already included in the DatabaseHandler class and in the database functions in place, the code in Catalog is very simple and straightforward. The GetDepartments method will be called from the presentation tier, which will display the returned data to the visitor. It starts by preparing the SQL query (you learned earlier about the advantages of preparing SQL statements), and then calling the appropriate DatabaseHandler method to execute the query. In this case, we're calling GetAll to retrieve the list of departments.

Right now, the database connection is opened when index.php starts processing and is closed at the end. All database operations that happen in one iteration of this file will be done through this connection.

Displaying the List of Departments

Now that everything is in place in the other tiers, all you have to do is create the presentation tier part—this is the final goal that we've been aiming toward from the beginning. As shown at the beginning of this chapter, the departments list needs to look something like Figure 3-14, when the site is loaded in the browser.

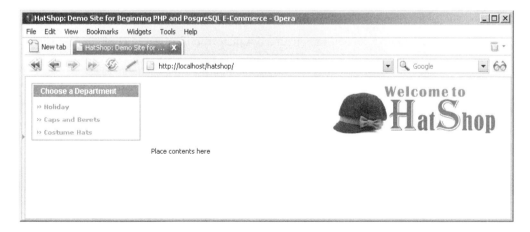

Figure 3-14. *HatShop with a dynamically generated list of departments*

You implement this as a separate componentized template named `departments_list` made up of two files: the Smarty design template (`templates/departments_list.tpl`) and the Smarty plugin file (`smarty_plugins/function.load_departments_list.php`). An additional helper class called `DepartmentsList` will also be used. You'll then just include this componentized template in the main Smarty template (`templates/index.tpl`).

Using Smarty Plugins

The Smarty plugin is the Smarty technology we'll use to implement the logic behind Smarty design template files (with the `.tpl` extension). This is not the only way to store the logic behind a Smarty design template, but it's the way the Smarty documentation recommends at `http://smarty.php.net/manual/en/tips.componentized.templates.php`.

For the departments list, the Smarty plugin file is `function.load_departments_list.php`, which contains the `smarty_function_load_departments_list` function that loads the list of departments from the database. The list is loaded into Smarty variables that are read from the Smarty design template file (`departments_list.tpl`) that generates the HTML output.

Smarty plugin files and functions must follow strict naming conventions to be located by Smarty. Smarty plugin files must be named as `type.name.php` (in our case, `function.load_departments_list.php`), and the functions inside them must be named as `smarty_type_name` (in our case, `smarty_function_load_departments_list`). The official page for Smarty plugins naming conventions is `http://smarty.php.net/manual/en/plugins.naming.conventions.php`. You can learn more about Smarty plugins at `http://smarty.php.net/manual/en/plugins.php`.

After the Smarty plugin file is in place, you can reference it from the Smarty design template file (`departments_list.tpl`) with a line like this:

```
{load_departments_list assign="departments_list"}
```

Given the correct naming conventions where used, this line is enough to get Smarty to load the plugin file and execute the function that loads the departments list. The Smarty design template file can then access the variables populated by the plugin function like this:

```
{$departments_list->mDepartments[i].name}
```

Before actually writing the componentized template, there's one more little detail to learn about.

Exercise: Creating the departments_list Componentized Template

1. Open the `hatshop.css` file in the `hatshop` folder, and add the styles shown in the following code listing. These styles refer to the way department names should look inside the departments list when they are unselected, unselected but with the mouse hovering over them, or selected.

```
.left_box p
{
  color: #ffffff;
  font-family: arial, tahoma, verdana;
  font-size: 12px;
  font-weight: bold;
```

```
      margin: 0px 0px 5px 0px;
      padding: 2px 0px 2px 12px;
    }
    #departments_box
    {
      position: relative;
      border: 1px solid #30b86e;
    }
    #departments_box p
    {
      background: #30b86e;
    }
    a
    {
      color: #a6a6a6;
      font-family: verdana, arial, tahoma;
      font-size: 10px;
      font-weight: bold;
      line-height: 20px;
      text-decoration: none;
    }
    a:hover
    {
      color: #000000;
    }
    a.selected
    {
      color: #000000;
      text-decoration: underline;
    }
    ol
    {
      list-style-type: none;
      margin: 0px 5px;
      padding: 0px;
    }
```

2. Edit the `presentation/page.php` file, and add the following two lines to the constructor of the `page` class. These lines configure the plugin folders used by Smarty. The first one is for the internal Smarty plug-ins, and the second specifies the `smarty_plugins` folder you'll create to hold the plugins you'll write for HatShop.

```
/* Class that extends Smarty, used to process and display Smarty
   files */
class Page extends Smarty
{
  // Class constructor
  public function __construct()
```

```
    {
      // Call Smarty's constructor
      parent::Smarty();

      // Change the default template directories
      $this->template_dir = TEMPLATE_DIR;
      $this->compile_dir = COMPILE_DIR;
      $this->config_dir = CONFIG_DIR;
      $this->plugins_dir[0] = SMARTY_DIR . 'plugins';
      $this->plugins_dir[1] = PRESENTATION_DIR . 'smarty_plugins';
    }
  }
```

3. Now create the Smarty template file for the departments_list componentized template. Write the following lines in presentation/templates/departments_list.tpl:

```
{* departments_list.tpl *}
{load_departments_list assign="departments_list"}
{* Start departments list *}
<div class="left_box" id="departments_box">
  <p>Choose a Department</p>
  <ol>
  {* Loop through the list of departments *}
  {section name=i loop=$departments_list->mDepartments}
    {assign var=selected_d value=""}
    {* Verify if the department is selected to decide what CSS style
       to use *}
    {if ($departments_list->mSelectedDepartment ==
         $departments_list->mDepartments[i].department_id)}
      {assign var=selected_d value="class=\"selected\""}
    {/if}
    <li>
      {* Generate a link for a new department in the list *}
      <a {$selected_d}
      href="{$departments_list->mDepartments[i].link|escape:"html"}">
        &raquo; {$departments_list->mDepartments[i].name}
      </a>
    </li>
  {/section}
  </ol>
</div>
{* End departments list *}
```

4. Create a folder named smarty_plugins in the presentation folder. This will contain the Smarty plugin files.

5. Inside the `smarty_plugins` folder, create a file named `function.load_departments_list.php`, and add the following code to it:

```php
<?php
// Plugin functions inside plugin files must be named: smarty_type_name
function smarty_function_load_departments_list($params, $smarty)
{
  // Create DepartmentsList object
  $departments_list = new DepartmentsList();
  $departments_list->init();

  // Assign template variable
  $smarty->assign($params['assign'], $departments_list);
}

// Manages the departments list
class DepartmentsList
{
  /* Public variables available in departments_list.tpl Smarty template */
  public $mDepartments;
  public $mSelectedDepartment;

  // Constructor reads query string parameter
  public function __construct()
  {
    /* If DepartmentID exists in the query string, we're visiting a
       department */
    if (isset ($_GET['DepartmentID']))
      $this->mSelectedDepartment = (int)$_GET['DepartmentID'];
    else
      $this->mSelectedDepartment = -1;
  }

  /* Calls business tier method to read departments list and create
     their links */
  public function init()
  {
    // Get the list of departments from the business tier
    $this->mDepartments = Catalog::GetDepartments();

    // Create the department links
    for ($i = 0; $i < count($this->mDepartments); $i++)
      $this->mDepartments[$i]['link'] =
        'index.php?DepartmentID=' .
        $this->mDepartments[$i]['department_id'];
  }
}
?>
```

6. Modify the `include/app_top.php` file to include a reference to the `Catalog` business tier class:

```php
<?php
// Include utility files
require_once 'include/config.php';
require_once BUSINESS_DIR . 'error_handler.php';

// Sets the error handler
ErrorHandler::SetHandler();

// Load the page template
require_once PRESENTATION_DIR . 'page.php';

// Load the database handler
require_once BUSINESS_DIR . 'database_handler.php';

// Load Business Tier
require_once BUSINESS_DIR . 'catalog.php';
?>
```

7. Make the following modification in `presentation/templates/index.tpl` to load the newly created `departments_list` componentized template. Search for the following code:

```
<div class="left_box">
  Place list of departments here
</div>
```

and replace it with this:

```
{include file="departments_list.tpl"}
```

8. Examine the result of your work with your favorite browser by loading `http://localhost/hatshop/index.php` (refer to Figure 3-14). Play a little with the page to see what happens when you click on a department or place the mouse over a link.

■**Note**   If you don't get the expected output, make sure your machine is configured correctly and all PHP required modules, such as PDO, were loaded successfully. Many errors will be reported in the Apache error log file (by default, `Apache2/logs/error.log`).

How It Works: The departments_list Smarty Template

If the page worked as expected from the start, you're certainly one lucky programmer! Most of the time, errors happen because of typos, so watch out for them! Database access problems are also common, so make sure you correctly configured the `hatshop` database and the hatshopadmin user, as shown in Chapter 2. In any case, we're lucky to have a good error-reporting mechanism, which shows a detailed error report if something goes wrong. Figure 3-15 shows the error message I received when mistyping the database password in `config.php`.

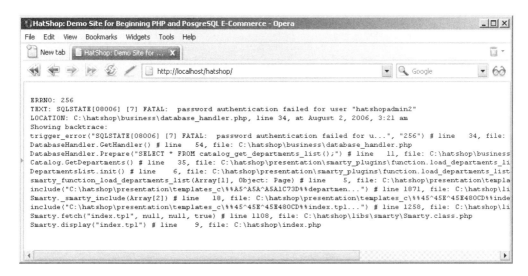

Figure 3-15. *The error-handling code you've written in Chapter 2 is helpful for debugging.*

If everything goes right, however, you'll get the neat page containing a list of departments generated using a Smarty template. Each department name in the list is a link to the department's page, which in fact is a link to the index.php page with a DepartmentID parameter in the query string that specifies which department was selected. Here's an example of such a link:

http://localhost/hatshop/index.php?DepartmentID=3

When clicking a department's link, the selected department will be displayed using a different CSS style in the list (see Figure 3-16).

Figure 3-16. *Selecting a department*

It is important to understand how the Smarty template file (presentation/templates/departments_list.tpl) and its associated plugin file (presentation/smarty_plugins/

`function.load_departments_list.php`) work together to generate the list of departments, and use the correct style for the currently selected one.

The processing starts at `function.load_departments_list.php`, which is included in the `index.tpl` file. The first line in `departments_list.tpl` loads the plugin:

```
{load_departments_list assign="departments_list"}
```

The `load_departments_list` plugin function creates and initializes a `DepartmentsList` object (this class is included in `function.load_departments_list.php`), which is then assigned to a variable accessible from the Smarty design template file:

```
function smarty_function_load_departments_list($params, $smarty)
{
  // Create DepartmentsList object
  $departments_list = new DepartmentsList();
  $departments_list->init();

  // Assign template variable
  $smarty->assign($params['assign'], $departments_list);
}
```

The `init()` method in `DepartmentsList` populates a public member of the class (`$mDepartments`) with an array containing the list of departments and another public member containing the index of the currently selected department (`$mSelectedDepartment`).

Back to the Smarty code now. Inside the HTML code that forms the layout of the Smarty template (`presentation/templates/departments_list.tpl`), you can see the Smarty tags that do the magic:

```
{section name=i loop=$departments_list->mDepartments}
  {assign var=selected_d value=""}
  {* Verify if the department is selected to decide what CSS style
     to use *}
  {if ($departments_list->mSelectedDepartment ==
       $departments_list->mDepartments[i].department_id)}
    {assign var=selected_d value="class=\"selected\""}
  {/if}
  {* Generate a link for a new department in the list *}
  <li>
    <a {$selected_d}
    href="{$departments_list->mDepartments[i].link|escape:"html"}">
      &raquo; {$departments_list->mDepartments[i].name}
    </a>
  </li>
{/section}
```

Smarty template sections are used for looping over arrays of data. In this case, you want to loop over the departments array kept in `$departmentsList->mDepartments`:

```
{section name=i loop=$departments_list->mDepartments}
  ...
{/section}
```

Inside the loop, you verify whether the current department in the loop (`$departments_list->mDepartments[i].department_id`) has the ID that was mentioned in the query string (`$departments_list->mSelectedDepartment`). Depending on this, you decide what style to apply to the name by saving the style name (`selected` or default style) to a variable named `selected_d`.

This variable is then used to generate the link:

```
<a {$selected_d}
  href="{$departments_list->mDepartments[i].link|escape:"html"}">
    &raquo; {$departments_list->mDepartments[i].name}
</a>
```

Planning Ahead for Secure Connections

At some point in the development process, you'll want certain pages of your site to be accessible only through secure HTTPS connections to ensure the confidentiality of the data passed from the client to the server and back. Such sensitive pages include user login forms, pages where the user enters credit card data, and so on.

We don't get into much detail here because you'll learn much more later in the book. However, what you do need to know is that pages accessed through HTTPS occupy much of a server's resources, and we only want to use a secure connection when visiting secure pages.

Implementing this is a bit trickier than it appears. Most of the time, it's more comfortable to use relative links inside the web site. For example, it's typical for the header image of a site to contain a link to `index.php` rather than `http://www.example.com/index.php`. In this case, clicking on the header image from a secure page would redirect the user to `https://www.example.com/index.php`, so the visitor would end up accessing through a secure connection a page that isn't supposed to be accessed like that (and in effect consumes much more server resources than necessary).

To avoid this problem and other similar ones, we'll write a bit of code that makes sure all the links in the web site are absolute links.

Exercise: Preparing Links

1. Create a new file named `presentation/smarty_plugins/modifier.prepare_link.php`, and add the following code to it:

```php
<?php
// Plugin functions inside plugin files must be named: smarty_type_name
function smarty_modifier_prepare_link($string, $link_type = 'http')
{
```

```php
    // Use SSL?
    if ($link_type == 'https' && USE_SSL == 'no')
      $link_type = 'http';

    switch ($link_type)
    {
      case 'http':
        $link = 'http://' . getenv('SERVER_NAME');

        // If HTTP_SERVER_PORT is defined and different than default
        if (defined('HTTP_SERVER_PORT') && HTTP_SERVER_PORT != '80')
        {
          // Append server port
          $link .= ':' . HTTP_SERVER_PORT;
        }

        $link .= VIRTUAL_LOCATION . $string;

        // Escape html
        return htmlspecialchars($link, ENT_QUOTES);
      case 'https':
        $link = 'https://' . getenv('SERVER_NAME') .
                VIRTUAL_LOCATION . $string;

        // Escape html
        return htmlspecialchars($link, ENT_QUOTES);
      default:
        return htmlspecialchars($string, ENT_QUOTES);
    }
  }
?>
```

2. Add two new constants to include/config.php:

```php
// Server HTTP port (can omit if the default 80 is used)
define('HTTP_SERVER_PORT', '80');
/* Name of the virtual directory the site runs in, for example:
   '/hatshop/' if the site runs at http://www.example.com/hatshop/
   '/' if the site runs at http://www.example.com/ */
define('VIRTUAL_LOCATION', '/hatshop/');
// We enable and enforce SSL when this is set to anything else than 'no'
define('USE_SSL', 'yes');
```

3. Modify presentation/templates/header.tpl like this:

```html
<div id="header">
  <a href="{"index.php"|prepare_link:"http"}">
    <img src="images/title.png" alt="Site title" />
  </a>
</div>
```

4. Modify `presentation/templates/departments_list.tpl` like this:

```
<li>
  <a {$selected_d}
   href="{$departments_list->mDepartments[i].link|prepare_link:"http"}">
     &raquo; {$departments_list->mDepartments[i].name}
  </a>
</li>
```

How It Works: Preparing Links

First of all, make sure the new entry you added to `config.php` is configured correctly. If you're running your web site on a different port than the default of 80 (say, if you're using port 8080), make sure you specify the correct port in the `HTTP_SERVER_PORT` constant.

We also defined a constant named `USE_SSL`, which specifies whether the site is supposed to generate HTTPS URLs. If the constant is set to `no`, your site won't generate any HTTPS links even for the places that should normally be secured. Let's see how this works.

The code you've just added to the presentation tier is a **Smarty modifier**. The Smarty modifier is used as shown by the modifications you've implemented in `header.tpl` and `departments_list.tpl`, and it transforms the relative links received as parameters to absolute links. The `prepare_link` Smarty modifier takes as parameter the name of the protocol that should be used to generate the links; if `http` is passed, an HTTP URL will be generated; if `https` is passed, an HTTPS URL will be generated.

Take the example of the link in the header:

```
<a href="{"index.php"|prepare_link:"http"}">
```

This link will be transformed to an absolute link by our Smarty modifier, which will arrive to the client like this:

```
<a href="http://www.example.com/index.php">
```

If you wanted that particular link to be accessed only through HTTPS, then you could use the Smarty modifier like this:

```
<a href="{"index.php"|prepare_link:"https"}">
```

This modifier would transform the link to

```
<a href="https://www.example.com/index.php">
```

Note that if the `USE_SSL` constant is set to `no`, then HTTP will be used even if the parameter is `https`.

You can reload the web site to ensure that nothing's broken.

■**Note** In case you aren't using the `hatshop` alias as explained in Chapter 2, you'll need to modify the `VIRTUAL_LOCATION` constant in `config.php` to reflect the real location of your web application.

Note that the Smarty modifier doesn't add the port if the HTTP_SERVER_PORT constant isn't defined or if it contains the default port 80:

```
// If HTTP_SERVER_PORT is defined and different than default
if (defined('HTTP_SERVER_PORT') && HTTP_SERVER_PORT != '80')
{
  // Append server port
  $link .= ':' . HTTP_SERVER_PORT;
}
```

However, you should add the HTTP_SERVER_PORT to config.php anyway to make it easier to modify in case you move the application to a server that runs on another port. If HTTP_SERVER_PORT would be, for example, 8080, the links to index.php specified earlier would be transformed to

```
<a href="http//www.example.com:8080/index.php">
```

Summary

This long chapter was well worth the effort when you consider how much theory you've learned and applied to the HatShop project! In this chapter, you accomplished the following:

- You created the department table and populated it with data.

- You learned how to access this data from the data tier using PDO, and then how to access the data tier method from the business tier.

- You learned how to use PHP 5 exceptions.

- You implemented the user interface using a Smarty template.

In the next chapter, you will finish creating the product catalog by displaying the site's categories and products!

Creating the Product Catalog: Part II

In the previous chapter, you implemented a selectable list of departments for the HatShop web site. However, a product catalog means much more than that list of departments. In this chapter, you'll add many new product catalog features. This chapter has a similar structure to the last chapter, but there's a lot of new functionality to add, which involves quite a bit of code.

Review Figures 3-1, 3-2, and 3-3 from Chapter 3 to get a visual feeling of the new functionality you'll implement in this chapter.

In this chapter, you will

- Learn about relational data and the types of relationships that occur between data tables, and then create the new data structures in your database.

- Understand how to join related data tables, how to use subqueries, how to implement paging at the data tier level, and even more theory about PL/pgSQLl functions and techniques.

- Complete the business tier to work with the new PL/pgSQL functions, send parameters, and pass requested data to the presentation tier.

- Complete the presentation tier to show your visitor details about the catalog's categories, products, and more.

Storing the New Data

Given the new functionality you are adding in this chapter, it's not surprising that you need to add more data tables to the database. However, this isn't just about adding new data tables. You also need to learn about relational data and the relationships that you can implement between the data tables, so that you can obtain more significant information from your database.

What Makes a Relational Database

It's no mystery that a database is something that stores data. However, today's modern **Relational Database Management Systems (RDBMS)**, such as PostgreSQL, MySQL, SQL Server, Oracle, DB2, and others, have extended this basic role by adding the capability to store and manage **relational data**. This is a concept that deserves some attention.

So what does *relational data* mean? It's easy to see that every piece of data ever written in a real-world database is somehow related to some already existing information. Products are related to categories and departments, orders are related to products and customers, and so on. A relational database keeps its information stored in data tables but is also aware of the relations between them.

These related tables form the *relational database*, which becomes an object with a significance of its own, rather than simply being a group of unrelated data tables. It is said that *data* becomes *information* only when we give significance to it, and establishing relations with other pieces of data is an ideal means of doing so.

Look at the product catalog to see what pieces of data it needs and how you can transform this data into information. For the product catalog, you'll need at least three data tables: one for departments, one for categories, and one for products. It's important to note that physically each data table is an independent database object, even if logically it's part of a larger entity—in other words, even though we say that a category *contains* products, the table that contains the products is not inside the table that contains categories. This is not in contradiction with the relational character of the database. Figure 4-1 depicts a simple representation of three data tables, including some selected sample data.

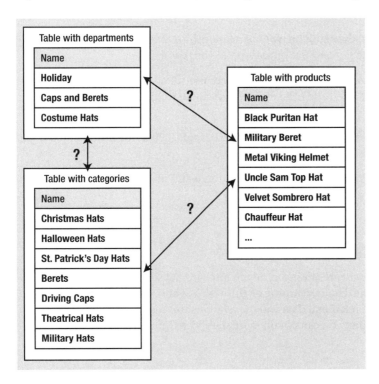

Figure 4-1. *Unrelated departments, categories, and products*

When two tables are said to be related, this more specifically means that the *records* of those tables are related. So, if the products table is related to the categories table, this translates into each product record being somehow related to one of the records in the categories table.

Figure 4-1 doesn't show the physical representation of the database, so we didn't list the table names there. Diagrams like this are used to decide *what* needs to be stored in the database. After you know *what* to store, the next step is to decide *how* the listed data is related, which leads to the physical structure for the database. Although Figure 4-1 shows three kinds of data that you want to store, you'll learn later that to implement this structure in the database, you'll actually use four tables.

So, now that you know the data you want to store, let's think about how the three parts relate to each other. Apart from knowing that the records of two tables are related *somehow*, you also need to know *the kind of relationship* between them. Let's now take a closer look at the different ways in which two tables can be related.

Relational Data and Table Relationships

To continue exploring the world of relational databases, let's further analyze the three logical tables we've been looking at so far. To make life easier, let's give them names now: the table containing products is `product`, the table containing categories is `category`, and the last one is our old friend, `department`. No surprises here! Luckily, these tables implement the most common kinds of relationships that exist between tables, the **One-to-Many** and **Many-to-Many** relationships, so you have the chance to learn about them.

■**Note** Some variations of these two relationship types exist, as well as the less popular *One-to-One* relationship. In the One-to-One relationship, each row in one table matches exactly one row in the other. For example, in a database that allowed patients to be assigned to beds, you would hope that there would be a One-to-One relationship between patients and beds! Database systems don't support enforcing this kind of relationship because you would have to add matching records in both tables at the same time. Moreover, two tables with a One-to-One relationship can be joined to form a single table.

One-to-Many Relationships

The One-to-Many relationship happens when one record in a table can be associated with multiple records in the related table but not vice versa. In our case, this happens for the `department` – `category` relation. A specific department can contain any number of categories, but each category belongs to *exactly one* department. Figure 4-2 better represents the One-to-Many relationship between departments and categories.

Another common scenario in which you see the One-to-Many relationship is with the `order` – `order_details` tables, where `order` contains general details about the order (such as date, total amount, and so on), and `order_details` contains the products related to the order.

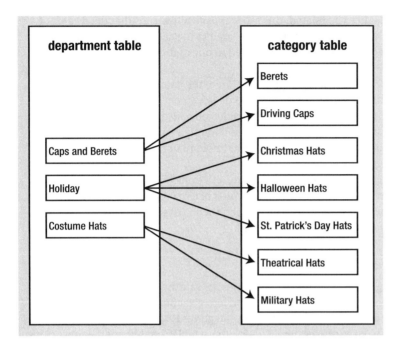

Figure 4-2. *A One-to-Many relationship between departments and categories*

The One-to-Many relationship is implemented in the database by adding an extra column in the table at the *many* side of the relationship, which references the ID column of the table in the *one* side of the relationship. Simply said, in the category table, you'll have an extra column (called department_id) that will hold the ID of the department the category belongs to. You'll implement this in your database a bit later, after you learn about the Many-to-Many relationships and the FOREIGN KEY constraint.

Many-to-Many Relationships

The other common type of relationship is the Many-to-Many relationship. This kind of relationship is implemented when records in both tables of the relationship can have multiple matching records in the other. In our scenario, this happens for the product and category tables because we know that a product can exist in more than one category (*one* product – *many* categories), and also a category can have more than one product (*one* category – *many* products).

This happens because we decided earlier that a product could be in more than one category. If a product could only belong to a single category, you would have another One-to-Many relationship, just like the one that exists between departments and categories (where a category can't belong to more than one department).

If you represent this relationship with a picture, as shown previously in Figure 4-2, but with generic names this time, you get something like what is shown in Figure 4-3.

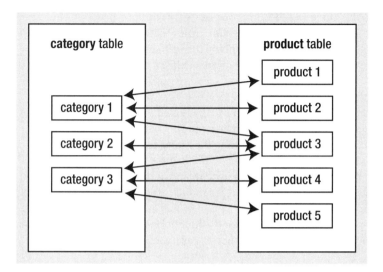

Figure 4-3. *The Many-to-Many relationship between categories and products*

Although logically the Many-to-Many relationship happens between two tables, databases (including PostgreSQL databases) don't have the means to physically implement this kind of relationship by using just two tables, so we cheat by adding a third table to the mix. This third table, called a **junction table** (also known as a *linking table* or an *associate table*) and two One-to-Many relationships will help achieve the Many-to-Many relationship. The junction table is used to associate products and categories, with no restriction on how many products can exist for a category, or how many categories a product can be added to. Figure 4-4 shows the role of the junction table.

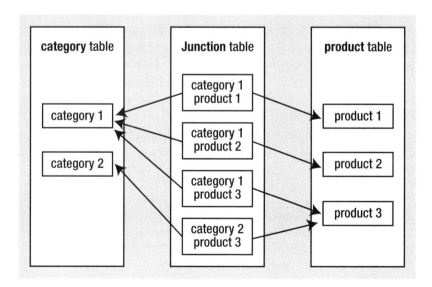

Figure 4-4. *The Many-to-Many relationship between categories and products*

Note that each record in the junction table links one category with one product. You can have as many records as you like in the junction table, linking any category to any product. The linking table contains two fields, each one referencing the primary key of one of the two linked tables. In our case, the junction table will contain two fields: a `category_id` field and a `product_id` field.

Each record in the junction table will consist of a (`product_id`, `category_id`) pair, which will be used to associate a particular product with a particular category. By adding more records to the `product_category` table, you can associate a product with more categories or a category with more products, effectively implementing the Many-to-Many relationship.

Because the Many-to-Many relationship is implemented using a third table that makes the connection between the linked tables, there is no need to add additional fields to the related tables in the way that we added the `department_id` to the `category` table for implementing the One-to-Many relationship.

There's no definitive naming convention to use for the junction table. Most of the time it's okay to just join the names of the two linked tables—in this case, the junction table is named `product_category`.

Enforcing Table Relationships with the FOREIGN KEY Constraint

Relationships between tables can be physically enforced in the database using `FOREIGN KEY` constraints, or simply *foreign keys*.

You learned in the previous chapter about the `PRIMARY KEY` and `UNIQUE` constraints. We covered them there because they apply to the table as an individual entity. Foreign keys, on the other hand, occur between two tables: the table in which the foreign key is defined (the *referencing table*) and the table the foreign key references (the *referenced table*).

■**Tip** Actually, the referencing table and the referenced table can be one and the same. This isn't seen too often in practice, but it's not unusual either. For example, you can have a table with employees, where each employee references the employee that is his or her boss (in this scenario the big boss would probably reference itself).

A **foreign key** is a column or combination of columns used to enforce a link between data in two tables (usually representing a One-to-Many relationship). Foreign keys are used both as a method of ensuring data integrity and to establish a relationship between tables.

To enforce database integrity, the foreign keys, like the other types of constraints, apply certain restrictions. Unlike `PRIMARY KEY` and `UNIQUE` constraints that apply restrictions to a single table, the `FOREIGN KEY` constraint applies restrictions on both the referencing and referenced tables. For example, if you enforce the One-to-Many relationship between the `department` and `category` tables by using a `FOREIGN KEY` constraint, the database will include this relationship as part of its integrity. It will not allow you to add a category to a nonexistent department, nor will it allow you to delete a department if there are categories that belong to it.

You now know the general theory of foreign keys. In the following exercises, you'll put into practice the new theory you learned on table relationships by creating and populating these tables:

- category

- product

- product_category

Adding Categories

The process of creating the category table is pretty much the same as for the department table you created in Chapter 2. The category table will have four fields, described in Table 4-1.

Table 4-1. *Designing the* category *Table*

Field Name	Data Type	Description
category_id	SERIAL	An integer that represents the unique ID for the category. It is the primary key of the table.
department_id	INTEGER	An integer that represents the department the category belongs to. It doesn't allow NULLs.
name	VARCHAR(50)	Stores the category name. It does not allow NULLs.
description	VARCHAR(1000)	Stores the category description. It allows NULLs.

There are two ways to create the category table and populate it. Either execute the SQL scripts from the Source Code/Download section of the Apress web site (http://www.apress.com/) or follow the steps in the following exercise.

Exercise: Creating the category Table

1. Start pgAdmin III, and connect to the hatshop database.

2. Select Tools ➤ Query Tool.

3. Enter the following code:

```
-- Create category table
CREATE TABLE category
(
  category_id   SERIAL       NOT NULL,
  department_id INTEGER       NOT NULL,
  name          VARCHAR(50) NOT NULL,
  description    VARCHAR(1000),
  CONSTRAINT pk_category_id   PRIMARY KEY (category_id),
  CONSTRAINT fk_department_id FOREIGN KEY (department_id)
          REFERENCES department (department_id)
          ON UPDATE RESTRICT ON DELETE RESTRICT
);
```

4. Execute the query by selecting Query ➤ Execute, or by pressing F5. The results can be seen in Figure 4-5.

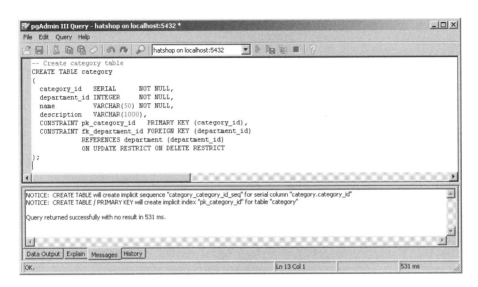

Figure 4-5. *Creating the* category *table using pgAdmin III*

■**Tip** When executing this command, the database will automatically create a sequence named category_category_id_seq that will generate the values for the category_id field. Also, as you know from Chapter 3, an index will be created on the primary key column.

How It Works: The One-to-Many Relationship

Okay, so you created and then enforced a relationship between the category and department tables. But how does it work, and how does it affect your life? Let's study how you implemented this relationship.

In the category table, apart from the primary key and the usual category_id, name, column, and description columns, you added a department_id column. This column stores the ID of the department the category belongs to. Because the department_id field in category doesn't allow NULLs, you must supply a department for each category. Furthermore, because of the foreign key relationship, the database won't allow you to specify a nonexistent department.

The foreign key's behavior is dictated by the command used to create it, which in our case is

```
CONSTRAINT fk_department_id FOREIGN KEY (department_id)
        REFERENCES department (department_id)
        ON UPDATE RESTRICT ON DELETE RESTRICT
```

The constraint can be instructed to act differently on update and delete operations. Here, in both cases the behavior is RESTRICT. Let's see the alternatives:

- **RESTRICT (similar to NO ACTION):** This is probably the most important of the options. It tells PostgreSQL to make sure that database operations on the tables involved in the relationship don't break the relationship. When this option is set, PostgreSQL won't allow you to add categories to nonexistent departments or delete departments that have related categories.

- **CASCADE**: Performs automatic data changes to maintain the data integrity. For example, changing the ID of an existing department would cause the change to propagate to the category table to keep the category-department associations intact. This way, even after you change the ID of the department, its categories would still belong to it. This option is dangerous because when deleting a department, PostgreSQL automatically deletes all the department's related categories. This is a sensitive option, so be very careful with it. You won't use it in the HatShop project.

- **SET NULL**: Sets the foreign key field to NULL when the parent is updated or deleted.

- **SET DEFAULT**: Sets the foreign key field to its default value when the parent is updated or deleted.

In the One-to-Many relationship (and implicitly the FOREIGN KEY constraint), you link two columns from two different tables. One of these columns is a primary key, and it defines the One part of the relationship. In our case, department_id is the primary key of department, so department is the one that connects to many categories. A primary key must be on the One part to ensure that it's unique—a category can't be linked to a department if you can't be sure that the department ID is unique. You must ensure that no two departments have the same ID; otherwise, the relationship wouldn't make much sense.

You'll find a very nice article on referential integrity with PostgreSQL at http://techdocs.postgresql.org/techdocs/hackingreferentialintegrity.php.

Now that you've created the category table, you can populate it with some data. We'll also try to add data that would break the relationship that you established between the department and category tables.

The sample data that we'll add to the category table is shown in Table 4-2.

Table 4-2. *Designing the* category *Table*

category_id	department_id	name	description
1	1	Christmas Hats	Enjoy browsing our collection of Christmas hats!
2	1	Halloween Hats	Find the hat you'll wear this Halloween!
3	1	St. Patrick's Day Hats	Try one of these beautiful hats on St. Patrick's Day!
4	2	Berets	An amazing collection of berets from all around the world!
5	2	Driving Caps	Be an original driver! Buy a driver's hat today!
6	3	Theatrical Hats	Going to a costume party? Try one of these hats to complete your costume!
7	3	Military Hats	This collection contains the most realistic replicas of military hats!

Exercise: Adding Categories

1. Start pgAdmin, and connect to the `hatshop` database.

2. Select Tools ➤ Query Tool.

3. Enter the following code:

```
-- Populate category table
INSERT INTO category (category_id, department_id, name, description)
 VALUES (1, 1, 'Christmas Hats',
 'Enjoy browsing our collection of Christmas hats!');
INSERT INTO category (category_id, department_id, name, description)
 VALUES (2, 1, 'Halloween Hats',
 'Find the hat you''ll wear this Halloween!');
INSERT INTO category (category_id, department_id, name, description)
 VALUES (3, 1, 'St. Patrick''s Day Hats',
 'Try one of these beautiful hats on St. Patrick''s Day!');
INSERT INTO category (category_id, department_id, name, description)
 VALUES (4, 2, 'Berets',
 'An amazing collection of berets from all around the world!');
INSERT INTO category (category_id, department_id, name, description)
 VALUES (5, 2, 'Driving Caps',
 'Be an original driver! Buy a driver''s hat today!');
INSERT INTO category (category_id, department_id, name, description)
 VALUES (6, 3, 'Theatrical Hats',
 'Going to a costume party? Try one of these hats to complete your costume!');
INSERT INTO category (category_id, department_id, name, description)
 VALUES (7, 3, 'Military Hats',
 'This collection contains the most realistic replicas of military hats!');

-- Update the sequence
ALTER SEQUENCE category_category_id_seq RESTART WITH 8;
```

■**Note** In the SQL code that creates the categories, we preferred not to rely on the `category_id` values automatically generated by the database, to make sure you end up having the same IDs as the ones we assume you have. This will be important later, when assigning particular category IDs with product IDs. When manually specifying IDs that would otherwise be generated by the sequence, you need to also update the sequence, as shown in the previous code snippet. If you plan on adding new categories, make sure the table is empty before executing the SQL `INSERT` statements. You can delete the contents of the `category` table using this command:

```
DELETE FROM category;
```

4. Execute the query by selecting Query ➤ Execute, or by pressing F5. The results can be seen in Figure 4-6.

Figure 4-6. *Adding sample categories*

5. Now, try to break the database integrity by adding a category to a nonexistent department (for example, set the DepartmentID to 500). Try executing this SQL command using pgAdmin III:

```
INSERT INTO category (department_id, name, description)
VALUES (500, 'New category', 'Executing this command should throw an error.');
```

6. If everything goes well, the database should deny adding the new record, throwing this error you can see in Figure 4-7.

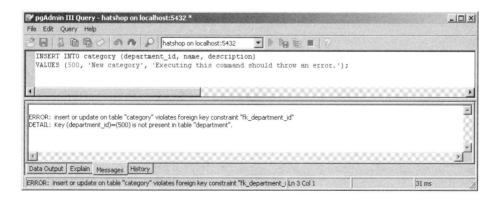

Figure 4-7. *The foreign key in action*

How It Works: Populating the categories Table

Adding data to your table should be a trivial task, given that you know the data that needs to be inserted. As pointed out earlier, you can find the SQL scripts in the book's code in the Source Code/Download section of the Apress web site (http://www.apress.com).

Note how we escaped the special characters in the category descriptions, such as the single quotes, which need to be doubled, so PostgreSQL will know to interpret that as a quote to be added to the description, instead of a string termination character.

When manually adding values to fields whose values would otherwise be generated by sequences, you need to manually update the sequence because the sequences are separate database objects that aren't automatically updated if they aren't used to generate data. If you don't change the sequence, it would probably end up generating values that have already been added to the database, and some or all of your INSERT commands would end up throwing errors.

Adding Products

You'll now go through the same steps as earlier, but this time, you'll create a bit more complicated table: product. The product table has the fields shown in Table 4-3.

Table 4-3. *Designing the* product *Table*

Field Name	Data Type	Description
product_id	SERIAL	An integer that represents the unique ID for the category. It is the primary key of the table.
name	VARCHAR(50)	Stores the product name. It doesn't allow NULLs.
description	VARCHAR(1000)	Stores the category description. It allows NULLs.
price	NUMERIC(10,2)	Stores the product price.
discounted_price	NUMERIC(10,2)	Stores the discounted product price. Will store 0.00 in case the product doesn't have a current discount price.
image	VARCHAR(150)	Stores the name of the product's picture file (or eventually the complete path), which gets displayed on the product details page. You could keep the picture directly in the table, but in most cases, it's much more efficient to store the picture files in the file system and have only their names stored into the database. If you have a high-traffic web site, you might even want to have the image files placed in a separate physical location (for example, another hard disk) to increase site performance.
thumbnail	VARCHAR(150)	Stores the name of the product's thumbnail picture. This image gets displayed in product lists when browsing the catalog.
display	INTEGER	Stores a value specifying in what areas of the catalog this product should be displayed. The possible values are 0 (default; the product shows only in the page of the category it's a part of), 1 (the product is also featured on the front catalog page), 2 (the product is also

Table 4-3. *Continued*

Field Name	Data Type	Description
		featured in the departments it's a part of), and 3 (the product is also featured on both the front page and on the department page). With the help of this field, the site administrators can highlight a set of products that will be of particular interest to visitors at a specific time. For example, before Halloween, you will want the Halloween hats to appear prominently on the front page of the site. Also if you want to promote products that have a discounted price, this feature is just what you need.

Follow the steps of the exercise to create the product table in your database.

Exercise: Creating the product Table

1. Start pgAdmin III, and connect to the hatshop database.

2. Select Tools ➤ Query tool.

3. Enter the following code:

```
-- Create product table
CREATE TABLE product
(
  product_id        SERIAL         NOT NULL,
  name              VARCHAR(50)    NOT NULL,
  description       VARCHAR(1000)  NOT NULL,
  price             NUMERIC(10, 2) NOT NULL,
  discounted_price  NUMERIC(10, 2) NOT NULL DEFAULT 0.00,
  image             VARCHAR(150),
  thumbnail         VARCHAR(150),
  display           SMALLINT       NOT NULL DEFAULT 0,
  CONSTRAINT pk_product PRIMARY KEY (product_id)
);
```

4. Execute the query by selecting Query ➤ Execute, or by pressing F5.

■**Note** When executing this command, the database will automatically create a sequence named product_product_id_seq that will generate the values for the product_id field. Also, an index will be created for the primary key column.

5. Let's now populate the table with products. Because there are so many of them, use the populate_product.sql script provided in the Source Code/Download section (http://www.apress.com).

Relating Products to Categories

The product_category table is the linking table that allows implementing the Many-to-Many relationship between product and category. It has two fields, product_id and category_id, which form the primary key of the table.

Create and populate the table following the steps in the exercise.

Exercise: Creating the product_category Table

1. Start pgAdmin III, and connect to the hatshop database.

2. Select Tools ➤ Query Tool.

3. Enter the following code:

```
-- Create product_category table
CREATE TABLE product_category
(
  product_id   INTEGER NOT NULL,
  category_id INTEGER NOT NULL,
  CONSTRAINT pk_product_id_category_id PRIMARY KEY (product_id, category_id),
  CONSTRAINT fk_product_id            FOREIGN KEY (product_id)
            REFERENCES product (product_id)
            ON UPDATE RESTRICT ON DELETE RESTRICT,
  CONSTRAINT fk_category_id           FOREIGN KEY (category_id)
            REFERENCES category (category_id)
            ON UPDATE RESTRICT ON DELETE RESTRICT
);
```

4. Execute the query by selecting Query ➤ Execute, or by pressing F5.

5. Populate the table with data. Because there are many rows, use the populate_product_category.sql script provided in the Source Code/Download section (http://www.apress.com).

How It Works: Many-to-Many Relationships

Many-to-Many relationships are created by adding a third table, called a junction table, which is named product_category in this case. This table contains (product_id, category_id) pairs, and each record in the table associates a particular product with a particular category. So, if you see a record such as (1,4) in product_category, you know that the product with the ID of 1 belongs to the category with the ID of 4.

The Many-to-Many relationship is physically enforced through two FOREIGN KEY constraints—one that links the table product to the table product_category, and the other that links the table product_category to the table category. In English, this means, "one product can be associated with many product-category entries, each of those being associated with one category." The foreign keys ensure that the products and categories that appear in the product_category table actually exist in the database and won't allow you to delete a product if you have a category associated with it and vice versa.

This is also the first time that you set a primary key consisting of more than one column. The primary key of product_category is formed by both its fields: product_id and category_id. This means that you won't be allowed to have two identical (`product_id`, `category_id`) pairs in the table. However, it's perfectly legal to have a `product_id` or `category_id` appear more than once, as long as it is part of a unique (`product_id`, `category_id`) pair. This makes sense because you don't want to have two identical records in the `product_category` table. A product can be associated with a particular category, or not; it cannot be associated with a category multiple times.

At first, all the theory about table relationships can be a bit confusing, until you get used to it. To understand the relationship more clearly, you can get a picture by using database diagrams.

Using Database Diagrams

A number of tools allow you to build database structures visually, implement them physically in the database for you, and generate the necessary SQL script. Although we won't present any particular tool in this book, it's good to know that they exist. You can find a list of the most popular tools at `http://www.databaseanswers.com/modelling_tools.htm`.

Database diagrams also have the capability to implement the relationships between tables. For example, if you had implemented the relationships between your four tables so far, the database diagram would look something like Figure 4-8.

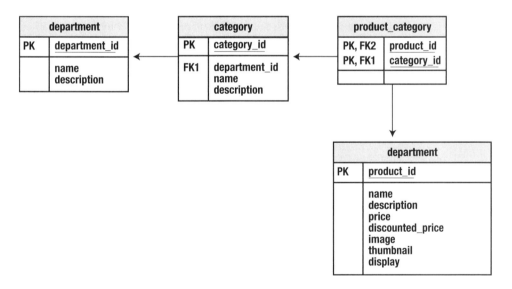

Figure 4-8. *Viewing tables and relationships using the database diagram*

In the diagram, the primary keys of each table are marked with the PK notation. Foreign keys are marked with FK (because there can be more of them in a table, they're numbered). The arrows between two tables point toward the table in the One part of the relationship.

Querying the New Data

Now you have a database with a wealth of information just waiting to be read by somebody. However, the new elements bring with them a set of new things you need to learn.

For this chapter, the data tier logic is a little bit more complicated than in the previous chapter because it must answer to queries like "give me the second page of products from the Cartoons category" or "give me the products on promotion for department X." Before moving on to writing the stored procedures that implement this logic, let's first cover the theory about

- Retrieving short product descriptions

- Joining data tables

- Implementing paging

Let's deal with these tasks one by one.

Getting Short Descriptions

In the product lists your visitor sees while browsing the catalog, we won't display full product descriptions but only a portion of them. In HatShop, we'll display the first 150 characters of every product description, after which we append "…".

In PostgreSQL, you can extract a substring from a string using the substring function. The following SELECT command returns products' descriptions trimmed at 30 characters, with "…" appended:

```
SELECT   name,
         substring(description, 1, 30) || '...' AS description
FROM     product
ORDER BY name;
```

The new column generated by the (substring(description, 1, 30) || '...') expression doesn't have a name, so we created an alias for it using the AS keyword. With your current data, this query would return something like this:

name	description
454 Black Pirate Hat	Our wool felt Pirate Hat comes...
9 Green MadHatter Top Hat	Each of our MadHatter hats is ...
Black Basque Beret	This is our tried and true men...
Black Puritan Hat	Haentze Hatcrafters has been m...
Black Wizard Hat	This cool Merlin-style wizard ...
...	...

Joining Data Tables

Because your data is stored in several tables, frequently not all of the information you'll need is in one table. Take a look at the following list, which contains data from both the department and category tables:

Department Name	Category Name
Holiday	Christmas Hats
Holiday	Halloween Hats
Holiday	St. Patrick's Day Hats
Caps and Berets	Berets
Caps and Berets	Driving Caps
Costume Hats	Theatrical Hats
Costume Hats	Military Hats

In other cases, all the information you need is in just one table, but you need to place conditions on it based on the information in another table. You cannot get this kind of result set with simple queries such as the ones you've used so far. Needing a result set based on data from multiple tables is a good indication that you might need to use **table joins**.

When extracting the products that belong to a category, the SQL query isn't the same as when extracting the categories that belong to a department. This is because products and categories are linked through the product_category associate table.

To get the list of products in a category, you first need to look in the product_category table and get all the (product_id, category_id) pairs where category_id is the ID of the category you're looking for. That list contains the IDs of the products in that category. Using these IDs, you'll be able to generate the required product list. Although this sounds pretty complicated, it can be done using a single SQL query. The real power of SQL lies in its capability to perform complex operations on large amounts of data using simple queries.

You'll learn how to make table joins by analyzing the product and product_category tables and by analyzing how you can get a list of products that belong to a certain category. Tables are joined in SQL using the JOIN clause. Joining one table with another results in the columns (not the rows) of those tables being joined. When joining two tables, there always must be a common column on which the join will be made.

Suppose you want to get all the products in the category where category_id = 5. The query that joins the product and product_category tables is as follows:

```
SELECT     product_category.product_id,
           product_category.category_id,
           product.name
FROM       product_category
INNER JOIN product
        ON product.product_id = product_category.product_id
ORDER BY   product.product_id;
```

The result will look something like this (to save space, the listing doesn't include all returned rows and columns):

```
product_id  category_id name
----------- ----------- --------------------------------------------------
1           1           Christmas Candy Hat
2           1           Hanukah Hat
3           1           Springy Santa Hat
4           1           Plush Santa Hat
5           1           Red Santa Cowboy Hat
6           1           Santa Jester Hat
7           1           Santa's Elf Hat
8           2           Chauffeur Hat
8           5           Chauffeur Hat
...
```

The resultant table is composed of the requested fields from the joined tables synchronized on the product_id column, which was specified as the column to make the join on. You can see that the products that exist in more categories are listed more than once, once for each category they belong in, but this problem will go away after we filter the results to get only the products for a certain category.

Note that in the SELECT clause, the column names are prefixed by the table name. This is a requirement if the columns exist in more tables that participate in the table join, such as product_id in our case. For the other column, prefixing its name with the table name is optional, although it's a good practice to avoid confusion.

The query that returns only the products that belong to category 5 is

```
SELECT     product.product_id, product.name
FROM       product_category
INNER JOIN product
           ON product.product_id = product_category.product_id
WHERE      product_category.category_id = 5;
```

The results are

```
product_id  Name
----------- --------------------------------------------------
8           Chauffeur Hat
27          Bond-Leather Driver
28          Moleskin Driver
29          Herringbone English Driver
```

A final thing worth discussing here is the use of **aliases**. Aliases aren't necessarily related to table joins, but they become especially useful (and sometimes necessary) when joining tables, and they assign different (usually) shorter names for the tables involved. Aliases are necessary when joining a table with itself, in which case, you need to assign different aliases for its different instances to differentiate them. The following query returns the same products as the query before, but it uses aliases:

```
SELECT    p.product_id, p.name
FROM      product_category pc
INNER JOIN product p
       ON p.product_id = pc.product_id
WHERE     pc.category_id = 5;
```

Showing Products Page by Page

If certain web sections need to list large numbers of products, it's useful to let the visitor browse them page by page, with a predefined (or configurable by the visitor) number of products per page.

Depending on the tier on your architecture where paging is performed, there are three main ways to implement paging:

Paging at the data tier level: In this case, the database returns only the page of products needed by the presentation tier.

Paging at the business tier level: The business tier requests the complete page of products from the database, performs filtering, and returns back to the presentation tier only the page of products that needs to be displayed.

Paging at the presentation tier level: In this scenario, the presentation tier receives the complete list of products and extracts the page that needs to be displayed for the visitor.

Paging at the business tier and presentation tier levels has potential performance problems, especially when dealing with large result sets, because they imply transferring unnecessarily large quantities of data from the database to the presentation tier. Additional data also needs to be stored on the server's memory, unnecessarily consuming server resources.

In our web site, we'll implement paging at the data tier level, not only because of its better performance, but also because it allows you to learn some tricks about database programming that you'll find useful when developing your web sites.

To implement paging at the data tier level, we need to find how to build a SELECT query that returns just a portion of records (products) from a larger set, and each database language seems to have different ways for doing this. To achieve this functionality in PostgreSQL, you need to use the LIMIT and OFFSET keywords together with the SELECT statement:

- OFFSET specifies how many records from the original rowset to skip. So if you want to retrieve the second page of products in a catalog that has four products per page, you would need to specify OFFSET 4. A query without an offset is the same as a query with OFFSET 0.

- LIMIT specifies the maximum number of rows to return.

When using OFFSET and LIMIT, it's highly recommended to also use ORDER BY. Without this clause, PostgreSQL doesn't guarantee the order in which the results are returned, so, theoretically, different requests for a certain page of products could deliver different results. The following SQL query tells PostgreSQL to return the rows 15, 16, 17, 18, and 19 from the list of alphabetically ordered products:

```
SELECT   name
FROM     product
ORDER BY name
LIMIT    5
OFFSET   14;
```

With the current database you should get these products:

```
name
-------------------------------------------------
Confederate Civil War Kepi
Confederate Slouch Hat
Cotton Beret
Green MadHatter Hat
Hanukah Hat
```

You'll use the LIMIT and OFFSET keywords to specify the range of records you're interested in when retrieving lists of products. For more details, you can always refer to the official documentation at http://www.postgresql.org/docs/current/interactive/queries-limit.html.

Writing the New Database Functions

Now you implement the data tier functions, which return data from the database. First you'll implement the PostgreSQL functions that retrieve department and category information:

- catalog_get_department_details
- catalog_get_categories_list
- catalog_get_category_details

Afterwards, you'll write the functions that deal with products. Only four functions effectively ask for products, but you'll also implement three helper functions (catalog_count_products_in_category, catalog_count_products_on_department, and catalog_count_products_on_catalog) to assist in implementing the paging functionality. The complete list of methods you need to implement is

- catalog_count_products_in_category
- catalog_get_products_in_category
- catalog_count_products_on_department
- catalog_get_products_on_department
- catalog_count_products_on_catalog
- catalog_get_products_on_catalog
- catalog_get_product_details

In the following sections, you'll be shown the code of each function and its return type. We won't go though individual exercises to create these functions. Use pgAdmin III to add them to your database.

catalog_get_department_details

The `catalog_get_category_details` function returns the name and description for a given department whose ID is received as parameter. This is needed when the user selects a department in the product catalog, and the database must be queried to find out the name and the description of the particular department.

The return data is packaged into an object of the type `department_details`. Next is the SQL code that creates the `catalog_get_department_details` function and the `department_details` type:

```
-- Create department_details type
CREATE TYPE department_details AS
(
  name         VARCHAR(50),
  description  VARCHAR(1000)
);

-- Create catalog_get_department_details function
CREATE FUNCTION catalog_get_department_details(INTEGER)
RETURNS department_details LANGUAGE plpgsql AS $$
  DECLARE
    inDepartmentId ALIAS FOR $1;
    outDepartmentDetailsRow department_details;
  BEGIN
    SELECT INTO outDepartmentDetailsRow
           name, description
    FROM   department
    WHERE  department_id = inDepartmentId;
    RETURN outDepartmentDetailsRow;
  END;
$$;
```

The `WHERE` clause (`WHERE department_id = inDepartmentId`) is used to request the details of a specific department.

catalog_get_categories_list

When a visitor selects a department, the categories that belong to that department must be displayed. The categories will be retrieved by the `catalog_get_categories_list` function, which returns the list of categories in a specific department. The function needs to know the ID of the department for which to retrieve the categories. The return type is `category_list`.

```
-- Create category_list type
CREATE TYPE category_list AS
(
  category_id INTEGER,
```

```
   name          VARCHAR(50)
);


-- Create catalog_get_categories_list function
CREATE FUNCTION catalog_get_categories_list(INTEGER)
RETURNS SETOF category_list LANGUAGE plpgsql AS $$
  DECLARE
    inDepartmentId ALIAS FOR $1;
    outCategoryListRow category_list;
  BEGIN
    FOR outCategoryListRow IN
      SELECT    category_id, name
      FROM      category
      WHERE     department_id = inDepartmentId
      ORDER BY category_id
    LOOP
      RETURN NEXT outCategoryListRow;
    END LOOP;
  END;
$$;
```

catalog_get_category_details

When the visitor selects a particular category, we need to display its name and description.

```
-- Create category_details type
CREATE TYPE category_details AS
(
  name         VARCHAR(50),
  description VARCHAR(1000)
);


-- Create catalog_get_category_details function
CREATE FUNCTION catalog_get_category_details(INTEGER)
RETURNS category_details LANGUAGE plpgsql AS $$
  DECLARE
    inCategoryId ALIAS FOR $1;
    outCategoryDetailsRow category_details;
  BEGIN
    SELECT INTO outCategoryDetailsRow
           name, description
    FROM    category
    WHERE   category_id = inCategoryId;
    RETURN outCategoryDetailsRow;
  END;
$$;
```

catalog_count_products_in_category

This function returns the number of products in a category. This data will be necessary when paginating the lists of products, when we'll need to be able to calculate how many pages of products we have in a category.

```
-- Create catalog_count_products_in_category function
CREATE FUNCTION catalog_count_products_in_category(INTEGER)
RETURNS INTEGER LANGUAGE plpgsql AS $$
  DECLARE
    inCategoryId ALIAS FOR $1;
    outCategoriesCount INTEGER;
  BEGIN
    SELECT     INTO outCategoriesCount
               count(*)
    FROM       product p
    INNER JOIN product_category pc
                 ON p.product_id = pc.product_id
    WHERE      pc.category_id = inCategoryId;
    RETURN outCategoriesCount;
  END;
$$;
```

catalog_get_products_in_category

This function returns the products that belong to a certain category. To obtain this list of products, you need to join the product and product_category tables, as explained earlier in this chapter. We also trim the product's description.

The function receives four parameters:

- inCategoryID represents the ID for which we're returning products.

- inShortProductDescriptionLength represents the maximum length allowed for the product's description. If the description is longer than this value, it will be truncated, and "…" is added at the end. Note this is only used when displaying product lists; in a product details page, the description won't be truncated.

- inProductsPerPage represent the maximum number of products our site can display on a catalog page. If the total number of products in the category is larger than this number, we only return a page containing inProductsPerPage products.

- inStartItem represents the index of the first product to return. When using pagination and displaying four products per page, inStartItem will be 5 and inProductsPerPage will be 4 when the visitor visits the second page of products. With these values, the catalog_get_products_in_category function will return the products from fifth to ninth.

```
-- Create product_list type
CREATE TYPE product_list AS
(
  product_id       INTEGER,
  name             VARCHAR(50),
  description      VARCHAR(1000),
  price            NUMERIC(10, 2),
  discounted_price NUMERIC(10, 2),
  thumbnail        VARCHAR(150)
);

-- Create catalog_get_products_in_category function
CREATE FUNCTION catalog_get_products_in_category(
                 INTEGER, INTEGER, INTEGER, INTEGER)
RETURNS SETOF product_list LANGUAGE plpgsql AS $$
  DECLARE
    inCategoryId                 ALIAS FOR $1;
    inShortProductDescriptionLength ALIAS FOR $2;
    inProductsPerPage            ALIAS FOR $3;
    inStartItem                  ALIAS FOR $4;
    outProductListRow product_list;
  BEGIN
    FOR outProductListRow IN
      SELECT    p.product_id, p.name, p.description, p.price,
                p.discounted_price, p.thumbnail
      FROM      product p
      INNER JOIN product_category pc
                ON p.product_id = pc.product_id
      WHERE     pc.category_id = inCategoryId
      ORDER BY  p.product_id
      LIMIT     inProductsPerPage
      OFFSET    inStartItem
    LOOP
      IF char_length(outProductListRow.description) >
         inShortProductDescriptionLength THEN
        outProductListRow.description :=
          substring(outProductListRow.description, 1,
                    inShortProductDescriptionLength) || '...';
      END IF;
      RETURN NEXT outProductListRow;
    END LOOP;
  END;
$$;
```

catalog_count_products_on_department

This function counts the number of products that are to be displayed in the page of a given department. Note that all the department's products aren't listed on the department's page, but only those products whose `display` value is 2 (product on department promotion) or 3 (product on department and catalog promotion).

```
-- Create catalog_count_products_on_department function
CREATE FUNCTION catalog_count_products_on_department(INTEGER)
RETURNS INTEGER LANGUAGE plpgsql AS $$
  DECLARE
    inDepartmentId ALIAS FOR $1;
    outProductsOnDepartmentCount INTEGER;
  BEGIN
    SELECT DISTINCT INTO outProductsOnDepartmentCount
                    count(*)
    FROM            product p
    INNER JOIN      product_category pc
                       ON p.product_id = pc.product_id
    INNER JOIN      category c
                       ON pc.category_id = c.category_id
    WHERE           (p.display = 2 OR p.display = 3)
                    AND c.department_id = inDepartmentId;
    RETURN outProductsOnDepartmentCount;
  END;
$$;
```

The SQL code is almost the same as the one in `catalog_get_products_on_department`, which we're discussing next.

catalog_get_products_on_department

When the visitor selects a particular department, apart from needing to list its name, description, and list of categories (you wrote the necessary code for these tasks earlier), you also want to display the list of featured products for that department.

`catalog_get_products_on_department` returns all the products that belong to a specific department and has the `display` set to 2 (product on department promotion) or 3 (product on department and catalog promotion).

In `catalog_get_products_in_category`, you needed to make a table join to find out the products that belong to a specific category. Now that you need to do this for departments, the task is a bit more complicated because you can't directly know what products belong to each department.

You know how to find categories that belong to a specific department (you did this in `catalog_get_categories_list`), and you know how to get the products that belong to a specific category (you did that in `catalog_get_products_in_category`). By combining these pieces of information, you can generate the list of products in a department. For this, you need two table joins.

You will also use the DISTINCT clause to filter the results to avoid getting the same record multiple times. This can happen when a product belongs to more than one category, and these categories are in the same department. In this situation, you would get the same product returned for each of the matching categories, unless the results are filtered using DISTINCT.

```
-- Create catalog_get_products_on_department function
CREATE FUNCTION catalog_get_products_on_department(
                  INTEGER, INTEGER, INTEGER, INTEGER)
RETURNS SETOF product_list LANGUAGE plpgsql AS $$
  DECLARE
    inDepartmentId                 ALIAS FOR $1;
    inShortProductDescriptionLength ALIAS FOR $2;
    inProductsPerPage              ALIAS FOR $3;
    inStartItem                    ALIAS FOR $4;
    outProductListRow product_list;
  BEGIN
    FOR outProductListRow IN
      SELECT DISTINCT p.product_id, p.name, p.description, p.price,
                      p.discounted_price, p.thumbnail
      FROM       product p
      INNER JOIN  product_category pc
                    ON p.product_id = pc.product_id
      INNER JOIN  category c
                    ON pc.category_id = c.category_id
      WHERE      (p.display = 2 OR p.display = 3)
                    AND c.department_id = inDepartmentId
      ORDER BY   p.product_id
      LIMIT      inProductsPerPage
      OFFSET     inStartItem
    LOOP
      IF char_length(outProductListRow.description) >
          inShortProductDescriptionLength THEN
        outProductListRow.description :=
          substring(outProductListRow.description, 1,
                    inShortProductDescriptionLength) || '...';
      END IF;
      RETURN NEXT outProductListRow;
    END LOOP;
  END;
$$;
```

Tip If the way table joins work looks too complicated, try following them on the diagram shown earlier in Figure 4-8.

---

catalog_count_products_on_catalog

The `catalog_count_products_on_catalog` catalog returns the number of products to be displayed on the catalog's front page. These are products whose `display` fields have the value of 1 (product is promoted on the first page) or 3 (product is promoted on the first page and on the department pages).

```
-- Create catalog_count_products_on_catalog function
CREATE FUNCTION catalog_count_products_on_catalog()
RETURNS INTEGER LANGUAGE plpgsql AS $$
  DECLARE
    outProductsOnCatalogCount INTEGER;
  BEGIN
      SELECT INTO outProductsOnCatalogCount
             count(*)
      FROM   product
      WHERE  display = 1 OR display = 3;
      RETURN outProductsOnCatalogCount;
  END;
$$;
```

catalog_get_products_on_catalog

The `catalog_get_products_on_catalog` function returns the products to be displayed on the catalog's front page. These are products whose `display` fields have the value of 1 (product is promoted on the first page) or 3 (product is promoted on the first page and on the department pages). The product description is trimmed at a specified number of characters. The pagination is implemented the same way as in the previous two functions that return lists of products.

```
-- Create catalog_get_products_on_catalog function
CREATE FUNCTION catalog_get_products_on_catalog(INTEGER, INTEGER, INTEGER)
RETURNS SETOF product_list LANGUAGE plpgsql AS $$
  DECLARE
    inShortProductDescriptionLength ALIAS FOR $1;
    inProductsPerPage               ALIAS FOR $2;
    inStartItem                     ALIAS FOR $3;
    outProductListRow product_list;
  BEGIN
    FOR outProductListRow IN
      SELECT    product_id, name, description, price,
                discounted_price, thumbnail
      FROM      product
      WHERE     display = 1 OR display = 3
      ORDER BY  product_id
      LIMIT     inProductsPerPage
      OFFSET    inStartItem
    LOOP
      IF char_length(outProductListRow.description) >
```

```
              inShortProductDescriptionLength THEN
          outProductListRow.description :=
             substring(outProductListRow.description, 1,
                       inShortProductDescriptionLength) || '...';
      END IF;
      RETURN NEXT outProductListRow;
    END LOOP;
  END;
$$;
```

catalog_get_product_details

The catalog_get_product_details function returns detailed information about a product and is called to get the data that will be displayed on the product's details page.

```
-- Create product_details type
CREATE TYPE product_details AS
(
  product_id       INTEGER,
  name             VARCHAR(50),
  description       VARCHAR(1000),
  price            NUMERIC(10, 2),
  discounted_price NUMERIC(10, 2),
  image            VARCHAR(150)
);

-- Create catalog_get_product_details function
CREATE FUNCTION catalog_get_product_details(INTEGER)
RETURNS product_details LANGUAGE plpgsql AS $$
  DECLARE
    inProductId ALIAS FOR $1;
    outProductDetailsRow product_details;
  BEGIN
    SELECT INTO outProductDetailsRow
          product_id, name, description,
          price, discounted_price, image
    FROM   product
    WHERE  product_id = inProductId;
    RETURN outProductDetailsRow;
  END;
$$;
```

Well, that's about it. Right now, your data store is ready to hold and process the product catalog information. It's time to move to the next step: implementing the business tier of the product catalog.

Completing the Business Tier Code

In the business tier, you'll add some new methods that will call the earlier created methods in the data tier. Remember that you started working on the Catalog class (located in the business/catalog.php file) in Chapter 3. The new methods that you'll add here are

- GetDepartmentDetails

- GetCategoriesInDepartment

- GetCategoryDetails

- HowManyPages

- GetProductsInCategory

- GetProductsOnDepartment

- GetProductsOnCatalog

- GetProductDetails

Defining Product List Constants and Activating Session

Before writing the business tier methods, let's first update the include/config.php file by adding the SHORT_PRODUCT_DESCRIPTION_LENGTH and PRODUCTS_PER_PAGE constants. These allow you to easily define the behavior of your site by specifying the length of product descriptions and how many products to be displayed per page.

```
...
// Server HTTP port (can omit if the default 80 is used)
define('HTTP_SERVER_PORT', '8080');
/* Name of the virtual directory the site runs in, for example:
   '/hatshop/' if the site runs at http://www.example.com/hatshop/
   '/' if the site runs at http://www.example.com/ */
define('VIRTUAL_LOCATION', '/hatshop/');
// We enable and enforce SSL when this is set to anything else than 'no'
define('USE_SSL', 'yes');

// Configure product lists display options
define('SHORT_PRODUCT_DESCRIPTION_LENGTH', 150);
define('PRODUCTS_PER_PAGE', 4);
?>
```

Then, modify include/app_top.php by adding these lines to it:

```
<?php
// Activate session
session_start();

// Include utility files
require_once 'include/config.php';
require_once BUSINESS_DIR . 'error_handler.php';
...
```

The SHORT_PRODUCT_DESCRIPTION_LENGTH constant specifies how many characters from the product's description should appear when displaying product lists. The complete description gets displayed in the product's details page, which you'll implement at the end of this chapter.

PRODUCTS_PER_PAGE specifies the maximum number of products that can be displayed in any catalog page. If the visitor's selection contains more than PRODUCTS_PER_PAGE products, the list of products is split into subpages, accessible through the navigation controls.

We also enabled the PHP session, which will help us improve performance when navigating through pages of products.

Note Session handling is a great PHP feature that allows you to keep track of variables specific to a certain visitor accessing the web site. While the visitor browses the catalog, its session variables are persisted by the web server and associated to a unique visitor identifier (which is stored by default in the visitor's browser as a **cookie**). The visitor's session object stores (name, value) pairs that are saved at server-side and are accessible for the entire visitor's session. In this chapter, we'll use the session feature for improving performance. When implementing the paging functionality, before requesting the list of products, you first ask the database for the total number of products that are going to be returned, so you can show the visitor how many pages of products are available. This number will be saved in the visitor's session, so if the visitor browses the pages of a list of products, the database wouldn't be queried multiple times for the total number of products—on subsequent calls, this number will be directly read from the session (this functionality is implemented in the HowManyPages method that you'll implement later). In this chapter, you'll also use the session to implement the Continue Shopping buttons in product details pages.

Let's work through each business tier method. All these methods need to be added to the Catalog class, located in the business/catalog.php file that you started writing in Chapter 3.

GetDepartmentDetails

GetDepartmentDetails is called from the presentation tier when a department is clicked to display its name and description. The presentation tier passes the ID of the selected department, and you need to send back the name and the description of the selected department.

```php
// Retrieves complete details for the specified department
public static function GetDepartmentDetails($departmentId)
{
  // Build SQL query
  $sql = 'SELECT *
          FROM catalog_get_department_details(:department_id);';
  // Build the parameters array
  $params = array (':department_id' => $departmentId);
  // Prepare the statement with PDO-specific functionality
  $result = DatabaseHandler::Prepare($sql);

  // Execute the query and return the results
  return DatabaseHandler::GetRow($result, $params);
}
```

GetCategoriesInDepartment

The GetCategoriesInDepartment method is called to retrieve the list of categories that belong
to a department. Add this method to the Catalog class:

```
// Retrieves list of categories that belong to a department
public static function GetCategoriesInDepartment($departmentId)
{
  // Build SQL query
  $sql = 'SELECT *
          FROM catalog_get_categories_list(:department_id);';
  // Build the parameters array
  $params = array (':department_id' => $departmentId);
  // Prepare the statement with PDO-specific functionality
  $result = DatabaseHandler::Prepare($sql);

  // Execute the query and return the results
  return DatabaseHandler::GetAll($result, $params);
}
```

GetCategoryDetails

GetCategoryDetails is called from the presentation tier when a category is clicked to display
its name and description. The presentation tier passes the ID of the selected category, and
you need to send back the name and the description of the selected category.

```
// Retrieves complete details for the specified category
public static function GetCategoryDetails($categoryId)
{
  // Build SQL query
  $sql = 'SELECT *
          FROM catalog_get_category_details(:category_id);';
  // Build the parameters array
  $params = array (':category_id' => $categoryId);
  // Prepare the statement with PDO-specific functionality
  $result = DatabaseHandler::Prepare($sql);

  // Execute the query and return the results
  return DatabaseHandler::GetRow($result, $params);
}
```

HowManyPages

As you know, our product catalog will display a fixed number of products in every page. When a
catalog page contains more than an established number of products, we display navigation controls that allow the visitor to browse back and forth through the subpages of products. You can
see the navigation controls in Figure 3-2 in Chapter 3 or later in this chapter in Figure 4-11.

When displaying the navigation controls, you need to calculate the number of subpages of products you have for a given catalog page; for this, we're creating the HowManyPages helper method.

This method receives as argument a SELECT query that counts the total number of products of the catalog page ($countSql) and returns the number of subpages. This will be done by simply dividing the total number of products by the number of products to be displayed in a subpage of products; this latter number is configurable through the PRODUCTS_PER_PAGE constant in include/config.php.

To improve the performance when the visitor browses back and forth through the subpages, after we calculate the number of subpages for the first time, we're saving it to the visitor's session. This way, the SQL query received as parameter won't need to be executed more than once on a single visit to a catalog page.

This method is called from the other data tier methods (GetProductsInCategory, GetProductsOnDepartment, GetProductsOnCatalog), which we'll cover next.

Add HowManyPages to the Catalog class.

```
/* Calculates how many pages of products could be filled by the
   number of products returned by the $countSql query */
private static function HowManyPages($countSql, $countSqlParams)
{
  // Create a hash for the sql query
  $queryHashCode = md5($countSql . var_export($countSqlParams, true));

  // Verify if we have the query results in cache
  if (isset ($_SESSION['last_count_hash']) &&
      isset ($_SESSION['how_many_pages']) &&
      $_SESSION['last_count_hash'] === $queryHashCode)
  {
    // Retrieve the the cached value
    $how_many_pages = $_SESSION['how_many_pages'];
  }
  else
  {
    // Execute the query
    $prepared = DatabaseHandler::Prepare($countSql);
    $items_count = DatabaseHandler::GetOne($prepared, $countSqlParams);

    // Calculate the number of pages
    $how_many_pages = ceil($items_count / PRODUCTS_PER_PAGE);

    // Save the query and its count result in the session
    $_SESSION['last_count_hash'] = $queryHashCode;
    $_SESSION['how_many_pages'] = $how_many_pages;
  }

  // Return the number of pages
  return $how_many_pages;
}
```

Let's analyze the function to see how it does its job.

The method is private because you won't access it from within other classes—it's a helper class for other methods of Catalog.

The method verifies whether the previous call to it was for the same SELECT query. If it was, the result cached from the previous call is returned. This small trick improves performance when the visitor is browsing subpages of the same list of products because the actual counting in the database is performed only once.

```
// Create a hash for the sql query
$queryHashCode = md5($countSql . var_export($countSqlParams, true));

// Verify if we have the query results in cache
if (isset ($_SESSION['last_count_hash']) &&
    isset ($_SESSION['how_many_pages']) &&
    $_SESSION['last_count_hash'] === $queryHashCode)
{
  // Retrieve the the cached value
  $how_many_pages = $_SESSION['how_many_pages'];
}
```

The number of pages associated with the received query and parameters is saved in the current visitor's session in a variable named how_many_pages. If the conditions aren't met, which means the results of the query aren't cached, we calculate them and save them to the session:

```
else
{
  // Execute the query
  $prepared = DatabaseHandler::Prepare($countSql);
  $items_count = DatabaseHandler::GetOne($prepared, $countSqlParams);

  // Calculate the number of pages
  $how_many_pages = ceil($items_count / PRODUCTS_PER_PAGE);

  // Save the query and its count result in the session
  $_SESSION['last_count_hash'] = $queryHashCode;
  $_SESSION['how_many_pages'] = $how_many_pages;
}
```

In the end, no matter if the number of pages was fetched from the session or calculated by the database, it is returned to the calling function:

```
// Return the number of pages
return $how_many_pages;
```

GetProductsInCategory

GetProductsInCategory returns the list of products that belong to a particular category. Add the following method to the Catalog class in business/catalog.php:

```
// Retrieves list of products that belong to a category
public static function GetProductsInCategory(
                        $categoryId, $pageNo, &$rHowManyPages)
{
  // Query that returns the number of products in the category
  $sql = 'SELECT catalog_count_products_in_category(:category_id);';
  $params = array (':category_id' => $categoryId);
  // Calculate the number of pages required to display the products
  $rHowManyPages = Catalog::HowManyPages($sql, $params);
  // Calculate the start item
  $start_item = ($pageNo - 1) * PRODUCTS_PER_PAGE;

  // Retrieve the list of products
  $sql = 'SELECT *
          FROM   catalog_get_products_in_category(
                    :category_id, :short_product_description_length,
                    :products_per_page, :start_item);';
  $params = array (
    ':category_id' => $categoryId,
    ':short_product_description_length' => SHORT_PRODUCT_DESCRIPTION_LENGTH,
    ':products_per_page' => PRODUCTS_PER_PAGE,
    ':start_item' => $start_item);
  $result = DatabaseHandler::Prepare($sql);

  // Execute the query and return the results
  return DatabaseHandler::GetAll($result, $params);
}
```

This function has two purposes:

- Calculate the number of subpages of products, and return this number through the &$rHowManyPages parameter. To calculate this number, the HowManyPages method you've added earlier is used. The SQL query that is used to retrieve the total number of products calls the catalog_count_products_in_category database function that you added earlier to your databases.

- Return the list of products in the mentioned category.

■**Note**   The ampersand (&) before a function parameter means it is passed by reference. When a variable is passed by reference, an alias of the variable is passed instead of creating a new copy of the value. This way, when a variable is passed by reference and the called function changes its value, its new value will reflect in the caller function, too. Passing by reference is an alternative method to receiving a return value from a called function and is particularly useful when you need to get multiple return values from the called function. CreateSubpageQuery returns the text of a SELECT query through its return value and the total number of subpages through the $rHowManyPages parameter that is passed by reference.

GetProductsOnDepartment

The GetProductsOnDepartment function returns the list of products featured for a particular department. The department's featured products must be displayed when the customer visits the home page of a department. Put it inside the Catalog class.

```
// Retrieves the list of products for the department page
public static function GetProductsOnDepartmentDisplay(
                        $departmentId, $pageNo, &$rHowManyPages)
{
  // Query that returns the number of products in the department page
  $sql = 'SELECT catalog_count_products_on_department(:department_id);';
  $params = array (':department_id' => $departmentId);
  // Calculate the number of pages required to display the products
  $rHowManyPages = Catalog::HowManyPages($sql, $params);
  // Calculate the start item
  $start_item = ($pageNo - 1) * PRODUCTS_PER_PAGE;

  // Retrieve the list of products
  $sql = 'SELECT *
          FROM   catalog_get_products_on_department(
                   :department_id, :short_product_description_length,
                   :products_per_page, :start_item);';
  $params = array (
    ':department_id' => $departmentId,
    ':short_product_description_length' => SHORT_PRODUCT_DESCRIPTION_LENGTH,
    ':products_per_page' => PRODUCTS_PER_PAGE,
    ':start_item' => $start_item);
  $result = DatabaseHandler::Prepare($sql);

  // Execute the query and return the results
  return DatabaseHandler::GetAll($result, $params);
}
```

GetProductsOnCatalog

The GetProductsOnCatalog function returns the list of products featured on the catalog's front page. It goes inside the Catalog class.

```
// Retrieves the list of products on catalog display
public static function GetProductsOnCatalogDisplay($pageNo, &$rHowManyPages)
{
  // Query that returns the number of products for the front catalog page
  $sql = 'SELECT catalog_count_products_on_catalog();';
  // Calculate the number of pages required to display the products
  $rHowManyPages = Catalog::HowManyPages($sql, null);
  // Calculate the start item
  $start_item = ($pageNo - 1) * PRODUCTS_PER_PAGE;
```

```
// Retrieve the list of products
$sql = 'SELECT *
        FROM   catalog_get_products_on_catalog(
                   :short_product_description_length,
                   :products_per_page, :start_item);';
$params = array (
  ':short_product_description_length' => SHORT_PRODUCT_DESCRIPTION_LENGTH,
  ':products_per_page' => PRODUCTS_PER_PAGE,
  ':start_item' => $start_item);
$result = DatabaseHandler::Prepare($sql);

// Execute the query and return the results
return DatabaseHandler::GetAll($result, $params);
}
```

GetProductDetails

Add the GetProductDetails method to the Catalog class:

```
// Retrieves complete product details
public static function GetProductDetails($productId)
{
  // Build SQL query
  $sql = 'SELECT *
          FROM catalog_get_product_details(:product_id);';
  // Build the parameters array
  $params = array (':product_id' => $productId);
  // Prepare the statement with PDO-specific functionality
  $result = DatabaseHandler::Prepare($sql);

  // Execute the query and return the results
  return DatabaseHandler::GetRow($result, $params);
}
```

Implementing the Presentation Tier

Believe it or not, right now the data and business tiers of the product catalog are complete for this chapter. All you have to do is use their functionality in the presentation tier. In this final section, you'll create a few Smarty templates and integrate them into the existing project.

Execute the HatShop project (or load http://localhost/hatshop in your favorite web browser) to see once again what happens when the visitor clicks a department. After the page loads, click one of the departments. The main page (index.php) is reloaded, but this time with a query string at the end:

http://localhost/hatshop/index.php?DepartmentID=1

Using this parameter, `DepartmentID`, you can obtain any information about the selected department, such as its name, description, list of products, and so on. In the following sections, you'll create the controls that display the list of categories associated with the selected department, and the products for the selected department, category, or main web page.

Displaying Department and Category Details

The componentized template responsible for showing the contents of a particular department is named `department`, and you'll build it in the exercise that follows. You'll first create the componentized template and then modify `index.php` and `templates/index.tpl` to load it when `DepartmentID` is present in the query string. After this exercise, when clicking a department in the list, you should see a page like the one in Figure 4-9.

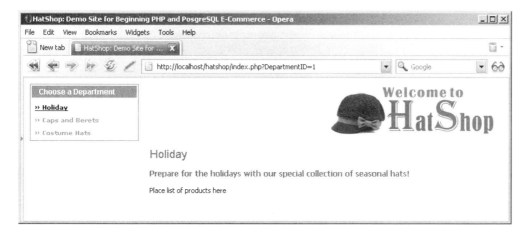

Figure 4-9. *Selecting the Holiday department*

Exercise: Displaying Department Details

1. Add the following two styles to the `hatshop.css` file. You'll need them for displaying the department's title and description:

```
.title
{
  color: #ff0000;
  font-family: arial, tahoma, verdana;
  font-size: 18px;
  margin: 0px;
}
.description
{
  color: #0583b5;
  font-size: 12px;
  font-weight: bold;
  margin: 0px;
}
```

2. Create a new template file named `blank.tpl` in the `presentation/templates` folder with the following contents:

```
{* Smarty blank page *}
```

Yes, this is a blank Smarty template file, which contains just a comment. You'll use it a bit later. Make sure you add that comment to the file; otherwise, if you leave it empty, you'll get an error when trying to use the template.

3. Create a new template file named `department.tpl` in the `presentation/templates` folder, and add the following code to it:

```
{* department.tpl *}
{load_department assign="department"}
<p class="title">{$department->mNameLabel}</p>
<br />
<p class="description">{$department->mDescriptionLabel}</p>
<br />
Place list of products here
```

The two variables, `$department->mNameLabel` and `$department->mDescriptionLabel`, contain the name and description of the selected department and are populated by the template plugin file, `function.load_department.php`.

4. Let's now create the template plugin file for `department.tpl`. Create the `presentation/smarty_plugins/function.load_department.php` file, and add the following code to it:

```php
<?php
// Plugin functions inside plugin files must be named: smarty_type_name
function smarty_function_load_department($params, $smarty)
{
  // Create Department object
  $department = new Department();
  $department->init();

  // Assign template variable
  $smarty->assign($params['assign'], $department);
}

// Deals with retrieving department details
class Department
{
  // Public variables for the smarty template
  public $mDescriptionLabel;
  public $mNameLabel;

  // Private members
  private $_mDepartmentId;
  private $_mCategoryId;
```

```php
    // Class constructor
    public function __construct()
    {
      // We need to have DepartmentID in the query string
      if (isset ($_GET['DepartmentID']))
        $this->_mDepartmentId = (int)$_GET['DepartmentID'];
      else
        trigger_error('DepartmentID not set');

      /* If CategoryID is in the query string we save it
         (casting it to integer to protect against invalid values) */
      if (isset ($_GET['CategoryID']))
        $this->_mCategoryId = (int)$_GET['CategoryID'];
    }

    public function init()
    {
      // If visiting a department ...
      $details = Catalog::GetDepartmentDetails($this->_mDepartmentId);
      $this->mNameLabel = $details['name'];
      $this->mDescriptionLabel = $details['description'];

      // If visiting a category ...
      if (isset ($this->_mCategoryId))
      {
        $details = Catalog::GetCategoryDetails($this->_mCategoryId);
        $this->mNameLabel =
          $this->mNameLabel . ' &raquo; ' . $details['name'];
        $this->mDescriptionLabel = $details['description'];
      }
    }
  }
?>
```

5. Now let's modify index.tpl and index.php to load the newly created componentized template when DepartmentID appears in the query string. If the visitor is browsing a department, you set the pageContentsCell variable to the componentized template you have just created.

Modify index.php as shown:

```php
<?php
// Load Smarty library and config files
require_once 'include/app_top.php';

// Load Smarty template file
$page = new Page();

// Define the template file for the page contents
$pageContentsCell = 'blank.tpl';
```

```
    // Load department details if visiting a department
    if (isset ($_GET['DepartmentID']))
    {
      $pageContentsCell = 'department.tpl';
    }

    // Assign a template file to the page contents cell
    $page->assign('pageContentsCell', $pageContentsCell);

    // Display the page
    $page->display('index.tpl');

    // Load app_bottom which closes the database connection
    require_once 'include/app_bottom.php';
    ?>
```

6. Open presentation/templates/index.tpl, and replace the text Place contents here with

   ```
   {include file="$pageContentsCell"}
   ```

7. Load your web site in a browser, and select one of the departments to ensure everything works as expected.

How It Works: The Department Componentized Template

Now that the most important functionality has already been implemented in the data and business tiers, implementing the visual part was an easy task.

After adding the CSS styles and creating the blank template file, you created the Smarty template file department.tpl, which contains the HTML layout for displaying a department's data. This template file is loaded in the page contents cell, just below the header, in index.tpl:

```
    {include file="header.tpl"}
  <div id="content">
    {include file="$pageContentsCell"}
  </div>
```

The $pageContentsCell variable is populated in index.php, depending on the query string parameters. At the moment, if the DepartmentID parameter is found in the query string, the page contents cell is populated with the department.tpl template file you just wrote. Otherwise (such as when being on the first page), the blank template file is used (you'll change this when creating a template to populate the contents cell for the first page). This is the code in index.php that assigns a value to $pageContentsCell:

```
// Define the template file for the page contents
$pageContentsCell = 'blank.tpl';

// Load department details if visiting a department
if (isset ($_GET['DepartmentID']))
{
```

```
  $pageContentsCell = 'department.tpl';
}
```

```
// Assign a template file to the page contents cell
$page->assign('pageContentsCell', $pageContentsCell);
```

The first interesting aspect to know about `department.tpl` is the way it loads the `load_department` function plugin.

```
{* department.tpl *}
{load_department assign="department"}
```

This allows you to access the instance of the `Department` class (that we'll discuss next) and its public members (`mNameLabel` and `mDescriptionLabel`) from the template file (`department.tpl`), like this:

```
<p class="title">{$department->mNameLabel}</p>
  <br />
  <p class="description">{$department->mDescriptionLabel}</p>
  <br />
Place list of products here
```

The next step now is to understand how the template plugin file (`function.load_department.php`) does its work to obtain the department's name and description. The file begins with a plugin function that is standard in our architecture. It creates a `Department` instance (the `Department` class is defined afterwards), initializes it calling its `init()` method, and then associates the `assign` plugin parameter with the earlier created `Department` instance.

```
// Plugin functions inside plugin files must be named: smarty_type_name
function smarty_function_load_department($params, $smarty)
{
  // Create Department object
  $department = new Department();
  $department->init();

  // Assign template variable
  $smarty->assign($params['assign'], $department);
}
```

Next, we have the `Department` class. The two public members of `Department` are the ones you access from the Smarty template (the department's name and description). The final role of this class is to populate these members, which are required to build the output for the visitor:

```
// Deals with retrieving department details
class Department
{
  // Public variables for the smarty template
  public $mDescriptionLabel;
  public $mNameLabel;
```

There are also two private members that are used for internal purposes. `$_mDepartmentId` and `$m_CategoryId` will store the values of the `DepartmentID` and `CategoryID` query string parameters:

```
// Private members
private $_mDepartmentId;
private $_mCategoryId;
```

And then comes the constructor. In any object-oriented language, the constructor of the class is executed when the class is instantiated, and the constructor is used to perform various initialization procedures. In our case, the constructor of Department reads the DepartmentID and CategoryID query string parameters into the _mDepartmentId and _mCategoryId private class members. You need these because if CategoryID actually exists in the query string, then you also need to display the name of the category and the category's description instead of the department's description.

```
// Class constructor
public function __construct()
{
  // We need to have DepartmentID in the query string
  if (isset ($_GET['DepartmentID']))
    $this->_mDepartmentId = (int)$_GET['DepartmentID'];
  else
    trigger_error('DepartmentID not set');

  /* If CategoryID is in the query string we save it
     (casting it to integer to protect against invalid values) */
  if (isset ($_GET['CategoryID']))
    $this->_mCategoryId = (int)$_GET['CategoryID'];
}
```

The real functionality of the class is hidden inside the init() method, which in our case gets executed immediately after the constructor. This method populates the mNameLabel and mDescriptionLabel public members with information from the business tier. The GetDepartmentDetails method of the business tier Catalog class is used to retrieve the details of the department; if necessary, the GetCategoryDetails method is also called to retrieve the details of the category. (The details of the department need to be retrieved even if visiting a category because the page heading would be composed of both the department name and the category name.)

```
public function init()
  {
    // If visiting a department ...
    $details = Catalog::GetDepartmentDetails($this->_mDepartmentId);
    $this->mNameLabel = $details['name'];
    $this->mDescriptionLabel = $details['description'];

    // If visiting a category ...
    if (isset ($this->_mCategoryId))
    {
      $details = Catalog::GetCategoryDetails($this->_mCategoryId);
      $this->mNameLabel =
        $this->mNameLabel . ' &raquo; ' . $details['name'];
      $this->mDescriptionLabel = $details['description'];
    }
  }
```

Displaying the List of Categories

When the visitor selects a department, the categories that belong to that department must appear. For this, you'll implement a new Smarty template named `categories_list`.

`categories_list` is very similar to the `department_list` componentized template. It consists of a template section used for looping over the array of categories data (category name and category ID). This template section will contain links to `index.php`, but this time their query string will also contain a `CategoryID`, showing that a category has been clicked, like this:

```
http://localhost/hatshop/index.php?DepartmentID=1&CategoryID=2
```

The steps in the following exercise are very much like the ones for the `departments_list` componentized template (created at the end of Chapter 3), so we'll move a bit more quickly this time.

Exercise: Creating the categories_list Componentized Template

1. First, update `hatshop.css` by adding the following styles, which you'll use for displaying categories:

```css
#categories_box
{
  border: 1px solid #ef8d0e;
}
#categories_box p
{
  background: #ef8d0e;
}
```

2. Create the Smarty template for the `categories_list` componentized template. Write the following lines in `presentation/templates/categories_list.tpl`:

```
{* categories_list.tpl *}
{load_categories_list assign="categories_list"}
{* Start categories list *}
<div class="left_box" id="categories_box">
  <p>Choose a Category</p>
  <ol>
  {section name=i loop=$categories_list->mCategories}
    {assign var=selected_c value=""}
    {if ($categories_list->mCategorySelected ==
        $categories_list->mCategories[i].category_id)}
      {assign var=selected_c value="class=\"selected\""}
    {/if}
    <li>
      <a {$selected_c}
       href="{$categories_list->mCategories[i].link|prepare_link:"http"}">
       &raquo; {$categories_list->mCategories[i].name}
      </a>
    </li>
```

```
    {/section}
    </ol>
  </div>
  {* End categories list *}
```

3. Create the presentation/smarty_plugins/function.load_categories_list.php file, and add
   the following code to it:

```php
<?php
// Plugin functions inside plugin files must be named: smarty_type_name
function smarty_function_load_categories_list($params, $smarty)
{
  // Create CategoriesList object
  $categories_list = new CategoriesList();
  $categories_list->init();

  // Assign template variable
  $smarty->assign($params['assign'], $categories_list);
}

// Manages the categories list
class CategoriesList
{
  // Public variables for the smarty template
  public $mCategorySelected   = 0;
  public $mDepartmentSelected = 0;
  public $mCategories;

  // Constructor reads query string parameter
  public function __construct()
  {
    if (isset ($_GET['DepartmentID']))
      $this->mDepartmentSelected = (int)$_GET['DepartmentID'];
    else
      trigger_error('DepartmentID not set');

    if (isset ($_GET['CategoryID']))
      $this->mCategorySelected = (int)$_GET['CategoryID'];
  }

  public function init()
  {
    $this->mCategories =
      Catalog::GetCategoriesInDepartment($this->mDepartmentSelected);

    // Building links for the category pages
    for ($i = 0; $i < count($this->mCategories); $i++)
      $this->mCategories[$i]['link'] =
```

```
             'index.php?DepartmentID=' . $this->mDepartmentSelected .
             '&CategoryID=' . $this->mCategories[$i]['category_id'];
      }
   }
   ?>
```

4. Modify `index.php` like this:

```php
<?php
// Load Smarty library and config files
require_once 'include/app_top.php';

// Load Smarty template file
$page = new Page();

// Define the template file for the page contents
$pageContentsCell = 'blank.tpl';

// Define the template file for the categories cell
$categoriesCell = 'blank.tpl';

// Load department details if visiting a department
if (isset ($_GET['DepartmentID']))
{
  $pageContentsCell = 'department.tpl';
  $categoriesCell = 'categories_list.tpl';
}

// Assign a template file to the page contents cell
$page->assign('pageContentsCell', $pageContentsCell);
$page->assign('categoriesCell', $categoriesCell);

// Display the page
$page->display('index.tpl');

// Load app_bottom which closes the database connection
require_once 'include/app_bottom.php';
?>
```

5. Now include the `categories_list` componentized template in `presentation/templates/index.tpl`, just below the list of departments:

```
{include file="departments_list.tpl"}
{include file="$categoriesCell"}
```

6. Load HatShop in a web browser. When the page loads, click on one of the departments. You'll see the categories list appear in the chosen place (see Figure 4-10).

Figure 4-10. *Selecting the Holiday department*

How It Works: The categories_list Componentized Template

The categories_list componentized template works similarly to the departments_list. The CategoriesList class (located in the function.load_categories_list.php plugin file) has three public members that can be accessed from the template file (categories_list.tpl):

```
// Public variables for the smarty template
public $mCategorySelected   = 0;
public $mDepartmentSelected = 0;
public $mCategories;
```

$mCategorySelected retains the category that is selected, which must be displayed with a different style than the other categories in the list. The same is true with $mDepartmentSelected. $mCategories is the list of categories you populate the categories list with. This list is obtained with a call to the business tier.

The links in the categories list are processed using the prepare_link Smarty modifier to ensure all characters are transformed to their HTML equivalents (such as & is transformed to &, and so on) and to compose the correct absolute links, as you learned in Chapter 3.

```
<a {$selected_c}
 href="{$categories_list->mCategories[i].link|prepare_link:"http"}">
   &raquo; {$categories_list->mCategories[i].name}
</a>
```

Displaying Product Lists

Whether on the main web page or browsing a category, some products should appear instead of the "Place list of products here" text. Here you create the products_list componentized template, which is capable of displaying a list containing detailed information about the products. When a large number of products are present to be browsed, navigation links will appear (see Figure 4-11).

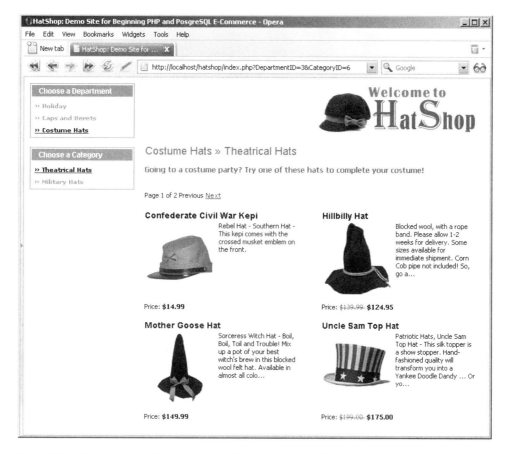

Figure 4-11. *The* products_list *componentized template with paging*

This componentized template will be used in multiple places within the web site. On the main page, it displays the products on catalog display (remember, the ones that have the display field set to 1 or 3). When a visitor selects a particular department, the products_list componentized template displays the products featured for the selected department. Finally, when the visitor clicks on a category, the componentized template displays all the products that belong to that category. Due to the way the database is implemented, you can feature a product in the departments it belongs to but not on the main page, or vice versa. If a product belongs to more than one department, it will appear on the main page of each of these departments.

The componentized template chooses which products to display after analyzing the query string. If both DepartmentID and CategoryID parameters are present in the query string, this means the products of that category should be listed. If only DepartmentID is present, the visitor is visiting a department, so its featured products should appear. If DepartmentID is not present, the visitor is on the main page, so the catalog featured products should appear.

To integrate the products_list componentized template with the first page, you'll need to create an additional template file (first_page_contents.tpl), which you'll implement later. After creating products_list in the following exercise, you'll be able to browse the products by department and by category. Afterwards, you'll see how to add products to the main web page.

Exercise: Creating the products_list Componentized Template

1. Copy the product_images directory from the Source Code/Download section (http://www.apress.com) to your project's hatshop folder.

2. Add the following styles to the hatshop.css file:

```css
.paging_text a
{
  color: #0000ff;
  font-size: 11px;
  font-weight: normal;
  text-decoration: underline;
}
.paging_text a:hover
{
  color: #0000ff;
}
p.right
{
  clear: right;
  float: right;
  width: 260px;
  margin: 0px 0px 15px 0px;
}
p.right br
{
  clear: left;
}
p.left
{
  clear: left;
  float:left;
  width: 260px;
  margin: 0px 0px 15px 0px;
  padding: 0px;
}
p.left br
```

```
{
  clear: left;
}
.product_image
{
  clear: none;
  float: left;
  margin: -10px 5px 0px 0px;
  padding: 10px 0px 0px 0px;
}
a.product_name
{
  color: #000000;
  font-family: arial, tahoma, verdana;
  font-size: 14px;
}
a.product_name:hover
{
  color: #ff0000;
  font-family: arial, tahoma, verdana;
  font-size: 14px;
}
.price
{
  font-weight: bold;
}
.old_price
{
  color: #ff0000;
  font-weight: normal;
  text-decoration: line-through;
}
```

3. Create a new Smarty design template named products_list.tpl inside the presentation/
   templates folder, and add the following code to it:

```
{* products_list.tpl *}
{load_products_list assign="products_list"}
{if $products_list->mrHowManyPages > 1}
<br />
<span class="paging_text">
  Page {$products_list->mPageNo} of {$products_list->mrHowManyPages}
  {if $products_list->mPreviousLink}
    <a href="{$products_list->mPreviousLink|prepare_link:"http"}">Previous</a>
  {else}
    Previous
  {/if}
  {if $products_list->mNextLink}
```

```
       <a href="{$products_list->mNextLink|prepare_link:"http"}">Next</a>
    {else}
      Next
    {/if}
  </span>
{/if}
<br />
{section name=k loop=$products_list->mProducts}
  {assign var=direction_p value="left"}
  {if  $smarty.section.k.index != 0 &&
       ($smarty.section.k.index + 1) % 2 == 0}
    {assign var=direction_p value="right"}
  {else}
    <br />
  {/if}
  <p class="{$direction_p}">
    <a class="product_name"
     href="{$products_list->mProducts[k].link|prepare_link:"http"}">
      {$products_list->mProducts[k].name}
    </a>
    <br />
    <a href="{$products_list->mProducts[k].link|prepare_link:"http"}">
      <img src="product_images/{$products_list->mProducts[k].thumbnail}"
       border="0" width="120" alt="Product image" class="product_image" />
    </a>
    <span class="product_description">
      {$products_list->mProducts[k].description}
    </span>
    <br /><br />
    <span>Price:</span>
    {if $products_list->mProducts[k].discounted_price == 0}
    <span class="price">
    {else}
    <span class="old_price">
    {/if}
      ${$products_list->mProducts[k].price}
    </span>
    {if $products_list->mProducts[k].discounted_price != 0}
    <span class="price">
       ${$products_list->mProducts[k].discounted_price}
    </span>
    {/if}
  </p>
{/section}
```

4. Now you must create the template plugin file for the `products_list.tpl` template. Create a new file named `function.load_products_list.php` in the `presentation/smarty_plugins` folder, and add the following code to it:

```php
<?php
// Plugin functions inside plugin files must be named: smarty_type_name
function smarty_function_load_products_list($params, $smarty)
{
  // Create ProductsList object
  $products_list = new ProductsList();
  $products_list->init();

  // Assign template variable
  $smarty->assign($params['assign'], $products_list);
}

class ProductsList
{
  // Public variables to be read from Smarty template
  public $mProducts;
  public $mPageNo;
  public $mrHowManyPages;
  public $mNextLink;
  public $mPreviousLink;

  // Private members
  private $_mDepartmentId;
  private $_mCategoryId;

  // Class constructor
  public function __construct()
  {
    // Get DepartmentID from query string casting it to int
    if (isset ($_GET['DepartmentID']))
      $this->_mDepartmentId = (int)$_GET['DepartmentID'];

    // Get CategoryID from query string casting it to int
    if (isset ($_GET['CategoryID']))
      $this->_mCategoryId = (int)$_GET['CategoryID'];

    // Get PageNo from query string casting it to int
    if (isset ($_GET['PageNo']))
      $this->mPageNo = (int)$_GET['PageNo'];
    else
      $this->mPageNo = 1;
  }

  public function init()
```

```
{
  /* If browsing a category, get the list of products by calling
     the GetProductsInCategory business tier method */
  if (isset ($this->_mCategoryId))
    $this->mProducts = Catalog::GetProductsInCategory(
      $this->_mCategoryId, $this->mPageNo, $this->mrHowManyPages);
  /* If browsing a department, get the list of products by calling
     the GetProductsOnDepartmentDisplay business tier method */
  elseif (isset ($this->_mDepartmentId))
    $this->mProducts = Catalog::GetProductsOnDepartmentDisplay(
      $this->_mDepartmentId, $this->mPageNo, $this->mrHowManyPages);
  /* If browsing the first page, get the list of products by
     calling the GetProductsOnCatalogDisplay business
     tier method */
  else
    $this->mProducts = Catalog::GetProductsOnCatalogDisplay(
                       $this->mPageNo, $this->mrHowManyPages);

  /* If there are subpages of products, display navigation
     controls */
  if ($this->mrHowManyPages > 1)
  {
    // Read the query string
    $query_string = getenv('QUERY_STRING');

    // Find if we have PageNo in the query string
    $pos = stripos($query_string, 'PageNo=');

    /* If there is no PageNo in the query string
       then we're on the first page */
    if ($pos == false)
    {
      $query_string .= '&PageNo=1';
      $pos = stripos($query_string, 'PageNo=');
    }

    // Read the current page number from the query string
    $temp = substr($query_string, $pos);
    sscanf($temp, 'PageNo=%d', $this->mPageNo);

    // Build the Next link
    if ($this->mPageNo >= $this->mrHowManyPages)
      $this->mNextLink = '';
    else
    {
      $new_query_string = str_replace('PageNo=' . $this->mPageNo,
                                      'PageNo=' . ($this->mPageNo + 1),
```

```
                                        $query_string);
          $this->mNextLink = 'index.php?' . $new_query_string;
        }


        // Build the Previous link
        if ($this->mPageNo == 1)
          $this->mPreviousLink = '';
        else
        {
          $new_query_string = str_replace('PageNo=' . $this->mPageNo,
                                          'PageNo=' . ($this->mPageNo - 1),
                                          $query_string);
          $this->mPreviousLink = 'index.php?' . $new_query_string;
        }
      }


      // Build links for product details pages
      $url = $_SESSION['page_link'];

      if (count($_GET) > 0)
        $url = $url . '&ProductID=';
      else
        $url = $url . '?ProductID=';

      for ($i = 0; $i < count($this->mProducts); $i++)
      {
        $this->mProducts[$i]['link'] =
          $url . $this->mProducts[$i]['product_id'];
      }
    }
  }
?>
```

5. Add the following code at the beginning of index.php, *after* the reference to app_top.php
   (app_top.php activates session handling, which is required for the following code to work). This code
   makes sure to always save the link to the current page if that page is not a product details page. In other
   words, $_SESSION['page_link'] will always contain the link to the last visited page which is not
   a product details page. You need to save this value to implement the Continue Shopping button in the
   product details page, which needs to forward the visitor to the previously visited page.

```
<?php
// Load Smarty library and config files
require_once 'include/app_top.php';


/* If not visiting a product page, save the link to the current page
   in the page_link session variable; it will be used to create the
   Continue Shopping link in the product details page and the links
   to product details pages */
```

```
if (!isset ($_GET['ProductID']))
  $_SESSION['page_link'] = substr(getenv('REQUEST_URI'),
                            strrpos(getenv('REQUEST_URI'), '/') + 1,
                            strlen(getenv('REQUEST_URI')) - 1);
```

```
// Load Smarty template file
$page = new Page();
```

6. Open presentation/templates/department.tpl and replace

```
<br />
Place list of products here
```

with

```
{include file="products_list.tpl"}
```

7. Load your project in your favorite browser, navigate to one of the departments, and then select a category from a department. Also, find a category with more than four products to test that the paging functionality works, as shown earlier in Figure 4-8.

How It Works: The products_list Componentized Template

Because most functionality regarding the products list has already been implemented in the data and business tiers, this task was fairly simple. The Smarty design template file (products_list.tpl) contains the layout to be used when displaying products, and its template plugin file (function.load_products_list.php) gets the correct list of products to display.

The constructor in function.load_products_list.php (the ProductsList class) creates a new instance of the business tier object (Catalog) and retrieves DepartmentID, CategoryID, and PageNo from the query string, casting them to int as a security measure. These values are used to decide which products to display:

```
// Class constructor
public function __construct()
{
  // Get DepartmentID from query string casting it to int
  if (isset ($_GET['DepartmentID']))
    $this->_mDepartmentId = (int)$_GET['DepartmentID'];

  // Get CategoryID from query string casting it to int
  if (isset ($_GET['CategoryID']))
    $this->_mCategoryId = (int)$_GET['CategoryID'];

  // Get PageNo from query string casting it to int
  if (isset ($_GET['PageNo']))
    $this->mPageNo = (int)$_GET['PageNo'];
  else
    $this->mPageNo = 1;
}
```

The `init()` method, which continues the constructor's job, starts by retrieving the requested list of products. It decides what method of the business tier to call by analyzing the `mCategoryId` and `mDepartmentId` members (which, thanks to the constructor, represent the values of the `CategoryID` and `DepartmentID` query string parameters).

If `CategoryID` is present in the query string, it means the visitor is browsing a category, so `GetProductsInCategory` is called to retrieve the products in that category. If only `DepartmentID` is present, `GetProductsOnDepartmentDisplay` is called to retrieve the department's featured products. If not even `DepartmentID` is present, this means the visitor is on the main page, and `GetProductsOnCatalogDisplay` is called to get the products to be featured on the first page of the site:

```
public function init()
{
  /* If browsing a category, get the list of products by calling
     the GetProductsInCategory business tier method */
  if (isset ($this->_mCategoryId))
    $this->mProducts = Catalog::GetProductsInCategory(
      $this->_mCategoryId, $this->mPageNo, $this->mrHowManyPages);
  /* If browsing a department, get the list of products by calling
     the GetProductsOnDepartmentDisplay business tier method */
  elseif (isset ($this->_mDepartmentId))
    $this->mProducts = Catalog::GetProductsOnDepartmentDisplay(
      $this->_mDepartmentId, $this->mPageNo, $this->mrHowManyPages);
  /* If browsing the first page, get the list of products by
     calling the GetProductsOnCatalogDisplay business
     tier method */
  else
    $this->mProducts = Catalog::GetProductsOnCatalogDisplay(
                         $this->mPageNo, $this->mrHowManyPages);
```

The next part of the function takes care of paging. If the business tier call tells you there is more than one page of products (so there are more products than what you specified in the `PRODUCTS_PER_PAGE` constant), you need to show the visitor the current subpage of products being visited, the total number of subpages, and the `Previous` and `Next` page links. The comments in code should make the functionality fairly clear so we won't reiterate the code here.

In the final part of the function, you added the `link` member to each `mProducts` record, which contains the link to the product's page. These values are used in the template file to create links to the product's pages on the product's name and picture. The links are created using the `page_link` session variable, which points to the last loaded page that is not a product details page (which in this case is the current page), and adds `ProductID` to the query string:

```
// Build links for product details pages
$url = $_SESSION['page_link'];

if (count($_GET) > 0)
  $url = $url . '&ProductID=';
else
  $url = $url . '?ProductID=';
```

```
for ($i = 0; $i < count($this->mProducts); $i++)
{
  $this->mProducts[$i]['link'] =
    $url . $this->mProducts[$i]['product_id'];
}
```

Displaying Front Page Contents

Apart from general information about the web site, you also want to show some promotional products on the first page of HatShop.

If the visitor browses a department or a category, the department Smarty template is used to build the output. For the main web page, we'll create the first_page_contents componentized template that will build the output.

Remember in index.tpl you have a cell named pageContentsCell that you fill with different details depending on what part of the site is being visited? When a department or a category is being visited, the department componentized template is loaded, and it takes care of filling that space. We still haven't done anything with that cell for the first page, when no department or category has been selected.

In the following exercise, you'll write a template file that contains some information about the web site and shows the products that have been set up as promotions on the first page. Remember that the product table contains a field named display. Site administrators will set this field to on_catalog for products that need to be displayed in the first page.

Exercise: Creating the first_page_contents Componentized Template

1. Start by creating the Smarty design template file. The presentation/templates/first_page_contents.tpl file should have these contents:

```
{* first_page_contents.tpl *}
<p class="first_page_text">
  We hope you have fun developing HatShop, the e-commerce store from
  <br />
  Beginning PHP and PostgreSQL E-Commerce: From Novice to Professional!
</p>
<br />
<p class="description">
  This week we have discounted prices for these fantastic products!
</p>
{include file="products_list.tpl"}
```

2. Enter the following style into hatshop.css:

```
.first_page_text
{
  color: #000080;
  font-size: 12px;
```

```
    font-weight: bold;
    margin: 0px;
  }
```

3. Open the `index.php` file, and replace the line

```
$pageContentsCell = 'blank.tpl';
```

with the line

```
$pageContentsCell = 'first_page_contents.tpl';
```

This way, when no `DepartmentID` and `CategoryID` are in the query string, `index.php` will load the `first_page_contents` componentized template.

4. Load your project in your favorite browser. The result should look like Figure 3-1 in Chapter 3.

How It Works: The first_page_contents Componentized Template

The actual list of products is still displayed using the `products_list` Smarty componentized template, which you built earlier in this chapter. However, this time it isn't loaded from `department.tpl` (like it loads when browsing a department or a category) but from a new template file named `first_page_contents.tpl`.

Showing Product Details

The last bit of code you'll implement in this chapter is about displaying product details. When the visitor clicks on any product, he or she will be forwarded to the product's details page, which shows the product's complete description and the secondary product image. In the later chapters, you'll add more features to this page, such as product recommendations or product reviews.

Let's do this in the following exercise.

Exercise: Creating the product Componentized Template

1. Edit `index.php` to load the `product.tpl` template using the `$pageContentsCell` variable if the `ProductID` parameter exists in the query string. Add the boldfaced lines to the `index.php` file as shown in the following code:

```
// Load department details if visiting a department
if (isset ($_GET['DepartmentID']))
{
  $pageContentsCell = 'department.tpl';
  $categoriesCell = 'categories_list.tpl';
}

// Load product details page if visiting a product
if (isset ($_GET['ProductID']))
```

```
$pageContentsCell = 'product.tpl';
```

```
// Assign a template file to the page contents cell
$page->assign('pageContentsCell', $pageContentsCell);
$page->assign('categoriesCell', $categoriesCell);
```

2. Okay, now create the componentized template for the product details page in which the product with full
    description and second image will display. Create a file named function.load_product.php in the
    presentation/smarty_plugins folder with the following contents:

```php
<?php
// Plugin function for the load_product function plugin
function smarty_function_load_product($params, $smarty)
{
  // Create Product object
  $product = new Product();
  $product->init();

  // Assign template variable
  $smarty->assign($params['assign'], $product);
}

// Handles product details
class Product
{
  // Public variables to be used in Smarty template
  public $mProduct;
  public $mPageLink = 'index.php';

  // Private stuff
  private $_mProductId;

  // Class constructor
  public function __construct()
  {
    // Variable initialization
    if (isset ($_GET['ProductID']))
      $this->_mProductId = (int)$_GET['ProductID'];
    else
      trigger_error('ProductID required in product.php');
  }
```

```
  public function init()
  {
    // Get product details from business tier
    $this->mProduct = Catalog::GetProductDetails($this->_mProductId);

    if (isset ($_SESSION['page_link']))
      $this->mPageLink = $_SESSION['page_link'];
  }
}
?>
```

3. Now get in touch with your artistic side, and spread these variables all over the page in an attempt to make the page more attractive to the visitor. To do that, you need to create a `product.tpl` file in the `presentation/templates` folder. Feel free to go wild and customize this page as you want.

```
{load_product assign="product"}
<span class="description">{$product->mProduct.name}</span>
<br /><br />
<img src="product_images/{$product->mProduct.image}"
     alt="Product image" width="190" border="0" />
<br /><br />
<span>
  {$product->mProduct.description}
  <br /><br />Price:
</span>
{if $product->mProduct.discounted_price == 0}
<span class="price">
{else}
<span class="old_price">
{/if}
  ${$product->mProduct.price}
</span>
{if $product->mProduct.discounted_price != 0}
<span class="price">
   ${$product->mProduct.discounted_price}
</span>
{/if}
<br /><br />
<input type="button" value="Continue Shopping"
 onclick="window.location='{$product->mPageLink|prepare_link:"http"}';" />
```

4. Load the web site, and click on the picture or name of any product. You should be forwarded to its details page. Figure 4-12 shows an example details page.

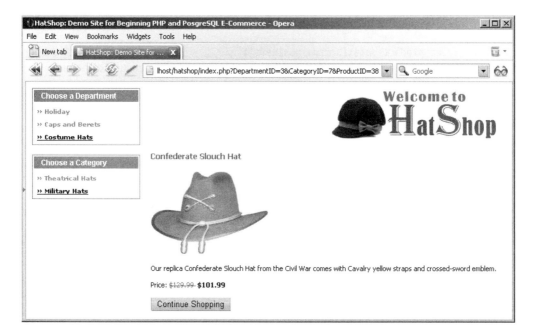

Figure 4-12. *Product details for the Confederate Slouch Hat*

How It Works: The product Componentized Template

It all starts in `index.php`, which loads the `product.tpl` Smarty template in case `ProductID` appears in the query string:

```
// Load product details page if visiting a product
if (isset ($_GET['ProductID']))
    $pageContentsCell = 'product.tpl';
```

The Smarty template gets the needed information through the members of the `Product` class, which is made available to the template by the function plugin it loads:

```
{load_product assign="product"}
```

The `Product` class gets the necessary data at its turn by calling the `GetProductDetails` method from the business tier class `Catalog`.

Summary

You've done a lot of work in this chapter. You finished building the product catalog by implementing the necessary logic in the data, business, and presentation tiers. On the way, you learned about many new theory issues, including

- Relational data and the types of relationships that can occur between tables

- How to obtain data from multiple tables in a single result set using `JOIN`, and how to filter the results using `WHERE`

- How to display the list of categories and products depending on what page the visitor is browsing

- How to display a product details page, and implement the Continue Shopping functionality

- How to implement paging in the products list when browsing pages containing many products

Chapter 5 will be at least as exciting as this one because you'll learn how to add search functionality to your web site!

CHAPTER 5
■ ■ ■

Searching the Catalog

"What are you looking for?" There are no places where you'll hear this question more frequently than in both brick-and-mortar stores and e-commerce stores. Like any other quality web store around, your HatShop will allow visitors to search through the product catalog. You'll see how easy it is to add new functionality to a working site by integrating the new components into the existing architecture.

In this chapter, you will

- Analyze the various ways in which the product catalog can be searched.

- Implement a custom search engine that works with PostgreSQL.

- Write the data and business tiers for the searching feature.

- Build the user interface for the catalog search feature using Smarty componentized templates.

Choosing How to Search the Catalog

As always, there are a few things you need to think about before starting to code. When designing a new feature, you should always begin by analyzing that feature from the final user's perspective.

For the visual part, you'll use a text box in which the visitor can enter one or more words to search for. In HatShop, the words entered by the visitor will be searched for in the products' names and descriptions. The text entered by the visitor can be searched for in several ways:

Exact-match search: If the visitor enters a search string composed of more words, this would be searched in the catalog as it is, without splitting the words and searching for them separately.

All-words search: The search string entered by the visitor is split into words, causing a search for products that contain every word entered by the visitor. This is like the exact-match search in that it still searches for all the entered words, but this time the order of the words is no longer important.

Any-words search: At least one of the words of the search string must find a matching product.

This simple classification isn't by any means complete. The search engine can be as complex as the one offered by modern search engines, which provides many options and features and shows a ranked list of results, or as simple as searching the database for the exact string provided by the visitor.

HatShop will support the any-words and all-words search modes. This decision leads to the visual design of the search feature (see Figure 5-1).

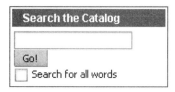

Figure 5-1. *The design of the search feature*

The text box is there, as expected, along with a check box that allows the visitor to choose between an all-words search and an any-words search.

Another decision you need to make here is the way in which the search results are displayed. How should the search results page look? You want to display, after all, a list of products that match the search criteria.

The simplest solution to display the search results would be to reuse the products_list componentized template you built in the previous chapter. A sample search page will look like Figure 5-2.

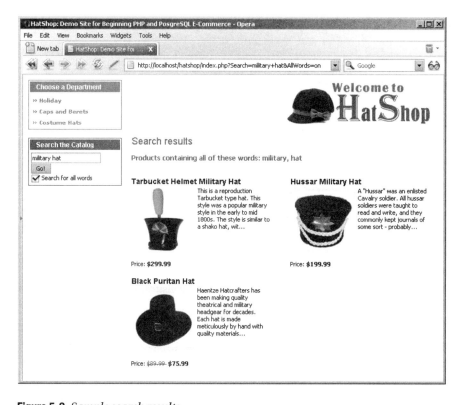

Figure 5-2. *Sample search results*

You can also see in the figure that the site employs paging. If there are a lot of search results, you'll only present a fixed (but configurable) number of products per page and allow the visitor to browse through the pages using `Previous` and `Next` links.

Let's begin implementing the functionality, by starting, as usual, with the data tier.

Teaching the Database to Search Itself

You have two main options to implement searching in the database:

- Implement searching using `WHERE` and `LIKE`.

- Search using the `tsearch2` module.

Let's analyze these options.

Searching Using WHERE and LIKE

The straightforward solution, frequently used to implement searching, consists of using `LIKE` in the `WHERE` clause of the `SELECT` statement. Let's take a look at a simple example that will return the products that have the word "war" somewhere in their description:

```
SELECT name FROM product WHERE description LIKE '%war%'
```

The `LIKE` operator matches parts of strings, and the percent wildcard (%) is used to specify any string of zero or more characters. That's why in the previous example, the pattern %war% matches all records whose description column has the word "war" somewhere in it. This search is case-insensitive.

If you want to retrieve all the products that contain the word "war" somewhere in the product's name or description, the query will look like this:

```
SELECT name FROM product
WHERE description LIKE '%war%' OR name LIKE '%war%';
```

This method of searching has three important drawbacks:

Speed: Because we need to search for text somewhere inside the description and name fields, the entire database must be searched on each query. This can significantly slow down the overall performance of HatShop when database searches are performed, especially if you have a large number of products in the database.

Quality of search results: This method doesn't make it easy for you to implement various advanced features, such as returning the matching products sorted by search relevance.

Advanced search features: These include searching using the Boolean operators (AND, OR) and searching for inflected forms of words, such as plurals and various verb tenses, or words located in close proximity.

So how can you do better searches that implement these features? If you have a large database that needs to be searched frequently, how can you search this database without killing your server?

The answer is using PostgreSQL's `tsearch2` module.

Searching Using the PostgreSQL tsearch2 Module

tsearch2 is the search module we'll be using to implement our site's search feature. This module ships with PostgreSQL, and it allows performing advanced searches of your database by using special search indexes. Read Appendix A for installation instructions.

There are two aspects to consider when building the data tier part of a catalog search feature:

- Preparing the database to be searched

- Using SQL to search the database

Creating Data Structures That Enable Searching

In our scenario, the table that we'll use for searches is product, because that's what our visitors will be looking for. To make the table searchable using the tsearch2 module, you need to prepare the table to be searched in three steps:

1. Add a new field to the product table, which will hold the *search vectors*. A search vector is a string that contains a prepared (searchable) version of the data you want to be searched (such as product names and descriptions). In our case, the command will look like this (don't execute it now, we'll take care of this using an exercise):

```
ALTER TABLE product ADD COLUMN search_vector tsvector;
```

2. Update the product table by adding a gist index on the newly added field. gist is the engine that performs the actual searches, and it is an implementation of the Berkeley Generalized Search Tree (find more details about gist at http://gist.cs.berkeley. edu/). The command for adding a gist index on the product table is

```
CREATE INDEX idx_search_vector ON product USING gist(search_vector);
```

3. Populate the search_vector field of product with the search vectors. These search vectors are lists of the words to be searchable for each product. For HatShop, we'll consider the words that appear in the product's name and the product's description, giving more relevance to those appearing in the name. This way, if more products match a particular search string, those with matches in the name will be shown at the top of the results list. At this step, we also filter the so-called *stop-words* (also called noise words), which aren't relevant for searches, such as "the," "or," "in," and so on. The following command sets the search vector for each product using the to_tsvector function (which creates the search vector) and setweight (used to give higher relevance to the words in the name):

```
UPDATE product
SET    search_vector =
         setweight(to_tsvector(name), 'A') || to_tsvector(description);
```

The '**A**' parameter of `setweight` gives highest relevance to words appearing in the product's name. For detailed information about how these functions work, refer to *The tsearch2 Reference* at `http://www.sai.msu.su/~megera/postgres/gist/tsearch/V2/docs/tsearch2-ref.html`. You can find a `tsearch2` guide at `http://rhodesmill.org/brandon/projects/tsearch2-guide.html` and an excellent article at `http://www.devx.com/opensource/Article/21674`.

For an example, see Table 5-1, which shows the search vector for the Santa Jester Hat. Note the vector retains the positions of the words (although we don't really need this), and the "A" relevance factor is added to the words from the product's name. Also note that various forms of the same word are recognized (see "fit" for example) and that the stop-words aren't taken into consideration.

Table 5-1. *The Search Vector for a Product*

Field	Value
`product_id`	6
`name`	Santa Jester Hat
`description`	This three-prong velvet jester is one size fits all and has an adjustable touch fastener back for perfect fitting.
`search_string`	`'fit':13,24 'hat':3A 'one':11 'back':21 'size':12 'prong':7 'santa':1A 'three':6 'touch':19 'adjust':18 'fasten':20 'jester':2A,9 'velvet':8 'perfect':23 'three-prong':5`

■**Note** When adding new products to the table or updating existing products, you'll need to be sure to also (re)create their search vectors. The index that parses these vectors does its job automatically, but the vector itself must be manually created. You'll take care of this in Chapter 7, where you'll add catalog administration features. Until then, if you change your products manually, just execute the previous SQL command to update the search vectors.

Searching the Database

Now that you've built the search vector for each product, let's see how to use it for searching. For performing the search, once again, there are three steps that you need to take:

1. Build a *search string* that expresses what exactly you are looking for. This can contain Boolean operators; we'll use & (AND) when doing all-words searches, and | (OR) when doing any-words searches.

2. Apply the `to_tsquery` function on the query string. This prepares the query string into a form that can be used for searching.

3. When performing the search, use the condition `search_vector @@`
`prepared_search_string`, which returns TRUE if there's a match and FALSE otherwise.
Here, `search_vector` is the one calculated earlier (step 3 of the previous section), and
`prepared_search_string` is the result of step 2.

Let's see how this would be applied in practice. The following query performs an all-
words search on the "yankee war" search string:

```
SELECT    product_id, name
FROM      product
WHERE     search_vector @@ to_tsquery('yankee & war')
ORDER BY product_id;
```

With the sample products database, this query should have the results shown in Table 5-2.

Table 5-2. *Hats That Match "yankee & war"*

product_id	name
40	Civil War Union Slouch Hat
44	Union Civil War Kepi Cap

To perform an any-words search, you should use | instead of & in the search string:

```
SELECT    product_id, name
FROM      product
WHERE     search_vector @@ to_tsquery('yankee | war')
ORDER BY product_id;
```

As expected, this time you'll have more matching products as shown in Table 5-3 (because
the list is unsorted, you may get these results in different order).

Table 5-3. *Hats That Match "yankee | war"*

product_id	name
26	Military Beret
30	Confederate Civil War Kepi
33	Uncle Sam Top Hat
38	Confederate Slouch Hat
40	Civil War Union Slouch Hat
41	Civil War Leather Kepi Cap
44	Union Civil War Kepi Cap

Sorting Results by Relevance

The previous queries show matching products without ordering them in any particular order.
The database engine will simply return the results in whatever order it finds easier. For

searches, we're interested in showing the more relevant matches first. Remember that we gave higher priority to matches from the product titles, so everything is set.

The `tsearch2` engine offers the rank function that can be used for ordering the results. The default order is to show the lower ranking matches first, so you'll also need to use the `DESC` option of `ORDER BY` to put the better matches at the top.

The following query performs a ranked any-words search for "yankee war":

```
SELECT   rank(search_vector, to_tsquery('yankee | war')) as rank, product_id, name
FROM     product
WHERE    search_vector @@ to_tsquery('yankee | war')
ORDER BY rank DESC;
```

This time, the results will come ordered. You can also see the search rankings. The products that have matches in the name have significantly higher ranks.

Table 5-4. *Search Results Ordered by Rank*

rank	product_id	name
0.341959	40	Civil War Union Slouch Hat
0.33436	44	Union Civil War Kepi Cap
0.31684	41	Civil War Leather Kepi Cap
0.303964	30	Confederate Civil War Kepi
0.0379954	26	Military Beret
0.0303964	38	Confederate Slouch Hat
0.0303964	33	Uncle Sam Top Hat

You should be ready now to implement your web site's search functionality. To learn more about the inner workings of the `tsearch2` engine, consult its official documentation.

Exercise: Writing the Database Searching Code

1. Load pgAdmin III, and connect to the `hatshop` database.

2. Click Tools ➤ Query Tools (or click the SQL button on the toolbar). A new query window should appear.

3. Write the following code in the query tool, and then execute it by pressing F5. This command prepares the product table to be searched using the `tsearch2` engine, as explained earlier in this chapter.

```
-- Alter product table adding search_vector field
ALTER TABLE product ADD COLUMN search_vector tsvector;

-- Create index for search_vector field in product table
CREATE INDEX idx_search_vector ON product USING gist(search_vector);

-- Update newly added search_vector field from product table
UPDATE product
SET     search_vector =
        setweight(to_tsvector(name), 'A') || to_tsvector(description);
```

4. Use the Query tool to execute this code, which creates the `catalog_flag_stop_words` function into your hatshop database:

```
-- Create catalog_flag_stop_words function
CREATE FUNCTION catalog_flag_stop_words(TEXT[])
RETURNS SETOF SMALLINT LANGUAGE plpgsql AS $$
  DECLARE
    inWords ALIAS FOR $1;
    outFlag SMALLINT;
    query   TEXT;
  BEGIN
    FOR i IN array_lower(inWords, 1)..array_upper(inWords, 1) LOOP
      SELECT INTO query
             to_tsquery(inWords[i]);
      IF query = '' THEN
        outFlag := 1;
      ELSE
        outFlag := 0;
      END IF;
      RETURN NEXT outFlag;
    END LOOP;
  END;
$$;
```

5. Use the Query tool to execute this code, which creates the `catalog_count_search_result` function into your hatshop database:

```
-- Function returns the number of products that match a search string
CREATE FUNCTION catalog_count_search_result(TEXT[], VARCHAR(3))
RETURNS INTEGER LANGUAGE plpgsql AS $$
  DECLARE
    -- inWords is an array with the words from user's search string
    inWords    ALIAS FOR $1;

    -- inAllWords is 'on' for all-words searches
    -- and 'off' for any-words searches
    inAllWords ALIAS FOR $2;

    outSearchResultCount INTEGER;
    query                TEXT;
    search_operator      VARCHAR(1);
  BEGIN
    -- Initialize query with an empty string
    query := '';
    -- Establish the operator to be used when preparing the search string
    IF inAllWords = 'on' THEN
      search_operator := '&';
    ELSE
      search_operator := '|';
```

```
      END IF;

      -- Compose the search string
      FOR i IN array_lower(inWords, 1)..array_upper(inWords, 1) LOOP
        IF i = array_upper(inWords, 1) THEN
          query := query || inWords[i];
        ELSE
          query := query || inWords[i] || search_operator;
        END IF;
      END LOOP;

      -- Return the number of matches
      SELECT INTO outSearchResultCount
             count(*)
      FROM   product,
             to_tsquery(query) AS query_string
      WHERE  search_vector @@ query_string;
      RETURN outSearchResultCount;
    END;
  $$;
```

6. Use the query tool to execute this code, which creates the `catalog_` search function into your `hatshop` database:

```
-- Create catalog_search function
CREATE FUNCTION catalog_search(TEXT[], VARCHAR(3), INTEGER, INTEGER, INTEGER)
RETURNS SETOF product_list LANGUAGE plpgsql AS $$
  DECLARE
    inWords                          ALIAS FOR $1;
    inAllWords                       ALIAS FOR $2;
    inShortProductDescriptionLength  ALIAS FOR $3;
    inProductsPerPage                ALIAS FOR $4;
    inStartPage                      ALIAS FOR $5;
    outProductListRow product_list;
    query            TEXT;
    search_operator  VARCHAR(1);
    query_string     TSQUERY;
  BEGIN
    -- Initialize query with an empty string
    query := '';
    -- All-words or Any-words?
    IF inAllWords = 'on' THEN
      search_operator := '&';
    ELSE
      search_operator := '|';
    END IF;

    -- Compose the search string
```

```
      FOR i IN array_lower(inWords, 1)..array_upper(inWords, 1) LOOP
        IF i = array_upper(inWords, 1) THEN
          query := query||inWords[i];
        ELSE
          query := query||inWords[i]||search_operator;
        END IF;
      END LOOP;
      query_string := to_tsquery(query);

      -- Return the search results
      FOR outProductListRow IN
        SELECT   product_id, name, description, price,
                 discounted_price, thumbnail
        FROM     product
        WHERE    search_vector @@ query_string
        ORDER BY rank(search_vector, query_string) DESC
        LIMIT    inProductsPerPage
        OFFSET   inStartPage
      LOOP
        IF char_length(outProductListRow.description) >
           inShortProductDescriptionLength THEN
          outProductListRow.description :=
            substring(outProductListRow.description, 1,
                     inShortProductDescriptionLength) || '...';
        END IF;
        RETURN NEXT outProductListRow;
      END LOOP;
    END;
  $$;
```

How It Works: The Catalog Search Functionality

In this exercise, you created the database functionality to support the product searching business tier logic. After adding the necessary structures as explained in the beginning of the chapter, you added three functions:

- `catalog_flag_stop_words`: As mentioned earlier, some words from the search string entered by the visitor may not be used for searching, because they are considered to be noise words. The `tsearch2` engine removes the noise words by default, but we need to find what words it removed, so we can report these words to our visitor. We do this using `catalog_flag_stop_words`, which will be called from the `FlagStopWords` method of the business tier.

- `catalog_count_search_result`: This function counts the number of search results. This is required so that the presentation tier will know how many search results pages to display.

- `catalog_search`: Performs the actual product search.

Implementing the Business Tier

The business tier of the search feature consists of two methods: FlagStopWords and Search. Let's implement them first and discuss how they work afterwards.

Exercise: Implementing the Business Tier

1. The full-text search feature automatically removes words that are shorter than a specified length. You need to tell the visitor which words have been removed when doing searches. First, find out which words are removed with the FlagStopWords method. This method receives as parameter an array of words and returns two arrays, one for the stop-words, and the other for the accepted words. Add this method to your Catalog class, located in business/catalog.php:

```php
// Flags stop words in search query
public static function FlagStopWords($words)
{
  // Build SQL query
  $sql = 'SELECT *
          FROM catalog_flag_stop_words(:words);';
  // Build the parameters array
  $params = array (':words' => '{' . implode(', ', $words) . '}');
  // Prepare the statement with PDO-specific functionality
  $result = DatabaseHandler::Prepare($sql);

  // Execute the query
  $flags = DatabaseHandler::GetAll($result, $params);

  $search_words = array ('accepted_words' => array (),
                         'ignored_words' => array ());

  for ($i = 0; $i < count($flags); $i++)
    if ($flags[$i]['catalog_flag_stop_words'])
      $search_words['ignored_words'][] = $words[$i];
    else
      $search_words['accepted_words'][] = $words[$i];

  return $search_words;
}
```

2. Finally, add the Search method to your Catalog class:

```php
// Search the catalog
public static function Search($searchString, $allWords,
                              $pageNo, &$rHowManyPages)
{
  // The search results will be an array of this form
  $search_result = array ('accepted_words' => array (),
                          'ignored_words' => array (),
```

```php
                                    'products' => array ());

  // Return void result if the search string is void
  if (empty ($searchString))
    return $search_result;

  // Search string delimiters
  $delimiters = ',.; ';
  // Use strtok to get the first word of the search string
  $word = strtok($searchString, $delimiters);
  $words = array ();

  // Build words array
  while ($word)
  {
    $words[] = $word;
    // Get the next word of the search string
    $word = strtok($delimiters);
  }

  // Split the search words in two categories: accepted and ignored
  $search_words = Catalog::FlagStopWords($words);
  $search_result['accepted_words'] = $search_words['accepted_words'];
  $search_result['ignored_words'] = $search_words['ignored_words'];

  // Return void result if all words are stop words
  if (count($search_result['accepted_words']) == 0)
    return $search_result;

  // Count the number of search results
  $sql = 'SELECT catalog_count_search_result(:words, :all_words);';
  $params = array (
    ':words' => '{' . implode(', ', $search_result['accepted_words']) . '}',
    ':all_words' => $allWords);
  // Calculate the number of pages required to display the products
  $rHowManyPages = Catalog::HowManyPages($sql, $params);
  // Calculate the start item
  $start_item = ($pageNo - 1) * PRODUCTS_PER_PAGE;

  // Retrieve the list of matching products
  $sql = 'SELECT *
          FROM   catalog_search(:words,
                                 :all_words,
                                 :short_product_description_length,
                                 :products_per_page,
                                 :start_page);';
  $params = array (
```

```
        ':words' => '{' . implode(', ', $search_result['accepted_words']) . '}',
        ':all_words' => $allWords,
        ':short_product_description_length' => SHORT_PRODUCT_DESCRIPTION_LENGTH,
        ':products_per_page' => PRODUCTS_PER_PAGE,
        ':start_page' => $start_item);

    // Prepare and execute the query, and return the results
    $result = DatabaseHandler::Prepare($sql);
    $search_result['products'] = DatabaseHandler::GetAll($result, $params);
    return $search_result;
}
```

How It Works: The Business Tier Search Method

The main purpose of the FlagStopWords method is to analyze which words will and will not be used for searching.

The full-text feature of PostgreSQL automatically filters the words that are less than four letters by default, and you don't interfere with this behavior in the business tier. However, you need to find out which words will be ignored by PostgreSQL so you can inform the visitor.

The Search method of the business tier is called from the presentation tier with the following parameters (notice all of them except the first one are the same as the parameters of the data tier Search method):

- $searchString contains the search string entered by the visitor.
- $allWords is "on" for all-words searches.
- $pageNo represents the page of products being requested.
- $rHowManyPages represents the number of pages.

The method returns the results to the presentation tier in an associative array.

Implementing the Presentation Tier

The catalog-searching feature has two separate interface elements that you need to implement:

- A componentized template named search_box, whose role is to provide the means to enter the search string for the visitor (refer to Figure 5-1).
- A componentized template named search_results, which displays the products matching the search criteria (refer to Figure 5-2).

You'll create the two componentized templates in two separate exercises.

Creating the Search Box

Follow the steps in the exercise to build the search_box componentized template, and integrate it into HatShop.

Exercise: Creating the search_box Componentized Template

1. Create a new template file named search_box.tpl in the presentation/templates folder, and add the following code to it:

```
{* search_box.tpl *}
{load_search_box assign="search_box"}
{* Start search box *}
<div  class="left_box" id="search_box">
  <p>Search the Catalog</p>
  <form action={"index.php"|prepare_link:"http"}>
    <input maxlength="100" id="Search" name="Search"
           value="{$search_box->mSearchString}" size="23" />
    <input type="submit" value="Go!" /><br />
    <input type="checkbox" id="AllWords" name="AllWords"
    {if $search_box->mAllWords == "on" } checked="checked" {/if}/>
      Search for all words
  </form>
</div>
{* End search box *}
```

2. Create a new Smarty function plugin file named function.load_search_box.php in the presentation/smarty_plugins folder with the following code in it:

```php
<?php
// Plugin functions inside plugin files must be named: smarty_type_name
function smarty_function_load_search_box($params, $smarty)
{
  // Create SearchBox object
  $search_box = new SearchBox();

  // Assign template variable
  $smarty->assign($params['assign'], $search_box);
}


// Manages the search box
class SearchBox
{
  // Public variables for the smarty template
  public $mSearchString = '';
  public $mAllWords = 'off';

  // Class constructor
  public function __construct()
  {
    if (isset ($_GET['Search']))
      $this->mSearchString = $_GET['Search'];
```

```
      if (isset ($_GET['AllWords']))
        $this->mAllWords = $_GET['AllWords'];
    }
  }
  ?>
```

3. Add the following styles needed in the search_box template file to the hatshop.css file:

```
#search_box
{
  border: 1px solid #0583b5;
}
#search_box p
{
  background: #0583b5;
}
form
{
  margin: 2px;
}
input
{
  font-family: tahoma, verdana, arial;
  font-size: 11px;
}
```

4. Modify the index.tpl file to load the newly created template file:

```
...
      {include file="departments_list.tpl"}
      {include file="$categoriesCell"}
      {include file="search_box.tpl"}
...
```

5. Load your project in a browser, and you'll see the search box resting nicely in its place (refer to Figure 5-1).

How It Works: The search_box Componentized Template

By now, you're used to the way we use function plugins in conjunction with Smarty templates. In this case, we use the plugin to maintain the state of the search box after performing a search. When the page is reloaded after clicking the Go! button, we want to keep the entered string in the text box and also maintain the state of the AllWords check box.

The load_search_box function plugin simply saves the values of the Search and AllWords query string parameters, while checking to make sure these parameters actually exist in the query string. These values are then used in the search_box.tpl Smarty template to recreate the previous state.

Note that we could have implemented this functionality by reading the values of the Search and AllWords query string parameters using $smarty.get.Search and $smarty.get.AllWords instead of a plugin. However, having a plugin gives you more control over the process and also avoids generating warnings in case the mentioned parameters don't exist in the query string.

Displaying the Search Results

In the next exercise, you'll create the componentized template that displays the search results. To make your life easier, you can reuse the product_list componentized template to display the actual list of products. This is the componentized template that we have used so far to list products for the main page, for departments, and for categories. Of course, if you want to have the search results displayed in another format, you must create another user control.

You'll need to modify the templates-logic file of the products list (products_list.php) to recognize when it's being called to display search results, so it calls the correct method of the business tier to get the list of products.

Let's create the search_result template and update the templates-logic file of the products_list componentized template in the following exercise:

Exercise: Creating the search_results Componentized Template

1. Create a new template file in the presentation/templates directory named search_results.tpl, and add the following to it:

```
{* search_results.tpl *}
<p class="title">Search results</p>
<br />
{include file="products_list.tpl"}
```

2. Modify the presentation/smarty_plugins/function.load_products_list.php file by adding the following lines at the end of the constructor method of the ProductList class (__construct):

```
    // Get search details from query string
    if (isset ($_GET['Search']))
        $this->mSearchString = $_GET['Search'];

    // Get all_words from query string
    if (isset ($_GET['AllWords']))
        $this->mAllWords = $_GET['AllWords'];
```

3. Add the $mSearchResultsTitle, $mSearch, $mAllWords, and $mSearchString members to the ProductsList class, located in the same file:

```
class ProductsList
{
  // Public variables to be read from Smarty template
  public $mProducts;
  public $mPageNo;
  public $mrHowManyPages;
  public $mNextLink;
  public $mPreviousLink;
  public $mSearchResultsTitle;
  public $mSearch = '';
  public $mAllWords = 'off';
  public $mSearchString;
```

```
    // Private members
    private $_mDepartmentId;
    private $_mCategoryId;
```

4. Modify the `init` method in `ProductsList` class like this:

```
public function init()
{
  /* If searching the catalog, get the list of products by calling
     the Search busines tier method */
  if (isset ($this->mSearchString))
  {
    // Get search results
    $search_results = Catalog::Search($this->mSearchString,
                                      $this->mAllWords,
                                      $this->mPageNo,
                                      $this->mrHowManyPages);
    // Get the list of products
    $this->mProducts = $search_results['products'];
    // Build the title for the list of products
    if (count($search_results['accepted_words']) > 0)
      $this->mSearchResultsTitle =
        'Products containing <font class="words">'
        . ($this->mAllWords == 'on' ? 'all' : 'any') . '</font>'
        . ' of these words: <font class="words">'
        . implode(', ', $search_results['accepted_words']) .
        '</font><br />';
    if (count($search_results['ignored_words']) > 0)
      $this->mSearchResultsTitle .=
        'Ignored words: <font class="words">'
        . implode(', ', $search_results['ignored_words']) .
        '</font><br />';
    if (!(count($search_results['products']) > 0))
      $this->mSearchResultsTitle .=
        'Your search generated no results.<br />';
  }
  /* If browsing a category, get the list of products by calling
     the GetProductsInCategory business tier method */
  elseif (isset ($this->_mCategoryId))
    $this->mProducts = Catalog::GetProductsInCategory(
          $this->mCategoryId, $this->mPageNo, $this->mrHowManyPages);
...
```

5. Add the following lines in the beginning of presentation/templates/products_list.tpl, just below
   the load_products_list line:

```
{* products_list.tpl *}
{load_products_list assign="products_list"}
{if $products_list->mSearchResultsTitle != ""}
  <p class="description">{$products_list->mSearchResultsTitle}</p>
{/if}
```

6. Modify the index.php file to load the search_results componentized template when a search is
   performed by adding these lines:

```
...
// Load department details if visiting a department
if (isset ($_GET['DepartmentID']))
{
  $pageContentsCell = 'department.tpl';
  $categoriesCell = 'categories_list.tpl';
}

// Load search result page if we're searching the catalog
if (isset ($_GET['Search']))
  $pageContentsCell = 'search_results.tpl';

// Load product details page if visiting a product
if (isset ($_GET['ProductID']))
  $pageContentsCell = 'product.tpl';
...
```

7. Add the following style to the hatshop.css file:

```
.words
{
  color: #ff0000;
}
```

8. Load your project in your favorite browser and type **yankee** to get an output similar to Figure 5-3.

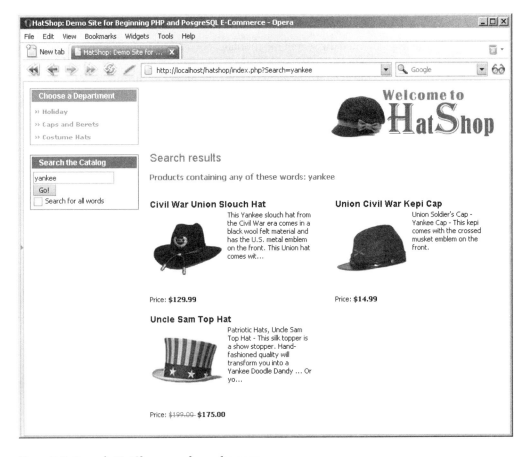

Figure 5-3. *Sample HatShop search results page*

How It Works: The Searchable Product Catalog

Congratulations, you have a searchable product catalog! There was quite a bit to write, but the code wasn't very complicated, was it?

Because you've used much of the already existing code and added bits to the already working architecture, there weren't any surprises. The list of products is still displayed by the `products_list` template you built earlier, which is now updated to recognize the `Search` element in the query string, in which case it uses the `Search` method of the business tier to get the list of products for the visitor.

The `Search` method of the business tier returns a `SearchResults` object that contains, apart from the list of returned products, the list of words that were used for searching and the list of words that were ignored (words shorter than a predefined number of characters). These details are shown to the visitor.

Summary

In this chapter, you implemented the search functionality of HatShop by using the full-text searching functionality of PostgreSQL. The search mechanism integrated very well with the current web site structure and the paging functionality built in Chapter 4. The most interesting new detail you learned in this chapter was about performing full-text searches with PostgreSQL. This was also the first instance where the business tier had some functionality of its own instead of simply passing data back and forth between the data tier and the presentation tier.

In Chapter 6, you'll learn how to sell your products using PayPal.

CHAPTER 6

■ ■ ■

Receiving Payments Using PayPal

Let's make some money! Your e-commerce web site needs a way to receive payments from customers. The preferred solution for established companies is to open a merchant account, but many small businesses choose to start with a solution that's simpler to implement, where they don't have to process credit card or payment information themselves.

A number of companies and web sites can help individuals or small businesses that don't have the resources to process credit cards and wire transactions. These companies can be used to intermediate the payment between online businesses and their customers. Many of these payment-processing companies are relatively new, and the handling of any individual's financial details is very sensitive. Additionally, a quick search on the Internet will produce reports from both satisfied and unsatisfied customers for almost all of these companies. For these reasons, we are not recommending any specific third-party company.

Instead, this chapter lists some of the companies currently providing these services, and then demonstrates some of the functionality they provide with PayPal. You'll learn how to integrate PayPal with HatShop in the first two stages of development. In this chapter, you will

- Learn how to create a new PayPal Website Payments Standard account.

- Learn how to integrate PayPal in stage 1 of development, where you'll need a shopping cart and custom checkout mechanism.

- Learn how to integrate PayPal in stage 2 of development, where you'll have your own shopping cart, so you'll need to guide the visitor directly to a payment page.

- Learn how to configure PayPal to automatically calculate shipping costs.

■**Note** This chapter is not a PayPal manual but a quick guide to using PayPal. For any complex queries about the services provided, visit PayPal (http://www.paypal.com) or the Internet Payment Service Provider you decide to use. Also, you can buy components that make it easier to interact with these systems, or use free ones such as ComponentOne PayPal eCommerce for ASP.NET by ComponentOne (http://www.componentone.com).

Considering Internet Payment Service Providers

Take a look at this list of Internet Payment Service Provider web sites. This is a diverse group, each having its advantages. Some of the providers transfer money person to person, and payments need to be verified manually; others offer sophisticated integration with your web site. Some work anywhere on the globe, whereas others work only for a single country.

The following list is not complete. You can find many other such companies by doing a Google search on "Internet Payment Service Providers."

- **2Checkout:** http://www.2checkout.com

- **AnyPay:** http://www.anypay.com

- **CCNow:** http://www.ccnow.com

- **Electronic Transfer:** http://www.electronictransfer.com

- **Moneybookers:** http://www.moneybookers.com

- **MultiCards:** http://www.multicards.com

- **Pay By Web:** http://www.paybyweb.com

- **Paymate:** https://www.paymate.com.au

- **PayPal:** http://www.paypal.com

- **PaySystems:** http://www.paysystems.com

- **ProPay:** http://www.propay.com

- **QuickPayPro:** http://www.quickpaypro.com

- **WorldPay:** http://www.worldpay.com

Apart from being popular, PayPal offers services that fit very well into our web site for the first two stages of development. PayPal is available in a number of countries—the most up-to-date list can be found at http://www.paypal.com.

For the first stage of development (the current stage)—where you only have a searchable product catalog—and with only a few lines of HTML code, PayPal enables you to add a shopping cart with checkout functionality. For the second stage of development, in which you will implement your own shopping cart, PayPal has a feature called Single Item Purchases that can be used to send the visitor directly to a payment page without the intermediate shopping cart. You'll use this feature of PayPal in Chapter 9.

For a summary of the features provided by PayPal, point your browser to http://www.paypal.com and click the Merchant Tools link. That page contains a few other useful links that will show you the main features available from PayPal.

Getting Started with PayPal

Probably the best description of this service is the one found on its web site: "PayPal is an account-based system that lets anyone with an email address securely send and receive online payments using their credit card or bank account."

Instead of paying the client directly, the visitor pays PayPal using a credit card or bank account. The client then uses its PayPal account to get the money received from the customers. At the time of writing, no cost is involved in creating a new PayPal account, and the service is free for the buyer. The fees involved when receiving money are shown at `http://www.paypal.com/cgi-bin/webscr?cmd=_display-fees-outside`.

PAYPAL LINKS AND RESOURCES

Check out these resources when you need more information than this short chapter provides:

- **Website Payments Standard Integration Guide:** Contains information previously contained in separate manuals, such as the Shopping Cart manual and the Instant Payments Notification manual. Get it at `https://www.paypal.com/en_US/pdf/PP_WebsitePaymentsStandard_IntegrationGuide.pdf`.

- **The PayPal Developer Network:** The official resource for PayPal developers, which you can access at `https://www.paypal.com/pdn`.

- **PayPalDev:** According to the site, this is an independent forum for PayPal developers. Access it at `http://www.paypaldev.org/`. You'll also find numerous links to various PayPal resources.

In the following exercise, you'll create a new PayPal account, and then integrate it with HatShop. (The steps to create a PayPal account are also described in more detail in the PayPal manuals mentioned earlier.)

Exercise: Creating the PayPal Account

To create your PayPal account, follow these steps:

1. Browse to `http://www.paypal.com` using your favorite web browser.

2. Click the `Sign Up` link.

3. PayPal supports three account types: Personal, Premier, and Business. To receive credit card payments, you need to open a Premier or Business account. Choose your country from the combo box, and click Continue.

4. Complete all of the requested information, and you will receive an email asking you to revisit the PayPal site to confirm the details you have entered.

How It Works: The PayPal Account

After the PayPal account is set up, the email address you provided will be your PayPal ID.

A lot of functionality is available within the PayPal service—because the site is easy to use and many of the functions are self-explanatory, we won't describe everything here. Remember that these sites are there for your business, so they're more than happy to assist with any of your queries.

Now let's see how you can actually use the new account for the web site.

Integrating the PayPal Shopping Cart and Checkout

In the first stage of development (the current stage), you need to integrate the shopping cart and checkout functionality from PayPal. In the second stage of development, after you create your own shopping cart, you'll only need to rely on PayPal's checkout mechanism.

To accept payments, you need to add two important elements to the user interface part of the site: Add to Cart buttons for each product and a View Cart button somewhere on the page. PayPal makes adding these buttons a piece of cake.

The functionality of those buttons is performed by secure links to the PayPal web site. For example, the following form represents the Add to Cart button for a product named "Black Puritan Hat" that costs $74.99:

```
<form target="paypal" action="https://www.paypal.com/cgi-bin/webscr"
     method="post">
<input type="hidden" name="cmd" value="_cart" />
<input type="hidden" name="business" value="youremail@example.com" />
<input type="hidden" name="item_name" value="Black Puritan Hat" />
<input type="hidden" name="amount" value="74.99" />
<input type="hidden" name="currency" value="USD" />
<input type="hidden" name="add" value="1" />
<input type="hidden" name="return" value="www.example.com" />
<input type="hidden" name="cancel_return" value="www.example.com" />
<input type="submit" name="submit" value="Add to Cart" />
</form>
```

The fields are predefined, and their names are self-explanatory. The most important is `business`, which must be the email address you used when you registered the PayPal account (the email address that will receive the money). Consult PayPal's Website Payments Standard Integration Guide for more details.

■**Tip** Although we won't use them for our site, it's good to know that PayPal provides button generators based on certain data you provide (product name, product price), giving you an HTML code block similar to the one shown previously. Click the `Developers` link at the bottom of the first page, and then click `PayPal Solutions` in the menu on the left to find the button generators.

You need to make sure this HTML code gets added to each product, so you'll have Add to Cart buttons for each product. To do this, you must modify the `products_list.tpl` file. Next, you'll add the View Cart button somewhere on `index.tpl`, so it will be accessible at any time for the visitor.

The View Cart button can be generated using a similar structure. An alternative way to generate the `Add to Cart` and `View Cart` links is to use links such as the following, instead of forms as shown earlier:

```
https://www.paypal.com/cgi-bin/webscr?cmd=_cart&business=your_email_address&
item_name=Black Puritan Hat&amount=74.99&amount=74.99&currency=USD&add=1&
return=www.example.com&cancel_return=www.example.com
```

■**Caution** Yes, it's just that simple to manufacture an Add to Cart link! The drawback of this simplicity is that it can be potentially used against you. After PayPal confirms the payment, you can ship the products to your customer. On each payment, you need to carefully check that the product prices correspond to the correct amounts because it's very easy for anyone to add a fake product to the shopping cart or an existing product with a modified price. This can be done simply by fabricating one of those PayPal Add to Cart links and navigating to it. You can read a detailed article about this problem at http://www.alphabetware.com/pptamper.asp.

After adding the Add to Cart and View Cart buttons, the web site will look like Figure 6-1.

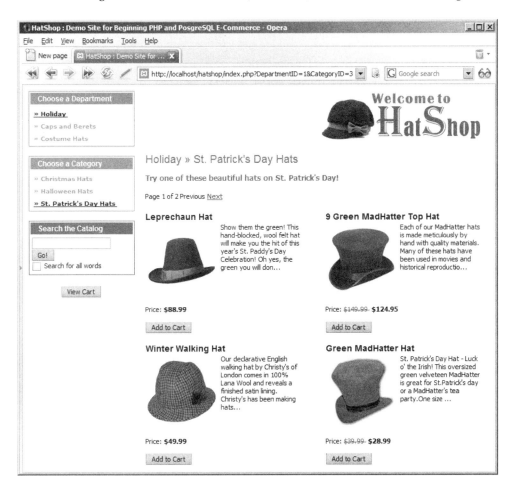

Figure 6-1. *HatShop with* Add to Cart *and* View Cart *buttons*

You'll implement the PayPal integration in the next exercise.

Exercise: Integrating the PayPal Shopping Cart and Custom Checkout

1. Open `index.tpl`, and add the `OpenPayPalWindow` JavaScript function inside the `<head>` element, as shown in the following code listing. This function is used to open the PayPal shopping cart window when the visitor clicks on one of the Add to Cart buttons.

```
<head>
  <title>{#site_title#}</title>
  <link href="hatshop.css" type="text/css" rel="stylesheet" />
  {literal}
  <script language="JavaScript" type="text/javascript">
  <!--
    var PayPalWindow = null;
    function OpenPayPalWindow(url)
    {
      if ((!PayPalWindow) || PayPalWindow.closed)
        // If the PayPal window doesn't exist, we open it
        PayPalWindow = window.open(url, "cart", "height=300, width=500");
      else
      {
        // If the PayPal window exists, we make it show
        PayPalWindow.location.href = url;
        PayPalWindow.focus();
      }
    }
  // -->
  </script>
  {/literal}
</head>
```

■Note Any JavaScript code you place in a Smarty template should be enclosed between {literal} and {/literal} elements because the JavaScript code uses { and } characters, which are the default delimiters for Smarty. This way, Smarty will not parse your JavaScript code.

2. Now, add the View Cart button on the main page, just below the search box. Modify `index.tpl` like this:

```
{include file="departments_list.tpl"}
{include file="$categoriesCell"}
{include file="search_box.tpl"}
<div class="left_box" id="view_cart">
  <input type="button" name="view_cart" value="View Cart"
  onclick="JavaScript:OpenPayPalWindow(
```

```
        &quot;https://www.paypal.com/cgi-bin/webscr?cmd=_cart
        &amp;business=youremail@example.com
        &amp;display=1&amp;return=www.example.com
        &amp;cancel_return=www.example.com&quot;)" />
  </div>
  {include file="header.tpl"}
  <div id="content">
    {include file="$pageContentsCell"}
  </div>
```

■**Caution** You must write the `OpenPayPalWindow` call on a single line in the HTML source. We split it on multiple lines in the code snippet to make it easier to read.

---

3. Add the following style code to `hatshop.css`:

```
#view_cart
{
  text-align: center;
}
```

4. Add the PayPal Add to Cart button in `presentation/templates/products_list.tpl`, just below the product price:

```
    <br /><br />
    <input type="button" name="add_to_cart" value="Add to Cart"
     onclick="{$products_list->mProducts[k].paypal}" />
  </p>
{/section}
```

5. Add the code that creates the PayPal `Add to Cart` link code at the end of the `init()` method in `presentation/smarty_plugins/function.load_products_list.php`:

```
    for ($i = 0; $i < count($this->mProducts); $i++)
    {
      $this->mProducts[$i]['link'] =
        $url . $this->mProducts[$i]['product_id'];

      // Create the PayPal link
      $this->mProducts[$i]['paypal'] =
        'JavaScript:OpenPayPalWindow(&quot;' .
        'https://www.paypal.com/cgi-bin/webscr?' .
        'cmd=_cart&amp;business=youremail@example.com' .
        '&amp;item_name=' . rawurlencode($this->mProducts[$i]['name']) .
        '&amp;amount=' .
```

```
            (($this->mProducts[$i]['discounted_price'] == 0) ?
             $this->mProducts[$i]['price'] :
             $this->mProducts[$i]['discounted_price']) .
            '&amp;currency=USD&amp;add=1&amp;return=www.example.com' .
            '&amp;cancel_return=www.example.com&quot;)';
      }
   }
```

6. Make sure you replace youremail@example.com with the email address you submitted when you created your PayPal account for both Add to Cart and View Cart buttons! Also, replace both instances of www.example.com with the address of your e-commerce store. Alternatively, you can remove the return and cancel_return variables if you don't want PayPal to redirect to your web site after the customer completes or cancels a payment.

■**Caution**   You need to use the correct email address if you want the money to get into your account!

---

7. Load the index.php page in a browser, and click one of the Add to Cart buttons. You should get the PayPal shopping cart, which looks like Figure 6-2.

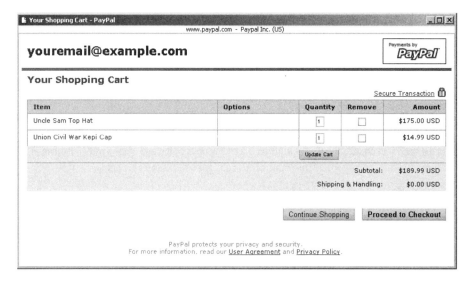

Figure 6-2. *Integrating the PayPal shopping cart*

Experiment with the PayPal shopping cart to see that it works as advertised.

How It Works: PayPal Integration

Yes, it was just that simple. Now, all visitors are potential customers! They can click the Checkout button of the PayPal shopping cart and then buy the products!

For building the PayPal call, we use Smarty's escaping functionality to ensure the product's name is correctly formed in case it contains nonportable characters (such as &, spaces, and so on). See more details about the escape method at `http://smarty.php.net/manual/en/language.modifier.escape.php`.

After a customer makes a payment on the web site, an email notification is sent to the email address registered on PayPal and also to the customer. Your PayPal account will reflect the payment, and you can view the transaction information in your account history or as a part of the history transaction log.

After PayPal confirms the payment, you can ship the products to your customer.

If you decide to use PayPal for your own web site, make sure you learn about all of its features. For example, you can teach PayPal to automatically calculate shipping costs and tax for each order.

Using the PayPal Single Item Purchases Feature

Single Item Purchases is a PayPal feature that allows you to send the visitor directly to a payment page instead of the PayPal shopping cart. The PayPal shopping cart will become useless in Chapter 8, where you'll create your own shopping cart.

In Chapter 9, you'll implement the Place Order button in the shopping cart, which saves the order into the database and forwards to a PayPal payment page. To call the PayPal payment page (bypassing the PayPal shopping cart), you redirect to a link like the following:

```
https://www.paypal.com/xclick/business=youremail@example.com&item_name=Order 123
&item_number=123&amount=123&currency=USD&return=www.example.com
&cancel_return=www.example.com
```

Review the PayPal Website Payments Standard Integration Guide for more details about the service.

■**Tip** You will create your own complete order-processing system in the third phase of development (starting with Chapter 12), where you'll process credit card transactions.

When you implement the PayPal Single Item Purchases in Chapter 9, you'll use code that looks like the following code snippet to create the URL of the PayPal Single Item Purchases page:

```
// Calculate the total amount for the shopping cart
$this->mTotalAmount = ShoppingCart::GetTotalAmount();
```

```
// If the Place Order button was clicked ...
if(isset ($_POST['place_order']))
{
  // Create the order and get the order ID
  $order_id = ShoppingCart::CreateOrder();

  // This will contain the PayPal link
  $redirect =
    'https://www.paypal.com/xclick/business=youremail@example.com' .
    '&item_name=HatShop Order ' . $order_id .
    '&item_number=' . $order_id .
    '&amount=' . $this->mTotalAmount .
    '&currency=USD&return=www.example.com' .
    '&cancel_return=www.example.com';

  // Redirection to the payment page
  header('Location: ' . $redirect);

  exit;
}
```

You'll learn how to work with this feature in Chapter 9.

Summary

In this chapter, you saw how to integrate PayPal into an e-commerce site—a simple payment solution that many small businesses choose so they don't have to process credit card or payment information themselves.

First, we listed some of the alternatives to PayPal, before guiding you through the creation of a new PayPal account. We then covered how to integrate PayPal in stages 1 and 2 of development, first discussing a shopping cart, a custom checkout mechanism, and then how to direct the visitor directly to the payment page.

In the next chapter, we will move on to look at a catalog administration page for HatShop.

CHAPTER 7

■■■

Catalog Administration

In the previous chapters, you worked with catalog information that already existed in the database. You have probably inserted some records yourself, or maybe you downloaded the department, category, and product information from the book's accompanying source code. Obviously, both ways are unacceptable for a real web site, so you need to write some code to allow easy management of the web store data. That said, the final detail to take care of before launching a web site is to create its administrative interface. Although visitors will never see this part, it's key to delivering a quality web site to your client.

In this chapter, you'll implement a catalog administration page. With this feature, you complete the first stage of your web site's development! Because this page can be implemented in many ways, a serious discussion with the client is required to get the specific list of required features. In our case, the catalog administration page should allow your client to do the following:

- Add and remove departments

- Modify existing departments' information (name, description)

- View the list of categories that belong to a department

- Manage department categories

- Edit existing categories' information (name, description)

- View the list of products in a specific category

- Edit product details

- Assign an existing product to an additional category (a product can belong to multiple categories), or move it to another category

- View the categories that a department is associated with

- Remove a product from a category

- Delete a product from the catalog

To secure sensitive pages, such as the administrative section of your site, you'll also do the following:

- Implement a login form where the administrator needs to supply a username and password.

- Learn how to secure the login form and the administrative pages using SSL.

Previewing the Catalog Administration Page

Although the long list of objectives might look intimidating at first, they will be easy to imple-ment. We have already covered most of the theory in the previous chapters, but you'll still learn quite a bit in this chapter.

The first step toward creating the catalog administration page is to create a login mecha-nism, which will be implemented as a simple login page that you can see in Figure 7-1.

Figure 7-1. *The HatShop login page*

Next, you build the site administration part of the site by creating its main page (admin.php), its associated Smarty template (admin.tpl), a main menu template (admin_menu.tpl) used to navigate through different sections of administration that we'll develop in the next chapters, a componentized template to manage the authentication (admin_login), and four componentized templates for catalog administration (admin_departments, admin_categories, admin_products, and admin_product).

After logging in, the administrator is presented with the list of departments (generated by the admin_departments Smarty template, which is loaded from the main admin page, admin.php), as shown in Figure 7-2.

The functionality you'll implement for departments is much the same as you'll see for categories and products. More specifically, the administrator can

- Edit the department's name or description by clicking the Edit button.

- Edit the categories for a specific department by clicking the Edit Categories button.

- Completely remove a department from the database by clicking the Delete button (this works only if the department has no related categories).

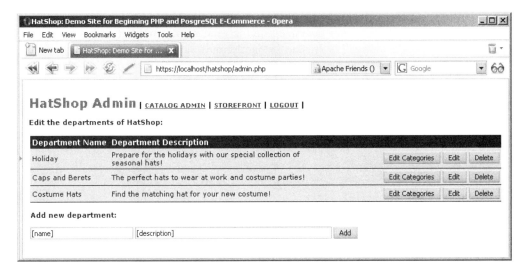

Figure 7-2. *The HatShop departments admin page*

When clicking the Edit button, the corresponding row from the table enters edit mode, and its fields become editable, as shown in Figure 7-3. Also, as you can see, instead of the Edit button, you get Update and Cancel buttons. Clicking Update updates the database with the changes, whereas clicking Cancel simply quits edit mode.

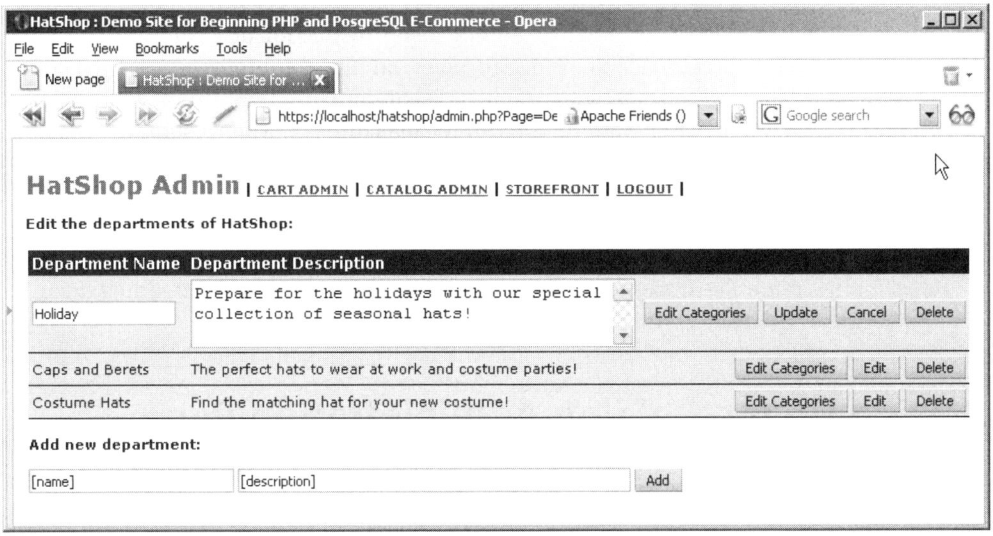

Figure 7-3. *Editing department information*

The administrator can add new departments by entering the new department's name and description in the text boxes below the table, and then clicking the Add button.

When the administrator clicks the Edit Categories button, the admin.php page is reloaded but with an additional parameter in the query string: DepartmentID. This parameter tells admin.php to load the admin_categories Smarty template, which lets the administrator edit the categories that belong to the selected department (see Figure 7-4).

Figure 7-4. *The HatShop categories admin page*

This page works similarly to the one for editing departments. You also get a link (back to departments...) that redirects back to the department's administration page.

The navigation logic among the department, category, and product administration pages is done using query string parameters. As you can see in Figure 7-4, when a department is selected, its ID is appended to the query string.

You already implemented this kind of functionality in the index.php page. There you decided which componentized template to load (at runtime) by analyzing the query string parameters.

We'll discuss more about admin.php and its templates later, while you're building them. For now, let's start by dealing with the security mechanism.

Setting Up the Catalog Administration Page

The catalog administration part of the site will consist of the admin.php page and a number of other PHP files and Smarty templates. You'll build each of these components one at a time. For each component, you'll first implement the presentation layer, then write the business tier code, and finally write the data tier methods.

Before building the admin pages, however, you need to put in place a mechanism to secure access to them. You don't want to give anyone access to your admin pages! Also, for an even increased level of security, if the admin pages are to be accessed through the Internet (and not only in a local intranet), you may also want to load them through SSL.

Your administrators will be able to log in and perform various administrative tasks. In this chapter, you're only implementing catalog administration features, but at stage two of development, you'll also have them manage customers' orders. When implementing your own order-processing system, you'll handle customer accounts yourself and store sensitive data such as customer credit cards, phone numbers, and so on.

This makes it obvious how important it is to plan ahead for implementing secure connections to the sensitive areas of your web site.

Using Secure Connections

HTTP isn't a secure protocol, and even if your site protects sensitive areas using passwords (or other forms of authentication), the transmitted data could be intercepted and stolen. To avoid this, you need to set up the application to work with SSL (Secure Socket Layer) connections, using the HTTPS protocol (Hypertext Transport Protocol - Secure).

To do this, you have a bit of groundwork to get through first. Unless you have already been using an SSL connection on your web server, you are unlikely to have the correct configuration to do so. This configuration involves obtaining a security certificate for your server and installing it on your Apache web server. (If the hosting service is provided by a third party, the hosting service probably also has an option of enabling SSL.)

Security certificates are basically public-private key pairs similar to those used in asynchronous encryption algorithms. You can generate these if your domain controller is configured as a certification authority, but if you're not a trusted certification authority, this method may be problematic. Digitally signed SSL certificates may cause browsers that use these certificates to be unable to verify the identity of your certification authority and therefore doubt your security.

When someone accesses secure pages whose certificate isn't issued by a trusted certification authority, the browser will show a warning message. This isn't disastrous when securing pages that are to be visited by your company personnel, but would certainly affect customer confidence if such a warning message shows up, for example, when they try to pay for their order.

To set up Apache on your own, we recommend you check out the article at `http://www.sitepoint.com/article/securing-apache-2-server-ssl`. Because enabling SSL can be a time-consuming process, for test purposes, you can get an already-configured Apache version from `http://www.devside.net/web/server/free/download`. Review Appendix A for more details.

The alternative is to obtain SSL certificates from a known and respected organization that specializes in web security, such as:

- VeriSign (`http://www.verisign.com/`)

- Thawte (`http://www.thawte.com/`)

- InstantSSL (`http://www.instantssl.com/`)

Web browsers have built-in root certificates from organizations such as these and are able to authenticate the digital signature of SSL certificates supplied by them. This means that no warning message will appear, and an SSL-secured connection will be available with a minimum of fuss.

For example, in Opera, you can see the name of the company that registered the SSL certificate next to the URL (see Figure 7-5).

Figure 7-5. *Opening a secured web page in Opera*

For the purpose of this chapter, I've installed the XAMPP package, with comes with an SSL-enabled Apache server. My local machine issued the certificate, which, as you can guess, isn't in the list of trusted certificate providers.

With this setup, I can show you what you get when loading an HTTPS address that doesn't have a trusted certificate (see Figure 7-6).

Figure 7-6. *Certificate signer not found*

If you click View, you can see that the certificate has been issued by localhost, for Apache Friends. Apache Friends (http://www.apachefriends.org) is the maker of the XAMPP package.

The warning message you get when using an untrusted certificate varies from browser to browser. In Internet Explorer 7, the message is even more obvious (see Figure 7-7).

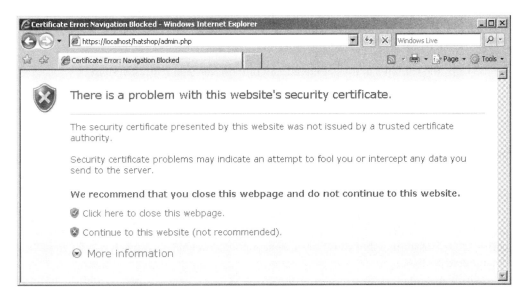

Figure 7-7. *Internet Explorer doesn't like untrusted certificates.*

Configuring HatShop for SSL

If you decide to use SSL, you'll need to install an SSL certificate, as shown in the next few pages. When using SSL, it's also advisable to enforce any sensitive page to be accessed through SSL; that is, in case anyone tries accessing a sensitive page (such as the login page) through http://, the request will be automatically redirected to an https:// URL.

However, if you want to postpone handling SSL and want to focus on building the admin pages for the moment, you can. To make the solution configurable, you added the following configuration option to your include/config.php file, back in Chapter 3.

```
// We enable and enforce SSL when this is set to anything else than 'no'
define('USE_SSL', 'yes')
```

If you prefer not to use SSL for now, simply set the USE_SSL constant to no.

Obtaining an SSL Certificate

Obtaining a certificate is a relatively painless experience. We're covering here the steps required to get a certificate from VeriSign, but the process is similar with the other providers as well. The full instructions are available on the VeriSign web site (http://www.verisign.com/). You can also get test certificates from VeriSign, which are free to use for a trial period. Here are the basic steps:

1. Sign up for a trial certificate on the VeriSign web site.

2. Generate a Certificate Signing Request (CSR) on your web server. This involves filling out various personal information, including the name of your web site, and so on. For this to work, you need to install an SSL module in your web server, as described in Appendix A.

3. Copy the contents of the generated CSR into the VeriSign request system.

4. Shortly afterwards, you will receive a certificate from VeriSign that you copy into your web server to install the certificate.

There is a little more to it than that, but as noted previously, detailed instructions are available on the VeriSign web site, and you shouldn't run into any difficulties.

Enforcing SSL Connections

After you've installed the certificate, you can access any web pages on your web server using an SSL connection, simply by replacing the http:// part of the URL used to access the page with https:// (assuming that your firewall is set up to allow an SSL connection, which by default uses port 443).

Obviously, you don't need SSL connections for all areas of the site and shouldn't enforce it in all places because that reduces performance. However, you do want to make sure that the sensitive pages are accessible only via SSL. Now you should enforce SSL for the administrator login page and for the admin pages of your site. (In later chapters, when we'll handle payments ourselves, we'll also want to enforce SSL for the checkout, customer login, customer registration, and customer detail modification pages.)

If you want to ensure that all requests to the admin script (admin.php) are done through HTTPS, you'll simply need to add this code at the beginning of admin.php:

```php
<?php
// Load Smarty library and config files
require_once 'include/app_top.php';

// Enforce page to be accessed through HTTPS
if (USE_SSL != 'no' and getenv('HTTPS') != 'on')
{
  header ('Location: https://' . getenv('SERVER_NAME') .
          getenv('REQUEST_URI'));
  exit();
}
```

Note that the secure connection isn't enforced if the USE_SSL constant defined in config.php is set to no. Setting the constant to no may be useful when developing the web site if you don't have access to an SSL-enabled server.

Authenticating Administrators

Because you want only certain users to access the catalog administration page, you need to implement some sort of security mechanism that controls access to the sensitive pages in the site.

Implementing security requires dealing with two important concepts: authentication and authorization. **Authentication** is the process in which users are uniquely identified (most often by supplying a username and password), whereas **authorization** refers to which resources the authenticated user can access.

Users who want to access the catalog administration page should first authenticate themselves. After you know who the user is, you decide whether the user is authorized to access the administration page.

In HatShop, you'll use an authentication method called **HTTP authentication**, which allows you to control the login process through an HTML form. After the client is authenticated, PHP automatically generates a cookie on the client, which is used to authenticate all subsequent requests. If the cookie is not found, the client is shown the login HTML form.

■**Note** We assume the administrator accesses the administrative pages from a client that has cookies enabled.

The username and password combinations can be physically stored in various ways. For example, in Chapter 11, you'll see how to store hashed (encrypted) customer passwords in the database.

■**Tip** **Hashing** is a common method for storing passwords. The hash value of a password is calculated by applying a mathematical function (hash algorithm) to it. When the user tries to authenticate, the password is hashed, and the resulting hash value is compared to the hash value of the original (correct) password. If the two values are identical, then the entered password is correct. The essential property about the hash algorithm is that theoretically you cannot obtain the original password from its hash value (the algorithm is one-way). In practice, scientists have recently found vulnerabilities with the popular MD5, SHA-0, and SHA-1 hashing algorithms.

A simpler method is to store the username and password combination in your PHP file. This method isn't as flexible as using the database, but it's fast and easy to implement.

When storing the username/password combination in your script file, you can choose to store the password either in clear text or as hashed text with a hashing algorithm such as MD5 or SHA-1.

In the following exercise, you'll simply store the password in clear text, but it's good to know you have other options as well. You'll learn more about hashing in Chapter 11.

Exercise: Implementing the Skeleton of the Admin Page

1. Modify the `presentation/templates/first_page_contents.tpl` file to add a link to the admin page:

    ```
    Beginning PHP and PostgreSQL E-Commerce: From Novice to Professional!
    <br /><br />
    Access the <a href="{"admin.php"|prepare_link:"https"}">admin page</a>.
    </p>
    ```

2. Add the following styles to `hatshop.css`:

    ```css
    .first_page_text a
    {
      color: #0000ff;
      font-size: 12px;
      text-decoration: underline;
    }
    #admin_login_box
    {
      border: dashed 1px #c9c9c9;
      display: block;
      margin: auto;
      padding: 10px;
      width: 368px;
    }
    .admin_title
    {
      color: #228aaa;
      font-family: verdana, arial, tahoma;
      font-size: 20px;
      font-weight: bold;
      text-align: left;
    }
    .admin_page_text
    {
      color: #000080;
      font-family: verdana, arial, tahoma;
      font-size: 11px;
      font-weight: bold;
      line-height: 12px;
    }
    .admin_page_text a
    {
      color: #0000ff;
      text-decoration: underline;
    }
    .admin_error_text
    {
    ```

```css
  color: #ff0000;
  font-family: verdana, arial, tahoma;
  font-size: 12px;
  font-weight: bold;
}
.menu_text
{
  color: #000000;
  font-family: verdana, arial, tahoma;
  font-size: 11px;
  font-weight: bold;
}
.menu_text a
{
  color: #0000ff;
  text-decoration: underline;
}
table
{
  border-collapse: collapse;
  table-layout: auto;
  width: 100%;
}
th
{
  background: #00008b;
  color: #ffffff;
  font-family: verdana, arial, tahoma;
  font-size: 12px;
  font-weight: bold;
  margin: 1px;
  padding: 3px;
  text-align: left;
}
td
{
  background: #e6e6e6;
  border-bottom: solid 1px #000000;
  font-family: verdana, arial, tahoma;
  font-size: 11px;
  margin: 1px;
  padding: 3px;
}
select
{
  font-family: tahoma, verdana, arial;
  font-size: 11px;
}
```

3. Modify include/app_top.php by adding the following two lines at its beginning. Calling ob_start()–see http://www.php.net/ob_start–turns on output buffering, which improves performance and ensures that page redirections with the header function (see admin.php at the next step) don't generate errors.

```php
<?php
// Turn on output buffering
ob_start();

// Activate session
session_start();
```

4. In your site's document root, create a new file named admin.php, and write the following code in it:

```php
<?php
// Load Smarty library and config files
require_once 'include/app_top.php';

// Enforce page to be accessed through HTTPS
if (USE_SSL != 'no' and getenv('HTTPS') != 'on')
{
  header ('Location: https://' . getenv('SERVER_NAME') .
          getenv('REQUEST_URI'));

  exit();
}

// Load Smarty template file
$page = new Page();

// Define the template file for the page menu
$pageMenuCell = 'blank.tpl';

// Define the template file for the page contents
$pageContentsCell = 'blank.tpl';

// If admin is not logged, assign admin_login template to $pageContentsCell
if (!(isset ($_SESSION['admin_logged'])) || $_SESSION['admin_logged'] != true)
  $pageContentsCell = 'admin_login.tpl';
else
{
  // If admin is logged, load the admin page menu
  $pageMenuCell = 'admin_menu.tpl';

  // If loggin out ...
  if (isset ($_GET['Page']) && ($_GET['Page'] == 'Logout'))
  {
    unset($_SESSION['admin_logged']);
    header('Location: admin.php');
```

```
      exit;
    }
  }

  // Assign templates file to be loaded
  $page->assign('pageMenuCell', $pageMenuCell);
  $page->assign('pageContentsCell', $pageContentsCell);

  // Display the page
  $page->display('admin.tpl');

  // Load app_bottom which closes the database connection
  require_once 'include/app_bottom.php';
?>
```

5. Create the `presentation/templates/admin.tpl` template file, which is loaded from the `admin.php` file we just created, and add the following code in it:

```
{* smarty *}
{config_load file="site.conf"}
<!DOCTYPE html PUBLIC "-//W3C//DTD XHTML 1.1//EN"
  "http://www.w3.org/TR/xhtml11/DTD/xhtml11.dtd">
<html>
  <head>
    <title>{#site_title#}</title>
    <link href="hatshop.css" type="text/css" rel="stylesheet" />
  </head>
  <body>
    <div>
      <br />
      {include file="$pageMenuCell"}
    </div>
    <div>
      {include file="$pageContentsCell"}
    </div>
  </body>
</html>
```

6. Add the administrator login information at the end of `include/config.php`:

```
// Administrator login information
define('ADMIN_USERNAME', 'hatshopadmin');
define('ADMIN_PASSWORD', 'hatshopadmin');
```

Note As stated earlier, in Chapter 11, you'll learn about hashing and how to work with hashed passwords stored in the database. If you want to use hashing now, you need to store the hash value of the password in the config file instead of storing the password in clear text (hatshopadmin, in this case). At login time, you compare the hash value of the string entered by the user to the hash value you saved in the config file. You can calculate the hash value of a string by applying the sha1 function to it (the sha1 function calculates the hash value using the SHA-1 algorithm). Don't worry if this sounds too advanced at this moment, Chapter 11 will show you the process in more detail.

7. Now we'll create the admin_login componentized template to supervise the login moment. Let's start by creating the presentation/templates/admin_login.tpl file and then add the following code to it:

```
{* admin_login.tpl *}
{load_admin_login assign="admin_login"}
<br /><br />
<div id="admin_login_box">
  <span class="admin_title">HatShop Login</span>
  <br /><br />
  <span class="admin_page_text">
    Enter login information or go back to
    <a href="{"index.php"|prepare_link:"http"}">storefront</a>
  </span>
  <br />
{if $admin_login->mLoginMessage neq ''}
  <br />
  <span class="admin_error_text">{$admin_login->mLoginMessage}</span>
  <br />
{/if}
  <br />
  <form method="post" action="{"admin.php"|prepare_link:"https"}">
    Username:
    <input type="text" name="username" value="{$admin_login->mUsername}" />
      
    Password:
    <input type="password" name="password" value="" />
    <br /><br />
    <input type="submit" name="submit" value="Login" />
  </form>
</div>
```

8. Create a new Smarty function plugin file named function.load_admin_login.php in the presentation/smarty_plugins folder with the following code in it:

```
<?php
/* Smarty plugin function that gets called when the
   load_admin_login function plugin is loaded from a template */
function smarty_function_load_admin_login($params, $smarty)
```

```
{
  // Create AdminLogin object
  $admin_login = new AdminLogin();

  // Assign template variable
  $smarty->assign($params['assign'], $admin_login);
}

// Class that deals with authenticating administrators
class AdminLogin
{
  // Public variables available in smarty templates
  public $mUsername;
  public $mLoginMessage = '';

  // Class constructor
  public function __construct()
  {
    // Verify if the correct username and password have been supplied
    if (isset ($_POST['submit']))
    {
      if ($_POST['username'] == ADMIN_USERNAME
          && $_POST['password'] == ADMIN_PASSWORD)
      {
        $_SESSION['admin_logged'] = true;
        header('Location: admin.php');
        exit;
      }
      else
        $this->mLoginMessage = 'Login failed. Please try again:';
    }
  }
}
?>
```

9. Create the `presentation/templates/admin_menu.tpl` file, and add the following code:

```
{* admin_menu.tpl *}
<span class="admin_title">HatShop Admin</span>
<span class="menu_text"> |
  <a href="{"admin.php"|prepare_link:"https"}">CATALOG ADMIN</a> |
  <a href="{"index.php"|prepare_link:"http"}">STOREFRONT</a> |
  <a href="{"admin.php?Page=Logout"|prepare_link:"https"}">LOGOUT</a> |
</span>
<br />
```

10. Load `index.php` in your favorite browser page, and you'll see the `admin page` link in the welcome message. Click it, and an HTML login form will be displayed; Figure 7-8 shows the message you'll get if you type in the wrong password.

Figure 7-8. *The login page*

After you supply the correct login info (hatshopadmin/hatshopadmin), you'll be redirected to the catalog admin page. Currently the catalog admin page contains only the main menu but we'll change this immediately.

How It Works: The admin Page

So far, you've created the admin.php that you'll continue to develop in the rest of the chapter to allow the user to administer catalog data and the admin_login componentized template that contains the admin authentication and authorization functionality.

All the fun begins in admin.php, which checks to see whether the visitor has been authenticated as administrator (by checking whether the admin_logged session variable is true). If the visitor is not logged in as administrator, the admin_login componentized template is loaded:

```
// If admin is not logged, assign admin_login template to $pageContentsCell
if (!(isset ($_SESSION['admin_logged'])) || $_SESSION['admin_logged'] != true)
  $pageContentsCell = 'admin_login.tpl';
```

The login mechanism in the AdminLogin helper class stores the current authentication state in the visitor's session under a variable named admin_logged. In the __construct function, we test whether the supplied username and password match the values stored in config.php as ADMIN_USERNAME and ADMIN_PASSWORD; if they match, we set the value of admin_logged to true and redirect to admin.php:

```
    // Verify if the correct username and password have been supplied
    if (isset ($_POST['submit']))
    {
      if ($_POST['username'] == ADMIN_USERNAME
          && $_POST['password'] == ADMIN_PASSWORD)
      {
        $_SESSION['admin_logged'] = true;
        header('Location: admin.php');
```

```
    exit;
  }
  else
    $this->mLoginMessage = 'Login failed. Please try again:';
}
```

The logout link in admin_menu.tpl simply unsets the admin_logged session variable in admin.php and redirects the administrator to index.php. This way, on the next attempt to access the admin page, the administrator will be redirected to the login page.

```
// If loggin out ...
if (isset ($_GET['Page']) && ($_GET['Page'] == 'Logout'))
{
  unset($_SESSION['admin_logged']);
  header('Location: admin.php');

  exit;
}
```

Administering Departments

The department administration section allows the client to add, remove, or change department information. To implement this functionality, you'll need to write the necessary code for the presentation, business, and data layers.

One fundamental truth regarding *n*-Tiered applications (which also applies to this particular case) is that the business and data tiers are ultimately created to support the presentation tier. Drawing on paper and establishing exactly how you want the site to look (in other words, what functionality needs to be supported by the UI) is a good indication of what the database and business tier will contain.

With the proper design work, you can know exactly what to place in each tier, so the order of writing the code doesn't matter. When the design is clearly established, a team of programmers can work at the same time and implement the three tiers concurrently, which is one of the benefits of having a tiered architecture.

However, this rarely happens in practice, except for the largest projects that really need very careful design and planning. In our case, usually the best way is to start with the lower levels (the database and data object) to have the basics established before creating the UI. For this to happen, first you need to analyze what functionality you'll need for the UI; otherwise, you won't know what to write in the data and business tiers.

In this chapter, we will always start with the presentation tier. You can do this because now you have a good overview of the architecture and know beforehand how you'll implement the other two tiers. This knowledge is necessary because in the presentation tier, you call methods from the business tier (which you haven't created yet), and in the business tier, you call the data tier (which, again, you haven't yet created). If you don't have a clear idea of how to implement the other tiers, starting with the presentation tier can be trickier in the long run.

Because you already have a working architecture, it will be simple to write components as needed for each tier. Of course, if you had to implement something new or more complicated, we would have spent some time analyzing the full implications, but here you won't do anything more complicated than the code in the previous chapters. You'll apply the same technique for all componentized templates you'll build in this chapter.

Implementing the Presentation Tier

Take another look at what the admin_departments componentized template looks like in action (see Figure 7-9).

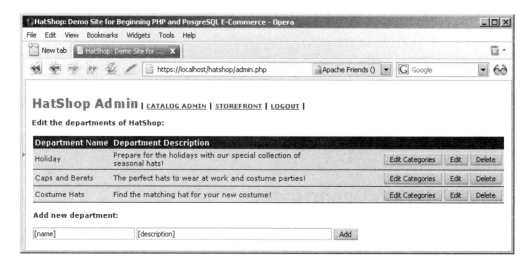

Figure 7-9. *The* admin_departments *componentized template in action*

This componentized template will generate a list populated with the departments' information, and it also has a label, two text boxes, and a button used to add new departments to the list.

When you click on a department's Edit button, the name and the description of that department becomes editable, and the Update and Cancel buttons appear in place of the Edit button, as you saw earlier in Figure 7-3.

Exercise: Implementing the admin_departments Componentized Template

1. Create a new template file named admin_departments.tpl in the presentation/templates folder, and add the following code to it:

```
{* admin_departments.tpl *}
{load_admin_departments assign="admin_departments"}
<span class="admin_page_text">Edit the departments of HatShop:</span>
<br /><br />
{if $admin_departments->mErrorMessage neq ""}
<span class="admin_error_text">
```

```
    {$admin_departments->mErrorMessage}<br /><br />
</span>
{/if}
<form method="post"
 action="{$admin_departments->mAdminDepartmentsTarget|prepare_link:"https"}">
{if $admin_departments->mDepartmentsCount eq 0}
  <strong>There are no departments in your database!</strong><br />
{else}
  <table>
    <tr>
      <th>Department Name</th>
      <th>Department Description</th>
      <th> </th>
    </tr>
  {section name=cDepartments loop=$admin_departments->mDepartments}
    {if $admin_departments->mEditItem ==
        $admin_departments->mDepartments[cDepartments].department_id}
    <tr>
      <td width="122">
        <input type="text" name="name"
         value="{$admin_departments->mDepartments[cDepartments].name}" />
      </td>
      <td>
      {strip}
        <textarea name="description" rows="3" cols="42">
          {$admin_departments->mDepartments[cDepartments].description}
        </textarea>
      {/strip}
      </td>
      <td align="right" width="280">
        <input type="submit"
         name="submit_edit_categ_{
              $admin_departments->mDepartments[cDepartments].department_id}"
         value="Edit Categories" />
        <input type="submit"
         name="submit_update_dep_{
              $admin_departments->mDepartments[cDepartments].department_id}"
         value="Update" />
        <input type="submit" name="cancel" value="Cancel" />
        <input type="submit"
         name="submit_delete_dep_{
              $admin_departments->mDepartments[cDepartments].department_id}"
         value="Delete" />
      </td>
    </tr>
    {else}
    <tr>
```

```
          <td width="122">
            {$admin_departments->mDepartments[cDepartments].name}
          </td>
          <td>{$admin_departments->mDepartments[cDepartments].description}</td>
          <td align="right" width="280">
            <input type="submit"
             name="submit_edit_categ_{
                   $admin_departments->mDepartments[cDepartments].department_id}"
             value="Edit Categories" />
            <input type="submit"
             name="submit_edit_dep_{
                   $admin_departments->mDepartments[cDepartments].department_id}"
             value="Edit" />
            <input type="submit"
             name="submit_delete_dep_{
                   $admin_departments->mDepartments[cDepartments].department_id}"
             value="Delete" />
          </td>
        </tr>
        {/if}
      {/section}
      </table>
    {/if}
      <br />
      <span class="admin_page_text">Add new department:</span>
      <br /><br />
      <input type="text" name="department_name" value="[name]" size="30" />
      <input type="text" name="department_description" value="[description]"
       size="60" />
      <input type="submit" name="submit_add_dep_0" value="Add" />
    </form>
```

2. Create a new plugin file named function.load_admin_departments.php in the
   presentation/smarty_plugins folder, and add the following to it:

```php
<?php
/* Smarty plugin function that gets called when the
   load_admin_departments function plugin is loaded from a template */
function smarty_function_load_admin_departments($params, $smarty)
{
  // Create AdminDepartments object
  $admin_departments = new AdminDepartments();
  $admin_departments->init();

  // Assign template variable
  $smarty->assign($params['assign'], $admin_departments);
}
```

```php
// Class that supports departments admin functionality
class AdminDepartments
{
  // Public variables available in smarty template
  public $mDepartmentsCount;
  public $mDepartments;
  public $mErrorMessage = '';
  public $mEditItem;
  public $mAdminDepartmentsTarget = 'admin.php?Page=Departments';

 // Private members
  public $mAction = '';
  public $mActionedDepartmentId;

  // Class constructor
  public function __construct()
  {
    // Parse the list with posted variables
    foreach ($_POST as $key => $value)
      // If a submit button was clicked ...
      if (substr($key, 0, 6) == 'submit')
      {
        /* Get the position of the last '_' underscore from submit
           button name e.g strtpos('submit_edit_dep_1', '_') is 16 */
        $last_underscore = strrpos($key, '_');

        /* Get the scope of submit button
           (e.g  'edit_dep' from 'submit_edit_dep_1') */
        $this->mAction = substr($key, strlen('submit_'),
                                $last_underscore - strlen('submit_'));

        /* Get the department id targeted by submit button
           (the number at the end of submit button name)
           e.g '1' from 'submit_edit_dep_1' */
        $this->mActionedDepartmentId = substr($key, $last_underscore + 1);

        break;
      }
  }

  public function init()
  {
    // If adding a new department ...
    if ($this->mAction == 'add_dep')
    {
      $department_name = $_POST['department_name'];
      $department_description = $_POST['department_description'];
```

```php
    if ($department_name == null)
      $this->mErrorMessage = 'Department name required';

    if ($this->mErrorMessage == null)
      Catalog::AddDepartment($department_name, $department_description);
  }

  // If editing an existing department ...
  if ($this->mAction == 'edit_dep')
    $this->mEditItem = $this->mActionedDepartmentId;

  // If updating a department ...
  if ($this->mAction == 'update_dep')
  {
    $department_name = $_POST['name'];
    $department_description = $_POST['description'];

    if ($department_name == null)
      $this->mErrorMessage = 'Department name required';

    if ($this->mErrorMessage == null)
      Catalog::UpdateDepartment($this->mActionedDepartmentId,
                                $department_name, $department_description);
  }

  // If deleting a department ...
  if ($this->mAction == 'delete_dep')
  {
    $status = Catalog::DeleteDepartment($this->mActionedDepartmentId);

    if ($status < 0)
      $this->mErrorMessage = 'Department not empty';
  }

  // If editing department's categories ...
  if ($this->mAction == 'edit_categ')
  {
    header('Location: admin.php?Page=Categories&DepartmentID=' .
           $this->mActionedDepartmentId);

    exit;
  }

  // Load the list of departments
  $this->mDepartments = Catalog::GetDepartmentsWithDescriptions();
  $this->mDepartmentsCount = count($this->mDepartments);
```

```
      }
    }
    ?>
```

3. Modify the `admin.php` file to load the newly created `admin_departments` componentized template:

```
    // If admin is logged, load the admin page menu
    $pageMenuCell = 'admin_menu.tpl';

    if (isset ($_GET['Page']))
      $admin_page = $_GET['Page'];
    // If Page is not explicitly set, assume the Departments page
    else
      $admin_page = 'Departments';

    // If logging out ...
    if (isset ($_GET['Page']) && ($_GET['Page'] == 'Logout'))
    {
      unset($_SESSION['AdminLogged']);
      header('Location: admin.php');

      exit;
    }

    // Choose what admin page to load ...
    if ($admin_page == 'Departments')
      $pageContentsCell = 'admin_departments.tpl';
    }
```

How It Works: The admin_departments Componentized Template

You wrote a lot of code in this exercise, and you still can't test anything. This is the tough part about creating the UI first. Still, the code is not that complicated if you look at it. Let's see how the `admin_departments.tpl` template is done.

Here's a scheme of the {section} construct used to build the rows of the table:

```
{section name=cDepartments loop=$admin_departments->mDepartments}
  {if $admin_departments->mEditItem ==
      $admin_departments->mDepartments[cDepartments].department_id}
  <!--
    Here goes a form where the administrator can edit the department name
    and description with Update/Cancel, Edit Categories, and Delete buttons.
  //-->
  {else}
  <!--
    Here goes a form that displays the department name and description, and
    also Edit, Edit Categories, and Delete buttons.
  //-->
  {/if}
{/section}
```

By default, the department name and description are not editable, but when you click the Edit button of one department, `$admin_departments->mEditItem` is set to the `department_id` value of the clicked department, and the Smarty presentation logic generates editable text boxes instead of labels. This will allow the administrator to edit the selected department's details (in edit mode, Update/Cancel buttons appear instead of the Edit button, as you saw in the earlier figures).

The Smarty plugin function loaded from the `admin_departments` template (in `function.load_admin_departments.php`) is executed whenever the user clicks any of these buttons and reacts to the visitor's action. The function recognizes what button was clicked and knows what to do after parsing the list of posted variables and reading the clicked button's name. In the departments admin page (see the `admin_departments.tpl` template file), buttons have names such as `submit_edit_dep_1`.

All button names start with `submit` and end with the ID of the department. In the middle of the name is the code for the button type, which specifies what operation to do with the mentioned department. A button named `submit_edit_dep_1` tells the plugin function to enter edit mode for the department with a `department_id` value of 1.

Note that with the Add department button, the department's ID specified in the button name becomes irrelevant, because its value is automatically generated by the database (`department_id` is a `SERIAL` column).

In our case, the button type can be

- `add_dep` for the Add department buttons
- `edit_dep` for the Edit department buttons
- `update_dep` for the Update buttons
- `delete_dep` for the Delete buttons
- `edit_categ` for the Edit Categories buttons

Depending on the type of the clicked button, one of the corresponding business tier methods is called. Let's consider these methods next.

Implementing the Business Tier

You called four middle-tier methods from the `AdminDepartments` class. Now it's time to add their business tier counterparts:

- `GetDepartmentsWithDescriptions` returns the list of departments to be displayed in the department's admin page.

- `UpdateDepartment` changes a department's details. Its parameters are the department's `department_id` value, its new name, and its new description.

- `DeleteDepartment` deletes the department specified by the `department_id` parameter.

- `AddDepartment` needs the name and description for the new department because the `department_id` value is automatically generated by the database (the `department_id` column in the `department` table is a `SERIAL` column).

Exercise: Implementing the Business Tier

Now it's time to implement the new methods. Add this code to the `Catalog` class in `business/catalog.php`:

```
// Retrieves all departments with their descriptions
public static function GetDepartmentsWithDescriptions()
{
  // Build the SQL query
  $sql = 'SELECT * FROM catalog_get_departments();';
  // Prepare the statement with PDO-specific functionality
  $result = DatabaseHandler::Prepare($sql);

  return DatabaseHandler::GetAll($result);
}

// Updates department details
public static function UpdateDepartment($departmentId, $departmentName,
                                     $departmentDescription)
{
  // Build the SQL query
  $sql = 'SELECT catalog_update_department(:department_id, :department_name,
                                    :department_description);';
  // Build the parameters array
  $params = array (':department_id' => $departmentId,
                   ':department_name' => $departmentName,
                   ':department_description' => $departmentDescription);
  // Prepare the statement with PDO-specific functionality
  $result = DatabaseHandler::Prepare($sql);

  // Execute the query
  return DatabaseHandler::Execute($result, $params);
}

// Deletes a department
public static function DeleteDepartment($departmentId)
{
  // Build the SQL query
  $sql = 'SELECT catalog_delete_department(:department_id);';
  // Build the parameters array
  $params = array (':department_id' => $departmentId);
  // Prepare the statement with PDO-specific functionality
  $result = DatabaseHandler::Prepare($sql);

  // Execute the query and return the results
  return DatabaseHandler::GetOne($result, $params);
}
```

```
// Add a department
public static function AddDepartment($departmentName, $departmentDescription)
{
  // Build the SQL query
  $sql = 'SELECT catalog_add_department(
                 :department_name, :department_description);';
  // Build the parameters array
  $params = array (':department_name' => $departmentName,
                 ':department_description' => $departmentDescription);
  // Prepare the statement with PDO-specific functionality
  $result = DatabaseHandler::Prepare($sql);

  // Execute the query
  return DatabaseHandler::Execute($result, $params);
}
```

Implementing the Data Tier

You'll add four methods in the data tier that correspond to the four business tier methods you wrote earlier. Let's see what this is all about.

Exercise: Adding Data Tier Functions to the Database

1. Load pgAdmin III, and connect to the hatshop database.

2. Click Tools ➤ Query tool (or click the SQL button on the toolbar). A new query window should appear.

3. Use the query tool to execute this code, which creates the catalog_get_departments function in your hatshop database:

```
-- Create catalog_get_departments function
CREATE FUNCTION catalog_get_departments()
RETURNS SETOF department LANGUAGE plpgsql AS $$
  DECLARE
    outDepartmentRow department;
  BEGIN
    FOR outDepartmentRow IN
      SELECT    department_id, name, description
      FROM      department
      ORDER BY department_id
    LOOP
```

```
      RETURN NEXT outDepartmentRow;
    END LOOP;
  END;
$$;
```

`catalog_get_departments` is the simplest function you'll implement here. It returns the complete list of departments with their identities, names, and descriptions. This is almost similar to the `catalog_get_departments_list` function called to fill the departments list from the storefront, but this one also returns the descriptions and doesn't need to create a type for the returned data because we already have it from the creation of the `department` table.

4. Use the query tool to execute this code, which creates the `catalog_update_department` function in your `hatshop` database:

```
-- Create catalog_update_department function
CREATE FUNCTION catalog_update_department(
                  INTEGER, VARCHAR(50), VARCHAR(1000))
RETURNS VOID LANGUAGE plpgsql AS $$
  DECLARE
    inDepartmentId ALIAS FOR $1;
    inName         ALIAS FOR $2;
    inDescription  ALIAS FOR $3;
  BEGIN
    UPDATE department
    SET    name = inName, description = inDescription
    WHERE  department_id = inDepartmentId;
  END;
$$;
```

The `catalog_update_department` function updates the name and description of an existing department using the UPDATE SQL statement.

5. Use the query tool to execute this code, which creates the `catalog_delete_department` function in your `hatshop` database:

```
-- Create catalog_delete_department function
CREATE FUNCTION catalog_delete_department(INTEGER)
RETURNS SMALLINT LANGUAGE plpgsql AS $$
  DECLARE
    inDepartmentId ALIAS FOR $1;
    categoryRowsCount INTEGER;
  BEGIN
    SELECT INTO categoryRowsCount
           count(*)
```

```
      FROM    category
      WHERE   department_id = inDepartmentId;
      IF categoryRowsCount = 0 THEN
        DELETE FROM department WHERE department_id = inDepartmentId;
        RETURN 1;
      END IF;
      RETURN -1;
    END;
$$;
```

catalog_delete_department deletes an existing department from the database, but only if no categories are related to it.

6. Use the query tool to execute this code, which creates the catalog_add_department function in your hatshop database:

```
-- Create catalog_add_department function
CREATE FUNCTION catalog_add_department(VARCHAR(50), VARCHAR(1000))
RETURNS VOID LANGUAGE plpgsql AS $$
  DECLARE
    inName        ALIAS FOR $1;
    inDescription ALIAS FOR $2;
  BEGIN
    INSERT INTO department (name, description)
           VALUES (inName, inDescription);
  END;
$$;
```

catalog_add_department inserts a new department into the database.

7. Finally, load the admin.php page in your browser, and admire your results. Check all the buttons carefully.

Administering Categories and Products

Because the pages that administer categories and products are based on the same steps and concepts as the departments' admin page, we'll quickly list the steps you need to follow.

As you saw earlier, when clicking the Edit Categories button in the departments page, you get the list of categories for that department. In the categories page, clicking an Edit Products button brings up the list of products for the selected category (see Figure 7-10).

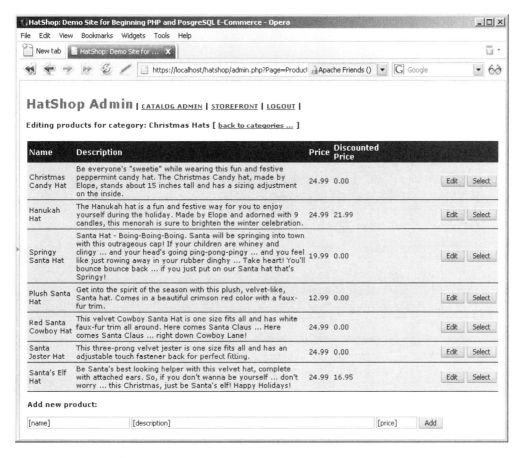

Figure 7-10. *Visiting the Christmas Hats category*

Exercise: Creating Admin Categories and Products Pages

1. Create a new template file named `admin_categories.tpl` in the `presentation/templates` folder, and add the following code to it:

```
{* admin_categories.tpl *}
{load_admin_categories assign="admin_categories"}
<span class="admin_page_text">
  Editing categories for department: {$admin_categories->mDepartmentName} [
  {strip}
  <a href="{$admin_categories->mAdminDepartmentsLink|prepare_link:"https"}">
    back to departments ...
  </a>
```

```
    {/strip}
    ]
  </span>
  <br /><br />
  {if $admin_categories->mErrorMessage neq ""}
  <span class="admin_error_text">
    {$admin_categories->mErrorMessage}<br /><br />
  </span>
  {/if}
  <form method="post"
   action="{$admin_categories->mAdminCategoriesTarget|prepare_link:"https"}">
  {if $admin_categories->mCategoriesCount eq 0}
    <strong>There are no categories in this department!</strong><br />
  {else}
    <table>
      <tr>
        <th>Category Name</th>
        <th>Category Description</th>
        <th> </th>
      </tr>
    {section name=cCategories loop=$admin_categories->mCategories}
      {if $admin_categories->mEditItem ==
          $admin_categories->mCategories[cCategories].category_id}
      <tr>
        <td width="122">
          <input type="text" name="name"
           value="{$admin_categories->mCategories[cCategories].name}" />
        </td>
        <td>
          {strip}
          <textarea name="description"rows="3" cols="42">
            {$admin_categories->mCategories[cCategories].description}
          </textarea>
          {/strip}
        </td>
        <td align="right" width="280">
          <input type="submit"
           name="submit_edit_products_{
                $admin_categories->mCategories[cCategories].category_id}"
           value="Edit Products" />
          <input type="submit"
           name="submit_update_categ_{
                $admin_categories->mCategories[cCategories].category_id}"
           value="Update" />
          <input type="submit" name="cancel" value="Cancel" />
          <input type="submit"
           name="submit_delete_categ_{
```

```
                    $admin_categories->mCategories[cCategories].category_id}"
            value="Delete" />
        </td>
      </tr>
      {else}
      <tr>
        <td width="122">
          {$admin_categories->mCategories[cCategories].name}
        </td>
        <td>{$admin_categories->mCategories[cCategories].description}</td>
        <td align="right" width="280">
          <input type="submit"
           name="submit_edit_products_{
                  $admin_categories->mCategories[cCategories].category_id}"
           value="Edit Products" />
          <input type="submit"
           name="submit_edit_categ_{
                  $admin_categories->mCategories[cCategories].category_id}"
           value="Edit" />
          <input type="submit"
           name="submit_delete_categ_{
                  $admin_categories->mCategories[cCategories].category_id}"
           value="Delete" />
        </td>
      </tr>
      {/if}
    {/section}
    </table>
  {/if}
    <br />
    <span class="admin_page_text">Add new category:</span>
    <br /><br />
    <input type="text" name="category_name" value="[name]" size="30" />
    <input type="text" name="category_description" value="[description]"
     size="60" />
    <input type="submit" name="submit_add_categ_0" value="Add" />
  </form>
```

2. Create a new plugin file named `function.load_admin_categories.php` in the `presentation/smarty_plugins` folder, and add the following to it:

```php
<?php
/* Smarty plugin function that gets called when the
   load_admin_categories function plugin is loaded from a template */
function smarty_function_load_admin_categories($params, $smarty)
{
  // Create AdminLogin object
  $admin_categories = new AdminCategories();
```

```php
    $admin_categories->init();

    // Assign template variable
    $smarty->assign($params['assign'], $admin_categories);
}

// Class that deals with departments admin
class AdminCategories
{
  // Public variables available in smarty template
  public $mCategoriesCount;
  public $mCategories;
  public $mEditItem = - 1;
  public $mErrorMessage = '';
  public $mDepartmentId;
  public $mDepartmentName;
  public $mAdminDepartmentsLink = 'admin.php?Page=Departments';
  public $mAdminCategoriesTarget = 'admin.php?Page=Categories';

  // Private members
  private $mAction = '';
  private $mActionedCategoryId;

  // Class constructor
  public function __construct()
  {
    if (isset ($_GET['DepartmentID']))
      $this->mDepartmentId = (int)$_GET['DepartmentID'];
    else
      trigger_error('DepartmentID not set');

    $department_details = Catalog::GetDepartmentDetails($this->mDepartmentId);
    $this->mDepartmentName = $department_details['name'];

    foreach ($_POST as $key => $value)
      // If a submit button was clicked ...
      if (substr($key, 0, 6) == 'submit')
      {
        /* Get the position of the last '_' underscore from submit
           button name e.g strtpos('submit_edit_categ_1', '_') is 18 */
        $last_underscore = strrpos($key, '_');

        /* Get the scope of submit button
           (e.g  'edit_categ' from 'submit_edit_categ_1') */
        $this->mAction = substr($key, strlen('submit_'),
                                $last_underscore - strlen('submit_'));
```

```php
        /* Get the category id targeted by submit button
           (the number at the end of submit button name)
           e.g '1' from 'submit_edit_categ_1' */
        $this->mActionedCategoryId = (int)substr($key, $last_underscore + 1);

        break;
      }
    }
  }

  public function init()
  {
    // If adding a new category ...
    if ($this->mAction == 'add_categ')
    {
      $category_name = $_POST['category_name'];
      $category_description = $_POST['category_description'];

      if ($category_name == null)
        $this->mErrorMessage = 'Category name is empty';

      if ($this->mErrorMessage == null)
        Catalog::AddCategory($this->mDepartmentId, $category_name,
                             $category_description);
    }

    // If editing an existing category ...
    if ($this->mAction == 'edit_categ')
    {
      $this->mEditItem = $this->mActionedCategoryId;
    }

    // If updating a category ...
    if ($this->mAction == 'update_categ')
    {
      $category_name = $_POST['name'];
      $category_description = $_POST['description'];

      if ($category_name == null)
        $this->mErrorMessage = 'Category name is empty';

      if ($this->mErrorMessage == null)
        Catalog::UpdateCategory($this->mActionedCategoryId, $category_name,
                                $category_description);
    }

    // If deleting a category ...
    if ($this->mAction == 'delete_categ')
```

```
        {
          $status = Catalog::DeleteCategory($this->mActionedCategoryId);

          if ($status < 0)
            $this->mErrorMessage = 'Category not empty';
        }

        // If editing category's products ...
        if ($this->mAction == 'edit_products')
        {
          header('Location: admin.php?Page=Products&DepartmentID=' .
                 $this->mDepartmentId . '&CategoryID=' .
                 $this->mActionedCategoryId);

          exit;
        }

        $this->mAdminCategoriesTarget .= '&DepartmentID=' . $this->mDepartmentId;

        // Load the list of categories
        $this->mCategories =
          Catalog::GetDepartmentCategories($this->mDepartmentId);
        $this->mCategoriesCount = count($this->mCategories);
      }
    }
    ?>
```

3. Create a new template file named admin_products.tpl in the presentation/templates folder,
   and add the following code to it:

```
{* admin_products.tpl *}
{load_admin_products assign="admin_products"}
<span class="admin_page_text">
  Editing products for category: {$admin_products->mCategoryName} [
  {strip}
  <a href="{$admin_products->mAdminCategoriesLink|prepare_link:"https"}">
    back to categories ...
  </a>
  {/strip}
  ]
</span>
<br /><br />
{if $admin_products->mErrorMessage neq ""}
<span class="admin_error_text">
  {$admin_products->mErrorMessage}<br /><br />
</span>
{/if}
<form  method="post"
```

```
 action="{$admin_products->mAdminProductsTarget|prepare_link:"https"}">
{if $admin_products->mProductsCount eq 0}
  <strong>There are no products in this category!</strong><br />
{else}
  <table>
    <tr>
      <th>Name</th>
      <th>Description</th>
      <th>Price</th>
      <th>Discounted Price</th>
      <th> </th>
    </tr>
  {section name=cProducts loop=$admin_products->mProducts}
    {if $admin_products->mEditItem ==
        $admin_products->mProducts[cProducts].product_id}
    <tr>
      <td>
        <input type="text" size="15" name="name"
         value="{$admin_products->mProducts[cProducts].name}" />
      </td>
      <td>
      {strip}
        <textarea name="description" rows="3" cols="39">
          {$admin_products->mProducts[cProducts].description}
        </textarea>
      {/strip}
      </td>
      <td>
        <input type="text" name="price"
         value="{$admin_products->mProducts[cProducts].price}" size="5" />
      </td>
      <td>
        <input type="text" name="discounted_price"
         value="{$admin_products->mProducts[cProducts].discounted_price}"
         size="5" />
      </td>
      <td align="right" width="180">
        <input type="submit"
         name="submit_update_prod_{
              $admin_products->mProducts[cProducts].product_id}"
         value="Update" />
        <input type="submit" name="cancel" value="Cancel" />
        <input type="submit"
         name="submit_select_prod_{
              $admin_products->mProducts[cProducts].product_id}"
         value="Select" />
      </td>
```

```
        </tr>
        {else}
        <tr>
          <td>{$admin_products->mProducts[cProducts].name}</td>
          <td>{$admin_products->mProducts[cProducts].description}</td>
          <td>{$admin_products->mProducts[cProducts].price}</td>
          <td>{$admin_products->mProducts[cProducts].discounted_price}</td>
          <td align="right" width="180">
            <input type="submit"
             name="submit_edit_prod_{
                   $admin_products->mProducts[cProducts].product_id}"
             value="Edit" />
            <input type="submit"
             name="submit_select_prod_{
                   $admin_products->mProducts[cProducts].product_id}"
             value="Select" />
          </td>
        </tr>
        {/if}
      {/section}
      </table>
   {/if}
     <br />
     <span class="admin_page_text">Add new product:</span>
     <br /><br />
     <input type="text" name="product_name" value="[name]" size="30" />
     <input type="text" name="product_description" value="[description]"
      size="75" />
     <input type="text" name="product_price" value="[price]" size="10" />
     <input type="submit" name="submit_add_prod_0" value="Add" />
   </form>
```

4. Create a new plugin file named function.load_admin_products.php in the presentation/smarty_plugins folder, and add the following to it:

```php
<?php
/* Smarty plugin function that gets called when the
   load_admin_products function plugin is loaded from a template */
function smarty_function_load_admin_products($params, $smarty)
{
  // Create AdminProducts object
  $admin_products = new AdminProducts();
  $admin_products->init();

  // Assign template variable
  $smarty->assign($params['assign'], $admin_products);
}
```

```php
// Class that deals with products administration from a specific category
class AdminProducts
{
  // Public variables available in smarty template
  public $mProducts;
  public $mProductsCount;
  public $mEditItem;
  public $mErrorMessage = '';
  public $mDepartmentId;
  public $mCategoryId;
  public $mProductId;
  public $mCategoryName;
  public $mAdminCategoriesLink = 'admin.php?Page=Categories';
  public $mAdminProductsTarget = 'admin.php?Page=Products';

  // Private attributes
  private $mCatalog;
  private $mAction = '';
  private $mActionedProductId;
  // Class constructor
  public function __construct()
  {
    if (isset ($_GET['DepartmentID']))
      $this->mDepartmentId = (int)$_GET['DepartmentID'];
    else
      trigger_error('DepartmentID not set');

    if (isset ($_GET['CategoryID']))
      $this->mCategoryId = (int)$_GET['CategoryID'];
    else
      trigger_error('CategoryID not set');

    $category_details = Catalog::GetCategoryDetails($this->mCategoryId);
    $this->mCategoryName = $category_details['name'];

    foreach ($_POST as $key => $value)
      // If a submit button was clicked ...
      if (substr($key, 0, 6) == 'submit')
      {
        /* Get the position of the last '_' underscore from submit button name
           e.g strtpos('submit_edit_prod_1', '_') is 17 */
        $last_underscore = strrpos($key, '_');

        /* Get the scope of submit button
           (e.g  'edit_dep' from 'submit_edit_prod_1') */
        $this->mAction = substr($key, strlen('submit_'),
                               $last_underscore - strlen('submit_'));
```

```
      /* Get the product id targeted by submit button
         (the number at the end of submit button name)
         e.g '1' from 'submit_edit_prod_1' */
      $this->mActionedProductId = (int)substr($key, $last_underscore + 1);

      break;
    }
  }
}

public function init()
{
  // If adding a new product
  if ($this->mAction == 'add_prod')
  {
    $product_name = $_POST['product_name'];
    $product_description = $_POST['product_description'];
    $product_price = $_POST['product_price'];

    if ($product_name == null)
      $this->mErrorMessage = 'Product name is empty';

    if ($product_description == null)
      $this->mErrorMessage = 'Product description is empty';

    if ($product_price == null || !is_numeric($product_price))
      $this->mErrorMessage = 'Product price must be a number!';

    if ($this->mErrorMessage == null)
      Catalog::AddProductToCategory($this->mCategoryId, $product_name,
        $product_description, $product_price, 'generic_image.jpg',
        'generic_thumbnail.jpg');
  }

  // If editing a product
  if ($this->mAction == 'edit_prod')
  {
    $this->mEditItem = $this->mActionedProductId;
  }

  // If we want to see a product details
  if ($this->mAction == 'select_prod')
  {
    header('Location: admin.php?Page=ProductDetails&DepartmentID=' .
           $this->mDepartmentId . '&CategoryID=' . $this->mCategoryId .
           '&ProductID=' . $this->mActionedProductId);
```

```
      exit;
    }

    // If updating a product
    if ($this->mAction == 'update_prod')
    {
      $product_name = $_POST['name'];
      $product_description = $_POST['description'];
      $product_price = $_POST['price'];
      $product_discounted_price = $_POST['discounted_price'];

      if ($product_name == null)
        $this->mErrorMessage = 'Product name is empty';

      if ($product_description == null)
        $this->mErrorMessage = 'Product description is empty';

      if ($product_price == null || !is_numeric($product_price))
        $this->mErrorMessage = 'Product price must be a number!';

      if ($product_discounted_price == null ||
          !is_numeric($product_discounted_price))
        $this->mErrorMessage = 'Product discounted price must be a number!';

      if ($this->mErrorMessage == null)
        Catalog::UpdateProduct($this->mActionedProductId, $product_name,
          $product_description, $product_price, $product_discounted_price);
    }

    $this->mAdminCategoriesLink .= '&DepartmentID=' . $this->mDepartmentId;
    $this->mAdminProductsTarget .= '&DepartmentID=' . $this->mDepartmentId .
                                  '&CategoryID=' . $this->mCategoryId;

    $this->mProducts = Catalog::GetCategoryProducts($this->mCategoryId);
    $this->mProductsCount = count($this->mProducts);
  }
}
?>
```

5. Open business/catalog.php to add the following business tier methods needed for admin_categories and admin_products to the Catalog class:

```
// Gets categories in a department
public static function GetDepartmentCategories($departmentId)
{
  // Build the SQL query
  $sql = 'SELECT * FROM catalog_get_department_categories(:department_id);';
  // Build the parameters array
```

```
    $params = array (':department_id' => $departmentId);
    // Prepare the statement with PDO-specific functionality
    $result = DatabaseHandler::Prepare($sql);

    // Execute the query and return the results
    return DatabaseHandler::GetAll($result, $params);
  }


  // Adds a category
  public static function AddCategory($departmentId, $categoryName,
                                     $categoryDescription)
  {
    // Build the SQL query
    $sql = 'SELECT catalog_add_category(:department_id, :category_name,
                                        :category_description);';
    // Build the parameters array
    $params = array (':department_id' => $departmentId,
                     ':category_name' => $categoryName,
                     ':category_description' => $categoryDescription);
    // Prepare the statement with PDO-specific functionality
    $result = DatabaseHandler::Prepare($sql);

    // Execute the query
    return DatabaseHandler::Execute($result, $params);
  }


  // Deletes a category
  public static function DeleteCategory($categoryId)
  {
    // Build the SQL query
    $sql = 'SELECT catalog_delete_category(:category_id);';
    // Build the parameters array
    $params = array (':category_id' => $categoryId);
    // Prepare the statement with PDO-specific functionality
    $result = DatabaseHandler::Prepare($sql);

    // Execute the query and return the results
    return DatabaseHandler::GetOne($result, $params);
  }


  // Updates a category
  public static function UpdateCategory($categoryId, $categoryName,
                                        $categoryDescription)
  {
    // Build the SQL query
    $sql = 'SELECT catalog_update_category(:category_id, :category_name,
                                           :category_description);';
```

```php
  // Build the parameters array
  $params = array (':category_id' => $categoryId,
                   ':category_name' => $categoryName,
                   ':category_description' => $categoryDescription);
  // Prepare the statement with PDO-specific functionality
  $result = DatabaseHandler::Prepare($sql);

  // Execute the query
  return DatabaseHandler::Execute($result, $params);
}

// Gets products in a category
public static function GetCategoryProducts($categoryId)
{
  // Build the SQL query
  $sql = 'SELECT * FROM catalog_get_category_products(:category_id);';
  // Build the parameters array
  $params = array (':category_id' => $categoryId);
  // Prepare the statement with PDO-specific functionality
  $result = DatabaseHandler::Prepare($sql);

  // Execute the query and return the results
  return DatabaseHandler::GetAll($result, $params);
}

// Creates a product and assigns it to a category
public static function AddProductToCategory($categoryId, $productName,
                        $productDescription, $productPrice)
{
  // Build the SQL query
  $sql = 'SELECT catalog_add_product_to_category(:category_id, :product_name,
                 :product_description, :product_price);';
  // Build the parameters array
  $params = array (':category_id' => $categoryId,
                   ':product_name' => $productName,
                   ':product_description' => $productDescription,
                   ':product_price' => $productPrice);
  // Prepare the statement with PDO-specific functionality
  $result = DatabaseHandler::Prepare($sql);

  // Execute the query
  return DatabaseHandler::Execute($result, $params);
}

// Updates a product
public static function UpdateProduct($productId, $productName,
                $productDescription, $productPrice,
```

```
                            $productDiscountedPrice)
    {
      // Build the SQL query
      $sql = 'SELECT catalog_update_product(:product_id, :product_name,
                          :product_description, :product_price,
                          :product_discounted_price);';
      // Build the parameters array
      $params = array (':product_id' => $productId,
                          ':product_name' => $productName,
                          ':product_description' => $productDescription,
                          ':product_price' => $productPrice,
                          ':product_discounted_price' => $productDiscountedPrice);
      // Prepare the statement with PDO-specific functionality
      $result = DatabaseHandler::Prepare($sql);

      // Execute the query
      return DatabaseHandler::Execute($result, $params);
    }
```

6. Modify the admin.php page to load the newly added componentized templates:

```
// Choose what admin page to load ...
if ($admin_page == 'Departments')
  $pageContentsCell = 'admin_departments.tpl';
elseif ($admin_page == 'Categories')
  $pageContentsCell = 'admin_categories.tpl';
elseif ($admin_page == 'Products')
  $pageContentsCell = 'admin_products.tpl';
```

7. Load pgAdmin III, and connect to the hatshop database. Use the query tool to execute this code, which creates the data tier functions into your hatshop database:

```
-- Create department_category type
CREATE TYPE department_category AS
(
  category_id INTEGER,
  name        VARCHAR(50),
  description VARCHAR(1000)
);


-- Create catalog_get_department_categories function
CREATE FUNCTION catalog_get_department_categories(INTEGER)
RETURNS SETOF department_category LANGUAGE plpgsql AS $$
  DECLARE
    inDepartmentId ALIAS FOR $1;
    outDepartmentCategoryRow department_category;
  BEGIN
    FOR outDepartmentCategoryRow IN
      SELECT   category_id, name, description
```

```
      FROM      category
      WHERE     department_id = inDepartmentId
      ORDER BY category_id
    LOOP
      RETURN NEXT outDepartmentCategoryRow;
    END LOOP;
  END;
$$;


-- Create catalog_add_category function
CREATE FUNCTION catalog_add_category(
                  INTEGER, VARCHAR(50), VARCHAR(1000))
RETURNS VOID LANGUAGE plpgsql AS $$
  DECLARE
    inDepartmentId ALIAS FOR $1;
    inName         ALIAS FOR $2;
    inDescription  ALIAS FOR $3;
  BEGIN
    INSERT INTO category (department_id, name, description)
          VALUES (inDepartmentId, inName, inDescription);
  END;
$$;


-- Create catalog_delete_category function
CREATE FUNCTION catalog_delete_category(INTEGER)
RETURNS SMALLINT LANGUAGE plpgsql AS $$
  DECLARE
    inCategoryId ALIAS FOR $1;
    productCategoryRowsCount INTEGER;
  BEGIN
    SELECT      INTO productCategoryRowsCount
                count(*)
    FROM        product p
    INNER JOIN  product_category pc
                  ON p.product_id = pc.product_id
    WHERE       pc.category_id = inCategoryId;
    IF productCategoryRowsCount = 0 THEN
      DELETE FROM category WHERE category_id = inCategoryId;
      RETURN 1;
    END IF;
    RETURN -1;
  END;
$$;


-- Create catalog_update_category function
CREATE FUNCTION catalog_update_category(
                  INTEGER, VARCHAR(50), VARCHAR(1000))
```

```
      RETURNS VOID LANGUAGE plpgsql AS $$
        DECLARE
          inCategoryId  ALIAS FOR $1;
          inName        ALIAS FOR $2;
          inDescription ALIAS FOR $3;
        BEGIN
          UPDATE category
          SET    name = inName, description = inDescription
          WHERE  category_id = inCategoryId;
        END;
      $$;

      -- Create category_product type
      CREATE TYPE category_product AS
      (
        product_id       INTEGER,
        name             VARCHAR(50),
        description       VARCHAR(1000),
        price            NUMERIC(10, 2),
        discounted_price NUMERIC(10, 2)
      );

      -- Create catalog_get_category_products function
      CREATE FUNCTION catalog_get_category_products(INTEGER)
      RETURNS SETOF category_product LANGUAGE plpgsql AS $$
        DECLARE
          inCategoryId ALIAS FOR $1;
          outCategoryProductRow category_product;
        BEGIN
          FOR outCategoryProductRow IN
            SELECT     p.product_id, p.name, p.description, p.price,
                       p.discounted_price
            FROM       product p
            INNER JOIN product_category pc
                       ON p.product_id = pc.product_id
            WHERE      pc.category_id = inCategoryId
            ORDER BY   p.product_id
          LOOP
            RETURN NEXT outCategoryProductRow;
          END LOOP;
        END;
      $$;
```

```
-- Create catalog_add_product_to_category function
CREATE FUNCTION catalog_add_product_to_category(INTEGER, VARCHAR(50),
                VARCHAR(1000), NUMERIC(10, 2))
RETURNS VOID LANGUAGE plpgsql AS $$
  DECLARE
    inCategoryId  ALIAS FOR $1;
    inName        ALIAS FOR $2;
    inDescription ALIAS FOR $3;
    inPrice       ALIAS FOR $4;
    productLastInsertId INTEGER;
  BEGIN
    INSERT INTO product (name, description, price, image, thumbnail,
                         search_vector)
          VALUES (inName, inDescription, inPrice, 'generic.jpg',
                  'generic.thumb.jpg',
                  (setweight(to_tsvector(inName), 'A')
                   || to_tsvector(inDescription)));
    SELECT INTO productLastInsertId currval('product_product_id_seq');
    INSERT INTO product_category (product_id, category_id)
          VALUES (productLastInsertId, inCategoryId);
  END;
$$;


-- Create catalog_update_product function
CREATE FUNCTION catalog_update_product(INTEGER, VARCHAR(50),
                VARCHAR(1000), NUMERIC(10, 2), NUMERIC(10, 2))
RETURNS VOID LANGUAGE plpgsql AS $$
  DECLARE
    inProductId       ALIAS FOR $1;
    inName            ALIAS FOR $2;
    inDescription     ALIAS FOR $3;
    inPrice           ALIAS FOR $4;
    inDiscountedPrice ALIAS FOR $5;
  BEGIN
    UPDATE product
    SET    name = inName, description = inDescription, price = inPrice,
           discounted_price = inDiscountedPrice,
           search_vector = (setweight(to_tsvector(inName), 'A')
                            || to_tsvector(inDescription))
    WHERE  product_id = inProductId;
  END;
$$;
```

8. Load `admin.php` in your browser, choose a department, and click its Edit Categories button. The `categories` componentized template loads, and a page like the one in Figure 7-11 appears.

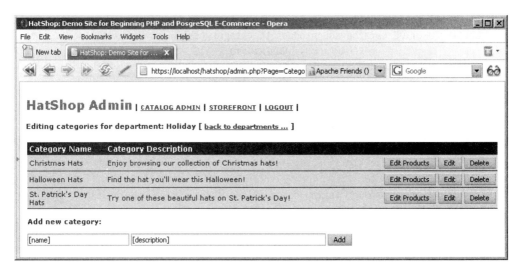

Figure 7-11. *The* admin_categories *componentized template*

How It Works: Administering Categories and Products

This time, we chose to quickly show you how to add the new functionality. We did this because the code for administering categories and products follows the same patterns as the code for administering departments.

Have a close look at the new code that you added to make sure you understand exactly how it works before moving on to administering product details.

Administering Product Details

The products list you built earlier is wonderful, but it lacks a few important features. The final componentized template you're implementing, admin_product, enables you to

- View the product's picture.

- Remove the product from a category.

- Remove the product from the database completely.

- Assign the current product to an additional category.

- Move the current product to another category.

When it comes to product removal, things aren't so straightforward. You can either unassign the product from a category by removing the record from the product_category table, or you can effectively remove the product from the product table. Because products are accessed in the catalog by selecting a category, you must make sure there are no orphaned products (products that don't belong to any category) because they couldn't be accessed using the current administration interface.

So, if you added a Delete button for a product, what would it actually do? Delete the product from the database? This would work, but it's a bit awkward if you have a product assigned to multiple categories, and you only want to remove it from a single category. On the other hand, if the Delete button removes the product from the current category, you can create orphaned products because they exist in the product table, but they don't belong to any category, so they can't be accessed. You could fix that by allowing the site administrator to see the complete list of products without locating them by department and category.

The simple solution implemented in this chapter is like that. There will be two delete buttons: a Remove from category button, which allows removing the product from a single category, and a Remove from catalog button, which completely removes the product from the catalog by deleting its entries in the product and product_category tables. If the product belongs to more categories, only the Remove from category button will be active. If the product belongs to a single category, only the Remove from catalog button will be available because removing it only from its category would generate an orphan product in the product table (a product that doesn't belongs to any category, thus is inaccessible through the current interface).

With this componentized template, apart from permitting the administrator to remove products, you'll also see how to assign the currently selected product to an additional category or to move the product to another category.

Implementing the Presentation Tier

Figure 7-12 shows how the product details admin page will look for the Black Basque Beret product.

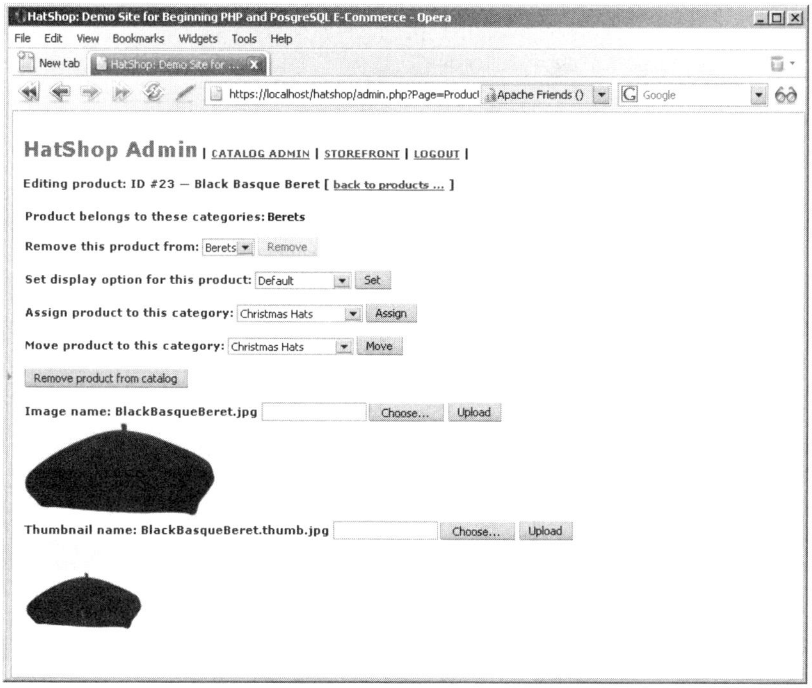

Figure 7-12. *Administering product details*

You'll implement the admin_product Smarty componentized template in the following exercise.

1. Create the presentation/templates/admin_product.tpl template file, and add the following in it:

```
{* admin_product.tpl *}
{load_admin_product assign="admin_product"}
<span class="admin_page_text">
  Editing product: ID #{$admin_product->mProductId} &mdash;
  {$admin_product->mProductName} [
  {strip}
  <a href="{$admin_product->mAdminProductsLink|prepare_link:"https"}">
    back to products ...
  </a>
  {/strip}
  ]
</span>
<form enctype="multipart/form-data" method="post"
 action="{$admin_product->mAdminProductTarget|prepare_link:"https"}">
  <br />
  <span class="admin_page_text">Product belongs to these categories:</span>
  <span><strong>{$admin_product->mProductCategoriesString}</strong></span>
  <br /><br />
  <span class="admin_page_text">Remove this product from:</span>
  {html_options name="TargetCategoryIdRemove"
   options=$admin_product->mRemoveFromCategories}
  <input type="submit" name="RemoveFromCategory" value="Remove"
  {if $admin_product->mRemoveFromCategoryButtonDisabled}
   disabled="disabled" {/if}/>
  <br /><br />
  <span class="admin_page_text">Set display option for this product:</span>
  {html_options name="ProductDisplay"
   options=$admin_product->mProductDisplayOptions
   selected=$admin_product->mProductDisplay}
  <input type="submit" name="SetProductDisplayOption" value="Set" />
  <br /><br />
  <span class="admin_page_text">Assign product to this category:</span>
  {html_options name="TargetCategoryIdAssign"
   options=$admin_product->mAssignOrMoveTo}
  <input type="submit" name="Assign" value="Assign" />
  <br /><br />
  <span class="admin_page_text">Move product to this category:</span>
  {html_options name="TargetCategoryIdMove"
   options=$admin_product->mAssignOrMoveTo}
  <input type="submit" name="Move" value="Move" />
```

```
<br /><br />
<input type="submit" name="RemoveFromCatalog"
 value="Remove product from catalog"
{if !$admin_product->mRemoveFromCategoryButtonDisabled}
 disabled="disabled" {/if} />
<br /><br />
<span class="admin_page_text">
  Image name: {$admin_product->mProductImage}
  <input name="ImageUpload" type="file" value="Upload" />
  <input type="submit" name="Upload" value="Upload" /><br />
  <img src="product_images/{$admin_product->mProductImage}"
   border="0" alt="Product image" />
  <br />
  Thumbnail name: {$admin_product->mProductThumbnail}
  <input name="ThumbnailUpload" type="file" value="Upload" />
  <input type="submit" name="Upload" value="Upload" /><br />
  <img src="product_images/{$admin_product->mProductThumbnail}"
   border="0" alt="Product thumbnail" />
</span>
</form>
```

2. Open business/catalog.php to add the $mProductDisplayOptions member to the Catalog class needed for admin_products as shown:

```
<?php
// Business tier class for reading product catalog information
class Catalog
{
  public static $mProductDisplayOptions = array ('Default',      // 0
                                                 'On Catalog',    // 1
                                                 'On Department', // 2
                                                 'On Both');      // 3


  // Retrieves all departments
  public static function GetDepartments()
```

3. Create the presentation/smarty_plugins/function.load_admin_product.php file, and add the following in it:

```
<?php
// Plugin function for the load_admin_product function plugin
function smarty_function_load_admin_product($params, $smarty)
{
  // Create AdminProduct object
  $admin_product = new AdminProduct();
  $admin_product->init();

  // Assign template variable
  $smarty->assign($params['assign'], $admin_product);
```

```php
    }

    // Class that deals with product administration
    class AdminProduct
    {
      // Public attributes
      public $mProductName;
      public $mProductImage;
      public $mProductThumbnail;
      public $mProductDisplay;
      public $mProductCategoriesString;
      public $mRemoveFromCategories;
      public $mProductDisplayOptions;
      public $mProductId;
      public $mCategoryId;
      public $mDepartmentId;
      public $mRemoveFromCategoryButtonDisabled = false;
      public $mAdminProductsLink = 'admin.php?Page=Products';
      public $mAdminProductTarget = 'admin.php?Page=ProductDetails';

      // Private attributes
      private $mTargetCategoryId;

      // Class constructor
      public function __construct()
      {
        // Need to have DepartmentID in the query string
        if (!isset ($_GET['DepartmentID']))
          trigger_error('DepartmentID not set');
        else
          $this->mDepartmentId = (int)$_GET['DepartmentID'];

        // Need to have CategoryID in the query string
        if (!isset ($_GET['CategoryID']))
          trigger_error('CategoryID not set');
        else
          $this->mCategoryId = (int)$_GET['CategoryID'];

        // Need to have ProductID in the query string
        if (!isset ($_GET['ProductID']))
          trigger_error('ProductID not set');
        else
          $this->mProductId = (int)$_GET['ProductID'];

        $this->mProductDisplayOptions = Catalog::$mProductDisplayOptions;
      }
```

```php
public function init()
{
  // If uploading a product picture ...
  if (isset ($_POST['Upload']))
  {
    /* Check whether we have write permission on the
       product_images folder */
    if (!is_writeable(SITE_ROOT . '/product_images/'))
    {
      echo "Can't write to the product_images folder";

      exit;
    }

    // If the error code is 0, the first file was uploaded ok
    if ($_FILES['ImageUpload']['error'] == 0)
    {
      /* Use the move_uploaded_file PHP function to move the file
         from its temporary location to the product_images folder */
      move_uploaded_file($_FILES['ImageUpload']['tmp_name'],
                         SITE_ROOT . '/product_images/' .
                         $_FILES['ImageUpload']['name']);

      // Update the product's information in the database
      Catalog::SetImage($this->mProductId,
                        $_FILES['ImageUpload']['name']);
    }

    // If the error code is 0, the second file was uploaded ok
    if ($_FILES['ThumbnailUpload']['error'] == 0)
    {
      // Move the uploaded file to the product_images folder
      move_uploaded_file($_FILES['ThumbnailUpload']['tmp_name'],
                         SITE_ROOT . '/product_images/' .
                         $_FILES['ThumbnailUpload']['name']);

      // Update the product's information in the database
      Catalog::SetThumbnail($this->mProductId,
                            $_FILES['ThumbnailUpload']['name']);
    }
  }

  // If removing the product from a category ...
  if (isset ($_POST['RemoveFromCategory']))
  {
    $target_category_id = $_POST['TargetCategoryIdRemove'];
    $still_exists = Catalog::RemoveProductFromCategory(
```

```
                          $this->mProductId, $target_category_id);

      if ($still_exists == 0)
      {
        header('Location: admin.php?Page=Products&DepartmentID=' .
                 $this->mDepartmentId . '&CategoryID=' . $this->mCategoryId);

        exit;
      }
    }

    // If setting product display option ...
    if (isset ($_POST['SetProductDisplayOption']))
    {
      $product_display = $_POST['ProductDisplay'];
      Catalog::SetProductDisplayOption($this->mProductId, $product_display);
    }

    // If removing the product from catalog ...
    if (isset ($_POST['RemoveFromCatalog']))
    {
      Catalog::DeleteProduct($this->mProductId);

      header('Location: admin.php?Page=Products&DepartmentID=' .
               $this->mDepartmentId . '&CategoryID=' . $this->mCategoryId);

      exit;
    }

    // If assigning the product to another category ...
    if (isset ($_POST['Assign']))
    {
      $target_category_id = $_POST['TargetCategoryIdAssign'];
      Catalog::AssignProductToCategory($this->mProductId,
                                       $target_category_id);
    }

    // If moving the product to another category ...
    if (isset ($_POST['Move']))
    {
      $target_category_id = $_POST['TargetCategoryIdMove'];
      Catalog::MoveProductToCategory($this->mProductId,
        $this->mCategoryId, $target_category_id);

      header('Location: admin.php?Page=ProductDetails&DepartmentID=' .
               $this->mDepartmentId . '&CategoryID=' .
               $target_category_id . '&ProductID=' . $this->mProductId);
```

```
    exit;
  }

  // Get product info and show it to user
  $product_info = Catalog::GetProductInfo($this->mProductId);
  $this->mProductName = $product_info['name'];
  $this->mProductImage = $product_info['image'];
  $this->mProductThumbnail = $product_info['thumbnail'];
  $this->mProductDisplay = $product_info['display'];
  $product_categories = Catalog::GetCategoriesForProduct($this->mProductId);

  if (count($product_categories) == 1)
    $this->mRemoveFromCategoryButtonDisabled = true;

  // Show the categories the product belongs to
  for ($i = 0; $i < count($product_categories); $i++)
    $temp1[$product_categories[$i]['category_id']] =
      $product_categories[$i]['name'];

  $this->mRemoveFromCategories = $temp1;
  $this->mProductCategoriesString = implode(', ', $temp1);
  $all_categories = Catalog::GetCategories();

  for ($i = 0; $i < count($all_categories); $i++)
    $temp2[$all_categories[$i]['category_id']] =
      $all_categories[$i]['name'];

  $this->mAssignOrMoveTo = array_diff($temp2, $temp1);

  $this->mAdminProductsLink .= '&DepartmentID=' . $this->mDepartmentId .
                               '&CategoryID=' . $this->mCategoryId;
  $this->mAdminProductTarget .= '&DepartmentID=' . $this->mDepartmentId .
                                '&CategoryID=' . $this->mCategoryId .
                                '&ProductID=' . $this->mProductId;
  }
}
?>
```

4. Modify the `admin.php` page to load the `admin_product` componentized template:

```
// Choose what admin page to load ...
if ($admin_page == 'Departments')
  $pageContentsCell = 'admin_departments.tpl';
elseif ($admin_page == 'Categories')
  $pageContentsCell = 'admin_categories.tpl';
elseif ($admin_page == 'Products')
  $pageContentsCell = 'admin_products.tpl';
```

```
elseif ($admin_page == 'ProductDetails')
   $pageContentsCell = 'admin_product.tpl';
```

How It Works: admin_product

Even though you can't execute the page yet, it's worth taking a look at the new elements the new template contains.

The admin_product.tpl template contains a single form with the enctype="multipart/form-data" attribute. This attribute is needed for uploading product pictures, and works in conjunction with the HTML code that enables file uploading:

```
...
  <input name="ImageUpload" type="file" value="Upload" />
  <input type="submit" name="Upload" value="Upload" /><br />
...
```

At the end of the admin_product.tpl template file, you'll find a similar piece of code used for uploading the thumbnail image of the product:

```
...
  <input name="ThumbnailUpload" type="file" value="Upload" />
  <input type="submit" name="Upload" value="Upload" /><br />
...
```

The reaction to clicking these Upload buttons is implemented in the init() method from the AdminProduct class (in presentation/smarty_plugins/function.load_admin_product.php):

```
// If uploading a product picture ...
if (isset ($_POST['Upload']))
{
  /* Check whether we have write permission on the
     product_images folder */
  if (!is_writeable(SITE_ROOT . '/product_images/'))
  {
    echo "Can't write to the product_images folder";

    exit;
  }

  // If the error code is 0, the first file was uploaded ok
  if ($_FILES['ImageUpload']['error'] == 0)
  {
    /* Use the move_uploaded_file PHP function to move the file
       from its temporary location to the product_images folder */
    move_uploaded_file($_FILES['ImageUpload']['tmp_name'],
                       SITE_ROOT . '/product_images/' .
                       $_FILES['ImageUpload']['name']);

    // Update the product's information in the database
```

```
    Catalog::SetImage($this->mProductId,
                    $_FILES['ImageUpload']['name']);
  }


  // If the error code is 0, the second file was uploaded ok
  if ($_FILES['ThumbnailUpload']['error'] == 0)
  {
    // Move the uploaded file to the product_images folder
    move_uploaded_file($_FILES['ThumbnailUpload']['tmp_name'],
                    SITE_ROOT . '/product_images/' .
                    $_FILES['ThumbnailUpload']['name']);

    // Update the product's information in the database
    Catalog::SetThumbnail($this->mProductId,
                    $_FILES['ThumbnailUpload']['name']);
  }
}
```

The $_FILES superglobal variable is a two-dimensional array that stores information about your uploaded file (or files). If the $_FILES['ImageUpload']['error'] variable is set to 0, then the main image of the product has uploaded successfully and must be handled. The $_FILES['ImageUpload']['tmp_name'] variable stores the temporary file name of the uploaded file on the server, and the $_FILES['ImageUpload']['name'] variable stores the name of the file as specified when uploaded to the server.

■**Note** A complete description of the $_FILES superglobal is available at http://www.php.net/manual/en/features.file-upload.php.

The move_uploaded_file PHP function is used to move the file from the temporary location to the product_images folder:

```
    /* Use the move_uploaded_file PHP function to move the file
       from its temporary location to the product_images folder */
    move_uploaded_file($_FILES['ImageUpload']['tmp_name'],
                    SITE_ROOT . '/product_images/' .
                    $_FILES['ImageUpload']['name']);
```

After uploading a product picture, the file name must be stored in the database (otherwise, the file upload has no effect):

```
    // Update the product's information in the database
    Catalog::SetImage($this->mProductId,
                    $_FILES['ImageUpload']['name']);
```

As you can see, it's pretty simple to handle file uploads with PHP.

Implementing the Business Tier

To implement the business tier, you'll need to add the following methods to the Catalog class:

- DeleteProduct completely removes a product from the catalog.

- RemoveProductFromCategory is called when the Remove from category button is clicked to unassign the product from a category.

- GetCategories returns all the categories from our catalog.

- GetProductInfo returns the product details.

- GetCategoriesForProduct is used to get the list of categories that are related to the specified product.

- SetProductDisplayOption sets the product's display setting.

- AssignProductToCategory assigns a product to a category.

- MoveProductToCategory moves a product from one category to another.

- SetImage changes the image file name in the database for a certain product.

- SetThumbnail changes the second image file name for a certain product.

Exercise: Implementing the Business Tier Methods

Because the functionality is better expressed by the data tier functions the methods call, we'll discuss more about them when implementing the data tier. Add the following code to the Catalog class inside of business/catalog.php:

```php
// Removes a product from the product catalog
public static function DeleteProduct($productId)
{
  // Build the SQL query
  $sql = 'SELECT catalog_delete_product(:product_id);';
  // Build the parameters array
  $params = array (':product_id' => $productId);
  // Prepare the statement with PDO-specific functionality
  $result = DatabaseHandler::Prepare($sql);

  // Execute the query
  return DatabaseHandler::Execute($result, $params);
}

// Unassigns a product from a category
public static function RemoveProductFromCategory($productId, $categoryId)
{
```

```
  // Build the SQL query
  $sql = 'SELECT catalog_remove_product_from_category(
                  :product_id, :category_id);';
  // Build the parameters array
  $params = array (':product_id' => $productId,
                  ':category_id' => $categoryId);
  // Prepare the statement with PDO-specific functionality
  $result = DatabaseHandler::Prepare($sql);

  // Execute the query and return the results
  return DatabaseHandler::GetOne($result, $params);
}

// Retrieves the list of categories a product belongs to
public static function GetCategories()
{
  // Build the SQL query
  $sql = 'SELECT * FROM catalog_get_categories();';
  // Prepare the statement with PDO-specific functionality
  $result = DatabaseHandler::Prepare($sql);

  // Execute the query and return the results
  return DatabaseHandler::GetAll($result);
}

// Retrieves product info
public static function GetProductInfo($productId)
{
  // Build the SQL query
  $sql = 'SELECT * FROM catalog_get_product_info(:product_id);';
  // Build the parameters array
  $params = array (':product_id' => $productId);
  // Prepare the statement with PDO-specific functionality
  $result = DatabaseHandler::Prepare($sql);

  // Execute the query and return the results
  return DatabaseHandler::GetRow($result, $params);
}

// Retrieves the list of categories a product belongs to
public static function GetCategoriesForProduct($productId)
{
  // Build the SQL query
  $sql = 'SELECT * FROM catalog_get_categories_for_product(:product_id);';
  // Build the parameters array
  $params = array (':product_id' => $productId);
  // Prepare the statement with PDO-specific functionality
  $result = DatabaseHandler::Prepare($sql);
```

```
  // Execute the query and return the results
  return DatabaseHandler::GetAll($result, $params);
}


// Assigns a product to a category
public static function SetProductDisplayOption($productId, $display)
{
  // Build the SQL query
  $sql = 'SELECT catalog_set_product_display_option(
              :product_id, :display);';
  // Build the parameters array
  $params = array (':product_id' => $productId,
              ':display' => $display);
  // Prepare the statement with PDO-specific functionality
  $result = DatabaseHandler::Prepare($sql);

  // Execute the query
  return DatabaseHandler::Execute($result, $params);
}


// Assigns a product to a category
public static function AssignProductToCategory($productId, $categoryId)
{
  // Build the SQL query
  $sql = 'SELECT catalog_assign_product_to_category(
              :product_id, :category_id);';
  // Build the parameters array
  $params = array (':product_id' => $productId,
              ':category_id' => $categoryId);
  // Prepare the statement with PDO-specific functionality
  $result = DatabaseHandler::Prepare($sql);

  // Execute the query
  return DatabaseHandler::Execute($result, $params);
}


// Moves a product from one category to another
public static function MoveProductToCategory($productId, $sourceCategoryId,
                                             $targetCategoryId)
{
  // Build the SQL query
  $sql = 'SELECT catalog_move_product_to_category(:product_id,
              :source_category_id, :target_category_id);';
  // Build the parameters array
```

```
  $params = array (':product_id' => $productId,
                    ':source_category_id' => $sourceCategoryId,
                    ':target_category_id' => $targetCategoryId);
  // Prepare the statement with PDO-specific functionality
  $result = DatabaseHandler::Prepare($sql);

  // Execute the query
  return DatabaseHandler::Execute($result, $params);
}

// Changes the name of the product image file in the database
public static function SetImage($productId, $imageName)
{
  // Build the SQL query
  $sql = 'SELECT catalog_set_image(:product_id, :image_name);';
  // Build the parameters array
  $params = array (':product_id' => $productId, ':image_name' => $imageName);
  // Prepare the statement with PDO-specific functionality
  $result = DatabaseHandler::Prepare($sql);

  // Execute the query
  return DatabaseHandler::Execute($result, $params);
}

// Changes the name of the product thumbnail file in the database
public static function SetThumbnail($productId, $thumbnailName)
{
  // Build the SQL query
  $sql = 'SELECT catalog_set_thumbnail(:product_id, :thumbnail_name);';
  // Build the parameters array
  $params = array (':product_id' => $productId,
                    ':thumbnail_name' => $thumbnailName);
  // Prepare the statement with PDO-specific functionality
  $result = DatabaseHandler::Prepare($sql);

  // Execute the query
  return DatabaseHandler::Execute($result, $params);
}
```

Implementing the Data Tier

In the data tier, you add the corresponding methods in the Catalog class for the business tier methods you have just seen.

1. Load pgAdmin III, and connect to the `hatshop` database.

2. Click Tools ➤ Query tool (or click the SQL button on the toolbar). A new query window should appear.

3. Use the query tool to execute this code, which creates the `catalog_delete_product` function to your `hatshop` database:

```
-- Create catalog_delete_product function
CREATE FUNCTION catalog_delete_product(INTEGER)
RETURNS VOID LANGUAGE plpgsql AS $$
  DECLARE
    inProductId ALIAS FOR $1;
  BEGIN
    DELETE FROM product_category WHERE product_id = inProductId;
    DELETE FROM product WHERE product_id = inProductId;
  END;
$$;
```

The `catalog_delete_product` function completely removes a product from the catalog by deleting its entries in the `product_category` and `product` tables.

4. Use the query tool to execute this code, which creates the `catalog_remove_product_from_category` function in your `hatshop` database:

```
-- Create catalog_remove_product_from_category function
CREATE FUNCTION catalog_remove_product_from_category(INTEGER, INTEGER)
RETURNS SMALLINT LANGUAGE plpgsql AS $$
  DECLARE
    inProductId  ALIAS FOR $1;
    inCategoryId ALIAS FOR $2;
    productCategoryRowsCount INTEGER;
  BEGIN
    SELECT INTO productCategoryRowsCount
           count(*)
    FROM   product_category
    WHERE  product_id = inProductId;
    IF productCategoryRowsCount = 1 THEN
      PERFORM catalog_delete_product(inProductId);
      RETURN 0;
    END IF;
    DELETE FROM product_category
    WHERE  category_id = inCategoryId AND product_id = inProductId;
    RETURN 1;
  END;
$$;
```

The catalog_remove_product_from_category function verifies how many categories the product exists in. If the product exists in more than one category, then it just removes the product from the specified category (ID received as a parameter). If the product is associated with a single category, it is removed completely from the database.

5. Use the query tool to execute this code, which creates the catalog_get_categories function in your hatshop database:

```
-- Create catalog_get_categories function
CREATE FUNCTION catalog_get_categories()
RETURNS SETOF department_category LANGUAGE plpgsql AS $$
  DECLARE
    outDepartmentCategoryRow department_category;
  BEGIN
    FOR outDepartmentCategoryRow IN
      SELECT    category_id, name, description
      FROM      category
      ORDER BY category_id
    LOOP
      RETURN NEXT outDepartmentCategoryRow;
    END LOOP;
  END;
$$;
```

catalog_get_categories simply returns all the categories from your catalog.

6. Use the query tool to execute this code, which creates the product_info type and catalog_get_product_info function in your hatshop database:

```
-- Create product_info type
CREATE TYPE product_info AS
(
  name      VARCHAR(50),
  image     VARCHAR(150),
  thumbnail VARCHAR(150),
  display   SMALLINT
);

-- Create catalog_get_product_info function
CREATE FUNCTION catalog_get_product_info(INTEGER)
RETURNS product_info LANGUAGE plpgsql AS $$
  DECLARE
    inProductId ALIAS FOR $1;
    outProductInfoRow product_info;
  BEGIN
    SELECT INTO outProductInfoRow
           name, image, thumbnail, display
    FROM   product
    WHERE  product_id = inProductId;
    RETURN outProductInfoRow;
  END;
$$;
```

The catalog_get_product_info function retrieves the product name, image, and thumbnail for the product identified by the product ID ($1).

7. Use the query tool to execute this code, which creates the product_category_details type and catalog_get_categories_for_product function in your hatshop database:

```
-- Create product_category_details type
CREATE TYPE product_category_details AS
(
  category_id    INTEGER,
  department_id INTEGER,
  name           VARCHAR(50)
);

-- Create catalog_get_categories_for_product function
CREATE FUNCTION catalog_get_categories_for_product(INTEGER)
RETURNS SETOF product_category_details LANGUAGE plpgsql AS $$
  DECLARE
    inProductId ALIAS FOR $1;
    outProductCategoryDetailsRow product_category_details;
  BEGIN
    FOR outProductCategoryDetailsRow IN
      SELECT   c.category_id, c.department_id, c.name
      FROM     category c
      JOIN     product_category pc
                 ON c.category_id = pc.category_id
      WHERE    pc.product_id = inProductId
      ORDER BY category_id
    LOOP
      RETURN NEXT outProductCategoryDetailsRow;
    END LOOP;
  END;
$$;
```

The catalog_get_categories_for_product function returns a list of the categories that belong to the specified product. Only their IDs and names are returned because this is the only information we're interested in.

8. Use the query tool to execute this code, which creates the catalog_set_product_display_option function in your hatshop database:

```
-- Create catalog_set_product_display_option function
CREATE FUNCTION catalog_set_product_display_option(INTEGER, SMALLINT)
RETURNS VOID LANGUAGE plpgsql AS $$
  DECLARE
    inProductId ALIAS FOR $1;
    inDisplay   ALIAS FOR $2;
  BEGIN
    UPDATE product SET display = inDisplay WHERE product_id = inProductId;
  END;
$$;
```

9. Use the query tool to execute this code, which creates the catalog_assign_product_to_category function in your hatshop database:

```
-- Create catalog_assign_product_to_category function
CREATE FUNCTION catalog_assign_product_to_category(INTEGER, INTEGER)
RETURNS VOID LANGUAGE plpgsql AS $$
  DECLARE
    inProductId  ALIAS FOR $1;
    inCategoryId ALIAS FOR $2;
  BEGIN
    INSERT INTO product_category (product_id, category_id)
          VALUES (inProductId, inCategoryId);
  END;
$$;
```

The catalog_assign_product_to_category function associates a product with a category by adding a (product_id, category_id) value pair into the product_category table.

10. Use the query tool to execute this code, which creates the catalog_assign_product_to_category function in your hatshop database:

```
-- Create catalog_move_product_to_category function
CREATE FUNCTION catalog_move_product_to_category(
                  INTEGER, INTEGER, INTEGER)
RETURNS VOID LANGUAGE plpgsql AS $$
  DECLARE
    inProductId        ALIAS FOR $1;
    inSourceCategoryId ALIAS FOR $2;
    inTargetCategoryId ALIAS FOR $3;
  BEGIN
    UPDATE product_category
    SET    category_id = inTargetCategoryId
    WHERE  product_id = inProductId
          AND category_id = inSourceCategoryId;
  END;
$$;
```

The catalog_move_product_to_category function removes a product from a category and places it in another one.

11. Use the query tool to execute this code, which creates the catalog_set_image and catalog_set_thumbnail functions in your hatshop database:

```
-- Create catalog_set_image function
CREATE FUNCTION catalog_set_image(INTEGER, VARCHAR(150))
RETURNS VOID LANGUAGE plpgsql AS $$
  DECLARE
    inProductId ALIAS FOR $1;
    inImage     ALIAS FOR $2;
  BEGIN
    UPDATE product SET image = inImage WHERE product_id = inProductId;
  END;
$$;
```

```
-- Create catalog_set_thumbnail function
CREATE FUNCTION catalog_set_thumbnail(INTEGER, VARCHAR(150))
RETURNS VOID LANGUAGE plpgsql AS $$
  DECLARE
    inProductId ALIAS FOR $1;
    inThumbnail ALIAS FOR $2;
  BEGIN
    UPDATE product
    SET    thumbnail = inThumbnail
    WHERE  product_id = inProductId;
  END;
$$;
```

We need these functions to change the image or thumbnail name of a product when uploading a new picture.

12. Load your product details page, and ensure everything works as it should. You have a lot of functionality to test! Figure 7-13 shows the product details admin page in action.

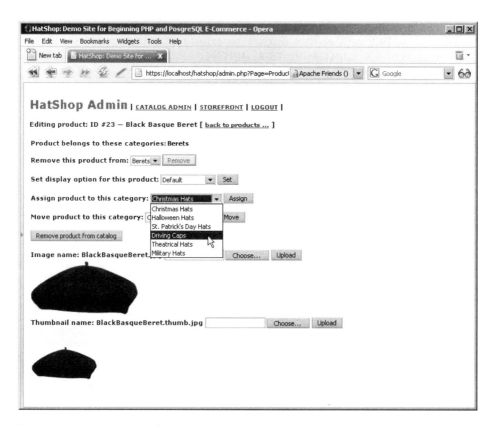

Figure 7-13. *Assigning a product to a new category*

Summary

You've done quite a lot of coding in this chapter. You implemented a number of componen-tized templates, along with their middle-tier methods and methods for the data tier. You learned how to implement a simple authentication scheme so only administrators are allowed to access the catalog administration page. At the conclusion of the chapter, you learned how to upload files from the client to the server using PHP.

In the next chapter, you enter the second stage of development by implementing a custom shopping basket into your web site.

PART 2

Phase II of Development

CHAPTER 8

■■■

The Shopping Cart

Welcome to the second stage of development! At this stage, you start improving and adding new features to the already existing, fully functional e-commerce site.

So, what exactly can you improve? Well, the answer to this question isn't hard to find if you take a quick look at the popular e-commerce sites on the web. They personalize the experience for the user, provide product recommendations, remember customers' preferences, and boast many other features that make the site easy to remember and hard to leave without first purchasing something.

In the first stage of development, you extensively relied on a third-party payment processor (PayPal) that supplied an integrated shopping cart, so you didn't record any shopping cart or order info in the database. Right now, your site isn't capable of displaying a list of "most wanted" products or any other information about the products that have been sold through the web site because, at this stage, you aren't tracking the products sold. This makes it impossible to implement any of these improvements.

Obviously, saving order information in the database is your first priority. In fact, most of the features you'll want to implement next rely on having a record of the products sold. To achieve this functionality, in this chapter, you'll implement a custom shopping cart, which will store data in the local `hatshop` database. This will provide you with more flexibility than the PayPal shopping cart over which you have no control and which cannot be easily saved into your database for further processing and analysis. With the custom shopping cart, when the visitor clicks the Add to Cart button for a product, the product is added to the visitor's shopping cart. When the visitor clicks the View Cart button, a page like the one shown in Figure 8-1 appears.

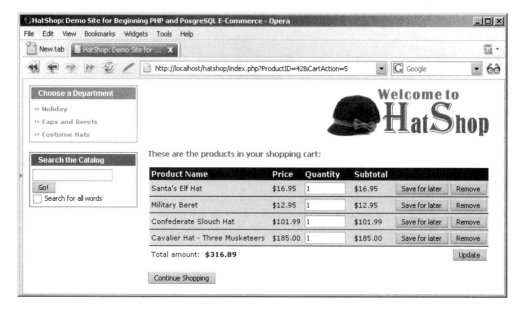

Figure 8-1. *The HatShop shopping cart*

Our shopping cart will have a "Save for Later" feature, which allows the visitor to move a shopping cart product to a separate list, in case he or she wants to buy only a part of the items (see Figure 8-2).

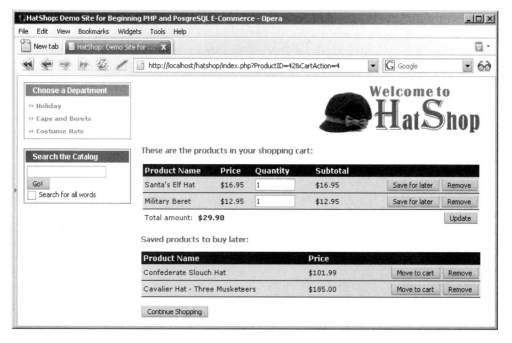

Figure 8-2. *The HatShop "Save for Later" feature*

In all the other pages except the shopping cart page, the visitor will be able to see a shopping cart summary in the left part of the screen as shown in Figure 8-3.

At the end of this chapter, you'll have a functional shopping cart, but the visitor will not yet be able to order the products contained in it. You'll add this functionality in the next chapter, when you implement a custom checkout—the Proceed to Checkout button. When the visitor clicks this button, the products in the shopping cart are saved as a separate order in the database, and the visitor is redirected to a page to pay. If you integrated the PayPal shopping cart for the first development stage, starting with the next chapter, PayPal will only be used to handle payments, and you won't rely on its shopping cart anymore.

Specifically, in this chapter, you'll learn how to

- Design a shopping cart

- Add a new database table to store shopping cart records

- Create the data tier functions that work with the new table

- Implement the business layer methods

- Implement the Add to Cart and View Cart buttons (or make them work with the new shopping cart if you already implemented them in the PayPal chapter)

- Implement the presentation layer part of the custom shopping cart

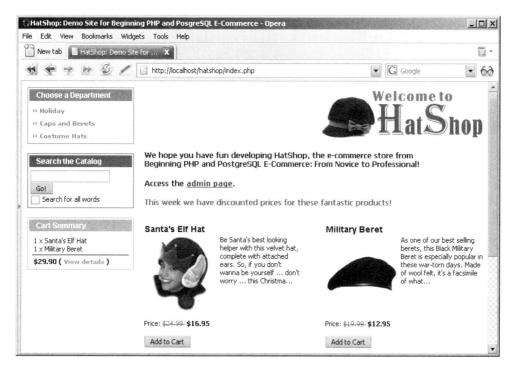

Figure 8-3. *Displaying the shopping cart summary*

Designing the Shopping Cart

Before starting to write the code for the shopping cart, let's take a closer look at what you're going to do.

First, note that you won't have any user personalization features at this stage of the site. It doesn't matter who buys your products at this point, you just want to know what products were sold and when. When you add user customization features in the later chapters, your task will be fairly simple: when the visitor authenticates, the visitor's temporary (anonymous) shopping cart will be associated with the visitor's account. Because you work with temporary shopping carts, even after implementing the customer account system, the visitor isn't required to supply additional information (log in) earlier than necessary.

Probably the best way to store shopping cart information is to generate a unique cart ID for each shopping cart and save it on the visitor's computer as a cookie. When the visitor clicks the Add to Cart button, the server first verifies whether the cookie exists on the client computer. If it does, the specified product is added to the existing cart. Otherwise, the server generates another cart ID, saves it to the client's cookie, and then adds the product to the newly generated shopping cart.

In the previous chapter, you created the componentized templates by starting with the presentation layer components. However, this strategy doesn't work here because now you need to do a bit more design work beforehand, so we'll take the more common approach and start with the database tier.

Storing Shopping Cart Information

You will store all the information from the shopping carts in a single table named shopping_cart. Follow the next exercise to create the shopping_cart table.

Exercise: Creating the shopping_cart Table

1. Load pgAdmin III, and connect to the hatshop database.

2. Click Tools ➤ Query tool (or click the SQL button on the toolbar). A new query window should appear.

3. Use the query tool to execute this code, which creates the shopping_cart table in your hatshop database:

```
-- Create shopping_cart table
CREATE TABLE shopping_cart
(
  cart_id      CHAR(32)  NOT NULL,
  product_id   INTEGER   NOT NULL,
  quantity     INTEGER   NOT NULL,
  buy_now      BOOLEAN   NOT NULL DEFAULT true,
  added_on     TIMESTAMP NOT NULL,
  CONSTRAINT pk_cart_id_product_id PRIMARY KEY (cart_id, product_id),
  CONSTRAINT fk_product_id         FOREIGN KEY (product_id)
             REFERENCES product (product_id)
             ON UPDATE RESTRICT ON DELETE RESTRICT
);
```

How It Works: The shopping_cart Table

Let's look at each field in `shopping_cart`:

- `cart_id` stores a unique ID that you'll generate for each shopping cart. This is not an integer field like other ID columns you've created so far. It is a char field and will be filled with an MD5 hash of a unique ID, which will be a 32-character string.

- `product_id` references the ID of an existing product.

- `quantity` stores the product's shopping cart quantity.

- `buy_now` helps you implement the Save for Later functionality. The `buy_now` field is a `boolean` type with the default value of `true`. When the customer proceeds to check out, only the products that have this value set to `true` are added to the order, whereas the Save for Later products remain in the shopping cart. This feature is useful because it allows the visitor to keep more products in the shopping cart than he or she can afford (or wants to buy) at the moment and allows the visitor to order only a selection of the products in the shopping cart.

- `added_on` will be populated with the current date when a new product is added to the cart and is useful when deleting old shopping carts from the database.

■Note The `shopping_cart` table has a composite primary key formed of both `cart_id` and `product_id` fields. This make sense because a particular product can exist only once in a particular shopping cart, so a (`cart_id`, `product_id`) pair shouldn't appear more than once in the table.

Implementing the Data Tier

In this section, you'll create the usual functions that query the database for the shopping cart operation. Before going further with the code, let's review the functions you'll add to the `hatshop` database:

- `shopping_cart_add_product` adds a product to the shopping cart.

- `shopping_cart_update` modifies shopping cart products' quantities.

- `shopping_cart_remove_product` deletes a record from the visitor's shopping cart.

- `shopping_cart_get_products` gets the list of products in the specified shopping cart and is called when you want to show the user his shopping cart.

- `shopping_cart_get_saved_products` gets the list of products saved in the shopping cart to buy later and is called when the user requests to view the shopping cart details page.

- `shopping_cart_get_total_amount` returns the total costs of the products in the specified product cart.

- shopping_cart_save_product_for_later saves a product to a shopping cart for later purchase.

- shopping_cart_move_product_to_cart moves a product from the Save for Later list back to the "main" shopping cart.

Now let's create each method one at a time in the following exercise.

Exercise: Implementing the Functions

1. Load pgAdmin III, and connect to the hatshop database.

2. Click Tools ➤ Query tool (or click the SQL button on the toolbar). A new query window should appear.

3. Use the query tool to execute this code, which creates the shopping_cart_add_product function in your hatshop database:

```
-- Create shopping_cart_add_product function
CREATE FUNCTION shopping_cart_add_product(CHAR(32), INTEGER)
RETURNS VOID LANGUAGE plpgsql AS $$
  DECLARE
    inCartId      ALIAS FOR $1;
    inProductId   ALIAS FOR $2;
    productQuantity INTEGER;
  BEGIN
    SELECT INTO productQuantity
             quantity
    FROM   shopping_cart
    WHERE  cart_id = inCartId AND product_id = inProductId;
    IF productQuantity IS NULL THEN
      INSERT INTO shopping_cart(cart_id, product_id, quantity, added_on)
           VALUES (inCartId, inProductId , 1, NOW());
    ELSE
      UPDATE shopping_cart
      SET    quantity = quantity + 1, buy_now = true
      WHERE  cart_id = inCartId AND product_id = inProductId;
    END IF;
  END;
$$;
```

The shopping_cart_add_product function is called when the visitor clicks on the Add to Cart button for one of the products. If the selected product already exists in the shopping cart, its quantity is increased by one; if the product doesn't exist, one unit is added to the shopping cart (a new shopping_cart record is created).

Not surprisingly, shopping_cart_add_product receives two parameters, namely inCartId and, of course, inProductId.

The function first determines whether the product mentioned by `inProductId` exists in the cart referred to by the `inCartId`. It does this by testing whether an (`inCartId`, `inProductId`) pair is in the `shopping_cart` table. If the product is in the cart, `shopping_cart_add_product` updates the current product quantity in the shopping cart by adding one unit. Otherwise, `shopping_cart_add_product` creates a new record for the product in `shopping_cart` with a default quantity of 1 but not before checking whether the mentioned `inProductId` is valid.

The `NOW()` PostgreSQL function retrieves the current date and manually populates the added_on field.

4. Use the query tool to execute the following code, which creates the `shopping_cart_update` function in your `hatshop` database:

```
-- Create shopping_cart_update function
CREATE FUNCTION shopping_cart_update(CHAR(32), INTEGER[], INTEGER[])
RETURNS VOID LANGUAGE plpgsql AS $$
  DECLARE
    inCartId    ALIAS FOR $1;
    inProductIds ALIAS FOR $2;
    inQuantities ALIAS FOR $3;
  BEGIN
    FOR i IN array_lower(inQuantities, 1)..array_upper(inQuantities, 1)
    LOOP
      IF inQuantities[i] > 0 THEN
        UPDATE shopping_cart
        SET    quantity = inQuantities[i], added_on = NOW()
        WHERE  cart_id = inCartId AND product_id = inProductIds[i];
      ELSE
        PERFORM shopping_cart_remove_product(inCartId, inProductIds[i]);
      END IF;
    END LOOP;
  END;
$$;
```

The `shopping_cart_update` function is used when you want to update the quantity of one or more existing shopping cart items. This function is called when the visitor clicks the Update button.

`shopping_cart_update` receives as parameters two array values: `inProductIds` and `inQuantities`. The value of `inQuantities[i]` represents the new quantity for the product specified by `inProductIDs[i]`.

If `inQuantities[i]` is zero or less, `shopping_cart_update` removes the mentioned product from the shopping cart. Otherwise, it updates the quantity of the product in the shopping cart and also updates added_on to accurately reflect the time the record was last modified.

Updating the added_on field is particularly useful for the administration page, when you'll want to remove shopping carts that haven't been updated in a long time.

5. Use the query tool to execute this code, which creates the `shopping_cart_remove_product` function in your `hatshop` database:

```
-- Create shopping_cart_remove_product function
CREATE FUNCTION shopping_cart_remove_product(CHAR(32), INTEGER)
```

```
RETURNS VOID LANGUAGE plpgsql AS $$
  DECLARE
    inCartId    ALIAS FOR $1;
    inProductId ALIAS FOR $2;
  BEGIN
    DELETE FROM shopping_cart
    WHERE  cart_id = inCartId AND product_id = inProductId;
  END;
$$;
```

The shopping_cart_remove_product function removes a product from the shopping cart when a visitor clicks the Remove button for one of the products in the shopping cart.

6. Use the query tool to execute this code, which creates the cart_product type and shopping_cart_get_products functions in your hatshop database:

```
-- Create cart_product type
CREATE TYPE cart_product AS
(
  product_id INTEGER,
  name       VARCHAR(50),
  price      NUMERIC(10, 2),
  quantity   INTEGER,
  subtotal   NUMERIC(10, 2)
);

-- Create shopping_cart_get_products function
CREATE FUNCTION shopping_cart_get_products(CHAR(32))
RETURNS SETOF cart_product LANGUAGE plpgsql AS $$
  DECLARE
    inCartId ALIAS FOR $1;
    outCartProductRow cart_product;
  BEGIN
    FOR outCartProductRow IN
      SELECT    p.product_id, p.name,
                COALESCE(NULLIF(p.discounted_price, 0), p.price) AS price,
                sc.quantity,
                COALESCE(NULLIF(p.discounted_price, 0),
p.price) * sc.quantity AS subtotal

      FROM       shopping_cart sc
      INNER JOIN product p
                  ON sc.product_id = p.product_id
      WHERE      sc.cart_id = inCartId AND buy_now
    LOOP
      RETURN NEXT outCartProductRow;
    END LOOP;
  END;
$$;
```

The `shopping_cart_get_products` function returns the products in the shopping cart mentioned by the `inCartId` parameter. Because the `shopping_cart` table only stores the `product_id` for each product it stores, you need to join the `shopping_cart` and `product` tables to get the information you need.

Note that some of the products can have discounted prices. When a product has a discounted price (which happens when its `discounted_price` value is different from 0), then its discounted price should be used for calculations. Otherwise, its list price should be used. The following expression returns `discounted_price` if different from 0; otherwise, it returns `price`.

```
COALESCE(NULLIF(p.discounted_price, 0), p.price)
```

Note This is the first time you've worked with the COALESCE and NULLIF PostgreSQL conditional expressions, so let's see what they do. COALESCE can receive any number of parameters, and it returns the first one that is not NULL. NULLIF receives two parameters and returns NULL if they're equal; otherwise, it returns the first of the parameters. In our case, we use NULLIF to test whether the `discounted_price` is 0; if this condition is true, NULLIF return false, and the COALESCE function will return p.price. If `discounted_price` is different from 0, the whole expression returns `discounted_price`.

---

7. Use the query tool to execute this code, which creates the `cart_saved_product` type and `shopping_cart_get_saved_products` functions in your `hatshop` database:

```
-- Create cart_saved_product type
CREATE TYPE cart_saved_product AS
(
  product_id INTEGER,
  name       VARCHAR(50),
  price      NUMERIC(10, 2)
);

-- Create shopping_cart_get_saved_products function
CREATE FUNCTION shopping_cart_get_saved_products(CHAR(32))
RETURNS SETOF cart_saved_product LANGUAGE plpgsql AS $$
  DECLARE
    inCartId ALIAS FOR $1;
    outCartSavedProductRow cart_saved_product;
  BEGIN
    FOR outCartSavedProductRow IN
      SELECT    p.product_id, p.name,
                COALESCE(NULLIF(p.discounted_price, 0), p.price) AS price
      FROM      shopping_cart sc
      INNER JOIN product p
                ON sc.product_id = p.product_id
      WHERE     sc.cart_id = inCartId AND NOT buy_now
```

```
    LOOP
      RETURN NEXT outCartSavedProductRow;
    END LOOP;
  END;
$$;
```

The shopping_cart_get_saved_products function returns the products saved for later in the shopping cart specified by the inCartId parameter.

8. Use the query tool to execute this code, which creates the shopping_cart_get_total_amount function in your hatshop database:

```
-- Create shopping_cart_get_total_amount function
CREATE FUNCTION shopping_cart_get_total_amount(CHAR(32))
RETURNS NUMERIC(10, 2) LANGUAGE plpgsql AS $$
  DECLARE
    inCartId ALIAS FOR $1;
    outTotalAmount NUMERIC(10, 2);
  BEGIN
    SELECT     INTO outTotalAmount
               SUM(COALESCE(NULLIF(p.discounted_price, 0), p.price)
                 * sc.quantity)
    FROM       shopping_cart sc
    INNER JOIN product p
                 ON sc.product_id = p.product_id
    WHERE      sc.cart_id = inCartId AND sc.buy_now;
    RETURN outTotalAmount;
  END;
$$;
```

The shopping_cart_get_total_amount function returns the total value of the products in the shopping cart. This is called when displaying the total amount for the shopping cart. If the cart is empty, total_amount will be 0.

9. Use the query tool to execute this code, which creates the shopping_cart_save_product_for_later function in your hatshop database:

```
-- Create shopping_cart_save_product_for_later function
CREATE FUNCTION shopping_cart_save_product_for_later(CHAR(32), INTEGER)
RETURNS VOID LANGUAGE plpgsql AS $$
  DECLARE
    inCartId    ALIAS FOR $1;
    inProductId ALIAS FOR $2;
  BEGIN
    UPDATE shopping_cart
    SET    buy_now = false, quantity = 1
    WHERE  cart_id = inCartId AND product_id = inProductId;
  END;
$$;
```

The shopping_cart_save_product_for_later function saves a shopping cart product to the Save for Later list so the visitor can buy it later (the product isn't sent to checkout when placing the order). This is done by setting the value of the buy_now field to false.

10. Use the query tool to execute this code, which creates the shopping_cart_move_product_to_cart function in your hatshop database:

```
-- Create shopping_cart_move_product_to_cart function
CREATE FUNCTION shopping_cart_move_product_to_cart(CHAR(32), INTEGER)
RETURNS VOID LANGUAGE plpgsql AS $$
  DECLARE
    inCartId    ALIAS FOR $1;
    inProductId ALIAS FOR $2;
  BEGIN
    UPDATE shopping_cart
    SET    buy_now = true, added_on = NOW()
    WHERE  cart_id = inCartId AND product_id = inProductId;
  END;
$$;
```

The shopping_cart_move_product_to_cart function sets a product's buy_now state to true, so the visitor can buy the product when placing the order.

Implementing the Business Tier

To implement the business tier, you'll need to create the usual methods that call the data object layer methods you've just written, and you'll add some new ones that manage business logic.

Exercise: Implementing the Shopping Cart Business Logic

1. First, add the following two lines at the end of your include/config.php file. These constants are used to differentiate between current shopping cart items and items that are saved for later:

```
// Shopping cart item types
define('GET_CART_PRODUCTS', 1);
define('GET_CART_SAVED_PRODUCTS', 2);
```

2. Include a reference to shopping_cart.php in include/app_top.php:

```
// Load Business Tier
require_once BUSINESS_DIR . 'catalog.php';
require_once BUSINESS_DIR . 'shopping_cart.php';
```

3. Create a new file called shopping_cart.php in the business folder. Add the following code to the file, and then we'll comment on it in the "How It Works" section:

```php
<?php
// Business tier class for the shopping cart
class ShoppingCart
{
  // Stores the visitor's Cart ID
  private static $_mCartId;

  // Private constructor to prevent direct creation of object
  private function __construct()
  {
  }

  /* This will be called by GetCartId to ensure we have the
     visitor's cart ID in the visitor's session in case
     $_mCartID has no value set */
  public static function SetCartId()
  {
    // If the cart ID hasn't already been set ...
    if (self::$_mCartId == '')
    {
      // If the visitor's cart ID is in the session, get it from there
      if (isset ($_SESSION['cart_id']))
      {
        self::$_mCartId = $_SESSION['cart_id'];
      }
      // If not, check if the cart ID was saved as a cookie
      elseif (isset ($_COOKIE['cart_id']))
      {
        // Save the cart ID from the cookie
        self::$_mCartId = $_COOKIE['cart_id'];
        $_SESSION['cart_id'] = self::$_mCartId;

        // Regenerate cookie to be valid for 7 days (604800 seconds)
        setcookie('cart_id', self::$_mCartId, time() + 604800);
      }
      else
      {
        /* Generate cart id and save it to the $_mCartId class member,
           the session and a cookie (on subsequent requests $_mCartId
           will be populated from the session) */
        self::$_mCartId = md5(uniqid(rand(), true));

        // Store cart id in session
        $_SESSION['cart_id'] = self::$_mCartId;

        // Cookie will be valid for 7 days (604800 seconds)
        setcookie('cart_id', self::$_mCartId, time() + 604800);
      }
```

```
    }
  }

  // Returns the current visitor's cart id
  public static function GetCartId()
  {
    // Ensure we have a cart id for the current visitor
    if (!isset (self::$_mCartId))
      self::SetCartId();

    return self::$_mCartId;
  }

  // Adds product to the shopping cart
  public static function AddProduct($productId)
  {
    // Build the SQL query
    $sql = 'SELECT shopping_cart_add_product(:cart_id, :product_id);';
    // Build the parameters array
    $params = array (':cart_id' => self::GetCartId(),
                     ':product_id' => $productId);
    // Prepare the statement with PDO-specific functionality
    $result = DatabaseHandler::Prepare($sql);

    // Execute the query
    return DatabaseHandler::Execute($result, $params);
  }

  /* Updates the shopping cart with new product quantities
     ($productId and $quantity are arrays that contain product ids
     and their respective quantities) */
  public static function Update($productId, $quantity)
  {
    // Build the SQL query
    $sql = 'SELECT shopping_cart_update(:cart_id, :product_id, :quantity);';
    // Build the parameters array
    $params = array (':cart_id' => self::GetCartId(),
                     ':product_id' => '{' . implode(', ', $productId) . '}',
                     ':quantity' =>  '{' . implode(', ', $quantity) . '}');
    // Prepare the statement with PDO-specific functionality
    $result = DatabaseHandler::Prepare($sql);

    // Execute the query
    return DatabaseHandler::Execute($result, $params);
  }
```

```php
// Removes product from shopping cart
public static function RemoveProduct($productId)
{
  // Build the SQL query
  $sql = 'SELECT shopping_cart_remove_product(:cart_id, :product_id);';
  // Build the parameters array
  $params = array (':cart_id' => self::GetCartId(),
                   ':product_id' => $productId);
  // Prepare the statement with PDO-specific functionality
  $result = DatabaseHandler::Prepare($sql);

  // Execute the query
  return DatabaseHandler::Execute($result, $params);
}

// Save product to the Save for Later list
public static function SaveProductForLater($productId)
{
  // Build the SQL query
  $sql = 'SELECT shopping_cart_save_product_for_later(
                 :cart_id, :product_id);';
  // Build the parameters array
  $params = array (':cart_id' => self::GetCartId(),
                   ':product_id' => $productId);
  // Prepare the statement with PDO-specific functionality
  $result = DatabaseHandler::Prepare($sql);

  // Execute the query
  return DatabaseHandler::Execute($result, $params);
}

// Get product from the Save for Later list back to the cart
public static function MoveProductToCart($productId)
{
  // Build the SQL query
  $sql = 'SELECT shopping_cart_move_product_to_cart(
                 :cart_id, :product_id);';
  // Build the parameters array
  $params = array (':cart_id' => self::GetCartId(),
                   ':product_id' => $productId);
  // Prepare the statement with PDO-specific functionality
  $result = DatabaseHandler::Prepare($sql);

  // Execute the query
  return DatabaseHandler::Execute($result, $params);
}
```

```php
  // Gets shopping cart products
  public static function GetCartProducts($cartProductsType)
  {
    $sql = '';
    // If retrieving "active" shopping cart products ...
    if ($cartProductsType == GET_CART_PRODUCTS)
    {
      // Build the SQL query
      $sql = 'SELECT * FROM shopping_cart_get_products(:cart_id);';
    }
    // If retrieving products saved for later ...
    elseif ($cartProductsType == GET_CART_SAVED_PRODUCTS)
    {
      // Build the SQL query
      $sql = 'SELECT * FROM shopping_cart_get_saved_products(:cart_id);';
    }
    else
      trigger_error($cartProductsType. ' value unknown', E_USER_ERROR);

    // Build the parameters array
    $params = array (':cart_id' => self::GetCartId());
    // Prepare the statement with PDO-specific functionality
    $result = DatabaseHandler::Prepare($sql);

    // Execute the query and return the results
    return DatabaseHandler::GetAll($result, $params);
  }

  /* Gets total amount of shopping cart products
     (not including the ones that are being saved for later) */
  public static function GetTotalAmount()
  {
    // Build the SQL query
    $sql = 'SELECT shopping_cart_get_total_amount(:cart_id);';
    // Build the parameters array
    $params = array (':cart_id' => self::GetCartId());
    // Prepare the statement with PDO-specific functionality
    $result = DatabaseHandler::Prepare($sql);

    // Execute the query and return the results
    return DatabaseHandler::GetOne($result, $params);
  }
}
?>
```

How It Works: The Business Tier Part of the Shopping Cart

When a visitor adds a product or requests any shopping cart operation, you'll have to generate a shopping cart ID for the visitor if he doesn't have one. You take care of this in the SetCartId method in the ShoppingCart class to ensure that the visitor's cart ID is saved in the $_mCartID member of the ShoppingCart class. The shopping cart ID is cached in the visitor's session and in a persistent cookie.

The function starts by verifying that the $_mCartId member was already set, in which case, we don't need to read it from external sources:

```
public static function SetCartId()
{
  // If the cart ID hasn't already been set ...
  if (self::$_mCartId == '')
  {
```

If we don't have the ID in the member variable, the next place to look is the visitor's session:

```
    // If the visitor's cart ID is in the session, get it from there
    if (isset ($_SESSION['cart_id']))
    {
      self::$_mCartId = $_SESSION['cart_id'];
    }
```

If the ID couldn't be found in the session either, we check whether it was saved as a cookie. If yes, we save the value both to the session and to the $_mCartId member, and we regenerate the cookie to reset its expiration date:

```
    // If not, check if the cart ID was saved as a cookie
    elseif (isset ($_COOKIE['cart_id']))
    {
      // Save the cart ID from the cookie
      self::$_mCartId = $_COOKIE['cart_id'];
      $_SESSION['cart_id'] = self::$_mCartId;

      // Regenerate cookie to be valid for 7 days (604800 seconds)
      setcookie('cart_id', self::$_mCartId, time() + 604800);
    }
```

Finally, if the cart ID can't be found anywhere, a new one is generated and saved to the session, to the $_mCartId member, and to the persistent cookie:

```
    else
    {
      /* Generate cart id and save it to the $_mCartId class member,
         the session and a cookie (on subsequent requests $_mCartId
         will be populated from the session) */
      self::$_mCartId = md5(uniqid(rand(), true));

      // Store cart id in session
      $_SESSION['cart_id'] = self::$_mCartId;
```

```
      // Cookie will be valid for 7 days (604800 seconds)
      setcookie('cart_id', self::$_mCartId, time() + 604800);
    }
  }
}
```

Three functions are used to generate the cart ID: md5, uniqid, and rand. The call to md5(uniqid(rand(),true)) generates a unique, difficult-to-predict, 32-byte value, which represents the cart ID.

▓Note If you're interested to know the details about generating the cart ID, here they are. The md5 function uses the MD5 Message-Digest Algorithm to calculate the hash value of the value it receives as parameter; it always returns a 32.The uniqid function returns a unique identifier based on the current time in microseconds; its first parameter is the prefix to be appended to its generated value, in this case, the rand() function that returns a pseudo-random value between 0 and RAND_MAX, which is platform dependent. If the second parameter of uniqid is true, uniqid adds an additional *combined LCG* (combined Linear Congruential Generator) entropy at the end of the return value, which should make the results even "more unique."

In short, uniquid(rand(), true) generates a "very unique" value, which is passed through md5 to ensure that it becomes a random sequence of characters that is 32 characters long.

The SetCartId method is used only by the GetCartId method that returns the cart ID. GetCartID first checks to see whether _mCartId has been set, and if not, it calls SetCartId before returning the value of $_mCartId:

```
  // Returns the current visitor's cart id
  public static function GetCartId()
  {
    // Ensure we have a cart id for the current visitor
    if (!isset (self::$_mCartId))
      self::SetCartId();

    return self::$_mCartId;
  }
```

Let's also take a look at the GetCartProducts method. This method returns the products in the shopping cart. It receives $cartProductsType as a parameter, which determines whether you're looking for the current shopping cart products or for the products saved for later.

If $cartProductsType is equal to the GET_CART_PRODUCTS constant, GetCartProducts will return the shopping cart products. If the $cartProductsType is equal to the GET_CART_SAVED_PRODUCTS constant, GetCartProducts will return the Save for Later products. If $cartProductsType is neither GET_CART_PRODUCTS nor GET_CART_SAVED_PRODUCTS, the method will raise an error.

All the other business tier methods you've written basically call their associated data tier functions to perform the various shopping cart tasks.

Implementing the Presentation Tier

Now let's build the user interface (UI) part of the shopping cart. After updating the storefront, you'll have Add to Cart buttons for each product and a View Cart link in the cart summary box in the left part of the page. If the visitor's cart is empty, the link isn't displayed anymore, as you can see in Figure 8-4.

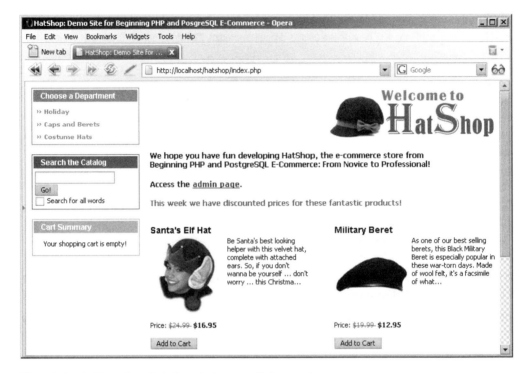

Figure 8-4. *The View Cart link doesn't show up if the cart is empty.*

If you added PayPal integration as presented in Chapter 6, you'll already have these buttons on your site, and you'll update their functionality here.

When clicking on View Cart, the shopping cart componentized template (which you'll build later) is loaded in `index.tpl`. You can see this componentized component in action in Figure 8-1, shown earlier.

The mechanism for loading the shopping cart componentized template is the same one you already used in `index.php` to load other components. When the Add to Cart button is clicked, `index.php` is reloaded with an additional parameter (`CartAction`) in the query string:

```
http://localhost/hatshop/index.php?CartAction=1&ProductID=10
```

When clicking on View Cart, the `CartAction` parameter added to the query string doesn't take any value.

The shopping cart will have five cart actions, which are described using the following self-explanatory constants in the configuration file (`include/config.php`): `ADD_PRODUCT`, `REMOVE_PRODUCT`, `UPDATE_PRODUCTS_QUANTITIES`, `SAVE_PRODUCT_FOR_LATER`, and `MOVE_PRODUCT_TO_CART`.

Before moving on, let's recap the main steps you'll take to implement the whole UI of the shopping cart:

1. Modify the Add to Cart buttons to use the custom shopping cart.

2. Add a "shopping cart summary" box to `index.tpl` instead of the View Cart button.

3. Modify `index.php` to recognize the `CartAction` query string parameter.

4. Implement the `cart_details` componentized template.

Updating the Add to Cart Buttons

You need to change the code of `products_list.tpl` so that each displayed product includes an Add to Cart button with a link like the ones shown earlier (a link to `index.php` with an additional `CartAction` parameter in the query string).

Exercise: Adding Products to the New Shopping Cart

1. Add the following code at the end of `include/config.php`:

```
// Cart actions
define('ADD_PRODUCT', 1);
define('REMOVE_PRODUCT', 2);
define('UPDATE_PRODUCTS_QUANTITIES', 3);
define('SAVE_PRODUCT_FOR_LATER', 4);
define('MOVE_PRODUCT_TO_CART', 5);
```

2. If you implemented the PayPal shopping cart, you need to change the Add to Cart buttons to link to the Hat-Shop web site instead of PayPal. Open `presentation/templates/products_list.tpl`, and replace the code that calls the `OpenPayPalWindow()` function:

```
<input type="button" name="add_to_cart" value="Add to Cart"
onclick="{$products_list->mProducts[k].paypal}" />
```

with the following code:

```
<input type="button" name="add_to_cart" value="Add to Cart"
onclick="javascript:window.location=
  '{$products_list->mProducts[k].add_to_cart|prepare_link:"http"}';" />
```

3. Open `presentation/smarty_plugins/function.load_products_list.php`; find the following code from the `init()` method of the `ProductList` class that builds PayPal links:

```
  // Create the PayPal link
  $this->mProducts[$i]['paypal'] =
    'JavaScript:OpenPayPalWindow(&quot;' .
    'https://www.paypal.com/cgi-bin/webscr?' .
    'cmd=_cart&amp;business=youremail@example.com' .
    '&amp;item_name=' . rawurlencode($this->mProducts[$i]['name']) .
    '&amp;amount=' .
```

```
(($this->mProducts[$i]['discounted_price'] == 0) ?
 $this->mProducts[$i]['price'] :
 $this->mProducts[$i]['discounted_price']) .
 '&amp;currency=USD&amp;add=1&amp;return=www.example.com' .
 '&amp;cancel_return=www.example.com&quot;)';
```

Replace it with the following code that builds the Add to Cart links for our shopping cart:

```
// Create the Add to Cart link
$this->mProducts[$i]['add_to_cart'] = $this->mProducts[$i]['link'] .
                                      '&CartAction=' . ADD_PRODUCT;
```

4. Let's also create Add to Cart links in product.tpl. First, add the following highlighted code to presentation/templates/product.tpl, just before the Continue Shopping button:

```
<br /><br />
<input type="button" name="add_to_cart" value="Add to Cart"
 onclick="window.location=
   '{$product->mAddToCartLink|prepare_link:"http"}';" />
<input type="button" value="Continue Shopping"
 onclick="window.location='{$product->mPageLink|prepare_link:"http"}';" />
```

5. Open presentation/smarty_plugins/function.load_product.php, and add the $mAddToCartLink member to the Product class:

```
// Public variables to be used in Smarty template
public $mProduct;
public $mPageLink = 'index.php';
public $mAddToCartLink;
```

6. In the same file, add the following code at the end of the init() method of the Product class. This creates the link for the Add to Cart button:

```
$this->mAddToCartLink = 'index.php?ProductID=' . $this->_mProductId .
                        '&CartAction=' . ADD_PRODUCT;
```

How It Works: Adding Products Links

You created Add to Cart buttons that link to index.php with an additional CartAction parameter to the original query string. After making this change, execute the page to make sure you have your button in place, although you can't really test how they work until finishing the presentation tier. If you browse now to your favorite department, and click the Add to Cart button of one of the products, index.php is reloaded with the additional CartAction parameter appended at the beginning of the query string: http://localhost/hatshop/ index.php?CartAction=1&ProductID=10.

At this moment, this links gets you to the product details page because your site doesn't know yet how to interpret the CartAction query string parameter. The value of the CartAction parameter represents the value of one of the constants you just added to include/config.php.

Displaying the Cart Summary in the Main Page

Instead of PayPal's View Cart buttons, we want to have a cart summary component with a view details link, as shown in the screenshots at the beginning of this chapter.

Now follow the steps to implement the cart_summary componentized template by following the steps of the exercise.

Exercise: Displaying the Cart Summary

1. Let's start by removing the View Cart button. Locate and delete the following code in presentation/ templates/index.tpl (feel free to also remove the OpenPayPalWindow function completely):

```
<div class="left_box" id="view_cart">
  <input type="button" name="view_cart" value="View Cart"
    onclick="JavaScript:OpenPayPalWindow(&quot;...&quot;)" />
</div>
```

2. In the same file, add a reference to the cart summary component:

```
{include file="departments_list.tpl"}
{include file="$categoriesCell"}
{include file="search_box.tpl"}
{include file="$cartSummaryCell"}
```

3. Open index.php, and update it as highlighted in the following code snippet. This way, index.php will recognize the CartAction query string parameter.

```
// Define the template file for the categories cell
$categoriesCell = 'blank.tpl';

// Define the template file for the cart summary cell
$cartSummaryCell = 'blank.tpl';

// Load department details if visiting a department
if (isset ($_GET['DepartmentID']))
{
  $pageContentsCell = 'department.tpl';
  $categoriesCell = 'categories_list.tpl';
}

// Load search result page if we're searching the catalog
if (isset ($_GET['Search']))
  $pageContentsCell = 'search_results.tpl';

// Load product details page if visiting a product
if (isset ($_GET['ProductID']))
  $pageContentsCell = 'product.tpl';

if (isset ($_GET['CartAction']))
{
```

```
      $pageContentsCell = 'cart_details.tpl';
    }
    else
      $cartSummaryCell = 'cart_summary.tpl';

    // Assign a template file to the cart summary cell
    $page->assign('cartSummaryCell', $cartSummaryCell);

    // Assign a template file to the page contents cell
    $page->assign('pageContentsCell', $pageContentsCell);
```

4. Create a new file named presentation/smarty_plugins/function.load_cart_summary.php,
   and add the following code to it:

```php
<?php
// Plugin functions inside plugin files must be named: smarty_type_name
function smarty_function_load_cart_summary($params, $smarty)
{
  // Create CartSummary object
  $cart_summary = new CartSummary();

  // Assign template variable
  $smarty->assign($params['assign'], $cart_summary);
}

// Class that deals with managing the shopping cart summary
class CartSummary
{
  // Public variables to be used in Smarty template
  public $mTotalAmount;
  public $mItems;
  public $mEmptyCart;

  // Class constructor
  public function __construct()
  {
    // Calculate the total amount for the shopping cart
    $this->mTotalAmount = ShoppingCart::GetTotalAmount();

    // Get shopping cart products
    $this->mItems = ShoppingCart::GetCartProducts(GET_CART_PRODUCTS);

    if (empty($this->mItems))
      $this->mEmptyCart = true;
    else
      $this->mEmptyCart = false;
  }
}
?>
```

5. Create a new file in the `presentation/templates` folder named `cart_summary.tpl`, and write the following code to it:

```
{* cart_summary.tpl *}
{load_cart_summary assign="cart_summary"}
{* Start cart summary *}
<div class="left_box" id="cart_summary_box">
  <p>Cart Summary</p>
{if $cart_summary->mEmptyCart}
  <span class="cart_empty">Your shopping cart is empty!</span>
{else}
  <ol class="cart_items_list">
  {section name=cCartSummary loop=$cart_summary->mItems}
    <li>
    {$cart_summary->mItems[cCartSummary].quantity} x
    {$cart_summary->mItems[cCartSummary].name}
    </li>
  {/section}
  </ol>
  <span class="cart_items_total">
    ${$cart_summary->mTotalAmount}
    ( <a href="{"index.php?CartAction"|prepare_link:"http"}">View details</a> )
  </span>
{/if}
</div>
{* End cart summary *}
```

6. Add the following styles to `hatshop.css`:

```
#cart_summary_box
{
  border: 1px solid #efba00;
}
#cart_summary_box p
{
  background: #efba00;
}
.cart_empty
{
  display: block;
  text-align: center;
  margin: 10px;
}
.cart_items_list
{
  border-bottom: 1px solid #000000;
  padding: 3px;
}
.cart_items_total
```

```
  {
    display: block;
    font-weight: bold;
    margin-left: 8px;
  }
```

How It Works: Displaying the Cart Summary

If you reload HatShop, you'll now see the cart summary box on the left side of the page. At this point, you still can't add new products to your cart yet because you need to create the cart details page. You'll be able to fully test your cart summary component after you implement the cart details page in the next exercise.

Displaying the Cart Details

Right now, clicking on the Add to Cart or View Cart buttons generates an error because you haven't written the cart_details componentized template yet (this displays the visitor's shopping cart details). To create the new componentized template, you first create a new template named cart_details.tpl in the Templates folder. Next, you create the function.load_cart_details.php file that will keep your function plugin and CartDetails class behind the cart_details.tpl template.

Exercise: Creating the shopping_cart Template

1. Update index.php to avoid saving the page_link session item (used for building the Continue Shopping links) when visiting the shopping cart:

```php
/* If not visiting a product page, save the link to the current page
   in the page_link session variable; it will be used to create the
   Continue Shopping link in the product details page and the links
   to product details pages */
if (!isset ($_GET['ProductID']) && !isset ($_GET['CartAction']))
  $_SESSION['page_link'] = substr(getenv('REQUEST_URI'),
                                  strrpos(getenv('REQUEST_URI'), '/') + 1,
                                  strlen(getenv('REQUEST_URI')) - 1);
```

2. Create a new file named presentation/smarty_plugins/function.load_cart_details.php, and add the following code to it:

```php
<?php
// Plugin functions inside plugin files must be named: smarty_type_name
function smarty_function_load_cart_details($params, $smarty)
{

  $cart_details = new CartDetails();
  $cart_details->init();
```

```
  // Assign template variable
  $smarty->assign($params['assign'], $cart_details);
}

// Class that deals with managing the shopping cart
class CartDetails
{
  // Public variables available in smarty template
  public $mCartProducts;
  public $mSavedCartProducts;
  public $mTotalAmount;
  public $mIsCartNowEmpty = 0; // Is the shopping cart empty?
  public $mIsCartLaterEmpty = 0; // Is the 'saved for later' list empty?
  public $mCartReferrer = 'index.php';
  public $mCartDetailsTarget;

  // Private attributes
  private $_mProductId;
  private $_mCartAction;

  // Class constructor
  public function __construct()
  {
    // Setting the "Continue shopping" button target
    if (isset ($_SESSION['page_link']))
      $this->mCartReferrer = $_SESSION['page_link'];

    if (isset ($_GET['CartAction']))
      $this->mCartAction = $_GET['CartAction'];
    else
      trigger_error('CartAction not set', E_USER_ERROR);

    // These cart operations require a valid product id
    if ($this->mCartAction == ADD_PRODUCT ||
        $this->mCartAction == REMOVE_PRODUCT ||
        $this->mCartAction == SAVE_PRODUCT_FOR_LATER ||
        $this->mCartAction == MOVE_PRODUCT_TO_CART)

    if (isset ($_GET['ProductID']))
      $this->mProductId = $_GET['ProductID'];
    else
      trigger_error('ProductID must be set for this type of request',
                    E_USER_ERROR);

    $this->mCartDetailsTarget = 'index.php?CartAction=' .
                                UPDATE_PRODUCTS_QUANTITIES;
  }
```

```php
public function init()
{
  switch ($this->mCartAction)
  {
    case ADD_PRODUCT:
      ShoppingCart::AddProduct($this->mProductId);
      header('Location: ' . $this->mCartReferrer);

      break;
    case REMOVE_PRODUCT:
      ShoppingCart::RemoveProduct($this->mProductId);

      break;
    case UPDATE_PRODUCTS_QUANTITIES:
      ShoppingCart::Update($_POST['productID'], $_POST['quantity']);

      break;
    case SAVE_PRODUCT_FOR_LATER:
      ShoppingCart::SaveProductForLater($this->mProductId);

      break;
    case MOVE_PRODUCT_TO_CART:
      ShoppingCart::MoveProductToCart($this->mProductId);

      break;
    default:
      // Do nothing
      break;
  }

  // Calculate the total amount for the shopping cart
  $this->mTotalAmount = ShoppingCart::GetTotalAmount();

  // Get shopping cart products
  $this->mCartProducts =
    ShoppingCart::GetCartProducts(GET_CART_PRODUCTS);

  // Gets the Saved for Later products
  $this->mSavedCartProducts =
    ShoppingCart::GetCartProducts(GET_CART_SAVED_PRODUCTS);

  // Check whether we have an empty shopping cart
  if (count($this->mCartProducts) == 0)
    $this->mIsCartNowEmpty = 1;

  // Check whether we have an empty Saved for Later list
```

```
      if (count($this->mSavedCartProducts) == 0)
        $this->mIsCartLaterEmpty = 1;

      // Build the links for cart actions
      for ($i = 0; $i < count($this->mCartProducts); $i++)
      {
        $this->mCartProducts[$i]['save'] = 'index.php?ProductID=' .
          $this->mCartProducts[$i]['product_id'] .
          '&CartAction=' . SAVE_PRODUCT_FOR_LATER;

        $this->mCartProducts[$i]['remove'] = 'index.php?ProductID=' .
          $this->mCartProducts[$i]['product_id'] .
          '&CartAction=' . REMOVE_PRODUCT;
      }

      for ($i = 0; $i < count($this->mSavedCartProducts); $i++)
      {
        $this->mSavedCartProducts[$i]['move'] = 'index.php?ProductID=' .
          $this->mSavedCartProducts[$i]['product_id'] .
          '&CartAction=' . MOVE_PRODUCT_TO_CART;

        $this->mSavedCartProducts[$i]['remove'] = 'index.php?ProductID=' .
          $this->mSavedCartProducts[$i]['product_id'] .
          '&CartAction=' . REMOVE_PRODUCT;
      }
    }
  }
}
?>
```

3. Create a new file named cart_details.tpl in the presentation/templates folder, and add the following code to it:

```
{* cart_details.tpl *}
{load_cart_details assign="cart_details"}
{if ($cart_details->mIsCartNowEmpty == 1)}
<span class="description">Your shopping cart is empty!</span>
<br /><br />
{else}
<span class="description">These are the products in your shopping cart:</span>
<br /><br />
<form method="post"
 action="{$cart_details->mCartDetailsTarget|prepare_link:"http"}">
  <table>
    <tr>
      <th>Product Name</th>
      <th>Price</th>
      <th>Quantity</th>
      <th>Subtotal</th>
```

```
        <th> </th>
      </tr>
    {section name=cCart loop=$cart_details->mCartProducts}
      <tr>
        <td>
          <input name="productID[]" type="hidden"
           value="{$cart_details->mCartProducts[cCart].product_id}" />
          {$cart_details->mCartProducts[cCart].name}
        </td>
        <td>${$cart_details->mCartProducts[cCart].price}</td>
        <td>
          <input type="text" name="quantity[]" size="10"
           value="{$cart_details->mCartProducts[cCart].quantity}" />
        </td>
        <td>${$cart_details->mCartProducts[cCart].subtotal}</td>
        <td align="right">
          <input type="button" name="saveForLater" value="Save for later"
           onclick="window.location=
             '{$cart_details->mCartProducts[cCart].save|prepare_link}';" />
          <input type="button" name="remove" value="Remove"
           onclick="window.location=
             '{$cart_details->mCartProducts[cCart].remove|prepare_link}';" />
        </td>
      </tr>
    {/section}
    </table>
    <table>
      <tr>
        <td class="cart_total">
          <span>Total amount:</span> 
          <span class="price">${$cart_details->mTotalAmount}</span>
        </td>
        <td class="cart_total" align="right">
          <input type="submit" name="update" value="Update" />
        </td>
      </tr>
    </table>
</form>
{/if}
{if ($cart_details->mIsCartLaterEmpty == 0)}
<br />
<span class="description">Saved products to buy later:</span>
<br /><br />
<table>
  <tr>
    <th>Product Name</th>
    <th>Price</th>
```

```
      <th> </th>
    </tr>
    {section name=cSavedCart loop=$cart_details->mSavedCartProducts}
    <tr>
      <td>{$cart_details->mSavedCartProducts[cSavedCart].name}</td>
      <td>
        ${$cart_details->mSavedCartProducts[cSavedCart].price}
      </td>
      <td align="right">
        <input type="button" name="moveToCart" value="Move to cart"
         onclick="window.location=
           '{$cart_details->mSavedCartProducts[cSavedCart].move|prepare_link}';"
         />
        <input type="button" name="remove" value="Remove"
         onclick="window.location=
         '{$cart_details->mSavedCartProducts[cSavedCart].remove|prepare_link}';"
         />
      </td>
    </tr>
    {/section}
  </table>
{/if}
<br />
<input type="button" name="continueShopping" value="Continue Shopping"
 onclick="window.location='{$cart_details->mCartReferrer}';" />
```

4. Add the following styles to `hatshop.css`:

```
.cart_total
{
  background: #ffffff;
  border: none;
}
```

You just finished the visitor's part of the code for this chapter, so now it's time to try it out and make sure everything works as expected. Test it by adding products to the shopping cart, changing the quantity, and removing items.

How It Works: The Shopping Cart

The actions that the shopping cart can execute are defined by the following constants defined in `include/config.php`: `ADD_PRODUCT`, `REMOVE_PRODUCT`, `UPDATE_PRODUCTS_QUANTITIES`, `SAVE_PRODUCT_FOR_LATER`, and `MOVE_PRODUCT_TO_CART`. Note that we didn't define any variable for viewing the shopping cart, so if `CartAction` does not take any value or its value is not equal to one of the action variables, it will simply display the shopping cart content.

Every shopping cart action, except viewing and updating the shopping cart, relies on the `ProductID` query string parameter (an error is raised if it isn't set). If the proper conditions are met, the business tier method that corresponds to the visitor's action is called.

Administering the Shopping Cart

Now that you've finished writing the shopping cart, there are two more things you need to take into account, both related to administration issues:

- How to delete from the catalog a product that exists in shopping carts.

- How to count or remove old shopping cart elements by building a simple shopping cart administration page. This is important because without this feature, the shopping_cart table keeps growing, filled with old temporary (and useless) carts.

Deleting Products Residing in the Shopping Cart

The catalog administration pages enable you to completely delete products from the catalog. Before removing a product, you should also remove its appearances in visitors' shopping carts.

Update the catalog_delete_product function from the hatshop database by following these steps:

1. Load pgAdmin III, and connect to the hatshop database.

2. Click Tools ➤ Query tool (or click the SQL button on the toolbar). A new query window should appear.

3. Use the query tool to execute this code, which updates the catalog_delete_product function from your hatshop database:

```
-- Updates catalog_delete_product function
CREATE OR REPLACE FUNCTION catalog_delete_product(INTEGER)
RETURNS VOID LANGUAGE plpgsql AS $$
  DECLARE
    inProductId ALIAS FOR $1;
  BEGIN
    DELETE FROM product_category WHERE product_id = inProductId;
    DELETE FROM shopping_cart WHERE product_id = inProductId;
    DELETE FROM product WHERE product_id = inProductId;
  END;
$$;
```

Building the Shopping Cart Admin Page

The second problem with the shopping cart is that at this moment no mechanism exists to delete the old records from the shopping_cart table. On a high-activity web site, the shopping_cart table can grow very large.

With the current version of the code, shopping cart IDs are stored at the client browser for seven days. As a result, you can assume that any shopping carts that haven't been updated in the last ten days are invalid and can be safely removed.

In the following exercise, you'll quickly implement a simple shopping cart administration page, where the administrator can see how many old shopping cart entries exist, and can delete them if he or she wants to. Figure 8-5 shows this page.

Figure 8-5. *Administering shopping carts*

The most interesting aspect you need to understand is the SQL logic that deletes all shopping carts that haven't been updated in a certain amount of time. This isn't as simple as it sounds—at first sight, you might think all you have to do is delete all the records in shopping_cart whose added_on is older than a specified date. However, this strategy doesn't work with shopping carts that are modified over time (say, the visitor has been adding items to the cart each week in the past three months). If the last change to the shopping cart is recent, none of its elements should be deleted, even if some are very old. In other words, you should either remove all elements in a shopping cart or none of them. The age of a shopping cart is given by the age of its most recently modified or added product.

This being said, implement the new functionality by following the exercise steps.

Exercise: Creating the Shopping Cart Admin Page

1. Load pgAdmin III, and connect to the hatshop database.

2. Add the following data tier functions to the hatshop database:

```
-- Create shopping_cart_count_old_carts function
CREATE FUNCTION shopping_cart_count_old_carts(INTEGER)
RETURNS INTEGER LANGUAGE plpgsql AS $$
  DECLARE
    inDays ALIAS FOR $1;
    outOldShoppingCartsCount INTEGER;
  BEGIN
    SELECT INTO outOldShoppingCartsCount
           COUNT(cart_id)
    FROM   (SELECT   cart_id
            FROM     shopping_cart
```

```
                  GROUP BY cart_id
                  HAVING    ((NOW() - ('1'||' DAYS')::INTERVAL) >= MAX(added_on)))
                AS old_carts;
          RETURN outOldShoppingCartsCount;
       END;
    $$;


    -- Create shopping_cart_delete_old_carts function
    CREATE FUNCTION shopping_cart_delete_old_carts(INTEGER)
    RETURNS VOID LANGUAGE plpgsql AS $$
       DECLARE
          inDays ALIAS FOR $1;
       BEGIN
          DELETE FROM shopping_cart
          WHERE cart_id IN
                (SELECT    cart_id
                   FROM    shopping_cart
                   GROUP BY cart_id
                   HAVING   ((NOW() - (inDays||' DAYS')::INTERVAL) >= MAX(added_on)));
       END;
    $$;
```

3. Add the following business tier method to business/shopping_cart.php:

```php
    // Count old shopping carts
    public static function CountOldShoppingCarts($days)
    {
      // Build SQL query
      $sql = 'SELECT shopping_cart_count_old_carts(:days);';
      // Build the parameters array
      $params = array (':days' => $days);
      // Prepare the statement with PDO-specific functionality
      $result = DatabaseHandler::Prepare($sql);

      // Execute the query and return the results
      return DatabaseHandler::GetOne($result, $params);
    }

    // Deletes old shopping carts
    public static function DeleteOldShoppingCarts($days)
    {
      // Build the SQL query
      $sql = 'SELECT shopping_cart_delete_old_carts(:days);';
      // Build the parameters array
      $params = array (':days' => $days);
      // Prepare the statement with PDO-specific functionality
      $result = DatabaseHandler::Prepare($sql);
```

```
    // Execute the query
    return DatabaseHandler::Execute($result, $params);
  }
```

4. Create a new file named presentation/smarty_plugins/function.load_admin_cart.php, and add the following code to it:

```php
<?php
/* Smarty plugin function that gets called when the
   load_admin_cart function plugin is loaded from a template */
function smarty_function_load_admin_cart($params, $smarty)
{
  // Create AdminCart object
  $admin_cart = new AdminCart();
  $admin_cart->init();

  // Assign template variable
  $smarty->assign($params['assign'], $admin_cart);
}

// Class that supports cart admin functionality
class AdminCart
{
  // Public variables available in smarty template
  public $mMessage;
  public $mDaysOptions = array (0  => 'All shopping carts',
                                1  => 'One day old',
                                10 => 'Ten days old',
                                20 => 'Twenty days old',
                                30 => 'Thirty days old',
                                90 => 'Ninety days old');
  public $mSelectedDaysNumber = 0;

  // Private members
  public $_mAction = '';

  // Class constructor
  public function __construct()
  {
    foreach ($_POST as $key => $value)
      // If a submit button was clicked ...
      if (substr($key, 0, 6) == 'submit')
      {
        // Get the scope of submit button
        $this->_mAction = substr($key, strlen('submit_'), strlen($key));

        // Get selected days number
        if (isset ($_POST['days']))
```

```
              $this->mSelectedDaysNumber = (int) $_POST['days'];
            else
              trigger_error('days value not set');
          }
      }

    public function init()
    {
      // If counting shopping carts ...
      if ($this->_mAction == 'count')
      {
        $count_old_carts =
          ShoppingCart::CountOldShoppingCarts($this->mSelectedDaysNumber);

        if ($count_old_carts == 0)
          $count_old_carts = 'no';

        $this->mMessage = 'There are ' . $count_old_carts .
                          ' old shopping carts (selected option: ' .
                          $this->mDaysOptions[$this->mSelectedDaysNumber] .
                          ').';
      }

      // If deleting shopping carts ...
      if ($this->_mAction == 'delete')
      {
        $this->mDeletedCarts =
          ShoppingCart::DeleteOldShoppingCarts($this->mSelectedDaysNumber);

        $this->mMessage = 'The old shopping carts were removed from the
          database (selected option: ' .
          $this->mDaysOptions[$this->mSelectedDaysNumber] .').').';
      }
    }
  }
?>
```

5. Create a new file in the presentation/templates folder named admin_cart.tpl, and type the
   following code:

```
{* admin_cart.tpl *}
{load_admin_cart assign='admin_cart'}
<span class="admin_page_text">Admin users&#039; shopping carts:</span>
<br /><br />
{if $admin_cart->mMessage neq ""}
<span  class="admin_page_text">{$admin_cart->mMessage}</span>
<br /><br />
{/if}
```

```
<form action="{"admin.php?Page=Cart"|prepare_link:"https"}" method="post">
  <span class="admin_page_text">Select carts</span>
  {html_options name="days" options=$admin_cart->mDaysOptions
              selected=$admin_cart->mSelectedDaysNumber}
  <input type="submit" name="submit_count" value="Count Old Shopping Carts" />
  <input type="submit" name="submit_delete" value="Delete Old Shopping Carts" />
</form>
```

6. Modify `presentation/templates/admin_menu.tpl` by adding the highlighted link code to the cart admin page:

```
<span class="menu_text"> |
  <a href="{"admin.php?Page=Cart"|prepare_link:"https"}">CART ADMIN</a> |
  <a href="{"admin.php"|prepare_link:"https"}">CATALOG ADMIN</a> |
```

7. Add the highlighted code that loads the `admin_cart.tpl` in `admin.php`:

```
elseif ($admin_page == 'ProductDetails')
  $pageContentsCell = 'admin_product.tpl';
elseif ($admin_page == 'Cart')
  $pageContentsCell = 'admin_cart.tpl';
```

How It Works: The Shopping Cart Admin Page

The hard work of the shopping cart admin page is done by the two functions you've added to the `hatshop` database: `shopping_cart_count_old_carts` and `shopping_cart_delete_old_carts`. They both receive as parameter the number of days that determine when a shopping cart is old, and they use the same logic to calculate the shopping cart elements that are old and should be removed.

The age of a shopping cart is given by the age of the most recently added or changed item and is calculated using the GROUP BY SQL clause. The condition that establishes whether a cart should be considered old is the following:

```
WHERE  cart_id IN
       (SELECT  cart_id
        FROM    shopping_cart
        GROUP BY cart_id
        HAVING ((NOW() - (inDays||' DAYS')::INTERVAL) >= MAX(added_on)));
```

Summary

In this chapter, you learned how to store the shopping cart information in the database, and you learned a few things in the process as well. Probably the most interesting was the way you can store the shopping cart ID as a cookie on the client because you haven't done anything similar so far in this book.

After working through the process of creating the shopping cart, starting with the database and ending with the presentation tier, we also touched on the new administrative challenges.

You'll complete the functionality offered by the custom shopping cart in the next chapter with a custom checkout system. You'll add a Place Order button to the shopping cart, which will allow you to save the shopping cart information as a separate order in the database.

CHAPTER 9

■■■

Dealing with Customer Orders

The good news is that your shopping cart looks good and is fully functional. The bad news is that it doesn't allow the visitor to actually place an order, which makes the cart totally useless in the context of a production system. We'll deal with that problem in this chapter in two separate stages. In the first part of the chapter, you'll implement the client-side part of the order-placing mechanism. More precisely, you'll add a Place Order button to the shopping cart control, which will allow the visitor to order the products in the shopping cart.

In the second part of the chapter, you'll implement a simple orders administration page where the site administrator can view and handle pending orders.

The code for each part of the site will be presented in the usual way, starting with the database tier, continuing with the business tier, and finishing with the user interface (UI).

Implementing an Order Placement System

The entire order-placement system is related to the Place Order button mentioned earlier. Figure 9-1 shows how this button will look after you update the `cart_details` componentized template in this chapter.

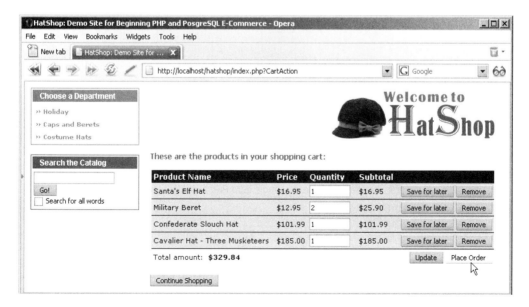

Figure 9-1. *The shopping cart with a Place Order button*

The button looks quite boring for something that we can honestly say is the center of this chapter's universe. Still, a lot of logic is hidden behind it, so let's talk about what should happen when the customer clicks that button. Remember that at this stage we don't care who places the order, but we do want to store information in the database about the products that were ordered.

Basically, two things need to happen when the customer clicks the Place Order button:

- First, the order must be stored somewhere in the database. This means that you must save the shopping cart's products to an order named HatShop Order ***nnn*** and clear the shopping cart.

- Secondly, the customer is redirected to a PayPal payment page where the customer pays the necessary amount for the order. You can see the PayPal payment page in Figure 9-2.

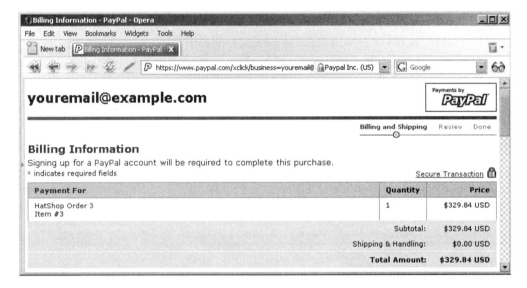

Figure 9-2. *The PayPal payment page*

■**Note** For the second development stage, we still don't process payments ourselves but use a third-party payment processor instead. Now we no longer need the PayPal shopping cart because we implemented our own in the previous chapter. Instead, we'll use the Single Item Purchases option of PayPal, which redirects the visitor directly to a payment page.

A problem that arises when using a third-party payment processor is that the customer can change his mind and cancel the order while at the checkout page. This can result in orders that are saved to the database (the order is saved before the page is redirected to the payment page) but for which payment wasn't completed. Obviously, we need a payment confirmation system, along with a database structure that is able to store status information about each order.

The confirmation system that you'll implement is simple. Every payment processor, including PayPal, can be instructed to send a confirmation message after a payment has been processed. We'll allow the site administrator to manually check, in the administration page, which orders have been paid for. These orders are known as verified orders. You'll see later in this chapter how to manage them in the orders-management part of the site.

■**Note** PayPal and its competitors offer automated systems that inform your web site when a payment has been completed or canceled. However, this book doesn't visit the intimate details of any of these payment systems—you'll need to do your homework and study the documentation of your company of choice. The PayPal Instant Payment Notification documentation is included in the Order Management Integration Guide, which can be downloaded at https://www.paypal.com/en_US/pdf/ PP_OrderManagement_IntegrationGuide.pdf.

Now that you have an idea of what to do with that Place Order button, the next major concerns are what order information to store in the database and how to store it. As you saw in previous chapters, deciding how to store information helps you get a better idea of how the whole system works.

Storing Orders in the Database

Two kinds of order information need to be stored:

- General details about the order, such as the date the order was created; whether and when the products have been shipped; whether the order is verified, completed, or canceled; and a few other details

- The products that belong to that order and their quantities

In the orders administration page that you'll create later in this chapter, you'll be able to see and modify the general order information.

Creating the New Data Tables

Due to the nature of the information that will be stored, you need two data tables: `orders` and `order_detail`. The `orders` table stores information regarding the order as a whole, while `order_detail` contains the products that belong to each order.

> **■Tip** So far we have been consistent about naming our tables in singular form (shopping_cart,
> department, and so on). However, here we make an exception for the orders table because ORDER is
> also an SQL keyword. For the purposes of this book, we prefer to break the naming convention to avoid any
> confusion while writing the SQL code, and generally speaking, it isn't good practice to use SQL keywords as
> object names.

These tables have a one-to-many relationship, enforced through a FOREIGN KEY constraint
on their order_id fields. One-to-many is the usual relationship implemented between an
orders table and an order_detail table. The order_detail table contains many records that
belong to one order. You might want to revisit Chapter 4 where the table relationships are
explained in more detail.

You'll implement the tables in the following exercise.

Exercise: Adding the orders and the order_detail Tables to the Database

1. Load pgAdmin III, and connect to the hatshop database.

2. Click Tools ➤ Query tool (or click the SQL button on the toolbar). A new query window should appear.

3. Use the query tool to execute this code, which creates the orders table in your hatshop database:

```
-- Create orders table
CREATE TABLE orders
(
    order_id         SERIAL         NOT NULL,
    total_amount     NUMERIC(10,2)  NOT NULL DEFAULT 0.00,
    created_on       TIMESTAMP      NOT NULL,
    shipped_on       TIMESTAMP,
    status           INTEGER        NOT NULL DEFAULT 0,
    comments         VARCHAR(255),
    customer_name    VARCHAR(50),
    shipping_address VARCHAR(255),
    customer_email   VARCHAR(50),
    CONSTRAINT pk_order_id PRIMARY KEY (order_id)
);
```

4. Use the query tool to execute this code, which creates the order_detail table in your hatshop database:

```
-- Create order_detail table
CREATE TABLE order_detail
(
    order_id     INTEGER       NOT NULL,
    product_id   INTEGER       NOT NULL,
    product_name VARCHAR(50)   NOT NULL,
    quantity     INTEGER       NOT NULL,
    unit_cost    NUMERIC(10, 2) NOT NULL,
```

```
        CONSTRAINT pk_order_id_product_id PRIMARY KEY (order_id, product_id),
        CONSTRAINT fk_order_id          FOREIGN KEY (order_id)
                REFERENCES orders (order_id)
                ON UPDATE RESTRICT ON DELETE RESTRICT
);
```

How It Works: The Data Tables

Now that you've created the tables, let's take a closer look at their structure and relationships.

The orders Table

The `orders` table contains two categories of information: data about the order itself (the first six fields) and data about the customer that made the order (last three fields).

An alternative would be to store the customer information in a separate table named `customer` and store only the `customer_id` value in the `orders` table. However, storing customer data is not one of the goals of this development stage. At this stage, we prefer to keep things simple because it doesn't matter who made the order, just what products have been sold. You'll deal with creating a separate `customer` table in Chapter 11.

Third-party payment processors such as PayPal store and manage the complete customer information, so it doesn't need to be stored in your database as well. We have added the `customer_name`, `shipping_address`, and `customer_email` fields as optional fields that can be filled by the administrator if it's easier to have this information at hand for certain (or all) orders.

The field names are self-explanatory. `order_id` is the primary key of the table. `total_amount` stores the total value of the order. `created_on` and `shipped_on` specify when the order was created and shipped (the latter supports `NULL`s if the order hasn't been shipped yet).

The status field contains an integer that can have these values:

- 0: The order has been *placed*. This is the initial status of an order after the Place Order button is clicked in the shopping cart.

- 1: The order is *verified*. The administrator marks the order as verified after the payment was confirmed.

- 2: The order is *completed*. The administrator marks the order as completed after the products have been shipped. At the same time, the `shipped_on` field is also populated.

- 3: The order is *canceled*. Typically, the administrator marks the order as canceled if the order has been placed (by clicking the Place Order button), but the payment wasn't processed, or in other scenarios that require canceling the order.

■**Note** PayPal can automatically tell your web site when a payment is completed through the Instant Payment Notification feature. Using this feature can make things easier for the site administrator because he or she wouldn't need to manually check orders for which payment was received; however, we won't use this feature in HatShop because it's too specific to PayPal. Consult the documentation of the payment provider you choose to check what specific features they have prepared for you to play with.

The order_detail Table

Let's see what information the order_detail table contains. Take a look at Figure 9-3 to see some typical order_detail records.

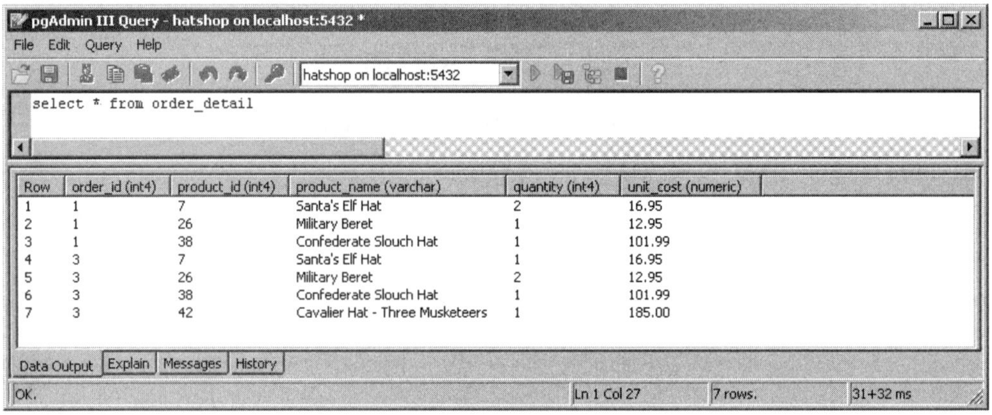

Figure 9-3. *Sample data in the* order_detail *table*

Each record in order_detail represents an ordered product that belongs to the order specified by order_id. The primary key is formed by both order_id and product_id because a particular product can be ordered only once in one order. A quantity field contains the number of ordered items, so it wouldn't make any sense to have one product_id recorded more than once for one order.

You might be wondering why the product_id *and* the price and product name are recorded in the order_detail table, especially because if you have the product id, you can get all of the product's details from the product table without having any duplicated information.

We chose to duplicate the product data (the product's name and price) in the order_detail table to guard against product information changes; products can be removed from the database, and their name and price can change, but this shouldn't affect the orders' data.

We store the product_id because apart from being the only programmatic way to link back to the original product info (if the product still exists), product_id is used to create the primary key of order_detail. product_id comes in very handy here because having it in the composite primary key in order_detail saves you from needing to add another primary key field, and also ensures that you won't have the same product more than once in a single order.

Implementing the Data Tier

At this stage, you need to add two additional data tier functions in the hatshop database. The most important is shopping_cart_create_order, which takes the products from the shopping cart and creates an order with them. The other function is shopping_cart_empty, which empties the visitor's cart after the order has been placed.

In the following exercise we'll implement those functions starting with shopping_cart_empty because this is called from shopping_cart_create_order.

Exercise: Implementing the Functions

1. Load pgAdmin III, and connect to the hatshop database.

2. Click Tools ➤ Query tool (or click the SQL button on the toolbar). A new query window should appear.

3. Use the query tool to execute this code, which creates the shopping_cart_empty function in your hatshop database:

```
-- Create shopping_cart_empty function
CREATE FUNCTION shopping_cart_empty(CHAR(32))
RETURNS VOID LANGUAGE plpgsql AS $$
  DECLARE
    inCartId ALIAS FOR $1;
  BEGIN
    DELETE FROM shopping_cart WHERE cart_id = inCartId;
  END;
$$;
```

When a customer places an order, shopping_cart_create_order will call shopping_cart_empty to delete the products from the customer's shopping cart.

4. Use the query tool to execute this code, which creates the shopping_cart_create_order function in your hatshop database:

```
-- Create shopping_cart_create_order function
CREATE FUNCTION shopping_cart_create_order(CHAR(32))
RETURNS INTEGER LANGUAGE plpgsql AS $$
  DECLARE
    inCartId ALIAS FOR $1;
    outOrderId       INTEGER;
    cartItem         cart_product;
    orderTotalAmount NUMERIC(10, 2);
  BEGIN
    -- Insert a new record into orders
    INSERT INTO orders (created_on) VALUES (NOW());
    -- Obtain the new Order ID
    SELECT INTO outOrderId
           currval('orders_order_id_seq');
    orderTotalAmount := 0;
    -- Insert order details in order_detail table
    FOR cartItem IN
      SELECT     p.product_id, p.name,
                 COALESCE(NULLIF(p.discounted_price, 0), p.price) AS price,
                 sc.quantity,
                 COALESCE(NULLIF(p.discounted_price, 0), p.price) * sc.quantity
                   AS subtotal
```

```
     FROM       shopping_cart sc
     INNER JOIN product p
                    ON sc.product_id = p.product_id
     WHERE      sc.cart_id = inCartId AND sc.buy_now
   LOOP
     INSERT INTO order_detail (order_id, product_id, product_name,
                                quantity, unit_cost)
          VALUES (outOrderId, cartItem.product_id, cartItem.name,
                   cartItem.quantity, cartItem.price);
     orderTotalAmount := orderTotalAmount + cartItem.subtotal;
   END LOOP;
   -- Save the order's total amount
   UPDATE orders
   SET    total_amount = orderTotalAmount
   WHERE  order_id = outOrderId;
   -- Clear the shopping cart
   PERFORM shopping_cart_empty(inCartId);
   -- Return the Order ID
   RETURN outOrderId;
 END;
$$;
```

This function gets called when the customer decides to buy the products in the shopping cart and clicks the Place Order button.

The role of shopping_cart_create_order is to create a new order based on the products in the customer's shopping cart. This implies adding a new record to the orders table and a number of records (one record for each product) in the order_detail table.

How It Works: Implementing Functions

The first step in shopping_cart_create_order involves creating the new record in the orders table. You need to do this at the beginning to find out what order_id was generated for the new order. Remember that the order_id field is an INTEGER column that has a sequence associated (orders_order_id_seq) and is automatically generated by the database, so you need to retrieve its value after inserting a record into orders:

```
-- Insert a new record into orders
INSERT INTO orders (created_on) VALUES (NOW());
-- Obtain the new Order ID
SELECT INTO outOrderId
       currval('orders_order_id_seq');
```

This is the basic mechanism of extracting the newly generated ID. After the INSERT statement, you save the value returned by currval to a variable. You must do this immediately after inserting the new row because the value returned by currval is incremented after the next successful insert operation. currval returns the current value of the sequence that is equivalent with the last inserted order_id.

Using the outOrderId variable, you add the order_detail records by gathering information from the product and shopping_cart tables. You get the list of the products and their quantities from shopping_cart, get their names and prices from product, and save these records one by one to the order_detail table.

```
-- Insert order details in order_detail table
FOR cartItem IN
  SELECT    p.product_id, p.name,
            COALESCE(NULLIF(p.discounted_price, 0), p.price) AS price,
            sc.quantity,
            COALESCE(NULLIF(p.discounted_price, 0), p.price) * sc.quantity
              AS subtotal
  FROM      shopping_cart sc
  INNER JOIN product p
              ON sc.product_id = p.product_id
  WHERE     sc.cart_id = inCartId AND sc.buy_now
LOOP
  INSERT INTO order_detail (order_id, product_id, product_name,
                            quantity, unit_cost)
        VALUES (outOrderId, cartItem.product_id, cartItem.name,
                cartItem.quantity, cartItem.price);
  orderTotalAmount := orderTotalAmount + cartItem.subtotal;
END LOOP;
```

Tip When joining product and shopping_cart, you get the product_id from product, but you could also get it from shopping_cart; the result would be the same because the table join is made on the product_id column.

While saving the products, the function also calculates the total amount of the order by adding each product's price multiplied by its quantity to orderTotalAmount. This value is then saved as the order's total_amount:

```
-- Save the order's total amount
UPDATE orders
SET    total_amount = orderTotalAmount
WHERE  order_id = outOrderId;
```

In the end, the function empties the visitor's shopping cart calling the shopping_cart_empty function and returns the order's ID:

```
-- Clear the shopping cart
PERFORM shopping_cart_empty(inCartId);
-- Return the Order ID
RETURN outOrderId;
```

Implementing the Business Tier

In this step, you only need a single method, `CreateOrder`, which you'll add to the `ShoppingCart` class inside `business/shopping_cart.php`:

```
// Create a new order
public static function CreateOrder()
{
  // Build SQL query
  $sql = 'SELECT shopping_cart_create_order(:cart_id);';
  // Build the parameters array
  $params = array (':cart_id' => self::GetCartId());
  // Prepare the statement with PDO-specific functionality
  $result = DatabaseHandler::Prepare($sql);

  // Execute the query and return the results
  return DatabaseHandler::GetOne($result, $params);
}
```

The method calls the `shopping_cart_create_order` data tier function, returning the `order_id` of the newly created order.

Implementing the Presentation Tier

You've finally arrived at the part of the process where you'll put the code you've written into action. The UI consists of the Place Order button along with all the logic behind it, which allows the visitor to become a customer.

This button is the only addition on the visitor side for the custom checkout. Let's first place the button on the `cart_details` template file, and then implement its functionality.

To get the desired functionality, you just follow a few simple steps. The first one involves adding the Place Order button to the shopping cart.

Adding the Place Order Button

Modify `presentation/templates/cart_details.tpl` by adding a new button just after the Update button, as highlighted in the following code snippet:

```
<table>
  <tr>
    <td class="cart_total">
      <span>Total amount:</span> 
      <span class="price">${$cart_details->mTotalAmount}</span>
    </td>
    <td class="cart_total" align="right">
      <input type="submit" name="update" value="Update" />
      <input type="submit" name="place_order" value="Place Order" />
    </td>
  </tr>
</table>
```

Cool, now you have a Place Order button in the shopping cart!

Implementing the Order Placement Functionality

Now it's time to implement the Place Order button's functionality. Because this functionality depends on the company that processes your payments, you might need to adapt it to the behavior of your payment processing company. If you use PayPal, the code that redirects the visitor to a payment was already presented in "Using the PayPal Single Item Purchases Feature" section of Chapter 6.

Add the following highlighted code in the init() method of the CartDetails class in presentation/smarty_plugins/function.load_cart_details.php:

```
// Calculate the total amount for the shopping cart
$this->mTotalAmount = ShoppingCart::GetTotalAmount();

// If the Place Order button was clicked ...
if(isset ($_POST['place_order']))
{
  // Create the order and get the order ID
  $order_id = ShoppingCart::CreateOrder();

  // This will contain the PayPal link
  $redirect =
    'https://www.paypal.com/xclick/business=youremail@example.com' .
    '&item_name=HatShop Order ' . $order_id .
    '&item_number=' . $order_id .
    '&amount=' . $this->mTotalAmount .
    '&currency=USD&return=www.example.com' .
    '&cancel_return=www.example.com';

  // Redirection to the payment page
  header('Location: ' . $redirect);

  exit;
}

// Get shopping cart products
$this->mCartProducts =
  ShoppingCart::GetCartProducts(GET_CART_PRODUCTS);
```

Of course, if you use another company to process your payments, you'll need to modify the code accordingly.

When a visitor clicks the Place Order button, two important actions happen. First, the order is created in the database by calling the CreateOrder method of the ShoppingCart class. This function calls the shopping_cart_create_order database function to create a new order with the products in the shopping cart and returns the ID of the new order:

```
// Create the order and get the order ID
$order_id = ShoppingCart::CreateOrder();
```

Second, the visitor is redirected to the payment page, which requests payment for an item named "HatShop Order *nnn*" with a value that amounts to the total value of the order.

Right now, your Place Order button is fully functional! Test it by adding some products to your cart, and clicking Place Order. Your shopping cart should be cleared, and you should be forwarded to a PayPal payment page like the one shown earlier in Figure 9-2.

Administering Orders

So your visitor just made an order. Now what?

After giving visitors the option to pay for your products, you need to make sure they actually get what they paid for. HatShop needs a carefully designed orders administration page, where the administrator can quickly see the status of pending orders.

■**Note**   This chapter doesn't intend to help you create a perfect order administration system but rather something that is simple and functional enough to get you on the right track.

The orders administration part of the site will consist of two componentized templates named admin_orders and admin_order_details.

When the administrator clicks on the ORDERS ADMIN link, the admin.php page loads the admin_orders componentized template that offers the capability to filter the orders. When first loaded, it offers you various ways of selecting orders, as shown in Figure 9-4.

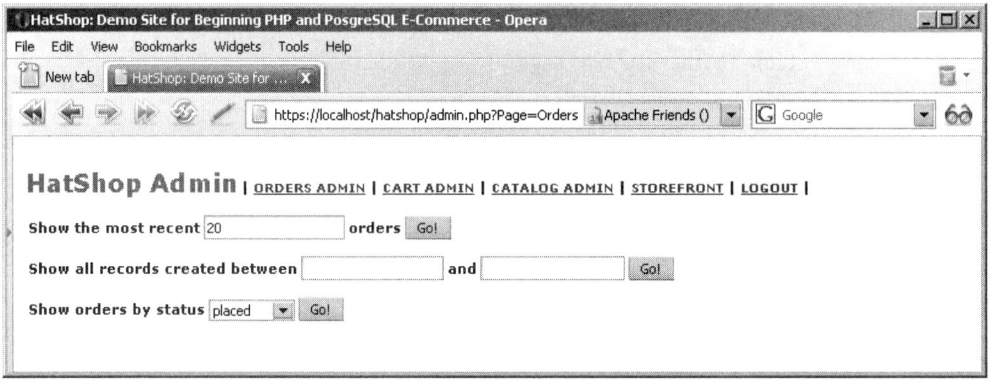

Figure 9-4. *The Orders Admin page*

After clicking one of the Go! buttons, the matching orders appear in a table (see Figure 9-5).

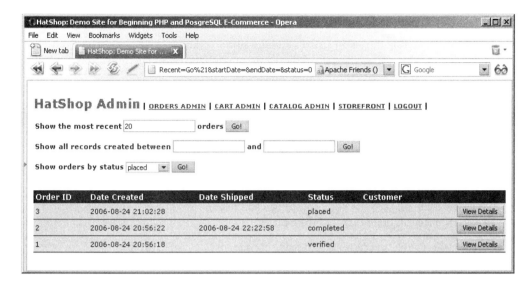

Figure 9-5. *Selecting the most recent orders in the Orders Admin page*

When you click the View Details button for an order, you are sent to a page where you can view and update order information, as shown in Figure 9-6.

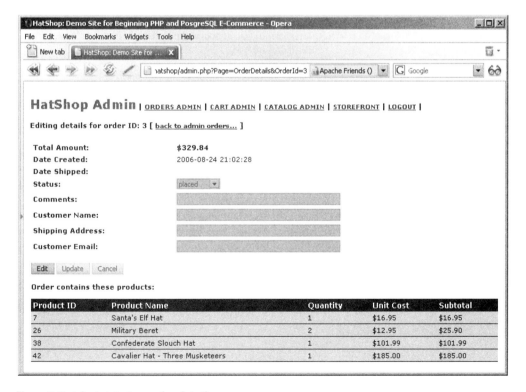

Figure 9-6. *Administering order details*

Setting Up the Orders Administration Page

Before you start creating the `admin_orders` and the `admin_order_details` componentized templates, let's modify `admin.php` to load these componentized templates and also modify `admin_menu.tpl` to display an `ORDERS ADMIN` link.

Exercise: Setting Up ADMIN ORDERS

1. Modify `admin.php` to include a reference to `include/app_top.php` that we'll later create:

```
// Load Business Tier
require_once BUSINESS_DIR . 'catalog.php';
require_once BUSINESS_DIR . 'shopping_cart.php';
require_once BUSINESS_DIR . 'orders.php';
```

2. In the `admin.php` file, add the highlighted code that loads `admin_orders.tpl` and `admin_order_details.tpl`:

```
  elseif ($admin_page == 'Cart')
    $pageContentsCell = 'admin_cart.tpl';
  elseif ($admin_page == 'Orders')
    $pageContentsCell = 'admin_orders.tpl';
  elseif ($admin_page == 'OrderDetails')
    $pageContentsCell = 'admin_order_details.tpl';
```

3. Modify `presentation/templates/admin_menu.tpl` by adding the highlighted link code to the cart admin page:

```
<span class="menu_text"> |
  <a href="{"admin.php?Page=Orders"|prepare_link:"https"}">ORDERS ADMIN</a>
  |
  <a href="{"admin.php?Page=Cart"|prepare_link:"https"}">CART ADMIN</a> |
```

Displaying Pending Orders

In the following pages, you'll implement the `admin_orders` componentized template and its supporting data tier and business tier functionality. `admin_orders` is the componentized template that allows the administrator to view the orders that have been placed on the web site. Because the orders list will become very long, it is important to have a few well-chosen filtering options.

The administrator will be able to select the orders using the following criteria:

- Show the most recent orders.

- Show orders that took place in a certain period of time.

- Show orders with a specified status value.

CHAPTER 9 ■ DEALING WITH CUSTOMER ORDERS   317

Okay, now that you know what you want, let's start writing some code. You'll start with the data tier.

Implementing the Data Tier

In the following exercise, you'll create the data tier functions one at a time, and we'll comment a little upon each one of them.

Exercise: Implementing the Functions

1. Load pgAdmin III, and connect to the `hatshop` database.

2. Click Tools ➤ Query tool (or click the SQL button on the toolbar). A new query window should appear.

3. Use the query tool to execute this code, which creates the `order_short_details` type and `orders_get_most_recent_orders` function in your `hatshop` database:

```
-- Create order_short_details type
CREATE TYPE order_short_details AS
(
  order_id      INTEGER,
  total_amount  NUMERIC(10, 2),
  created_on    TIMESTAMP,
  shipped_on    TIMESTAMP,
  status        INTEGER,
  customer_name VARCHAR(50)
);

-- Create orders_get_most_recent_orders function
CREATE FUNCTION orders_get_most_recent_orders(INTEGER)
RETURNS SETOF order_short_details LANGUAGE plpgsql AS $$
  DECLARE
    inHowMany ALIAS FOR $1;
    outOrderShortDetailsRow order_short_details;
  BEGIN
    FOR outOrderShortDetailsRow IN
      SELECT    order_id, total_amount, created_on,
                shipped_on, status, customer_name
      FROM      orders
      ORDER BY created_on DESC
      LIMIT     inHowMany
    LOOP
      RETURN NEXT outOrderShortDetailsRow;
    END LOOP;
  END;
$$;
```

The `orders_get_most_recent_orders` function retrieves a list of the most recent orders. The `SELECT` SQL statement used in this method uses the `LIMIT` clause to limit the number of returned rows to `inHowMany` rows.

The `ORDER BY` clause is used to sort the results. The default sorting mode is ascending, but by adding `DESC`, the descending sort mode is set (so the most recent orders will be listed first).

4. Use the query tool to execute this code, which creates the `orders_get_orders_between_dates` function in your `hatshop` database:

```
-- Create orders_get_orders_between_dates function
CREATE FUNCTION orders_get_orders_between_dates(TIMESTAMP, TIMESTAMP)
RETURNS SETOF order_short_details LANGUAGE plpgsql AS $$
  DECLARE
    inStartDate ALIAS FOR $1;
    inEndDate   ALIAS FOR $2;
    outOrderShortDetailsRow order_short_details;
  BEGIN
    FOR outOrderShortDetailsRow IN
      SELECT   order_id, total_amount, created_on,
               shipped_on, status, customer_name
      FROM     orders
      WHERE    created_on >= inStartDate AND created_on <= inEndDate
      ORDER BY created_on DESC
    LOOP
      RETURN NEXT outOrderShortDetailsRow;
    END LOOP;
  END;
$$;
```

This function returns all the records in which the current date is between `inStartDate` and `inEndDate` that are supplied as parameters. The results are sorted descending by date.

5. Use the query tool to execute this code, which creates the `orders_get_orders_by_status` function in your `hatshop` database:

```
-- Create orders_get_orders_by_status function
CREATE FUNCTION orders_get_orders_by_status(INTEGER)
RETURNS SETOF order_short_details LANGUAGE plpgsql AS $$
  DECLARE
    inStatus ALIAS FOR $1;
    outOrderShortDetailsRow order_short_details;
  BEGIN
    FOR outOrderShortDetailsRow IN
      SELECT   order_id, total_amount, created_on,
               shipped_on, status, customer_name
      FROM     orders
      WHERE    status = inStatus
      ORDER BY created_on DESC
    LOOP
```

```
        RETURN NEXT outOrderShortDetailsRow;
      END LOOP;
    END;
  $$;
```

This function is used to return the orders that have the status value specified by the inStatus parameter.

Implementing the Business Tier

The business tier consists of a new class named Orders, whose methods call their data tier counterparts. This class is pretty straightforward with no particularly complex logic, so we'll just list the code. Create the business/orders.php file, and add the following code to it:

```php
<?php
// Business tier class for the orders
class Orders
{
  public static $mOrderStatusOptions = array ('placed',     // 0
                                              'verified',  // 1
                                              'completed', // 2
                                              'canceled'); // 3

  // Get the most recent $how_many orders
  public static function GetMostRecentOrders($how_many)
  {
    // Build the SQL query
    $sql = 'SELECT * FROM orders_get_most_recent_orders(:how_many);';
    // Build the parameters array
    $params = array (':how_many' => $how_many);
    // Prepare the statement with PDO-specific functionality
    $result = DatabaseHandler::Prepare($sql);

    // Execute the query and return the results
    return DatabaseHandler::GetAll($result, $params);
  }

  // Get orders between two dates
  public static function GetOrdersBetweenDates($startDate, $endDate)
  {
    // Build the SQL query
    $sql = 'SELECT * FROM orders_get_orders_between_dates(
                      :start_date, :end_date);';
    // Build the parameters array
    $params = array (':start_date' => $startDate, ':end_date' => $endDate);
    // Prepare the statement with PDO-specific functionality
    $result = DatabaseHandler::Prepare($sql);
```

```php
    // Execute the query and return the results
    return DatabaseHandler::GetAll($result, $params);
  }

  // Gets orders by status
  public static function GetOrdersByStatus($status)
  {
    // Build the SQL query
    $sql = 'SELECT * FROM orders_get_orders_by_status(:status);';
    // Build the parameters array
    $params = array (':status' => $status);
    // Prepare the statement with PDO-specific functionality
    $result = DatabaseHandler::Prepare($sql);

    // Execute the query and return the results
    return DatabaseHandler::GetAll($result, $params);
  }
}
?>
```

Implementing the Presentation Tier

Now it's time to implement the admin_orders componentized template. Follow the steps from the next exercise to make the magic happen.

Exercise: Creating the admin_orders Componentized Template

1. Create a new file named admin_orders.tpl in the presentation/templates folder with the following code in it:

```smarty
{* admin_orders.tpl *}
{load_admin_orders assign="admin_orders"}
{if $admin_orders->mErrorMessage neq ""}
<span class="admin_error_text">{$admin_orders->mErrorMessage}</span>
<br /><br />
{/if}
<form action="{"admin.php"|prepare_link:"https"}" method="get">
  <input name="Page" type="hidden" value="Orders" />
  <span class="admin_page_text">Show the most recent</span>
  <input name="recordCount" type="text" value="{$admin_orders->mRecordCount}" />
  <span class="admin_page_text">orders</span>
  <input type="submit" name="submitMostRecent" value="Go!" />
  <br /><br />
  <span class="admin_page_text">Show all records created between</span>
  <input name="startDate" type="text" value="{$admin_orders->mStartDate}" />
  <span class="admin_page_text">and</span>
  <input name="endDate" type="text" value="{$admin_orders->mEndDate}" />
```

```
      <input type="submit" name="submitBetweenDates" value="Go!" />
      <br /><br />
      <span class="admin_page_text">Show orders by status</span>
      {html_options name="status" options=$admin_orders->mOrderStatusOptions
       selected=$admin_orders->mSelectedStatus}
      <input type="submit" name="submitOrdersByStatus" value="Go!" />
      <br /><br />
   </form>
   <br />
   {if $admin_orders->mOrders}
   <table>
     <tr>
      <th>Order ID</th>
      <th>Date Created</th>
      <th>Date Shipped</th>
      <th>Status</th>
      <th>Customer</th>
      <th> </th>
     </tr>
     {section name=cOrders loop=$admin_orders->mOrders}
       {assign var=status value=$admin_orders->mOrders[cOrders].status}
     <tr>
       <td>{$admin_orders->mOrders[cOrders].order_id}</td>
       <td>
         {$admin_orders->mOrders[cOrders].created_on|date_format:"%Y-%m-%d %T"}
       </td>
       <td>
         {$admin_orders->mOrders[cOrders].shipped_on|date_format:"%Y-%m-%d %T"}
       </td>
       <td>{$admin_orders->mOrderStatusOptions[$status]}</td>
       <td>{$admin_orders->mOrders[cOrders].customer_name}</td>
       <td align="right">
         <input type="button" value="View Details"
           onclick="window.location='{
             $admin_orders->mOrders[cOrders].onclick|prepare_link:"https"}';" />
       </td>
     </tr>
     {/section}
   </table>
   {/if}
```

2. Create a new file named `presentation/smarty_plugins/function.load_admin_orders.php`,
   and add the following code to it:

```php
<?php
// Plugin functions inside plugin files must be named: smarty_type_name
function smarty_function_load_admin_orders($params, $smarty)
{
```

```php
    // Create AdminOrders object
    $admin_orders = new AdminOrders();
    $admin_orders->init();

    // Assign template variable
    $smarty->assign($params['assign'], $admin_orders);
}

/* Presentation tier class that supports order administration
   functionality */
class AdminOrders
{
  // Public variables available in smarty template
  public $mOrders;
  public $mStartDate;
  public $mEndDate;
  public $mRecordCount = 20;
  public $mOrderStatusOptions;
  public $mSelectedStatus = 0;
  public $mErrorMessage = '';

  // Class constructor
  public function __construct()
  {
    /* Save the link to the current page in the AdminOrdersPageLink
       session variable; it will be used to create the
       "back to admin orders ..." link in admin order details pages */
    $_SESSION['admin_orders_page_link'] =
      str_replace(VIRTUAL_LOCATION, '', getenv('REQUEST_URI'));

    $this->mOrderStatusOptions = Orders::$mOrderStatusOptions;
  }

  public function init()
  {
    // If the "Show the most recent x orders" filter is in action ...
    if (isset ($_GET['submitMostRecent']))
    {
      // If the record count value is not a valid integer, display error
      if ((string)(int)$_GET['recordCount'] == (string)$_GET['recordCount'])
      {
        $this->mRecordCount = (int)$_GET['recordCount'];
        $this->mOrders = Orders::GetMostRecentOrders($this->mRecordCount);
      }
      else
        $this->mErrorMessage = $_GET['recordCount'] . ' is not a number.';
    }
```

```php
/* If the "Show all records created between date_1 and date_2"
   filter is in action ... */
if (isset ($_GET['submitBetweenDates']))
{
  $this->mStartDate = $_GET['startDate'];
  $this->mEndDate = $_GET['endDate'];

  // Check if the start date is in accepted format
  if (($this->mStartDate == '') ||
      ($timestamp = strtotime($this->mStartDate)) == -1)
    $this->mErrorMessage = 'The start date is invalid. ';
  else
    // Transform date to YYYY/MM/DD HH:MM:SS format
    $this->mStartDate =
      strftime('%Y/%m/%d %H:%M:%S', strtotime($this->mStartDate));

  // Check if the end date is in accepted format
  if (($this->mEndDate == '') ||
      ($timestamp = strtotime($this->mEndDate)) == -1)
    $this->mErrorMessage .= 'The end date is invalid.';
  else
    // Transform date to YYYY/MM/DD HH:MM:SS format
    $this->mEndDate =
      strftime('%Y/%m/%d %H:%M:%S', strtotime($this->mEndDate));

  // Check if start date is more recent than the end date
  if ((empty ($this->mErrorMessage)) &&
      (strtotime($this->mStartDate) > strtotime($this->mEndDate)))
    $this->mErrorMessage .=
      'The start date should be more recent than the end date.';

  // If there are no errors, get the orders between the two dates
  if (empty($this->mErrorMessage))
    $this->mOrders = Orders::GetOrdersBetweenDates(
                       $this->mStartDate, $this->mEndDate);
}

// If "Show orders by status" filter is in action ...
if (isset ($_GET['submitOrdersByStatus']))
{
  $this->mSelectedStatus = $_GET['status'];
  $this->mOrders = Orders::GetOrdersByStatus($this->mSelectedStatus);
}

// Build View Details link
for ($i = 0; $i < count($this->mOrders); $i++)
```

```
    {
      $this->mOrders[$i]['onclick'] =
        'admin.php?Page=OrderDetails&OrderId=' .
        $this->mOrders[$i]['order_id'];
    }
  }
}
?>
```

3. Load `admin.php` into the browser and introduce the username/password combination if you logged out. Click on the ORDERS ADMIN menu link, then click one of the Go! buttons, and see the results that should be similar to those found earlier in Figure 9-4.

How It Works: The admin_orders Componentized Template

Each of the Go! buttons calls one of the business tier methods (in the `Orders` class) and populates the table with the returned orders information.

When processing the request, we test the data the visitor entered to make sure it's valid. When the first Go! button is clicked, we verify that the entered value is a number (how many records to show). We also verify whether the dates entered in the Start Date and End Date text boxes are valid. We process them first with `strtotime` that parses a string and transforms it into a Unix timestamp. This function is useful because it also accepts entries such as "now," "tomorrow," "last week," and so on as input values. The resulting timestamp is then processed with the `strftime` function, which transforms it into the YYYY/MM/DD HH:MM:SS format. Have a look at how these date/time values are parsed:

```
// Check if the start date is in accepted format
if (($this->mStartDate == '') ||
    ($timestamp = strtotime($this->mStartDate)) == -1)
  $this->mErrorMessage = 'The start date is invalid. ';
else
  // Transform date to YYYY/MM/DD HH:MM:SS format
  $this->mStartDate =
    strftime('%Y/%m/%d %H:%M:%S', strtotime($this->mStartDate));
```

■**Note** Check `http://www.php.net/strtotime` to see what input formats are supported by the `strtotime` function and `http://www.php.net/strftime` for more details about `strftime`.

Apart from this detail, the `admin_orders.tpl` template file is pretty simple and doesn't introduce any new theoretical elements for you.

Displaying Order Details

In this section, you'll create the `admin_order_details` componentized template, which allows the administrator to edit the details of a particular order. The most common tasks are to mark a placed order as either verified or canceled, and to mark a verified order as completed when the shipment is dispatched. Take a look at Figure 9-5 (shown earlier) to see the `admin_order_details` template in action.

The site administrator marks an order as verified when the payment for that order is confirmed by PayPal and marks the order as completed when the order is assembled, addressed, and mailed to the purchaser. The administrator can mark an order as canceled if, for example, PayPal does not confirm the payment in a reasonable amount of time (the exact meaning of "reasonable" is up to the administrator).

The other buttons—Edit, Update, and Cancel—allow the administrator to manually edit any of the details of an order. When the Edit button is clicked, the select box and the text boxes become editable.

Now that you have an idea of what this control will do, let's implement it in the usual style by starting with the data tier.

Implementing the Data Tier

Here you'll implement the data tier logic that supports the functionality required by the UI. You'll enable the administrator to do three operations, and you'll implement them with the following functions:

- `orders_get_order_info` gets back the data needed to populate the form with general order information, such as the total amount, date created, date shipped, and so on. You can see the complete list in Figure 9-6, shown previously.

- `orders_get_order_details` returns all the products that belong to the selected order, and its return data is used to fill the grid at the bottom of the form.

- `orders_update_order` is called when the administrator updates an order in edit mode.

Now implement each of these functions by following the steps from the next exercise.

Exercise: Implementing the Functions

1. Load pgAdmin III, and connect to the `hatshop` database.

2. Click Tools ➤ Query tool (or click the SQL button on the toolbar). A new query window should appear.

3. Use the query tool to execute this code, which creates the `orders_get_order_info` function in your `hatshop` database:

```
-- Create orders_get_order_info function
CREATE FUNCTION orders_get_order_info(INTEGER)
RETURNS orders LANGUAGE plpgsql AS $$
  DECLARE
    inOrderId ALIAS FOR $1;
    outOrdersRow orders;
  BEGIN
```

```
    SELECT INTO outOrdersRow
                order_id, total_amount, created_on, shipped_on, status,
                comments, customer_name, shipping_address, customer_email
    FROM    orders
    WHERE   order_id = inOrderId;
    RETURN outOrdersRow;
  END;
$$;
```

This function returns the information necessary to fill the form in the admin_order_details componentized template.

4. Use the query tool to execute this code, which creates the order_details type and the orders_get_order_details function in your hatshop database:

```
-- Create order_details type
CREATE TYPE order_details AS
(
  order_id      INTEGER,
  product_id    INTEGER,
  product_name  VARCHAR(50),
  quantity      INTEGER,
  unit_cost     NUMERIC(10, 2),
  subtotal      NUMERIC(10, 2)
);

-- Create orders_get_order_details function
CREATE FUNCTION orders_get_order_details(INTEGER)
RETURNS SETOF order_details LANGUAGE plpgsql AS $$
  DECLARE
    inOrderId ALIAS FOR $1;
    outOrderDetailsRow order_details;
  BEGIN
    FOR outOrderDetailsRow IN
      SELECT order_id, product_id, product_name, quantity,
             unit_cost, (quantity * unit_cost) AS subtotal
      FROM    order_detail
      WHERE   order_id = inOrderId
    LOOP
      RETURN NEXT outOrderDetailsRow;
    END LOOP;
  END;
$$;
```

The orders_get_order_details function returns the list of products that belong to a specific order. This will be used to populate the table containing the order details, situated at the bottom of the page.

5. Use the query tool to execute this code, which creates the orders_update_order function in your hatshop database:

```
-- Create orders_update_order function
CREATE FUNCTION orders_update_order(INTEGER, INTEGER, VARCHAR(255),
                 VARCHAR(50), VARCHAR(255), VARCHAR(50))
RETURNS VOID LANGUAGE plpgsql AS $$
  DECLARE
    inOrderId         ALIAS FOR $1;
    inStatus          ALIAS FOR $2;
    inComments        ALIAS FOR $3;
    inCustomerName    ALIAS FOR $4;
    inShippingAddress ALIAS FOR $5;
    inCustomerEmail   ALIAS FOR $6;
    currentStatus INTEGER;
  BEGIN
    SELECT INTO currentStatus
           status
    FROM   orders
    WHERE  order_id = inOrderId;
    IF  inStatus != currentStatus AND (inStatus = 0 OR inStatus = 1) THEN
      UPDATE orders SET shipped_on = NULL WHERE order_id = inOrderId;
    ELSEIF inStatus != currentStatus AND inStatus = 2 THEN
      UPDATE orders SET shipped_on = NOW() WHERE order_id = inOrderId;
    END IF;
    UPDATE orders
    SET    status = inStatus, comments = inComments,
           customer_name = inCustomerName,
           shipping_address = inShippingAddress,
           customer_email = inCustomerEmail
    WHERE  order_id = inOrderId;
  END;
$$;
```

The orders_update_order function updates the details of an order.

Implementing the Business Tier

The business tier part for the admin_order_details componentized template is very simple and consists of the following methods that you need to add to the Orders class inside of the business/orders.php file:

```
// Gets the details of a specific order
public static function GetOrderInfo($orderId)
{
  // Build the SQL query
  $sql = 'SELECT * FROM orders_get_order_info(:order_id);';
  // Build the parameters array
  $params = array (':order_id' => $orderId);
  // Prepare the statement with PDO-specific functionality
```

```
    $result = DatabaseHandler::Prepare($sql);

    // Execute the query and return the results
    return DatabaseHandler::GetRow($result, $params);
  }

  // Gets the products that belong to a specific order
  public static function GetOrderDetails($orderId)
  {
    // Build the SQL query
    $sql = 'SELECT * FROM orders_get_order_details(:order_id);';
    // Build the parameters array
    $params = array (':order_id' => $orderId);
    // Prepare the statement with PDO-specific functionality
    $result = DatabaseHandler::Prepare($sql);

    // Execute the query and return the results
    return DatabaseHandler::GetAll($result, $params);
  }

  // Updates order details
  public static function UpdateOrder($orderId, $status, $comments,
                          $customerName, $shippingAddress, $customerEmail)
  {
    // Build the SQL query
    $sql = 'SELECT orders_update_order(:order_id, :status, :comments,
                  :customer_name, :shipping_address, :customer_email);';
    // Build the parameters array
    $params = array (':order_id' => $orderId,
                    ':status' => $status,
                    ':comments' => $comments,
                    ':customer_name' => $customerName,
                    ':shipping_address' => $shippingAddress,
                    ':customer_email' => $customerEmail);
    // Prepare the statement with PDO-specific functionality
    $result = DatabaseHandler::Prepare($sql);

    // Execute the query
    return DatabaseHandler::Execute($result, $params);
  }
```

Implementing the Presentation Tier

Once again, you've reached the stage where you wrap up all the data tier and business tier functionality and package it into a nice-looking UI. The presentation tier consists of the admin_order_details componentized template. Let's create this componentized template in the following exercise.

Exercise: Creating the admin_order_details Componentized Template

1. Create a new template file named admin_order_details.tpl in the presentation/templates folder, and add the following code to it:

```
{* admin_order_details.tpl *}
{load_admin_order_details assign="admin_order_details"}
<span class="admin_page_text">
  Editing details for order ID:
  {$admin_order_details->mOrderInfo.order_id} [
  {strip}
  <a href="{$admin_order_details->mAdminOrdersPageLink|prepare_link:"https"}">
    back to admin orders...
  </a>
  {/strip}
  ]
</span>
<br /><br />
<form action="{"admin.php"|prepare_link:"https"}" method="get">
  <input type="hidden" name="Page" value="OrderDetails" />
  <input type="hidden" name="OrderId"
   value="{$admin_order_details->mOrderInfo.order_id}" />
  <table class="edit">
    <tr>
      <td class="admin_page_text">Total Amount: </td>
      <td class="price">
        ${$admin_order_details->mOrderInfo.total_amount}
      </td>
    </tr>
    <tr>
      <td class="admin_page_text">Date Created: </td>
      <td>
        {$admin_order_details->mOrderInfo.created_on|date_format:"%Y-%m-%d %T"}
      </td>
    </tr>
    <tr>
      <td class="admin_page_text">Date Shipped: </td>
      <td>
        {$admin_order_details->mOrderInfo.shipped_on|date_format:"%Y-%m-%d %T"}
      </td>
    </tr>
    <tr>
      <td class="admin_page_text">Status: </td>
      <td>
        <select name="status"
         {if ! $admin_order_details->mEditEnabled}
         disabled="disabled"
```

```
            {/if} >
              {html_options options=$admin_order_details->mOrderStatusOptions
                selected=$admin_order_details->mOrderInfo.status}
            </select>
          </td>
        </tr>
        <tr>
          <td class="admin_page_text">Comments: </td>
          <td>
            <input name="comments" type="text" size="50"
            value="{$admin_order_details->mOrderInfo.comments}"
            {if ! $admin_order_details->mEditEnabled}
            disabled="disabled"
            {/if} />
          <td>
        </tr>
        <tr>
          <td class="admin_page_text">Customer Name: </td>
          <td>
            <input name="customerName" type="text" size="50"
            value="{$admin_order_details->mOrderInfo.customer_name}"
            {if ! $admin_order_details->mEditEnabled}
            disabled="disabled"
            {/if} />
          <td>
        </tr>
        <tr>
          <td class="admin_page_text">Shipping Address: </td>
          <td>
            <input name="shippingAddress" type="text" size="50"
            value="{$admin_order_details->mOrderInfo.shipping_address}"
            {if ! $admin_order_details->mEditEnabled}
            disabled="disabled"
            {/if} />
          </td>
        </tr>
        <tr>
          <td class="admin_page_text">Customer Email: </td>
          <td>
            <input name="customerEmail" type="text" size="50"
            value="{$admin_order_details->mOrderInfo.customer_email}"
            {if ! $admin_order_details->mEditEnabled}
            disabled="disabled"
            {/if} />
          </td>
        </tr>
      </table>
```

```
    <br />
    <input type="submit" name="submitEdit" value="Edit"
     {if $admin_order_details->mEditEnabled}
     disabled="disabled"
     {/if} />
    <input type="submit" name="submitUpdate" value="Update"
     {if ! $admin_order_details->mEditEnabled}
     disabled="disabled"
     {/if} />
    <input type="submit" name="submitCancel" value="Cancel"
     {if ! $admin_order_details->mEditEnabled}
     disabled="disabled"
     {/if} />
    <br /><br />
    <span class="admin_page_text">Order contains these products:</span>
    <br /><br />
    <table>
      <tr>
        <th>Product ID</th>
        <th>Product Name</th>
        <th>Quantity</th>
        <th>Unit Cost</th>
        <th>Subtotal</th>
      </tr>
    {section name=cOrder loop=$admin_order details->mOrderDetails}
      <tr>
        <td>{$admin_order_details->mOrderDetails[cOrder].product_id}</td>
        <td>{$admin_order_details->mOrderDetails[cOrder].product_name}</td>
        <td>{$admin_order_details->mOrderDetails[cOrder].quantity}</td>
        <td>${$admin_order_details->mOrderDetails[cOrder].unit_cost}</td>
        <td>${$admin_order_details->mOrderDetails[cOrder].subtotal}</td>
      </tr>
    {/section}
    </table>
  </form>
```

2. Create a new file named `function.load_admin_order_details.php` in the
   `presentation/smarty_plugins` folder, and write the following code in it:

```php
<?php
// Plugin functions inside plugin files must be named: smarty_type_name
function smarty_function_load_admin_order_details($params, $smarty)
{
  // Create AdminOrderDetils object
  $admin_order_details = new AdminOrderDetails();
  $admin_order_details->init();
```

```
    // Assign the template variable
    $smarty->assign($params['assign'], $admin_order_details);
}

// Presentation tier class that deals with administering order details
class AdminOrderDetails
{
    // Public variables available in smarty template
    public $mOrderId;
    public $mOrderInfo;
    public $mOrderDetails;
    public $mEditEnabled;
    public $mOrderStatusOptions;
    public $mAdminOrdersPageLink;

    // Class constructor
    public function __construct()
    {
        // Get the back link from session
        $this->mAdminOrdersPageLink = $_SESSION['admin_orders_page_link'];

        // We receive the order ID in the query string
        if (isset ($_GET['OrderId']))
            $this->mOrderId = (int) $_GET['OrderId'];
        else
            trigger_error('OrderId paramater is required');

        $this->mOrderStatusOptions = Orders::$mOrderStatusOptions;
    }

    // Initializes class members
    public function init()
    {
        if (isset ($_GET['submitUpdate']))
        {
            Orders::UpdateOrder($this->mOrderId, $_GET['status'],
                $_GET['comments'], $_GET['customerName'], $_GET['shippingAddress'],
                $_GET['customerEmail']);
        }

        $this->mOrderInfo = Orders::GetOrderInfo($this->mOrderId);
        $this->mOrderDetails = Orders::GetOrderDetails($this->mOrderId);

        // Value which specifies whether to enable or disable edit mode
        if (isset ($_GET['submitEdit']))
```

```
          $this->mEditEnabled = true;
        else
          $this->mEditEnabled = false;
      }
    }
    ?>
```

3. Open hatshop.css, and add the following styles:

```
.edit tr td
{
  background: #ffffff;
  border: none;
}
```

4. Add some fictional orders to the database, and then load the admin.php file in your browser. Click on the ORDERS ADMIN menu link, click on a Go! button to show some orders, and click the View Details button for one of the orders. The order details admin page will show up allowing you to edit the order's details, as advertised earlier in this chapter.

How It Works: The admin_order_details Componentized Template

The three files you just wrote, admin_order_details.tpl, function.load_admin_order_details.php, and admin_order_details.php, allow you to view and update the details of a particular order.

The function plugin is loaded from the template file using the usual mechanism. The constructor of the AdminOrderDetails class (the __construct method) ensures that there's an OrderId parameter in the query string because without it this componentized template doesn't make sense:

```
// Class constructor
public function __construct()
{
  // Get the back link from session
  $this->mAdminOrdersPageLink = $_SESSION['admin_orders_page_link'];

  // We receive the order ID in the query string
  if (isset ($_GET['OrderId']))
    $this->mOrderId = (int) $_GET['OrderId'];
  else
    trigger_error('OrderId paramater is required');

  $this->mOrderStatusOptions = Orders::$mOrderStatusOptions;
}
```

The init() method reacts to user's actions and calls various business tier methods to accomplish the user's requests.

It populates the form with data it gets from the Orders::GetOrderInfo and the Orders::GetOrderDetails business tier methods.

The `mEditEnabled` class member enters or exits edit mode depending on whether the `submitEdit` parameter from the query string is set or not. When entering edit mode, all text boxes and the Update and Cancel buttons become enabled, but the Edit button is disabled. The reverse happens when exiting edit mode, which happens when either the Cancel or Update button is clicked.

Summary

We covered a lot of ground in this chapter. In two separate stages, you implemented a system for taking orders and manually administering them. You added a Place Order button to the shopping cart control to allow the visitor to order the products in the shopping cart. You implemented a simple orders administration page, in which the site administrator can view and handle pending orders.

Because order data is now stored in the database, you can do various statistics and calculations based on the items sold. In the next chapter, you'll learn how to implement a "Visitors who bought this also bought…" feature, which wouldn't have been possible without the order data stored in the database.

■■■

CHAPTER 10

Product Recommendations

One of the most important advantages of an Internet store compared to a brick-and-mortar location is the capability to customize the web site for each visitor based on his or her preferences or based on data gathered from other visitors with similar preferences. If your web site knows how to suggest additional products to your visitor in a clever way, he or she might end up buying more than initially planned.

In this chapter, you'll implement a simple, but efficient, product recommendations system in your HatShop web store. You can implement a product recommendations system in several ways, depending on your kind of store. Here are a few popular ones:

Up-Selling: Up-selling is defined as the strategy of offering consumers the opportunity to purchase an "upgrade" or a little extra based on their requested purchase. Perhaps the most famous example of up-selling—"Would you like to super-size that?"—is mentioned to customers when they order a value meal at McDonalds. This seemingly innocent request greatly increases the profit margin.

Cross-Selling: Cross-selling is defined as the practice of offering customers complementary products. Continuing with the McDonalds analogy, you'll always hear the phrase "Would you like fries with that?" when someone orders a hamburger. Because it's widely acknowledged that fries go with burgers, and the consumer is ordering a burger, then its likely that the consumer also likes french fries—the mere mention of french fries is likely to generate a new sale.

Featured products on the home page: HatShop already permits the site administrator to choose the products featured on the main page and on the department pages.

In this chapter, you'll implement a dynamic recommendations system with both up-selling and cross-selling strategies. This system has the advantage of not needing manual maintenance. Because at this point HatShop retains what products were sold, you will implement a "customers who bought this product also bought..." feature in this chapter.

Increasing Sales with Dynamic Recommendations

In HatShop, you'll implement the dynamic recommendations system in the visitor's shopping cart and in the product details page. After adding the new bits to your shop, the product details page will contain the product recommendations list at the bottom of the page, as shown in Figure 10-1.

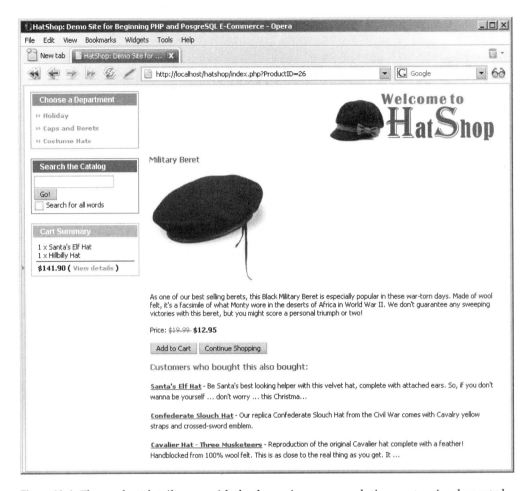

Figure 10-1. *The product details page with the dynamic recommendations system implemented*

The shopping cart page gets a similar addition, as shown in Figure 10-2.

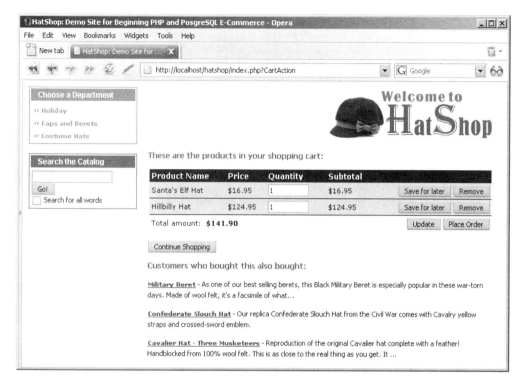

Figure 10-2. *The shopping cart details page with the dynamic recommendations system implemented*

Implementing the Data Tier

Before writing any code, you first need to understand the logic you'll implement for making product recommendations. We'll focus here on the logic of recommending products that were ordered together with another specific product. Afterward, the recommendations for the shopping cart page will function in a similar way but will take more products into consideration.

So, you need to find out what other products were bought by customers who also bought the product for which you're calculating the recommendations (in other words, determine the "customer who bought this product also bought…" information). Let's develop the SQL logic to achieve the list of product recommendations step by step.

■**Tip** Because SQL is very powerful, you can actually implement the same functionality in several ways. Here, we'll cover just one of the options, but when implementing the actual database functions, you'll be shown other options as well.

To determine what other products were ordered together with a specific product, you need to join two instances of the order_detail table on their order_id fields. Feel free to review the "Joining Data Tables" section in Chapter 4 for a quick refresher about table joins. Joining multiple instances of a single table is just like joining different data tables, which contain the same data.

You join two instances of order_detail—called od1 and od2—on their order_id fields, while filtering the product_id value in od1 for the ID of the product you're looking for. This way, you'll get in the od2 side of the relationship all the products that were ordered in the orders that contain the product you're looking for.

The SQL code that retrieves all the products that were ordered together with the product identified by a product_id of 4 is

```
SELECT od2.product_id
FROM   order_detail od1
JOIN   order_detail od2
         ON od1.order_id = od2.order_id
WHERE  od1.product_id = 4;
```

This code returns a long list of products, which includes the product with the product_id of 4, such as this one:

```
product_id
----------
         4
         5
        10
        43
         4
         5
        10
        23
        25
        28
         4
        10
        12
        14
        43
```

Starting from this list of results, you need to get the products that are most frequently bought along with this product. The first problem with this list of products is that it includes the product with the product_id of 4. To eliminate it from the list (because, of course, you can't put it in the recommendations list), you simply add one more rule to the WHERE clause:

```
SELECT od2.product_id
FROM   order_detail od1
JOIN   order_detail od2
       ON od1.order_id = od2.order_id
WHERE  od1.product_id = 4 AND od2.product_id != 4;
```

Not surprisingly, you get a list of products that is similar to the previous one, except it doesn't contain the product with a product_id of 4 any more:

```
product_id
----------
         5
        10
        43
         5
        10
        23
        25
        28
        10
        12
        14
        43
```

Now the list of returned products is much shorter, but it contains multiple entries for the products that were ordered more than once in the orders that contain the product identifier 4. To get the most relevant recommendations, you need to see which products appear more frequently in this list. You do this by grouping the results of the previous query by product_id and sorting in descending order by how many times each product appears in the list (this number is given by the rank calculated column in the following code snippet):

```
SELECT    od2.product_id, COUNT(od2.product_id) AS rank
FROM      order_detail od1
JOIN      order_detail od2
          ON od1.order_id = od2.order_id
WHERE     od1.product_id = 4 AND od2.product_id != 4
GROUP BY  od2.product_id
ORDER BY  rank DESC;
```

This query now returns a list such as the following:

product_id	rank
10	3
5	2
43	2
23	1
25	1
28	1
12	1
14	1

If you don't need the rank to be returned, you can rewrite this query by using the COUNT aggregate function directly in the ORDER BY clause. You can also use the LIMIT keyword to specify how many records you're interested in. If you want the top five products of the list, this query does the trick:

```
SELECT   od2.product_id
FROM     order_detail od1
JOIN     order_detail od2
             ON od1.order_id = od2.order_id
WHERE    od1.product_id = 4 AND od2.product_id != 4
GROUP BY od2.product_id
ORDER BY COUNT(od2.product_id) DESC
LIMIT 5;
```

The results of this query are

product_id
10
43
5
23
28

Because this list of numbers doesn't make much sense to the human eye, you'll also want to know the name and the description of the recommended products. The following query does exactly this by querying the product table for the IDs returned by the previous query (the description isn't requested because of space reasons):

```
SELECT product_id, name
FROM    product
WHERE   product_id IN
          (
```

```
    SELECT   od2.product_id
    FROM     order_detail od1
    JOIN     order_detail od2 ON od1.order_id = od2.order_id
    WHERE    od1.product_id = 4 AND od2.product_id != 4
    GROUP BY od2.product_id
    ORDER BY COUNT(od2.product_id) DESC
    LIMIT 5
);
```

Based on the data from the previous fictional results, this query returns something like this:

product_id	name
10	Vinyl Policeman Cop Hat
43	Hussar Military Hat
5	Red Santa Cowboy Hat
23	Black Basque Beret
28	Moleskin Driver

Alternatively, you might want to calculate the product recommendations only using data from the orders that happened in the last *n* days. For this, you need an additional join with the orders table, which contains the date_created field. The following query calculates product recommendations based on orders placed in the past 30 days:

```
SELECT product_id, name
FROM    product
WHERE   product_id IN
    (
        SELECT   od2.product_id
        FROM     order_detail od1
        JOIN     order_detail od2
                    ON od1.order_id = od2.order_id
        JOIN     orders o
                    ON od1.order_id = o.order_id
        WHERE    od1.product_id = 7
                 AND od2.product_id != 7
                 AND (NOW() - o.created_on) < 30
        GROUP BY od2.product_id
        ORDER BY COUNT(od2.product_id) DESC
        LIMIT 5
    );
```

We won't use this trick in HatShop, but it's worth keeping in mind as a possibility.

Adding Product Recommendations

Make sure you understand the data tier logic explained earlier because you'll implement it in the catalog_get_recommendations database function. The only significant difference from the queries shown earlier is that you'll also ask for the product description, which will be truncated at a specified number of characters.

The catalog_get_recommendations database function is called when displaying what products were ordered together with the selected product. Follow the steps in the next exercise to add the catalog_get_recommendations function to the hatshop database.

Exercise: Adding the catalog_get_recommendations Function

1. Load pgAdmin III, and connect to the hatshop database.

2. Click Tools ➤ Query tool (or click the SQL button on the toolbar). A new query window should appear.

3. Use the query tool to execute this code, which creates the product_recommendation type and the catalog_get_recommendations function in your hatshop database:

```
-- Create product_recommendation type
CREATE TYPE product_recommendation AS
(
  product_id   INTEGER,
  name         VARCHAR(50),
  description  VARCHAR(1000)
);


-- Create catalog_get_recommend+ations function
CREATE FUNCTION catalog_get_recommendations(INTEGER, INTEGER)
RETURNS SETOF product_recommendation LANGUAGE plpgsql AS $$
  DECLARE
     inProductId                   ALIAS FOR $1;
     inShortProductDescriptionLength ALIAS FOR $2;
     outProductRecommendationRow product_recommendation;
  BEGIN
     FOR outProductRecommendationRow IN
       SELECT product_id, name, description
       FROM   product
       WHERE  product_id IN
              (SELECT   od2.product_id
               FROM     order_detail od1
               JOIN     order_detail od2
                        ON od1.order_id = od2.order_id
               WHERE    od1.product_id = inProductId
                        AND od2.product_id != inProductId
               GROUP BY od2.product_id
               ORDER BY COUNT(od2.product_id) DESC
               LIMIT    5)
     LOOP
```

```
      IF char_length(outProductRecommendationRow.description) >
         inShortProductDescriptionLength THEN
        outProductRecommendationRow.description :=
          substring(outProductRecommendationRow.description, 1,
                    inShortProductDescriptionLength) || '...';
      END IF;
      RETURN NEXT outProductRecommendationRow;
    END LOOP;
  END;
$$;
```

An Alternate Solution Using Subqueries

Because SQL is so versatile, catalog_get_recommendations can be written in a variety of ways. In our case, one popular alternative to using table joins is using subqueries. Here's a version of catalog_get_recommendations that uses subqueries instead of joins. The commented code is self-explanatory:

```
-- Create catalog_get_recommendations function
CREATE OR REPLACE FUNCTION catalog_get_recommendations(INTEGER, INTEGER)
RETURNS SETOF product_recommendation LANGUAGE plpgsql AS $$
  DECLARE
    inProductId                     ALIAS FOR $1;
    inShortProductDescriptionLength ALIAS FOR $2;
    outProductRecommendationRow product_recommendation;
  BEGIN
    FOR outProductRecommendationRow IN
      -- Returns the product recommendations
      SELECT product_id, name, description
      FROM   product
      WHERE  product_id IN
            (-- Returns the products that were ordered
             -- together with inProductId
             SELECT    product_id
             FROM      order_detail
             WHERE     order_id IN
                   (-- Returns the orders that contain inProductId
                    SELECT DISTINCT order_id
                    FROM            order_detail
                    WHERE           product_id = inProductId
                    LIMIT           5)
                    -- Must not include products that already
                    -- exist in the visitor's cart
                    AND product_id != inProductId
             -- Group the product_id so we can calculate the rank
             GROUP BY product_id
```

```
                    -- Order descending by rank
                    ORDER BY COUNT(product_id) DESC
                    LIMIT    5)
      LOOP
        IF char_length(outProductRecommendationRow.description) >
             inShortProductDescriptionLength THEN
           outProductRecommendationRow.description :=
               substring(outProductRecommendationRow.description, 1,
                         inShortProductDescriptionLength) || '...';
        END IF;
        RETURN NEXT outProductRecommendationRow;
      END LOOP;
  END;
$$;
```

Adding Shopping Cart Recommendations

The logic for showing shopping cart recommendations is very similar to what you did earlier,
except now you need to take into account all products that exist in the shopping cart, instead
of a single product. Follow the steps in the next exercise to add the shopping_cart_get_
recommendations function to the hatshop database.

Exercise: Adding the shopping_cart_get_recommendations Function

1. Load pgAdmin III, and connect to the hatshop database.

2. Click Tools ➤ Query tool (or click the SQL button on the toolbar). A new query window should appear.

3. Use the query tool to execute this code, which creates the shopping_cart_get_recommendations
   function in your hatshop database:

```
-- Create shopping_cart_get_recommendations function
CREATE FUNCTION shopping_cart_get_recommendations(CHAR(32), INTEGER)
RETURNS SETOF product_recommendation LANGUAGE plpgsql AS $$
  DECLARE
     inCartId                       ALIAS FOR $1;
     inShortProductDescriptionLength ALIAS FOR $2;
     outProductRecommendationRow product_recommendation;
  BEGIN
    FOR outProductRecommendationRow IN
       -- Returns the product recommendations
       SELECT product_id, name, description
       FROM   product
       WHERE  product_id IN
             (-- Returns the products that exist in a list of orders
              SELECT   od1.product_id
              FROM     order_detail od1
              JOIN     order_detail od2
```

```
                              ON od1.order_id = od2.order_id
                JOIN      shopping_cart
                              ON od2.product_id = shopping_cart.product_id
                WHERE     shopping_cart.cart_id = inCartId
                          -- Must not include products that already exist
                          -- in the visitor's cart
                          AND od1.product_id NOT IN
                        (-- Returns the products in the specified
                          -- shopping cart
                          SELECT product_id
                          FROM   shopping_cart
                          WHERE  cart_id = inCartId)
                -- Group the product_id so we can calculate the rank
                GROUP BY od1.product_id
                -- Order descending by rank
                ORDER BY COUNT(od1.product_id) DESC
                LIMIT    5)
      LOOP
        IF char_length(outProductRecommendationRow.description) >
            inShortProductDescriptionLength THEN
          outProductRecommendationRow.description :=
            substring(outProductRecommendationRow.description, 1,
                      inShortProductDescriptionLength) || '...';
        END IF;
        RETURN NEXT outProductRecommendationRow;
      END LOOP;
    END;
  $$;
```

The alternate version of this function, which uses subqueries instead of table joins, looks like this:

```
-- Create shopping_cart_get_recommendations function
CREATE OR REPLACE FUNCTION shopping_cart_get_recommendations(CHAR(32), INTEGER)
RETURNS SETOF product_recommendation LANGUAGE plpgsql AS $$
  DECLARE
    inCartId                        ALIAS FOR $1;
    inShortProductDescriptionLength ALIAS FOR $2;
    outProductRecommendationRow product_recommendation;
  BEGIN
    FOR outProductRecommendationRow IN
      -- Returns the product recommendations
      SELECT product_id, name, description
      FROM   product
      WHERE  product_id IN
            (-- Returns the products that exist in a list of orders
            SELECT   product_id
            FROM     order_detail
            WHERE    order_id IN
```

```
                        (-- Returns the orders that contain certain products
                         SELECT DISTINCT order_id
                         FROM            order_detail
                         WHERE           product_id IN
                                        (-- Returns the products in the
                                         -- specified shopping cart
                                         SELECT product_id
                                         FROM   shopping_cart
                                         WHERE  cart_id = inCartId))
                        -- Must not include products that already
                        -- exist in the visitor's cart
                        AND product_id NOT IN
                       (-- Returns the products in the specified
                        -- shopping cart
                        SELECT product_id
                        FROM   shopping_cart
                        WHERE  cart_id = inCartId)
                  -- Group the product_id so we can calculate the rank
                  GROUP BY product_id
                  -- Order descending by rank
                  ORDER BY COUNT(product_id) DESC
                  LIMIT    5)
      LOOP
        IF char_length(outProductRecommendationRow.description) >
           inShortProductDescriptionLength THEN
          outProductRecommendationRow.description :=
            substring(outProductRecommendationRow.description, 1,
                      inShortProductDescriptionLength) || '...';
        END IF;
        RETURN NEXT outProductRecommendationRow;
      END LOOP;
    END;
$$;
```

Implementing the Business Tier

The business tier of the product recommendations system consists of two methods both named GetRecommendations. One of them is located in the Catalog class and retrieves recommendations for a product details page, and the other one is located in the ShoppingCart class and retrieves recommendations to be displayed in the visitor's shopping cart.

Exercise: Implementing the Business Logic

1. Add the following code to the `business/catalog.php` file:

```
// Get product recommendations
public static function GetRecommendations($productId)
{
  // Build the SQL query
  $sql = 'SELECT * FROM catalog_get_recommendations(
                      :product_id, :short_product_description_length);';
  // Build the parameters array
  $params = array (':product_id' => $productId,
                   ':short_product_description_length' =>
                     SHORT_PRODUCT_DESCRIPTION_LENGTH);
  // Prepare the statement with PDO-specific functionality
  $result = DatabaseHandler::Prepare($sql);

  // Execute the query and return the results
  return DatabaseHandler::GetAll($result, $params);
}
```

2. Open the `shopping_cart.php` file located in the `business` folder, and add the following code:

```
// Get product recommendations for the shopping cart
public static function GetRecommendations()
{
  // Build the SQL query
  $sql = 'SELECT * FROM shopping_cart_get_recommendations(
                      :cart_id, :short_product_description_length);';
  // Build the parameters array
  $params = array (':cart_id' => self::GetCartId(),
                   ':short_product_description_length' =>
                     SHORT_PRODUCT_DESCRIPTION_LENGTH);
  // Prepare the statement with PDO-specific functionality
  $result = DatabaseHandler::Prepare($sql);

  // Execute the query and return the results
  return DatabaseHandler::GetAll($result, $params);
}
```

Implementing the Presentation Tier

The next exercise shows you how to update the product and cart_details componentized templates to display the product recommendations.

Exercise: Updating the product and cart_details Componentized Templates

1. Open the `presentation/smarty_plugins/function.load_product.php` file, and add the `$mRecommendation` member to the `Product` class:

   ```
   // Public variables to be used in Smarty template
   public $mProduct;
   public $mPageLink = 'index.php';
   public $mAddToCartLink;
   public $mRecommendations;
   ```

2. Now you have to get the recommended products data in `$mRecommendations`, and create links to their home pages. Modify the `init()` method of the `Product` class as highlighted here:

   ```
   $this->mAddToCartLink = 'index.php?ProductID=' . $this->_mProductId .
                           '&CartAction=' . ADD_PRODUCT;

   // Get product recommendations
   $this->mRecommendations =
     Catalog::GetRecommendations($this->_mProductId);

   // Create recommended product links
   for ($i = 0; $i < count($this->mRecommendations); $i++)
     $this->mRecommendations[$i]['link'] = 'index.php?ProductID=' .
       $this->mRecommendations[$i]['product_id'];
   ```

3. The last step to complete the product recommendations system for the product details page is to update the `product` template to display the list of recommendations. Add the following lines at the end of `presentation/templates/product.tpl`:

   ```
   {if $product->mRecommendations}
   <br /><br />
   <span class="description">Customers who bought this also bought:</span>
     {section name=m loop=$product->mRecommendations}
   <br /><br />
       {strip}
   <a class="product_recommendation"
      href="{$product->mRecommendations[m].link|prepare_link:"http"}">
      {$product->mRecommendations[m].name}
   </a>
       {/strip}
    -
   <span>{$product->mRecommendations[m].description}</span>
     {/section}
   {/if}
   ```

4. Open hatshop.css, and add the following style:

```
.product_recommendation
{
  color: #0000ff;
  text-decoration: underline;
}
```

5. Now let's modify the cart_details componentized template to show product recommendations. Open function.load_cart_details.php located in the presentation/smarty_plugins folder to add the $mRecommendation member to the CartDetails class:

```
public $mCartReferrer = 'index.php';
public $mCartDetailsTarget;
public $mRecommendations;
```

6. Now you have to get the recommended products data in $mRecommendations, and create links to their home pages. Modify the init() method of the CartDetails class as highlighted here:

```
        $this->mSavedCartProducts[$i]['remove'] = 'index.php?ProductID=' .
          $this->mSavedCartProducts[$i]['product_id'] .
          '&CartAction=' . REMOVE_PRODUCT;
      }

    // Get product recommendations for the shopping cart
    $this->mRecommendations =
      ShoppingCart::GetRecommendations();

    // Create recommended product links
    for ($i = 0; $i < count($this->mRecommendations); $i++)
      $this->mRecommendations[$i]['link'] = 'index.php?ProductID=' .
        $this->mRecommendations[$i]['product_id'];
  }
}
?>
```

7. And, finally, the last step is to update the cart_details template to display the list of recommendations. Add the following lines at the end of presentation/templates/cart_details.tpl:

```
{if $cart_details->mRecommendations}
<br /><br />
<span class="description">Customers who bought this also bought:</span>
  {section name=m loop=$cart_details->mRecommendations}
<br /><br />
    {strip}
<a class="product_recommendation"
   href="{$cart_details->mRecommendations[m].link|prepare_link:"http"}">
   {$cart_details->mRecommendations[m].name}
</a>
    {/strip}
  -
<span>{$cart_details->mRecommendations[m].description}</span>
  {/section}
{/if}
```

8. Load HatShop, place some orders, and then check the product and shopping cart details pages display recommendations based on the ordered products! The results should look like Figures 10-1 and 10-2 shown earlier in this chapter.

Summary

Showing product recommendations is a great way to encourage sales, and we succeeded in implementing this functionality throughout this short chapter. The greatest challenge was to build the SQL query that gets the list of recommended products, and we analyzed how to create it, step by step.

In the next chapter, you'll enter the third stage of development by adding customer accounts functionality.

PART 3

Phase III of Development

CHAPTER 11

■■■

Managing Customer Details

So far in this book you've built a basic, but functional site, and integrated it with PayPal for accepting payments and confirming orders. In this section of the book, you'll take things a little further. By cutting out PayPal from your ordering process, you can obtain much better control—as well as reduce overhead costs. It isn't as complicated as you might think, but we do have to be careful to do things right.

In this chapter, we'll be laying the groundwork for this by implementing a customer account system.

To make e-commerce sites more user friendly, you usually store details such as credit card numbers in a database, so that users don't have to retype this information each time they place an order. The customer account system you'll implement will store this information and include all of the web pages required for the entry of such details.

As well as implementing these web pages, we'll need to take several other factors into account. First, simply placing credit card numbers, expiry dates, and other important information into a database in plain text isn't ideal because it raises the possibility that this data could be stolen should the server be compromised. This could occur remotely or be perpetrated by individuals within our organization. In addition to enforcing a prohibitively restrictive access policy to such data, it can be a lot easier simply to encrypt sensitive information and retrieve it programmatically when required. We'll create a security library to ease this functionality.

Secondly, secure communications are important because you'll be capturing sensitive information such as credit card details via the web. We can't just put a form up for people to access via HTTP and allow them to send it to us because the information could be intercepted. Instead, we'll use SSL over HTTPS connections. You'll take the HatShop application to the point where you can move on and implement your own back-end order pipeline in the next chapter.

In this chapter, you'll learn how to

- Store customer accounts

- Implement the security classes

- Add customer accounts functionality to HatShop

- Create the checkout page

Storing Customer Accounts

You can handle customer account functionality in web sites in many ways. In general, however, the methods share the following features:

- Customers log in to access secured areas of the web site.

- Once logged in, the web application remembers the customer until the customer logs out (either manually via a Log Out link, or automatically if the session times out or a server error occurs).

- All secure pages in a web application need to check whether a customer is logged in before allowing access.

First, let's look at the general implementation details for the HatShop e-commerce site.

The HatShop Customer Account Scheme

One simple way to determine whether a customer is logged in is to store the customer ID in the session state. You can then verify whether a value is present at the start of the secured pages, and warn the user if not. The login form itself can then authenticate the user and store a value in the session state if successful, ready for later retrieval. To log a user out, you simply remove the ID from the session state.

To log in, a customer needs to supply a username (we'll use the customer's email address here because it is guaranteed to be unique) and a password. Sending this information over the Internet is a sensitive issue because third parties can eavesdrop and capture it. Later in this chapter, we'll look at how to enable secure communications over the Internet. For now, though, we'll concentrate on the authentication side of things, which is unaffected by the type of connection used to transmit the email address and password of the customer.

Another issue related to security concerns storing user passwords. It isn't a good idea to store user passwords in your database in plain text because this information is a potential target for attack. Instead, you should store what is known as the **hash** of the password. A hash is a unique string that represents the password but cannot be converted back into the password itself. To validate the password entered by the user, then, you simply need to generate a hash for the password entered and compare it with the hash stored in your database. If the hashes match, then the passwords entered match as well, so you can be sure that the customer is genuine.

This leads to another important task—you need to supply a way for new users to register. The result of registration is to add a new customer to your database, including username and password hash information.

To implement this scheme in your application, you'll complete the following tasks:

- Create two new database tables, the first called `customer` to hold customer details, and the second called `shipping_region`, which stores possible shipping regions that a customer can reside in.

- Implement the associated methods in data and business tiers that add, modify, and retrieve information from `customer` and `shipping_region`.

- Modify the `cart_details` componentized template, which will now redirect the user to a checkout page that will be implemented in a new componentized template called `checkout_info`.

- Create a componentized template for customer login called `customer_login`.

- Create a componentized template for customer registration or for editing basic account details called `customer_details`.

- Create a componentized template named `customer_credit_card` that allows customers to enter credit card details.

- Create a componentized template named `customer_address` for customers to enter a shipping address.

Creating customer and shipping_region Tables

Now you can build the `customer` and `shipping_region` tables by following the steps in the next exercise.

Exercise: Creating the Database Tables

1. Load pgAdmin III, and connect to the `hatshop` database.

2. Click Tools ➤ Query tool (or click the SQL button on the toolbar). A new query window should appear.

3. Use the query tool to execute this code, which creates the `shipping_region` table in your `hatshop` database:

```
-- Create shipping_region table
CREATE TABLE shipping_region
(
  shipping_region_id SERIAL      NOT NULL,
  shipping_region    VARCHAR(100) NOT NULL,
  CONSTRAINT pk_shipping_region_id PRIMARY KEY (shipping_region_id)
);
```

4. Now add the values "`Please select`", "`US / Canada`", "`Europe`", and "`Rest of the World`" to the `shipping_region` table. "`Please Select`" should always have a `shipping_region_id` value of `1`—this is important! Execute the following SQL code using the query tool to add the mentioned values to the `shipping_region` table:

```
-- Populate shipping_region table
INSERT INTO shipping_region (shipping_region_id, shipping_region)
     VALUES (1, 'Please Select');
INSERT INTO shipping_region (shipping_region_id, shipping_region)
     VALUES (2, 'US / Canada');
INSERT INTO shipping_region (shipping_region_id, shipping_region)
     VALUES (3, 'Europe');
```

```
INSERT INTO shipping_region (shipping_region_id, shipping_region)
      VALUES (4, 'Rest of World');
-- Update the sequence
ALTER SEQUENCE shipping_region_shipping_region_id_seq RESTART WITH 5;
```

5. Use the query tool to execute this code, which creates the `customer` table in your `hatshop` database:

```
-- Create customer table
CREATE TABLE customer
(
  customer_id          SERIAL        NOT NULL,
  name                 VARCHAR(50)   NOT NULL,
  email                VARCHAR(100)  NOT NULL,
  password             VARCHAR(50)   NOT NULL,
  credit_card          TEXT,
  address_1            VARCHAR(100),
  address_2            VARCHAR(100),
  city                 VARCHAR(100),
  region               VARCHAR(100),
  postal_code          VARCHAR(100),
  country              VARCHAR(100),
  shipping_region_id   INTEGER       NOT NULL  DEFAULT 1,
  day_phone            VARCHAR(100),
  eve_phone            VARCHAR(100),
  mob_phone            VARCHAR(100),
  CONSTRAINT pk_customer_id        PRIMARY KEY (customer_id),
  CONSTRAINT fk_shipping_region_id FOREIGN KEY (shipping_region_id)
            REFERENCES shipping_region (shipping_region_id)
            ON UPDATE RESTRICT ON DELETE RESTRICT,
  CONSTRAINT uk_email              UNIQUE (email)
);
```

Customers' credit card information will be stored in an encrypted format so that no one will be able to access this information. However, unlike with passwords, you need to be able to retrieve this credit card information when required by the order pipeline, so you can't simply use a hash (the hash algorithm is one-way). You'll implement the credit card data encryption functionality using a number of business tier classes, which you'll see next.

Implementing the Security Classes

So far, the following two areas need security functionality:

- Password hashing

- Credit card encryption

Both these tasks are carried out by business tier classes that you'll save in the `business` directory in the following files:

`password_hasher.php`: Contains the `PasswordHasher` class, which contains the static method `Hash()` that returns the hash value for the password supplied.

`secure_card.php`: Contains the `SecureCard` class, which represents a credit card. This class can be supplied with credit card information, which is then accessible in encrypted format. This class can also take encrypted credit card data and supply access to the decrypted information.

`symmetric_crypt.php`: The class contained in this file, `SymmetricCrypt`, is used by `SecureCard` to encrypt and decrypt data. This means that if you ever want to change the encryption method, you only need to modify the code here, leaving the `SecureCard` class untouched.

We'll look at the code for hashing first, followed by encryption.

Implementing Hashing Functionality in the Business Tier

Hashing is a means by which you can obtain a unique value that represents an object. The algorithm used to convert the source byte array into a hashed byte array varies. The most used hashing algorithm is called MD5 (Message Digest, another name for the hash code generated), which generates a 128-bit hash value. Unfortunately, many kinds of attacks are based on word dictionaries constructed against MD5 hashes. Another popular hashing algorithm is called SHA1 (Secure Hash Algorithm), which generates a 160-bit hash value. SHA1 is generally agreed to be more secure (although slower) than MD5.

In the HatShop implementation, you'll use SHA1, although it is easy to change this if you require another type of security. Now, you'll implement the `PasswordHasher` class in the following exercise.

■Note PHP doesn't come by default with support for `mhash` and `mcrypt`, the libraries we're using in this chapter for hashing and encryption. See Appendix A to learn how to enable support for `mhash` and `mcrypt`.

Exercise: Implementing the PasswordHasher Class

To implement the `PasswordHasher` class, follow these steps:

1. Add the following line at the end of the `include/config.php` file. This defines a random value (feel free to change it) to add to the passwords before hashing them.

```
// Random value used for hashing
define('HASH_PREFIX', 'K1-');
```

2. Create a new file named password_hasher.php in the business directory, and write the PasswordHasher class in it:

```php
<?php
class PasswordHasher
{
  public static function Hash($password, $withPrefix = true)
  {
    if ($withPrefix)
      $hashed_password = sha1(HASH_PREFIX . $password);
    else
      $hashed_password = sha1($password);

    return $hashed_password;
  }
}
?>
```

3. Next, write a simple test page to test the PasswordHasher class. Create a new file named test_hasher.php in the hatshop folder with the following code in it:

```php
<?php
if (isset ($_GET['to_be_hashed']))
{
  require_once 'include/config.php';
  require_once BUSINESS_DIR . 'password_hasher.php';

  $original_string = $_GET['to_be_hashed'];

  echo 'The hash of "' . $original_string . '" is ' .
      PasswordHasher::Hash($original_string, false);

  echo '<br />';

  echo '... and the hash of "' . HASH_PREFIX . $original_string .
      '" (secret prefix concateneted with password) is ' .
      PasswordHasher::Hash($original_string, true);
}
?>

<br /><br />
<form action="test_hasher.php">
  Write your password:
  <input type="text" name="to_be_hashed" /><br />
  <input type="submit" value="Hash it" />
</form>
```

4. Load the `test_hasher.php` file in your favorite browser, enter a password to hash, and admire the results as shown in Figure 11-1.

Figure 11-1. *Testing the password hashing functionality*

How It Works: The Hashing Functionality

The code in the `PasswordHasher` class is pretty simple. By default, the static `Hash()` method returns the hash of a string representing the secret prefix concatenated with the password.

You might be wondering what the secret prefix is all about. As you might have already guessed, it has to do with security. If your database is stolen, the thief could try to match the hashed password values with a large dictionary of hashed values that looks something like this:

```
word1     .... sha1(word1)
word2     .... sha1(word2)
...
word10000 .... sha1(word10000)
```

If two hash values match, it means the original strings (which, in our case, are the customers' passwords) also match.

Appending a secret prefix to the password before hashing it reduces the risk of dictionary attacks on the hashed passwords database because the resulting string being hashed (secret prefix + password) is less likely to be found in a large dictionary of "password – hash value" pairs.

The `test_hasher.php` page tests your newly created `PasswordHasher` class.

> **■Note** You can also handle hashing at the database level by using PostgreSQL cryptographic functions. First, you need to add cryptographic functions to PostgreSQL. Unix users should look in the `contrib/pgcrypto` directory from PostgreSQL sources and follow the instructions (for detailed instructions please see Appendix A). Then, for example, you could execute the following PostgreSQL statement to see the PostgreSQL SHA1 in action:
>
> ```
> SELECT ENCODE(DIGEST('freedom', 'sha1'), 'hex');
> ```
>
> Of course, when relying on PostgreSQL's hashing functionality, the passwords travel in "plain format" to your PostgreSQL server, so if the PostgreSQL server is on another network (which is quite unlikely, however), you must secure the connection between your web server and the PostgreSQL server by using SSL connections. This can be avoided by handling hashing in the PHP code, which also offers better portability because it doesn't rely on PostgreSQL-specific functions. Remember that for the same portability reason, we chose to use PDO instead of using PHP PostgreSQL-specific functions.

Implementing the Encryption Functionality in the Business Tier

Encryption comes in many shapes and sizes and continues to be a hot topic. There is no definitive solution to encrypting data, although there is plenty of advice on the subject. In general, the two forms of encryption are

Symmetric encryption: A single key is used both to encrypt and decrypt data.

Asymmetric encryption: Separate keys are used to encrypt and decrypt data. The encryption key is commonly known as the **public key**, and anyone can use it to encrypt information. The decryption key is known as the **private key** because it can only be used to decrypt data that has been encrypted using the public key. The encryption key (public key) and the decryption key (private key) are mathematically related and are always generated in pairs. The public key and private key can't be obtained one from another. If you have a public key/private key pair, you can send the public key to parties that need to encrypt information for you. You will be the only one who knows the private key associated with that public key, thus the only one able to decrypt the information.

Although asymmetric encryption is more secure, it also requires much more processing power. Symmetric encryption is faster but can be less secure because both the encryptor and decryptor have knowledge of a single key. With symmetric encryption, the encryptor needs to send the key to the decryptor. With Internet communications, there is often no way of ensuring that this key remains a secret from third parties when it is sent to the encryptor.

Asymmetric encryption gets around this by using key pairs. There is never a need for the decryption key to be divulged, so it's much more difficult for a third party to break the encryption. Because it requires a lot more processing power, however, the practical method of operation is to use asymmetric encryption to exchange a symmetric key over the Internet, which is then used for symmetric encryption safe in the knowledge that this key has not been exposed to third parties.

In the HatShop application, things are much simpler than with Internet communications. You just need to encrypt data for storage in the database and decrypt it again when required, so you can use a symmetric encryption algorithm.

■Note Behind the scenes, some asymmetric encryption is also going on, however, because that is the method implemented by HTTPS communication.

As with hashing, several algorithms can be used for both symmetric and asymmetric encryption. PHP's `mcrypt` library contains implementations of the most important symmetric algorithms. No library in PHP deals with asymmetric encryption, but if you ever need to do asymmetric encryption, you can use the PGP (Pretty Good Privacy) family of software (for more information, see `http://www.pgp.com`) and GnuPG (`http://www.gnupg.org`).

Two of the more commonly used asymmetric algorithms are DSA (Digital Signature Algorithm) and RSA (Rivest-Shamir-Adleman, from the names of its inventors, Ronald Rivest, Adi Shamir, and Leonard Adleman). Of these, DSA can only be used to "sign" data so that its authenticity can be verified, whereas RSA is more versatile (although slower than DSA when used to generate digital signatures). DSA is the current standard for digital authentication used by the U.S. government. Both the DSA and the RSA asymmetric algorithms are implemented in the PGP family of software (PGP and GnuPG).

Some popular symmetric algorithms found in the `mcrypt` library are DES (Data Encryption Standard), Triple DES (3DES), RC2 (Ron's Code, or Rivest's Cipher, depending on who you ask, also from Ronald Rivest), and Rijndael (from the names of its inventors, Joan Daemen and Vincent Rijmen).

DES AND RIJNDAEL

DES has been the standard for some time now, although this is gradually changing. It uses a 64-bit key, however, in practice only 56 of these bits are used (8 bits are "parity" bits), which are not strong enough to avoid being broken using today's computers.

Both Triple DES and RC2 are variations of DES. Triple DES effectively encrypts data using three separate DES encryptions with three keys totaling 168 bits when parity bits are subtracted. The RC2 variant can have key lengths up to 128 bits (longer keys are also possible using RC3, RC4, and so on), so it can be made weaker or stronger than DES depending on the key size.

Rijndael is a completely separate encryption method and has now been accepted as the new AES (Advanced Encryption Standard) standard (several competing algorithms were considered before Rijndael was chosen). This standard is intended to replace DES and is gradually becoming the most used (and secure) symmetric encryption algorithm.

The tasks associated with encrypting and decrypting data are a little more involved than hashing. The `mcrypt` functions are optimized to work with raw data, so you have some work to do with data conversion. You also have to define both a key and an initialization vector (IV) to perform encryption and decryption. The IV is required due to the nature of encryption: the data blocks are usually encrypted in sequence, and calculating the encrypted values for one sequence of bits involves using some data from the preceding sequence of bits. Because there are no such values at the start of encryption, an IV is used instead. For AES encryption (Rijndael_128), the IV and the key must be 32 bytes long.

■Note At `http://en.wikipedia.org/wiki/Block_cipher_modes_of_operation`, you can learn more about the various modes of encryption.

The general steps required for encrypting a string are as follows:

1. Create a 32-byte random IV.

2. Convert the IV (which you keep as a hexadecimal string) into a byte array.

3. Encrypt the string using AES encryption by supplying the IV in byte array format.

4. Convert the resulting encrypted data from a byte array into a hexadecimal string.

Decryption follows a similar scheme:

1. Convert the IV (which you keep as a hexadecimal string) into a byte array (the same with the encryption first step).

2. Convert the string to decrypt into a byte array.

3. Decrypt the binary string from the previous step by supplying the IV in a byte array.

In your code, you'll use AES, but the code in the `SymmetricCrypt` class can be modified to use any of the supported encryption algorithms.

Exercise: Implementing the SymmetricCrypt Class

1. Add a new file in the `business` directory called `symmetric_crypt.php` with the following code in it:

```php
<?php
class SymmetricCrypt
{
    // Encryption/decryption key
    private static $_msSecretKey = 'From Dusk Till Dawn';

    // The initialization vector
    private static $_msHexaIv = 'c7098adc8d6128b5d4b4f7b2fe7f7f05';

    // Use the Rijndael Encryption Algorithm
    private static $_msCipherAlgorithm = MCRYPT_RIJNDAEL_128;

    /* Function encrypts plain-text string received as parameter
       and returns the result in hexadecimal format */
```

```php
    public static function Encrypt($plainString)
    {
      // Pack SymmetricCrypt::_msHexaIv into a binary string
      $binary_iv = pack('H*', self::$_msHexaIv);

      // Encrypt $plainString
      $binary_encrypted_string = mcrypt_encrypt(
                                 self::$_msCipherAlgorithm,
                                 self::$_msSecretKey,
                                 $plainString,
                                 MCRYPT_MODE_CBC,
                                 $binary_iv);

      // Convert $binary_encrypted_string to hexadecimal format
      $hexa_encrypted_string = bin2hex($binary_encrypted_string);

      return $hexa_encrypted_string;
    }

    /* Function decrypts hexadecimal string received as parameter
       and returns the result in hexadecimal format */
    public static function Decrypt($encryptedString)
    {
      // Pack Symmetric::_msHexaIv into a binary string
      $binary_iv = pack('H*', self::$_msHexaIv);

      // Convert string in hexadecimal to byte array
      $binary_encrypted_string = pack('H*', $encryptedString);

      // Decrypt $binary_encrypted_string
      $decrypted_string = mcrypt_decrypt(
                          self::$_msCipherAlgorithm,
                          self::$_msSecretKey,
                          $binary_encrypted_string,
                          MCRYPT_MODE_CBC,
                          $binary_iv);

      return $decrypted_string;
    }
  }
?>
```

2. Add a test file in the `hatshop` folder called `test_encryption.php` with the following code:

```php
<?php
if (isset ($_GET['my_string']))
{
  require_once 'include/config.php';
```

```
    require_once BUSINESS_DIR . 'symmetric_crypt.php';

    $string = $_GET['my_string'];

    echo 'The string is:<br />' . $string . '<br /><br />';

    $encrypted_string = SymmetricCrypt::Encrypt($string);

    echo 'Encrypted string: <br />' . $encrypted_string . '<br /><br />';

    $decrypted_string = SymmetricCrypt::Decrypt($encrypted_string);

    echo 'Decrypted string:<br />' . $decrypted_string;
  }
  ?>

  <br /><br />
  <form action="test_encryption.php">
    Enter string to encrypt:
    <input type="text" name="my_string" /><br />
    <input type="submit" value="Encrypt" />
  </form>
```

3. Load the newly created test_encryption.php file in your favorite browser and give a string to encrypt/decrypt (see Figure 11-2).

■**Note** If the mcrypt library wasn't installed or configured correctly, you'll receive a fatal error about the call to mcrypt_encrypt(). If that happens, check the installation instructions in Appendix A.

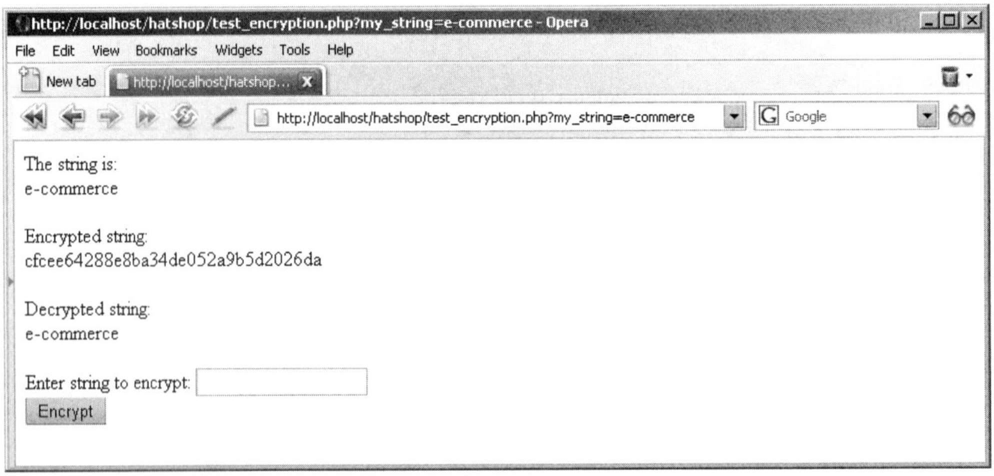

Figure 11-2. *Testing encryption*

■**Caution** As you might have noticed after running the test page, the decrypted string always has a length that is a multiple of 32 bytes. If the original string is less than 32 bytes, null characters are appended until the string's length becomes a multiple of 32 bytes. You need to be careful with this detail because it means the decrypted value of the string may not be identical to the encrypted value. For our HatShop project, because we'll encrypt XML data and the values of interest are between XML tags, we won't need to worry about having additional void characters at the end of the string.

How It Works: Encryption Functionality in the Business Tier

The SymmetricCrypt class has two static methods, Encrypt() and Decrypt(), which encrypt and decrypt data, and a number of encryption configurations parameters stored as static members:

```
// Encryption/decryption key
private static $_msSecretKey = 'From Dusk Till Dawn';

// The initialization vector
private static $_msHexaIv = 'c7098adc8d6128b5d4b4f7b2fe7f7f05';

// Use the Rijndael Encryption Algorithm
private static $_msCipherAlgorithm = MCRYPT_RIJNDAEL_128;
```

The secret key is 16 characters (bytes) long for AES algorithms. Using a smaller key is allowed by the mcrypt library but will reduce the encryption security. The IV should be exactly 16 bytes long for AES and will be kept as a hexadecimal string (2x16=32 chars long). Both $_msSecretKey and $_msHexaIv variables are set to temporary values here. They could just as easily take any other values, depending on the key you want to use.

Encrypt() starts by converting the IV from its hexadecimal value to a byte array because this is the format expected by the mcrypt_encrypt function (the one that does the actual encryption):

```
// Pack SymmetricCrypt::_msHexaIv into a binary string
$binary_iv = pack('H*', self::$_msHexaIv);
```

The conversion is done using PHP's pack function (learn more about it at http://www.php.net/pack).

The call to mcrypt_encrypt follows:

```
// Encrypt $plainString
$binary_encrypted_string = mcrypt_encrypt(
                        self::$_msCipherAlgorithm,
                        self::$_msSecretKey,
                        $plainString,
                        MCRYPT_MODE_CBC,
                        $binary_iv);
```

This is the call that performs the actual encryption. Its parameters are obvious, and you can find more detail about the mcrypt_encrypt function at http://www.php.net/mcrypt. The MCRYPT_MODE_CBC specifies the "cipher block chaining" encryption method; this method uses a chaining mechanism in which the encryption of each block of data depends on the encryption results of preceding blocks, except for the first block in which the IV is used instead.

At the end, the encrypted string is transformed into hexadecimal format, which is easier to work with (for example, to save in the database or in a configuration file):

```
// Convert $binary_encrypted_string to hexadecimal format
$hexa_encrypted_string = bin2hex($binary_encrypted_string);
```

The Decrypt() method is very similar to the Encrypt() method. First, you need the IV to be in a binary form (the same first step you took in the Encrypt() method).

As the Encrypt() method returns the encrypted string as a hexadecimal string, the input parameter of Decrypt() is also a hexadecimal string. You must convert this string to a byte array, which is the format that mcrypt_decrypt needs:

```
// Convert string in hexadecimal to byte array
$binary_encrypted_string = pack('H*', $encryptedString);

// Decrypt $binary_encrypted_string
$decrypted_string = mcrypt_decrypt(
                    self::$_msCipherAlgorithm,
                    self::$_msSecretKey,
                    $binary_encrypted_string,
                    MCRYPT_MODE_CBC,
                    $binary_iv);

return $decrypted_string;
```

The test_encryption.php test file for this class simply encrypts and decrypts data, demonstrating that things are working properly. The code for this is very simple, so we won't detail it here.

Now that you have the SymmetricCrypt class code, the last step in creating the security-related classes is to add the SecureCard class.

Storing Credit Cart Information Using the SecureCard Class

In the following exercise, you'll build the SecureCard class, which represents the credit card of a customer. This class will use the functionality you implemented in the previous two exercises to ensure that its data will be stored securely in the database.

Exercise: Implementing the SecureCard Class

1. Create a new file named secure_card.php in the business folder, and add the following code to it:

```
<?php
// Represents a credit card
class SecureCard
{
```

```php
// Private members containing credit card's details
private $_mIsDecrypted = false;
private $_mIsEncrypted = false;
private $_mCardHolder;
private $_mCardNumber;
private $_mIssueDate;
private $_mExpiryDate;
private $_mIssueNumber;
private $_mCardType;
private $_mEncryptedData;
private $_mXmlCardData;

// Class constructor
public function __construct()
{
  // Nothing here
}

// Decrypt data
public function LoadEncryptedDataAndDecrypt($newEncryptedData)
{
  $this->_mEncryptedData = $newEncryptedData;
  $this->DecryptData();
}

// Encrypt data
public function LoadPlainDataAndEncrypt($newCardHolder, $newCardNumber,
                                        $newIssueDate, $newExpiryDate,
                                        $newIssueNumber, $newCardType)
{
  $this->_mCardHolder = $newCardHolder;
  $this->_mCardNumber = $newCardNumber;
  $this->_mIssueDate = $newIssueDate;
  $this->_mExpiryDate = $newExpiryDate;
  $this->_mIssueNumber = $newIssueNumber;
  $this->_mCardType = $newCardType;
  $this->EncryptData();
}

// Create XML with credit card information
private function CreateXml()
{
  // Encode card details as XML document
  $xml_card_data = &$this->_mXmlCardData;
  $xml_card_data = new DOMDocument();

  $document_root = $xml_card_data->createElement('CardDetails');
```

```php
    $child = $xml_card_data->createElement('CardHolder');
    $child = $document_root->appendChild($child);
    $value = $xml_card_data->createTextNode($this->_mCardHolder);
    $value = $child->appendChild($value);

    $child = $xml_card_data->createElement('CardNumber');
    $child = $document_root->appendChild($child);
    $value = $xml_card_data->createTextNode($this->_mCardNumber);
    $value = $child->appendChild($value);

    $child = $xml_card_data->createElement('IssueDate');
    $child = $document_root->appendChild($child);
    $value = $xml_card_data->createTextNode($this->_mIssueDate);
    $value = $child->appendChild($value);

    $child = $xml_card_data->createElement('ExpiryDate');
    $child = $document_root->appendChild($child);
    $value = $xml_card_data->createTextNode($this->_mExpiryDate);
    $value = $child->appendChild($value);

    $child = $xml_card_data->createElement('IssueNumber');
    $child = $document_root->appendChild($child);
    $value = $xml_card_data->createTextNode($this->_mIssueNumber);
    $value = $child->appendChild($value);

    $child = $xml_card_data->createElement('CardType');
    $child = $document_root->appendChild($child);
    $value = $xml_card_data->createTextNode($this->_mCardType);
    $value = $child->appendChild($value);

    $document_root = $xml_card_data->appendChild($document_root);
  }

  // Extract information from XML credit card data
  private function ExtractXml($decryptedData)
  {
    $xml = simplexml_load_string($decryptedData);
    $this->_mCardHolder = (string) $xml->CardHolder;
    $this->_mCardNumber = (string) $xml->CardNumber;
    $this->_mIssueDate = (string) $xml->IssueDate;
    $this->_mExpiryDate = (string) $xml->ExpiryDate;
    $this->_mIssueNumber = (string) $xml->IssueNumber;
    $this->_mCardType = (string) $xml->CardType;
  }

  // Encrypts the XML credit card data
  private function EncryptData()
  {
```

```php
  // Put data into XML doc
  $this->CreateXml();

  // Encrypt data
  $this->_mEncryptedData =
    SymmetricCrypt::Encrypt($this->_mXmlCardData->saveXML());

  // Set encrypted flag
  $this->_mIsEncrypted = true;
}

// Decrypts XML credit card data
private function DecryptData()
{
  // Decrypt data
  $decrypted_data = SymmetricCrypt::Decrypt($this->_mEncryptedData);

  // Extract data from XML
  $this->ExtractXml($decrypted_data);

  // Set decrypted flag
  $this->_mIsDecrypted = true;
}

public function __get($name)
{
  if ($name == 'EncryptedData')
  {
    if ($this->_mIsEncrypted)
      return $this->_mEncryptedData;
    else
      throw new Exception('Data not encrypted');
  }
  elseif ($name == 'CardNumberX')
  {
    if ($this->_mIsDecrypted)
      return 'XXXX-XXXX-XXXX-' .
        substr($this->_mCardNumber, strlen($this->_mCardNumber) - 4, 4);
    else
      throw new Exception('Data not decrypted');
  }
  elseif (in_array($name, array ('CardHolder', 'CardNumber', 'IssueDate',
                                 'ExpiryDate', 'IssueNumber', 'CardType')))
  {
    $name = '_m' . $name;

    if ($this->_mIsDecrypted)
```

```
        return $this->$name;
      else
        throw new Exception('Data not decrypted');
    }
    else
    {
      throw new Exception('Property ' . $name . ' not found');
    }
  }
}
?>
```

2. Create a new file named test_card.php file in the hatshop folder:

```php
<?php
require_once 'include/config.php';
require_once BUSINESS_DIR . 'symmetric_crypt.php';
require_once BUSINESS_DIR . 'secure_card.php';

$card_holder = 'Mihai Bucica';
$card_number = '1234567890123456';
$expiry_date = '01/09';
$issue_date = '01/01';
$issue_number = 100;
$card_type = 'Mastercard';

echo '<br />Credit card data:<br />' .
     $card_holder . ', ' . $card_number . ', ' .
     $issue_date . ', ' . $expiry_date . ', ' .
     $issue_number . ', ' . $card_type . '<br />';

$credit_card = new SecureCard();

try
{
  $credit_card->LoadPlainDataAndEncrypt($card_holder, $card_number,
                 $issue_date, $expiry_date, $issue_number, $card_type);

  $encrypted_data = $credit_card->EncryptedData;
}
catch(Exception $e)
{
  echo '<font color="red">Exception: ' . $e->getMessage() . '</font>';

  exit;
}

echo '<br />Encrypted data:<br />' . $encrypted_data . '<br />';
```

```php
$our_card = new SecureCard();

try
{
  $our_card->LoadEncryptedDataAndDecrypt($encrypted_data);

  echo '<br/>Decrypted data:<br/>' .
       $our_card->CardHolder . ', ' . $our_card->CardNumber . ', ' .
       $our_card->IssueDate . ', ' . $our_card->ExpiryDate . ', ' .
       $our_card->IssueNumber . ', ' . $our_card->CardType;
}
catch(Exception $e)
{
  echo '<font color="red">Exception: ' . $e->getMessage() . '</font>';

  exit;
}
?>
```

3. Load `test_card.php` file in your favorite browser to see the results (see Figure 11-3). You may change the data from this file as you want.

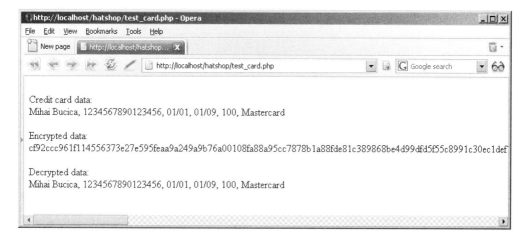

Figure 11-3. *Encrypting and decrypting credit card information*

How It Works: The SecureCard Class

There's a bit more code here than in previous examples, but it's all quite simple. First you have the private member variables to hold the card details as individual strings, as an encrypted string, and in an intermediate XML document. You also have Boolean flags indicating whether the data has been successfully encrypted or decrypted:

```php
<?php
// Represents a credit card
```

```
class SecureCard
{
  // Private members containing credit card's details
  private $_mIsDecrypted = false;
  private $_mIsEncrypted = false;
  private $_mCardHolder;
  private $_mCardNumber;
  private $_mIssueDate;
  private $_mExpiryDate;
  private $_mIssueNumber;
  private $_mCardType;
  private $_mEncryptedData;
  private $_mXmlCardData;
```

Next you have two important public methods. Public members are part of the public interface of the class, which provides the functionality for external clients. LoadEncryptedDataAndDecrypt receives an encrypted string and performs the decryption; LoadPlainDataAndEncrypt receives the credit card data in plain format and encrypts it:

```
  // Decrypt data
  public function LoadEncryptedDataAndDecrypt($newEncryptedData)
  {
    $this->_mEncryptedData = $newEncryptedData;
    $this->DecryptData();
  }

  // Encrypt data
  public function LoadPlainDataAndEncrypt($newCardHolder, $newCardNumber,
                                          $newIssueDate, $newExpiryDate,
                                          $newIssueNumber, $newCardType)
  {
    $this->_mCardHolder = $newCardHolder;
    $this->_mCardNumber = $newCardNumber;
    $this->_mIssueDate = $newIssueDate;
    $this->_mExpiryDate = $newExpiryDate;
    $this->_mIssueNumber = $newIssueNumber;
    $this->_mCardType = $newCardType;
    $this->EncryptData();
  }
```

The main work is carried out by the private EncryptData() and DecryptData() methods, which you'll come to shortly. First, you have two utility methods for packaging and unpackaging data in XML format (which makes it easier to get at the bits you want when exchanging data with the encrypted format).

XML is a very powerful, tag-based format in which you can store various kinds of information. The SecureCard class stored a customer's credit card data in a structure like the following:

```
<?xml version="1.0"?>
<CardDetails>
  <CardHolder>Mihai Bucica</CardHolder>
```

```
  <CardNumber>1234567890123456</CardNumber>
  <IssueDate>01/04</IssueDate>
  <ExpiryDate>01/07</ExpiryDate>
  <IssueNumber>100</IssueNumber>
  <CardType>Mastercard</CardType>
</CardDetails>
```

The DOMDocument class is used to work with XML data; this class knows how to create, read, and manipulate XML documents without much effort from the developer. DOM (Document Object Model) is the most important and versatile tree model XML parsing API (Application Programming Interface).

Tip The World Wide Web Consortium manages the DOM standard; its official web page is http://www.w3.org/DOM/.

With the new PHP 5 DOM extension, reading, creating, editing, saving, and searching XML documents from PHP has never been easier. The DOM extension in PHP 5 was entirely rewritten from scratch to fully comply with the DOM specifications. You can see this extension in action in the CreateXml() method, which creates an XML document with the structure shown earlier by creating nodes and setting their values:

```
  // Create XML with credit card information
  private function CreateXml()
  {
    // Encode card details as XML document
    $xml_card_data = &$this->_mXmlCardData;
    $xml_card_data = new DOMDocument();

    $document_root = $xml_card_data->createElement('CardDetails');

    $child = $xml_card_data->createElement('CardHolder');
    $child = $document_root->appendChild($child);
    $value = $xml_card_data->createTextNode($this->_mCardHolder);
    $value = $child->appendChild($value);

    ...

    $document_root = $xml_card_data->appendChild($document_root);
  }
```

For reading the XML document, you can use the DOMDocument object, but in the ExtractXml() method, we preferred to use a new and unique feature of PHP 5 called SimpleXML. Although less complex and powerful than DOMDocument, the SimpleXML extension makes parsing XML data a piece of cake by transforming it into a data structure you can simply iterate through:

```
  // Extract information from XML credit card data
  private function ExtractXml($decryptedData)
  {
```

```
    $xml = simplexml_load_string($decryptedData);
    $this->_mCardHolder = (string) $xml->CardHolder;
    $this->_mCardNumber = (string) $xml->CardNumber;
    $this->_mIssueDate = (string) $xml->IssueDate;
    $this->_mExpiryDate = (string) $xml->ExpiryDate;
    $this->_mIssueNumber = (string) $xml->IssueNumber;
    $this->_mCardType = (string) $xml->CardType;
  }
```

The EncryptData() method starts by using the CreateXml() method to package the details supplied in the SecureCard constructor into XML format:

```
  // Encrypts the XML credit card data
  private function EncryptData()
  {
    // Put data into XML doc
    $this->CreateXml();
```

Next, the XML string contained in the resultant XML document is encrypted into a single string and stored in the _mEncryptedData member:

```
  // Encrypt data
  $this->_mEncryptedData =
    SymmetricCrypt::Encrypt($this->_mXmlCardData->saveXML());
```

Finally, the _mIsEncrypted flag is set to true to indicate that the credit card data has been encrypted:

```
  // Set encrypted flag
  $this->_mIsEncrypted = true;
  }
```

The DecryptData() method gets the XML credit card data from its encrypted form, decrypts it, and populates class attributes with the ExtractXml() method:

```
  // Decrypts XML credit card data
  private function DecryptData()
  {
    // Decrypt data
    $decrypted_data = SymmetricCrypt::Decrypt($this->_mEncryptedData);

    // Extract data from XML
    $this->ExtractXml($decrypted_data);

    // Set decrypted flag
    $this->_mIsDecrypted = true;
  }
```

Next, we define a few properties for the class. Starting with PHP 5, you can define a public __get function that is called automatically whenever you try to call a method or read a member that isn't defined in the class. Take, for example, this code snippet:

```
$card = new SecureCard();
$encrypted = $card->EncryptedData;
```

Because there's no member named `EncryptedData` in the `SecureCard` class, the `__get` function is called. In `__get`, you can check which property is accessed, and you can include code that returns the value for that property. This technique is particularly useful when you want to define "virtual" members of the class whose values need to be calculated on the spot, as an alternative to using get functions, such as `getEncryptedData()`.

In our case, the `__get` function handles eight "virtual" members. The first is `EncryptedData`, whose value is returned only if `_mIsEncrypted` is true:

```
public function __get($name)
{
  if ($name == 'EncryptedData')
  {
    if ($this->_mIsEncrypted)
      return $this->_mEncryptedData;
    else
      throw new Exception('Data not encrypted');
  }
```

Then there's `CardNumberX`, which needs to return a version of the card number where all digits are obfuscated (replaced with 'X') except the last four. This is handy when showing a user existing details and is becoming standard practice because it lets customers know what card they have stored without exposing the details to prying eyes:

```
  elseif ($name == 'CardNumberX')
  {
    if ($this->_mIsDecrypted)
      return 'XXXX-XXXX-XXXX-' .
        substr($this->_mCardNumber, strlen($this->_mCardNumber) - 4, 4);
    else
      throw new Exception('Data not decrypted');
  }
```

The last six properties (`CardHolder`, `CardNumber`, `IssueDate`, `ExpiryDate`, `IssueNumber`, and `CardType`) are handled in a single block:

```
  elseif (in_array($name, array ('CardHolder', 'CardNumber', 'IssueDate',
                                 'ExpiryDate', 'IssueNumber', 'CardType')))
  {
    $name = '_m' . $name;

    if ($this->_mIsDecrypted)
      return $this->$name;
    else
      throw new Exception('Data not decrypted');
  }
  else
  {
```

```
        throw new Exception('Property ' . $name . ' not found');
    }
}
```

Note that in all cases, the data is only accessible when _mIsDecrypted is true; otherwise, an exception is thrown.

Also, note that the data isn't accessible after encryption—the data used to initialize a SecureCard object is only accessible in encrypted form. This is more a use-case decision than anything else because this class is only really intended for encryption and decryption, not for persistently representing credit card details. After a SecureCard instance has been used to encrypt card details, we shouldn't subsequently need access to the unencrypted data, only the encrypted string.

■**Note** Before moving on to the client code, it is worth explaining and emphasizing one important design consideration that you have probably already noticed. At no point are any of the card details validated. In fact, this class will work perfectly well with empty strings for any properties. This is so the class can remain as versatile as possible. It is more likely that credit card details will be validated as part of the UI used to enter them, or even not at all. This isn't at all dangerous—if invalid details are used, then the credit card transaction will simply fail, and we handle that using very similar logic to that required to deal with lack of funds (that is, we notify the customer of failure and ask them to try another card). Of course, there are also simple data-formatting issues (dates are usually MM/YY for example), but as noted, these can be dealt with externally to the SecureCard class.

The test page (test_cart.php) for this class simply allows you to see how an encrypted card looks. As you can see, quite a lot of data is generated, hence the rather large column size in the customer database. You can also see that both encryption and decryption are working perfectly, so you can now move on to the customer account section of this chapter.

Adding Customer Accounts Functionality to HatShop

Before implementing the visual bits of the customer accounts functionality, let's preview what we're going to do in the final part of this chapter.

First, we want to have a login form on the front of the site. We also want to let users register on the site and edit their profiles. You'll create a componentized template for the login form and place it just on top of the departments list, as shown in Figure 11-4.

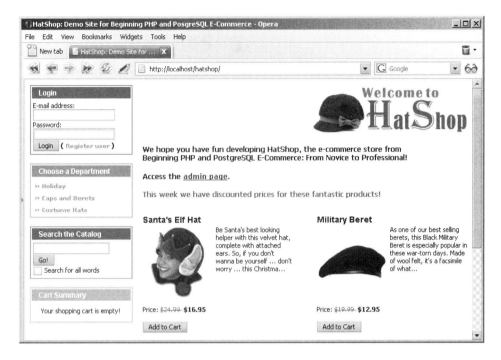

Figure 11-4. *HatShop with a login box*

The new user registration page looks like Figure 11-5.

Figure 11-5. *The new user registration page in HatShop*

After the user logs in to the site, a new componentized template appears on top of the departments list to display the logged user's name and a number of links for manipulating his or her account (see Figure 11-6).

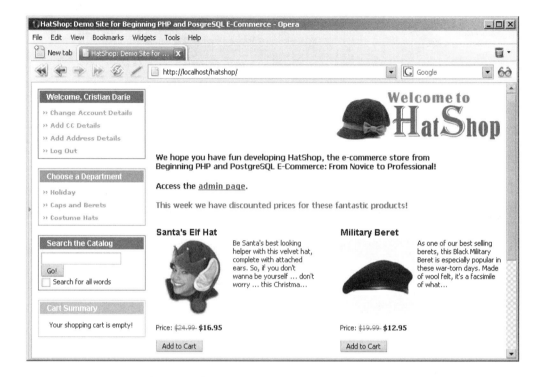

Figure 11-6. *Sample HatShop page for a logged-in user*

Clicking the Add CC Details link leads you to the page shown in Figure 11-7.

Figure 11-7. *Adding credit card information*

A similar form will be shown to you when clicking the Add Address Details link. When the user already has a credit card and an address listed, the Add... links in the Welcome box change into Change... links.

You'll start implementing the new functionality by writing the data tier code that will support the UI.

Implementing the Data Tier

You'll create the usual data tier functions supporting customer accounts functionality in the following exercise, and we'll comment on each one.

Exercise: Creating the Database Functions

1. Load pgAdmin III, and connect to the `hatshop` database.

2. Click Tools ➤ Query tool (or click the SQL button on the toolbar). A new query window should appear.

3. Use the query tool to execute this code, which creates the `customer_login` type and `customer_get_login_info` function in your `hatshop` database:

```
-- Create customer_login_info type
CREATE TYPE customer_login_info AS
(
  customer_id INTEGER,
  password    VARCHAR(50)
);


-- Create customer_get_login_info function
CREATE FUNCTION customer_get_login_info(VARCHAR(100))
RETURNS customer_login_info LANGUAGE plpgsql AS $$
  DECLARE
    inEmail ALIAS FOR $1;
    outCustomerLoginInfoRow customer_login_info;
  BEGIN
    SELECT INTO outCustomerLoginInfoRow
               customer_id, password
    FROM   customer
    WHERE  email = inEmail;
    RETURN outCustomerLoginInfoRow;
  END;
$$;
```

When a user logs in to the site, you must check his or her password. The `customer_get_login_info` function returns the customer ID and the hashed password for a user with a specific email.

4. Use the query tool to execute this code, which creates the `customer_add` function in your `hatshop` database:

```
-- Create customer_add function
CREATE FUNCTION customer_add(
                  VARCHAR(50), VARCHAR(100), VARCHAR(50))
RETURNS INTEGER LANGUAGE plpgsql AS $$
  DECLARE
    inName     ALIAS FOR $1;
    inEmail    ALIAS FOR $2;
    inPassword ALIAS FOR $3;
    outCustomerId INTEGER;
  BEGIN
    INSERT INTO customer (name, email, password)
           VALUES (inName, inEmail, inPassword);
    SELECT INTO outCustomerId
           currval('customer_customer_id_seq');
```

```
      RETURN outCustomerId;
    END;
  $$;
```

The `customer_add` function is called when a user registers on the site. This method returns the customer ID for that user to be saved in the session.

5. Use the query tool to execute this code, which creates the `customer_get_customer` function in your hatshop database:

```
-- Create customer_get_customer function
CREATE FUNCTION customer_get_customer(INTEGER)
RETURNS customer LANGUAGE plpgsql AS $$
  DECLARE
    inCustomerId ALIAS FOR $1;
    outCustomerRow customer;
  BEGIN
    SELECT INTO outCustomerRow
              customer_id, name, email, password, credit_card,
              address_1, address_2, city, region, postal_code, country,
              shipping_region_id, day_phone, eve_phone, mob_phone
    FROM    customer
    WHERE   customer_id = inCustomerId;
    RETURN outCustomerRow;
  END;
$$;
```

The `customer_get_customer` function returns full customer details for a given customer ID.

6. Use the query tool to execute this code, which creates the `customer_update_account` function in your hatshop database:

```
-- Create customer_update_account function
CREATE FUNCTION customer_update_account(INTEGER, VARCHAR(50), VARCHAR(100),
                VARCHAR(50), VARCHAR(100), VARCHAR(100), VARCHAR(100))
RETURNS VOID LANGUAGE plpgsql AS $$
  DECLARE
    inCustomerId ALIAS FOR $1;
    inName       ALIAS FOR $2;
    inEmail      ALIAS FOR $3;
    inPassword   ALIAS FOR $4;
    inDayPhone   ALIAS FOR $5;
    inEvePhone   ALIAS FOR $6;
    inMobPhone   ALIAS FOR $7;
  BEGIN
    UPDATE customer
    SET    name = inName, email = inEmail,
           password = inPassword, day_phone = inDayPhone,
           eve_phone = inEvePhone, mob_phone = inMobPhone
    WHERE  customer_id = inCustomerId;
  END;
$$;
```

The `customer_update_account` function updates the customer's account details in the database.

7. Use the query tool to execute this code, which creates the `customer_update_credit_card` function in your `hatshop` database:

```
-- Create customer_update_credit_card function
CREATE FUNCTION customer_update_credit_card(INTEGER, TEXT)
RETURNS VOID LANGUAGE plpgsql AS $$
  DECLARE
    inCustomerId ALIAS FOR $1;
    inCreditCard ALIAS FOR $2;
  BEGIN
    UPDATE customer
    SET    credit_card = inCreditCard
    WHERE  customer_id = inCustomerId;
  END;
$$;
```

The `customer_update_credit_card` function updates the customer's credit card information in the database. It only updates the `credit_card` column for the customer, which contains the encrypted version of the XML document containing the customer's complete credit card details.

8. Use the query tool to execute this code, which creates the `customer_get_shipping_regions` function in your `hatshop` database:

```
-- Create customer_get_shipping_regions function
CREATE FUNCTION customer_get_shipping_regions()
RETURNS SETOF shipping_region LANGUAGE plpgsql AS $$
  DECLARE
    outShippingRegion shipping_region;
  BEGIN
    FOR outShippingRegion IN
      SELECT shipping_region_id, shipping_region
      FROM   shipping_region
    LOOP
      RETURN NEXT outShippingRegion;
    END LOOP;
    RETURN;
  END;
$$;
```

The `customer_get_shipping_regions` function returns the shipping regions in the database for the customer address details page.

9. Use the query tool to execute this code, which creates the `customer_update_address` function in your `hatshop` database:

```
-- Create customer_update_address function
CREATE FUNCTION customer_update_address(INTEGER, VARCHAR(100),
                VARCHAR(100), VARCHAR(100), VARCHAR(100),
                VARCHAR(100), VARCHAR(100), INTEGER)
```

```
    RETURNS VOID LANGUAGE plpgsql AS $$
      DECLARE
        inCustomerId       ALIAS FOR $1;
        inAddress1         ALIAS FOR $2;
        inAddress2         ALIAS FOR $3;
        inCity             ALIAS FOR $4;
        inRegion           ALIAS FOR $5;
        inPostalCode       ALIAS FOR $6;
        inCountry          ALIAS FOR $7;
        inShippingRegionId ALIAS FOR $8;
      BEGIN
        UPDATE customer
        SET    address_1 = inAddress1, address_2 = inAddress2, city = inCity,
               region = inRegion, postal_code = inPostalCode,
               country = inCountry, shipping_region_id = inShippingRegionId
        WHERE  customer_id = inCustomerId;
      END;
    $$;
```

The customer_update_address function updates the customer's address in the database.

Implementing the Business Tier

In the business folder, create a new file named customer.php that will contain the Customer class. The Customer class is a little longer, and it mainly accesses the data tier functionality to respond to requests that come from the presentation tier. Write the following code in the business/customer.php file:

```php
<?php
// Business tier class that manages customer accounts functionality
class Customer
{
  // Checks if a customer_id exists in session
  public static function IsAuthenticated()
  {
    if (!(isset ($_SESSION['hatshop_customer_id'])))
      return 0;
    else
      return 1;
  }

  // Returns customer_id and password for customer with email $email
  public static function GetLoginInfo($email)
  {
    // Build the SQL query
    $sql = 'SELECT * FROM customer_get_login_info(:email);';
```

```
  // Build the parameters array
  $params = array (':email' => $email);
  // Prepare the statement with PDO-specific functionality
  $result = DatabaseHandler::Prepare($sql);

  // Execute the query and return the results
  return DatabaseHandler::GetRow($result, $params);
}

public static function IsValid($email, $password)
{
  $customer = self::GetLoginInfo($email);

  if (empty ($customer['customer_id']))
    return 2;

  $customer_id = $customer['customer_id'];
  $hashed_password = $customer['password'];

  if (PasswordHasher::Hash($password) != $hashed_password)
    return 1;
  else
  {
    $_SESSION['hatshop_customer_id'] = $customer_id;

    return 0;
  }
}

public static function Logout()
{
  unset($_SESSION['hatshop_customer_id']);
}

public static function GetCurrentCustomerId()
{
  if (self::IsAuthenticated())
    return $_SESSION['hatshop_customer_id'];
  else
    return 0;
}

/* Adds a new customer account, log him in if $addAndLogin is true
   and returns customer_id */
public static function Add($name, $email, $password, $addAndLogin = true)
{
  $hashed_password = PasswordHasher::Hash($password);
```

```
  // Build the SQL query
  $sql = 'SELECT customer_add(:name, :email, :password);';
  // Build the parameters array
  $params = array (':name' => $name, ':email' => $email,
                   ':password' => $hashed_password);
  // Prepare the statement with PDO-specific functionality
  $result = DatabaseHandler::Prepare($sql);

  // Execute the query and get the customer_id
  $customer_id = DatabaseHandler::GetOne($result, $params);

  if ($addAndLogin)
    $_SESSION['hatshop_customer_id'] = $customer_id;

  return $customer_id;
}

public static function Get($customerId = null)
{
  if (is_null($customerId))
    $customerId = self::GetCurrentCustomerId();

  // Build the SQL query
  $sql = 'SELECT * FROM customer_get_customer(:customer_id);';
  // Build the parameters array
  $params = array (':customer_id' => $customerId);
  // Prepare the statement with PDO-specific functionality
  $result = DatabaseHandler::Prepare($sql);

  // Execute the query and return the results
  return DatabaseHandler::GetRow($result, $params);
}

public static function UpdateAccountDetails($name, $email, $password,
                         $dayPhone, $evePhone, $mobPhone,
                         $customerId = null)
{
  if (is_null($customerId))
    $customerId = self::GetCurrentCustomerId();

  $hashed_password = PasswordHasher::Hash($password);

  // Build the SQL query
  $sql = 'SELECT customer_update_account(:customer_id, :name, :email,
                 :password, :day_phone, :eve_phone, :mob_phone);';
  // Build the parameters array
```

```php
    $params = array (':customer_id' => $customerId, ':name' => $name,
                     ':email' => $email, ':password' => $hashed_password,
                     ':day_phone' => $dayPhone, ':eve_phone' => $evePhone,
                     ':mob_phone' => $mobPhone);
    // Prepare the statement with PDO-specific functionality
    $result = DatabaseHandler::Prepare($sql);

    // Execute the query
    return DatabaseHandler::Execute($result, $params);
  }

  public static function DecryptCreditCard($encryptedCreditCard)
  {
    $secure_card = new SecureCard();
    $secure_card->LoadEncryptedDataAndDecrypt($encryptedCreditCard);

    $credit_card = array();
    $credit_card['card_holder'] = $secure_card->CardHolder;
    $credit_card['card_number'] = $secure_card->CardNumber;
    $credit_card['issue_date'] = $secure_card->IssueDate;
    $credit_card['expiry_date'] = $secure_card->ExpiryDate;
    $credit_card['issue_number'] = $secure_card->IssueNumber;
    $credit_card['card_type'] = $secure_card->CardType;
    $credit_card['card_number_x'] = $secure_card->CardNumberX;

    return $credit_card;
  }

  public static function GetPlainCreditCard()
  {
    $customer_data = self::Get();

    if (!(empty ($customer_data['credit_card'])))
      return self::DecryptCreditCard($customer_data['credit_card']);
    else
      return array('card_holder' => '', 'card_number' => '',
                   'issue_date' => '', 'expiry_date' => '',
                   'issue_number' => '', 'card_type' => '',
                   'card_number_x' => '');
  }

  public static function UpdateCreditCardDetails($plainCreditCard,
                                                 $customerId = null)
  {
    if (is_null($customerId))
      $customerId = self::GetCurrentCustomerId();
```

```php
  $secure_card = new SecureCard();
  $secure_card->LoadPlainDataAndEncrypt($plainCreditCard['card_holder'],
    $plainCreditCard['card_number'], $plainCreditCard['issue_date'],
    $plainCreditCard['expiry_date'], $plainCreditCard['issue_number'],
    $plainCreditCard['card_type']);
  $encrypted_card = $secure_card->EncryptedData;

  // Build the SQL query
  $sql = 'SELECT customer_update_credit_card(
                  :customer_id, :credit_card);';
  // Build the parameters array
  $params = array (':customer_id' => $customerId,
                  ':credit_card' => $encrypted_card);
  // Prepare the statement with PDO-specific functionality
  $result = DatabaseHandler::Prepare($sql);

  // Execute the query
  return DatabaseHandler::Execute($result, $params);
}

public static function GetShippingRegions()
{
  // Build the SQL query
  $sql = 'SELECT * FROM customer_get_shipping_regions();';
  // Prepare the statement with PDO-specific functionality
  $result = DatabaseHandler::Prepare($sql);

  // Execute the query and return the results
  return DatabaseHandler::GetAll($result);
}

public static function UpdateAddressDetails($address1, $address2, $city,
                       $region, $postalCode, $country,
                       $shippingRegionId, $customerId = null)
{
  if (is_null($customerId))
    $customerId = self::GetCurrentCustomerId();

  // Build the SQL query
  $sql = 'SELECT customer_update_address(:customer_id, :address_1,
                  :address_2, :city, :region, :postal_code, :country,
                  :shipping_region_id);';
  // Build the parameters array
  $params = array (':customer_id' => $customerId,
                  ':address_1' => $address1, ':address_2' => $address2,
                  ':city' => $city, ':region' => $region,
                  ':postal_code' => $postalCode,
```

```
                    ':country' => $country,
                    ':shipping_region_id' => $shippingRegionId);
    // Prepare the statement with PDO-specific functionality
    $result = DatabaseHandler::Prepare($sql);

    // Execute the query
    return DatabaseHandler::Execute($result, $params);
  }
}
?>
```

Implementing the Presentation Tier

The presentation tier for the HatShop customer account system consists of the following componentized templates:

customer_login: The login box.

customer_logged: After a user is logged in, this componentized template takes the place of the customer_login componentized template to show the currently logged-in user and displays account management and logout links.

customer_details: For registering a new user or for editing the basic details of an existing user.

customer_address: Allows a user to add/edit address information.

customer_credit_card: Allows a user to add/edit credit card information.

Now follow the steps of the exercise to implement these new componentized templates.

Exercise: Implementing the Componentized Templates

1. Create a new template file named customer_login.tpl in the presentation/templates folder, and add the following code to it:

```
{* customer_login.tpl *}
{load_customer_login assign="customer_login"}
<div class="left_box" id="login_box">
  <p>Login</p>
    <form method="post"
    action="{$customer_login->mCustomerLoginTarget|prepare_link:"https"}">
    {if $customer_login->mLoginMessage}
    <span class="error_text">
      {$customer_login->mLoginMessage}
    </span>
    <br />
    {/if}
    <span>E-mail address:</span><br />
```

```
        <input type="text" maxlength="50" name="email"
         size="25" value="{$customer_login->mEmail}" /><br />
        <span>Password:</span><br />
        <input type="password" maxlength="50"
         name="password" size="25" />
        <br />
        <input type="submit" name="Login" value="Login" />
        <strong>(
          {strip}
          <a href="{$customer_login->mRegisterUser|prepare_link:"https"}">
            Register user
          </a>
          {/strip} )
        </strong>
      </form>
    </div>
```

2. Create a new plugin file named `function.load_customer_login.php` in the
   `presentation/smarty_plugins` folder, and add the following to it:

```php
<?php
/* Smarty plugin function that gets called when the
   load_customer_login function plugin is loaded from a template */
function smarty_function_load_customer_login($params, $smarty)
{
  // Create CustomerLogin object
  $customer_login = new CustomerLogin();
  $customer_login->init();

  // Assign template variable
  $smarty->assign($params['assign'], $customer_login);
}

class CustomerLogin
{
  // Public stuff
  public $mLoginMessage;
  public $mCustomerLoginTarget;
  public $mRegisterUser;
  public $mEmail = '';

  // Private stuff
  private $_mHaveData = 0;

  // Class constructor
  public function __construct()
  {
    // Decide if we have submitted
```

```
      if (isset ($_POST['Login']))
        $this->_mHaveData = 1;
  }

  public function init()
  {
    $url_base = substr(getenv('REQUEST_URI'),
                         strrpos(getenv('REQUEST_URI'), '/') + 1,
                         strlen(getenv('REQUEST_URI')) - 1);

    $url_parameter_prefix = (count($_GET) == 0 ? '?' : '&');

    $this->mCustomerLoginTarget = $url_base;

    if (strpos($url_base, 'RegisterCustomer', 0) === false)
      $this->mRegisterUser = $url_base . $url_parameter_prefix .
                             'RegisterCustomer';
    else
      $this->mRegisterUser = $url_base;

    if ($this->_mHaveData)
    {
      // Get login status
      $login_status = Customer::IsValid($_POST['email'], $_POST['password']);

      switch ($login_status)
      {
        case 2:
          $this->mLoginMessage = 'Unrecognized Email.';
          $this->mEmail = $_POST['email'];

          break;
        case 1:
          $this->mLoginMessage = 'Unrecognized password.';
          $this->mEmail = $_POST['email'];

          break;
        case 0:
          // Valid login... build redirect link and redirect
          if (isset($_GET['Checkout']) && USE_SSL != 'no')
          {
            $redirect_link = 'https://' . getenv('SERVER_NAME');
          }
          else
          {
            $redirect_link = 'http://' . getenv('SERVER_NAME');
```

```
            // If HTTP_SERVER_PORT is defined and different than default
            if (defined('HTTP_SERVER_PORT') && HTTP_SERVER_PORT != '80')
            {
              // Append server port
              $redirect_link .= ':' . HTTP_SERVER_PORT;
            }
          }

          $redirect_link .= VIRTUAL_LOCATION . $this->mCustomerLoginTarget;

          header('Location:' . $redirect_link);

          exit;
        }
      }
    }
  }
?>
```

3. Create a new template file named `customer_logged.tpl` in the `presentation/templates` folder, and
    add the following code to it:

```
{* customer_logged.tpl *}
{load_customer_logged assign="customer_logged"}
<div class="left_box" id="login_box">
  <p>Welcome, {$customer_logged->mCustomerName}</p>
  <ol>
    <li>
      <a href="{$customer_logged->mUpdateAccount|prepare_link:"https"}">
        &raquo; Change Account Details
      </a>
    </li>
    <li>
      <a href="{$customer_logged->mUpdateCreditCard|prepare_link:"https"}">
        &raquo; {$customer_logged->mCreditCardAction} CC Details
      </a>
    </li>
    <li>
      <a href="{$customer_logged->mUpdateAddress|prepare_link:"https"}">
        &raquo; {$customer_logged->mAddressAction} Address Details
      </a>
    </li>
    <li>
      <a href="{$customer_logged->mLogout|prepare_link}">
        &raquo; Log Out
      </a>
    </li>
  </ol>
</div>
```

4. Create a new plugin file named function.load_customer_logged.php in the presentation/smarty_plugins folder, and add the following to it:

```php
<?php
/* Smarty plugin function that gets called when the
   load_customer_logged function plugin is loaded from a template */
function smarty_function_load_customer_logged($params, $smarty)
{
  // Create CustomerLogged object
  $customer_logged = new CustomerLogged();
  $customer_logged->init();

  // Assign template variable
  $smarty->assign($params['assign'], $customer_logged);
}

class CustomerLogged
{
  // Public attributes
  public $mCustomerName;
  public $mCreditCardAction = 'Add';
  public $mAddressAction = 'Add';
  public $mUpdateAccount;
  public $mUpdateCreditCard;
  public $mUpdateAddress;
  public $mLogout;

  // Class constructor
  public function __construct()
  {
  }

  public function init()
  {
    $url_base = substr(getenv('REQUEST_URI'),
                       strrpos(getenv('REQUEST_URI'), '/') + 1,
                       strlen(getenv('REQUEST_URI')) - 1);

    $url_parameter_prefix = (count($_GET) == 1 ? '?' : '&');

    if (isset($_GET['Logout']))
      $url_base = str_replace($url_parameter_prefix . 'Logout', '',
                              $url_base);
    elseif (isset($_GET['UpdateAccountDetails']))
      $url_base = str_replace($url_parameter_prefix .
                     'UpdateAccountDetails', '', $url_base);
    elseif (isset($_GET['UpdateCreditCardDetails']))
      $url_base = str_replace($url_parameter_prefix .
```

```php
                    'UpdateCreditCardDetails', '', $url_base);
elseif (isset($_GET['UpdateAddressDetails']))
  $url_base = str_replace($url_parameter_prefix .
                'UpdateAddressDetails', '', $url_base);


if (strpos($url_base, '?', 0) === false)
  $url_parameter_prefix = '?';
else
  $url_parameter_prefix = '&';


if (isset($_GET['Logout']))
{
  Customer::Logout();

  // Redirect
  if (isset($_GET['Checkout']) && USE_SSL != 'no')
  {
    $redirect_link = 'https://' . getenv('SERVER_NAME');
  }
  else
  {
    $redirect_link = 'http://' . getenv('SERVER_NAME');

    // If HTTP_SERVER_PORT is defined and different than default
    if (defined('HTTP_SERVER_PORT') && HTTP_SERVER_PORT != '80')
    {
      // Append server port
      $redirect_link .= ':' . HTTP_SERVER_PORT;
    }
  }

  $redirect_link .= VIRTUAL_LOCATION . $url_base;

  header('Location:' . $redirect_link);

  exit;
}

$url_base .= $url_parameter_prefix;
$this->mUpdateAccount = $url_base . 'UpdateAccountDetails';
$this->mUpdateCreditCard = $url_base . 'UpdateCreditCardDetails';
$this->mUpdateAddress = $url_base . 'UpdateAddressDetails';
$this->mLogout = $url_base . 'Logout';

$customer_data = Customer::Get();
$this->mCustomerName = $customer_data['name'];
```

```
        if (!(empty($customer_data['credit_card'])))
          $this->mCreditCardAction = 'Change';

        if (!(empty($customer_data['address_1'])))
          $this->mAddressAction = 'Change';
    }
  }
?>
```

5. Create a new template file named `customer_details.tpl` in the `presentation/templates` folder, and add the following code to it:

```
{* customer_details.tpl *}
{load_customer_details assign="customer_details"}
<form method="post"
 action="{$customer_details->mCustomerDetailsTarget|prepare_link:"https"}">
  <span class="description">Please enter your details:</span>
  {if $customer_details->mEmailAlreadyTaken}
  <br /><br />
  <span class="error_text">
    A user with that e-mail address already exists.
  </span>
  {/if}
  <br /><br />
  <table class="form_table">
    <tr>
      <td>E-mail Address:</td>
      <td>
        <input type="text" name="email"
         value="{$customer_details->mEmail}"
         {if $customer_details->mEditMode}readonly="readonly"{/if} />
      </td>
      <td>
      {if $customer_details->mEmailError}
        <span class="error_text">
          You must enter an e-mail address.
        </span>
      {/if}
      </td>
    </tr>
    <tr>
      <td>Name:</td>
      <td>
        <input type="text" name="name"
         value="{$customer_details->mName}" />
      </td>
      <td>
        {if $customer_details->mNameError}
```

```
      <span class="error_text">You must enter your name.</span>
      {/if}
    </td>
  </tr>
  <tr>
    <td>Password:</td>
    <td><input type="password" name="password" /></td>
    <td>
      {if $customer_details->mPasswordError}
      <span class="error_text">You must enter a password.</span>
      {/if}
    </td>
  </tr>
  <tr>
    <td>Re-enter Password:</td>
    <td><input type="password" name="passwordConfirm" /></td>
    <td>
      {if $customer_details->mPasswordConfirmError}
      <span class="error_text">
        You must re-enter your password.
      </span>
      {elseif $customer_details->mPasswordMatchError}
      <span class="error_text">
        You must re-enter the same password.
      </span>
      {/if}
    </td>
  </tr>
  {if $customer_details->mEditMode}
  <tr>
    <td>Day phone:</td>
    <td>
      <input type="text" name="dayPhone"
       value="{$customer_details->mDayPhone}" />
    </td>
  </tr>
  <tr>
    <td>Eve phone:</td>
    <td>
      <input type="text" name="evePhone"
       value="{$customer_details->mEvePhone}" />
    </td>
  </tr>
  <tr>
    <td>Mob phone:</td>
    <td>
      <input type="text" name="mobPhone"
```

```
              value="{$customer_details->mMobPhone}" />
        </td>
      </tr>
      {/if}
    </table>
    <br />
    <input type="submit" name="sended" value="Confirm" />
    <input type="button" value="Cancel"
     onclick="window.location='{
        $customer_details->mReturnLink|prepare_link:$customer_details->➥
   mReturnLinkProtocol}';" />
  </form>
```

6. Create a new plugin file named function.load_customer_details.php in the presentation/smarty_plugins folder, and add the following to it:

```php
<?php
/* Smarty plugin function that gets called when the
   load_customer_details function plugin is loaded from a template */
function smarty_function_load_customer_details($params, $smarty)
{
  // Create CustomerDetails object
  $customer_details = new CustomerDetails();
  $customer_details->init();

  // Assign template variable
  $smarty->assign($params['assign'], $customer_details);
}

class CustomerDetails
{
  // Public attributes
  public $mEditMode = 0;
  public $mCustomerDetailsTarget;
  public $mReturnLink;
  public $mReturnLinkProtocol = 'http';
  public $mEmail;
  public $mName;
  public $mPassword;
  public $mDayPhone = null;
  public $mEvePhone = null;
  public $mMobPhone = null;
  public $mNameError = 0;
  public $mEmailError = 0;
  public $mPasswordError = 0;
  public $mPasswordConfirmError = 0;
  public $mPasswordMatchError = 0;
  public $mEmailAlreadyTaken = 0;
```

```php
// Private attributes
private $_mErrors = 0;
private $_mHaveData = 0;

// Class constructor
public function __construct()
{
  // Check if we have new user or editing existing customer details
  if (Customer::IsAuthenticated())
    $this->mEditMode = 1;

  $url_base = substr(getenv('REQUEST_URI'),
                     strrpos(getenv('REQUEST_URI'), '/') + 1,
                     strlen(getenv('REQUEST_URI')) - 1);

  $url_parameter_prefix = (count($_GET) == 1 ? '?' : '&');

  $this->mCustomerDetailsTarget = $url_base;

  if ($this->mEditMode == 0)
    $this->mReturnLink = str_replace($url_parameter_prefix .
                           'RegisterCustomer', '', $url_base);
  else
    $this->mReturnLink = str_replace($url_parameter_prefix .
                           'UpdateAccountDetails', '', $url_base);

  if (isset($_GET['Checkout']) && USE_SSL != 'no')
    $this->mReturnLinkProtocol = 'https';

  // Check if we have submitted data
  if (isset ($_POST['sended']))
    $this->_mHaveData = 1;

  if ($this->_mHaveData == 1)
  {
    // Name cannot be empty
    if (empty ($_POST['name']))
    {
      $this->mNameError = 1;
      $this->_mErrors++;
    }
    else
      $this->mName = $_POST['name'];

    if ($this->mEditMode == 0 && empty ($_POST['email']))
    {
```

```php
      $this->mEmailError = 1;
      $this->_mErrors++;
    }
    else
      $this->mEmail = $_POST['email'];

    // Password cannot be empty
    if (empty ($_POST['password']))
    {
      $this->mPasswordError = 1;
      $this->_mErrors++;
    }
    else
      $this->mPassword = $_POST['password'];

    // Password confirm cannot be empty
    if (empty ($_POST['passwordConfirm']))
    {
      $this->mPasswordConfirmError = 1;
      $this->_mErrors++;
    }
    else
      $password_confirm = $_POST['passwordConfirm'];

    // Password and password confirm should be the same
    if (!isset ($password_confirm) ||
        $this->mPassword != $password_confirm)
    {
      $this->mPasswordMatchError = 1;
      $this->_mErrors++;
    }

    if ($this->mEditMode == 1)
    {
      if (!empty ($_POST['dayPhone']))
        $this->mDayPhone = $_POST['dayPhone'];

      if (!empty ($_POST['evePhone']))
        $this->mEvePhone = $_POST['evePhone'];

      if (!empty ($_POST['mobPhone']))
        $this->mMobPhone = $_POST['mobPhone'];
    }
  }
}

  public function init()
```

```
{
  // If we have submitted data and no errors in submitted data
  if (($this->_mHaveData == 1) && ($this->_mErrors == 0))
  {
    // Check if we have any customer with submitted email...
    $customer_read = Customer::GetLoginInfo($this->mEmail);

    /* ...if we have one and we are in 'new user' mode then
       email already taken error */
    if ((!(empty ($customer_read['customer_id']))) &&
        ($this->mEditMode == 0))
    {
      $this->mEmailAlreadyTaken = 1;

      return;
    }

    // We have a new user or we are updating an exisiting user details
    if ($this->mEditMode == 0)
      Customer::Add($this->mName, $this->mEmail, $this->mPassword);
    else
      Customer::UpdateAccountDetails($this->mName, $this->mEmail,
        $this->mPassword, $this->mDayPhone, $this->mEvePhone,
        $this->mMobPhone);

    // Redirect
    if (isset($_GET['Checkout']) && USE_SSL != 'no')
    {
      $redirect_link = 'https://' . getenv('SERVER_NAME');
    }
    else
    {
      $redirect_link = 'http://' . getenv('SERVER_NAME');

      // If HTTP_SERVER_PORT is defined and different than default
      if (defined('HTTP_SERVER_PORT') && HTTP_SERVER_PORT != '80')
      {
        // Append server port
        $redirect_link .= ':' . HTTP_SERVER_PORT;
      }
    }

    $redirect_link .= VIRTUAL_LOCATION . $this->mReturnLink;

    header('Location:' . $redirect_link);

    exit;
```

```php
        }

        if ($this->mEditMode == 1 && $this->_mHaveData == 0)
        {
          // We are editing an existing customer's details
          $customer_data = Customer::Get();

          $this->mName = $customer_data['name'];
          $this->mEmail = $customer_data['email'];
          $this->mDayPhone = $customer_data['day_phone'];
          $this->mEvePhone = $customer_data['eve_phone'];
          $this->mMobPhone = $customer_data['mob_phone'];
        }
      }
    }
?>
```

7. Create a new template file named `customer_address.tpl` in the `presentation/templates` folder, and add the following code to it:

```smarty
{* customer_address.tpl *}
{load_customer_address assign="customer_address"}
<form method="post"
 action="{$customer_address->mCustomerAddressTarget|prepare_link:"https"}">
  <span class="description">Please enter your address details:</span>
  <br /><br />
  <table class="form_table">
    <tr>
      <td>Address 1:</td>
      <td>
        <input type="text" name="address1"
         value="{$customer_address->mAddress1}" />
      </td>
      <td>
        {if $customer_address->mAddress1Error}
        <span class="error_text">You must enter an address.</span>
        {/if}
      </td>
    </tr>
    <tr>
      <td>Address 2:</td>
      <td>
        <input type="text" name="address2"
         value="{$customer_address->mAddress2}" />
      </td>
    </tr>
    <tr>
      <td>Town/City:</td>
```

```
    <td>
      <input type="text" name="city"
       value="{$customer_address->mCity}" />
    </td>
    <td>
      {if $customer_address->mCityError}
      <span class="error_text">You must enter a city.</span>
      {/if}
    </td>
  </tr>
  <tr>
    <td>Region/State:</td>
    <td>
      <input type="text" name="region"
       value="{$customer_address->mRegion}" />
    </td>
    <td>
      {if $customer_address->mRegionError}
      <span class="error_text">You must enter a region/state.</span>
      {/if}
    </td>
  </tr>
  <tr>
    <td>Postal Code/ZIP:</td>
    <td>
      <input type="text" name="postalCode"
       value="{$customer_address->mPostalCode}" />
    </td>
    <td>
      {if $customer_address->mPostalCodeError}
      <span class="error_text">You must enter a postal code/ZIP.</span>
      {/if}
    </td>
  </tr>
  <tr>
    <td>Country:</td>
    <td>
      <input type="text" name="country"
       value="{$customer_address->mCountry}" />
    </td>
    <td>
      {if $customer_address->mCountryError}
      <span class="error_text">You must enter a country.</span>
      {/if}
    </td>
  </tr>
  <tr>
```

```
        <td>Shipping region:</td>
        <td>
          <select name="shippingRegion">
            {html_options options=$customer_address->mShippingRegions
              selected=$customer_address->mShippingRegion}
          </select>
        </td>
        <td>
          {if $customer_address->mShippingRegionError}
          <span class="error_text">You must select a shipping region.</span>
          {/if}
        </td>
      </tr>
    </table>
    <br />
    <input type="submit" name="sended" value="Confirm" />
    <input type="button" value="Cancel"
      onclick="window.location='{
        $customer_address->mReturnLink|prepare_link:$customer_address->➥
mReturnLinkProtocol}';" />
    </form>
```

8. Create a new plugin file named function.load_customer_address.php in the presentation/smarty_plugins folder, and add the following to it:

```php
<?php
/* Smarty plugin function that gets called when the
   load_customer_address function plugin is loaded from a template */
function smarty_function_load_customer_address($params, $smarty)
{
  // Create CustomerAddress object
  $customer_address = new CustomerAddress();
  $customer_address->init();

  // Assign template variable
  $smarty->assign($params['assign'], $customer_address);
}

class CustomerAddress
{
  // Public attributes
  public $mCustomerAddressTarget;
  public $mReturnLink;
  public $mReturnLinkProtocol = 'http';
  public $mAddress1 = '';
  public $mAddress2 = '';
  public $mCity = '';
  public $mRegion = '';
```

```php
public $mPostalCode = '';
public $mCountry = '';
public $mShippingRegion = '';
public $mShippingRegions = array ();
public $mAddress1Error = 0;
public $mCityError = 0;
public $mRegionError = 0;
public $mPostalCodeError = 0;
public $mCountryError = 0;
public $mShippingRegionError = 0;

// Private attributes
private $_mErrors = 0;
private $_mHaveData = 0;

// Class constructor
public function __construct()
{
  $url_base = substr(getenv('REQUEST_URI'),
                     strrpos(getenv('REQUEST_URI'), '/') + 1,
                     strlen(getenv('REQUEST_URI')) - 1);

  $url_parameter_prefix = (count($_GET) == 1 ? '?' : '&');

  // Set form action target
  $this->mCustomerAddressTarget = $url_base;

  // Set the return page
  $this->mReturnLink = str_replace($url_parameter_prefix .
                       'UpdateAddressDetails', '', $url_base);

  if (isset($_GET['Checkout']) && USE_SSL != 'no')
    $this->mReturnLinkProtocol = 'https';

  if (isset ($_POST['sended']))
    $this->_mHaveData = 1;

  if ($this->_mHaveData == 1)
  {
    // Address 1 cannot be empty
    if (empty ($_POST['address1']))
    {
      $this->mAddress1Error = 1;
      $this->_mErrors++;
    }
    else
      $this->mAddress1 = $_POST['address1'];
```

```php
      if (isset ($_POST['address2']))
        $this->mAddress2 = $_POST['address2'];

      if (empty ($_POST['city']))
      {
        $this->mCityError = 1;
        $this->_mErrors++;
      }
      else
        $this->mCity = $_POST['city'];

      if (empty ($_POST['region']))
      {
        $this->mRegionError = 1;
        $this->_mErrors++;
      }
      else
        $this->mRegion = $_POST['region'];

      if (empty ($_POST['postalCode']))
      {
        $this->mPostalCodeError = 1;
        $this->_mErrors++;
      }
      else
        $this->mPostalCode = $_POST['postalCode'];

      if (empty ($_POST['country']))
      {
        $this->mCountryError = 1;
        $this->_mErrors++;
      }
      else
        $this->mCountry = $_POST['country'];

      if ($_POST['shippingRegion'] == 1)
      {
        $this->mShippingRegionError = 1;
        $this->_mErrors++;
      }
      else
        $this->mShippingRegion = $_POST['shippingRegion'];
    }
  }

  public function init()
  {
    $shipping_regions = Customer::GetShippingRegions();
```

```php
    foreach ($shipping_regions as $item)
      $this->mShippingRegions[$item['shipping_region_id']] =
        $item['shipping_region'];

    if ($this->_mHaveData == 0)
    {
      $customer_data = Customer::Get();

      if (!(empty ($customer_data)))
      {
        $this->mAddress1 = $customer_data['address_1'];
        $this->mAddress2 = $customer_data['address_2'];
        $this->mCity = $customer_data['city'];
        $this->mRegion = $customer_data['region'];
        $this->mPostalCode = $customer_data['postal_code'];
        $this->mCountry = $customer_data['country'];
        $this->mShippingRegion = $customer_data['shipping_region_id'];
      }
    }
    elseif ($this->_mErrors == 0)
    {
      Customer::UpdateAddressDetails($this->mAddress1, $this->mAddress2,
        $this->mCity, $this->mRegion, $this->mPostalCode,
        $this->mCountry, $this->mShippingRegion);

      if (isset($_GET['Checkout']) && USE_SSL != 'no')
      {
        $redirect_link = 'https://' . getenv('SERVER_NAME');
      }
      else
      {
        $redirect_link = 'http://' . getenv('SERVER_NAME');

        // If HTTP_SERVER_PORT is defined and different than default
        if (defined('HTTP_SERVER_PORT') && HTTP_SERVER_PORT != '80')
        {
          // Append server port
          $redirect_link .= ':' . HTTP_SERVER_PORT;
        }
      }

      $redirect_link .= VIRTUAL_LOCATION . $this->mReturnLink;

      header('Location:' . $redirect_link);

      exit;
    }
  }
}
?>
```

9. Create a new template file named `customer_credit_card.tpl` in the `presentation/templates` folder, and add the following code to it:

```
{* customer_credit_card.tpl *}
{load_customer_credit_card assign="customer_credit_card"}
<form method="post"
 action="{$customer_credit_card-
>mCustomerCreditCardTarget|prepare_link:"https"}">
  <span class="description">
    Please enter your credit card details:
  </span>
  <br /><br />
  <table class="form_table">
    <tr>
      <td>Card Holder:</td>
      <td>
        <input type="text" name="cardHolder"
         value="{$customer_credit_card->mPlainCreditCard.card_holder}" />
      </td>
      <td>
        {if $customer_credit_card->mCardHolderError}
        <span class="error_text">You must enter a card holder.</span>
        {/if}
      </td>
    </tr>
    <tr>
      <td>Card Number (digits only):</td>
      <td>
        <input type="text" name="cardNumber"
         value="{$customer_credit_card->mPlainCreditCard.card_number}" />
      </td>
      <td>
        {if $customer_credit_card->mCardNumberError}
        <span class="error_text">You must enter a card number.</span>
        {/if}
      </td>
    </tr>
    <tr>
      <td>Expiry Date (MM/YY):</td>
      <td>
        <input type="text" name="expDate"
         value="{$customer_credit_card->mPlainCreditCard.expiry_date}" />
      </td>
      <td>
        {if $customer_credit_card->mExpDateError}
        <span class="error_text">You must enter an expiry date</span>
        {/if}
      </td>
```

```
      </tr>
      <tr>
        <td>Issue Date (MM/YY if applicable):</td>
        <td>
          <input type="text" name="issueDate"
           value="{$customer_credit_card->mPlainCreditCard.issue_date}" />
        </td>
      </tr>
      <tr>
        <td>Issue Number (if applicable):</td>
        <td>
          <input type="text" name="issueNumber"
           value="{$customer_credit_card->mPlainCreditCard.issue_number}" />
        </td>
      </tr>
      <tr>
        <td>Card Type:</td>
        <td>
          <select name="cardType">
            {html_options options=$customer_credit_card->mCardTypes
             selected=$customer_credit_card->mPlainCreditCard.card_type}
          </select>
        </td>
        <td>
          {if $customer_credit_card->mCardTypesError}
          <span  class="error_text">You must enter a card type.</span>
          {/if}
        </td>
      </tr>
    </table>
    <br />
    <input type="submit" name="sended" value="Confirm" />
    <input type="button" value="Cancel"
     onclick="window.location='{
        $customer_credit_card->mReturnLink|prepare_link:$customer_credit_card->➥
   mReturnLinkProtocol}';" />
    </form>
```

10. Create a new plugin file named function.load_customer_credit_card.php in the presentation/smarty_plugins folder, and add the following to it:

```php
<?php
/* Smarty plugin function that gets called when the
   load_customer_credit_card function plugin is loaded from a template */
function smarty_function_load_customer_credit_card($params, $smarty)
{
  // Create CustomerCreditCard object
  $customer_credit_card = new CustomerCreditCard();
```

```php
    $customer_credit_card->init();

    // Assign template variable
    $smarty->assign($params['assign'], $customer_credit_card);
}

class CustomerCreditCard
{
  // Public attributes
  public $mCustomerCreditCardTarget;
  public $mReturnLink;
  public $mReturnLinkProtocol = 'http';
  public $mCardHolderError;
  public $mCardNumberError;
  public $mExpDateError;
  public $mCardTypesError;
  public $mPlainCreditCard;
  public $mCardTypes;

  // Private attributes
  private $_mErrors = 0;
  private $_mHaveData = 0;

  public function __construct()
  {
    $this->mPlainCreditCard = array('card_holder' => '',
      'card_number'  => '', 'issue_date' => '', 'expiry_date'  => '',
      'issue_number' => '', 'card_type'  => '', 'card_number_x' => '');

    $url_base = substr(getenv('REQUEST_URI'),
                       strrpos(getenv('REQUEST_URI'), '/') + 1,
                       strlen(getenv('REQUEST_URI')) - 1);

    $url_parameter_prefix = (count($_GET) == 1 ? '?' : '&');

    // Set form action target
    $this->mCustomerCreditCardTarget = $url_base;

    // Set the return page
    $this->mReturnLink = str_replace($url_parameter_prefix .
                           'UpdateCreditCardDetails', '', $url_base);

    if (isset($_GET['Checkout']) && USE_SSL != 'no')
      $this->mReturnLinkProtocol = 'https';

    if (!(empty ($_POST['sended'])))
      $this->_mHaveData = 1;
```

```php
$this->mCardTypes = array ('Mastercard' => 'Mastercard',
  'Visa' => 'Visa', 'Mastercard' => 'Mastercard',
  'Switch' => 'Switch', 'Solo' => 'Solo',
  'American Express' => 'American Express');

if ($this->_mHaveData == 1)
{
  // Initialization/validation stuff
  if (empty ($_POST['cardHolder']))
  {
    $this->mCardHolderError = 1;
    $this->_mErrors++;
  }
  else
    $this->mPlainCreditCard['card_holder'] = $_POST['cardHolder'];

  if (empty ($_POST['cardNumber']))
  {
    $this->mCardNumberError = 1;
    $this->_mErrors++;
  }
  else
    $this->mPlainCreditCard['card_number'] = $_POST['cardNumber'];

  if (empty ($_POST['expDate']))
  {
    $this->mExpDateError = 1;
    $this->_mErrors++;
  }
  else
    $this->mPlainCreditCard['expiry_date'] = $_POST['expDate'];

  if (isset ($_POST['issueDate']))
    $this->mPlainCreditCard['issue_date'] = $_POST['issueDate'];

  if (isset ($_POST['issueNumber']))
    $this->mPlainCreditCard['issue_number'] = $_POST['issueNumber'];

  $this->mPlainCreditCard['card_type'] = $_POST['cardType'];

  if (empty ($this->mPlainCreditCard['card_type']))
  {
    $this->mCardTypeError = 1;
    $this->_mErrors++;
  }
}
```

```
          }

          public function init()
          {
            if ($this->_mHaveData == 0)
            {
              // Get credit card information
              $this->mPlainCreditCard = Customer::GetPlainCreditCard();
            }
            elseif ($this->_mErrors == 0)
            {
              // Update credit card information
              Customer::UpdateCreditCardDetails($this->mPlainCreditCard);

              if (isset($_GET['Checkout']) && USE_SSL != 'no')
              {
                $redirect_link = 'https://' . getenv('SERVER_NAME');
              }
              else
              {
                $redirect_link = 'http://' . getenv('SERVER_NAME');

                // If HTTP_SERVER_PORT is defined and different than default
                if (defined('HTTP_SERVER_PORT') && HTTP_SERVER_PORT != '80')
                {
                  // Append server port
                  $redirect_link .= ':' . HTTP_SERVER_PORT;
                }
              }

              $redirect_link .= VIRTUAL_LOCATION . $this->mReturnLink;

              header('Location:' . $redirect_link);

              exit;
            }
          }
        }
        ?>
```

11. Update `include/app_top.php` by adding a reference to the symmetric crypting, secure card, and customer accounts business tier classes as highlighted:

```
// Load Business Tier
require_once BUSINESS_DIR . 'catalog.php';
require_once BUSINESS_DIR . 'shopping_cart.php';
```

```
require_once BUSINESS_DIR . 'orders.php';
require_once BUSINESS_DIR . 'password_hasher.php';
require_once BUSINESS_DIR . 'symmetric_crypt.php';
require_once BUSINESS_DIR . 'secure_card.php';
require_once BUSINESS_DIR . 'customer.php';
```

12. Update index.php by adding the new interface elements:

```
// Load search result page if we're searching the catalog
if (isset ($_GET['Search']))
  $pageContentsCell = 'search_results.tpl';

// Load product details page if visiting a product
if (isset ($_GET['ProductID']))
  $pageContentsCell = 'product.tpl';

if (isset ($_GET['CartAction']))
{
  $pageContentsCell = 'cart_details.tpl';
}
else
  $cartSummaryCell = 'cart_summary.tpl';

// Customer account functionality
$customerLoginOrLogged = 'customer_login.tpl';

if (Customer::IsAuthenticated())
  $customerLoginOrLogged = 'customer_logged.tpl';

if (isset($_GET['RegisterCustomer']) || isset($_GET['UpdateAccountDetails']))
  $pageContentsCell = 'customer_details.tpl';
elseif (isset($_GET['UpdateAddressDetails']))
  $pageContentsCell = 'customer_address.tpl';
elseif (isset($_GET['UpdateCreditCardDetails']))
  $pageContentsCell = 'customer_credit_card.tpl';

$page->assign('customerLoginOrLogged', $customerLoginOrLogged);

// Assign a template file to the cart summary cell
$page->assign('cartSummaryCell', $cartSummaryCell);

// Assign a template file to the page contents cell
$page->assign('pageContentsCell', $pageContentsCell);
$page->assign('categoriesCell', $categoriesCell);

// Display the page
$page->display('index.tpl');
```

13. Update `presentation/templates/index.tpl` by adding the following:

```
{include file="$customerLoginOrLogged"}
{include file="departments_list.tpl"}
{include file="$categoriesCell"}
```

14. Add the following styles to `hatshop.css`:

```
#login_box
{
  border: 1px solid #dc143c;
}
#login_box p
{
  background: #dc143c;
}
.error_text
{
  color: #ff0000;
  font-style: italic;
}
.form_table
{
  width: auto;
}
.form_table tr td
{
  background: #ffffff;
  border: none;
}
```

15. You can now load the web site to check that the functionality shown in Figures 11-4 through 11-7 works.

Creating the Checkout Page

You are now ready to add the checkout page. This page will look similar to the `cart_details` componentized template because you are displaying the items ordered, but it will also display additional information such as the shipping address or the type of the credit card. For new customers, neither address nor credit card information will be available yet, so you can also disable the order button until this information has been added.

Let's take a look now at what you'll be doing (see Figure 11-8).

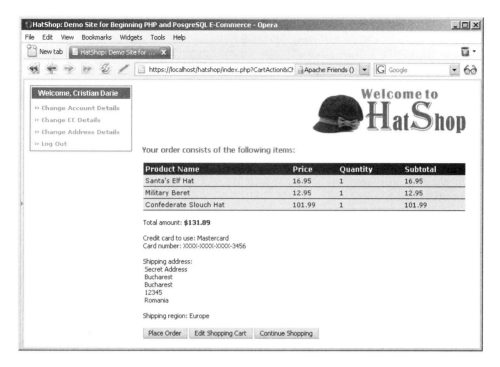

Figure 11-8. *The Checkout Page*

If you try to check out without entering all of your personal data, the Place Order button won't be active, and you'll be notified through an error message such as the one you can see in Figure 11-9.

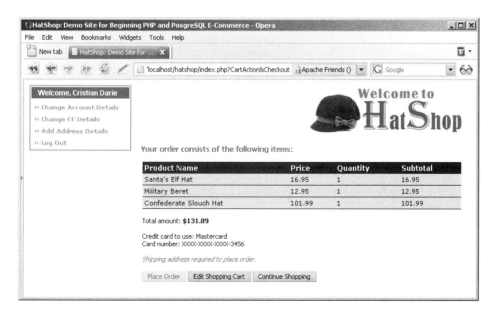

Figure 11-9. *Customers with incomplete details cannot place orders*

At this point, the customer also has the option to change the credit card or address details, using the functionality you implemented earlier.

Let's implement the checkout_info componentized template that you saw in Figure 11-9.

Exercise: Implementing the checkout_info Componentized Template

1. Create a new file named checkout_info.tpl in the presentation/templates folder, and add the following code to it:

```
{* cart_details.tpl *}
{load_checkout_info assign="checkout_info"}
<span class="description">
  Your order consists of the following items:
</span>
<br /><br />
<form method="post"
 action="{$checkout_info->mCheckoutInfoLink|prepare_link:"https"}">
  <table>
    <tr>
      <th>Product Name</th>
      <th>Price</th>
      <th>Quantity</th>
      <th>Subtotal</th>
    </tr>
  {section name=cCartItems loop=$checkout_info->mCartItems}
    <tr>
      <td>{$checkout_info->mCartItems[cCartItems].name}</td>
      <td>{$checkout_info->mCartItems[cCartItems].price}</td>
      <td>{$checkout_info->mCartItems[cCartItems].quantity}</td>
      <td>{$checkout_info->mCartItems[cCartItems].subtotal}</td>
    </tr>
  {/section}
  </table>
  <br />
  <span>Total amount:</span>
  <span class="price">${$checkout_info->mTotalAmountLabel}</span>
  <br /><br />
  {if $checkout_info->mNoCreditCard == 'yes'}
  <span class="error_text">No credit card details stored.</span>
  {else}
  <span>{$checkout_info->mCreditCardNote}</span>
  {/if}
  <br /><br />
  {if $checkout_info->mNoShippingAddress == 'yes'}
  <span class="error_text">Shipping address required to place order.</span>
  {else}
  <span>
```

```
      Shipping address: <br />
       {$checkout_info->mCustomerData.address_1}<br />
      {if $checkout_info->mCustomerData.address_2}
         {$checkout_info->mCustomerData.address_2}<br />
      {/if}
       {$checkout_info->mCustomerData.city}<br />
       {$checkout_info->mCustomerData.region}<br />
       {$checkout_info->mCustomerData.postal_code}<br />
       {$checkout_info->mCustomerData.country}<br /><br />
      Shipping region: {$checkout_info->mShippingRegion}
    </span>
    {/if}
    <br /><br />
    <input type="submit" name="sended" value="Place Order"
     {$checkout_info->mOrderButtonVisible} />
    <input type="button" value="Edit Shopping Cart"
     onclick="window.location='{
        $checkout_info->mEditCart|prepare_link:"http"}';" />
    <input type="button" value="Continue Shopping"
     onclick="window.location='{
        $checkout_info->mContinueShopping|prepare_link:"http"}';" />
</form>
```

2. Create the `presentation/smarty_plugins/function.load_checkout_info.php` file, and fill it with the following code:

```php
<?php
/* Smarty plugin function that gets called when the
   load_checkout_info function plugin is loaded from a template */
function smarty_function_load_checkout_info($params, $smarty)
{
  // Create CheckoutInfo object
  $checkout_info = new CheckoutInfo();
  $checkout_info->init();

  // Assign template variable
  $smarty->assign($params['assign'], $checkout_info);
}

// Class that supports the checkout page
class CheckoutInfo
{
  // Public attributes
  public $mCartItems;
  public $mTotalAmountLabel;
  public $mCreditCardNote;
  public $mEditCart = 'index.php?CartAction';
  public $mOrderButtonVisible;
```

```php
    public $mNoShippingAddress = 'no';
    public $mNoCreditCard = 'no';
    public $mContinueShopping;
    public $mCheckoutInfoLink;
    public $mPlainCreditCard;
    public $mShippingRegion;

    // Private attributes
    private $_mPlaceOrder = 0;

    // Class constructor
    public function __construct()
    {
      if (isset ($_POST['sended']))
        $this->_mPlaceOrder = 1;
    }

    public function init()
    {
      // If the Place Order button was clicked, save the order to database
      if ($this->_mPlaceOrder == 1)
      {
        $order_id = ShoppingCart::CreateOrder();

        // Redirect to index.php
        $redirect_link = 'http://' . getenv('SERVER_NAME');

        // If HTTP_SERVER_PORT is defined and different than default
        if (defined('HTTP_SERVER_PORT') && HTTP_SERVER_PORT != '80')
        {
          // Append server port
          $redirect_link .= ':' . HTTP_SERVER_PORT;
        }

        $redirect_link .= VIRTUAL_LOCATION . 'index.php';

        header('Location:' . $redirect_link);

        exit;
      }

      $this->mCheckoutInfoLink = substr(getenv('REQUEST_URI'),
                          strrpos(getenv('REQUEST_URI'), '/') + 1,
                          strlen(getenv('REQUEST_URI')) - 1);

      // Set members for use in the Smarty template
      $this->mCartItems = ShoppingCart::GetCartProducts(GET_CART_PRODUCTS);
```

```
      $this->mTotalAmountLabel = ShoppingCart::GetTotalAmount();
      $this->mContinueShopping = $_SESSION['page_link'];
      $this->mCustomerData = Customer::Get();

      // We allow placing orders only if we have complete customer details
      if (empty ($this->mCustomerData['credit_card']))
      {
        $this->mOrderButtonVisible = 'disabled="disabled"';
        $this->mNoCreditCard = 'yes';
      }
      else
      {
        $this->mPlainCreditCard = Customer::DecryptCreditCard(
                               $this->mCustomerData['credit_card']);

        $this->mCreditCardNote = 'Credit card to use: ' .
                               $this->mPlainCreditCard['card_type'] .
                               '<br />Card number: ' .
                               $this->mPlainCreditCard['card_number_x'];
      }

      if (empty ($this->mCustomerData['address_1']))
      {
        $this->mOrderButtonVisible = 'disabled="disabled"';
        $this->mNoShippingAddress = 'yes';
      }
      else
      {
        $shipping_regions = Customer::GetShippingRegions();

        foreach ($shipping_regions as $item)
          if ($item['shipping_region_id'] ==
              $this->mCustomerData['shipping_region_id'])
          $this->mShippingRegion = $item['shipping_region'];
      }
    }
  }
}
?>
```

3. Create the checkout_not_logged.tpl file in the presentation/templates folder, and add the following code:

```
{* checkout_not_logged.tpl *}
<h3>
  You must be logged in to CHECKOUT <br />
  If you don't have an account please register <br />
</h3>
```

4. Modify `index.php` to load the `checkout_info` componentized template and the `checkout_not_logged` template by adding the highlighted code:

```
// Customer account functionality
$customerLoginOrLogged = 'customer_login.tpl';

if (Customer::IsAuthenticated())
  $customerLoginOrLogged = 'customer_logged.tpl';

$hide_boxes = false;

if (isset ($_GET['Checkout']))
{
  if (Customer::IsAuthenticated())
    $pageContentsCell = 'checkout_info.tpl';
  else
    $pageContentsCell = 'checkout_not_logged.tpl';

  $hide_boxes = true;
}

if (isset($_GET['RegisterCustomer']) || isset($_GET['UpdateAccountDetails']))
  $pageContentsCell = 'customer_details.tpl';
elseif (isset($_GET['UpdateAddressDetails']))
  $pageContentsCell = 'customer_address.tpl';
elseif (isset($_GET['UpdateCreditCardDetails']))
  $pageContentsCell = 'customer_credit_card.tpl';

$page->assign('hide_boxes', $hide_boxes);
$page->assign('customerLoginOrLogged', $customerLoginOrLogged);
```

5. Modify `presentation/templates/index.tpl` to show only the login or logged box on the left when showing the checkout page by adding the highlighted code:

```
{if !$hide_boxes}
  {include file="departments_list.tpl"}
  {include file="$categoriesCell"}
  {include file="search_box.tpl"}
  {include file="$cartSummaryCell"}
{/if}
  {include file="header.tpl"}
```

6. Modify your `presentation/templates/cart_details.tpl` file to redirect the user to the `checkout_info` page instead of PayPal. The Place Order button becomes the Checkout button:

```
...
    <td class="cart_total" align="right">
      <input type="submit" name="update" value="Update" />
```

```
            <input type="button" name="Checkout" value="Checkout"
             {if $cart_details->mTotalAmount eq 0}disabled="disabled"{/if}
             onclick="window.location='{
               $cart_details->mCheckoutLink|prepare_link:"https"}';" />
         </td>
...
```

7. Modify the constructor of the CartDetails class in presentation/smarty_plugins/
   function.load_cart_details.php to add checkout functionality as highlighted:

```
...
  public $mRecommendations;
  public $mCheckoutActive = false;
  public $mCheckoutLink;

  // Private attributes
  private $_mProductId;
...
  // Class constructor
  public function __construct()
  {
    $url_base = substr(getenv('REQUEST_URI'),
                       strrpos(getenv('REQUEST_URI'), '/') + 1,
                       strlen(getenv('REQUEST_URI')) - 1);

    $url_parameter_prefix = (empty ($_GET) ? '?' : '&');

    $this->mCheckoutLink = $url_base . $url_parameter_prefix . 'Checkout';

    // Setting the "Continue shopping" button target
    if (isset ($_SESSION['page_link']))
      $this->mCartReferrer = $_SESSION['page_link'];
```

8. Update the init() method of the CartDetails class in presentation/smarty_plugins/
   function.load_cart_details.php as highlighted:

```
...
    // Calculate the total amount for the shopping cart
    $this->mTotalAmount = ShoppingCart::GetTotalAmount();

    if ($this->mTotalAmount != 0 && Customer::IsAuthenticated())
      $this->mCheckoutActive = true;

    // Get shopping cart products
    $this->mCartProducts =
      ShoppingCart::GetCartProducts(GET_CART_PRODUCTS);
...
```

9. Now everything is in its place, and you can see the results. Log in to your site, add some products to your shopping cart, and then click the Checkout button on your shopping cart page. Your page will look something like Figure 11-9 shown earlier.

How It Works: The checkout_info Componentized Template

In the init() method of the CheckoutInfo class, you start by checking whether the customer clicked the Place Order button. If so, you save the order into the database and redirect the customer to the home page:

```
// If the Place Order button was clicked, save the order to database
if ($this->_mPlaceOrder == 1)
{
  $order_id = ShoppingCart::CreateOrder();

  // Redirect to index.php
  $redirect_link = 'http://' . getenv('SERVER_NAME');

  // If HTTP_SERVER_PORT is defined and different than default
  if (defined('HTTP_SERVER_PORT') && HTTP_SERVER_PORT != '80')
  {
    // Append server port
    $redirect_link .= ':' . HTTP_SERVER_PORT;
  }

  $redirect_link .= VIRTUAL_LOCATION . 'index.php';

  header('Location:' . $redirect_link);

  exit;
}
```

You then need to set up some variables for the template to use:

```
// Set members for use in the Smarty template
$this->mCartItems = ShoppingCart::GetCartProducts(GET_CART_PRODUCTS);
$this->mTotalAmountLabel = ShoppingCart::GetTotalAmount();
$this->mContinueShopping = $_SESSION['page_link'];
$this->mCustomerData = Customer::Get();
```

If the customer didn't enter credit card information or a shipping address yet, a notice is displayed, and the Place Order button is disabled. If credit card information exists for the customer, you decrypt it and prepare to display the credit card type and the last four digits of its number:

```
// We allow placing orders only if we have complete customer details
if (empty ($this->mCustomerData['credit_card']))
{
  $this->mOrderButtonVisible = 'disabled="disabled"';
  $this->mNoCreditCard = 'yes';
}
```

```
else
{
  $this->mPlainCreditCard = Customer::DecryptCreditCard(
                       $this->mCustomerData['credit_card']);

  $this->mCreditCardNote = 'Credit card to use: ' .
                        $this->mPlainCreditCard['card_type'] .
                        '<br />Card number: ' .
                        $this->mPlainCreditCard['card_number_x'];
}

if (empty ($this->mCustomerData['address_1']))
{
  $this->mOrderButtonVisible = 'disabled="disabled"';
  $this->mNoShippingAddress = 'yes';
}
```

The rest of the code is straightforward.

Enforcing SSL Connections

When building the catalog admin pages, you also learned that it's good to use SSL for securing the data that passes between your server and the client's browser. Back then, SSL was semi-optional because the administrative pages could have been restricted for local access only.

However, now that you have customers sending you extremely sensitive data, using SSL isn't optional anymore! Depending on the settings you've implemented in Chapter 7, the customer details pages should be protected already. Remember that you have the config.php file that you can use to set the behavior of your site regarding SSL.

You still need to *force* the sensitive pages to be accessed through SSL. Say, if someone tried to access http://localhost/hatshop/index.php?UpdateCreditCardDetails, the visitor should be redirected automatically to https://localhost/hatshop/index. php?UpdateCreditCardDetails.

Obviously, you don't need SSL connections for all areas of the site, and you shouldn't enforce it in all places because that reduces performance. However, you *do* want to make sure that the checkout, customer login, customer registration, and customer detail modification pages are accessible only via SSL.

Assuming that your site is working correctly with SSL, you should make some updates to ensure that the pages can't be accessed via HTTP. Add the following code at the beginning of index.php:

```
// Load Smarty library and config files
require_once 'include/app_top.php';

// Is the page being accessed through an HTTPS connection?
if (getenv('HTTPS') != 'on')
  $is_https = false;
```

```php
else
  $is_https = true;

// Visiting a sensitive page?
if (isset($_GET['RegisterCustomer']) ||
    isset($_GET['UpdateAccountDetails']) ||
    isset($_GET['UpdateAddressDetails']) ||
    isset($_GET['UpdateCreditCardDetails']) ||
    isset($_GET['Checkout']) ||
    isset($_POST['Login']))
  $is_sensitive_page = true;
else
  $is_sensitive_page = false;

// Use HTTPS when accessing sensitive pages
if ($is_sensitive_page && $is_https == false && USE_SSL != 'no')
{
   header ('Location: https://' . getenv('SERVER_NAME') .
           getenv('REQUEST_URI'));

   exit;
}

// Don't use HTTPS for nonsensitive pages
if (!$is_sensitive_page && $is_https == true)
{

  $link = 'http://' . getenv('SERVER_NAME');

  // If HTTP_SERVER_PORT is defined and different than default
  if (defined('HTTP_SERVER_PORT') && HTTP_SERVER_PORT != '80')
  {
    // Append server port
    $link .= ':' . HTTP_SERVER_PORT;
  }

  $link .= getenv('REQUEST_URI');

   header ('Location: ' . $link);

   exit;
}

/* If not visiting a product page, save the link to the current page
   in the page_link session variable; it will be used to create the
   Continue Shopping link in the product details page and the links
   to product details pages */
if (!isset ($_GET['ProductID']) && !isset ($_GET['CartAction']))
```

Right now, trying to load `http://localhost/hatshop/index.php?UpdateCreditCardDetails` would redirect you to `https://localhost/hatshop/index.php?UpdateCreditCardDetails`, provided that you're logged in.

Summary

In this chapter, you've implemented a customer account system that customers can use to store their details for use during order processing. You've looked at many aspects of the customer account system, including encrypting sensitive data and securing web connections for obtaining it.

You started by looking at a new table in your database, `customer`, with fields for storing customer information.

Next, you created the security classes in your business tier, which handle hashing and encrypting strings, and a secure credit card representation that makes it easy to exchange credit card details between the encrypted and decrypted format.

After this, you used these classes to create the login, registration, and customer detail editing web pages. This required a bit more code, but the result turned out to be simple to understand.

In the next chapter, we'll be looking at how to create the framework for the order-processing pipeline, enabling you to automate even more of the supply process.

CHAPTER 12

Storing Customer Orders

The HatShop e-commerce application is shaping up nicely. You've added customer account management capabilities, and you're keeping track of customer addresses and credit card information, which is stored in a secure way. However, you're not currently using this information—you're delegating responsibility to PayPal.

In this chapter, you'll make the modifications required for customers to place orders that are associated with their user profiles. The main modification here is that the customer associated with an order will be identified by a new piece of information in the orders table, and much of the rest of the modifications will be made to use this information.

Also in this chapter, you'll take a look at dealing with another common feature of e-commerce sites: tax and shipping charges. Many options are available for implementing this functionality, but we'll just examine a simple way of doing things and lay the groundwork for your own further development.

This chapter is divided into three parts as follows:

- Enable customers to place orders through their accounts.

- Modify the orders admin section to integrate the new features.

- Add tax and shipping charges.

In the next chapter, you'll start to implement a more sophisticated order system, and the code you'll write in this chapter will facilitate this. Because of this, you'll be making some modifications that won't seem necessary at this stage, but they'll make your life easier later on.

Adding Orders to Customer Accounts

To enable customers to place orders, you need to make several modifications. You'll modify the database and business tier to enable customer orders to be placed and provide new code in the presentation tier to expose this functionality.

First, we'll modify the database to make it ready to hold information about customer orders. You'll first modify the orders table and then the shopping_cart_create_order function.

Currently the orders table doesn't allow for as much information as you'll need to implement customer orders. You'll also make some modifications in later chapters, so you need to add new columns to the orders table.

▪**Caution** The new `orders` table isn't totally compatible with the previous data in this table, and you'll be required to delete all the existing data. You need to back up your database and eventually save your current data before making these changes.

More specifically, these are the changes you'll make to the `orders` table:

- Clear all the existing data.

- Remove the `customer_name`, `shipping_address`, and `customer_email` fields.

- Add `customer_id`, `auth_code`, and `reference` fields. The `customer_id` field references the customer table, specifying the customer who made the order. The other two fields are related to processing credit card data, and will be discussed in Chapter 14.

You'll also modify the `shopping_cart_create_order` function to reflect the changes in the `orders` table.

Follow the steps in the following exercise to change your `orders` table and the `shopping_cart_create_order` function.

Exercise: Adding Orders to Customer Accounts

1. Load pgAdmin III, and connect to the `hatshop` database.

2. Click Tools ➤ Query tool (or click the SQL button on the toolbar). A new query window should appear.

3. Be sure to back up your data. Then use the query tool to execute this code, which deletes the data stored in the `order_details` and `orders` tables from your `hatshop` database.

   ```
   -- Delete all records from order_detail table
   DELETE FROM order_detail;

   -- Delete all records from orders table
   DELETE FROM orders;
   ```

4. Drop the `customer_name`, `shipping_address`, and `customer_email` fields from the `orders` table, which are no longer required. This data is now held in the `customer` table.

   ```
   -- Drop customer_name field from orders table
   ALTER TABLE orders DROP COLUMN customer_name;

   -- Drop shipping_address field from orders table
   ALTER TABLE orders DROP COLUMN shipping_address;

   -- Drop customer_email field from orders table
   ALTER TABLE orders DROP COLUMN customer_email;
   ```

5. Add the new fields (`customer_id`, `auth_code`, and `reference`), and a constraint that checks the value in the `customer_id` field will reference an existing customer.

```
-- Adding a new field named customer_id to orders table
ALTER TABLE orders ADD COLUMN customer_id INTEGER;

-- Adding a new field named auth_code to orders table
ALTER TABLE orders ADD COLUMN auth_code VARCHAR(50);

-- Adding a new field named reference to orders table
ALTER TABLE orders ADD COLUMN reference VARCHAR(50);

-- Adding a new foreign key constraint to orders table
ALTER TABLE orders
  ADD CONSTRAINT fk_customer_id FOREIGN KEY (customer_id)
                 REFERENCES customer (customer_id)
                 ON UPDATE RESTRICT ON DELETE RESTRICT;
```

6. Delete the old `shopping_cart_create_order` function and create a new one by executing the following code:

```
-- Drop shopping_cart_create_order function
DROP FUNCTION shopping_cart_create_order(CHAR(32));

-- Create shopping_cart_create_order function
CREATE FUNCTION shopping_cart_create_order(CHAR(32), INTEGER)
RETURNS INTEGER LANGUAGE plpgsql AS $$
  DECLARE
    inCartId    ALIAS FOR $1;
    inCustomerId ALIAS FOR $2;
    outOrderId INTEGER;
    cartItem cart_product;
    orderTotalAmount NUMERIC(10, 2);
  BEGIN
    -- Insert a new record into orders
    INSERT INTO orders (created_on, customer_id)
          VALUES (NOW(), inCustomerId);
    -- Obtain the new Order ID
    SELECT INTO outOrderId
          currval('orders_order_id_seq');
    orderTotalAmount := 0;
    -- Insert order details in order_detail table
    FOR cartItem IN
      SELECT    p.product_id, p.name,
                COALESCE(NULLIF(p.discounted_price, 0), p.price) AS price,
                sc.quantity,
                COALESCE(NULLIF(p.discounted_price, 0), p.price) * sc.quantity
                  AS subtotal
      FROM      shopping_cart sc
      INNER JOIN product p
                ON sc.product_id = p.product_id
```

```
            WHERE       sc.cart_id = inCartId AND sc.buy_now
          LOOP
            INSERT INTO order_detail (order_id, product_id, product_name,
                                    quantity, unit_cost)
                VALUES (outOrderId, cartItem.product_id, cartItem.name,
                            cartItem.quantity, cartItem.price);
            orderTotalAmount := orderTotalAmount + cartItem.subtotal;
          END LOOP;
          -- Save the order's total amount
          UPDATE orders
          SET    total_amount = orderTotalAmount
          WHERE  order_id = outOrderId;
          -- Clear the shopping cart
          PERFORM shopping_cart_empty(inCartId);
          -- Return the Order ID
          RETURN outOrderId;
        END;
      $$;
```

7. Modify the `CreateOrder` method from the `ShoppingCart` class in `business/shopping_cart.php` as follows:

```php
// Create a new order
public static function CreateOrder($customerId)
{
  // Build the SQL query
  $sql = 'SELECT shopping_cart_create_order(:cart_id, :customer_id);';
  // Build the parameters array
  $params = array (':cart_id' => self::GetCartId(),
                   ':customer_id' => $customerId);
  // Prepare the statement with PDO-specific functionality
  $result = DatabaseHandler::Prepare($sql);

  // Execute the query and return the results
  return DatabaseHandler::GetOne($result, $params);
}
```

8. Modify the `init()` method in `presentation/smarty_plugins/function.load_checkout_info.php` as highlighted:

```php
public function init()
{
  // If the Place Order button was clicked, save the order to database
  if ($this->_mPlaceOrder == 1)
  {
    $order_id =
      ShoppingCart::CreateOrder(Customer::GetCurrentCustomerId());

    // Redirect to index.php
    $redirect_link = 'http://' . getenv('SERVER_NAME');
```

9. Place an order or two using the new system to check that the code works. You'll need to log on to do this and supply enough details to get past the validation on the checkout page.

■**Note** At this stage, the orders administration page isn't functional anymore. We'll need to update it as well.

How It Works: Adding Customer Orders to HatShop

The code added in this exercise is very simple and hardly merits much discussion. The orders handling functions in the data and business tiers now take as parameter a customer ID, which is assigned to the order.

After you've implemented more of the new ordering code, you'll be able to provide more information to customers, such as sending them confirmation emails. For now, however, this is as far as we can take things.

Administering Customer Orders

After orders have been placed, you'll need to access them. This involves various modifications to the database and business tiers to provide new data structures and access code in the admin orders we developed in Chapter 9. Although essential in the next chapter and beyond, for now, you'll implement a simple (admin only) test form to access customer order data. Because the changes are extensive, we'll deal with them separately for the data, business, and presentation tiers.

Database Modifications

You only need to make several changes here. You'll update these database functions:

- orders_get_most_recent_orders
- orders_get_orders_between_dates
- orders_get_orders_by_status
- orders_get_order_info

You'll create three new functions:

- orders_get_by_customer_id
- orders_get_order_short_details
- customer_get_customers_list

You'll also drop the orders_update_order function, which we don't need anymore.

1. Load pgAdmin III, and connect to the `hatshop` database.

2. Click Tools ➤ Query tool (or click the SQL button on the toolbar). A new query window should appear.

3. Update the `orders_get_most_recent_orders` function:

```
-- Update orders_get_most_recent_orders function
CREATE OR REPLACE FUNCTION orders_get_most_recent_orders(INTEGER)
RETURNS SETOF order_short_details LANGUAGE plpgsql AS $$
  DECLARE
    inHowMany ALIAS FOR $1;
    outOrderShortDetailsRow order_short_details;
  BEGIN
    FOR outOrderShortDetailsRow IN
      SELECT     o.order_id, o.total_amount, o.created_on,
                 o.shipped_on, o.status, c.name
      FROM       orders o
      INNER JOIN customer c
                   ON o.customer_id = c.customer_id
      ORDER BY   o.created_on DESC
      LIMIT      inHowMany
    LOOP
      RETURN NEXT outOrderShortDetailsRow;
    END LOOP;
  END;
$$;
```

4. Update the `orders_get_orders_between_dates` function:

```
-- Update orders_get_orders_between_dates function
CREATE OR REPLACE FUNCTION orders_get_orders_between_dates(TIMESTAMP, TIMESTAMP)
RETURNS SETOF order_short_details LANGUAGE plpgsql AS $$
  DECLARE
    inStartDate ALIAS FOR $1;
    inEndDate   ALIAS FOR $2;
    outOrderShortDetailsRow order_short_details;
  BEGIN
    FOR outOrderShortDetailsRow IN
      SELECT     o.order_id, o.total_amount, o.created_on,
                 o.shipped_on, o.status, c.name
      FROM       orders o
      INNER JOIN customer c
                   ON o.customer_id = c.customer_id
      WHERE      o.created_on >= inStartDate AND o.created_on <= inEndDate
      ORDER BY   o.created_on DESC
    LOOP
      RETURN NEXT outOrderShortDetailsRow;
    END LOOP;
  END;
$$;
```

5. Update the `orders_get_orders_by_status` function:

```
-- Update orders_get_orders_by_status function
CREATE OR REPLACE FUNCTION orders_get_orders_by_status(INTEGER)
RETURNS SETOF order_short_details LANGUAGE plpgsql AS $$
  DECLARE
    inStatus ALIAS FOR $1;
    outOrderShortDetailsRow order_short_details;
  BEGIN
    FOR outOrderShortDetailsRow IN
      SELECT    o.order_id, o.total_amount, o.created_on,
                o.shipped_on, o.status, c.name
      FROM      orders o
      INNER JOIN customer c
                ON o.customer_id = c.customer_id
      WHERE     o.status = inStatus
      ORDER BY  o.created_on DESC
    LOOP
      RETURN NEXT outOrderShortDetailsRow;
    END LOOP;
  END;
$$;
```

6. Update the `orders_get_order_info` function:

```
-- Update orders_get_order_info function
CREATE OR REPLACE FUNCTION orders_get_order_info(INTEGER)
  RETURNS orders LANGUAGE plpgsql AS $$
  DECLARE
    inOrderId ALIAS FOR $1;
    outOrdersRow orders;
  BEGIN
    SELECT INTO outOrdersRow
                order_id, total_amount, created_on, shipped_on, status,
                comments, customer_id, auth_code, reference
    FROM   orders
    WHERE  order_id = inOrderId;
    RETURN outOrdersRow;
  END;
$$;
```

7. Create the `orders_get_orders_by_customer_id` function:

```
-- Create orders_get_by_customer_id function
CREATE FUNCTION orders_get_by_customer_id(INTEGER)
RETURNS SETOF order_short_details LANGUAGE plpgsql AS $$
  DECLARE
    inCustomerId ALIAS FOR $1;
    outOrderShortDetailsRow order_short_details;
  BEGIN
```

```
        FOR outOrderShortDetailsRow IN
           SELECT      o.order_id, o.total_amount, o.created_on,
                       o.shipped_on, o.status, c.name
           FROM        orders o
           INNER JOIN customer c
                        ON o.customer_id = c.customer_id
           WHERE       o.customer_id = inCustomerId
           ORDER BY    o.created_on DESC
        LOOP
          RETURN NEXT outOrderShortDetailsRow;
        END LOOP;
     END;
  $$;
```

8. Create the `orders_get_order_short_details` function:

```
-- Create orders_get_order_short_details function
CREATE FUNCTION orders_get_order_short_details(INTEGER)
RETURNS order_short_details LANGUAGE plpgsql AS $$
  DECLARE
    inOrderId ALIAS FOR $1;
    outOrderShortDetailsRow order_short_details;
  BEGIN
    SELECT INTO outOrderShortDetailsRow
                o.order_id, o.total_amount, o.created_on,
                o.shipped_on, o.status, c.name
    FROM        orders o
    INNER JOIN  customer c
                  ON o.customer_id = c.customer_id
    WHERE       o.order_id = inOrderId;
    RETURN outOrderShortDetailsRow;
  END;
$$;
```

9. Create the `customer_list` type and the `customer_get_customers_list` function:

```
-- Create customer_list type
CREATE TYPE customer_list AS
(
  customer_id INTEGER,
  name        VARCHAR(50)
);

-- Create customer_get_customers_list function
CREATE FUNCTION customer_get_customers_list()
RETURNS SETOF customer_list LANGUAGE plpgsql AS $$
```

```
  DECLARE
    outCustomerListRow customer_list;
  BEGIN
    FOR outCustomerListRow IN
      SELECT customer_id, name FROM customer ORDER BY name ASC
    LOOP
      RETURN NEXT outCustomerListRow;
    END LOOP;
  END;
$$;
```

10. Delete the old `orders_update_order` function, and create a new one:

```
-- Drop orders_update_order function
DROP FUNCTION orders_update_order(INTEGER, INTEGER, VARCHAR(255),
                                  VARCHAR(50), VARCHAR(255), VARCHAR(50));


-- Create orders_update_order function
CREATE FUNCTION orders_update_order(INTEGER, INTEGER, VARCHAR(255),
                                    VARCHAR(50), VARCHAR(50))
RETURNS VOID LANGUAGE plpgsql AS $$
  DECLARE
    inOrderId    ALIAS FOR $1;
    inStatus     ALIAS FOR $2;
    inComments   ALIAS FOR $3;
    inAuthCode   ALIAS FOR $4;
    inReference  ALIAS FOR $5;
    currentStatus INTEGER;
  BEGIN
    SELECT INTO currentStatus
           status
    FROM   orders
    WHERE  order_id = inOrderId;
    IF  inStatus != currentStatus AND (inStatus = 0 OR inStatus = 1) THEN
      UPDATE orders SET shipped_on = NULL WHERE order_id = inOrderId;
    ELSEIF inStatus != currentStatus AND inStatus = 2 THEN
      UPDATE orders SET shipped_on = NOW() WHERE order_id = inOrderId;
    END IF;
    UPDATE orders
    SET    status = inStatus, comments = inComments,
           auth_code = inAuthCode, reference = inReference
    WHERE  order_id = inOrderId;
  END;
$$;
```

Business Layer Modifications

We need to make a few changes to the business tier as well. We need to modify the UpdateOrder method of the Orders class, and add three new methods to the same class:

- GetByCustomerId

- GetOrderShortDetails

- GetCustomersList

These new methods support the new administrative functionality you'll need in the admin_orders.tpl presentation tier template.

Exercise: Modifying the Business Tier

1. Add a new method named GetByCustomerId to the Orders class in business/Orders.php:

```
// Gets all orders placed by a specified customer
public static function GetByCustomerId($customerId)
{
  // Build the SQL query
  $sql = 'SELECT * FROM orders_get_by_customer_id(:customer_id);';
  // Build the parameters array
  $params = array (':customer_id' => $customerId);
  // Prepare the statement with PDO-specific functionality
  $result = DatabaseHandler::Prepare($sql);

  // Execute the query and return the results
  return DatabaseHandler::GetAll($result, $params);
}
```

2. Add a new method named GetOrderShortDetails to the Orders class:

```
// Get short details for an order
public static function GetOrderShortDetails($orderId)
{
  // Build the SQL query
  $sql = 'SELECT * FROM orders_get_order_short_details(:order_id);';
  // Build the parameters array
  $params = array (':order_id' => $orderId);
  // Prepare the statement with PDO-specific functionality
  $result = DatabaseHandler::Prepare($sql);

  // Execute the query and return the results
  return DatabaseHandler::GetAll($result, $params);
}
```

3. Modify the UpdateOrder method of the Orders class as follows:

```
// Updates order details
public static function UpdateOrder($orderId, $status, $comments,
                                   $authCode, $reference)
{
  // Build the SQL query
  $sql = 'SELECT orders_update_order(:order_id, :status, :comments,
                                     :auth_code, :reference);';
  // Build the parameters array
  $params = array (':order_id' => $orderId,
                   ':status' => $status,
                   ':comments' => $comments,
                   ':auth_code' => $authCode,
                   ':reference' => $reference);
  // Prepare the statement with PDO-specific functionality
  $result = DatabaseHandler::Prepare($sql);

  // Execute the query
  return DatabaseHandler::Execute($result, $params);
}
```

4. Add a new method named GetCustomersList to the Customer class in business/customer.php:

```
// Gets all customers names with their associated id
public static function GetCustomersList()
{
  // Build the SQL query
  $sql = 'SELECT * FROM customer_get_customers_list();';
  // Prepare the statement with PDO-specific functionality
  $result = DatabaseHandler::Prepare($sql);

  // Execute the query and return the results
  return DatabaseHandler::GetAll($result);
}
```

Presentation Tier Modifications

Now you need to update the presentation tier to make use of the new data tier and business tier features. You're not going to implement massive changes to the order administration code at this stage because you'll just end up modifying it later after you've finished the new order-processing system.

Figure 12-1 shows the admin_orders template. This page gives administrators various means of filtering current orders.

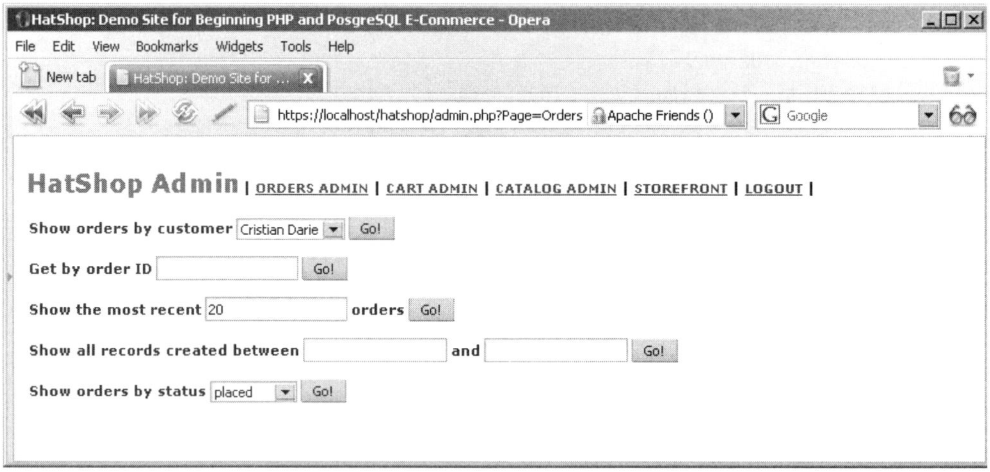

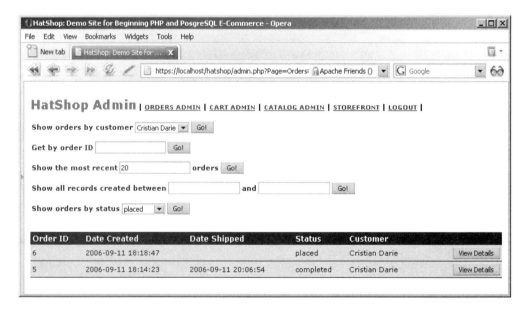

Figure 12-1. *The orders_admin template in action*

No matter what selection method you use, you'll get a list with the orders that match the criteria. In Figure 12-2, you can see the two orders I've just placed.

Figure 12-2. *The orders admin page*

The `admin_order_details` template looks like Figure 12-3. Notice also the Tax and Shipping data, which you'll add later in this chapter.

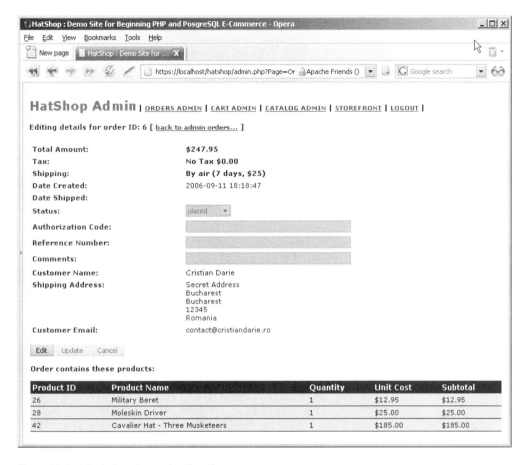

Figure 12-3. *Administering order details*

Exercise: Modifying the Presentation Tier

1. Add the highlighted piece of code to `presentation/templates/admin_orders.tpl`:

```
<form action="{"admin.php"|prepare_link:"https"}" method="get">
  <input name="Page" type="hidden" value="Orders" />
  <span class="admin_page_text">Show orders by customer</span>
  <select name="customer_id">
  {section name=cCustomers loop=$admin_orders->mCustomers}
    <option value="{$admin_orders->mCustomers[cCustomers].customer_id}"
      {if $admin_orders->mCustomers[cCustomers].customer_id ==
          $admin_orders->mCustomerId}selected="selected"{/if}>
      {$admin_orders->mCustomers[cCustomers].name}
    </option>
  {/section}
  </select>
```

```
<input type="submit" name="submitByCustomer" value="Go!" />
<br /><br />
<span class="admin_page_text">Get by order ID</span>
<input name="orderId" type="text"
 value="{$admin_orders->mOrderId}" />
<input type="submit" name="submitByOrderId" value="Go!" />
<br /><br />
<span class="admin_page_text">Show the most recent</span>
<input name="recordCount" type="text" value="{$admin_orders->mRecordCount}" />
```

2. Add the highlighted members to the `AdminOrders` class in `presentation/smarty_plugins/function.load_admin_orders.php`:

```php
public $mErrorMessage = '';
public $mCustomers;
public $mCustomerId;
public $mOrderId;
```

3. Add the highlighted code to the `init()` method of the `AdminOrders` class in `presentation/smarty_plugins/function.load_admin_orders.php`:

```php
// If "Show orders by status" filter is in action ...
if (isset ($_GET['submitOrdersByStatus']))
{
  $this->mSelectedStatus = $_GET['status'];
  $this->mOrders = Orders::GetOrdersByStatus($this->mSelectedStatus);
}

// If the "Show orders by customer ID" filter is in action ...
if (isset ($_GET['submitByCustomer']))
{
  if (empty ($_GET['customer_id']))
    $this->mErrorMessage = 'No customer has been selected';
  else
  {
    $this->mCustomerId = $_GET['customer_id'];
    $this->mOrders = Orders::GetByCustomerId($this->mCustomerId);
  }
}

// If the "Get order by ID" filter is in action ...
if (isset ($_GET['submitByOrderId']))
{
  if (empty ($_GET['orderId']))
    $this->mErrorMessage = 'You must enter an order ID.';
  else
  {
    $this->mOrderId = $_GET['orderId'];
    $this->mOrders = Orders::GetOrderShortDetails($this->mOrderId);
```

```
      }
   }

   $this->mCustomers = Customer::GetCustomersList();

   // Build View Details link
   for ($i = 0; $i < count($this->mOrders); $i++)
```

4. Add a new member to the `AdminOrderDetails` class in `presentation/smarty_plugins/function.load_admin_order_details.php`:

   ```
   public $mCustomerInfo;
   ```

5. Modify the line that updates an order in the `init()` function of `AdminOrderDetails` as highlighted:

   ```
   if (isset ($_GET['submitUpdate']))
   {
     Orders::UpdateOrder($this->mOrderId, $_GET['status'],
       $_GET['comments'], $_GET['authCode'], $_GET['reference']);
   }
   ```

6. Also in `AdminOrderDetails`, add a line that reads the data of the customer who made the order:

   ```
   $this->mOrderInfo = Orders::GetOrderInfo($this->mOrderId);
   $this->mOrderDetails = Orders::GetOrderDetails($this->mOrderId);
   $this->mCustomerInfo = Customer::Get($this->mOrderInfo['customer_id']);
   ```

7. Modify `presentation/templates/admin_order_details.tpl` like this:

   ```
   <tr>
     <td class="admin_page_text">Status: </td>
     <td>
       <select name="status"
        {if ! $admin_order_details->mEditEnabled}
        disabled="disabled"
        {/if} >
         {html_options options=$admin_order_details->mOrderStatusOptions
           selected=$admin_order_details->mOrderInfo.status}
       </select>
     </td>
   </tr>
   <tr>
     <td class="admin_page_text">Authorization Code: </td>
     <td>
       <input name="authCode" type="text" size="50"
        value="{$admin_order_details->mOrderInfo.auth_code}"
        {if ! $admin_order_details->mEditEnabled}
        disabled="disabled"
        {/if} />
     <td>
   </tr>
   ```

```
  <tr>
    <td class="admin_page_text">Reference Number: </td>
    <td>
      <input name="reference" type="text" size="50"
       value="{$admin_order_details->mOrderInfo.reference}"
       {if ! $admin_order_details->mEditEnabled}
       disabled="disabled"
       {/if} />
    <td>
  </tr>
  <tr>
    <td class="admin_page_text">Comments: </td>
    <td>
      <input name="comments" type="text" size="50"
       value="{$admin_order_details->mOrderInfo.comments}"
       {if ! $admin_order_details->mEditEnabled}
       disabled="disabled"
       {/if} />
    <td>
  </tr>
  <tr>
    <td class="admin_page_text">Customer Name: </td>
    <td>
      {$admin_order_details->mCustomerInfo.name}
    <td>
  </tr>
  <tr>
    <td class="admin_page_text" valign="top">Shipping Address: </td>
    <td>
      {$admin_order_details->mCustomerInfo.address_1}<br />
      {if $admin_order_details->mCustomerInfo.address_2}
        {$admin_order_details->mCustomerInfo.address_2}<br />
      {/if}
      {$admin_order_details->mCustomerInfo.city}<br />
      {$admin_order_details->mCustomerInfo.region}<br />
      {$admin_order_details->mCustomerInfo.postal_code}<br />
      {$admin_order_details->mCustomerInfo.country}<br />
    </td>
  </tr>
  <tr>
    <td class="admin_page_text">Customer Email: </td>
    <td>
      {$admin_order_details->mCustomerInfo.email}
    </td>
  </tr>
</table>
<br />
```

How It Works: Presentation Tier Changes

This was a long exercise, wasn't it? And yet, to make the most out of it, you still need to go through a few more exercises to implement tax and shipping charges. At that moment, all your customer-handling functionality will be completed, and you'll only be left with adding an order pipeline and credit card processing support.

Load your web site to make sure your newly added code works, and then proceed by adding tax and shipping charges support.

Handling Tax and Shipping Charges

One feature that is common to many e-commerce web sites is adding charges for tax and/or shipping. Obviously, this isn't always the case—digital download sites have no need to charge for shipping, for example, because no physical shipment is involved. However, you'll probably want to include additional charges of one kind or another in your orders.

In fact, this can be very simple, although not always. It really depends on how complicated you want to make things. In this chapter, we'll keep things simple and provide basic but extensible functionality for both tax and shipping charges. First, let's discuss the issues.

Tax Issues

The subject of tax and e-commerce web sites has a complicated history. Early on, you could usually get away with anything. Taxing was poorly enforced, and many sites simply ignored tax completely. This was especially true for international orders, where it was often possible for customers to avoid paying tax much of the time—unless orders were intercepted by customs officers!

Then more people started to become aware of e-commerce web sites, taxation bodies such as the IRS realized that they were losing a lot of money—or at least not getting all that they could. A flurry of activity ensued as various organizations worldwide attempted to hook into this revenue stream. A range of solutions was proposed; some solutions were implemented with mixed results. Now, things are becoming a little more settled.

The key concept to be aware of when thinking about tax is a nexus. A *nexus* is a "a sufficient presence in the taxing jurisdiction to justify the collection of tax." Effectively, this means that when shipping internationally, you may, in most situations, not be responsible for what happens unless your company has a significant presence in the destination country. When shipping internally to a country (or within, say, the European Union), you probably will be responsible. The legislation is a little unclear, and we certainly haven't examined the laws for every country in the world, but this general rule tends to hold true.

The other key issues can be summed up by the following:

- Taxation depends on where you are shipping from and where you are shipping to.

- National rules apply.

- The type of product you are selling is important.

Some countries have it easier than others. Within the United Kingdom, for example, you can charge the current VAT rate on all purchases where it applies (some types of product are exempt or charged at a reduced rate) and be relatively happy that you've done all you can. If you want to take things one step further, you can consider an offshore business to ship your goods (Amazon does it, so why shouldn't you?). The United States (and other countries) has a much more complex system to deal with. Within the United States, sales tax varies not just from state to state, but often within states as well. In fact, pretty much the only time you'll know exactly what to do is when you are shipping goods to a customer in the same tax area as your business. At other times...well, to be perfectly honest, your guess is as good as ours.

Many states are aware of the issue, and may well have resolved things by the time you read this, but this is far from certain. Recent estimates (from `http://www.offshore-e-com.com/`) put the loss of revenue from e-commerce trading at between $300 million and $3.8 billion annually; the margin of error here probably informs you that the officials are as confused about all this as we are. Calls have gone out to provide a "taxation calculator" where a source and target ZIP code could be used to obtain a tax rate, but as far as we know, no such service exists yet.

In this book, the taxation scheme you add is as simple as possible. A database table will include information concerning various tax rates that can be applied, and the choice of these will for now depend on the shipping region of the customer. All products are considered to be taxable at the same rate. This does leave a lot to be desired, but at least tax will be calculated and applied. You can replace it with your own system later.

Shipping Issues

Shipping is somewhat simpler to deal with than tax, although again you can make things as complicated as you want. Because sending out orders from a company that trades via an e-commerce front end is much the same as sending out orders from, say, a mail-order company, the practices are very much in place and relatively easy to come to understand. There may be new ways of doing things at your disposal, but the general principles are well known.

You may have an existing relationship with a postal service from pre-online trading times, in which case, it's probably easiest to keep things as close to the "old" way of doing things as possible. However, if you're just starting out or revising the way you do things, you have plenty of options to consider.

The simplest option is not to worry about shipping costs at all, which makes sense if there are no costs, for example, in the case of digital downloads. Alternatively, you could simply include the cost of shipping in the cost of your products. Or you could impose a flat fee regardless of the items ordered or the destination. However, some of these options could involve customers either overpaying or underpaying, which isn't ideal.

The other extreme involved is accounting for the weight and dimensions of all the products ordered and calculating the exact cost yourself. This can be simplified slightly because some shipping companies (including FedEx, and others) provide useful APIs to help you. In some cases, you can use a dynamic system to calculate the shipping options available (overnight, three to four days, and so on) based on a number of factors, including package weight and delivery location. The exact methods for doing this, however, can vary a great deal among shipping companies, and we'll leave it to you to implement such a solution if you require it.

In this book, we'll again take a simple line. For each shipping region in the database, you'll provide a number of shipping options for the user to choose from, each of which will have an associated cost. This cost is simply added to the cost of the order. This is the reason why, in Chapter 11, you included a `shipping_region` table—its use will soon become apparent.

Implementing Tax and Shipping Charges

As expected, you need to make several modifications to HatShop to enable the tax and shipping schemes outlined previously. You have two more database tables to add, `tax` and `shipping`, as well as modifications to make to the `orders` table. You'll need to add new database functions and make some modifications to existing ones. Some of the business tier classes need modifications to account for these changes, and the presentation tier must include a method for users to select a shipping method (the taxing scheme is selected automatically).

So, let's get started.

Database Modifications

In this section, you'll add the new tables and modify the `orders` table and database functions.

Exercise: Adding the Database Structures

1. Load pgAdmin III, and connect to the `hatshop` database.

2. Click Tools ➤ Query tool (or click the SQL button on the toolbar). A new query window should appear.

3. Use the query tool to execute this code, which adds the `shipping` table to your `hatshop` database:

```
-- Create shipping table
CREATE TABLE shipping
(
  shipping_id        SERIAL        NOT NULL,
  shipping_type      VARCHAR(100)  NOT NULL,
  shipping_cost      NUMERIC(10, 2) NOT NULL,
  shipping_region_id INTEGER       NOT NULL,
  CONSTRAINT pk_shipping_id          PRIMARY KEY (shipping_id),
  CONSTRAINT fk_shipping_region_id FOREIGN KEY (shipping_region_id)
            REFERENCES shipping_region (shipping_region_id)
            ON UPDATE RESTRICT ON DELETE RESTRICT
);
```

4. Use the query tool to execute this code, which populates the `shipping` table from your `hatshop` database:

```
-- Populate shipping table
INSERT INTO shipping (shipping_id, shipping_type,
                      shipping_cost, shipping_region_id)
       VALUES(1, 'Next Day Delivery ($20)', 20.00, 2);

INSERT INTO shipping (shipping_id, shipping_type,
                      shipping_cost, shipping_region_id)
       VALUES(2, '3-4 Days ($10)', 10.00, 2);

INSERT INTO shipping (shipping_id, shipping_type,
                      shipping_cost, shipping_region_id)
       VALUES(3, '7 Days ($5)', 5.00, 2);
```

```
INSERT INTO shipping (shipping_id, shipping_type,
                      shipping_cost, shipping_region_id)
       VALUES(4, 'By air (7 days, $25)', 25.00, 3);

INSERT INTO shipping (shipping_id, shipping_type,
                      shipping_cost, shipping_region_id)
       VALUES(5, 'By sea (28 days, $10)', 10.00, 3);

INSERT INTO shipping (shipping_id, shipping_type,
                      shipping_cost, shipping_region_id)
       VALUES(6, 'By air (10 days, $35)', 35.00, 4);

INSERT INTO shipping (shipping_id, shipping_type,
                      shipping_cost, shipping_region_id)
       VALUES(7, 'By sea (28 days, $30)', 30.00, 4);
```

5. Use the query tool to execute this code, which adds the tax table to your hatshop database:

```
-- Create tax table
CREATE TABLE tax
(
  tax_id         SERIAL         NOT NULL,
  tax_type       VARCHAR(100)   NOT NULL,
  tax_percentage NUMERIC(10, 2) NOT NULL,
  CONSTRAINT pk_tax_id PRIMARY KEY (tax_id)
);
```

6. Use the query tool to execute this code, which populates the tax table from your hatshop database:

```
-- Populate tax table
INSERT INTO tax (tax_id, tax_type, tax_percentage)
       VALUES(1, 'Sales Tax at 8.5%', 8.50);

INSERT INTO tax (tax_id, tax_type, tax_percentage)
       VALUES(2, 'No Tax', 0.00);
```

7. Execute this code, which adds the shipping_id column and a new constraint to the orders table from your hatshop database:

```
-- Adding a new field named shipping_id to orders table
ALTER TABLE orders ADD COLUMN shipping_id INTEGER;

-- Adding a new foreign key constraint to orders table
ALTER TABLE orders
  ADD CONSTRAINT fk_shipping_id FOREIGN KEY (shipping_id)
              REFERENCES shipping (shipping_id)
              ON UPDATE RESTRICT ON DELETE RESTRICT;
```

8. Use the query tool to execute this code, which adds the `tax_id` column and a new constraint to the `orders` table from your `hatshop` database:

```
-- Adding a new field named tax_id to orders table
ALTER TABLE orders ADD COLUMN tax_id INTEGER;

-- Adding a new foreign key constraint to orders table
ALTER TABLE orders
  ADD CONSTRAINT fk_tax_id FOREIGN KEY (tax_id)
                 REFERENCES tax (tax_id)
                 ON UPDATE RESTRICT ON DELETE RESTRICT;
```

9. Delete the current `shopping_cart_create_order` function, and create a new one that takes into consideration the new changes made to the `orders` table:

```
-- Drop shopping_cart_create_order function
DROP FUNCTION shopping_cart_create_order(CHAR(32), INTEGER);

-- Create shopping_cart_create_order function
CREATE FUNCTION shopping_cart_create_order(CHAR(32), INTEGER,
                                            INTEGER, INTEGER)
RETURNS INTEGER LANGUAGE plpgsql AS $$
  DECLARE
    inCartId     ALIAS FOR $1;
    inCustomerId ALIAS FOR $2;
    inShippingId ALIAS FOR $3;
    inTaxId      ALIAS FOR $4;
    outOrderId INTEGER;
    cartItem cart_product;
    orderTotalAmount NUMERIC(10, 2);
  BEGIN
    -- Insert a new record into orders
    INSERT INTO orders (created_on, customer_id, shipping_id, tax_id)
         VALUES (NOW(), inCustomerId, inShippingId, inTaxId);
    -- Obtain the new Order ID
    SELECT INTO outOrderId
         currval('orders_order_id_seq');
    orderTotalAmount := 0;
    -- Insert order details in order_detail table
    FOR cartItem IN
      SELECT     p.product_id, p.name,
                 COALESCE(NULLIF(p.discounted_price, 0), p.price) AS price,
                 sc.quantity,
                 COALESCE(NULLIF(p.discounted_price, 0), p.price) * sc.quantity
                  AS subtotal
      FROM       shopping_cart sc
      INNER JOIN product p
                 ON sc.product_id = p.product_id
      WHERE      sc.cart_id = inCartId AND sc.buy_now
```

```
      LOOP
        INSERT INTO order_detail (order_id, product_id, product_name,
                                  quantity, unit_cost)
              VALUES (outOrderId, cartItem.product_id, cartItem.name,
                      cartItem.quantity, cartItem.price);
        orderTotalAmount := orderTotalAmount + cartItem.subtotal;
      END LOOP;
      -- Save the order's total amount
      UPDATE orders
      SET    total_amount = orderTotalAmount
      WHERE  order_id = outOrderId;
      -- Clear the shopping cart
      PERFORM shopping_cart_empty(inCartId);
      -- Return the Order ID
      RETURN outOrderId;
    END;
  $$;
```

10. Create `order_info` type, and modify the `orders_get_order_info` function by deleting the old version and creating a new one. We can't simply replace it because the return data type is different.

```
-- Create order_info type
CREATE TYPE order_info AS
(
  order_id         INTEGER,
  total_amount     NUMERIC(10, 2),
  created_on       TIMESTAMP,
  shipped_on       TIMESTAMP,
  status           VARCHAR(9),
  comments         VARCHAR(255),
  customer_id      INTEGER,
  auth_code        VARCHAR(50),
  reference        VARCHAR(50),
  shipping_id      INTEGER,
  shipping_type    VARCHAR(100),
  shipping_cost    NUMERIC(10, 2),
  tax_id           INTEGER,
  tax_type         VARCHAR(100),
  tax_percentage   NUMERIC(10, 2)
);

-- Drop orders_get_order_info function
DROP FUNCTION orders_get_order_info(INTEGER);

-- Create orders_get_order_info function
CREATE FUNCTION orders_get_order_info(INTEGER)
RETURNS order_info LANGUAGE plpgsql AS $$
  DECLARE
```

```
    inOrderId ALIAS FOR $1;
    outOrderInfoRow order_info;
  BEGIN
    SELECT INTO outOrderInfoRow
                o.order_id, o.total_amount, o.created_on, o.shipped_on,
                o.status, o.comments, o.customer_id, o.auth_code,
                o.reference, o.shipping_id, s.shipping_type, s.shipping_cost,
                o.tax_id, t.tax_type, t.tax_percentage
    FROM        orders o
    INNER JOIN tax t
                ON t.tax_id = o.tax_id
    INNER JOIN shipping s
                ON s.shipping_id = o.shipping_id
    WHERE       o.order_id = inOrderId;
    RETURN outOrderInfoRow;
  END;
$$;
```

11. Add the orders_get_shipping_info function to your hatshop database:

```
-- Create orders_get_shipping_info function
CREATE FUNCTION orders_get_shipping_info(INTEGER)
RETURNS SETOF shipping LANGUAGE plpgsql AS $$
  DECLARE
    inShippingRegionId ALIAS FOR $1;
    outShippingRow shipping;
  BEGIN
    FOR outShippingRow IN
      SELECT shipping_id, shipping_type, shipping_cost, shipping_region_id
      FROM    shipping
      WHERE  shipping_region_id = inShippingRegionId
    LOOP
      RETURN NEXT outShippingRow;
    END LOOP;
  END;
$$;
```

Business Layer Modifications

To work with the new database tables and stored procedures, you need to make several changes to business/shopping_cart.php. You must modify CreateOrder in ShoppingCart to configure tax and shipping for new orders as well.

Exercise: Modifying the Business Tier

1. Modify the `CreateOrder` method in `business/shopping_cart.php` like this:

```
// Create a new order
public static function CreateOrder($customerId, $shippingId, $taxId)
{
  // Build the SQL query
  $sql = 'SELECT shopping_cart_create_order(:cart_id, :customer_id,
                                     :shipping_id, :tax_id);';
  // Build the parameters array
  $params = array (':cart_id' => self::GetCartId(),
                   ':customer_id' => $customerId,
                   ':shipping_id' => $shippingId,
                   ':tax_id' => $taxId);
  // Prepare the statement with PDO-specific functionality
  $result = DatabaseHandler::Prepare($sql);

  // Execute the query and return the results
  return DatabaseHandler::GetOne($result, $params);
}
```

2. Add the `GetShippingInfo` method to the `Orders` class in `business/orders.php`:

```
// Retrieves the shipping details for a given $shippingRegionId
public static function GetShippingInfo($shippingRegionId)
{
  // Build the SQL query
  $sql = 'SELECT * FROM orders_get_shipping_info(:shipping_region_id);';
  // Build the parameters array
  $params = array (':shipping_region_id' => $shippingRegionId);
  // Prepare the statement with PDO-specific functionality
  $result = DatabaseHandler::Prepare($sql);

  // Execute the query and return the results
  return DatabaseHandler::GetAll($result, $params);
}
```

Presentation Layer Modifications

Finally, we come to the presentation layer. In fact, due to the changes we've made, the only changes to make here are to the checkout and the orders admin pages.

Exercise: Modifying the Presentation Tier

1. Modify `presentation/templates/checkout_info.tpl`:

```
  Shipping region: {$checkout_info->mShippingRegion}
</span>
{/if}
<br /><br />
{if $checkout_info->mNoCreditCard!= 'yes' &&
    $checkout_info->mNoShippingAddress != 'yes'}
Shipping type:
<select name="shipping">
{section name=cShippings loop=$checkout_info->mShippings}
  <option value="{$checkout_info->mShippings[cShippings].shipping_id}">
    {$checkout_info->mShippings[cShippings].shipping_type}
  </option>
{/section}
</select>
<br /><br />
{/if}
<input type="submit" name="sended" value="Place Order"
 {$checkout_info->mOrderButtonVisible} />
<input type="button" value="Edit Shopping Cart"
```

2. Add a new member to the `CheckoutInfo` class in `presentation/smarty_plugins/function.load_checkout_info.php` as follows:

```
public $mPlainCreditCard;
public $mShippingRegion;
public $mShippings;
```

3. Modify the `init()` method in the `CheckoutInfo` class in `function.load_checkout_info.php`:

```
// If the Place Order button was clicked, save the order to database
if ($this->_mPlaceOrder == 1)
{
  $this->mCustomerData = Customer::Get();
  $tax_id = '';

  switch ($this->mCustomerData ['shipping_region_id'])
  {
    case 2:
      $tax_id = 1;

      break;
    default:
      $tax_id = 2;
  }
```

```
        $order_id = ShoppingCart::CreateOrder(
                        $this->mCustomerData['customer_id'],
                        (int)$_POST['shipping'], $tax_id);


        // Redirect to index.php
        $redirect_link = 'http://' . getenv('SERVER_NAME');
```

4. In the same method, make this change:

```
        foreach ($shipping_regions as $item)
          if ($item['shipping_region_id'] ==
              $this->mCustomerData['shipping_region_id'])
            $this->mShippingRegion = $item['shipping_region'];
        }

        if ($this->mNoCreditCard == 'no' && $this->mNoShippingAddress == 'no')
        {
          $this->mShippings = Orders::GetShippingInfo(
                              $this->mCustomerData['shipping_region_id']);
        }
      }
    }
  }
  ?>
```

5. Continue modifying the `AdminOrderDetails` class from the `presentation/smarty_plugins/` `function.load_admin_order_details.php` file by adding two members:

```
    public $mCustomerInfo;
    public $mTotalCost;
    public $mTaxCost = 0.0;
```

6. Add these lines to the `AdminOrderDetails` class in the `init()` method:

```
        $this->mOrderDetails = Orders::GetOrderDetails($this->mOrderId);
        $this->mCustomerInfo = Customer::Get($this->mOrderInfo['customer_id']);
        $this->mTotalCost = $this->mOrderInfo['total_amount'];

        if ($this->mOrderInfo['tax_percentage'] !== 0.0)
          $this->mTaxCost = round((float)$this->mTotalCost *
                              (float)$this->mOrderInfo['tax_percentage'], 2)
                            / 100.00;

        $this->mTotalCost += $this->mOrderInfo['shipping_cost'];
        $this->mTotalCost += $this->mTaxCost;

        // Format the values
        $this->mTotalCost = number_format($this->mTotalCost, 2, '.', '');
        $this->mTaxCost = number_format($this->mTaxCost, 2, '.', '');

        // Value which specifies whether to enable or disable edit mode
        if (isset ($_GET['submitEdit']))
```

7. Modify the `presentation/templates/admin_order_details.tpl` template as highlighted:

```
<form action="{"admin.php"|prepare_link:"https"}" method="get">
  <input type="hidden" name="Page" value="OrderDetails" />
  <input type="hidden" name="OrderId"
   value="{$admin_order_details->mOrderInfo.order_id}" />
  <table class="edit">
    <tr>
      <td class="admin_page_text">Total Amount: </td>
      <td class="price">
        ${$admin_order_details->mTotalCost}
      </td>
    </tr>
    <tr>
      <td class="admin_page_text">Tax: </td>
      <td class="price">
        {$admin_order_details->mOrderInfo.tax_type}
        ${$admin_order_details->mTaxCost}
      </td>
    </tr>
    <tr>
      <td class="admin_page_text">Shipping: </td>
      <td class="price">
        {$admin_order_details->mOrderInfo.shipping_type}
      </td>
    </tr>
    <tr>
      <td class="admin_page_text">Date Created: </td>
      <td>
        {$admin_order_details->mOrderInfo.created_on|date_format:"%Y-%m-%d %T"}
```

How It Works: Handling Tax and Shipping Issues

Note that this is one of the most crucial pieces of code in this chapter. Here, you'll most likely make any modifications to the tax and shipping systems if you decide to add your own system because choices are made on this page. The database and business layer changes are far more generic—although that's not to say that modifications wouldn't be necessary.

Before testing that the new system is working for tax and shipping charges, use the orders admin page to check that old orders are unaffected. The information retrieved for an old order should be unaffected because the data is unchanged.

Place a new order, preferably with a customer in the United States/Canada shipping region (as this is currently the only region where tax is applied). Notice that on the checkout page, you must select a shipping option.

After placing the order, check the new order in the database. The result is shown in Figure 12-3.

In this chapter leading up to this example, you've pretty much examined how the tax and shipping charges operate, but let's recap.

First, the customer is required to select a shipping region for his or her address. Without this shipping region being selected, visitors cannot place orders because they cannot select a shipping option. When a visitor places an order, the shipping region selected is attached to the order in the `orders` table. The tax requirement for the order is also attached, although this requires no user input and is currently selected using a very simple algorithm (although this wouldn't be difficult to change).

Further Development

There are several ways to proceed from here. Perhaps the first might be to add an administration system for tax and shipping options. This hasn't been implemented here partly because it would be trivial given the experience you've had so far in this book and partly because the techniques laid out here are more of a template for development than a fully developed way of doing things. There are so many options to choose from for both tax and shipping calculations that only the basics are discussed here.

Hooking into online services for tax and shipping cost calculations is an attractive option; for shipping services, this is very much a possibility. In fact, the services offered by shipping companies such as FedEx use a similar process to the credit card gateway companies we'll look at later in this book. Much of the code you would have to write to access these services will be very similar to that for credit card processing, although, of course, you'll have to adapt it to get the specifics right. Sadly, there may be more major changes required, such as adding weights and dimensions to products, but that very much depends on what products you are selling. For items in the HatShop catalog, many products are lighter than air, so shipping could be very cheap.

Summary

In this chapter, you've extended the HatShop site to enable customers to place orders using all the new data and techniques introduced in Chapter 11. Much of the modification made in this chapter lays the groundwork for the order pipeline to be used in the rest of this book. You've also included a quick way to examine customer orders, although this is by no means a fully fleshed-out administration tool—that will come later.

You also implemented a simple system for adding tax and shipping charges to orders. This system is far from being a universal solution, but it works, and it's simple. More importantly, the techniques can easily be built on to introduce more complex algorithms and user interaction to select tax and shipping options and price the order accordingly.

From the next chapter onward, you'll be expanding on the customer ordering system even more by starting to develop a professional order pipeline for order processing.

■■■

Implementing the Order Pipeline: Part I

Your e-commerce application is shaping up nicely. You have added customer account functionality, and you are keeping track of customer addresses and credit card information, which is stored securely. However, you are not currently using this information—instead, you are delegating responsibility for this to PayPal.

In this and the next chapter, you'll build your own order-processing pipeline that deals with credit card authorization, stock checking, shipping, email notification, and so on. We'll leave the credit card processing specifics until Chapter 15, but in this chapter, we'll show you where this process fits into the picture.

Order pipeline functionality is an extremely useful capability for an e-commerce site. Order pipeline functions let you keep track of orders at every stage in the process and provide auditing information that you can refer to later or if something goes wrong during the order processing. You can do all this without relying on a third-party accounting system, which can also reduce costs. The first section of this chapter discusses what an order pipeline is and the specifics that apply to the HatShop application.

The bulk of this chapter deals with constructing the order pipeline system, which also involves a small amount of modification to the way things currently work, and some additions to the database you've been using. However, the code in this chapter isn't much more complicated than the code you've already been using. The real challenges are in designing your system.

By the end of the next chapter, customers will be able to place orders into your pipeline, and you'll be able to follow the progress of these orders as they pass through various stages. Although no real credit card processing will take place, you'll end up with a fairly complete system, including a new administration web page that can be used by suppliers to confirm that they have items in stock and to confirm that orders have been shipped. To start with, however, you need a bit more background about what you're actually trying to achieve.

What Is an Order Pipeline?

Any commercial transaction, whether in a shop on the street, over the Internet, or anywhere else, has several related tasks that must be carried out before it can be considered complete. For example, you can't simply remove an item of clothing from a fashion boutique (without paying) and say that you've bought it—remuneration is an integral part of any purchase. In addition, a transaction only completes successfully if each of the tasks carried out completes successfully. If a customer's credit card is rejected, for example, then no funds can be taken from it, so a purchase can't be made.

The sequence of tasks in a transaction is often thought of in terms of a pipeline. In this analogy, orders start at one end of the pipe and come out of the other end when they are completed. Along the way, they must pass through several pipeline sections, each of which is responsible for a particular task or a related group of tasks. If any pipeline section fails to complete, then the order "gets stuck" and might require outside interaction before it can move further along the pipeline, or it might be canceled completely.

For example, the simple pipeline shown in Figure 13-1 applies to transactions in a brick-and-mortar store.

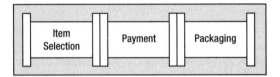

Figure 13-1. *Transactions for a brick-and-mortar store*

The last section might be optional and might involve additional tasks such as gift-wrapping. The payment stage might also take one of several methods of operation because the customer could pay using cash, a credit card, gift certificates, and so on.

When you consider e-commerce purchasing, the pipeline becomes longer, but it isn't really any more complicated.

Designing the Order Pipeline

In the HatShop e-commerce application, the pipeline will look like the one in Figure 13-2.

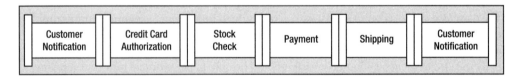

Figure 13-2. *The HatShop order pipeline*

The tasks carried out in these pipeline sections are as follows:

Customer Notification: An email notification is sent to the customer stating that order processing has started and confirming the items to be sent and the address that goods will be sent to.

Credit Card Authorization: The credit card used for purchasing is checked, and the total order amount is set aside (although no payment is taken at this stage).

Stock Check: An email is sent to the supplier with a list of the items that have been ordered. Processing continues when the supplier confirms that the goods are available.

Payment: The credit card transaction is completed using the funds set aside earlier.

Shipping: An email is sent to the supplier confirming that payment for the items ordered has been taken. Processing continues when the supplier confirms that the goods have been shipped.

Customer Notification: An email is sent notifying the customer that the order has been shipped and thanking the customer for using the HatShop web site.

▪**Note** In terms of implementation, as you'll see shortly, there are more stages than this because the stock check and shipping stages actually consist of two pipeline sections—one for sending the email and one that waits for confirmation.

As orders flow through this pipeline, entries are added to a new database table called `audit`. These entries can be examined to see what has happened to an order and are an excellent way to identify problems if they occur. Each entry in the `orders` table is also flagged with a status, identifying which point in the pipeline it has reached.

To process the pipeline, you'll create classes representing each stage. These classes carry out the required processing and then modify the status of the order in the `orders` table to advance the order. You'll also need a coordinating class (or processor), which can be called for any order and executes the appropriate pipeline stage class. This processor is called once when the order is placed and, in normal operation, is called twice more—once for stock confirmation and once for shipping confirmation.

To make life easier, you'll also define a common interface supported by each pipeline stage class. This enables the order processor class to access each stage in a standard way. You'll also define several utility functions and expose several common properties in the order processor class, which will be used as necessary by the pipeline stages. For example, the ID of the order should be accessible to all pipeline stages, so to save code duplication, you'll put that information in the order processor class.

Now, let's get on to the specifics. You'll build a number of files in the `business` folder containing all the new classes, which you'll reference from HatShop. The new files you'll create are the following:

`OrderProcessor`: Main class for processing orders.

`IPipelineSection`: Interface definition for pipeline sections.

`PsInitialNotification`, `PsCheckFunds`, `PsCheckStock`, `PsStockOk`, `PsTakePayment`, `PsShipGoods`, `PsShipOk`, `PsFinalNotification`: Pipeline section classes. We'll create these classes in Chapter 14; here we'll use a dummy (`PsDummy`) class instead.

The progress of an order through the pipeline as mediated by the order processor relates to the pipeline shown earlier (see Figure 13-3).

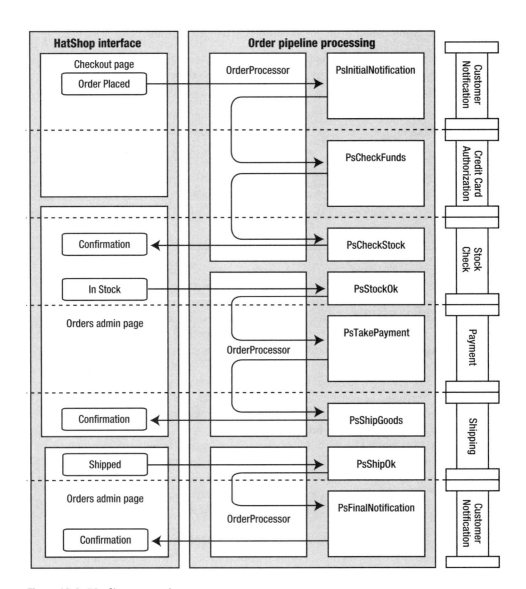

Figure 13-3. *Pipeline processing*

The process shown in this diagram is divided into three sections:

- Customer places order.
- Supplier confirms stock.
- Supplier confirms shipping.

The first stage is as follows:

1. When the customer confirms an order, `presentation/smarty_plugins/function.load_checkout_info.php` creates the order in the database and calls `OrderProcessor` to begin order processing.

2. `OrderProcessor` detects that the order is new and calls `PsInitialNotification`.

3. `PsInitialNotification` sends an email to the customer confirming the order and advances the order stage. It also instructs `OrderProcessor` to continue processing.

4. `OrderProcessor` detects the new order status and calls `PsCheckFunds`.

5. `PsCheckFunds` checks that funds are available on the customer's credit card and stores the details required to complete the transaction if funds are available. If this is successful, then the order stage is advanced, and `OrderProcessor` is told to continue.

6. `OrderProcessor` detects the new order status and calls `PsCheckStock`.

7. `PsCheckStock` sends an email to the supplier with a list of the items ordered, instructs the supplier to confirm via `ORDERS ADMIN` from the `admin` section, and advances the order status.

8. `OrderProcessor` terminates.

The second stage is as follows:

1. When the supplier logs in to the orders admin page to confirm that stock is available, `presentation/smarty_plugins/function.load_admin_order_details.php` calls `OrderProcessor` to continue order processing.

2. `OrderProcessor` detects the new order status and calls `PsStockOk`.

3. `PsStockOk` advances the order status and tells `OrderProcessor` to continue.

4. `OrderProcessor` detects the new order status and calls `PsTakePayment`.

5. `PsTakePayment` uses the transaction details stored earlier by `PsCheckFunds` to complete the transaction, then advances the order status, and tells `OrderProcessor` to continue.

6. `OrderProcessor` detects the new order status and calls `PsShipGoods`.

7. `PsShipGoods` sends an email to the supplier with a confirmation of the items ordered, instructs the supplier to ship these goods to the customer, and advances the order status.

8. `OrderProcessor` terminates.

The third stage is as follows:

1. When the supplier confirms that the goods have been shipped, `presentation/smarty_plugins/function.load_admin_order_details.php` calls `OrderProcessor` to continue order processing.

2. `OrderProcessor` detects the new order status and calls `PsShipOk`.

3. PsShipOk enters the shipment date in the database, advances the order status, and tells OrderProcessor to continue.

4. OrderProcessor detects the new order status and calls PsFinalNotification.

5. PsFinalNotification sends an email to the customer confirming that the order has been shipped and advances the order stage.

6. OrderProcessor terminates.

If anything goes wrong at any point in the pipeline processing, such as a credit card being declined, an email is sent to an administrator. The administrator then has all the information necessary to check what has happened, get in contact with the customer involved, and cancel or replace the order if necessary.

No point in this process is particularly complicated; it's just that a lot of code is required to put this into action!

Laying the Groundwork

Before you start building the components just described, you need to make a few modifications to the HatShop database and web application.

During order processing, one of the most important functions of the pipeline is to maintain an up-to-date audit trail. The implementation of this audit trail involves adding records to a new database table called audit. We'll add the audit table in the following exercise.

To implement the functionality just described, you'll also need to add a new function named orders_create_audit to the hatshop database. The orders_create_audit function adds an entry to the audit table.

We'll also create the OrderProcessor class (the class responsible for moving an order through the pipeline), which contains a lot of code. However, you can start simply, and build up additional functionality as needed. To start with, you'll create a version of the OrderProcessor class with the following functionality:

- Dynamically selects a pipeline section supporting the IPipelineSection interface

- Adds basic auditing data

- Gives access to the current order details

- Gives access to the customer for the current order

- Gives access to administrator mailing

- Mails the administrator in case of error

You'll create a single pipeline section, PsDummy, which uses some of this functionality. PsDummy is used in the code of this chapter in place of the real pipeline section classes, which you'll implement in the next chapter.

Exercise: Implementing the Skeleton of the Order-Processing Functionality

1. Load pgAdmin III, and connect to the `hatshop` database.

2. Click Tools ➤ Query tool (or click the SQL button on the toolbar). A new query window should appear.

3. Use the query tool to execute this code, which creates the `audit` table in your `hatshop` database:

```
-- Create audit table
CREATE TABLE audit
(
  audit_id        SERIAL     NOT NULL,
  order_id        INTEGER    NOT NULL,
  created_on      TIMESTAMP  NOT NULL,
  message         TEXT       NOT NULL,
  message_number  INTEGER    NOT NULL,
  CONSTRAINT pk_audit_id PRIMARY KEY (audit_id),
  CONSTRAINT fk_order_id FOREIGN KEY (order_id)
            REFERENCES orders (order_id)
            ON UPDATE RESTRICT ON DELETE RESTRICT
);
```

4. Use the query tool to execute this code, which creates the `orders_create_audit` function in your `hatshop` database:

```
-- Create orders_create_audit function
CREATE FUNCTION orders_create_audit(INTEGER, TEXT, INTEGER)
RETURNS VOID LANGUAGE plpgsql AS $$
  DECLARE
    inOrderId       ALIAS FOR $1;
    inMessage       ALIAS FOR $2;
    inMessageNumber ALIAS FOR $3;
  BEGIN
    INSERT INTO audit (order_id, created_on, message, message_number)
          VALUES (inOrderId, NOW(), inMessage, inMessageNumber);
  END;
$$;
```

5. Moving to the business tier, add the following method to the `Orders` class from `business/orders.php`:

```
// Creates audit record
public static function CreateAudit($orderId, $message, $messageNumber)
{
  // Build the SQL query
  $sql = 'SELECT orders_create_audit(:order_id, :message,
                                      :message_number);';
  // Build the parameters array
  $params = array (':order_id' => $orderId,
                   ':message' => $message,
                   ':message_number' => $messageNumber);
```

```php
  // Prepare the statement with PDO-specific functionality
  $result = DatabaseHandler::Prepare($sql);

  // Execute the query
  return DatabaseHandler::Execute($result, $params);
}
```

6. Add a new file to the business directory called order_processor.php with the following code:

```php
<?php
/* Main class, used to obtain order information,
   run pipeline sections, audit orders, etc. */
class OrderProcessor
{
  public  $mOrderInfo;
  public  $mOrderDetailsInfo;
  public  $mCustomerInfo;
  public  $mContinueNow;

  private $_mCurrentPipelineSection;
  private $_mOrderProcessStage;

  // Class constructor
  public function __construct($orderId)
  {
    // Get order
    $this->mOrderInfo = Orders::GetOrderInfo($orderId);

    if (empty ($this->mOrderInfo['shipping_id']))
      $this->mOrderInfo['shipping_id'] = -1;

    if (empty ($this->mOrderInfo['tax_id']))
      $this->mOrderInfo['tax_id'] = -1;

    // Get order details
    $this->mOrderDetailsInfo = Orders::GetOrderDetails($orderId);

    // Get customer associated with the processed order
    $this->mCustomerInfo = Customer::Get($this->mOrderInfo['customer_id']);

    $credit_card = new SecureCard();
    $credit_card->LoadEncryptedDataAndDecrypt(
      $this->mCustomerInfo['credit_card']);

    $this->mCustomerInfo['credit_card'] = $credit_card;
  }

  /* Process is called from
```

```php
    presentation/smarty_plugins/function.load_checkout_info.php and
    presentation/smarty_plugins/function.load_admin_orders.php
    to process an order */
public function Process()
{
  // Configure processor
  $this->mContinueNow = true;

  // Log start of execution
  $this->CreateAudit('Order Processor started.', 10000);

  // Process pipeline section
  try
  {
    while ($this->mContinueNow)
    {
      $this->mContinueNow = false;

      $this->GetCurrentPipelineSection();
      $this->_mCurrentPipelineSection->Process($this);
    }
  }
  catch(Exception $e)
  {
    $this->MailAdmin('Order Processing error occurred.',
                     'Exception: "' . $e->getMessage() . '" on ' .
                     $e->getFile() . ' line ' . $e->getLine(),
                     $this->_mOrderProcessStage);

    $this->CreateAudit('Order Processing error occurred.', 10002);

    throw new Exception('Error occurred, order aborted. ' .
                        'Details mailed to administrator.');
  }

  $this->CreateAudit('Order Processor finished.', 10001);
}

// Adds audit message
public function CreateAudit($message, $messageNumber)
{
  Orders::CreateAudit($this->mOrderInfo['order_id'], $message,
                      $messageNumber);
}

// Builds email message
public function MailAdmin($subject, $message, $sourceStage)
```

```
    {
      $to = ADMIN_EMAIL;
      $headers = 'From: ' . ORDER_PROCESSOR_EMAIL . "\r\n";
      $body = 'Message: ' . $message . "\n" .
              'Source: ' . $sourceStage . "\n" .
              'Order ID: ' . $this->mOrderInfo['order_id'];

      $result = mail($to, $subject, $body, $headers);

      if ($result === false)
      {
        throw new Exception ('Failed sending this mail to administrator:' .
                             "\n" . $body);
      }
    }

    // Gets current pipeline section
    private function GetCurrentPipelineSection()
    {
      $this->_mOrderProcessStage = 100;
      $this->_mCurrentPipelineSection = new PsDummy();
    }
  }
?>
```

7. Create the IPipelineSection interface in a new file named business/i_pipeline_section.php as follows:

```
<?php
interface IPipelineSection
{
  public function Process($processor);
}
?>
```

8. Add a new file in the business directory called ps_dummy.php with the following code. The PsDummy class is used in this chapter for testing purposes in place of the real pipeline sections that you'll implement in the next chapter.

```
<?php
class PsDummy implements IPipelineSection
{
  public function Process($processor)
  {
    $processor->CreateAudit('PsDoNothing started.', 99999);

    $processor->CreateAudit('Customer: ' .
      $processor->mCustomerInfo['name'], 99999);

    $processor->CreateAudit('Order subtotal: ' .
```

```
        $processor->mOrderInfo['total_amount'], 99999);

      $processor->MailAdmin('Test.', 'Test mail from PsDummy.', 99999);

      $processor->CreateAudit('PsDoNothing finished', 99999);
    }
  }
?>
```

9. Add the following code to `include/config.php`, customizing the data with your own email addresses:

```
// Constant definitions for order handling related messages
define('ADMIN_EMAIL', 'Admin@example.com');
define('CUSTOMER_SERVICE_EMAIL', 'CustomerService@example.com');
define('ORDER_PROCESSOR_EMAIL', 'OrderProcessor@example.com');
define('SUPPLIER_EMAIL', 'Supplier@example.com');
```

■**Note** The values of `ADMIN_EMAIL` and `SUPPLIER_EMAIL` will actually be used to send emails to. In other words, these must be existing, real email addresses that you can verify. You can leave `CUSTOMER_SERVICE_EMAIL` and `ORDER_PROCESSOR_EMAIL` as they are because they're used in the `FROM` field of the emails, and they don't need to be valid email addresses.

---

10. Add the highlighted lines to the `app_top.php` file located in the `include` folder:

```
// Load Business Tier
...
require_once BUSINESS_DIR . 'customer.php';
require_once BUSINESS_DIR . 'i_pipeline_section.php';
require_once BUSINESS_DIR . 'ps_dummy.php';
require_once BUSINESS_DIR . 'order_processor.php';
```

11. Modify `presentation/templates/admin_order_details.tpl` by adding the highlighted line:

```
    <input type="submit" name="submitCancel" value="Cancel"
    {if ! $admin_order_details->mEditEnabled}
    disabled="disabled"
    {/if} />
    <input type="submit" name="submitProcessOrder" value="Process Order" />
    <br /><br />
    <span class="admin_page_text">Order contains these products:</span>
    <br /><br />
```

12. Modify `presentation/smarty_plugins/function.load_admin_order_details.php` as highlighted here:

```
    // Initializes class members
    public function init()
    {
```

```
if (isset ($_GET['submitUpdate']))
{
  Orders::UpdateOrder($this->mOrderId, $_GET['status'],
    $_GET['comments'], $_GET['authCode'], $_GET['reference']);
}

if (isset ($_GET['submitProcessOrder']))
{
  $processor = new OrderProcessor($this->mOrderId);
  $processor->Process();
}

$this->mOrderInfo = Orders::GetOrderInfo($this->mOrderId);
$this->mOrderDetails = Orders::GetOrderDetails($this->mOrderId);
$this->mCustomerInfo = Customer::Get($this->mOrderInfo['customer_id']);
$this->mTotalCost = $this->mOrderInfo['total_amount'];
```

13. Load the `admin orders` section in your browser, and select an order to view its details. In the order details page, click the Process Order button (see Figure 13-4).

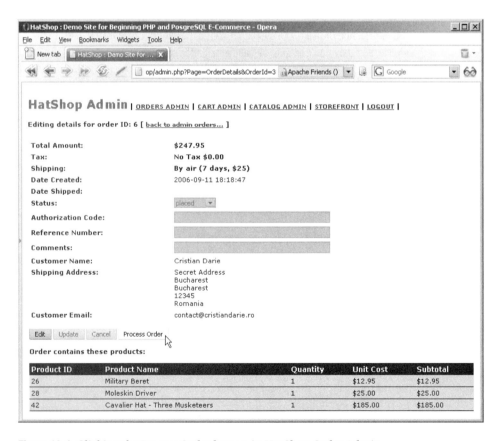

Figure 13-4. *Clicking the Process Order button in HatShop Order Admin*

■ **Note** If you haven't configured your SMTP server correctly, you'll get an error when the code tries to send the email. If that happens, check Appendix A for installation and configuration instructions.

14. Check your inbox for a new email that should read "Test mail from PsDummy."
15. Examine the `audit` table in the database to see the new entries (see Figure 13-5).

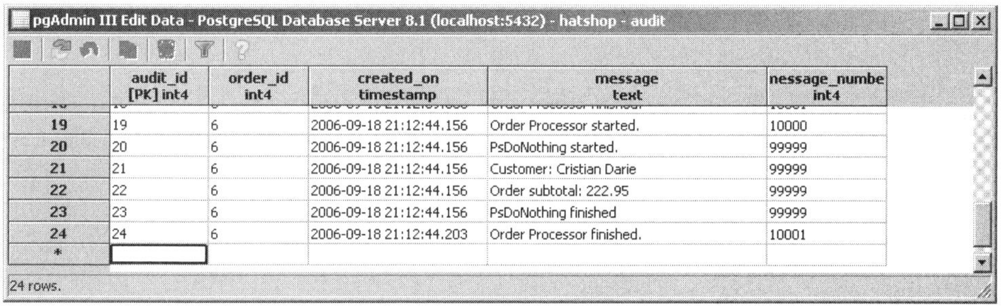

pgAdmin III Edit Data - PostgreSQL Database Server 8.1 (localhost:5432) - hatshop - audit

	audit_id [PK] int4	order_id int4	created_on timestamp	message text	nessage_numbe int4
19	19	6	2006-09-18 21:12:44.156	Order Processor started.	10000
20	20	6	2006-09-18 21:12:44.156	PsDoNothing started.	99999
21	21	6	2006-09-18 21:12:44.156	Customer: Cristian Darie	99999
22	22	6	2006-09-18 21:12:44.156	Order subtotal: 222.95	99999
23	23	6	2006-09-18 21:12:44.156	PsDoNothing finished	99999
24	24	6	2006-09-18 21:12:44.203	Order Processor finished.	10001
*					

24 rows.

Figure 13-5. *Audit table entries from PsDummy*

How It Works: The Skeleton of the Order-Processing Functionality

Entries will be added by `OrderProcessor` and by individual pipeline stages to indicate successes and failures. These entries can then be examined to see what has happened to an order, which is an important function when it comes to error checking.

The message number column is interesting because it allows you to associate specific messages with an identifying number. You can have another database table that matches these message numbers with descriptions, although this isn't really necessary because the scheme used for numbering (as you'll see later in the chapter) is quite descriptive. In addition, you have the message column, which already provides human-readable information.

For demonstration purposes, we set the administrator and supplier email addresses to fictive email address, which should also be the address of the customer used to generate test orders. You should do this to ensure everything is working properly before sending mail to the outside world.

Let's now look at the `OrderProcessor` class. The main body of the `OrderProcessor` class is the `Process()` method, which is now called from `function.load_admin_order_details.php` to process an order.

```
public function Process()
{
  // Configure processor
  $this->mContinueNow = true;
```

Next you used the `CreateAudit()` method to add an `audit` entry indicating that `OrderProcessor` has started:

```
  // Log start of execution
  $this->CreateAudit('Order Processor started.', 10000);
```

■**Note** 10000 is the message number to store for the `audit` entry. We'll look at these codes in more detail shortly.

Next you come to the order processing itself. The model used here is to check the Boolean $mContinueNow field before processing a pipeline section. This allows sections to specify either that processing should continue when they're finished with the current task (by setting $mContinueNow to `true`) or that processing should pause (by setting $mContinueNow to `false`). This is necessary because you need to wait for external input at certain points along the pipeline when checking whether the products are in stock and whether the funds are available on the customer's credit card.

The pipeline section to process is selected by the private `GetCurrentPipelineSection` method, which eventually returns a pipeline section class (you'll build these classes in the next chapter) corresponding to the current status of the order. However, at this moment, the `GetCurrentPipelineSection` has the job of setting the process stage and returning an instance of `PsDummy`. In the next chapter, you'll implement classes representing each pipeline section, and you'll return one of those classes instead of `PsDummy`.

```
// Gets current pipeline section
private function GetCurrentPipelineSection()
{
  $this->_mOrderProcessStage = 100;
  $this->_mCurrentPipelineSection = new PsDummy();
}
```

Back to `Process()`, you see this method being called in a `try` block:

```
// Process pipeline section
try
{
  while ($this->mContinueNow)
  {
    $this->mContinueNow = false;

    $this->GetCurrentPipelineSection();
    $this->_mCurrentPipelineSection->Process($this);
  }
}
```

Note that $mContinueNow is set to `false` in the `while` loop—the default behavior is to stop after each pipeline section. However, the call to the `Process` method of the current pipeline section class (which receives a parameter of the current `OrderProcessor` instance, thus having access to the $mContinueNow member) changes the value of $mContinueNow back to `true`, in case processing should go to the next pipeline section without waiting for user interaction.

Note that in the previous code snippet, the `Process` method is called without knowing what kind of object $this->_mCurrentPipelineSection references. Each pipeline section is represented by a different class, but all these classes need to expose a method named `Process`. When such behavior is needed, the standard technique is to create an interface that defines the common behavior you need in that set of classes.

All order pipeline section classes support the simple `IPipelineSection` interface, defined as follows:

```php
<?php
interface IPipelineSection
{
  public function Process($processor);
}
?>
```

■**Note** An interface is a set of method signatures that serves as a contract for classes that implement that interface. When a class implements an interface, the class guarantees that it will implement every signature defined in that interface. An interface cannot be instantiated like a normal class because it doesn't contain any method implementations, only their signatures. By implementing `IPipelineSection` in all order pipeline section classes (you'll write them in the next chapter), you guarantee that they all will export a public method named `Process`. This way, you can safely call the `Process` method on any pipeline section class from your `OrderProcessor` class without the risk of generating an error.

All pipeline sections use a `Process` method to perform their work. This method requires an `OrderProcessor` reference as a parameter because the pipeline sections need access to the public fields and methods exposed by the `OrderProcessor` class.

The last part of the `Process` method in `OrderProcessor` involves catching exceptions. Here, you catch any exceptions that may be thrown by the order pipeline section classes and react to them by sending an email to the administrator using the `MailAdmin` method, adding an `audit` entry, and throwing a new exception that can be caught by PHP pages that use the `OrderProcessor` class:

```php
    catch(Exception $e)
    {
      $this->MailAdmin('Order Processing error occurred.',
                      'Exception: "' . $e->getMessage() . '" on ' .
                      $e->getFile() . ' line ' . $e->getLine(),
                      $this->_mOrderProcessStage);

      $this->CreateAudit('Order Processing error occurred.', 10002);

      throw new Exception('Error occurred, order aborted. ' .
                          'Details mailed to administrator.');
    }
```

Regardless of whether processing is successful, you add a final `audit` entry saying that the processing has completed:

```php
    $this->CreateAudit('Order Processor finished.', 10001);
  }
```

Let's now look at the `AdminMail` method that simply takes a few parameters for the basic email properties:

```
// Builds email message
public function MailAdmin($subject, $message, $sourceStage)
{
  $to = ADMIN_EMAIL;
  $headers = 'From: ' . ORDER_PROCESSOR_EMAIL . "\r\n";
  $body = 'Message: ' . $message . "\n" .
          'Source: ' . $sourceStage . "\n" .
          'Order ID: ' . $this->mOrderInfo['order_id'];

  $result = mail($to, $subject, $body, $headers);

  if ($result === false)
  {
    throw new Exception ('Failed sending this mail to administrator:' .
                         "\n" . $body);
  }
}
```

The `CreateAudit` method is also a simple one and calls the `CreateAudit` business tier method shown earlier:

```
// Adds audit message
public function CreateAudit($message, $messageNumber)
{
  Orders::CreateAudit($this->mOrderInfo['order_id'], $message,
                      $messageNumber);
}
```

At this point, it's worth examining the message number scheme we've chosen for order-processing audits. In all cases, the audit message number will be a five-digit number. The first digit of this number is either 1 if an audit is being added by `OrderProcessor` or 2 if the audit is added by a pipeline section. The next two digits are used for the pipeline stage that added the audit (which maps directly to the status of the order when the audit was added). The final two digits uniquely identify the message within this scope. For example, so far you've seen the following message numbers:

- 10000: Order processor started.
- 10001: Order processor finished.
- 10002: Order processor error occurred.

Later, you'll see a lot of these numbers that start with 2, as you get on to pipeline sections and include the necessary information for identifying the pipeline section as noted previously. We hope you'll agree that this scheme allows for plenty of flexibility, although you can, of course, use whatever numbers you see fit. As a final note, numbers ending in 00 and 01 are used for starting and finishing messages for both the order processor and pipeline stages, whereas 02 and above are for other messages. There is no real reason for this apart from consistency between the components.

The `PsDummy` class that is used in this skeleton processor performs some basic functions to check that things are working correctly:

```php
<?php
class PsDummy implements IPipelineSection
{
  public function Process($processor)
  {
    $processor->CreateAudit('PsDoNothing started.', 99999);

    $processor->CreateAudit('Customer: ' .
      $processor->mCustomerInfo['name'], 99999);

    $processor->CreateAudit('Order subtotal: ' .
      $processor->mOrderInfo['total_amount'], 99999);

    $processor->MailAdmin('Test.', 'Test mail from PsDummy.', 99999);

    $processor->CreateAudit('PsDoNothing finished', 99999);
  }
}
?>
```

The code here uses the `CreateAudit` and `MailAdmin` methods of `OrderProcessor` to generate something to show that the code has executed correctly. Note that the numbering schemes outlined previously aren't used there because this isn't a real pipeline section!

That was a lot of code to get through, but it did make the client code very simple.

Short of setting all the configuration details, there is very little to do because `OrderProcessor` does a lot of the work for you. Note that the code you have ended up with is, for the most part, a consequence of the design choices made earlier. This is an excellent example of how a strong design can lead you straight to powerful and robust code.

Adding More Functionality to OrderProcessor

You need to add a few more bits and pieces to the `OrderProcessor` class, but it hardly seems worth going through another "Exercise" section to do so. Instead, we'll simply go through the code briefly.

We need to look at the following:

- Updating the status of an order

- Setting credit card authentication details

- Setting the order shipment date

- Sending emails to customers and suppliers

- Retrieving order details and the customer address

Updating the Status of an Order

Each pipeline section needs the capability to change the status of an order, advancing it to the next pipeline section. Rather than simply incrementing the status, this functionality is kept flexible, just in case you end up with a more complicated branched pipeline. This requires a new function in the database, named orders_update_status, and a data tier method, UpdateOrderStatus, which you need to add to the Orders class (located in business/orders.php):

Start by creating the orders_update_status function in your hatshop database:

```
-- Create orders_update_status function
CREATE FUNCTION orders_update_status(INTEGER, INTEGER)
RETURNS VOID LANGUAGE plpgsql AS $$
  DECLARE
    inOrderId ALIAS FOR $1;
    inStatus  ALIAS FOR $2;
  BEGIN
    UPDATE orders SET status = inStatus WHERE order_id = inOrderId;
  END;
$$;
```

Then, add the UpdateOrderStatus method to the Orders class in business/order.php:

```
// Updates the order pipeline status of an order
public static function UpdateOrderStatus($orderId, $status)
{
  // Build the SQL query
  $sql = 'SELECT orders_update_status(:order_id, :status);';
  // Build the parameters array
  $params = array (':order_id' => $orderId, ':status' => $status);
  // Prepare the statement with PDO-specific functionality
  $result = DatabaseHandler::Prepare($sql);

  // Execute the query
  return DatabaseHandler::Execute($result, $params);
}
```

The method in OrderProcessor (in business/order_processor.php) that calls businessdata tier method is also called UpdateOrderStatus:

```
// Set order status
public function UpdateOrderStatus($status)
{
  Orders::UpdateOrderStatus($this->mOrderInfo['order_id'], $status);
  $this->mOrderInfo['status'] = $status;
}
```

Setting Credit Card Authentication Details

In the next chapter, when we deal with credit card usage, you'll need to set data in the auth_code and reference fields in the orders table.

To support that functionality, first add the orders_set_auth_code function to your database:

```
-- Create orders_set_auth_code function
CREATE FUNCTION orders_set_auth_code(INTEGER, VARCHAR(50), VARCHAR(50))
RETURNS VOID LANGUAGE plpgsql AS $$
  DECLARE
    inOrderId   ALIAS FOR $1;
    inAuthCode  ALIAS FOR $2;
    inReference ALIAS FOR $3;
  BEGIN
    UPDATE orders
    SET    auth_code = inAuthCode, reference = inReference
    WHERE  order_id = inOrderId;
  END;
$$;
```

Then, add the SetOrderAuthCodeAndReference method to your Orders class in business/order.php:

```
// Sets order's authorization code
public static function SetOrderAuthCodeAndReference ($orderId, $authCode,
                                                     $reference)
{
  // Build the SQL query
  $sql = 'SELECT orders_set_auth_code(:order_id, :auth_code, :reference);';
  // Build the parameters array
  $params = array (':order_id' => $orderId,
                   ':auth_code' => $authCode,
                   ':reference' => $reference);
  // Prepare the statement with PDO-specific functionality
  $result = DatabaseHandler::Prepare($sql);

  // Execute the query
  return DatabaseHandler::Execute($result, $params);
}
```

The code to set these values in the database is the SetOrderAuthCodeAndReference method, which you need to add to your OrderProcessor class in business/order_processor.php:

```
// Set order's authorization code and reference code
public function SetAuthCodeAndReference($authCode, $reference)
{
  Orders::SetOrderAuthCodeAndReference($this->mOrderInfo['order_id'], $authCode,
                                       $reference);
```

```
    $this->mOrderInfo['auth_code'] = $authCode;
    $this->mOrderInfo['reference'] = $reference;
}
```

This code also sets the corresponding elements from the $mOrderInfo array, just in case they are required before OrderProcessor terminates. In this situation, it wouldn't make much sense to get these values from the database when we already know what the result will be.

Setting the Order Shipment Date

When an order is shipped, you should update the shipment date in the database, which can simply be the current date. Add the orders_set_date_shipped function to your hatshop database:

```
-- Create orders_set_date_shipped function
CREATE FUNCTION orders_set_date_shipped(INTEGER)
RETURNS VOID LANGUAGE plpgsql AS $$
  DECLARE
    inOrderId ALIAS FOR $1;
  BEGIN
    UPDATE orders SET shipped_on = NOW() WHERE order_id = inOrderId;
  END;
$$;
```

Add the new data tier method, SetDateShipped, to your Orders class in business/orders.php as follows:

```
// Set order's ship date
public static function SetDateShipped($orderId)
{
  // Build the SQL query
  $sql = 'SELECT orders_set_date_shipped(:order_id);';
  // Build the parameters array
  $params = array (':order_id' => $orderId);
  // Prepare the statement with PDO-specific functionality
  $result = DatabaseHandler::Prepare($sql);

  // Execute the query
  return DatabaseHandler::Execute($result, $params);
}
```

Add the following method to the OrderProcessor class in business/order_processor.php:

```
// Set order's ship date
public function SetDateShipped()
{
  Orders::SetDateShipped($this->mOrderInfo['order_id']);

  $this->mOrderInfo['shipped_on'] = date('Y-m-d');
```

Sending Emails to Customers and Suppliers

We need two methods to handle sending emails to customers and suppliers. Add the
MailCustomer and MailSupplier methods to the OrderProcessor class, located in
business/order_processor.php:

```php
public function MailCustomer($subject, $body)
{
  $to = $this->mCustomerInfo['email'];
  $headers = 'From: ' . CUSTOMER_SERVICE_EMAIL . "\r\n";
  $result = mail($to, $subject, $body, $headers);

  if ($result === false)
  {
    throw new Exception ('Unable to send e-mail to customer.');
  }
}

public function MailSupplier($subject, $body)
{
  $to = SUPPLIER_EMAIL;
  $headers = 'From: ' . ORDER_PROCESSOR_EMAIL . "\r\n";
  $result = mail($to, $subject, $body, $headers);

  if ($result === false)
  {
    throw new Exception ('Unable to send email to supplier.');
  }
}
```

Retrieving Order Details and the Customer Address

You'll need to retrieve a string representation of your order and the customer address.
For these tasks, add the GetCustomerAddressAsString and GetOrderAsString methods to
your OrderProcessor class, located in business/order_processor.php:

```php
public function GetCustomerAddressAsString()
{
  $new_line = "\n";

  $address_details = $this->mCustomerInfo['name'] . $new_line .
                     $this->mCustomerInfo['address_1'] . $new_line;

  if (!empty ($this->mOrderInfo['address_2']))
    $address_details .= $this->mCustomerInfo['address_2'] . $new_line;

  $address_details .= $this->mCustomerInfo['city'] . $new_line .
                      $this->mCustomerInfo['region'] . $new_line .
```

```
                              $this->mCustomerInfo['postal_code'] . $new_line .
                              $this->mCustomerInfo['country'];

      return $address_details;
    }

    public function GetOrderAsString($withCustomerDetails = true)
    {
      $total_cost = 0.00;
      $order_details = '';
      $new_line = "\n";

      if ($withCustomerDetails)
      {
        $order_details = 'Customer address:' . $new_line .
                          $this->GetCustomerAddressAsString() .
                          $new_line . $new_line;

        $order_details .= 'Customer credit card:' . $new_line .
                          $this->mCustomerInfo['credit_card']->CardNumberX .
                          $new_line . $new_line;
      }

      foreach ($this->mOrderDetailsInfo as $order_detail)
      {
        $order_details .= $order_detail['quantity'] . ' ' .
                          $order_detail['product_name'] . ' $' .
                          $order_detail['unit_cost'] . ' each, total cost $' .
                          number_format($order_detail['subtotal'],
                                        2, '.', '') . $new_line;

        $total_cost += $order_detail['subtotal'];
      }

      // Add shipping cost
      if ($this->mOrderInfo['shipping_id'] != -1)
      {
        $order_details .= 'Shipping: ' . $this->mOrderInfo['shipping_type'] .
                          $new_line;

        $total_cost += $this->mOrderInfo['shipping_cost'];
      }

      // Add tax
      if ($this->mOrderInfo['tax_id'] != -1 &&
          $this->mOrderInfo['tax_percentage'] != 0.00)
      {
```

```
    $tax_amount = round((float)$total_cost *
                       (float)$this->mOrderInfo['tax_percentage'], 2)
                       / 100.00;

    $order_details .= 'Tax: ' . $this->mOrderInfo['tax_type'] . ', $' .
                       number_format($tax_amount, 2, '.', '') .
                       $new_line;

    $total_cost += $tax_amount;
  }

  $order_details .= $new_line . 'Total order cost: $' .
                     number_format($total_cost, 2, '.', '');

  return $order_details;
}
```

Summary

You've begun to build the backbone of the application, and prepared it for the lion's share of the order pipeline processing functionality, which you'll implement in the next chapter.

Specifically, we've covered

- Modifications to the HatShop application to enable your own pipeline processing

- The basic framework for your order pipeline

- The database additions for auditing data and storing additional required data in the orders table

In the next chapter, you'll go on to fully implement the order pipeline.

■ ■ ■

Implementing the Order Pipeline: Part II

In the previous chapter, you completed the basic functionality of the OrderProcessor class, which is responsible for moving orders through the pipeline stages. You've seen a quick demonstration of this using a dummy pipeline section, but you haven't yet implemented the pipeline discussed at the beginning of the previous chapter.

In this chapter, you'll add the required pipeline sections so that you can process orders from start to finish, although you won't be adding full credit card transaction functionality until the next chapter.

We'll also look at the web administration of orders by modifying the order admin pages added earlier in the book to take into account the new order-processing system.

Implementing the Pipeline Sections

In the previous chapter, you completed the OrderProcessor class, except for one important section—the pipeline stage selection. Rather than forcing the processor to use PsDummy (the class you used instead of the real pipeline section classes that you'll build in this chapter), you actually want to select one of the pipeline stages outlined in Chapter 13, depending on the status of the order.

Let's run through the code for each of the pipeline sections in turn, which will take you to the point where the order pipeline will be complete, apart from actual credit card authorization that you'll implement in Chapter 15. You'll implement eight new classes with the following names:

- PsInitialNotification

- PsCheckFunds

- PsCheckStock

- PsStockOk

- PsTakePayment

- PsShipGoods

- PsShipOk

- PsFinalNotification

We'll discuss the classes you're creating as we go. Before moving on, remember that this code is available in the Source Code/Download section of the Apress web site (http://www.apress.com).

PsInitialNotification

This is the first pipeline stage, which is responsible for sending an email to the customer confirming that the order has been placed. Create a new file named ps_initial_notification.php in the business folder, and start adding code to it as shown here. This class starts off in what will soon become a very familiar fashion:

```php
<?php
class PsInitialNotification implements IPipelineSection
{
  private $_mProcessor;

  public function Process($processor)
  {
    // Set processor reference
    $this->_mProcessor = $processor;

    // Audit
    $processor->CreateAudit('PsInitialNotification started.', 20000);
```

The class implements the IPipelineSection interface, then a private field for storing a reference to OrderProcessor that invoked the PsInitialNotification, and finally the Process method implementation. This method starts by storing the reference to OrderProcessor, which some of your pipeline sections will do because using the methods it exposes (either in the Process method or in other methods) is essential. We also add an audit entry using the numbering scheme introduced in Chapter 13 (the initial 2 indicates it's coming from a pipeline section, the next 00 shows that it's the first pipeline section, and the final 00 means that it's the start message for the pipeline section).

The remainder of the Process method sends the notification email. This requires information from the customer, which you have easy access to. You also use a private method to build a message body, which we'll look at shortly:

```php
    // Send mail to customer
    $processor->MailCustomer('HatShop order received.',
                        $this->GetMailBody());
```

The mail is sent, you add an audit message and change the status of the order, and tell the order processor that it's okay to move straight on to the next pipeline section:

```php
    // Audit
    $processor->CreateAudit('Notification e-mail sent to customer.', 20002);

    // Update order status
    $processor->UpdateOrderStatus(1);

    // Continue processing
```

```
    $processor->mContinueNow = true;
```

If all goes according to plan, the Process method finishes by adding a final audit entry:

```
    // Audit
    $processor->CreateAudit('PsInitialNotification finished.', 20001);
  }
```

The GetMailBody method is used to build up an email body to send to the customer. The text uses customer and order data but follows a generally accepted e-commerce email format. Continue by adding this method to the PsInitialNotification class:

```
  private function GetMailBody()
  {
    $body = 'Thank you for your order! ' .
            'The products you have ordered are as follows:';
    $body.= "\n\n";

    $body.= $this->_mProcessor->GetOrderAsString(false);
    $body.= "\n\n";

    $body.= 'Your order will be shipped to:';
    $body.= "\n\n";

    $body.= $this->_mProcessor->GetCustomerAddressAsString();
    $body.= "\n\n";

    $body.= 'Order reference number: ';
    $body.= $this->_mProcessor->mOrderInfo['order_id'];
    $body.= "\n\n";

    $body.= 'You will receive a confirmation e-mail when this order ' .
            'has been dispatched. Thank you for shopping at HatShop!';

    return $body;
  }
}
?>
```

When this pipeline stage finishes, processing moves straight on to PsCheckFunds.

PsCheckFunds

This pipeline stage is responsible for making sure that the customer has the required funds available on a credit card. For now, you'll provide a dummy implementation of this and just assume that these funds are available. You'll implement the real functionality in the next chapter, which deals with credit card transactions.

Add the following code to a new file in the business folder named ps_check_funds.php. The code of the Process method starts almost in the same way as PsInitialNotification:

```php
<?php
class PsCheckFunds implements IPipelineSection
{
  public function Process($processor)
  {
    // Audit
    $processor->CreateAudit('PsCheckFunds started.', 20100);
```

Even though you aren't actually performing a check, set the authorization and reference codes for the transaction to make sure that the code in OrderProcessor works properly:

```php
    /* Check customer funds assume they exist for now
       set order authorization code and reference */
    $processor->SetAuthCodeAndReference('DummyAuthCode',
                                        'DummyReference');
```

You finish up with some auditing and the code required for continuation:

```php
    // Audit
    $processor->CreateAudit('Funds available for purchase.', 20102);

    // Update order status
    $processor->UpdateOrderStatus(2);

    // Continue processing
    $processor->mContinueNow = true;

    // Audit
    $processor->CreateAudit('PsCheckFunds finished.', 20101);
  }
}
?>
```

When this pipeline stage finishes, processing moves on to PsCheckStock.

PsCheckStock

This pipeline stage sends an email instructing the supplier to check stock availability. Add the following code to a new file in the business folder named ps_check_stock.php:

```php
<?php
class PsCheckStock implements IPipelineSection
{
  private $_mProcessor;

  public function Process($processor)
  {
    // Set processor reference
    $this->_mProcessor = $processor;
```

```
// Audit
$processor->CreateAudit('PsCheckStock started.', 20200);
```

Mail is sent in a similar way to PsInitialNotification, using a private method to build up the body:

```
// Send mail to supplier
$processor->MailSupplier('HatShop stock check.',
                         $this->GetMailBody());
```

As before, you finish by auditing and updating the status, although this time you don't tell the order processor to continue straight away:

```
// Audit
$processor->CreateAudit('Notification email sent to supplier.', 20202);

// Update order status
$processor->UpdateOrderStatus(3);

// Audit
$processor->CreateAudit('PsCheckStock finished.', 20201);
}
```

The code for building the message body is simple; it just lists the items in the order and tells the supplier to confirm via the HatShop web site (using the order administration page, which you'll modify later):

```
private function GetMailBody()
{
  $body = 'The following goods have been ordered:';
  $body .= "\n\n";

  $body .= $this->_mProcessor->GetOrderAsString(false);
  $body .= "\n\n";

  $body .= 'Please check availability and confirm via ' .
           'http://www.hatshop.com/admin.php';
  $body .= "\n\n";

  $body .= 'Order reference number: ';
  $body .= $this->_mProcessor->mOrderInfo['order_id'];

  return $body;
  }
}
?>
```

When this pipeline stage finishes, processing pauses. Later, when the supplier confirms that stock is available, processing moves on to PsStockOk.

PsStockOk

This pipeline section just confirms that the supplier has the product in stock and moves on. Its Process method is called for orders whose stock was confirmed and that need to move on to the next pipeline section. Add the following code to a new file in the business folder named ps_stock_ok.php:

```php
<?php
class PsStockOk implements IPipelineSection
{
  public function Process($processor)
  {
    // Audit
    $processor->CreateAudit('PsStockOk started.', 20300);

    /* The method is called when the supplier confirms that stock is
       available, so we don't have to do anything here except audit */
    $processor->CreateAudit('Stock confirmed by supplier.', 20302);

    // Update order status
    $processor->UpdateOrderStatus(4);

    // Continue processing
    $processor->mContinueNow = true;

    // Audit
    $processor->CreateAudit('PsStockOk finished.', 20301);
  }
}
?>
```

When this pipeline stage finishes, processing moves straight on to PsTakePayment.

PsTakePayment

This pipeline section completes the transaction started by PsCheckFunds. As with that section, you only provide a dummy implementation here. Add the following code to a new file in the business folder named ps_take_payment.php:

```php
<?php
class PsTakePayment implements IPipelineSection
{
  public function Process($processor)
  {
    // Audit
    $processor->CreateAudit('PsTakePayment started.', 20400);

    // Take customer funds assume success for now
```

```php
    // Audit
    $processor->CreateAudit('Funds deducted from customer credit card account.',
                            20402);

    // Update order status
    $processor->UpdateOrderStatus(5);

    // Continue processing
    $processor->mContinueNow = true;

    // Audit
    $processor->CreateAudit('PsTakePayment finished.', 20401);
  }
}
?>
```

When this pipeline stage finishes, processing moves straight on to PsShipGoods.

PsShipGoods

This pipeline section is remarkably similar to PsCheckStock, as it sends an email to the supplier and stops the pipeline until the supplier has confirmed that stock has shipped. This time you do need customer information, however, because the supplier needs to know where to ship the order! Add the following code to a new file in the business folder named ps_ship_goods.php:

```php
<?php
class PsShipGoods implements IPipelineSection
{
  private $_mProcessor;

  public function Process($processor)
  {
    // Set processor reference
    $this->_mProcessor = $processor;

    // Audit
    $processor->CreateAudit('PsShipGoods started.', 20500);

    // Send mail to supplier
    $processor->MailSupplier('HatShop ship goods.',
                            $this->GetMailBody());

    // Audit
    $processor->CreateAudit('Ship goods e-mail sent to supplier.', 20502);

    // Update order status
    $processor->UpdateOrderStatus(6);
```

```
  // Audit
  $processor->CreateAudit('PsShipGoods finished.', 20501);
}
```

As before, a private method called GetMailBody is used to build the message body for the email sent to the supplier:

```
private function GetMailBody()
{
  $body = 'Payment has been received for the following goods:';
  $body.= "\n\n";

  $body.= $this->_mProcessor->GetOrderAsString(false);
  $body.= "\n\n";

  $body.= 'Please ship to:';
  $body.= "\n\n";

  $body.= $this->_mProcessor->GetCustomerAddressAsString();
  $body.= "\n\n";

  $body.= 'When goods have been shipped, please confirm via ' .
          'http://www.hatshop.com/admin.php';
  $body.= "\n\n";

  $body.= 'Order reference number: ';
  $body.= $this->_mProcessor->mOrderInfo['order_id'];

  return $body;
}
}
?>
```

When this pipeline stage finishes, processing pauses. Later, when the supplier confirms that the order has been shipped, processing moves on to PsShipOk.

PsShipOk

This pipeline section is very similar to PsStockOk, although it has slightly more to do. Because you know that items have shipped, you can add a shipment date value to the orders table. Technically, this isn't really necessary because all audit entries are dated. However, this method means that you have all the information easily accessible in one database table. Add the following code to a new file in the business folder named ps_ship_ok.php:

```
<?php
class PsShipOk implements IPipelineSection
{
  public function Process($processor)
```

```
  {
    // Audit
    $processor->CreateAudit('PsShipOk started.', 20600);

    // Set order shipment date
    $processor->SetDateShipped();

    // Audit
    $processor->CreateAudit('Order dispatched by supplier.', 20602);

    // Update order status
    $processor->UpdateOrderStatus(7);

    // Continue processing
    $processor->mContinueNow = true;

    // Audit
    $processor->CreateAudit('PsShipOk finished.', 20601);
  }
}
?>
```

When this pipeline stage finishes, processing moves straight on to PsFinalNotification.

PsFinalNotification

This last pipeline section is very similar to the first because it sends an email to the customer. This time, you're confirming that the order has shipped. Add the following code to a new file in the business folder named ps_final_notification.php:

```
<?php
class PsFinalNotification implements IPipelineSection
{
  private $_mProcessor;

  public function Process($processor)
  {
    // Set processor reference
    $this->_mProcessor = $processor;

    // Audit
    $processor->CreateAudit('PsFinalNotification started.', 20700);

    // Send mail to customer
    $processor->MailCustomer('HatShop order dispatched.',
                             $this->GetMailBody());

    // Audit
```

```
    $processor->CreateAudit('Dispatch e-mail send to customer.', 20702);

    // Update order status
    $processor->UpdateOrderStatus(8);

    // Audit
    $processor->CreateAudit('PsFinalNotification finished.', 20701);
  }
```

It uses a familiar-looking GetMailBody method to build the body of the email:

```
private function GetMailBody()
{
  $body = 'Your order has now been dispatched! ' .
          'The following products have been shipped:';
  $body .= "\n\n";

  $body .= $this->_mProcessor->GetOrderAsString(false);
  $body .= "\n\n";

  $body .= 'Your order has been shipped to:';
  $body .= "\n\n";

  $body .= $this->_mProcessor->GetCustomerAddressAsString();
  $body .= "\n\n";

  $body .= 'Order reference number: ';
  $body .= $this->_mProcessor->mOrderInfo['order_id'];
  $body .= "\n\n";

  $body .= 'Thank you for shopping at HatShop.com!';

  return $body;
  }
}
?>
```

When this pipeline section finishes, the order status is changed to 8, which represents a completed order. Further attempts to process the order using OrderProcessor will result in an exception being thrown.

Testing the Pipeline

Now let's do a simple test to make sure the code you just wrote is working as expected.

1. Add the following highlighted lines in the include/app_top.php file. (Also feel free to remove the reference to ps_dummy.php, which is no longer required.)

```
require_once BUSINESS_DIR . 'order_processor.php';
require_once BUSINESS_DIR . 'ps_initial_notification.php';
require_once BUSINESS_DIR . 'ps_check_funds.php';
require_once BUSINESS_DIR . 'ps_check_stock.php';
require_once BUSINESS_DIR . 'ps_stock_ok.php';
require_once BUSINESS_DIR . 'ps_take_payment.php';
require_once BUSINESS_DIR . 'ps_ship_goods.php';
require_once BUSINESS_DIR . 'ps_ship_ok.php';
require_once BUSINESS_DIR . 'ps_final_notification.php';
```

2. Modify the code of the GetCurrentPipelineSection method in OrderProcessor (inside business/order_processor.php) as follows:

```
// Gets current pipeline section
private function GetCurrentPipelineSection()
{
  switch($this->mOrderInfo['status'])
  {
    case 0:
      $this->_mOrderProcessStage = $this->mOrderInfo['status'];
      $this->_mCurrentPipelineSection = new PsInitialNotification();

      break;
    case 1:
      $this->_mOrderProcessStage = $this->mOrderInfo['status'];
      $this->_mCurrentPipelineSection = new PsCheckFunds();

      break;
    case 2:
      $this->_mOrderProcessStage = $this->mOrderInfo['status'];
      $this->_mCurrentPipelineSection = new PsCheckStock();

      break;
    case 3:
      $this->_mOrderProcessStage = $this->mOrderInfo['status'];
      $this->_mCurrentPipelineSection = new PsStockOk();

      break;
```

```php
      case 4:
        $this->_mOrderProcessStage = $this->mOrderInfo['status'];
        $this->_mCurrentPipelineSection = new PsTakePayment();

        break;
      case 5:
        $this->_mOrderProcessStage = $this->mOrderInfo['status'];
        $this->_mCurrentPipelineSection = new PsShipGoods();

        break;
      case 6:
        $this->_mOrderProcessStage = $this->mOrderInfo['status'];
        $this->_mCurrentPipelineSection = new PsShipOk();

        break;
      case 7:
        $this->_mOrderProcessStage = $this->mOrderInfo['status'];
        $this->_mCurrentPipelineSection = new PsFinalNotification();

        break;
      case 8:
        $this->_mOrderProcessStage = 100;
        throw new Exception('Order already been completed.');

        break;
      default:
        $this->_mOrderProcessStage = 100;
        throw new Exception('Unknown pipeline section requested.');
    }
  }
```

3. Open business/orders.php and modify the $mOrdersStatusOptions member of the Orders class to manage the new order status codes. Note that this change affects the old orders, which used different status codes:

```php
public static $mOrderStatusOptions = array (
                 'Order placed, notifying customer', // 0
                 'Awaiting confirmation of funds',   // 1
                 'Notifying supplier-stock check',   // 2
                 'Awaiting stock confirmation',      // 3
                 'Awaiting credit card payment',     // 4
                 'Notifying supplier-shipping',      // 5
                 'Awaiting shipment confirmation',   // 6
                 'Sending final notification',       // 7
                 'Order completed',                  // 8
                 'Order canceled');                  // 9
```

4. Open `presentation/smarty_plugins/function.load_admin_order_details.php`, and add the highlighted new member to the `AdminOrderDetails` class:

   ```
   public $mTaxCost = 0.0;
   public $mOrderProcessMessage;
   ```

5. Modify the code of the `init` method in the `AdminOrderDetails` class located in `presentation/smarty_plugins/function.load_admin_order_details.php` as highlighted. This will handle the functionality necessary when the visitor clicks the Process button.

   ```
   if (isset ($_GET['submitProcessOrder']))
   {
     $processor = new OrderProcessor($this->mOrderId);

     try
     {
       $processor->Process();
       $this->mOrderProcessMessage = 'Order processed, status now: ' .
                                     $processor->mOrderInfo['status'];
     }
     catch (Exception $e)
     {
       $this->mOrderProcessMessage = 'Processing error, status now: ' .
                                     $processor->mOrderInfo['status'];
     }
   }
   ```

6. Open the `presentation/templates/admin_order_details.tpl` file, and add the highlighted code:

   ```
   <span class="admin_page_text">
     Editing details for order ID:
     {$admin_order_details->mOrderInfo.order_id} [
     {strip}
     <a href="{$admin_order_details->mAdminOrdersPageLink|prepare_link:"https"}">
       back to admin orders...
     </a>
     {/strip}
     ]
   </span>
   <br /><br />
   {if $admin_order_details->mOrderProcessMessage}
     <strong>{$admin_order_details->mOrderProcessMessage}</strong>
     <br /><br />
   {/if}
   <form action="{"admin.php"|prepare_link:"https"}" method="get">
   ```

7. Execute the code, create a new order, and then open that order in the orders admin page. In the orders admin page, click the Process Order button.

8. You should get a customer notification email (see Figure 14-1).

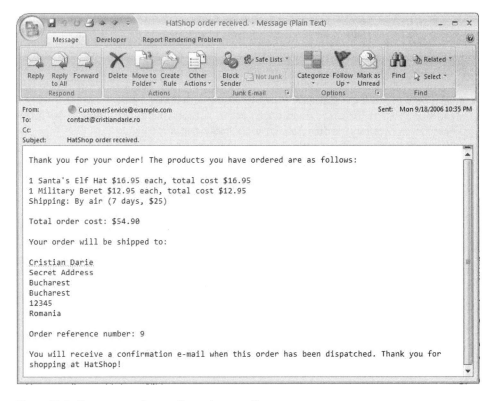

Figure 14-1. *Customer order confirmation email*

9. Check your supplier email for the stock check email (see Figure 14-2).

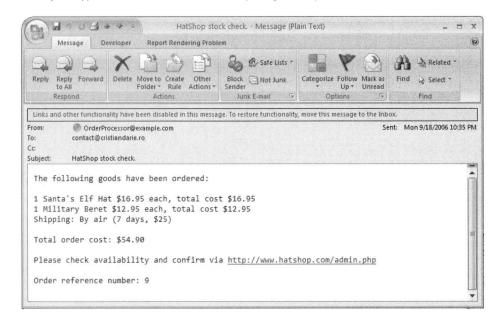

Figure 14-2. *Stock check email*

10. Continue processing in the admin order details page by clicking the Process Order button again, calling the Process method of the OrderProcessor class for the second time.

11. Check your email for the ship goods email (see Figure 14-3).

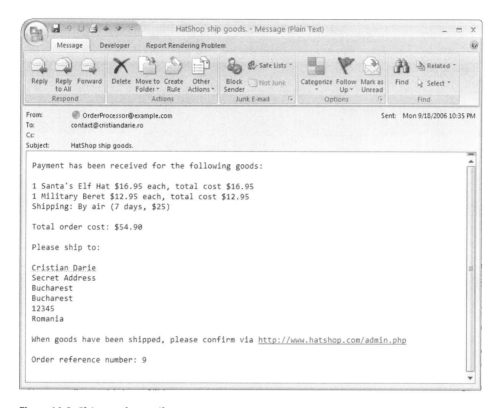

Figure 14-3. *Ship goods email*

12. Continue processing in the admin order details page by clicking Process and calling the Process method of the OrderProcessor class for the third and last time.

13. Check your email for the shipping confirmation email (see Figure 14-4).

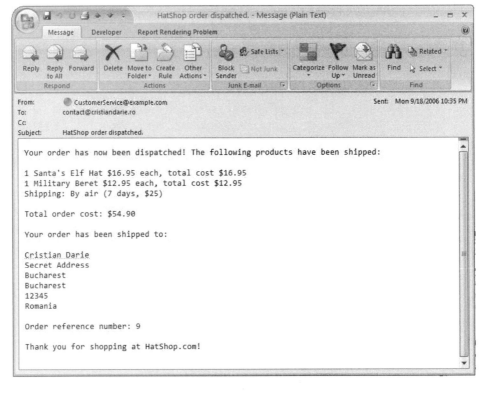

Figure 14-4. *Customer shipping notification email (dispatched.png)*

14. Examine the new `audit` entries for the order as shown in Figure 14-5.

pgAdmin III Edit Data - PostgreSQL Database Server 8.1 (localhost:5432) - hatshop - audit

	audit_id [PK] int4	order_id int4	created_on timestamp	message text	message_number int4
129	129	9	2006-09-18 22:34:49.234	Order Processor started.	10000
130	130	9	2006-09-18 22:34:49.25	PsInitialNotification started.	20000
131	131	9	2006-09-18 22:34:49.281	Notification e-mail sent to customer.	20002
132	132	9	2006-09-18 22:34:49.281	PsInitialNotification finished.	20001
133	133	9	2006-09-18 22:34:49.281	PsCheckFunds started.	20100
134	134	9	2006-09-18 22:34:49.296	Funds available for purchase.	20102
135	135	9	2006-09-18 22:34:49.296	PsCheckFunds finished.	20101
136	136	9	2006-09-18 22:34:49.296	PsCheckStock started.	20200
137	137	9	2006-09-18 22:34:49.312	Notification email sent to supplier.	20202
138	138	9	2006-09-18 22:34:49.312	PsCheckStock finished.	20201
139	139	9	2006-09-18 22:34:49.312	Order Processor finished.	10001
140	140	9	2006-09-18 22:34:50.75	Order Processor started.	10000
141	141	9	2006-09-18 22:34:50.75	PsStockOk started.	20300
142	142	9	2006-09-18 22:34:50.75	Stock confirmed by supplier.	20302
143	143	9	2006-09-18 22:34:50.765	PsStockOk finished.	20301
144	144	9	2006-09-18 22:34:50.765	PsTakePayment started.	20400
145	145	9	2006-09-18 22:34:50.765	Funds deducted from customer credit card account.	20402
146	146	9	2006-09-18 22:34:50.781	PsTakePayment finished.	20401
147	147	9	2006-09-18 22:34:50.781	PsShipGoods started.	20500
148	148	9	2006-09-18 22:34:50.796	Ship goods e-mail sent to supplier.	20502
149	149	9	2006-09-18 22:34:50.796	PsShipGoods finished.	20501
150	150	9	2006-09-18 22:34:50.796	Order Processor finished.	10001
151	151	9	2006-09-18 22:34:52.14	Order Processor started.	10000
152	152	9	2006-09-18 22:34:52.14	PsShipOk started.	20600
153	153	9	2006-09-18 22:34:52.156	Order dispatched by supplier.	20602
154	154	9	2006-09-18 22:34:52.156	PsShipOk finished.	20601
155	155	9	2006-09-18 22:34:52.156	PsFinalNotification started.	20700
156	156	9	2006-09-18 22:34:52.171	Dispatch e-mail send to customer.	20702
157	157	9	2006-09-18 22:34:52.171	PsFinalNotification finished.	20701
158	158	9	2006-09-18 22:34:52.171	Order Processor finished.	10001
159	159	9	2006-09-18 22:40:35.687	Order Processor started.	10000
*					

159 rows.

Figure 14-5. *Audit entries for completed order*

How It Works: The Order Pipeline

We've covered how the order pipeline works, so now we only need to explain the new code added to `OrderProcessor`. We changed the code in the `GetCurrentPipelineSection` method, which is responsible for selecting the pipeline section that needs to be executed.

The change is simply a switch block that assigns a pipeline section to the $_mCurrentPipelineSection member:

```
// Gets current pipeline section
private function GetCurrentPipelineSection()
{
  switch($this->mOrderInfo['status'])
  {
    case 0:
      $this->_mOrderProcessStage = $this->mOrderInfo['status'];
      $this->_mCurrentPipelineSection = new PsInitialNotification();

      break;
    case 1:
      $this->_mOrderProcessStage = $this->mOrderInfo['status'];
      $this->_mCurrentPipelineSection = new PsCheckFunds();

      break;
    case 2:
      $this->_mOrderProcessStage = $this->mOrderInfo['status'];
      $this->_mCurrentPipelineSection = new PsCheckStock();

      break;
    case 3:
      $this->_mOrderProcessStage = $this->mOrderInfo['status'];
      $this->_mCurrentPipelineSection = new PsStockOk();

      break;
    case 4:
      $this->_mOrderProcessStage = $this->mOrderInfo['status'];
      $this->_mCurrentPipelineSection = new PsTakePayment();

      break;
    case 5:
      $this->_mOrderProcessStage = $this->mOrderInfo['status'];
      $this->_mCurrentPipelineSection = new PsShipGoods();

      break;
    case 6:
      $this->_mOrderProcessStage = $this->mOrderInfo['status'];
      $this->_mCurrentPipelineSection = new PsShipOk();

      break;
    case 7:
      $this->_mOrderProcessStage = $this->mOrderInfo['status'];
      $this->_mCurrentPipelineSection = new PsFinalNotification();

      break;
    case 8:
```

```
        $this->_mOrderProcessStage = 100;
        throw new Exception('Order already been completed.');

        break;
    default:
        $this->_mOrderProcessStage = 100;
        throw new Exception('Unknown pipeline section requested.');
    }
}
```

If the order has been completed or an unknown section is requested, then you generate an exception.

The test code gives you the additional opportunity of testing this exception generation because if you run it again, you'll be processing an already completed order. Click the Process Order button for an order that's already complete (has the status 8), and you should get an error email as shown in Figure 14-6.

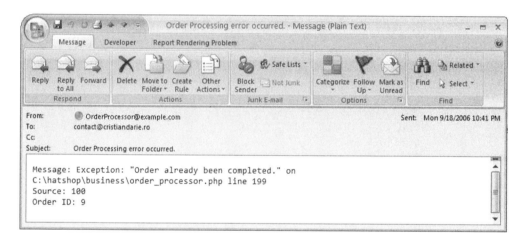

Figure 14-6. *Order completion error email*

The error message mailed to the administrator should be enough to get started on your way to finding out what happened.

Updating the Checkout Page

In the previous example, you were forced to call the OrderProcessor::Process() method three times in a row from the order details admin page. In practice, this won't happen—it will be called once by presentation/smarty_plugins/function.load_checkout_info.php when a customer places an order and twice more by the supplier in presentation/smarty_plugin/function.load_admin_order_details.php. You'll need to modify these web pages accordingly.

You also need to add a reference to your new classes in index.php. Follow the steps in this exercise to have function.load_checkout_info.php work with the new order pipeline.

Exercise: Updating the Checkout Process

1. Modify the init method in the CheckoutInfo class in presentation/smarty_plugins/ function.load_checkout_info.php by adding the highlighted code:

```php
public function init()
{
  // If the Place Order button was clicked, save the order to database
  if ($this->_mPlaceOrder == 1)
  {
    $this->mCustomerData = Customer::Get();
    $tax_id = '';

    switch ($this->mCustomerData['shipping_region_id'])
    {
      case 2:
        $tax_id = 1;

        break;
      default:
        $tax_id = 2;
    }

    $order_id = ShoppingCart::CreateOrder(
                $this->mCustomerData['customer_id'],
                (int)$_POST['shipping'], $tax_id);

    $redirect_page = '';

    // Create new OrderProcessor instance
    $processor = new OrderProcessor($order_id);

    try
    {
      $processor->Process();
    }
    catch (Exception $e)
    {
      // If an error occurs, head to an error page
      $redirect_page = 'index.php?OrderError';
    }

    // On success head to an order successful page
    $redirect_page = 'index.php?OrderDone';
```

```
        // Redirect to index.php
        $redirect_link = 'http://' . getenv('SERVER_NAME');

        // If HTTP_SERVER_PORT is defined and different than default
        if (defined('HTTP_SERVER_PORT') && HTTP_SERVER_PORT != '80')
        {
          // Append server port
          $redirect_link .= ':' . HTTP_SERVER_PORT;
        }

        $redirect_link .= VIRTUAL_LOCATION . $redirect_page;

        header('Location:' . $redirect_link);

        exit;
      }
  ...
```

2. Create a new file named order_done.tpl in the presentation/templates folder, and add the following code to its body:

```
{* order_done.tpl *}
<br />
<span class="description">Thank you for your order!</span>
<br /><br />
<strong>A confirmation email should arrive shortly.</strong>
```

3. If an error occurs while ordering, redirect to another page. Create presentation/templates/order_error.tpl with the following in it:

```
{* order_error.tpl *}
<br />
<span class="description">
An error has occurred during the processing of your order.</span>
<br /><br />
<strong>
  If you have an enquiry regarding this message please email
  <a class="mail" href="mailto:CustomerService@example.com">
  CustomerService@example.com</a>
</strong>
```

4. Add the following style to hatshop.css:

```
a.mail
{
  color: #0000ff;
  font-size: 11px;
  text-decoration: underline;
}
```

5. Modify `index.php` by adding the highlighted code to load either `order_done.tpl` or `order_error.tpl`, depending on whether the order processed successfully or not:

```
if (isset($_GET['RegisterCustomer']) || isset($_GET['UpdateAccountDetails']))
    $pageContentsCell = 'customer_details.tpl';
elseif (isset($_GET['UpdateAddressDetails']))
    $pageContentsCell = 'customer_address.tpl';
elseif (isset($_GET['UpdateCreditCardDetails']))
    $pageContentsCell = 'customer_credit_card.tpl';

if (isset($_GET['OrderDone']))
    $pageContentsCell = 'order_done.tpl';
elseif (isset($_GET['OrderError']))
    $pageContentsCell = 'order_error.tpl';

$page->assign('hide_boxes', $hide_boxes);
$page->assign('customerLoginOrLogged', $customerLoginOrLogged);
```

You can now use the HatShop web store to place orders, but they will pause when it gets to stock confirmation. To continue, you'll implement the interface for suppliers and administrators to use to force orders to continue processing.

Updating the Orders Admin Page

The basic functionality of this page is to allow suppliers and administrators to view a list of orders that need attention and advance them in the pipeline manually. This is simply a case of calling the `OrderProcess::Process` method as described earlier.

This page could be implemented in many ways. In fact, in some setups, it might be better to implement this as a standalone application, for example, if your suppliers are in-house and on the same network. Or, it might be better to combine this approach with Web Services.

To simplify things in this section, you'll supply a single page for both administrators and suppliers. This might not be ideal in all situations because you might not want to expose all order details and audit information to external suppliers. However, for demonstration purposes, this reduces the amount of code you have to get through. You'll also tie in the security for this page with the administrator forms-based security used earlier in the book, assuming that people with permission to edit the site data will also have permission to administer orders. In a more advanced setup, you could modify this slightly, providing roles for different types of users and restricting the functionality available to users in different roles.

Implementing the Data Tier

We need to add a new data tier function to the `hatshop` database, `orders_get_audit_trail`, and update an existing function, `orders_update_order`, to take into account the new status codes.

Using pgAdmin III, connect to the `hatshop` database, and use the query tool to execute this code, which creates the `orders_update_order` function in your `hatshop` database:

```
-- Update orders_update_order function
CREATE OR REPLACE FUNCTION orders_update_order(INTEGER, INTEGER,
                           VARCHAR(255), VARCHAR(50), VARCHAR(50))
RETURNS VOID LANGUAGE plpgsql AS $$
  DECLARE
    inOrderId    ALIAS FOR $1;
    inStatus     ALIAS FOR $2;
    inComments   ALIAS FOR $3;
    inAuthCode   ALIAS FOR $4;
    inReference  ALIAS FOR $5;
    currentDateShipped TIMESTAMP;
  BEGIN
    SELECT INTO currentDateShipped
                shipped_on
    FROM   orders
    WHERE  order_id = inOrderId;

    UPDATE orders
    SET    status = inStatus, comments = inComments,
           auth_code = inAuthCode, reference = inReference
    WHERE  order_id = inOrderId;

    IF inStatus < 7 AND currentDateShipped IS NOT NULL THEN
      UPDATE orders SET shipped_on = NULL WHERE order_id = inOrderId;
    ELSEIF inStatus > 6 AND currentDateShipped IS NULL THEN
      UPDATE orders SET shipped_on = NOW() WHERE order_id = inOrderId;
    END IF;
  END;
$$;
```

Then, use the query tool to execute this code, which creates the orders_get_audit_trail function in your hatshop database:

```
-- Create orders_get_audit_trail function
CREATE FUNCTION orders_get_audit_trail(INTEGER)
RETURNS SETOF audit LANGUAGE plpgsql AS $$
  DECLARE
    inOrderId ALIAS FOR $1;
    outAuditRow audit;
  BEGIN
    FOR outAuditRow IN
      SELECT audit_id, order_id, created_on, message, message_number
      FROM   audit
      WHERE  order_id = inOrderId
    LOOP
      RETURN NEXT outAuditRow;
    END LOOP;
  END;
$$;
```

Implementing the Business Tier

You also have to add a new method to the Orders class from business/orders.php to cater to the new data tier function added in the previous section.

Add the GetAuditTrail method to the Orders class in business/orders.php, as follows:

```
// Gets the audit table entries associated with a specific order
public static function GetAuditTrail($orderId)
{
  // Build the SQL query
  $sql = 'SELECT * FROM orders_get_audit_trail(:order_id);';
  // Build the parameters array
  $params = array (':order_id' => $orderId);
  // Prepare the statement with PDO-specific functionality
  $result = DatabaseHandler::Prepare($sql);

  // Execute the query and return the results
  return DatabaseHandler::GetAll($result, $params);
}
```

Implementing the Presentation Tier

You need to update the admin_order_details componentized template, which shows the details of an order. Earlier in the book, this componentized template also included the capability to test the order process, but we're removing this here. Instead, you'll provide the capability for orders to be pushed along the pipeline when they are stuck at the Awaiting confirmation of stock and Awaiting confirmation of shipment stages.

Now, you can also display all the audit information for the order in another new table. Let's look at what you're going to achieve, as shown in Figure 14-7.

You can split the orders admin page into three sections:

- In the first section, we'll change the Process button to a confirmation button for suppliers.

- In the second section, a table is filled with the items data from the order.

- In the third section, a table shows the audit trail for the order.

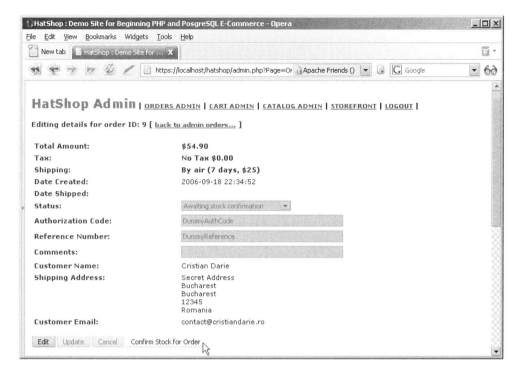

Figure 14-7. *The new Order Details Admin page*

You implement the new functionality in the next exercise.

Exercise: Modifying the Order Details Admin Section

1. Remove the following lines from `presentation/templates/admin_order_details.tpl`:

```
{if $admin_order_details->mOrderProcessMessage}
  <strong>{$admin_order_details->mOrderProcessMessage}</strong>
  <br /><br />
{/if}
```

2. Also in `presentation/templates/admin_order_details.tpl`, replace the Process Order button code with the highlighted code:

```
<input type="submit" name="submitCancel" value="Cancel"
{if ! $admin_order_details->mEditEnabled}
disabled="disabled"
{/if} />
{if $admin_order_details->mProcessButtonText}
<input type="submit" name="submitProcessOrder"
 value="{$admin_order_details->mProcessButtonText}" />
{/if}
<br /><br />
<span class="admin_page_text">Order contains these products:</span>
<br /><br />
```

3. In the `presentation/templates/admin_order_details.tpl` file, add the following highlighted code:

```
{section name=cOrder loop=$admin_order_details->mOrderDetails}
  <tr>
    <td>{$admin_order_details->mOrderDetails[cOrder].product_id}</td>
    <td>{$admin_order_details->mOrderDetails[cOrder].product_name}</td>
    <td>{$admin_order_details->mOrderDetails[cOrder].quantity}</td>
    <td>${$admin_order_details->mOrderDetails[cOrder].unit_cost}</td>
    <td>${$admin_order_details->mOrderDetails[cOrder].subtotal}</td>
  </tr>
{/section}
</table>
<br /><br />
<span class="admin_page_text">Order audit trail:</span>
<br /><br />
<table>
  <tr>
    <th>Audit ID</th>
    <th>Created On</th>
    <th>Message Number</th>
    <th>Message</th>
  </tr>
{section name=cOrder loop=$admin_order_details->mAuditTrail}
  <tr>
    <td>{$admin_order_details->mAuditTrail[cOrder].audit_id}</td>
    <td>{$admin_order_details->mAuditTrail[cOrder].created_on}</td>
    <td>{$admin_order_details->mAuditTrail[cOrder].message_number}</td>
    <td>{$admin_order_details->mAuditTrail[cOrder].message}</td>
  </tr>
{/section}
</table>
</form>
```

4. Open the `presentation/smarty_plugins/function.load_admin_order_details.php` file, and remove the definition of the `$mOrderProcessMessage` member of the `AdminOrderDetails` class shown here:

```
public $mOrderProcessMessage;
```

5. Also in the `function.load_admin_order_details.php` file, add two new members in the `AdminOrderDetails` class:

```
public $mProcessButtonText;
public $mAuditTrail;
```

6. In the same file, modify the `init` method of the `AdminOrderDetails` class by adding the code highlighted here:

```
if (isset ($_GET['submitUpdate']))
{
  Orders::UpdateOrder($this->mOrderId, $_GET['status'],
    $_GET['comments'], $_GET['authCode'], $_GET['reference']);
```

```
    }

    if (isset ($_GET['submitProcessOrder']))
    {
      $processor = new OrderProcessor($this->mOrderId);
      $processor->Process();
    }
...
    $this->mOrderInfo = Orders::GetOrderInfo($this->mOrderId);
    $this->mOrderDetails = Orders::GetOrderDetails($this->mOrderId);
    $this->mAuditTrail = Orders::GetAuditTrail($this->mOrderId);
    $this->mCustomerInfo = Customer::Get($this->mOrderInfo['customer_id']);
    $this->mTotalCost = $this->mOrderInfo['total_amount'];
...
    // Format the values
    $this->mTotalCost = number_format($this->mTotalCost, 2, '.', '');
    $this->mTaxCost = number_format($this->mTaxCost, 2, '.', '');

    if ($this->mOrderInfo['status'] == 3)
      $this->mProcessButtonText = 'Confirm Stock for Order';
    elseif ($this->mOrderInfo['status'] == 6)
      $this->mProcessButtonText = 'Confirm Shipment for Order';

    // Value which specifies whether to enable or disable edit mode
    if (isset ($_GET['submitEdit']))
      $this->mEditEnabled = true;
    else
      $this->mEditEnabled = false;
```

6. Load HatShop, make a new order, and then load the order details admin page to test the new changes.

How It Works: Order Details Admin

The init method found in AdminOrderDetails advances the pipeline to the next section if the Process button is clicked; the presence of this button on the page depends on the value of the mProcessButtonText member. This value is set to "Confirm Stock" if the current pipeline section is 3 (awaiting stock confirmation), or to "Confirm Shipment" if the current pipeline section is 6 (awaiting shipment confirmation). If the current pipeline section is not set to 3 or 6, it means that the order has been completed successfully, and the button is not shown. The administrator can always check what happened to the order by checking the audit trail that is displayed on the page.

All that remains now is to check that everything is working properly. To do this, use the web interface to place an order, and then check it out via the orders details admin section. You should see that the order is awaiting confirmation of stock, as shown earlier in Figure 14-7.

Click the Confirm Stock for Order button and the order is processed. Because this happens very quickly, you are soon presented with the next stage, where the Confirm Stock for Order button is replaced by a new button named Confirm Shipment, and the audit trail shows a new set of data.

Clicking the Confirm Shipment button completes the order. If you scroll down the page, you can see all audit trail messages that have been stored in the database concerning this order.

Summary

You've taken giant strides toward completing the HatShop e-commerce application in this chapter. Now you have a fully audited, secure backbone for the application.

Specifically, we've covered

- Modifications to the HatShop application to enable your own pipeline processing

- The basic framework for your order pipeline

- The database additions for auditing data and storing additional required data in the orders table

- The implementation of most of the order pipeline, apart from those sections that deal with credit cards

The only thing missing that you need to add before delivering this application to the outside world is credit card processing functionality, which we'll look at in the next chapter.

CHAPTER 15

■■■

Credit Card Transactions

The last thing you need to do before launching the e-commerce site is to enable credit card processing. In this chapter, we examine how you can build this into the pipeline you created in the previous chapter.

We'll start by looking at the theory behind credit card transactions, the sort of organizations that help you achieve credit card processing, and the sort of transactions that are possible. Moving on, we'll take two example organizations and discuss the specifics of their transaction APIs (Application Program Interfaces, the means by which you access credit card transaction functionality). After this, you'll build a new class library that helps you use one of these transaction APIs via some simple test code.

Finally, you'll integrate the API with the HatShop e-commerce application and order-processing pipeline.

Credit Card Transaction Fundamentals

Banks and other financial institutions use secure networks for their transactions based on the X.25 protocol rather than TCP/IP (Transmission Control Protocol/Internet Protocol, the primary means by which data is transmitted across the Internet). X.25 isn't something you need to know anything about, apart from the fact that it's a different protocol for networking and isn't compatible with TCP/IP. As such, X.25 networks are completely separate from the Internet, and although it's possible to get direct access to them, this isn't likely to be a reasonable option. To do so, you might have to enter into some serious negotiation with the owner of the network you want to use. The owner will want to be completely sure that you are a reliable customer who is capable of enforcing the necessary safeguards to prevent an attack on their system. Accordingly, the network owner won't be handing out these licenses to just anyone because most people can't afford the security measures required (which include locking your servers in a cage, sending daily backup tapes down a secure chute, having three individuals with separate keys to access these tapes, and so on).

The alternative is to access these networks via a gateway provider. This enables you to perform your side of the credit card transaction protocol over the Internet (using a secure protocol), while relying on your chosen gateway to communicate with X.25 networks. Although there is likely to be a cost involved with this, the provider should have a deal with financial institutions to keep costs low and pass the savings on to you (after the gateway takes its share), so it's likely to be much cheaper than having your own X.25 connection. This method is also likely to be cheaper than using a third party such as PayPal because you only need the minimum functionality when you are handling your own order pipeline. There is no need, for example, to use all the order-auditing functionality offered by a company such as PayPal because you already built all this functionality in the previous chapter.

Working with Credit Card Payment Gateways

To work with a gateway organization, you first need to open a merchant bank account. This can be done at most banks, and will get you a merchant ID that you can use when signing up with the gateway. The next step is to find a suitable gateway. Unfortunately, this can be a lot of hard work!

Although it isn't hard to find a gateway, the challenge lies in finding a competent one that offers services at a price and quality acceptable to you. Literally hundreds of companies are eager to take a cut of your sales. A quick search on the Internet for "credit card gateway" will produce a long list. The web sites of these companies are for the most part pure brochure-ware—you'll find yourself reading through pages of text about how they are the best and most secure at what they do, only to end up with a form to fill in so that a customer service representative can call you to "discuss your needs." In the long run, you can rest assured that at least you will probably only have to go through the procedure once.

You'll probably find that most of the organizations offering this service offer similar packages. However, key points to look for include the banks they do business with (your merchant bank account will have to be at one of these), the currencies they deal in, and, of course, the costs.

In this chapter, we'll look at two of the few organizations that are easy to deal with—DataCash and Authorize.net.

Table 15-1 shows some of the gateway services available.

Table 15-1. *Gateway Services*

United States	URL	United Kingdom	URL
Authorize.net	`http://www.authorize.net/`	Arcot	`http://www.arcot.com/`
First Data	`http://www.firstdata.com/`	WorldPay	`http://www.worldpay.com/`
Cardservice	`http://cardservice.com/`	DataCash	`http://www.datacash.com/`
ICVerify	`http://www.icverify.com/`		

DataCash and Authorize.net

In this chapter, we'll demonstrate implementing credit card transactions with two online services: DataCash and Authorize.net.

DataCash is a UK-based credit card gateway organization. You'll need a UK merchant bank account if you want to use it in your final application. However, you don't have to worry about this for now: it's very easy to get access to a rather useful test account—you don't even need a merchant bank account.

Authorize.net, as mentioned on its official web site at `http://www.authorize.net`, "provides Internet Protocol (IP) payment gateway services that enable merchants to authorize, settle and manage credit card or electronic check transactions anytime, anywhere." In other words, Authorize.net also offers the services that you need to process the credit cards yourself when someone buys one of your hats.

The important point to remember is that the techniques covered in this chapter apply to ˙ery credit card gateway. The specifics might change slightly if you switch to a different ˙ization, but you'll have done most of the hard work already.

As you'll see later in this chapter, both Authorize.net and DataCash let you perform test transactions using so-called "magic" credit card numbers (supplied separately by Authorize.net and DataCash), which will accept or decline transactions without performing any actual financial transactions. This is fantastic for development purposes because you don't want to use your own credit cards for testing!

■**Note** The authors of this book are in no way affiliated with Authorize.net or DataCash.

Understanding Credit Card Transactions

Whichever gateway you use, the basic principles of credit card transactions are the same. First, the sort of transactions you'll be dealing with in an e-commerce web site are known as Card Not Present (CNP) transactions, which means you don't have the credit card in front of you, and you can't verify the customer signature. This isn't a problem; after all you've probably been performing CNP transactions for some time now online, over the phone, by mail, and so on. It's just something to be aware of should you see the CNP acronym.

Several advanced services are offered by various gateways, including cardholder address verification, security code checking, fraud screening, and so on. Each of these adds an additional layer of complexity to your credit card processing, and we're not covering those details here. Rather, this chapter provides a starting point from which you can add these services if required. Whether to choose these optional extra services depends on how much money is passing through your system and the trade-off between the costs of implementing the services and the potential costs if something goes wrong that could have been prevented by these extra services. If you are interested in these services, the "customer service representative" mentioned previously will be happy to explain things.

You can perform several types of transactions, including

Authorization: Checks card for adequate funds and performs deduction.

Pre-authorization: Checks cards for funds and allocates them if available, but doesn't deduct them immediately.

Fulfillment: Completes a pre-authorization transaction, deducting the funds already allocated.

Refund: Refunds a completed transaction or simply puts money on a credit card.

Again, the specifics vary, but these are the basic types.

In this chapter, you'll use the pre/fulfill model, which means you don't take payment until just before you instruct your supplier to ship goods. This has been hinted at previously by the structure of the pipeline you created in the previous chapter.

Working with DataCash

Now that we've covered the basics, let's consider how you'll get things working in the HatShop application using the DataCash system. The first thing to do is to get a test account with DataCash by following these steps:

1. Go to `http://www.datacash.com/`.

2. Head to the Support – Integration Info section of the web site.

3. Enter your details and submit.

4. From the email you receive, make a note of your account username and password, as well as the additional information required for accessing the DataCash reporting system.

Normally, the next step would be to download one of DataCash's toolkits for easy integration. However, because DataCash doesn't provide a PHP-compatible implementation, you need to use the XML API for performing transactions. Basically, this involves sending XML requests to a certain URL using an SSL connection and then deciphering the XML result. This is easy to do in PHP if you have the CURL (Client URL Library Functions) library installed on your computer, and PHP is aware of it (see Appendix A).

You'll be doing a lot of XML manipulation when communicating with DataCash because you'll need to create XML documents to send to DataCash and to extract data from XML responses. In the following few pages, we'll take a quick look at the XML required for the operations you'll be performing and the responses you can expect.

Pre-Authentication Request

When you send a pre-authentication request to DataCash, you need to include the following information:

- DataCash username (known as the DataCash Client)

- DataCash password

- A unique transaction reference number (explained later in this section)

- The amount of money to be debited

- The currency used for the transaction (USD, GBP, and so on)

- The type of transaction (the code `pre` for pre-authentication, and the code `fulfil` for fulfillment)

- The credit card number

- The credit card expiry date

- The credit card issue date (if applicable to the type of credit card being used)

- The credit card issue number (if applicable to the type of credit card being used)

The unique transaction reference number must be a number between 6 and 12 digits long, which you choose to uniquely identify the transaction with an order. Because you can't use a short number, you can't just use the order ID values you've been using until now for orders. However, you can use this order ID as the starting point for creating a reference number simply by adding a high number, such as 1,000,000. You can't duplicate the reference number in any future transactions, so you can be sure that after a transaction is completed, it won't execute again, which might otherwise result in charging the customer twice. This does mean, however, that if a credit card is rejected, you might need to create a whole new order for the customer, but that shouldn't be a problem if required.

The XML request is formatted in the following way, with the values detailed previously shown in bold:

```xml
<?xml version="1.0" encoding="UTF-8"?>
<Request>
  <Authentication>
    <password>DataCash password</password>
    <client>DataCash client</client>
  </Authentication>
  <Transaction>
    <TxnDetails>
      <merchantreference>Unique reference number</merchantreference>
      <amount currency='Currency Type'>Cash amount</amount>
    </TxnDetails>
    <CardTxn>
      <method>pre</method>
      <Card>
        <pan>Credit card number</pan>
        <expirydate>Credit card expiry date</expirydate>
      </Card>
    </CardTxn>
  </Transaction>
</Request>
```

Response to Pre-Authentication Request

The response to a pre-authentication request includes the following information:

- A status code number indicating what happened; 1 if the transaction was successful, or one of several other codes if something else happens. For a complete list of return codes for a DataCash server, see https://testserver.datacash.com/software/returncodes.shtml.

- A reason for the status, which is basically a string explaining the status in English. For a status of 1, this string is ACCEPTED.

- An authentication code and a reference number that will be used to fulfill the transaction in the fulfillment request stage (discussed next).

- The time that the transaction was processed.

- The mode of the transaction, which is TEST when using the test account.

- Confirmation of the type of credit card used.

- Confirmation of the country that the credit card was issued in.

- The authorization code used by the bank (for reference only).

The XML for this is formatted as follows:

```
<?xml version="1.0" encoding="utf-8"?>
<Response>
  <status>Status code</status>
  <reason>Reason</reason>
  <merchantreference>Authentication code</merchantreference>
  <datacash_reference>Reference number</datacash_reference>
  <time>Time</time>
  <mode>TEST</mode>
  <CardTxn>
    <card_scheme>Card Type</card_scheme>
    <country>Country</country>
    <issuer>Card issuing bank</issuer>
    <authcode>Bank authorization code</authcode>
  </CardTxn>
</Response>
```

Fulfillment Request

For a fulfillment request, you need to send the following information:

- DataCash username (the DataCash Client)

- DataCash password

- The type of the transaction (for fulfillment, the code fulfil)

- The authentication code received earlier

- The reference number received earlier

Optionally, you can include additional information, such as a confirmation of the amount to be debited from the credit card, although this isn't really necessary.

This is formatted as follows:

```
<?xml version="1.0" encoding="UTF-8"?>
<Request>
  <Authentication>
    <password>DataCash password</password>
    <client>DataCash client</client>
  </Authentication>
  <Transaction>
    <HistoricTxn>
```

```
        <reference>Reference Number</reference>
        <authcode>Authentication code</authcode>
        <method>fulfil</method>
      </HistoricTxn>
    </Transaction>
  </Request>
```

Fulfillment Response

The response to a fulfillment request includes the following information:

- A status code number indicating what happened; 1 if the transaction was successful, or one of several other codes if something else happens. Again, for a complete list of the codes, see `https://testserver.datacash.com/software/returncodes.shtml`.

- A reason for the status, which is basically a string explaining the status in English. For a status of 1, this string is `FULFILLED OK`.

- Two copies of the reference code for use by DataCash.

- The time that the transaction was processed.

- The mode of the transaction, which is `TEST` when using the test account.

The XML for this is formatted as follows:

```
<?xml version="1.0" encoding="utf-8"?>
<Response>
  <status>Status code</status>
  <reason>Reason</reason>
  <merchantreference>Reference Code</merchantreference>
  <datacash_reference>Reference Code</datacash_reference>
  <time>Time</time>
  <mode>TEST</mode>
</Response>
```

Exchanging XML Data with DataCash

Because the XML data you need to send to DataCash has a simple and standard structure, we'll build it manually in a string, without using the XML support offered by PHP 5. We will, however, take advantage of PHP 5's SimpleXML extension, which makes reading simple XML data a piece of cake.

Although less complex and powerful than DOMDocument, the SimpleXML extension makes parsing XML data easy by transforming it into a data structure you can simply iterate through. You first met the SimpleXML extension in Chapter 11.

■Note For the code that communicates with DataCash, we use the CURL library (http://curl. haxx.se/). Read Appendix A for complete installation instructions. Under Linux, the process can be more complicated, but if you are running PHP under Windows, you just need to copy libeay32.dll and ssleay32.dll from the PHP package to the System32 folder of your Windows installation and uncomment the following line in php.ini (by default, located in your Windows installation folder) by removing the leading semicolon, and then restarting Apache: extension=php_curl.dll.

For more details about the CURL library, check out the excellent tutorial at http://www.zend.com/ pecl/tutorials/curl.php. The official documentation of PHP's CURL support is located at http://www.php.net/curl.

Exercise: Communicating with DataCash

1. Create a new file named datacash_request.php in the business folder, and add the following code to it:

```php
<?php
class DataCashRequest
{
  // DataCash Server URL
  private $_mUrl;

  // Will hold the current XML document to be sent to DataCash
  private $_mXml;

  // Constructor initializes the class with URL of DataCash
  public function __construct($url)
  {
    // Datacash URL
    $this->_mUrl = $url;
  }

  /* Compose the XML structure for the pre-authentication
     request to DataCash */
  public function MakeXmlPre($dataCashClient, $dataCashPassword,
                            $merchantReference, $amount, $currency,
                            $method, $cardNumber, $expiryDate,
                            $startDate = '', $issueNumber = '')
  {
    $this->_mXml =
      "<?xml version=\"1.0\" encoding=\"UTF-8\"\x3F>
       <Request>
         <Authentication>
           <password>$dataCashPassword</password>
```

```
            <client>$dataCashClient</client>
          </Authentication>
          <Transaction>
            <TxnDetails>
              <merchantreference>$merchantReference</merchantreference>
              <amount currency=\"$currency\">$amount</amount>
            </TxnDetails>
            <CardTxn>
              <method>pre</method>
              <Card>
                <pan>$cardNumber</pan>
                <expirydate>$expiryDate</expirydate>
                <startdate>$startDate</startdate>
                <issuenumber>$issueNumber</issuenumber>
              </Card>
            </CardTxn>
          </Transaction>
        </Request>";
}

// Compose the XML structure for the fulfillment request to DataCash
public function MakeXmlFulfill($dataCashClient, $dataCashPassword,
                              $method, $authCode, $reference)
{
  $this->_mXml =
    "<?xml version=\"1.0\" encoding=\"UTF-8\"\x3F>
      <Request>
        <Authentication>
          <password>$dataCashPassword</password>
          <client>$dataCashClient</client>
        </Authentication>
        <Transaction>
          <HistoricTxn>
            <reference>$reference</reference>
            <authcode>$authCode</authcode>
            <method>$method</method>
          </HistoricTxn>
        </Transaction>
      </Request>";
}

// Get the current XML
public function GetRequest()
{
  return $this->_mXml;
}
```

```php
    // Send an HTTP POST request to DataCash using CURL
    public function GetResponse()
    {
      // Initialize a CURL session
      $ch = curl_init();

      // Prepare for an HTTP POST request
      curl_setopt($ch, CURLOPT_POST, 1);

      // Prepare the XML document to be POSTed
      curl_setopt($ch, CURLOPT_POSTFIELDS, $this->_mXml);

      // Set the URL where we want to POST our XML structure
      curl_setopt($ch, CURLOPT_URL, $this->_mUrl);

      /* Do not verify the Common name of the peer certificate in the SSL
         handshake */
      curl_setopt($ch, CURLOPT_SSL_VERIFYHOST, 0);

      // Prevent CURL from verifying the peer's certificate
      curl_setopt($ch, CURLOPT_SSL_VERIFYPEER, 0);

      /* We want CURL to directly return the transfer instead of
         printing it */
      curl_setopt($ch, CURLOPT_RETURNTRANSFER, 1);

      // Perform a CURL session
      $result = curl_exec($ch);

      // Close a CURL session
      curl_close ($ch);

      // Return the response
      return $result;
    }
  }
?>
```

2. Define the DataCash URL and login data at the end of your `include/config.php` file:

```php
// Constant definitions for datacash
define('DATACASH_URL', 'https://testserver.datacash.com/Transaction');
define('DATACASH_CLIENT', 'your account client number');
define('DATACASH_PASSWORD', 'your account password');
```

3. Create the `test_datacash.php` file in your project's home (the `hatshop` folder), and add the following in it:

```php
<?php
session_start();

if (empty ($_GET['step']))
{
  require_once 'include/config.php';
  require_once BUSINESS_DIR . 'datacash_request.php';

  $request = new DataCashRequest(DATACASH_URL);
  $request->MakeXmlPre(DATACASH_CLIENT, DATACASH_PASSWORD,
                       8880000 + rand(0, 10000), 49.99, 'GBP',
                       'pre', '3528000000000007', '11/08');

  $request_xml = $request->GetRequest();
  $_SESSION['pre_request'] = $request_xml;

  $response_xml = $request->GetResponse();
  $_SESSION['pre_response'] = $response_xml;

  $xml = simplexml_load_string($response_xml);
  $request->MakeXmlFulfill(DATACASH_CLIENT, DATACASH_PASSWORD,
                           'fulfill', $xml->merchantreference,
                           $xml->datacash_reference);

  $response_xml = $request->GetResponse();
  $_SESSION['fulfill_response'] = $response_xml;
}
else
{
  header('Content-type: text/xml');

  switch ($_GET['step'])
  {
    case 1:
      print $_SESSION['pre_request'];

      break;
    case 2:
      print $_SESSION['pre_response'];

      break;
    case 3:
```

```
        print $_SESSION['fulfill_response'];

        break;
    }
    exit;
}
?>
<frameset cols="33%, 33%, 33%">
    <frame src="test_datacash.php?step=1">
    <frame src="test_datacash.php?step=2">
    <frame src="test_datacash.php?step=3">
</frameset>
```

4. Load the test_datacash.php file in your browser to see the results. If you use Opera, the output should look like Figure 15-1 because Opera only shows the contents of the XML elements. If you use another web browser, you would see properly formatted XML documents.

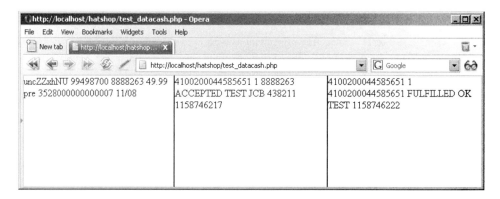

Figure 15-1. *DataCash transaction results*

5. Log on to https://testserver.datacash.com/reporting2 to see the transaction log for your DataCash account (note that this view takes a while to update, so you might not see the transaction right away). This report is shown in Figure 15-2.

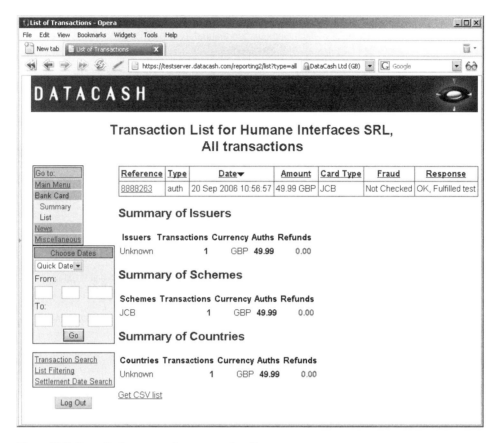

Figure 15-2. *DataCash transaction report details*

How It Works: The Code That Communicates with DataCash

The DataCashRequest class is quite simple. First the constructor sets the HTTPS address where you send your requests:

```
// Constructor initializes the class with URL of DataCash
public function __construct($url)
{
  // Datacash URL
  $this->_mUrl = $url;
}
```

When you want to make a pre-authentication request, you first need to call the MakeXmlPre method to create the required XML for this kind of request. Some XML elements are optional (such as startdate or issuenumber, which get default values in case you don't provide your own—have a look at the definition of the MakeXmlPre method), but the others are mandatory.

> ■**Note** If you want to see exactly which elements are mandatory and which are optional for each kind of request, check the XML API FAQ document from DataCash.

The next kind of request you must be able to make to the DataCash system is a fulfill request. The XML for this kind of request is prepared in the MakeXmlFulfill method.

You then have the GetRequest method that returns the last XML document built by either MakeXmlPre or MakeXmlFulfill:

```
// Get the current XML
public function GetRequest()
{
  return $this->_mXml;
}
```

Finally, the GetResponse method actually sends the latest XML request file, built by a call to either MakeXmlPre or MakeXmlFulfill, and returns the response XML. Let's take a closer look at this method.

GetResponse starts by initializing a CURL session and setting the POST method to send your data:

```
// Send an HTTP POST request to DataCash using CURL
public function GetResponse()
{
  // Initialize a CURL session
  $ch = curl_init();

  // Prepare for an HTTP POST request
  curl_setopt($ch, CURLOPT_POST, 1);

  // Prepare the XML document to be POSTed
  curl_setopt($ch, CURLOPT_POSTFIELDS, $this->_mXml);

  // Set the URL where we want to POST our XML structure
  curl_setopt($ch, CURLOPT_URL, $this->_mUrl);

  /* Do not verify the Common name of the peer certificate in the SSL
     handshake */
  curl_setopt($ch, CURLOPT_SSL_VERIFYHOST, 0);

  // Prevent CURL from verifying the peer's certificate
  curl_setopt($ch, CURLOPT_SSL_VERIFYPEER, 0);
```

To return the transfer into a PHP variable, we set the CURLOPT_RETURNTRANSFER parameter to 1, send the request, and close the CURL session:

```
  /* We want CURL to directly return the transfer instead of
     printing it */
  curl_setopt($ch, CURLOPT_RETURNTRANSFER, 1);
```

```
    // Perform a CURL session
    $result = curl_exec($ch);

    // Close a CURL session
    curl_close ($ch);

    // Return the response
    return $result;
  }
```

The `test_datacash.php` file acts like this. When you load it in the browser, the script makes a pre-authentication request and a fulfill request and then saves the pre-authentication request XML, the pre-authentication response XML, and the fulfill response XML data in the session:

```
session_start();

if (empty ($_GET['step']))
{
  require_once 'include/config.php';
  require_once BUSINESS_DIR . 'datacash_request.php';

  $request = new DataCashRequest(DATACASH_URL);
  $request->MakeXmlPre(DATACASH_CLIENT, DATACASH_PASSWORD,
                       8880000 + rand(0, 10000), 49.99, 'GBP',
                       'pre', '3528000000000007', '11/08');

  $request_xml = $request->GetRequest();
  $_SESSION['pre_request'] = $request_xml;

  $response_xml = $request->GetResponse();
  $_SESSION['pre_response'] = $response_xml;

  $xml = simplexml_load_string($response_xml);
  $request->MakeXmlFulfill(DATACASH_CLIENT, DATACASH_PASSWORD,
                           'fulfill', $xml->merchantreference,
                           $xml->datacash_reference);

  $response_xml = $request->GetResponse();
  $_SESSION['fulfill_response'] = $response_xml;
}
```

The `test_datacash.php` page will be loaded three more times because you have three frames that you want to fill with data:

```
<frameset cols="33%, 33%, 33%">
  <frame src="test_datacash.php?step=1">
  <frame src="test_datacash.php?step=2">
  <frame src="test_datacash.php?step=3">
</frameset>
```

Depending on the value, you decide which of the XMLs that you previously saved in the user session should be displayed as follows:

```
else
{
  header('Content-type: text/xml');

  switch ($_GET['step'])
  {
    case 1:
      print $_SESSION['pre_request'];

      break;
    case 2:
      print $_SESSION['pre_response'];

      break;
    case 3:
      print $_SESSION['fulfill_response'];

      break;
  }
  exit;
}
```

Integrating DataCash with HatShop

Now that you have a new class that performs credit card transactions, all you need to do is integrate its functionality into the order pipeline you built in the previous chapters. To fully integrate DataCash with HatShop, you'll need to update the existing PsCheckFunds and PsTakePayments classes.

You need to modify the pipeline section classes that deal with credit card transactions. We've already included the infrastructure for storing and retrieving authentication codes and reference information, via the OrderProcessor.SetOrderAuthCodeAndReference method.

Exercise: Implementing the Order Pipeline Classes

1. First modify business/ps_check_funds.php to work with DataCash:

```php
<?php
class PsCheckFunds implements IPipelineSection
{
  public function Process($processor)
  {
    // Audit
    $processor->CreateAudit('PsCheckFunds started.', 20100);
```

```php
      $order_total_cost = $processor->mOrderInfo['total_amount'];
      $order_total_cost += $processor->mOrderInfo['shipping_cost'];
      $order_total_cost +=
        round((float)$order_total_cost *
              (float)$processor->mOrderInfo['tax_percentage'], 2) / 100.00;

      $request = new DataCashRequest(DATACASH_URL);
      $request->MakeXmlPre(DATACASH_CLIENT, DATACASH_PASSWORD,
        $processor->mOrderInfo['order_id'] + 1000006,
        $order_total_cost, 'GBP', 'pre',
        $processor->mCustomerInfo['credit_card']->CardNumber,
        $processor->mCustomerInfo['credit_card']->ExpiryDate,
        $processor->mCustomerInfo['credit_card']->IssueDate,
        $processor->mCustomerInfo['credit_card']->IssueNumber);

      $responseXml = $request->GetResponse();
      $xml = simplexml_load_string($responseXml);

      if ($xml->status == 1)
      {
        $processor->SetAuthCodeAndReference(
          $xml->merchantreference, $xml->datacash_reference);

        // Audit
        $processor->CreateAudit('Funds available for purchase.', 20102);

        // Update order status
        $processor->UpdateOrderStatus(2);

        // Continue processing
        $processor->mContinueNow = true;
      }
      else
      {
        // Audit
        $processor->CreateAudit('Funds not available for purchase.', 20103);

        throw new Exception('Credit card check funds failed for order ' .
                            $processor->mOrderInfo['order_id'] . "\n\n" .
                            'Data exchanged:' . "\n" .
                            $request->GetResponse() . "\n" . $responseXml);
      }

      // Audit
      $processor->CreateAudit('PsCheckFunds finished.', 20101);
  }
}
?>
```

2. Modify the business/ps_take_payment.php file as follows:

```php
<?php
class PsTakePayment implements IPipelineSection
{
  public function Process($processor)
  {
    // Audit
    $processor->CreateAudit('PsTakePayment started.', 20400);

    $request = new DataCashRequest(DATACASH_URL);
    $request->MakeXmlFulFill(DATACASH_CLIENT, DATACASH_PASSWORD, 'fulfill',
                             $processor->mOrderInfo['auth_code'],
                             $processor->mOrderInfo['reference']);

    $responseXml = $request->GetResponse();
    $xml = simplexml_load_string($responseXml);

    if ($xml->status == 1)
    {
      // Audit
      $processor->CreateAudit(
       'Funds deducted from customer credit card account.', 20402);

      // Update order status
      $processor->UpdateOrderStatus(5);

      // Continue processing
      $processor->mContinueNow = true;
    }
    else
    {
      // Audit
      $processor->CreateAudit('Could not deduct funds from credit card.',
                              20403);

      throw new Exception('Credit card take payment failed for order ' .
                          $processor->mOrderInfo['order_id'] . "\n\n" .
                          'Data exchanged:' . "\n" .
                          $request->GetResponse() . "\n" . $responseXml);
    }

    // Audit
    $processor->CreateAudit('PsTakePayment finished.', 20401);
  }
}
?>
```

3. Add a reference to the `business/datacash_request.php` file in `include/app_top.php` as high-lighted:

```
require_once BUSINESS_DIR . 'ps_ship_ok.php';
require_once BUSINESS_DIR . 'ps_final_notification.php';
require_once BUSINESS_DIR . 'datacash_request.php';
```

Testing DataCash Integration

Now that you have all this in place, it's important to test with a few orders. You can do this easily by making sure you create a customer with "magic" credit card details. As mentioned earlier in the chapter, DataCash supplies these numbers for testing purposes and to obtain specific responses from DataCash. A sample of these numbers is shown in Table 15-2; a full list is available on the DataCash web site.

Table 15-2. *DataCash Credit Card Test Numbers*

Card Type	Card Number	Return Code	Description	Sample Message
Switch	4936000000000000001	1	Authorized with random auth code.	AUTH CODE ??????
	4936000000000000019	7	Decline the transaction.	DECLINED
	6333000000000005	1	Authorized with random auth code.	AUTH CODE ??????
	6333000000000013	7	Decline the transaction.	DECLINED
	6333000000123450	1	Authorized with random auth code.	AUTH CODE ??????
Visa	4242424242424242	7	Decline the transaction.	DECLINED
	4444333322221111	1	Authorized with random auth code.	AUTH CODE ??????
	4546389010000131	1	Authorized with random auth code.	AUTH CODE ??????

At this moment, you can experiment with your new fully featured e-commerce web site by placing orders with the test credit card numbers, checking the emails the web site sends, and finding out how it reacts in certain situation, such as how it logs errors, how orders are administered using the orders administration page, and so on.

Going Live

Moving from the test account to the live one is now simply a matter of replacing the DataCash login info in `include/config.php`. After you set up a merchant bank account, you can use the new details to set up a new DataCash account, obtaining new client and password data along the way. You also need to change the URL for the DataCash server that you send data to because it needs to be the production server instead of the testing server. Other than removing the test user accounts from the database and moving your web site to an Internet location (see Appendix B for more details), this is all you need to do before exposing your newly completed e-commerce application to customers.

Working with Authorize.net

To use Authorize.net, you need to sign up for a developer test account via `http://developer.authorize.net/testaccount/`. The main page where developers can get information on Authorize.net integration is `http://developer.authorize.net/`.

Communicating with Authorize.net is different from communicating with DataCash. Instead of sending and receiving XML files, you send strings consisting of name-value pairs, separated by ampersands. Effectively, you use a similar syntax to query strings appended to URLs.

Authorize.net returns the transaction results in the form of a string that contains the return values (without their names) separated by a character that you specify when making the initial request. In our examples, we'll use the pipe (|) character. The return values come in a predetermined order, and their significance is given by their position in the returned string.

■**Note** The complete documentation for the Authorize.net API can be found in the Advanced Integration Method (AIM) Implementation Guide Card-Not-Present Transactions at `http://www.authorize.net/support/AIM_guide.pdf`. Even more documents are available in the document library at `http://www.authorize.net/resources/documentlibrary/`.

The default transaction type is `AUTH_CAPTURE`, where you request and deduct the funds from the credit card using a single request. For HatShop, we'll use two other transaction types: `AUTH_ONLY`, which checks if the necessary funds are available (this happened in the `PsCheckFunds` pipeline stage), and `PRIOR_AUTH_CAPTURE`, which deducts the amount of money that was previously checked using `AUTH_ONLY` (this happens in the `PsTakePayment` pipeline stage).

To perform an `AUTH_ONLY` transaction, you'll first create an array such as the following, which contains the necessary transaction data.

```
// Auth
$transaction = array ('x_invoice_num' => '99999', // Invoice number
                      'x_amount'      => '45.99', // Amount
                      'x_card_num'    => '4007000000027', // Credit card number
                      'x_exp_date'    => '1209', // Expiration date
                      'x_method'      => 'CC', // Payment method
                      'x_type'        => 'AUTH_ONLY'); // Transaction type
```

For PRIOR_AUTH_CAPTURE transactions, you don't need to specify all this information again; instead, you only need to pass the transaction ID that was returned in response of the AUTH_ONLY request.

```
// Capture
$transaction = array (
 'x_ref_trans_id' => $ref_trans_id, // Transaction id
 'x_method' => 'CC', // Payment method
 'x_type' => 'PRIOR_AUTH_CAPTURE'); // Transaction type
```

We'll transform these arrays into a string of name-value pairs and submit them to the Authorize.net server. The response comes in the form of a string whose values are separated by a configurable character. In Figure 15-3, you can see a sample response for an AUTH_ONLY request (left part of the window) and a sample response for a PRIOR_AUTH_CAPTURE request (right part of the window).

We'll write a simple test with this transaction type before implementing any modifications to HatShop. Follow the steps in the exercise to test Authorize.net.

Exercise: Testing Authorize.net

1. Create a new file named authorize_net_request.php in the business folder, and add the following code to it:

```php
<?php
class AuthorizeNetRequest
{
  // Authorize Server URL
  private $_mUrl;

  // Will hold the current request to be sent to Authorize.net
  private $_mRequest;

  // Constructor initializes the class with URL of Authorize.net
  public function __construct($url)
  {
    // Authorize.net URL
    $this->_mUrl = $url;
  }

  public function SetRequest($request)
  {
    $this->_mRequest = '';

    $request_init = array ('x_login'          => AUTHORIZE_NET_LOGIN_ID,
                           'x_tran_key'       =>
                           AUTHORIZE_NET_TRANSACTION_KEY,
                           'x_version'        => '3.1',
                           'x_test_request'   => AUTHORIZE_NET_TEST_REQUEST,
                           'x_delim_data'     => 'TRUE',
```

```php
                              'x_delim_char'      => '|',
                              'x_relay_response'  => 'FALSE');

    $request = array_merge($request_init, $request);

    foreach($request as $key => $value )
      $this->_mRequest .= $key . '=' . urlencode($value) . '&';
  }

  // Send an HTTP POST request to Authorize.net using CURL
  public function GetResponse()
  {

    // Initialize a CURL session
    $ch = curl_init();

    // Prepare for an HTTP POST request
    curl_setopt($ch, CURLOPT_POST, 1);

    // Prepare the request to be POSTed
    curl_setopt($ch, CURLOPT_POSTFIELDS, rtrim($this->_mRequest, '& '));

    // Set the URL where we want to POST our data
    curl_setopt($ch, CURLOPT_URL, $this->_mUrl);

    /* Do not verify the Common name of the peer certificate in the SSL
       handshake */
    curl_setopt($ch, CURLOPT_SSL_VERIFYHOST, 0);

    // Prevent CURL from verifying the peer's certificate
    curl_setopt($ch, CURLOPT_SSL_VERIFYPEER, 0);

    /* We want CURL to directly return the transfer instead of
       printing it */
    curl_setopt($ch, CURLOPT_RETURNTRANSFER, 1);

    // Perform a CURL session
    $result = curl_exec($ch);

    // Close a CURL session
    curl_close ($ch);

    // Return the response
    return $result;
  }
}
?>
```

2. Add the following at the end of the `include/config.php` file, modifying the constant data with the details of your Authorize.net account:

```
// Constant definitions for authorize.net
define('AUTHORIZE_NET_URL', 'https://test.authorize.net/gateway/transact.dll');
define('AUTHORIZE_NET_LOGIN_ID', '[Your Login ID]');
define('AUTHORIZE_NET_TRANSACTION_KEY', '[Your Transaction Key]');
define('AUTHORIZE_NET_TEST_REQUEST', 'FALSE');
```

3. Add the following `test_authorize_net.php` test file in your site root folder:

```
<?php
session_start();

if (empty ($_GET['step']))
{
  require_once 'include/config.php';
  require_once BUSINESS_DIR . 'authorize_net_request.php';

  $request = new AuthorizeNetRequest(AUTHORIZE_NET_URL);

  // Auth
  $transaction = array ('x_invoice_num' => '99999', // Invoice number
                        'x_amount'      => '45.99', // Amount
                        'x_card_num'    => '4007000000027', // Credit card no
                        'x_exp_date'    => '1209', // Expiration date
                        'x_method'      => 'CC', // Payment method
                        'x_type'        => 'AUTH_ONLY'); // Transaction type

  $request->SetRequest($transaction);
  $auth_only_response = $request->GetResponse();

  $_SESSION['auth_only_response'] = $auth_only_response;

  $auth_only_response = explode('|', $auth_only_response);

  // Read the transaction ID, which will be necessary for taking the payment
  $ref_trans_id = $auth_only_response[6];

  // Capture
  $transaction = array ('x_ref_trans_id' => $ref_trans_id, // Transaction id
                        'x_method'       => 'CC', // Payment method
                        'x_type'         => 'PRIOR_AUTH_CAPTURE'); //
                        Transaction type

  $request->SetRequest($transaction);
  $prior_auth_capture_response = $request->GetResponse();
```

```
        $_SESSION['prior_auth_capture_response'] = $prior_auth_capture_response;
    }
    else
    {
      switch ($_GET['step'])
      {
        case 1:
          print $_SESSION['auth_only_response'];

          break;
        case 2:
          print $_SESSION['prior_auth_capture_response'];

          break;
      }

      exit;
    }
    ?>
    <frameset cols="50%, 50%">
      <frame src="test_authorize_net.php?step=1">
      <frame src="test_authorize_net.php?step=2">
    </frameset>
```

4. Load the test_authorize_net.php page in your favorite browser to see the results (see Figure 15-3).

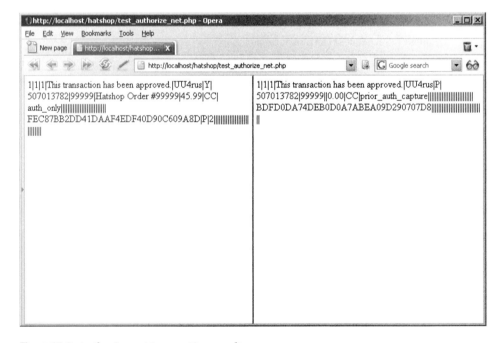

Figure 15-3. *Authorize.net transaction results*

5. Go to Authorize.net, log in to Merchant Interface (`https://test.authorize.net/`), and you can see the transaction you just performed in the Unsettled Transactions section under the Search tab. This report is shown in Figure 15-4.

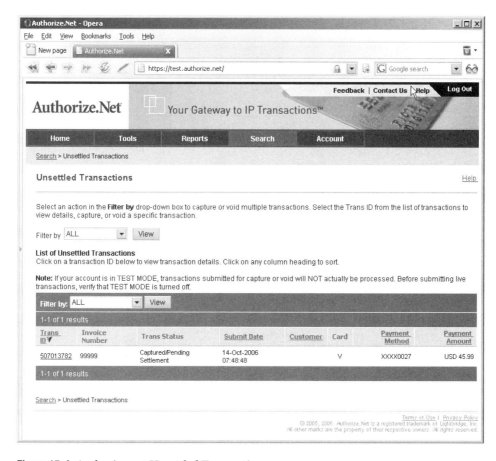

Figure 15-4. *Authorize.net Unsettled Transactions*

How It Works: Authorize.net Transactions

The hard work is done by the `AuthorizeNetRequest` class, which has two important methods: `SetRequest` is used to set up transaction details, and `GetResponse` is used to send the request to, and retrieve the response from, Authorize.net. The following code snippet shows how they are used:

```
// Auth
$transaction = array ('x_invoice_num' => '99999', // Invoice number
                      'x_amount'      => '45.99', // Amount
                      'x_card_num'    => '4007000000027', // Credit card number
                      'x_exp_date'    => '1209', // Expiration date
                      'x_method'      => 'CC', // Payment method
```

```
                              'x_type'          => 'AUTH_ONLY'); // Transaction type

$request->SetRequest($transaction);
$response = $request->GetResponse();
```

■**Note** The credit card data mentioned in this transaction is one of the "magic card numbers" provided by Authorize.net for testing purposes. Review the AIM Implementation Guide for the complete list of such credit card numbers.

We send an array with transaction details as a parameter to SetRequest. SetRequest then joins this array with another array that contains the Authorize.net account details:

```
public function SetRequest($request)
{
  $this->_mRequest = '';

  $request_init = array ('x_login'           => AUTHORIZE_NET_LOGIN_ID,
                         'x_tran_key'         => AUTHORIZE_NET_TRANSACTION_KEY,
                         'x_version'          => '3.1',
                         'x_test_request'     => AUTHORIZE_NET_TEST_REQUEST,
                         'x_delim_data'       => 'TRUE',
                         'x_delim_char'       => '|',
                         'x_relay_response'   => 'FALSE');
  $request = array_merge($request_init, $request);
```

The array data is merged into a name-value string that can be sent to Authorize.net. The values are encoded for inclusion in the URL using the urlencode() function:

```
  foreach($request as $key => $value )
    $this->_mRequest .= $key . '=' . urlencode($value) . '&';
}
```

The GetResponse() method of AuthorizeNetRequest does the actual request, using the CURL library.

```
// Send an HTTP POST request to Authorize.net using CURL
public function GetResponse()
{
  ...

  // Perform a CURL session
  $result = curl_exec($ch);

  // Close a CURL session
  curl_close ($ch);

  // Return the response
```

```
        return $result;
    }
}
?>
```

When executing the `GetResponse()` function to perform an `AUTH_ONLY` transaction, the response will contain a transaction ID. If the authorization is successful, we can then use this transaction ID to perform a `PRIOR_AUTH_CAPTURE` transaction, which effectively takes the money from the customer's account.

As explained earlier, the response from Authorize.net comes in the form of a string that contains values delimited by a configurable character, which in our case is the pipe character (|). To read a particular value from the string, we transform the string into an array using the `explode()` PHP function (`http://www.php.net/manual/en/function.explode.php`):

```
    $auth_only_response = $request->GetResponse();

    $_SESSION['auth_only_response'] = $auth_only_response;

    $auth_only_response = explode('|', $auth_only_response);
```

After this piece of code executes, `$auth_only_response` will contain an array whose elements are the values that were delimited by the pipe character in the original string. From this array, we're interested in the seventh element, which, according to the Authorize.net documentation, is the transaction ID. (Read the Gateway Response API details from `http://www.authorize.net/support/AIM_guide.pdf` for the complete details about the Authorize.net response.)

```
    // Read the transaction ID, which will be necessary for taking the payment
    $ref_trans_id = $auth_only_response[6];
```

■ Note The `$auth_only_response` array created by `explode()` is zero-based, so `$auth_only_response[6]` represents the seventh element of the array.

The code that takes the money using this transaction ID is straightforward. Because the transaction has already been authorized, we only need to specify the transaction ID received after authorization to complete the transaction:

```
    // Capture
    $transaction = array ('x_ref_trans_id' => $ref_trans_id, // Transaction id
                          'x_method'       => 'CC', // Payment method
                          'x_type'         => 'PRIOR_AUTH_CAPTURE'); // Transaction
                          type

    $request->SetRequest($transaction);
    $prior_auth_capture_response = $request->GetResponse();
```

Integrating Authorize.net with HatShop

As with DataCash, you'll have to modify the PsCheckFunds and PsTakePayment classes to use the new Authorize.net functionality.

Remember that you can use the files from the Source Code Download section of the Apress web site (http://www.apress.com/) instead of typing the code yourself.

The final modifications involve changing the pipeline section classes that deal with credit card transactions (PsCheckFunds and PsTakePayment). We've already included the infrastructure for storing and retrieving authentication code and reference information via the OrderProcessor::SetOrderAuthCodeAndReference method.

Exercise: Implementing the Order Pipeline Classes

1. First, modify business/ps_check_funds.php to work with Authorize.net:

```php
<?php
class PsCheckFunds implements IPipelineSection
{
  public function Process($processor)
  {
    // Audit
    $processor->CreateAudit('PsCheckFunds started.', 20100);

    $order_total_cost = $processor->mOrderInfo['total_amount'];
    $order_total_cost += $processor->mOrderInfo['shipping_cost'];
    $order_total_cost +=
      round((float)$order_total_cost *
           (float)$this->mOrderInfo['tax_percentage'], 2) / 100.00;

    $exp_date = str_replace('/', '',
      $processor->mCustomerInfo['credit_card']->ExpiryDate);


    $transaction =
      array (
        'x_invoice_num' => $processor->mOrderInfo['order_id'],
        'x_amount' => $order_total_cost, // Amount to charge
        'x_card_num' => $processor->mCustomerInfo['credit_card']->CardNumber,
        'x_exp_date' => $exp_date, // Expiry (MMYY)
        'x_method' => 'CC',
        'x_type' => 'AUTH_ONLY');

    // Process Transaction
    $request = new AuthorizeNetRequest(AUTHORIZE_NET_URL);
    $request->SetRequest($transaction);

    $response = $request->GetResponse();
```

```php
    $response = explode('|', $response);

    if ($response[0] == 1)
    {
      $processor->SetAuthCodeAndReference($response[4], $response[6]);

      // Audit
      $processor->CreateAudit('Funds available for purchase.', 20102);

      // Update order status
      $processor->UpdateOrderStatus(2);

      // Continue processing
      $processor->mContinueNow = true;
    }
    else
    {
      // Audit
      $processor->CreateAudit('Funds not available for purchase.', 20103);

      throw new Exception('Credit card check funds failed for order ' .
                          $processor->mOrderInfo['order_id'] . ".\n\n" .
                          'Data exchanged:' . "\n" .
                          var_export($transaction, true) . "\n" .
                          var_export($response, true));
    }

    // Audit
    $processor->CreateAudit('PsCheckFunds finished.', 20101);
  }
}
?>
```

2. Modify business/ps_take_payment.php as follows:

```php
<?php
class PsTakePayment implements IPipelineSection
{
  public function Process($processor)
  {
    // Audit
    $processor->CreateAudit('PsTakePayment started.', 20400);

    $transaction =
      array ('x_ref_trans_id' => $processor->mOrderInfo['reference'],
             'x_method'       => 'CC',
             'x_type'         => 'PRIOR_AUTH_CAPTURE');
```

```php
    // Process Transaction
    $request = new AuthorizeNetRequest(AUTHORIZE_NET_URL);
    $request->SetRequest($transaction);

    $response = $request->GetResponse();

    $response = explode('|', $response);

    if ($response[0] == 1)
    {
      // Audit
      $processor->CreateAudit(
        'Funds deducted from customer credit card account.',
        20402);

      // Update order status
      $processor->UpdateOrderStatus(5);

      // Continue processing
      $processor->mContinueNow = true;

      // Audit
      $processor->CreateAudit('PsTakePayment finished.', 20401);
    }
    else
    {
      // Audit
      $processor->CreateAudit(
        'Error taking funds from customer credit card.', 20403);

      throw new Exception('Credit card take payment failed for order ' .
                          $processor->mOrderInfo['order_id'] . ".\n\n" .
                          'Data exchanged:' . "\n" .
                          var_export($transaction, true) . "\n" .
                          var_export($response, true));
    }
  }
}
?>
```

3. Add a reference to the business/authorize_net_request.php file in include/app_top.php as highlighted:

```php
require_once BUSINESS_DIR . 'ps_ship_ok.php';
require_once BUSINESS_DIR . 'ps_final_notification.php';
require_once BUSINESS_DIR . 'authorize_net_request.php';
```

Testing Authorize.net Integration

All you have to do now is run some tests with your new web site. Retrieve the list of "magic" Authorize.net credit card numbers from the Advanced Integration Method (AIM) Implementation Guide, and experiment doing transactions with them.

Summary

In this chapter, you have completed your e-commerce application by integrating it with credit card authorization. Short of putting your own products in, hooking it up with your suppliers, getting a merchant bank account, and putting it on the web, you're ready to go. Okay, so that's still quite a lot of work, but none of it is particularly difficult. The hard work is behind you now.

Specifically, in this chapter, we have looked at the theory behind credit card transactions on the web and looked at one full implementation—DataCash. We created a library that can be used to access DataCash and integrated it with our application. We also looked at Authorize.net.

■■■

CHAPTER 16

Product Reviews

At this point, you have a complete and functional e-commerce web site. However, this doesn't stop you from adding even more features to it, making it more useful and pleasant for visitors.

By adding a product review system to your web site, you increase the chances that visitors will get back to your site, either to write a review for a product they bought, or to see what other people think about that product.

A review system can also help you learn your customers' tastes, which enables you to improve the product recommendations, and even make changes in the web site or the structure of the product catalog based on customer feedback.

To make things easy for both you and the customer, you'll add the list of product reviews and the form to add a new product review to the products' details pages. The form to add a new product shows up only for registered users because we decided not to allow anonymous reviews (however, you can easily change this if you like). You'll create the code for this new feature in the usual way, starting from the database and finishing with the user interface (UI). The final result of your work in this chapter will look like Figure 16-1.

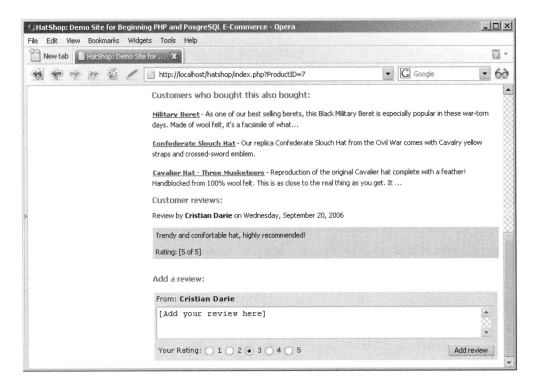

Figure 16-1. *The product details page containing product reviews*

Implementing the Data Tier

For your review system, you have to create a `review` table and two data tier functions in your `hatshop` database. The `catalog_get_product_reviews` function retrieves the reviews for a specific product, and the `catalog_create_product_review` method adds a review to a product.

Exercise: Adding Support for Customer Reviews to the Database

1. Load pgAdmin III, and connect to the `hatshop` database.

2. Click Tools ➤ Query tool (or click the SQL button on the toolbar). A new query window should appear.

3. Use the query tool to execute this code, which adds the `review` table in your `hatshop` database:

```
-- Create review table
CREATE TABLE review
(
  review_id    SERIAL   NOT NULL,
  customer_id  INTEGER  NOT NULL,
  product_id   INTEGER  NOT NULL,
```

```
   review      TEXT      NOT NULL,
   rating      SMALLINT  NOT NULL,
   created_on  TIMESTAMP NOT NULL,
   CONSTRAINT pk_review_id PRIMARY KEY (review_id),
   CONSTRAINT fk_customer_id FOREIGN KEY (customer_id)
              REFERENCES customer (customer_id)
              ON UPDATE RESTRICT ON DELETE RESTRICT,
   CONSTRAINT fk_product_id FOREIGN KEY (product_id)
              REFERENCES product (product_id)
              ON UPDATE RESTRICT ON DELETE RESTRICT
);
```

4. Execute the following code, which creates the `review_info` type and the `catalog_get_product_review` function in your hatshop database:

```
-- Create review_info type
CREATE TYPE review_info AS
(
  customer_name VARCHAR(50),
  review        TEXT,
  rating        SMALLINT,
  created_on    TIMESTAMP
);

-- Create catalog_get_product_reviews function
CREATE FUNCTION catalog_get_product_reviews(INTEGER)
RETURNS SETOF review_info LANGUAGE plpgsql AS $$
  DECLARE
    inProductId ALIAS FOR $1;
    outReviewInfoRow review_info;
  BEGIN
    FOR outReviewInfoRow IN
      SELECT    c.name, r.review, r.rating, r.created_on
      FROM      review r
      INNER JOIN customer c
                 ON c.customer_id = r.customer_id
      WHERE     r.product_id = inProductId
      ORDER BY  r.created_on DESC
    LOOP
      RETURN NEXT outReviewInfoRow;
    END LOOP;
  END;
$$;
```

The `catalog_get_product_review` function retrieves the reviews for the product identified by the `inProductId` parameter. You also need the name of the reviewer so we made an INNER JOIN with the `customer` table.

5. Use the query tool to execute this code, which adds the `catalog_create_product_review` function in your `hatshop` database:

```
-- Create catalog_create_product_review function
CREATE FUNCTION catalog_create_product_review(INTEGER, INTEGER, TEXT,
                                              SMALLINT)
RETURNS VOID LANGUAGE plpgsql AS $$
  DECLARE
    inCustomerId ALIAS FOR $1;
    inProductId  ALIAS FOR $2;
    inReview     ALIAS FOR $3;
    inRating     ALIAS FOR $4;
  BEGIN
    INSERT INTO review (customer_id, product_id, review, rating, created_on)
        VALUES (inCustomerId, inProductId, inReview, inRating, NOW());
  END;
$$;
```

When a registered visitor adds a product review, the `catalog_create_product_review` function is called.

Implementing the Business Tier

Add the corresponding business tier methods to the `Catalog` class from the `business/catalog.php` file:

```
// Gets the reviews for a specific product
public static function GetProductReviews($productId)
{
  // Build the SQL query
  $sql = 'SELECT * FROM catalog_get_product_reviews(:product_id);';
  // Build the parameters array
  $params = array (':product_id' => $productId);
  // Prepare the statement with PDO-specific functionality
  $result = DatabaseHandler::Prepare($sql);

  // Execute the query and return the results
  return DatabaseHandler::GetAll($result, $params);
}

// Creates a product review
public static function CreateProductReview($customer_id, $productId,
                                           $review, $rating)
{
  // Build the SQL query
  $sql = 'SELECT catalog_create_product_review(:customer_id, :product_id,
```

```
                                          :review, :rating);';
  // Build the parameters array
  $params = array (':customer_id' => $customer_id,
                   ':product_id' => $productId,
                   ':review' => $review,
                   ':rating' => $rating);
  // Prepare the statement with PDO-specific functionality
  $result = DatabaseHandler::Prepare($sql);

  // Execute the query
  return DatabaseHandler::Execute($result, $params);
}
```

Implementing the User Interface

Now it's time to see the code you've written so far in action. The UI consists of the reviews
componentized template that will be placed on the product details page. You'll create it in the
following exercise.

1. Create the file `presentation/templates/reviews.tpl`, and add the following to it:

```
{* reviews.tpl *}
{load_reviews assign="reviews"}
{if $reviews->mTotalReviews != 0}
<span class="description">Customer reviews:</span><br />
<ul>
  {section name=cReviews loop=$reviews->mReviews}
  <li>
    Review by
    <strong>{$reviews->mReviews[cReviews].customer_name}</strong> on
    {$reviews->mReviews[cReviews].created_on|date_format:"%A, %B %e, %Y"}
    <br /><br />
    <span>
    {$reviews->mReviews[cReviews].review}
    <br /><br />
    Rating: [{$reviews->mReviews[cReviews].rating} of 5]
    </span>
    <br />
  </li>
  {/section}
</ul>
{else}
<span class="description">
  Be the first person to voice your opinion!<br /><br />
```

```
</span>
{/if}
{if $reviews->mEnableAddProductReviewForm}
{* add review form *}
<span class="description"> Add a review:</span><br /><br />
<form method="post"
 action="{$reviews->mAddProductReviewTarget|prepare_link:"http"}">
  <table class="add_review">
    <tr>
      <td>
        From: <strong>{$reviews->mReviewerName}</strong>
      </td>
    </tr>
    <tr>
      <td>
        <textarea name="review"
         rows="3" cols="65">[Add your review here]</textarea>
      </td>
    </tr>
    <tr>
      <td>
        <table class="add_review">
          <tr>
            <td>
              Your Rating:
              <input type="radio" name="rating" value="1" /> 1
              <input type="radio" name="rating" value="2" /> 2
              <input type="radio" name="rating" value="3" checked="checked" /> 3
              <input type="radio" name="rating" value="4" /> 4
              <input type="radio" name="rating" value="5" /> 5
            </td>
            <td align="right">
              <input type="submit" name="AddProductReview" value="Add review" />
            </td>
          </tr>
        </table>
      </td>
    </tr>
  </table>
</form>
{else}
<span>
  <strong>You must log in to add a review.<strong/>
</span>
```

```
    {/if}
```

2. Create the `presentation/smarty_plugins/function.load_reviews.php` file, and add the
   following in it:

```php
<?php
// Plugin functions inside plugin files must be named: smarty_type_name
function smarty_function_load_reviews($params, $smarty)
{
  // Create Reviews object
  $reviews = new Reviews();
  $reviews->init();

  // Assign template variable
  $smarty->assign($params['assign'], $reviews);
}


// Class that handles product reviews
class Reviews
{
  public $mProductId;
  public $mReviews;
  public $mTotalReviews;
  public $mReviewerName;
  public $mEnableAddProductReviewForm = false;
  public $mAddProductReviewTarget = 'index.php';

  public function __construct()
  {
    if (isset ($_GET['ProductID']))
      $this->mProductId = (int)$_GET['ProductID'];
    else
      trigger_error('ProductID not set', E_USER_ERROR);

    $this->mAddProductReviewTarget .= '?ProductID=' . $this->mProductId;
  }

  public function init()
  {
    // If visitor is logged in ...
    if (Customer::IsAuthenticated())
    {
      // Check if visitor is adding a review
      if (isset($_POST['AddProductReview']))
        Catalog::CreateProductReview(Customer::GetCurrentCustomerId(),
                                     $this->mProductId, $_POST['review'],
                                     $_POST['rating']);
```

```
            // Display "add review" form because visitor is registered
            $this->mEnableAddProductReviewForm = true;

            // Get visitor's (reviewer's) name
            $customer_data = Customer::Get();
            $this->mReviewerName = $customer_data['name'];
        }

        // Get reviews for this product
        $this->mReviews = Catalog::GetProductReviews($this->mProductId);

        // Get the number of the reviews
        $this->mTotalReviews = count($this->mReviews);
    }
}
?>
```

3. Open presentation/templates/product.tpl, and add the following lines at the end of it:

```
<br /><br />
{include file="reviews.tpl"}
```

4. Add the following styles at the end of hatshop.css:

```
ul
{
  list-style-type: none;
  padding: 0px;
}
li span
{
  background: #ccddff;
  display: block;
  padding: 5px;
}
.add_review tr td
{
  background: #e6e6e6;
  border: none;
}
```

5. Load `index.php` in your browser, click on a product to view its product details page, and admire the results (refer to Figure 16-1 at the beginning of this chapter). You must be logged in to add new reviews.

How It Works: The reviews Componentized Template

The reviews componentized template takes care of both displaying the reviews and adding a new review. The first part of the `reviews.tpl` file determines whether you have any reviews to display for the current product. If you don't, a short message appears encouraging your visitor to write the first review.

```
{if $reviews->mTotalReviews != 0}
<span class="description">Customer reviews:</span><br />
[a list with reviews]
{else}
<span class="description">
  Be the first person to voice your opinion!<br /><br />
</span>
{/if}
```

The second part of the template displays a form to add a review or a message that invites your visitor to "log in" to be able to add a review:

```
{if $reviews->mEnableAddProductReviewForm}
{* add review form *}
<span class="description"> Add a review:</span><br /><br />
[add review form]
{else}
<span>
  <strong>You must log in to add a review.<strong/>
</span>
{/if}
```

The code from the function plugin is pretty straightforward and should not be a problem for you.

Summary

Yep, it was that simple. Although you might want to add certain improvements for your own solution (for example, allow the visitors to edit their reviews, or forbid them from adding more reviews), the base is there, and it works as expected.

You're now all set to proceed to the final chapter of this book, where you'll learn how to sell items to your customer from Amazon.com by using XML Web Services.

CHAPTER 17

■■■

Connecting to Web Services

In the dynamic world of the Internet, sometimes it isn't enough to just have an important web presence; you also need to interact with functionality provided by third parties to achieve your goals. So far in this book, you already saw how to integrate external functionality to process payments from your customers.

In this chapter, you'll learn new possibilities for integrating features from an external source through a Web Service. A **Web Service** is a piece of functionality that is exposed through a web interface using standard Internet protocols such as HTTP. The messages exchanged by the client and the server are encoded using an XML-based protocol named SOAP (Simple Object Access Protocol) or by using REST (Representational State Transfer). These messages are sent over HTTP. You'll learn more about these technologies a bit later.

The beauty of using Web Services is that the client and the server can use any technology, any language, and any platform. As long as they exchange information with a standard protocol such as SOAP over HTTP, there is no problem if the client is a cell phone, and the server is a Java application running on Solaris, for example.

The possibilities are exciting, and we recommend you purchase a book that specializes in Web Services to discover more about their world. Have a look at the list of public Web Services at http://www.xmethods.net/ to get an idea of the kinds of external functionality you can integrate into your application.

In this chapter, you'll learn how to integrate the **Amazon E-Commerce Service** (ECS; Web Services interface provided by Amazon.com, formerly known as Amazon Web Services—AWS) to sell Amazon.com products through your HatShop web site.

You already have an e-commerce web site that sells hats to its customers. You can go further and make some more money from their passion for hats by incorporating some other kinds of hats-related gifts from Amazon.com into your site. For free? Oh no . . . You'll display Amazon.com's details on your site, but the final checkout will be processed by Amazon.com, and Amazon.com will deliver in your bank account a small commission fee for purchases made from your web site. Sounds like easy money, doesn't it?

In this chapter, you'll learn how to use ECS to add a special department called Amazon Super Hats to your web store, which you can see in Figure 17-1. This will be a "special" department in that it will be handled differently from others—for example, payment is handled directly by Amazon when the visitor wants to buy a product. This chapter explores just a small subset of ECS's capabilities, so if you really want to make a fortune from this service, you should dig deeper to find more substance.

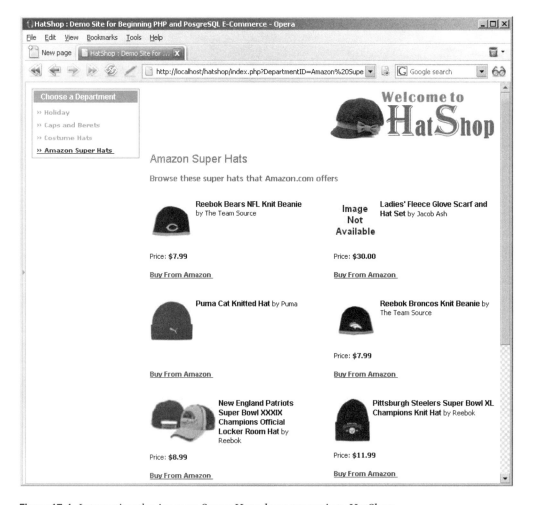

Figure 17-1. *Integrating the Amazon Super Hats department into HatShop*

The rest of the chapter is divided into two parts. In the first part, you'll learn how to access the Amazon E-Commerce Service (ECS); in the second part, you'll integrate ECS into the HatShop web site.

■**Tip** The code in this chapter is independent of the rest of the site, so all you need to get started integrating Amazon functionality is the code from the first four chapters (so you have a working product catalog). Of course, with minor adjustments you can also adapt this code to your own personal solutions.

Accessing the Amazon E-Commerce Service

Most service providers (including Amazon.com) use SOAP or REST (or both) to expose Web Services to Internet client programs. You can choose to make a Web Service request by using either REST or SOAP, and you get the exact same results with both options. In this chapter, you'll learn how to access ECS 4.0 using both REST and SOAP.

REST (Representational State Transfer) uses carefully crafted URLs with specific name-value pairs to call specific methods on the servers. You can find two useful articles about REST at `http://www.xml.com/pub/a/2004/08/11/rest.html` and `http://www.onlamp.com/pub/a/php/2003/10/30/amazon_rest.html`.

REST is considered to be the easiest way to communicate with the Web Services that expose this interface. Nonofficial sources say that 85% of ECS clients went the REST way. When using REST, all you have to do to perform an Amazon search is to make a classical HTTP `GET` request, and you'll receive the response in XML format.

SOAP (Simple Object Access Protocol) is an XML-based standard for encoding the information transferred in a Web Service request or response. SOAP is fostered by a number of organizations, including powerful companies such as Microsoft, IBM, and Sun.

When accessing ECS, you can send the request either through REST or by sending a SOAP message. The Web Service will return an XML response with the data you requested.

You'll learn more about REST and SOAP by playing with ECS.

■**Note** You need to understand that in this chapter we'll touch just a bit of the functionality provided by the Amazon ECS. A serious discussion on the subject would probably need a separate book, but what you'll see in this chapter is enough to get you on the right track. Also, be aware that in this chapter we integrate functionality from Amazon.com, but using the same Amazon ECS account, you can access services from `Amazon.fr`, `Amazon.ca`, `Amazon.de`, `Amazon.co.jp`, and `Amazon.co.uk`.

Creating Your Amazon E-Commerce Service Account

The official ECS web site is located at `http://www.amazon.com/webservices`. You can find the latest version of the documentation at `http://developer.amazonwebservices.com/connect/`— be sure to bookmark this URL because you'll find it very useful.

Before moving on, you need to create your account with the Amazon ECS. To access ECS, you need an *Access Key ID*, which identifies your account in the ECS system. If you don't already have one, apply now at `http://www.amazon.com/gp/aws/registration/registration-form.html`. The Access Key ID is a 20-character alphanumeric string.

■**Note** Before October 11, 2005, Amazon used to provide something called a Subscription ID, instead of an Access Key ID. The purpose is similar, and if you already have a Subscription ID, you may continue using it. For any new applications, Amazon encourages you to use the Access Key ID.

The Access Key ID gives you access to more Amazon Web Services and Alexa Web Services (Alexa is a service owned by Amazon), as you can see in Figure 17-2. To access some of these services, you'll also need a *Secret Access Key*, which you also get upon registration, but the Secret Access Key isn't required when working with ECS.

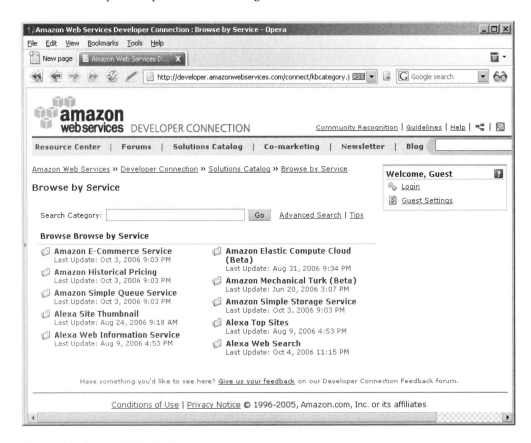

Figure 17-2. *Amazon Web Services*

Obtaining an Amazon Associate ID

The Access Key ID you created earlier is your key to retrieving data through the Amazon ECS. This data allows you to compose the Amazon Super Hats department that you saw in Figure 17-1.

What the Access Key ID can't do is give you a commission from the Amazon.com products that you sell through your web site. To obtain your money, you need to apply for an **Associate ID**. The Associate ID is used in the Buy From Amazon links you'll display in your special Amazon department, and it's the key that Amazon uses to identify you as the origin of that sale.

The Associate ID can even be used in the static web pages that contain links to Amazon.com products, and it doesn't require you to also have an ECS Access Key ID, which has different purposes.

So before moving further, if you want to make any money out of your Amazon Super Hats department, go get your Associate ID from http://associates.amazon.com/gp/associates/apply/main.html. Otherwise, if at the moment you're just interested in learning about the ECS, feel free to skip this step now.

Accessing Amazon E-Commerce Service Using REST

REST Web Services are accessed by requesting a properly formed URL. Try the following link in your browser (don't forget to replace the string [Your Access Key ID] with your real Access Key ID that you obtained earlier):

```
http://webservices.amazon.com/onca/xml?Service=AWSECommerceService
&AWSAccessKeyId=[Your Access Key ID]
&Operation=ItemLookup
&IdType=ASIN
&ItemId=159059648X
```

■**Tip** Make sure you type the entire URL on a single line; we've broken it down to individual elements to make them easier to read.

Your browser will display an XML structure with information about the book you are reading now. Figure 17-3 shows this XML structure in Firefox, which nicely displays the XML document tree.

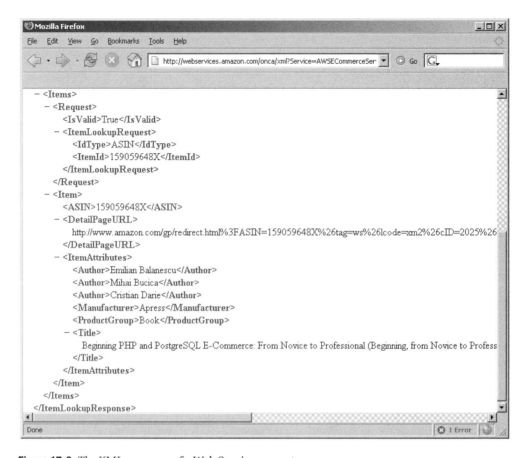

Figure 17-3. *The XML response of a Web Service request*

Pretty cool, huh? You have just seen REST in action. Every product in the Amazon database has a unique identifier called an ASIN (Amazon.com Standard Item Number). For books, the ASIN is the book's ISBN (this book has the ASIN 159059648X).

The Web Service request you just made tells ECS the following: I have an Access Key ID (AWSAccessKeyId=[Your Access Key ID]), and I want to make an item lookup operation (&Operation=ItemLookup) to learn more about the product with the 159059648X ASIN (&IdType=ASIN&ItemId=159059648X).

You didn't get much information about this book in this example—no price or availability information and no links to the cover picture or customer reviews. ECS 4.0 introduced a finer control of the data you want to receive using response groups (a response group is a set of information about the product).

■**Note** At the time of writing, ECS offers a list of more than 35 possible response groups. In this book, we'll only explain the purpose of the response groups we're using for HatShop; for the complete list, visit the ECS documentation.

So let's ask for some more data by using response groups. At the end of the link you've composed earlier, add the following string to get more specific information about the book: `&ResponseGroup=Request,SalesRank,Small,Images,OfferSummary`. The complete link should look like this:

```
http://webservices.amazon.com/onca/xml?Service=AWSECommerceService
&AWSAccessKeyId=[Your Access Key ID]
&Operation=ItemLookup
&IdType=ASIN
&ItemId=159059648X
&ResponseGroup=Request,SalesRank,Small,Images,OfferSummary
```

The new XML response from Amazon.com includes more details about the Amazon.com item, as shown in Figure 17-4.

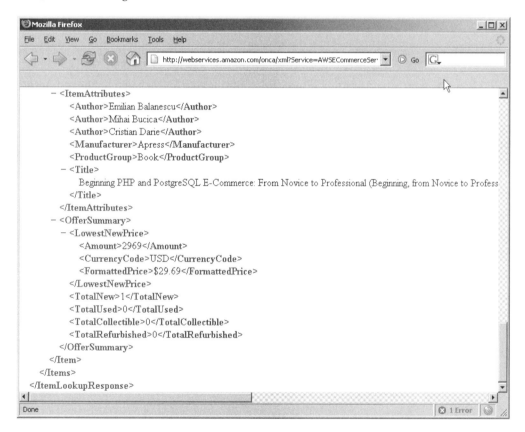

Figure 17-4. *The XML response of a Web Service request*

We have just mixed five response groups: Request, SalesRank, Small, Images, and OfferSummary. To learn more about the response groups, go to `http://developer.` `amazonwebservices.com/connect/kbcategory.jspa?categoryID=5`, and click the Latest Tech. Docs button. Alternatively, you can click the `Technical Documentation` link, and then click the link of the latest documentation version. You can download the documentation in PDF format, or you can read it online here: `http://docs.amazonwebservices.com/ AWSEcommerceService/2006-09-13/`.

In the ECS documentation, find the response groups details under the API Reference, Response Groups section. Here's the description for the five response groups used in the previous example:

- Request response group is a default response group in every kind of operation, and it returns the list of name-value pairs you used to make the request.

- Sales Rank response group returns data about the current Amazon.com sales rank of the product.

- Small response group returns general item data (ASIN, item name, URL, and so on) about items included in the response. This is a default response group for an `Item-Lookup` operation (like we have in this example).

- Images response group gives you the addresses for the three pictures (small, medium, and large) for each item in the response.

- OfferSummary response group returns price information for each item in the response.

Let's continue by learning how to make a REST request from PHP. To populate the future Amazon Super Hats department, you'll search the Amazon.com Apparel department for the "super hats" keywords. One trivial way is to use the PHP `file_get_contents` function, as you can see in the following script.

To test accessing Web Services using REST, create a new file named `test_rest.php` in your `hatshop` directory, and write the following code in it:

```php
<?php
// Tell the browser it is going to receive an XML document.
header('Content-type: text/xml');

/* DON'T FORGET to replace the string '[Your Access Key ID]' with your
   Access Key ID in the following line */
$url = 'http://webservices.amazon.com/onca/xml?Service=AWSECommerceService' .
       '&AWSAccessKeyId=[Your Access Key ID]' .
       '&Operation=ItemSearch' .
       '&Keywords=super+hats' .
       '&SearchIndex=Apparel' .
       '&ResponseGroup=Request,Medium';

echo file_get_contents($url);
?>
```

■Note Some PHP installations and web hosting providers may not allow this code to run by default. In that case, you can change this setting in php.ini:

```
allow_url_fopen = On
```

Alternatively, you can add the following line to `include/config.php`. This second solution is preferred because it only affects your application, and it remains set if you need to move the application to another server.

```
ini_set('allow_url_fopen', 'On');
```

Loading `http://localhost/hatshop/test_rest.php` will show you XML data about Amazon's Super Hats (see Figure 17-5).

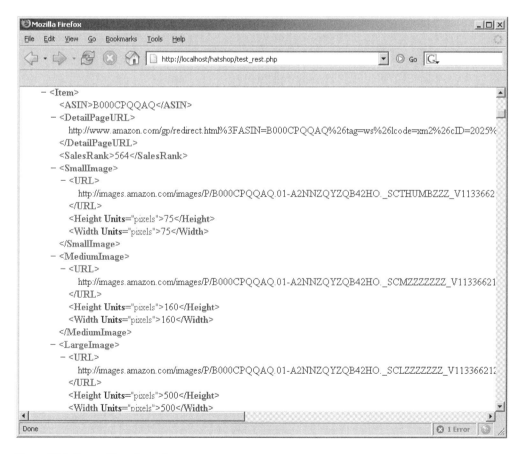

Figure 17-5. *Super Hats from Amazon*

To exercise and build more XML links, just study the examples in the "API Reference" section of the ECS 4.0 documentation. The material will show you how to do a variety of Amazon operations using REST.

Accessing Amazon E-Commerce Service Using SOAP

Using SOAP, you use a complex API to access the needed Amazon.com functionality. The following code, which performs the same search operation for hats that you did earlier with REST, is using the `AWSECommerceService`, `ItemSearch`, and `ItemSearchRequest` objects from the Amazon API to perform the operation.

■Tip To access the Amazon server using SOAP, we use the PHP SOAP extension. The documentation of the PHP SOAP functionality can be found at `http://www.php.net/soap/`. Consult Appendix A to ensure you have SOAP support enabled in your PHP installation.

To test accessing Web Services using SOAP, create a new file named `test_soap.php` in your hatshop directory, and write the following code in it:

```php
<?php
try
{
  // Initialize SOAP client object
  $client = new SoapClient(
    'http://webservices.amazon.com/AWSECommerceService/AWSECommerceService.wsdl');

  /* DON'T FORGET to replace the string '[Your Access Key ID]' with your
     subscription ID in the following line */
  $request = array ('Service' => 'AWSECommerceService',
                    'AWSAccessKeyId' => '[Your Access Key ID]',
                    'Request' => array ('Operation' => 'ItemSearchRequest',
                                        'Keywords' => 'super+hats',
                                        'SearchIndex' => 'Apparel',
                                        'ResponseGroup' => array ('Request',
                                                                  'Medium')));

  $result = $client->ItemSearch($request);

  echo '<pre>';
  print_r($result);
  echo '</pre>';
}
catch (SoapFault $fault)
{
  trigger_error('SOAP Fault: (faultcode: ' . $fault->faultcode . ', ' .
                'faultstring: ' . $fault->faultstring . ')', E_USER_ERROR);
}
?>
```

The whole SOAP request code is enclosed in a `try` block. If the SOAP request fails, it throws an exception of the `SoapFault` type, which we transform into an error using the `trigger_error()` function. Read more on the SOAP exception at `http://www.php.net/manual/en/function.is-soap-fault.php`.

The result of the SOAP request is an object containing the requested data. If you load `test_soap.php` in your browser (don't forget to put your Access Key ID in it), it should display the data in a text format that's not easy to read by the human eye.

The code starts by creating a SOAP client object to the Amazon SOAP Web Service:

```
// Initialize SOAP client object
$client = new SoapClient(
  'http://webservices.amazon.com/AWSECommerceService/AWSECommerceService.wsdl');
```

The referenced WSDL (Web Services Definition Language) file describes all the functions and their parameters' types that Amazon SOAP server understands. The earlier created Amazon SOAP client object knows about all these functions, and you can call them now using something like this:

```
$result = $client->ItemSearch($request);
```

Alternatively, you can make the exact same call, and implicitly obtain the same results, by using the `__soapCall` function (`http://www.php.net/manual/en/function.soap-soapclient-soapcall.php`), like this:

```
$result->__soapCall('ItemSearch', array ($request));
```

The Web Service request does an `ItemSearch` operation on the "super+hats" keywords in the "Apparel" store. The whole request is placed in a `try-catch` block that catches any potential exceptions and generates an error. Read more on the SoapFault exception class, which contains the details of the SOAP error, at `http://www.php.net/manual/en/function.is-soap-fault.php`. Loading `test_soap.php` would generate the result shown in Figure 17-6.

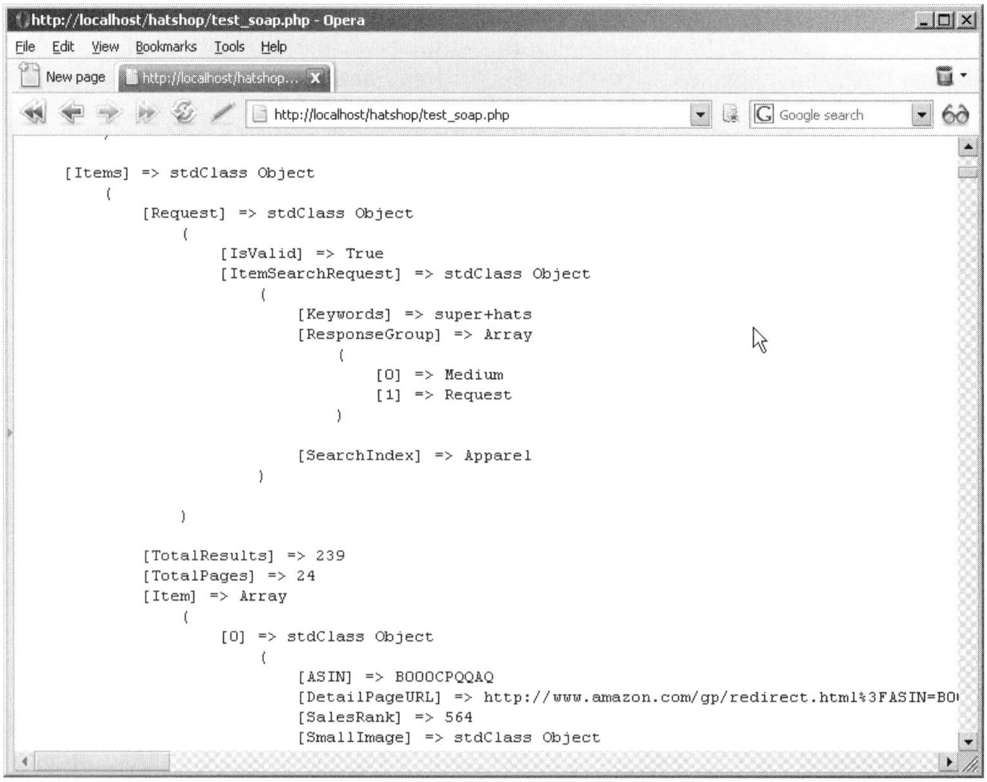

Figure 17-6. *The results of the SOAP request*

Integrating Amazon E-Commerce Service with HatShop

The goal is to bring some books related to "super hats" from Amazon to your store. You'll build a special department with no categories that will display some book info (cover image, title, authors, and price). Each book will have a Buy from Amazon link that allows your visitor to buy the book from Amazon.com. If you apply for an Amazon Associates ID account, you'll get a small commission from this. After following the exercises, you'll implement the Amazon integration as shown earlier in Figure 17-1.

The following link engages a REST search for Amazon Books on the "super hats" keywords and returns the first ten products' data sorted by their sales rank:

```
http://webservices.amazon.com/onca/xml?Service=AWSECommerceService
&Operation=ItemSearch
&AWSAccessKeyId=[Your Access Key ID]
&Keywords=super+hat
```

```
&SearchIndex=Apparel
&ResponseGroup=Request%2CMedium%2CImages%2COffers&Sort=salesrank
```

From these products, we will place on our site only the ones available for purchase and with cover images.

Implementing the Business Tier

In the business tier, you'll add the code that accesses the ECS system.

Exercise: Adding ECS Communication Code to the Business Tier

1. Add the following code in your `include/config.php` file:

```php
// Amazon E-Commerce Service
// define('AMAZON_METHOD', 'REST');
define('AMAZON_METHOD', 'SOAP');
define('AMAZON_WSDL',
  'http://webservices.amazon.com/AWSECommerceService/AWSECommerceService.wsdl');
define('AMAZON_REST_BASE_URL',
  'http://webservices.amazon.com/onca/xml?Service=AWSECommerceService');

// Set Amazon Access Key ID
define('AMAZON_ACCESS_KEY_ID', '[Your Access Key ID]');

// Set Amazon Associates ID
define('AMAZON_ASSOCIATES_ID', '[Your amazon associates ID]');

// Set Amazon request options
define('AMAZON_SEARCH_KEYWORDS', 'super hat');
define('AMAZON_SEARCH_NODE', 'Apparel');
define('AMAZON_RESPONSE_GROUPS', 'Request,Medium');
```

2. Create a new file named `amazon.php` in the `business` folder, and add the following code to it. The single public method, which will be called from the upper tiers, is `GetProducts`, whereas the others are private methods for internal use that support the functionality of `GetProducts`.

```php
<?php
// Class for accessing ECS
class Amazon
{
  public function Amazon()
  {
  }

  // Retrieves Amazon products for sending to presentation tier
  public function GetProducts()
  {
```

```php
  // Use SOAP to get data
  if (AMAZON_METHOD == 'SOAP')
    $result = $this->GetDataWithSoap();
  // Use REST to get data
  else
    $result = $this->GetDataWithRest();

  // Initializes Array object
  $results = array ();

  // Format results
  $results = $this->DataFormat($result);

  // Returns results
  return $results;
}

// Call ECS using REST
private function GetDataWithRest()
{
  $params = array ('Operation'      => 'ItemSearch',
                   'SubscriptionId' => AMAZON_ACCESS_KEY_ID,
                   'Keywords'       => AMAZON_SEARCH_KEYWORDS,
                   'SearchIndex'    => AMAZON_SEARCH_NODE,
                   'ResponseGroup'  => AMAZON_RESPONSE_GROUPS,
                   'Sort'           => 'salesrank');

  $query_string = '&';
  foreach ($params as $key => $value)
    $query_string .= $key . '=' . urlencode($value) . '&';

  $amazon_url = AMAZON_REST_BASE_URL . $query_string;

  // Get the XML response using REST
  $amazon_xml = file_get_contents($amazon_url);

  // Unserialize the XML and return
  return simplexml_load_string($amazon_xml);
}

// Call ECS using SOAP
private function GetDataWithSoap()
{
  try
  {
    $client = new SoapClient(AMAZON_WSDL);
```

```
      /* Set up an array containing input parameters to be
         passed to the remote procedure */
      $request = array ('SubscriptionId' => AMAZON_ACCESS_KEY_ID,
                        'Request' => array ('Operation' => 'ItemSearchRequest',
                                            'Keywords' =>
                                              AMAZON_SEARCH_KEYWORDS,
                                            'SearchIndex' => AMAZON_SEARCH_NODE,
                                            'ResponseGroup' =>
                                              AMAZON_RESPONSE_GROUPS,
                                            'Sort' => 'salesrank'));

      // Invoke the method
      $result = $client->ItemSearch($request);

      return $result;
    }
    catch (SoapFault $fault)
    {
      trigger_error('SOAP Fault: (faultcode: ' . $fault->faultcode . ', ' .
                    'faultstring: ' . $fault->faultstring . ')', E_USER_ERROR);
    }
  }

  /* Places an "image not available" picture for products with no image,
     and saves the results in an array with a simple structure for easier
     handling at the upper levels */
  private function DataFormat($result)
  {
    /* Variable k is the index of the $new_result array, which will
       contain the Amazon products to be displayed in HatShop */
    $k = 0;

    $new_result = array ();

    /* Analyze all products retrieved from ECS
       and save them into the $new_result array */
    for ($i = 0; $i < count($result->Items->Item); $i++)
    {
      // Make a temporary copy for product data
      $temp = $result->Items->Item[$i];

      /* Set product's image to images/not_available.jpg,
         if image url is empty */
      if (property_exists($temp, 'SmallImage') &&
          ((string) $temp->SmallImage->URL) != '')
        $new_result[$k]['image'] = (string) $temp->SmallImage->URL;
      else
```

```
            $new_result[$k]['image'] = 'images/not_available.jpg';

        // Save asin, brand, name, and price into the $new_result array
        $new_result[$k]['asin'] = (string) $temp->ASIN;
        $new_result[$k]['brand'] = (string) $temp->ItemAttributes->Brand;
        $new_result[$k]['item_name'] = (string) $temp->ItemAttributes->Title;

        if (property_exists($temp->OfferSummary, 'LowestNewPrice'))
          $new_result[$k]['price'] =
            (string) $temp->OfferSummary->LowestNewPrice->FormattedPrice;
        elseif (property_exists($temp->ItemAttributes, 'ListPrice'))
          $new_result[$k]['price'] =
            (string) $temp->ItemAttributes->ListPrice->FormattedPrice;
        else
          $new_result[$k]['price'] = '';

        $k++;
      }

    return $new_result;
    }
  }
?>
```

<hr>

How It Works: Communicating with ECS

The only public Amazon business tier method is GetProducts() that takes care to retrieve data. Its functionality is quite clear, as it uses a number of helper methods to get the work done. First, it decides whether it should use SOAP or REST depending on the configuration setting you've added to include/config.php.

The AMAZON_METHOD constant you defined in include/config.php instructs whether ECS will be contacted through REST or SOAP. The value of that constant (which should be REST or SOAP) decides whether GetDataWithRest() or GetDataWithSoap() will be used to contact Amazon. No matter which method you choose, the results should be the same:

```
// Retrieves Amazon products for sending to presentation tier
public function GetProducts()
{
  // Use SOAP to get data
  if (AMAZON_METHOD == 'SOAP')
    $result = $this->GetDataWithSoap();
  // Use REST to get data
  else
    $result = $this->GetDataWithRest();
```

GetDataWithSoap() and GetDataWithRest() return the list of products as an object. Then, we use the DataFormat() method to parse the data from this object and return that data in the form of an associative array. The DataFormat() method also places an "image not available" image for the Amazon products that don't have a product image.

```
  // Initializes Array object
  $results = array ();

  // Format results
  $results = $this->DataFormat($result);

  // Returns results
  return $results;
}
```

Let's have a look now at `GetAmazonDataWithRest()` and `GetAmazonDataWithSoap()`, which are the methods that do the actual communication with ECS. `GetAmazonDataWithRest()` retrieves Web Service data using REST. It starts by constructing the required query string by joining the individual parameters you want to send to Amazon:

```
// Call ECS using REST
private function GetDataWithRest()
{
  $params = array ('Operation'      => 'ItemSearch',
                   'SubscriptionId' => AMAZON_ACCESS_KEY_ID,
                   'Keywords'       => AMAZON_SEARCH_KEYWORDS,
                   'SearchIndex'    => AMAZON_SEARCH_NODE,
                   'ResponseGroup'  => AMAZON_RESPONSE_GROUPS,
                   'Sort'           => 'salesrank');
  $query_string = '&';
  foreach ($params as $key => $value)
    $query_string .= $key . '=' . urlencode($value) . '&';
```

The complete Amazon URL that you need to call is composed of the base URL (which you saved as a constant in `include/config.php`) to which you append the query string you just built:

```
$amazon_url = AMAZON_REST_BASE_URL . $query_string;
```

Using the `file_get_contents()` function, you make a simple HTTP GET request to Amazon. It's just like typing the address in your browser:

```
// Get the XML response using REST
$amazon_xml = file_get_contents($amazon_url);
```

The `$amazon_xml` variable will contain a string with the returned XML data. To further process it, we use the `simplexml_load_string()` function that parses the XML text and returns a `SimpleXMLElement` object representing the XML document. Read more details at `http://www.php.net/manual/en/function.simplexml-load-string.php`.

```
// Unserialize the XML and return
return simplexml_load_string($amazon_xml);
}
```

The `GetAmazonDataWithSoap()` method has similar functionality as `GetAmazonDataWithRest()`, but it makes the `ItemSearch` operation using SOAP. The logic this method uses to contact ECS is the same as in the page you wrote earlier in this chapter.

Implementing the Presentation Tier

Let's create the componentized template that will display the hats and then modify the
departments_list componentized template to include this new department.

Exercise: Displaying Amazon.com Products in HatShop

1. Add a new file named amazon_products_list.tpl in the presentation/templates folder of your
project, and add the following code in it:

```
{* amazon_products_list.tpl *}
{load_amazon_products_list assign="amazon_products_list"}
<p class="title">{$amazon_products_list->mDepartmentName}</p>
<br />
<p class="description">{$amazon_products_list->mDepartmentDescription}</p>
{section name=k loop=$amazon_products_list->mProducts}
  {assign var=direction_p value="left"}
  {if  $smarty.section.k.index != 0 &&
      ($smarty.section.k.index + 1) % 2 == 0}
    {assign var=direction_p value="right"}
  {else}
    <br />
  {/if}
  <p class="{$direction_p}">
    <br />
    <img src="{$amazon_products_list->mProducts[k].image}"
     border="0" height="70" alt="Product image" class="product_image" />
    <span class="small_title">
      {$amazon_products_list->mProducts[k].item_name}
    </span>
    <span>
      by {$amazon_products_list->mProducts[k].brand}
    </span>
    <br /><br />
    {if $amazon_products_list->mProducts[k].price}
    <span>Price:</span>
    <span class="price">
      {$amazon_products_list->mProducts[k].price}
    </span>
    {/if}
    <br /><br />
    <a class="small_link" target="_blank"
     href="{$amazon_products_list->mProducts[k].link}">
      Buy From Amazon
    </a>
  </p>
{/section}
```

2. Create a new file named function.load_amazon_products_list.php in the presentation/smarty_plugins folder, and add the following code in it:

```php
<?php
// Plugin functions inside plugin files must be named: smarty_type_name
function smarty_function_load_amazon_products_list($params, $smarty)
{
  // Create AmazonProductsList object
  $amazon_products_list = new AmazonProductsList();
  $amazon_products_list->init();

  // Assign template variable
  $smarty->assign($params['assign'], $amazon_products_list);
}

// Class that handles receiving ECS data
class AmazonProductsList
{
  // Public variables available in smarty template
  public $mProducts;
  public $mDepartmentName;
  public $mDepartmentDescription;

  // Constructor
  public function __construct()
  {
    $this->mDepartmentName = AMAZON_DEPARTMENT_TITLE;
    $this->mDepartmentDescription = AMAZON_DEPARTMENT_DESCRIPTION;
  }

  public function init()
  {
    $amazon = new Amazon();
    $this->mProducts = $amazon->GetProducts();

    for ($i = 0;$i < count($this->mProducts); $i++)
      $this->mProducts[$i]['link'] =
        'http://www.amazon.com/exec/obidos/ASIN/' .
        $this->mProducts[$i]['asin'] .
        '/ref=nosim/' . AMAZON_ASSOCIATES_ID;
  }
}
?>
```

3. Add the following styles at the end of hatshop.css:

```css
.small_title
{
  font-family: arial, tahoma, verdana;
```

```
      font-size: 12px;
      font-weight: bold;
    }
    a.small_link
    {
      color: #0000ff;
      font-family: arial, tahoma, verdana;
      font-size: 11px;
      text-decoration: underline;
    }
    a.small_link:hover
    {
      color: #0000ff;
      font-family: arial, tahoma, verdana;
      font-size: 11px;
    }
```

4. Add the following two configuration lines at the end of your `include/config.php` file:

```
// Amazon.com department configuration options
define('AMAZON_DEPARTMENT_TITLE', 'Amazon Super Hats');
define('AMAZON_DEPARTMENT_DESCRIPTION',
        'Browse these super hats that Amazon.com offers');
```

5. Modify the `presentation/templates/departments_list.tpl` template file to add the Amazon Super Hats department. Add the highlighted code as shown here:

```
        {* Generate a link for a new department in the list *}
        <a {$selected_d}
         href="{$departments_list->mDepartments[i].link|prepare_link:"http"}">
          &raquo; {$departments_list->mDepartments[i].name}
        </a>
      </li>
    {/section}
      {assign var=selected_d value=""}
      {if $departments_list->mAmazonSelected}
        {assign var=selected_d value="class=\"selected\""}
      {/if}
      <li>
        <a {$selected_d}
         href="{$departments_list->mAmazonDepartmentLink|prepare_link:"http"}">
          &raquo; {$departments_list->mAmazonDepartmentName}
        </a>
      </li>
    </ol>
</div>
{* End departments list *}
```

6. Update `presentation/smarty_plugins/function.load_departments_list.php` as highlighted in this code snippet:

```
...
// Manages the departments list
class DepartmentsList
{
  /* Public variables available in departments_list.tpl Smarty template */
  public $mDepartments;
  public $mSelectedDepartment;
  public $mAmazonSelected = false;
  public $mAmazonDepartmentName;
  public $mAmazonDepartmentLink;

  // Constructor reads query string parameter
  public function __construct()
  {
    /* If DepartmentID exists in the query string, we're visiting a
       department */
    if (isset ($_GET['DepartmentID']))
      $this->mSelectedDepartment = (int)$_GET['DepartmentID'];
    else
      $this->mSelectedDepartment = -1;

    // Set Amazon department name and build the link for department
    $this->mAmazonDepartmentName = AMAZON_DEPARTMENT_TITLE;
    $this->mAmazonDepartmentLink = 'index.php?DepartmentID=' .
                                   AMAZON_DEPARTMENT_TITLE;

    // Check if the Amazon department is selected
    if ((isset ($_GET['DepartmentID'])) &&
        ((string) $_GET['DepartmentID'] == AMAZON_DEPARTMENT_TITLE))
      $this->mAmazonSelected = true;
  }
...
```

7. Update `include/app_top.php` to reference the new business tier class by adding the following code at the end of the file:

```
require_once BUSINESS_DIR . 'amazon.php';
```

8. Modify the `index.php` file to load the newly created componentized template:

```
...
// Load department details if visiting a department
if (isset ($_GET['DepartmentID']))
{
  if ((string) $_GET['DepartmentID'] == AMAZON_DEPARTMENT_TITLE)
    $pageContentsCell = 'amazon_products_list.tpl';
```

```
      else
      {
        $pageContentsCell = 'department.tpl';
        $categoriesCell = 'categories_list.tpl';
      }
    }
    ...
```

9. Load `index.php` in your browser, and then click on your newly created Amazon Super Hats department.

How It Works: Displaying Amazon.com Products in HatShop

In this exercise, you simply updated HatShop to display Amazon.com products by employing the techniques you studied in the first part of the chapter. The new functionality isn't especially complex, but the possibilities are exciting.

To change the access method, modify the following in `include/config.php`:

```
// Amazon E-Commerce Service
 define('AMAZON_METHOD', 'REST');
//define('AMAZON_METHOD', 'SOAP');
```

When `Buy From Amazon` links are clicked, Amazon.com associates that customer and what he or she purchases to your Associate ID (which is mentioned in the links). In the `init` method from the `AmazonProductsList` class, the `GetProducts` method from the `Amazon` class is called to get the data to populate the list of products. This data is read to build the Amazon links to the retrieved products:

```
  public function init()
  {
    $amazon = new Amazon();
    $this->mProducts = $amazon->GetProducts();

    for ($i = 0;$i < count($this->mProducts); $i++)
      $this->mProducts[$i]['link'] =
        'http://www.amazon.com/exec/obidos/ASIN/' .
        $this->mProducts[$i]['asin'] .
        '/ref=nosim/' . AMAZON_ASSOCIATES_ID;
  }
```

However, you must know that Amazon offers many ways in which you can allow your visitors to buy their products. If you log in to the Associates page, you'll see a number of link types you can build and integrate into your web site.

Perhaps the most interesting and powerful is the possibility to create and manage Amazon shopping carts from your PHP code by using the Amazon API. If you're really into integrating Amazon.com into your web site, you should study the ECS documentation carefully and make the most of it.

Summary

In this chapter, you learned how to access Amazon E-Commerce Service using REST and SOAP. You will be able to use the same techniques when accessing any kind of external functionality exposed through these protocols.

Congratulations, you have just finished your journey into learning about building e-commerce web sites with PHP and PostgreSQL. You have the knowledge to build your own customized solutions, perhaps even more interesting and powerful than what we showed you in this book. We hope you enjoyed reading this book, and we wish you good luck with your own personal PHP and PostgreSQL projects!

APPENDIX A

■ ■ ■

Installing Apache, PHP, and PostgreSQL

In this appendix, you'll learn how to install

- Apache 2.2

- PHP 5.1 and the extra modules required for this book

- PostgreSQL 8.1

These are the software versions this appendix has been tested with. You should, however, install the latest version of all software packages, understanding that the installation steps might slightly differ. We'll discuss installation under Windows and under Linux separately.

The HatShop application you'll develop in the book may work with older versions of the software too. It is very important that the PHP version is PHP 5.0 or more recent; the code uses OOP syntax that isn't recognized by older versions of PHP.

Because highly sensitive data such as credit card information must travel safely over the Web, it's critical to host your application on an SSL-powered web server. Also, the PHP installation must have these modules installed: CURL, mcrypt, mhash, SOAP, PDO, and PDO driver for PostgreSQL.

Preparing Your Windows Playground

In this section, you'll learn how to install Apache 2.2, PHP 5.1, and PostgreSQL 8.1 on your development machine.

In Windows, installing an SSL-enabled Apache is a little bit more complicated than installing Apache without SSL. You can follow this book even if you don't have an SSL-enabled Apache; if you choose to do so, you can skip to the upcoming "Installing Apache (No SSL)" section.

Installing SSL-Enabled Apache

The steps that follow will install Apache on port 80, so you must make sure you don't have another web server, such as IIS, running on port 80.

1. Download `httpd-2.2.3-win32-x86-ssl.zip`, or a more recent version, from `http://www.apachelounge.com/download/`.

2. Unpack the archive, and follow the steps in `Read Me First.txt`. Your Apache installation will reside in `C:\Apache2`, but `https://localhost` will not respond yet—there are still a few steps to follow.

3. Copy `ssleay32.dll` and `libeay32.dll` from `C:\Apache2\bin` to the `System32` folder of your Windows installation. (Typically, the full path to it is `C:\Windows\System32`).

4. Open a command prompt window, and navigate to the `C:\Apache2\bin` folder of your Apache installation, with a command that looks like

   ```
   cd C:\Apache2\bin
   ```

5. Execute the following command, eventually replacing `hatshop.csr` with another name (but be sure to keep the `.csr` extension):

   ```
   openssl req -config C:\Apache2\conf\openssl.cnf -new -out hatshop.csr
   ```

6. When asked for "Common Name (that is, your web site's domain name)," give the exact domain name of your web server (for example, `www.example.com`). If the name in the certificate doesn't match with the URL perfectly, the browsers will alert the users with a warning message.

7. Execute the following command:

   ```
   openssl rsa -in privkey.pem -out hatshop.key
   ```

8. Execute the following command:

   ```
   openssl x509 -in hatshop.csr -out hatshop.crt -req -signkey hatshop.key -days
   365
   ```

9. Create a directory in the Apache folder named `C:\Apache2\conf\ssl`, and move `hatshop.key` and `hatshop.crt` to it.

10. Open `C:\Apache2\conf\httpd.conf`, and uncomment the following lines:

    ```
    LoadModule ssl_module modules/mod_ssl.so
    Include conf/extra/httpd-ssl.conf
    ```

11. Open `C:\Apache2\conf\extra\httpd-ssl.conf`, find

    ```
    SSLCertificateFile c:/Apache2/conf/server.crt
    ```

    and change it to

    ```
    SSLCertificateFile c:/Apache2/conf/ssl/hatshop.crt
    ```

12. Also in `httpd-ssl.conf`, find

`SSLCertificateKeyFile c:/Apache2/conf/server.key`

and change it to

`SSLCertificateKeyFile c:/Apache2/conf/ssl/hatshop.key`

12. Restart Apache, and load `https://localhost`. You should get a simple "It Works" page.

Installing Apache (No SSL)

If you already have an SSL-enabled Apache installation, you don't need to go through these steps; instead, simply skip to installing PHP, in the next section.

Download the latest Win32 Binary (MSI Installer) version of the Apache HTTP Server from `http://httpd.apache.org/download.cgi`. The file will be named something like `apache_2.x.y-win32-x86-no_ssl.msi`. Execute the file.

At install time, you'll be given the option to choose the location to which your Apache web server should be installed. By default, this location is `C:\Program Files\Apache Software Foundation\Apache2.2\`, but you can choose a more convenient location (such as `C:\Apache2`) that will make your life working with Apache a tad easier.

After accepting the license agreement and reading the introductory text, you're asked to enter your server's information (see Figure A-1).

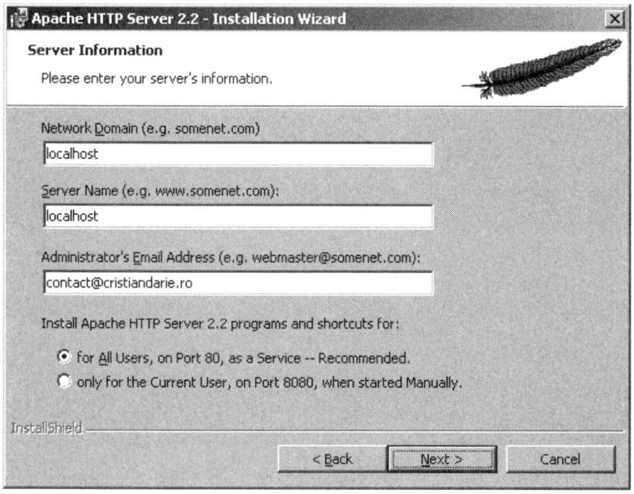

Figure A-1. *Installing Apache*

If you're not sure about how to complete the form, just use **localhost** for the first two fields, and enter an email address for the last. You can change this information later by editing the `httpd.conf` file (located in `C:\Program Files\Apache Software Foundation\ApacheX.Y\conf\httpd.conf` by default).

If you already have a web server (such as IIS) working on port 80, you'll need to install Apache on a different port. During installation, you have an option that specifies Apache should work "only for Current User, on Port 8080, when started manually." If you choose that option, you will need to start the Apache service manually by going to the folder you installed Apache to (by default, `C:\Program Files\Apache Software Foundation\Apache2.2\bin`), and typing the following:

```
apache -k install
```

You can use the default options in the other screens.

After installing the Apache service, you'll be able to see it in the Apache Service Monitor program (accessible from the taskbar), which also allows you to start, stop, or restart the Apache service. You'll need to restart (or stop and then start) the service after making changes to the `httpd.conf` configuration file.

After making sure the Apache2 service is started and running, test to make sure it works okay. If you installed it on port 80, browse to `http://localhost/`. If you installed it on 8080, go to `http://localhost:8080/`. You should see a welcome message that, for Apache 2.2, reads "It works!"

Installing PHP 5

Start by downloading the Windows binaries of the latest version of PHP from `http://www.php.net/downloads.php`. Don't use a PHP installer because it won't include the external extensions needed for HatShop.

Caution The code doesn't work with PHP 4 or older versions!

After you download the Windows binaries, follow these steps to install PHP:

1. Unzip the file (which should be named something like `php-5.x.y-win32.zip`) into a folder named `C:\PHP`. You can choose another name or location for this folder if you want.

2. Copy `php5ts.dll` from `C:\PHP` to `C:\Windows\System32` (or to your `System32` folder, if it has a different location).

3. Copy `php.ini-recommended` from `C:\PHP` to your Windows folder, renaming it as `php.ini`.

4. Uncomment the following lines from `php.ini` to enable the `mhash`, `mcrypt`, `curl`, `pdo`, and `soap` extensions. If any of these lines isn't present in the file, simply add it.

   ```
   extension=php_mhash.dll
   extension=php_mcrypt.dll
   extension=php_curl.dll

   extension=php_pdo.dll
   extension=php_pdo_pgsql.dll
   extension=php_soap.dll
   ```

5. Also in `php.ini`, find this line:

```
extension_dir = "./"
```

and change it to

```
extension_dir = "C:\PHP\ext"
```

6. Copy `libmhash.dll`, `libeay32.dll`, `ssleay32.dll`, and `libmcrypt.dll` from your PHP folder to the Windows System32 folder.

7. Open for editing, with any text editor (even Notepad), the Apache configuration file. The default location of this file is `conf\httpd.conf` under the Apache installation folder.

8. In `httpd.conf`, find the portion with many `LoadModule` entries, and add the following lines (the names may vary depending on your specific Apache and PHP versions):

```
LoadModule php5_module c:/php/php5apache2_2.dll
AddType application/x-httpd-php .php
```

▪**Note** If you don't have the `php5apach2_2.dll` file in your PHP folder, you can get it in the packages you can download from `http://snaps.php.net/`.

---

9. Also in `httpd.conf`, find the `DirectoryIndex` entry, and add `index.php` at the end of the line, like this:

```
DirectoryIndex index.html index.php
```

10. Save your changes in `httpd.conf`, then restart Apache 2. If you get any errors at this stage, you should check that you correctly implemented the previous steps.

11. To test that your PHP installation works, create a file named `test.php` in the `htdocs` folder of your Apache installation with a call to PHP's `phpinfo()` function:

```
<?php
phpinfo();
?>
```

12. Point your web browser to `http://localhost/test.php` (or `http://localhost:8080/test.php` if you installed Apache to work on port 8080) to test whether everything went okay with the installation. You should get a PHP information page similar to Figure 2-7 from Chapter 2.

Installing PostgreSQL

To install PostgreSQL, follow these simple steps. We tested these steps with PostgreSQL 8.1, but you should download the latest available version of PostgreSQL.

1. Visit http://www.postgresql.org/, and click the Downloads link from the menu.

3. Under the Download Core Distribution box, click Via FTP.

4. Select the binary directory from the list.

5. Select the folder for the latest available stable version.

6. Select win32.

7. Download the installer file, which is named something like postgresql-*version*.zip. You will then probably be asked to select a mirroring location. Choose one close to your current location.

8. Unzip the downloaded file, and execute the installer executable file.

9. In the first setup screen, choose your language, and click Start.

10. Use the default options in the first setup screens, but be sure to set the Account password in the Service configuration screen (see Figure A-2).

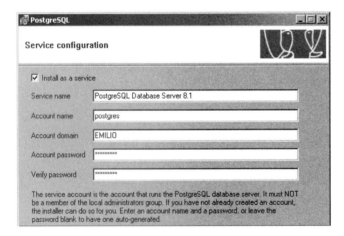

Figure A-2. *Testing the PHP installation*

11. After clicking Next, confirm the creation of the postgres user account in Windows. If you are warned about your password being weak, it's probably safe to say No when asked about replacing it with a random password during development on your local machine.

12. In the next screen, you're asked to configure the database cluster. Choose the settings depending on your particular requirements. For example, it may be safe to choose the default encoding to UTF-8 if you intend to store text that's not supported by the default encoding.

13. Click Next, make sure the selected procedural language PL/pgsql is selected, and click Next again.

14. In the Enable Contrib Modules screen, select TSearch2, which will be used for full-text searching, and click Next twice to install PostgreSQL.

Preparing Your Unix Playground

Almost all the Linux distributions include Apache, PHP, and PostgreSQL, however, you may have out-of-date versions of these programs. Before trying to download anything, you should check first whether you can find what you need on your system, online, or on the installation CDs of your Linux distribution. We don't have high requirements for Apache and PostgreSQL, so you can do a binary installation for them, but you'll have to compile PHP from sources to enable all the libraries you will need.

Installing Apache 2

The most common way to create an SSL-powered web server is to use Apache and OpenSSL. You probably have them installed on your system.

You should first check whether you have OpenSSL RPMs installed on your system with the following command:

```
rpm -qa | grep openssl
```

If you don't have OpenSSL, grab the following RPMs from a resource such as http://www.rpmfind.net/, and install them. Be sure to take the latest available versions.

```
openssl-version.rpm
openssl-devel-version.rpm
```

We decided to build the latest Apache Web Server (version 2.2.3 at the moment of writing) from sources. First, you should download the latest Unix Apache source from http://httpd.apache.org/download.cgi, and uncompress it with something like this:

```
tar -zxvf httpd-2.2.3.tar.gz
```

Now you can move on to actually compile and install the Apache Web Server on your system. Go to the root of the Apache sources, and execute the following commands (you need to be logged in as root when executing make install):

```
./configure --prefix=/usr/local/apache2 --enable-so --enable-ssl --with-ssl --
enable-auth-digest
make
make install
```

To enable SSL, you'll need to install an SSL certificate into Apache. If you host your application with a hosting company that offers SSL, you can do all testing on your development machine with a "fake" SSL certificate that you generate on your own. You can do this by making yourself a certificate authority. To generate your own certificate, you should follow some of the excellent tutorials you can find on the Internet, such as the one at http://www.linux.com/howtos/SSL-Certificates-HOWTO/index.shtml (you can also find many more using a simple web search). Otherwise, if you want to install an SSL certificate for production, you'll need to get a "real" SSL certificate from a certification authority such as VeriSign, as explained in Chapter 7.

Make any changes you need in the httpd.conf configuration file, and then start your Apache server with

```
/usr/local/apache2/bin/apachectl start
```

■**Note** If you get errors such as "module access_module is built in and can't be loaded," try to comment out the LoadModule line from the httpd.conf that corresponds to the module that generated the error. An even better method is to try to comment out every module that you don't need.

Now load http://localhost/ in your browser to make sure your Apache Web Server is up and running, and then browse to https://localhost/ to test that you can also access Apache through SSL.

Installing PostgreSQL 8

Follow these steps to install PostgreSQL on your system:

1. Download the PostgreSQL source code from http://www.postgresql.org/ftp/source/. For the purposes of this installation guide, we're using postgresql-8.1.5.tar.gz, but you should download the latest available version instead.

2. Unpack the archive with a command such as the following:

   ```
   tar -zxvf postgresql-8.1.5.tar.gz
   ```

3. Change context to the postgresq-8.1.5 folder:

   ```
   cd postgresql-8.1.5
   ```

4. Execute the following command to prepare PostgreSQL to install to /usr/local/pgsql:

   ```
   ./configure --prefix=/usr/local/pgsql
   ```

5. Make sure you're logged in as root (use the su command if necessary), and execute:

   ```
   make install
   ```

6. For security reasons, PostgreSQL won't allow root to start the server. Execute the following command to change the owner of all the files to `postgres`:

```
chown -R postgres:postgres /usr/local/pgsql
```

7. Log in as postgres, or use the `su` command, and then change the directory to `/usr/local/pgsql`:

```
cd /usr/local/pgsql
```

8. Initialize a database cluster with this command:

```
bin/initdb -D ./data
```

9. Start PostgreSQL with this command:

```
bin/pg_ctl -D ./data -l data/logfile start
```

10. Now that PostgreSQL is started, you need to create a database and another user before going any further. You should use a separate database for each of the projects to make things a little cleaner and easier to understand. You should also use separate users for each database. This keeps everything separate and "project a" won't be able to modify any of "project b's" data. To create a new user in PostgreSQL, it's pretty simple. Just use the following command and then follow the prompts:

```
/usr/local/pgsql/bin/createuser
```

The new user should not be able to create new databases or create new users. To create a database, it's a little different:

```
/usr/local/pgsql/bin/createdb --owner=username databasename
```

Installing pgAdmin III

pgAdmin III doesn't ship with the Linux version of PostgreSQL, as it does with the Windows version. Keeping in mind to replace the file names with the actual ones in case you use newer versions, here are the steps you should follow to install pgAdmin III on your Linux machine.

1. Download the source code for the pgAdmin III dependency wxWidgets from `http://wxwidgets.org/downloads/#latest_stable` (currently the version for pgAdmin III v1.4.3 is wxWidgets 2.6.3).

2. Unpack, build, and install the source code:

```
tar -zvxf wxWidgets*
cd wxWidgets*
./configure --with-gtk --enable-gtk2 --enable-unicode --enable-mimetype=no
make
make install
```

```
# Install wxWidgets contrib modules.
cd contrib/
make
make install
```

3. Download the latest version of pgAdmin III source code from `http://www.postgresql.org/ftp/pgadmin3/release`.

4. Unpack, build, and install the source code:

```
tar -zvxf pgadmin3-1.4.3.tar.gz
cd pgadmin3-1.4.3
./configure
make all
make install
```

Installing PHP 5

Every time you want to get a new PHP library working on Linux, you need to recompile the PHP module. That's why it's recommended to make a "good" compilation, with all the needed libraries, from the start.

Go to `http://www.php.net/downloads.php`, get the complete source code archive of PHP 5.x, and extract the contents in a directory.

Before compiling PHP and making Apache aware of it (by updating Apache's configuration file `httpd.conf`), you need to install the extra modules you'll need to work under PHP. Let's deal with them one by one.

mhash

The `mhash` library provides a uniform interface to a large number of hashing algorithms. You used it to hash customers' passwords in Chapter 11. Refer to that chapter to learn more about hashing.

Download `mhash` from `http://mhash.sourceforge.net/`, unpack it (using `tar -zxvf`), and install it by executing the following commands:

```
./configure
./make
./make install
```

Alternatively, if you use Red Hat, you can download the RPMs from `http://www.ottolander.nl/opensource/mhash/libmhash.html` and install them. We installed both `libmhash-0.8.18-2a.i386.rpm` and `libmhash-devel-0.8.18-2a.i386.rpm` RPMs.

mcrypt

This library allows you to use a wide range of encryption functions. You'll need it to encrypt highly sensitive information such as credit card details as discussed in Chapter 11. (Refer to Chapter 11 for more details about this.)

Download `mcrypt` from `http://mcrypt.sourceforge.net/`, unpack it (using `tar -zxvf`), and install it by executing the following commands:

```
./configure
./make
./make install
```

Alternatively, you can find the RPMs for Red Hat at `http://www.ottolander.nl/opensource/mcrypt/mcrypt.html`. We installed both `libmcrypt-2.5.7-1a.i386.rpm` and `libmcrypt-devel-2.5.7-1a.i386.rpm` RPMs.

Alternatively, you can use the source code from `http://mcrypt.sourceforge.net`.

CURL (Client URL Library) Functions

You'll use `libcurl`, a library that allows you to connect and communicate to many different types of servers with many different types of protocols. You need it to communicate through SSL with the payment gateways in Chapter 14. You can take a fresh version of the `curl` library from `http://curl.haxx.se/download.html`, but you can also use `http://www.rpmfind.net` to find the RPM packages for your system.

libxml2

PHP 5 requires a `libxml2` library version 2.5.10 or greater. If your Unix or Linux system doesn't have a recent enough version, go get fresh RPMs of `libxml2` and `libxml2-devel` from `http://xmlsoft.org/` and install them.

You can check for your `libxml2` library with the following command:

```
rpm -qa | grep libxml2
```

Compiling and Installing PHP 5

To compile and install PHP 5, follow these steps:

1. Go to the folder where you extracted the PHP source and execute the following commands:

```
./configure --with-config-file-path=/etc
            --with-pdo-pgsql=/usr/local/pgsql/bin/pg_config
            --with-apxs2=/usr/local/apache2/bin/apsx2
            --with-mcrypt --with-mhash
            --with-openssl-dir --with-curl --with-zlib
            --with-pdo --enable-soap
make
make install
```

2. Copy php.ini-recommended to /etc/php.ini by executing the following command:

```
cp php.ini-recommended /etc/php.ini
```

3. In httpd.conf, find the portion with many LoadModule entries, and add the following lines (the names may vary depending on your specific Apache and PHP versions):

```
LoadModule php5_module modules/libphp5.so
AddType application/x-httpd-php .php
```

4. Open the Apache configuration file (httpd.conf), find the DirectoryIndex entry, and make sure you have index.php at the end of the line:

```
DirectoryIndex index.html index.html.var index.php
```

5. Restart your Apache Web Server, and everything should be okay. To make sure your PHP installation works, create a file named test.php in the htdocs folder (by default, /usr/local/apache2/htdocs/), with the following content:

```
<?php
phpinfo();
?>
```

Finally, point your web browser to http://localhost/test.php to ensure PHP was correctly installed under Apache.

APPENDIX B

■■■

Project Management Considerations

It feels great to finish building a complete e-commerce store, doesn't it? For the purposes of this book, we dealt with many design issues on a chapter-by-chapter basis, while also covering the theory concepts. However, in real-world projects, many times, you'll need to consider the complete picture from the very start. This appendix discusses how to effectively manage building complete solutions.

Maybe it seems easier to just start coding without any upfront design, and with some luck, you might even create something that works on the second day; however, when it comes to large projects, you'll face a lot of problems in the long term by taking this route.

A project's life cycle includes much more than simply coding—it should not be done hastily. For example, for almost any real-world software project, a critical part of its success is the database design, even if it only counts for a small part of the project's development cycle. This makes perfect sense if you consider that e-commerce sites, web portals, search engines, and customer interfaces for service providers (banking, IT, insurance, and so on) are all basically interfaces to a backend database.

Of course, the way you display the data and the reports you present to the client also plays an important role in the success of the software. However, you can think of the database as the foundation of a house; if you make mistakes in the foundation, no matter how nice or trendy the house looks, it will still be torn down by the first gust of wind.

Developing Software Solutions

In fact, the software solution's technical design is only a part of the software project's life cycle. To give you an idea of the steps involved in managing a complete software solution, imagine a real-world example, such as building an ERP (Enterprise Resource Planning) application for a clothing factory.

For starters, you need to know exactly what the client requires from the software, so you talk to the client about the goals of implementing such software in the network. This involves gathering both system requirements and software requirements for the application you will eventually build.

After you (as the project manager) fully understand the customer's requirements and discuss a budget allocation and a timeline for the project, a team of analysts works with the customer to compile information about the tasks performed in the factory, the work schedule, and the manufacturing equipment. Your analysts must become knowledgeable of the region's economic regime, the employer's legal obligations, the import-export conditions, and so on—facts that are clarified with the commercial, economic, and personnel departments of the company. The analysts build the database and describe the reports and the operations that the software must accomplish.

After the customer reviews and comments upon this assemblage of material, the analytical stage ends with the addition of a written annex to the contract with all these features and a timeline that is agreed to by the customer. After this, any modifications in the database structure, the reports, or software functionality are typically handled with additional charges to the customer.

Next, the design team creates a user-friendly, attractive interface that can be presented to the customer and changed to fit the customer's artistic taste. After this phase is completed, the coding stage begins. This shouldn't take long because the programmers know exactly what they need to do. When they finish coding, the software is installed on a test platform at the customer site, and the customer team simulates using the software for a definite period of time. During the testing period, the eventual programming and design bugs are revealed and fixed by the programmers. At the end of this phase, the customer should have a software application that runs by the agreed specifications and deploys on the production machines. That's the end of the project; the final payments are made, and every modification the customer asks for in the future is billed.

That was a short version of a story about commercial software. Of course, the theory doesn't apply the same for all software projects. For smaller projects, such as many e-commerce sites, several, if not all, the tasks can be performed by a single person.

Considering the Theory Behind Project Management

Many theories exist about how to manage the software development life cycle (SDLC). No model can be deemed a silver bullet because choosing an SDLC model depends on the particularities of your project. You'll learn about the most popular project-management theories in the following pages.

The Waterfall (or Traditional) Method

The Waterfall method, also known as the traditional method, is the father of all methodologies. Now, it's considered by many to be a rather outdated development technology for software, but it's still the cornerstone of modern software development. It consists of breaking the software project into six or seven phases that must be processed in sequential order to deliver the final product. The input of each phase consists of the output of the preceding phase (see Figure B-1).

Establishing the requirements is the first phase and can be divided in two as shown in Figure B-1. First, you must establish the system requirements of the project; at the end of this phase, you have a paper describing all the hardware needed for implementing, testing, and deploying the application. You also need the software platforms your application will be developed and tested on. The first two phases must include an opportunity study at the beginning and a feasibility study at the end. Basically, the first question is "Do we really need this from the business point of view?" After you establish the requirements, the feasibility study provides a high-level cost and benefit analysis so that a ROI (return on investment) can be estimated.

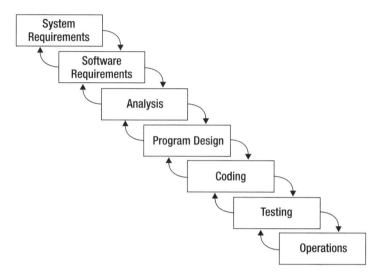

Figure B-1. *The Waterfall model*

In the Analysis phase, the analysts work with the customer to fully understand the customer needs. They have to spend time with the customer's staff to define the software functionalities, transcribing them in a professional analysis for the software engineers.

In the Program Design phase, the design team reads the specifications of the analysis and develops some prototypes that the customer must agree on. Usually, that is throwaway code.

In the Coding phase, programmers effectively code the application. This happens after the customer agrees on the software design delivered by the Program Design phase.

If a testing platform is provided, the programmers install the application there and test all the functionalities of the software. All the bugs discovered are corrected, and at the end of the Testing phase, the software must be ready to go into production. If a testing platform is not provided, the programmers have to simulate or conduct the testing on the actual platform the software will run on; however, at the end of the testing phase, the programmers have to install a fresh copy of the bug-free software they created.

Everything is completed after deployment at the beginning of the Operations phase.

■**Note** Every phase has a feedback to the preceding phase where new ideas can be added and errors are corrected.

Advantages of the Waterfall Method

The main advantages of the Waterfall method are its simplicity and the fact that everything is documented and agreed upon with the customer. This leads to some important benefits:

- Because everything is planned from the start, it's easy for the project manager to correctly estimate project costs and timelines.

- The rigorous initial planning makes the project goals clear.

- All requirements are analyzed and validated by the customer, so the customer can estimate the benefits incurred by the software application before it's actually implemented.

Disadvantages of the Waterfall Method

The disadvantages of the Waterfall method are

- The customer is not able to see the product until it's completely finished. At that stage, it can be very expensive to make any changes to the project.

- It has little flexibility for scope changes during the project's development.

- The architecture limitations are often not discovered until late in the development cycle.

- Because testing happens at the end of the Coding phase, unexpected problems with the code might force developers to find quick fixes at the expense of the planned architecture.

- The Waterfall method doesn't work on projects whose requirements can't be rigorously planned from the start.

The Spiral Method

As a development of the Waterfall method, the Spiral method is more suitable for large, expensive, and complicated projects. Barry Boehm first described it in 1988 as an iterative waterfall in which every iteration provides increased software capability (see Figure B-2, which represents the diagram created by Barry Boehm).

The diagram consists of a spiral divided into four quadrants. Each quadrant represents a management process: Identify, Design, Construct, and Evaluate. The system goes through four cycles of these four processes:

Proof-of-concept cycle: Define the business goals, capture the requirements, develop a conceptual design, construct a "proof-of-concept," establish test plans, and conduct a risk analysis. Share results with user.

First-build cycle: Derive system requirements, develop logic design, construct first build, and evaluate results. Share results with user.

Second-build cycle: Derive subsystem requirements, produce physical design, construct second build, and evaluate results. Share results with user.

Final-build cycle: Derive unit requirements, produce final design, construct final build, and test all levels. Seek user acceptance.

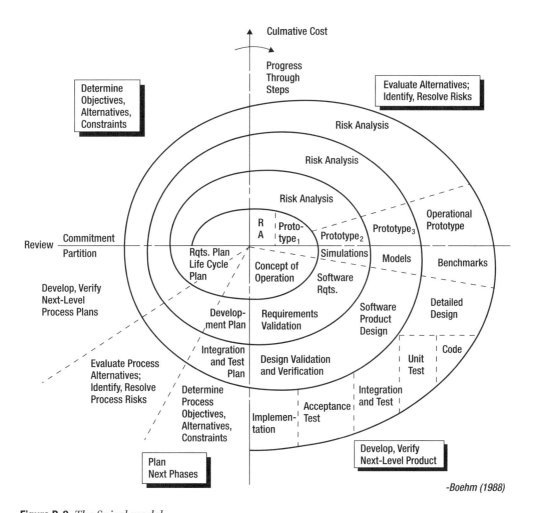

Figure B-2. *The Spiral model*

The main advantages of the Spiral method proposed by Boehm are

- The entire application is built on working with the client.

- Any gaps in the Requirement phase of the Waterfall method are identified as work progresses.

- The spiral representation conveys very clearly the cyclic nature of the project and the progression through its lifespan.

However, the Spiral method has some disadvantages as well:

- Requires serious discipline on the part of the client.

- Executive control can be difficult because in most projects, the client is not responsible for the schedule and budget.

■**Note** The Spiral method is more suitable for software in which the entire problem is well defined from the start, such as modeling and simulating software.

The Rapid Application Development (RAD) Method

RAD is another common project-management method that is, in essence, "try before you buy." Whereas in the Waterfall and even Spiral methods, the client was working with a lot of documentation, in the RAD approach, the client works with the software as it's being developed. The belief is that the client can produce better feedback when working with a live system as opposed to working strictly with documentation. When using RAD as a project-management method, customer rejection cases are significantly less when going into production.

The RAD method consists of the following phases:

- Business modeling

- Data modeling

- Process modeling

- Application generation

- Testing and turnover

The RAD approach allows rapid generation and change of UI features. The client works with the software just like in the production environment.

The main disadvantage of RAD is that the client will always want more enhancements to the software—not always important ones—and the developer must try to satisfy the client's needs. This can result in an unending cycle of requirements, going away from the main purpose of the project.

Extreme Programming (XP) Methodology

Extreme Programming (XP) is a controversial method because it eliminates a lot of phases from the traditional Waterfall methodology. XP, an *agile development methodology*, is simple and based on communication, feedback, and courage.

> ■**Note** XP is one of the *agile development methodologies*, but there are more. These methodologies try to overcome the essential problem of the Waterfall method: you can't always predict the evolution of a project from the beginning. If you don't have previous exposure to agile methods, I recommend you start by reading the great article at `http://www.martinfowler.com/articles/newMethodology.html`.

The professional analysts are replaced with the client, who is very active in the process. The client writes a document named "User Stories," which is a simple description of the desired functionality of the software. The programmers read the document and give an estimated time frame for implementing each functionality. After receiving the time estimates, the customer chooses a group of functionalities to be developed first. This is called an **iteration**.

The developers use a **test-driven** design in the implementation phase, meaning that a testing method for the desired functionality is conceived before the code is actually written. Usually, every piece of code is written by a programmer under the supervision of another programmer who tests the functionality of the code.

After the code for the entire iteration is complete, it's then given an acceptance test with the customer, who approves (or disapproves) the iteration. The programmer keeps developing or improving code for that iteration until it passes the acceptance test.

The software is deployed in a number of **releases**, composed of one or more iterations; the software gets to the final release when all iterations that contain all the functionalities described in the User Stories document pass the acceptance test.

Picking a Method

More project management methods are available to you than the ones described so far. Because no single method is best, a good project manager must know in theory a little about all of them to choose the best one for the current project. Choosing the wrong tactic for a project might lead to failure, so the project manager needs to carefully consider all options before choosing how to deal with a particular project. A strategy like this will never work: "Okay, we have to build an e-commerce site. Let's do XP with this one, and maybe we'll spiral the next one!"

In many cases, it's best to use a mix of methods to suit your project. For example, if the client doesn't know for sure what she wants, you can use bits of XP and collaborate closely with the client during the development based on a User Stories document, add a few steps from the Waterfall method, and do some RAD on the way.

Anyway, it's very important to keep some of these procedures in mind for your next projects because the way you manage your projects can save you time, money, and stress.

Understanding the E-Commerce Project Cycle

If you have some knowledge about management and a good artistic spirit for web design, after you read this book, the e-commerce project can be a "one man show." First of all, you need to organize the tasks so that they take place in a logical, sequential order.

Understanding the customer needs should not be difficult. The customer wants an e-store where a range of products can be advertised and bought. You need to know the type of products the customer wants on the site and a little about future strategy (today the customer is only selling hardware components, but in the future, the customer might want to sell laptops). This is very important because the database and the whole architecture must be designed from the start to support future changes. You might also want to find out about how the shipping department is organized to optimize the handling and shipping process.

Most customers require artistic and functional design, so, in most cases, the next phase is **creating a web prototype**. Whether you do it yourself or hire a web designer, the prototype should be only a web site template—only HTML code with something like "Product name Here" instead of an actual product, without the need for any databases. Depending on the artistic taste of the customer, you might have to build several prototypes until you agree on a design.

Designing the database is, as I said, a critical phase of the project. The logical database design is developed from the Requirements gathering phase, and is agreed on with the customer. The database's logical design describes what data you need to store and the relationships between different entities of data (such as the relationship between products and departments), but it doesn't include strict implementation details such as the associate table used to physically implement Many-to-Many relationships. If you're an advanced database designer, you'll create an optimal physical database structure yourself.

A number of tools (such as the ones presented at `http://www.infogoal.com/dmc/dmcdmd.htm`) enable you to design the database visually. (You can find even more useful links with a Google search on "data modeling.") These tools have very powerful features for designing relational database structures and even generate the SQL code to turn them into real databases. Regardless of the database engine you're using, design your tables in a visual way (even with a pen and paper) rather than start by writing SQL queries.

Next, you **implement the data tier objects**. This is the place you start playing with your database because you need to implement the data access logic that will support the other tiers in your application. In the process, you'll probably want to populate the database with some fictive examples to have a base for testing your queries. Before writing the queries as data tier objects, test them using a visual interface to the database engine that allows executing and debugging SQL queries. This will make your life easier when debugging the SQL code because, as all SQL developers know, the code doesn't always work as you expect it to the first time.

After the data tier is in place, you can continue by **building the middle tier** of your application. In this book, you learned some techniques about implementing the middle tier for various parts of the site, but you might want to choose other techniques for your particular project.

Building the user interface is obviously the next step. You already have a prototype that is usable only for design because, at the stage you created the prototypes, you didn't have a functional foundation. Usually, interface prototypes in software projects are throwaway code, but here you build the UI logic (preferably using Smarty or another templating engine) that generates the actual look of your web site with the design the customer agreed on.

A **final testing phase** is very important at the end of the project. The database will be populated with real records, and a simulation is made to test the efficiency of the ordering process. Every process should be tested before production, so you must give your customer enough time to test every functionality of the site, to make some test orders, and to evaluate the shipping process. During this stage, any programming errors should be revealed for you to correct.

After the code is ready and tested on your local machine, the next step is to **find/provide a hosting solution**. Perhaps the best strategy is to host the project at a specialized provider, and if the site proves to be successful, the customer can invest in its own hosting solution.

Maintaining Relationships with Your Customers

In the ideal project, you include all the possible clauses in a contract; after you deliver the site and finish the project, you never want to hear from the customer again, except for developing new functionalities or changing the design, in which case, you charge the customer extra.

The most unwanted thing would be for the customer to ask you to make changes without paying for them, which is possible if you are not careful with the contract and with the tools you provide the customer for administration.

For example, many e-commerce sites have poor catalog admin pages, which are nightmares for the programmers. Avoiding such a nightmare can be possible by providing proper tools and interfaces for the customer and, most importantly, describing how they work (eventually a user's manual). Many programmers don't take this detail seriously and prefer to bring the site up with an incomplete or hard-to-use catalog admin page, not knowing what's coming.

If the database is complicated, you must describe in a manual all the fields and how they must be completed; if an error occurs when the customer tries to submit a form to a database, you have to make the error page as eloquent as possible. Also, try to work with those who will use the tools you provide in the Design phase, and take a couple of hours to instruct them personally on how to use the tools. This will save you a lot of explanations over the phone or even going to the customer's office without being paid.

Summary

Different kinds of projects require different kinds of approaches. The methodology you and your team are using for a software project can significantly affect the team efficiency, especially in large projects. Building a small e-commerce web site such as HatShop can be a "one man show" for an experienced Web Developer, but it's always good to be prepared for the more challenging experiences!

Index

You Need the Companion eBook

We believe this Apress title will prove so indispensable that you'll want to carry it with you everywhere, which is why we are offering the companion eBook (in PDF format) for $10 to customers who purchase this book now. Convenient and fully searchable, the PDF version of any content-rich, page-heavy Apress book makes a valuable addition to your programming library. You can easily find and copy code—or perform examples by quickly toggling between instructions and the application. Even simultaneously tackling a donut, diet soda, and complex code becomes simplified with hands-free eBooks!

Once you purchase your book, getting the $10 companion eBook is simple:

1. Visit **www.apress.com/promo/tendollars/**.

2. Complete a basic registration form to receive a randomly generated question about this title.

3. Answer the question correctly in 60 seconds, and you will receive a promotional code to redeem for the $10.00 eBook.

2560 Ninth Street • Suite 219 • Berkeley, CA 94710

eBookshop

THE EXPERT'S VOICE™

Offer valid through 06/07.